CONTRACTOR'S MANAGEMENT HANDBOOK

Other McGraw-Hill Reference Books of Interest

Handbooks

American Water Works Association • WATER QUALITY AND TREATMENT: A HANDBOOK FOR PUBLIC WATER SUPPLIES

Brater and King • HANDBOOK OF HYDRAULICS

Brock • FIELD INSPECTION HANDBOOK

Corbitt • STANDARD HANDBOOK OF ENVIRONMENTAL ENGINEERING

Faherty and Williamson • WOOD ENGINEERING AND CONSTRUCTION HANDBOOK

Gaylord and Gaylord • STRUCTURAL ENGINEERING HANDBOOK

Merritt • BUILDING DESIGN AND CONSTRUCTION HANDBOOK

Merritt • STANDARD HANDBOOK FOR CIVIL ENGINEERS

Parmley • FIELD ENGINEERS' MANUAL

Rossnagel, MacDonald, and Higgins • HANDBOOK OF RIGGING

Other

Alfeld • CONSTRUCTION PRODUCTIVITY

Breyer • DESIGN OF WOOD STRUCTURES

Coombs and Palmer • CONSTRUCTION ACCOUNTING AND FINANCIAL MANAGEMENT

Grigg • WATER RESOURCES PLANNING

Horonjeff and McKelvey • PLANNING AND DESIGN OF AIRPORTS

Millman • GENERAL CONTRACTING

O'Brien • CPM IN CONSTRUCTION MANAGEMENT

CONTRACTOR'S MANAGEMENT HANDBOOK

James J. O'Brien, P.E.

Chairman of the Board
O'Brien-Kreitzberg & Associates, Inc.
Pennsauken, New Jersey

Robert G. Zilly, P.E., M.A.S.C.E.

Professor of Construction Management Emeritus
University of Nebraska
Lincoln, Nebraska

Second Edition

McGRAW-HILL, INC.

New York St. Louis San Francisco Auckland Bogotá
Caracas Hamburg Lisbon London Madrid
Mexico Milan Montreal New Delhi Paris
San Juan São Paulo Singapore
Sydney Tokyo Toronto

Library of Congress Cataloging-in-Publication Data

Contractor's management handbook / editors, James J. O'Brien, Robert
   G. Zilly.—2nd ed.
   p.   cm.
   Includes index.
   ISBN 0-07-047797-3
   1. Construction industry—Management.   2. Building trades—
Management.   3. Contractors' operations—Management.   I. O'Brien,
James Jerome.   II. Zilly, Robert G.
HD9715.A2C656   1991
624'.068—dc20

90-47465

CIP

1 2 3 4 5 6 7 8 9 0   DOC/DOC   9 6 5 4 3 2 1

ISBN   0-07-047797-3

*The sponsoring editor for this book was Joel E. Stein, the editing
supervisor was Caroline Levine, the designer was Naomi Auerbach, and
the production supervisor was Suzanne W. Babeuf. It was set in Times
Roman by McGraw-Hill's Professional Publishing composition unit.*

Printed and bound by R. R. Donnelley & Sons Company.

While the text of this book takes on masculine gender in many
cases for convenience, there is no intent on the part of the authors
to slight or ignore women, whose role in the construction industry
has seen tremendous growth in recent years.

CONTENTS

CONTRIBUTORS

Joseph Alcabes, D.E., B.C.E., M.B.A. *483 Stevens Avenue, West Hampton, New York* (CHAP. 15)

Stephen Beinfest, CPA *O'Brien-Kreitzberg & Associates, Inc., San Francisco, California* (CHAP. 11, SECOND EDITION)

Walter T. Derk, Vice President *Fred S. James & Co., Chicago, Illinois* (CHAP. 11, FIRST EDITION)

Robert D. Falese *President and Chief Executive Officer, Sterling Bank, Mt. Laurel, New Jersey* (CHAP. 19)

Paul E. Harmon, P.E., N.S.P.E., A.S.C.E., A.C.I. *Associate Professor of Construction Management, University of Nebraska, Lincoln, Nebraska* (CHAP. 14)

Robert B. Hemphill *Barclay White, Philadelphia, Pennsylvania* (CHAP. 6, FIRST EDITION)

Fred C. Kreitzberg *President and Chief Executive Officer, O'Brien-Kreitzberg & Associates, Inc, San Francisco, California* (CHAP. 16)

Verner M. Meyers, Architect *Associate Professor of Construction Management, Emeritus, University of Nebraska, Lincoln, Nebraska* (CHAP. 5)

Wesley F. Mikes, *Senior Vice President, O'Brien-Kreitzberg & Associates, Inc., Pennsauken, New Jersey* (CHAP. 15, SECOND EDITION)

James J. O'Brien, P.E. *Chairman of the Board, O'Brien-Kreitzberg & Associates, Inc., Pennsauken, New Jersey* (CHAPS. 2, 9, 10, 18, 20, AND 25)

Rita G. O'Brien *Executive Vice President, Personnel & Administration, O'Brien-Kreitzberg & Associates, Inc., Pennsauken, New Jersey* (CHAP. 21)

Thomas P. O'Callaghan, Esq. *O'Brien-Kreitzberg & Associates, Inc., Pennsauken, New Jersey* (CHAP. 20)

Matthew J. O'Rourke *Price Waterhouse & Company, Independence Mall West, Philadelphia, Pennsylvania* (CHAP. 17, FIRST EDITION)

Arnold S. Page, CPA *Page, Weaver & Carter, P.A., 106F Centre Boulevard, Marlton, New Jersey* (CHAP. 24)

William R. Park, P.E. *Consulting Engineer-Economist, Overland Park, Kansas* (CHAP. 8)

Terry D. Peters *Equipment Consultant, Elkhorn, Nebraska* (CHAP. 13)

Paul P. Poppler *College of Business Administration, University of Nebraska, Lincoln, Nebraska* (CHAP. 4)

Harold D. Robertson, AIC, AIA *Associate Professor of Construction Management, University of Nebraska, Lincoln, Nebraska* (CHAP. 3)

George B. Roscoe *6609 Rosecroft Place, Falls Church, Virginia* (CHAP. 2)

Lillian Watson, CPE *O'Brien-Kreitzberg & Associates, Pennsauken, New Jersey* (CHAP. 6, SECOND EDITION)

Jack Weaver   *Page, Weaver & Carter, North Crossing, Marlton, New Jersey* (CHAP. 17, SECOND EDITION)

Robert G. Zilly, P.E., M.A.S.C.E., A.I.C.   *Professor of Construction Management, Emeritus, University of Nebraska, Lincoln, Nebraska* (CHAPS. 1, 7, 12, 22, AND 23)

PREFACE

As the twenty-first century draws closer, the United States is facing a major breakdown in its infrastructure. The roads and streets, bridges and tunnels, water and sewage treatment plants, and airports and railroads that helped to make this nation the most productive in the world are suffering from neglect by both the general public and the federal government. Dedicated funds remain unspent, a backlog of construction work that could inundate the industry if properly funded.

Meanwhile, the 80s were not kind to the construction industry. Early in the decade, a recession wiped out many firms and forced others to retrench. Bid-rigging scandals in highway and electrical construction eroded public confidence in the constructor. Added to these woes was the realization that the glamour of working in construction that had attracted a steady flow of new employees into the industry was fading.

The 90s appear enigmatic to the professional forecasters, but there are many indicators displaying the resilience of an industry as old as civilization. New and stronger companies have been formed by combining the best elements of failed firms, and many old firms have reorganized to better face the problems of an erratic market. Ethics has again become a popular topic at constructors' meetings, and a number of construction firms have sponsored programs on the subject at leading universities. It is also to the industry's credit that it has set in motion programs to attract new recruits to the construction trades.

As the twenty-first century nears, construction firms must be ready to meet the pent-up demand for their services. This book was prepared to assist contractors to meet the challenges of today, tomorrow, and the coming years.

James J. O'Brien
Robert G. Zilly

CONTRACTOR'S MANAGEMENT HANDBOOK

CHAPTER 1
CONSTRUCTION INDUSTRY

Robert G. Zilly, P.E., M.A.S.C.E.
Professor of Construction Management
Emeritus
University of Nebraska
Lincoln, Nebraska

THE INDUSTRY

The roster of U.S. construction firms constitutes a heterogeneous collection ranging from the "one man with a toolbox and pickup truck" operation to huge companies with thousands of employees and millions of dollars invested in capital equipment. Services offered by these firms range from general contracting to specialty contracting to design-build and construction management for residential, commercial, industrial, and a broad range of civil engineering projects. *Engineering News-Record*'s list of the top 400 general contractors ranges from companies with annual contracts measured in the billions to those with just over $40 million in contracts. The top 40 companies on this list captured about half the revenues, the bottom 40 about 3 percent. A similar disparity in size and revenue is typical of other types of firms.

The construction business is easy to enter but extremely sensitive to the economic climate. Because profits are low, many firms are not financially sound enough to weather recessions such as the one that occurred in the early 1980s. According to records from Dun and Bradstreet, the effects of this recession began to appear in 1981 but did not peak until 1986. In that year, 2634 firms failed, but 33,079 firms entered the market as economic conditions continued to improve.

Size

The 1982 Census of Construction Industries reported the existence of almost 1,400,000 establishments with 4,275,000 employees. However, it must be quickly pointed out that less than 460,000 of these establishments had a payroll, leaving more than 900,000 "one man" operations. In 1982 establishments with payroll took in over 90 percent of the $365.5 billion in receipts. By late 1988, the annual rate of new construction put in place was running just over $422 billion (Table 1.1).

According to the Bureau of Labor Statistics, in 1988 one worker in twenty was

TABLE 1.1 Value of New Construction Put in Place in the United States*,†

(Seasonally adjusted annual rate in billions of dollars)

| | Jan. 1989 (p) | Dec. 1988 (r) | Nov. 1988 (r) | Oct. 1988 | Sep. 1988 | Aug. 1988 | Jul. 1988 | Jan. 1988 | Percent change Jan. 1989 from | |
Type of construction									Dec. 1988	Jan. 1988
					Current dollars					
Total new construction	424.0	422.3	413.6	408.2	406.9	403.2	404.2	395.3	(Z)	7
Private construction‡	342.3	336.4	333.3	330.3	327.2	326.8	324.7	321.5	2	6
Residential buildings§	204.6	202.3	201.8	199.6	196.9	195.4	194.2	195.2	1	5
New housing units	144.5	143.7	142.7	140.4	138.7	137.1	136.4	140.8	1	3
One unit structures	122.2	122.2	121.0	118.7	116.8	115.5	114.5	117.0	(Z)	4
Two or more unit structures	22.3	21.5	21.7	21.7	21.8	21.7	21.9	23.8	4	−6
Nonresidential buildings	99.1	95.0	93.1	93.2	91.7	93.3	93.3	91.1	4	9
Industrial	16.2	15.1	15.9	15.2	13.5	14.0	13.9	13.5	8	20
Office	28.3	27.7	27.2	27.6	27.2	28.4	28.1	26.8	2	6
Hotels and motels	7.5	6.9	6.6	6.2	5.8	6.3	6.5	7.1	8	5
Other commercial	29.6	28.2	26.6	27.1	28.7	28.0	28.6	26.8	5	11
Religious	3.0	2.7	2.6	2.5	2.7	2.8	2.7	2.9	12	3
Educational	3.0	3.1	2.9	3.0	3.0	2.6	2.3	3.1	−2	−2
Hospital and institutional	7.3	7.3	7.1	7.5	6.7	7.0	6.9	7.0	1	−5
Miscellaneous buildings	4.1	4.1	4.2	4.1	4.3	4.2	4.2	4.0	(Z)	3
Telephone and telegraph	(NA)	9.0	8.7	8.2	8.7	8.5	8.3	8.0	(NA)	(NA)
All other private	2.1	2.1	2.0	1.9	1.8	1.9	1.9	2.7	(Z)	−24
Public construction	81.7	85.9	80.3	77.9	79.7	76.4	79.5	73.7	−5	11
Housing and redevelopment	1.5	1.6	1.8	1.7	1.7	1.4	1.6	1.5	−7	1
Industrial	.7	1.3	1.4	1.4	2.1	1.6	1.4	1.3	−43	−43
Educational	12.2	11.8	11.3	11.0	11.3	11.1	10.4	9.1	4	35
Hospital	1.7	2.3	2.1	2.2	2.6	2.5	2.3	1.9	−23	−7
Other public buildings	11.5	11.4	10.7	10.5	11.2	11.7	11.4	10.7	1	8
Highways and streets	27.8	30.9	26.4	26.0	23.8	23.5	27.7	24.8	−10	12
Military facilities	3.8	4.1	3.9	3.7	4.9	4.0	4.3	4.2	−10	−10
Conservation and development	4.1	4.3	3.8	3.9	5.0	4.8	4.9	4.0	−6	1
Sewer systems	8.8	8.5	8.8	8.5	7.9	7.5	7.4	7.8	3	13
Water supply facilities	4.9	4.8	4.6	4.2	4.2	3.5	3.7	3.8	4	31
Miscellaneous public	4.6	5.0	5.3	4.9	5.1	4.8	4.5	4.8	−6	−3

1982 dollars

Total new construction	363.8	361.4	354.7	350.1	349.7	346.9	348.0	343.9	1	6
Private construction‡	296.0	290.4	288.1	285.5	283.3	283.0	281.4	280.6	2	5
Residential buildings§	180.6	178.3	177.9	176.0	174.0	172.6	171.7	172.6	1	5
New housing units	127.6	126.6	125.9	123.8	122.5	121.1	120.6	124.5	1	2
One unit structures	107.9	107.6	106.7	104.7	103.2	102.0	101.2	103.5	(Z)	4
Two or more unit structures	19.7	19.0	19.1	19.1	19.3	19.1	19.3	21.0	4	-6
Nonresidential buildings	82.6	79.1	77.6	77.7	76.6	77.9	77.9	76.9	4	7
Industrial	13.5	12.5	13.2	12.7	11.3	11.7	11.6	11.4	8	19
Office	23.6	23.1	22.7	23.0	22.7	23.7	23.4	22.6	2	4
Hotels and motels	6.2	5.8	5.5	5.1	4.8	5.2	5.4	6.0	8	4
Other commercial	24.7	23.5	22.2	22.6	23.9	23.4	23.9	22.6	5	9
Religious	2.5	2.2	2.1	2.1	2.2	2.3	2.3	2.5	13	2
Educational	2.5	2.6	2.4	2.5	2.5	2.1	2.0	2.6	-2	-3
Hospital and institutional	6.1	6.1	5.9	6.3	5.6	5.9	5.8	5.9	-1	4
Miscellaneous buildings	3.4	3.4	3.5	3.4	3.6	3.5	3.5	3.3	1	2
Telephone and telegraph	(NA)	7.8	7.5	7.1	7.5	7.4	7.2	7.0	(NA)	(NA)
All other private	1.7	1.7	1.6	1.6	1.5	1.6	1.6	2.4	(Z)	-27
Public construction	67.8	71.0	66.6	64.6	66.4	63.9	66.6	63.3	-4	7
Housing and redevelopment	1.3	1.4	1.6	1.5	1.5	1.3	1.4	1.3	-7	1
Industrial	.6	1.1	1.2	1.2	1.7	1.3	1.2	1.1	-43	-44
Educational	10.2	9.8	9.4	9.1	9.4	9.3	8.7	7.7	4	33
Hospital	1.5	1.9	1.7	1.8	2.1	2.1	1.9	1.6	-23	-9
Other public buildings	9.6	9.5	8.9	8.8	9.4	9.8	9.5	9.0	1	7
Highways and streets	21.8	24.2	20.7	20.4	18.7	18.7	22.2	20.7	-10	5
Military facilities	3.0	3.3	3.2	3.0	4.0	3.2	3.6	3.5	-9	-13
Conservation and development	3.6	3.9	3.4	3.5	4.5	4.3	4.4	3.7	-6	-2
Sewer systems	7.9	7.6	7.9	7.6	7.1	6.8	6.7	7.2	3	10
Water supply facilities	4.4	4.2	4.1	3.7	3.7	3.1	3.3	3.4	4	28
Miscellaneous public	3.9	4.1	4.5	4.1	4.2	4.1	3.8	4.2	-6	-7

*Detail may not add to total due to rounding. Percent changes based on unrounded figures.

†(NA) Not available. (p) Preliminary. (r) Revised. (Z) Less than 0.5 percent.

‡Includes the following categories of private construction not shown separately: residential improvements, railroads, electric light and power, gas, petroleum pipelines, and farm nonresidential.

§Includes improvements.

Source: U.S. Department of Commerce, Bureau of the Census.

employed in the construction industry, for a total of about 5.63 million. In 1982 the total was about 4.25 million, even though the industry was suffering from a severe recession. Overall, about 10.4 percent of employers in each state are members of the construction industry.

U.S. Department of Labor studies indicate a serious shortage of construction workers by the year 2000. Based on projected growth rates, total employment in the industry at the turn of the century will be from 5.64 to 6.08 million.

The Associated General Contractors of America estimated that in 1988 the construction industry's contribution to the gross national product (GNP) was 9 percent. This compares to a figure of close to 11 percent in the early 1960s, a figure which fell to about 10 percent by 1970. It should be noted that the extent of the construction industry's contribution to the GNP is vigorously debated by the "experts," because it depends on how it is calculated and which numbers are included, but there is a general consensus that the trend is down. However, a growing awareness of the decay of the U.S. "infrastructure"—e.g., roads, bridges, dams, water and sewage treatment plants—could reverse this trend in the foreseeable future.

Participants in the Construction Process

The Owner.   The marketing capabilities of construction firms have shown slow but steady improvement over the past several decades. This has led to the development of some significant construction projects initiated by creative promotional and sales efforts on the part of individual construction firms. However, it is the owner, whether government agency, company, or private individual, who is usually responsible for the conception of a construction project. In view of the high risk involved in guiding a construction project from conception to completion, it is surprising that owners have not developed better methods to help them deal with the problems presented by a new project. However, this is not to say that owners are at the mercy of the architects, engineers, and contractors who design and build their projects. In fact, today's owner displays an increasing level of sophistication in his relationship with the providers of construction services.

Perhaps the greatest impact ever exerted by owners on the construction industry resulted from studies by The Business Round Table's Construction Industry Cost Effectiveness Task Force. In its summary report "More Construction for the Money," the task force reported on the work of over 250 people from 125 companies, including both suppliers and users of construction services as well as universities and industry organizations. The thrust of this report can best be summarized by a quotation from the foreward written by Roger M. Blough, former CEO of the United States Steel Corporation:

> To some the construction industry may seem to be a relatively narrow special interest. It is not, and it has not been treated as such by The Business Roundtable, whose member companies spend enormous amounts of capital, talent and effort in the construction of plants, office buildings, and other facilities. The Construction Industry Cost Effectiveness Project was approached as an effort to improve one major aspect of a great economic system, to advance the market philosophy of production and distribution, to improve work methods to the end of creating more for more people. It was approached with the realization that construction in one way or another touches the lives of all.
>
> The rationale for this effort, then, can be summed up succinctly:

1. Construction is important to the economy as a whole and therefore to everybody. It affects costs, prices, and our international competitiveness both in our own and foreign markets.
2. Construction dollars are not being used effectively.
3. Declining cost effectiveness is not the fault of any one group. Owners, managers, contractors, unions, workers, suppliers, and governments all share the responsibility.
4. Cost-effectiveness in construction can be improved to the advantage of all without inequality to any group, if we recognize it as a national problem and seek cooperative instead of adversarial solutions.

In addition to the summary report, 23 additional reports were published covering specific problems discovered and analyzed by the Task Force. A series of regional meetings followed the January 1983 publication, and copies of the reports were widely distributed. They may be obtained by writing to

The Business Roundtable

200 Park Avenue

New York, New York 10166

There were many spinoffs from the work of this Business Roundtable group, among them the Construction Industry Institute at the University of Texas, Austin. While several large construction firms were and continue to be active in this work, major credit must be given to the impetus provided by large corporate buyers of construction services. In fact, through creative approaches to contracting procedures, sophisticated owners have been instrumental in pushing the use of critical path scheduling, job-site productivity studies, formalized worker motivation programs, and promotion of safe working practices. Overall, it is safe to say that during the past decade contractors have felt increasing pressure from their customers in the private sector to deliver projects faster and cheaper. Similar pressures from governmental agencies at all levels have been felt for even longer.

The Designer.   According to *Civil Engineering* magazine there were over 50,000 architectural and consulting engineering firms in the United States in 1988. This count probably neglects the large number of small, often "one man," operations that are still providing a variety of design services at the local level. The lion's share of the billing for design services is the $14.9 billion claimed by the top 500 design firms listed in *Engineering Record*'s report for the year 1987. Of the total 1987 billings, 46 percent went to engineer-architect (EA) firms, 29 to consulting engineering firms, 15 to architect-engineer (AE) firms, 7 to architectural firms, and 3 to soils engineering firms. These percentages show little change from those reported for 1984, with the exception of a significant shift of billing from AE firms to EA firms.

Even though the revenues of design firms were growing as the 1980s drew to a close, their profits grew at slightly less than 8 percent while direct labor hour costs rose by more than 8 percent, or $14.93 per hour, in 1987 according to *Professional Services Management Journal.* There was also evidence that a growing shortage of design professionals was beginning to strangle growth for some firms. In addition to rising labor and overhead costs, design firms continue to face the problem of increasing costs for professional liability insurance.

Pressured by rising costs and the emergence of new areas of specialization, not to mention manpower shortages, a number of design firms have gone the merger route in an attempt to solve their problems. Once a rare phenomenon in the design field, mergers and acquisitions have grown to the point where *Engineering News-Record* runs frequent columns to keep its readers abreast of changes. In addition, many design firms are actively engaged in construction management, an activity that would have been frowned on as unethical not too many years ago. It is also not uncommon to find design firms in joint ventures with contractors in the field of speculative building.

The Contractor. Over 1.4 million contractors are in the business of converting the drawings and specifications of architects and engineers into the "built environment"—commercial, residential, industrial, and institutional buildings; highways, bridges, and dams; and a variety of other projects ranging from sewage treatment plants to golf courses. Their success or failure depends on a combination of technological and business skills involving the management of people, machines, materials, products, money, and time. For the successful contractor in a highly competitive market, the rewards are often small; for the unsuccessful, the penalty is bankruptcy.

According to the U.S. Bureau of the Census, the total number of contractors can be quickly reduced to about half a million by weeding out those establishments without payroll. Further, the remaining one-third of all firms—those with payroll—account for over 90 percent of the total receipts each year. These ratios are approximately correct for the four broad contractor groups established by the Bureau of the Census—general building contractors and operative builders, heavy construction general contractors, special trade contractors, and subdividers and developers. While the total number of construction firms in the 1977 census count was smaller than that in the 1982 census, it is interesting to note that there were more firms with payroll in 1977 than in 1982 in all categories except heavy construction general contractors and subdividers and developers. This can probably be attributed to the impact of the early 1980s recession.

In late 1988, the annual rate of construction was running at over $422 billion in current dollars as opposed to just over $350 billion in 1982 dollars. Compared to the $312 billion total for 1982, it is obvious that while growth in dollars appears strong, the physical volume of construction produced is rising at a much slower rate. The 1988 annual rate included about $330 billion in private construction (mostly buildings) and $80 billion in public construction, representing about $27 billion in buildings with the balance being in areas such as highways, military projects, and water and sewage treatment plants.

Building construction is not only the largest segment of the industry, it is probably the most complicated in terms of both technology and management. It includes general contractors who control the entire construction process under a single contract, general contractors who operate under separate contracts along with specialty contractors who have direct contracts with the owner for such areas as mechanical and electrical work, and general contractors who function as design-build firms that can offer an owner a complete package which often includes site selection, design, construction, and "shakedown" operation. A significant amount of building construction, as well as other types, also involves the construction management approach where a firm representing the owner is responsible for holding design work within budget and putting together bid packages that go out for competitive bids as the design work progresses. On private building projects any of these approaches may be selected by the owner. On government work, from federal to local, the separate contract approach may well be mandated by law.

Few general contractors have the capability of handling a total building project with their own staff. They depend on a variety of specialty (sub)contractors who specialize in such areas as sheet metal work, piping, electrical, masonry, and many others. As a matter of fact, there has been a long-range trend on the part of many large general contractors to increase their use of specialty contractors as their own firms move more strongly into the management area.

There are about 1 million specialty contractors in the Census Bureau count, but only 30 percent of them have payroll. The total group accounts for just over a third of all construction receipts, some $130 billion in 1982. In 1987, about 400 specialty contractors covered by *Engineering News-Record*'s (ENR) annual survey accounted for over $13 billion in revenue, a 15 percent increase over the previous year. Included in the ENR group are mechanical, electrical, demolition and wrecking, excavation and foundation, roofing and sheet metal, glazing and curtain wall, and steel erection specialty firms.

About one-third of all specialty contractors with payroll are in the mechanical and electrical fields. In 1987, about 48,000 electrical firms with payroll did $34.5 billion in construction work with half a million employees. This represents an increase of about 25 percent over 1982 figures in both dollars and employees. The top electricals in ENR's 1987 list posted a 12 percent gain over 1986, the top mechanicals 4 percent.

As the 1980s drew to a close, the major problems of construction companies were low net profits, difficulty in obtaining bonding, dwindling physical volume of work, and a potential shortage of skilled craftsmen. On the upside, the industry appeared to have trimmed the fat from its management structure and could look forward to an increasing volume of work created by the general decline of the nation's infrastructure.

Government.   From federal to state to local levels, government affects the construction industry as both regulator and client. Regulation by various agencies at all levels is often mandated through legislative action. However, the agencies also exert regulatory power through their role of client. The power of taxation is not incidental. The government funds construction projects, either directly or by funds passed from higher to lower levels (e.g., federal fuel tax funds passed to the states for highway construction), and thus is able to exert various kinds of regulatory pressures.

The Occupational Safety and Health Act (OSHA) of 1970 was passed by the Congress to improve safety in all industries, but the construction industry was designated as a "target" because of its poor safety record. Thus, it is of major concern to contractors and OSHA has been named by some as a contributing factor in rising construction costs. Similarly, the Davis-Bacon Act has been blamed for increasing the cost of construction because it requires the Department of Labor to set "prevailing" wages for federally funded construction projects. Since prevailing wages are most easily determined in metropolitan areas, which are often union oriented, contractors complain that they are generally higher than established wages in rural or small town locations. A counter to these cost increase factors through most of the 1980s was the National Labor Relations Board (NLRB). According to *Builder and Contractor,* the NLRB moved from a prolabor majority to one that was more sympathetic to management by 1984. Many other controls over the construction industry have been legislated by the Congress and many have counterparts at the state level.

In their role as client, many federal agencies have had a major impact on the construction industry. For example, the General Services Administration (GSA) strongly promoted the construction management system of project delivery in the

1970s, abandoned it for a time in the 1980s, and then returned to it on a selective basis. It is probably safe to say that without the strong promotional backing of the GSA, the construction management approach would not be as strongly entrenched in the industry as it is today. Similarly, the GSA, the Veterans Administration, and a number of other federal agencies specified that contractors performing work for them use the critical path method (CPM) for construction planning and scheduling. While perhaps not a major factor, this did help to promote the adoption of CPM by many contractors for their major projects. Another technique promoted by federal agencies was value engineering, a system for getting the most construction for the least cost. It is being used today by many firms that function as construction managers. With construction labor shortages predicted for the early 1990s, the Bureau of Apprentice Training in the Department of Labor will likely play a significant role in the future success of the industry.

On the state level, registration and licensing are tools used by the states to control the quality of design and construction work. In addition, many state highway departments, strongly dependent on federal pass-along revenues, have implemented methods espoused by federal agencies and introduced a number of their own devising. Also, in the absence of federal building codes, state and local governments have enacted into law one or more of the widely accepted building codes—sometimes creating confusion and conflict via jurisdictional disputes between several levels of state and local government.

Through the 1980s, federal investment in the nation's infrastructure has been declining as a percentage of the gross national product. Although some of the slack has been taken up by the states, there is little doubt that roads, bridges, sewage and water treatment plants, and a variety of other public service facilities are in extreme danger of becoming unserviceable. Thus, a major sector of the construction industry has been at best holding its own in recent years. This has affected not only construction productivity, but also the overall productivity of our nation's business and industry.

Industry Associations. The American Institute of Architects, which is a mixed bag of individual and company members, represents the architectural profession. The American Consulting Engineers Council is its counterpart and represents engineering firms. Both deal extensively with government and other industry organizations, both to improve the construction industry and to protect its vested interests. In addition to these groups, there are individual membership organizations such as the National Society of Professional Engineers, the American Society of Civil Engineers, the American Society of Mechanical Engineers, the Construction Specifications Institute, and the American Society of Heating, Air Conditioning and Refrigeration Engineers. All affect the construction industry in a variety of ways.

Contractor organizations are usually strongly business oriented, with membership by company rather than by individual. The lone exception is the American Institute of Constructors, which has strongly influenced construction education and the movement toward professional status for practitioners in construction. Perhaps the most powerful contractor organization is the Associated General Contractors of America, formed in 1917 as the result of a meeting called by President Wilson to solve wartime labor problems in the industry. Originally strongly oriented toward the union-shop contractor, the organization now includes both union- and open-shop operators. To meet the special needs of open shop contractors, the Associated Builders and Constructors came into existence in the 1950s in Maryland. Its current membership is made up of both general and specialty contractors. The National Association of Home Builders represents home builders.

A number of contractor organizations are organized by specialty: the mechanical field, sheet metal, roofing, electrical, and a variety of others. Because these firms operated primarily as subcontractors and their organizations had no formal ties with each other, their power and influence were limited. This led to the formation of the American Subcontractors Association, an organization with the major goals of prompt payment and fairer treatment from general contractors.

All of these industry organizations are active in lobbying the Congress and other legislative bodies, and most are politically involved through PACs. In addition they promote education and sponsor training programs for both management and trade personnel. Many have been particularly supportive of bachelor degree programs in construction management at the university level and have made significant financial contributions to scholarship programs. Although some research and development work is funded, the construction industry is notoriously weak in this area and more needs to be done to stem the tide of declining productivity that threatens the industry.

CONTRACTOR RESOURCES

As the construction industry moves closer to the twenty-first century, its role as manager of people, products, and production equipment within a tight time and money framework is beset by problems. New workers must be recruited from the reduced pool created by low birth rates of the 1970s to replace dropouts from an aging work force. In addition, the "romance" of working construction has lost its allure and younger workers are looking to other industries to provide career opportunities. While there have been some notable advances in the products that go into a construction project, the asbestos scare, troubles with roofing and insulation products, and other environmental concerns have complicated the building process and contributed to the negative image that the industry has always battled. Meanwhile, the cost of production equipment has continued to rise and the rate of capital investment by contractors has declined to the point where productivity is being seriously affected.

Construction Labor

As the 1980s drew to a close, the battle between open-shop and union proponents continued unabated. Estimates of open-shop market control ranged as high as 80 percent, but unions were still strong in the major metropolitan areas. Table 1.2 presents a breakdown of employed wage and salary workers by occupation, industry, and union affiliation. Overshadowing the union versus open-shop debate was the prediction that the 1990s would usher in a serious shortage of skilled construction workers. The problem of a declining pool of candidates moving into the job market will apparently be compounded by the failure of new training programs designed to replace the traditional apprenticeship training programs run by union and management.

When 1988 construction employment peaked at almost 5.75 million, it was predicted that about 265,000 new workers would be needed each year in the fore-

TABLE 1.2 Employed Wage and Salary Workers by Occupation, Industry, and Union Affiliation (in Thousands)

Occupation and industry	1987					1988				
	Total employed	Members of unions*		Represented by unions†		Total employed	Members of unions*		Represented by unions†	
		Total	Percent of employed	Total	Percent of employed		Total	Percent of employed	Total	Percent of employed
Occupation										
Managerial and professional specialty	23,378	3,512	15.0	4,286	18.3	24,369	3,644	15.0	4,470	18.3
Executive, administrative, and managerial	10,770	726	6.7	944	8.8	11,337	734	6.5	977	8.6
Professional specialty	12,607	2,786	22.1	3,342	26.5	13,032	2,910	22.3	3,493	26.8
Technical, sales, and administrative support	31,801	3,265	10.3	3,868	12.2	32,271	3,312	10.3	3,976	12.3
Technicians and related support	3,243	341	10.5	412	12.7	3,462	391	11.3	469	13.5
Sales occupations	10,860	612	5.6	691	6.4	11,019	587	5.3	689	6.2
Administrative support, including clerical	17,698	2,311	13.1	2,765	15.6	17,790	2,333	13.1	2,818	15.8
Service occupations	13,876	1,953	14.1	2,187	15.8	14,178	1,989	14.0	2,225	15.7
Protective service	1,909	725	38.0	795	41.7	1,969	765	38.9	839	42.6
Service, except protective service	11,967	1,228	10.3	1,392	11.6	12,209	1,224	10.0	1,387	11.4
Precision production, craft, and repair	11,567	3,132	27.1	3,364	29.1	11,766	3,164	26.9	3,374	28.7
Operators, fabricators, and laborers	16,920	4,956	29.3	5,234	30.9	17,010	4,815	28.3	5,105	30.0
Machine operators, assemblers, and inspectors	7,882	2,423	30.7	2,538	32.2	7,879	2,327	29.5	2,453	31.1
Transportation and material moving occupations	4,351	1,349	31.0	1,430	32.9	4,418	1,330	30.1	1,407	31.8
Handlers, equipment cleaners, helpers, and laborers	4,686	1,183	25.2	1,266	27.0	4,713	1,158	24.6	1,245	26.4
Farming, forestry, and fishing	1,763	96	5.4	113	6.4	1,813	77	4.2	91	5.0

Industry										
Agricultural wage and salary workers	1,469	33	2.2	37	2.5	1,492	30	2.0	35	2.4
Private nonagricultural wage and salary workers	80,993	10,826	13.4	11,850	14.6	82,741	10,674	12.9	11,723	14.2
Mining	782	143	18.3	153	19.5	711	133	18.7	146	20.5
Construction	5,052	1,060	21.0	1,123	22.2	5,193	1,096	21.1	1,151	22.2
Manufacturing	20,235	4,691	23.2	5,008	24.7	20,430	4,516	22.1	4,854	23.8
Durable goods	12,005	2,969	24.7	3,162	26.3	12,170	2,875	23.6	3,095	25.4
Nondurable goods	8,231	1,722	20.9	1,846	22.4	8,260	1,641	19.9	1,759	21.3
Transportation and public utilities	5,819	1,947	33.5	2,106	36.2	6,053	2,001	33.1	2,144	35.4
Transportation	3,274	1,051	32.1	1,113	34.0	3,412	1,104	32.3	1,153	33.8
Communications and public utilities	2,545	897	35.2	993	39.0	2,640	897	34.0	992	37.6
Wholesale and retail trade	20,401	1,440	7.1	1,572	7.7	20,597	1,386	6.7	1,559	7.6
Wholesale trade	3,935	330	8.4	359	9.1	3,873	290	7.5	336	8.7
Retail trade	16,466	1,110	6.7	1,213	7.4	16,724	1,095	6.6	1,223	7.3
Finance, insurance, and real estate	6,738	158	2.3	217	3.2	6,812	178	2.6	238	3.5
Services	21,965	1,387	6.3	1,673	7.6	22,944	1,365	5.9	1,631	7.1
Government workers	16,841	6,055	36.0	7,164	42.5	17,175	6,298	36.7	7,483	43.6

*Data refer to members of a labor union or an employee association similar to a union.

†Data refer to members of a labor union or an employee association similar to a union as well as workers who report no union affiliation but whose jobs are covered by a union or an employee association contract.

Note: Data refer to the sole or principal job of full- and part-time workers. Excluded are self-employed workers whose business are incorporated although they technically qualify as wage and salary workers.

Source: U.S. Department of Labor, Bureau of Labor Statistics.

seeable future. About 70 percent of these new workers will be needed to replace retirees and dropouts and 30 percent to meet a predicted 2 percent annual growth. In broader terms, this means that the construction industry will have to attract almost 6 percent of all workers entering the labor market in 1995.

The pressing need to recruit new workers into construction is coupled with the problem of equipping these workers with the necessary skills to maintain an acceptable level of quality. For a long time, open-shop contractors were able to attract union-trained workers by promising them more hours of work per year. Today, the industry faces the anomaly of not enough union craftsmen in Massachusetts and not enough nonunion workers in Alabama! Some industry observers point to the decline in union-run apprenticeship programs, suggesting that reviving these programs would be of benefit to the industry while helping the unions to regain their dominant position. On the other hand, the growth of open-shop training programs has brought with it a new involvement on the part of management, which has always decried the long duration of the union-sponsored training program. While newer training programs have not yet begun to meet the demands of the industry, they will probably develop growing numbers of skilled workers.

In the late 1980s it was generally conceded that the union-shop contractor was suffering a wage disadvantage in comparison to the open-shop contractor. However, the spread began to narrow: there was an over 5 percent increase in hourly wages for open-shop workers as opposed to about 3 percent for union workers. (See Table 1.3 for a summary of average hours and earnings of production or nonsupervisory workers.) Fringe benefits for union workers increased this spread, but many open-shop companies improved their benefits package. Meanwhile, unions were beginning to realize that concessions in work rules and wages were necessary if they wished to survive. There are many examples of a union working with a single company to help it survive against open-shop competition. On a larger scale, the National Joint Heavy and Highway Committee began to track and target work that it could obtain with union cooperation. Members of this group have occasionally gained major reductions in hourly rates, but work rule elimination has often been sufficient to make them competitive.

Aside from the proliferation of work rules on union construction projects, the concept of "one man–one trade" has probably been the largest factor reducing union-labor productivity. Studies seem to indicate that the time it takes to perform a specific task varies little around the globe. But, a bricklayer crew forced to wait until a steel worker is found to set a steel lintel over an opening is doomed to low overall efficiency. Thus, there is some validity to the open-shop approach which operates on the principle that every worker can achieve a necessary level of competence in more than one trade. Since this concept flies in the face of traditional union apprenticeship programs, new worker training programs are necessary to achieve the goal of multitrade workers.

Construction Management Personnel

Graduation from a traditional civil engineering program or rising through the ranks based on experience have been the traditional routes for development of construction management personnel. However, as engineering moved closer to science, the management aspect of engineering education was minimized. With the exception of a few civil engineering programs which offered construction options, the engineering route to construction management was increasingly inef-

TABLE 1.3 Annual Data: Average Hours and Earnings of Production or Nonsupervisory Workers on Nonagricultural Payrolls, by Industry.

Industry	1978	1979	1980	1981	1982	1983	1984	1985	1986
Private sector									
Average weekly hours	35.8	35.7	35.3	35.2	34.8	35.0	35.2	34.9	34.8
Average hourly earnings, dollars	5.69	6.16	6.66	7.25	7.68	8.02	8.32	8.57	8.76
Average weekly earnings, dollars	203.70	219.91	235.10	255.20	267.26	280.70	292.86	299.09	304.85
Mining									
Average weekly hours	43.4	43.0	43.3	43.7	42.7	42.5	43.3	43.4	42.3
Average hourly earnings, dollars	7.67	8.49	9.17	10.04	10.77	11.28	11.63	11.98	12.45
Average weekly earnings, dollars	332.88	365.07	397.06	438.75	459.88	479.40	503.58	519.93	526.64
Construction									
Average weekly hours	36.8	37.0	37.0	36.9	36.7	37.1	37.8	37.7	37.5
Average hourly earnings, dollars	8.66	9.27	9.94	10.82	11.63	11.94	12.13	12.31	12.42
Average weekly earnings, dollars	318.69	342.99	367.78	399.26	426.82	442.97	458.51	464.09	465.75
Manufacturing									
Average weekly hours	40.4	40.2	39.7	39.8	38.9	40.1	40.7	40.5	40.7
Average hourly earnings, dollars	6.17	6.70	7.27	7.99	8.49	8.83	9.19	9.53	9.73
Average weekly earnings, dollars	249.27	269.34	288.62	318.00	330.26	354.08	374.03	385.97	396.01

Source: U.S. Department of Labor, Bureau of Labor Statistics.

fective. This led to the development of construction management programs in many universities, and a growing number of managers are coming from this new source. Meanwhile, promotion from the ranks is still viable, primarily because of the growth of training programs provided by various contractor organizations and independent consultants.

While the technological aspects of the construction process can always be improved, the industry has most often been faulted for its failures in people and money management. Advances in annual compensation for field personnel hopefully are the indicators that point to improvement in these areas. According to Personnel Administration Services, Inc., the salary for project superintendents jumped from $38,400 to $46,554 between 1985 and 1988 and for assistant superintendents from $27,600 to $32,771.

Plant and Engineering

Compared to a 2.7 percent average increase in the cost of construction machinery for 1988, increases from 3 to 10 percent were predicted for 1989. The worst-case scenario would accentuate what some researchers claim is a continuing decline in capital investment in the construction industry. This parallels a decline in public capital investment (roads, bridges, and sewage and water treatment plants) sponsored by the federal government. Together, these trends undoubtedly are contributing to poor productivity in the construction industry. However, it is difficult to quantify their impact.

Elimination of the investment tax credit has also contributed to reduced equipment ownership by construction companies. It should be pointed out, however, that the availability of rented and leased equipment is growing and may actually be making it easier for contractors to take advantage of productivity gains via a shift from manpower to machine power. Again, there are no definitive studies to quantify this, and it contradicts the concept of declining capital investment mentioned above.

As the 1980s drew to a close, construction equipment sales were strong, and there were indications that research and development expenditures were rising. Robotics received a major boost in applications ranging from excavation and grading to rebar placement to painting. How quickly these concepts can move into the workplace is anyone's guess, but the implications for cost reduction are enormous. What is needed most at this point is for contractors to tailor construction to automation rather than to tailor automation to traditional methods of construction.

Advances in construction plant and equipment continue to be made in terms of size and speed, and manufacturers continue to improve their products to gain a greater share of the market. Some contractors continue to work with their equipment suppliers in an effort to develop special equipment that would solve special problems, but manufacturers are continuing to play the lead role.

Construction Products

In a highly competitive and flat market, price has been a major concern for a contractor purchasing the products specified for a construction project. In the late 1980s metals were a major problem, with strong inflation for copper, steel, and aluminum. However, inflation in the 1990s will probably average between 5 and 6 percent, barring some unforeseen surge in construction activity. With the dollar holding its position, imports of steel and concrete may well decline, allowing domestic producers to hold and possibly gain market share. Although new products continue to flow into the marketplace, the pace seems to have slowed, probably as a result of the recession of the early 1980s and the growing trend toward litigation over unsatisfactory product performance. It is evident that the asbestos problem and the problem with some synthetic insulation materials have left their mark on all participants in the construction process.

Meanwhile, glowing predictions for prefabrication and modular construction made in the 1960s are no longer receiving much attention in the industry press. However, from prehung doors to package boilers, there is evidence that those earlier predictions have had an impact on the construction industry. In fact, 2500-metric-ton modules are not uncommon, and a number of substantial assemblies were barged from stateside plants to the North Slope oil fields. However, research into robotics may make field construction activities more economical and at the same time may have an impact on new product development.

Overall, architects and engineers seem to be more conservative in specifying products, and contractors are depending on the tried and true to help them maintain quality control on the job. However, as price pressure begins to build up in future years, the industry will again be forced to consider innovative products that are lower in cost and cheaper and easier to install.

EXTERNAL BUSINESS CLIMATE

With the possible exception of those engaged in design and build projects and speculative building, there are many external forces affecting the contractor. On the majority of his projects, the contractor is not given the opportunity to comment of the constructability of the drawings and specifications prepared by the designers. In addition, he must often function as the owner's banker, financing a high percentage of construction cost until the project is completed and accepted by the owner. This is in spite of the fact that he is also called upon to provide the owner with a variety of bonds and certificates of insurance.

Financial Requirements

Few construction companies are able to accumulate sufficient capital to finance their projects without recourse to lenders. Thus it is vital for the constructor to keep his financial house in order so that he can clearly present his position if and when he needs financial support from his banker. "High risk, high rate" is the banker's stern rule, and even the financially stable contractor will probably find that he cannot borrow at the rate of interest he is willing to pay.

Because some construction contracts call for retainage as high as 10 percent, the contractor is in reality playing the role of owner's banker in addition to building the project. Though he may lighten this burden by retaining payments due his subcontractors, he must still carry the lion's share himself. In fact, on some government work, the general contractor's payments to his subs are tightly controlled. Thus, the cost of money expended in construction, whether it is the contractor's or the banker's money, is a significant part of the cost of construction. One of the most important causes of contractor bankruptcy is failure to include the cost of money tied up in a specified project. As interest rates started to rise in early 1979, this cost had a growing impact on the contractor's ability to survive in a highly competitive market.

Control over cash flow is another important financial consideration for contractors working several projects concurrently. Delays or speedups can create large surges in demand for funds to meet payroll or equipment and materials purchases. If the contractor is without an open line of credit when this occurs, bankruptcy may be the final solution. Adding to this problem is the owner's demand that the contractor use critical path scheduling techniques over which the owner is allowed excessive control. The manipulation of noncritical activities, which may be delayed by the contractor with no influence on the final project completion date, can be useful in solving cash flow problems. However, if the owner exercises control, the contractor may be denied this opportunity with no recourse.

It is obvious that most construction companies are dependent on lenders some or all of the time. Thus, they have to be prepared to present their financial position for scrutiny on a continuous basis. Yet, there are still too many firms that make no use of business ratios as tools for internal use and for presentation to potential lenders. In part this is due to the wide variation in company operations, ranging from design/build to narrow technical specialty work. However, there is a growing number of construction consultants, large accounting firms, and associations which can offer comparative figures based on size, type of firm, and geographic area. The contractor who can present a set of business ratios, from current assets–current liabilities to return on investment, that stack up well with comparable firms is the one who will be best served by the lending agencies with which he chooses to deal.

Construction Contract Documents

On competitively bid projects, the contractor has little or no input into the documents with which he agrees to comply. It therefore behooves him to read them with care to be sure that their demands are reasonable. They include the invitation to bid or notice (by invitation on private work, publication on public), instructions to bidders, the bid or proposal form, the contract, the general and/or special conditions of contract, the technical specifications, and the drawings. All but the last-named are usually bound together and are properly called the "project manual."

Although it took almost 20 years to gain widespread acceptance, the Construction Specification Institute's standard format for construction specifications has been a boon to both those who must prepare them and those who must read them. While many consulting engineers are still resentful of what they consider to be a lack of emphasis on engineering aspects of a project, the CSI format is widely accepted for building construction and is frequently used for heavy and highway projects. Properly used, it can minimize the debate between general and specialty contractors over who is responsible for what and reduce the time it takes to locate specific information items. It is unfortunate that the CSI membership is still strongly architect and engineer oriented, with only minimal participation by contractors.

Because most public projects require "open" specifications and many private project owners opt to use them, the "or equal" specification has a long and continuing history in construction. The usual approach is to specify one or more products by brand name, followed by the expression "or approved equal." This seemingly innocuous statement has cost the industry wasted hours in argument and wasted dollars when the argument becomes a legal battle. In general, the courts have come to the conclusion that "equal" does not mean "identical" and that a substitute for the named brand must only meet the same quality and performance standards established for the named brand. But the problem continues, and many contractors are frustrated by what they consider wasted time and effort to get approval for a substitute for the named brand.

In a competitive bid situation in private work, a closed specification clearly identifying products by brand name would seem to put all bidders on an equal footing and ensure the owner the best price for a specific level of quality. However, then suppliers have a monopoly position via the closed specification, so they are unlikely to quote their lowest price. Hence the designer and owner sometimes resort to the "base bid plus alternates." Here the contractor may opt to quote on the base bid and select all or some alternates which he feels he can use to reduce cost. Again, theory is better than practice, for excessive use of alternates can muddy the bidding process and open the door to manipulation by both owner and contractor.

Since it was first copyrighted in 1911, the American Institute of Architects document "General Conditions of the Contract for Construction" (AIA Document A201) has been one of the standards of the industry. For just as long and despite numerous revisions, it has been an irritant to many contractors who see it as a vehicle for relieving the architect of his fair share of responsibility for the success of a project. The most recent edition, the 14th (1987), continues that tradition even though for many years AIA has worked on revisions with the Associated General Contractors of America.

Aside from some reorganization—insurance and bonds are now covered in the same article—and general improvement in language, some legal authorities see the 1987 edition as a retreat by architects from their traditional responsibilities on the job site. Language covering the architect's site visitation responsibility is criticized as vague, and the contractor's responsibility to notify the architect of design errors is seemingly increased. No doubt stimulated by some disastrous structural collapses attributed to the designer's failure to review shop drawings properly, the new document seems to further limit the architect's responsibility. On the positive side, the 1987 edition does seem to have reduced, or at least clarified, the contractor's warranty obligations. In addition, the contractor's position when requesting evidence of the owner's financial capacity is strengthened.

Risk Analysis

On the face of it, the contractor appears to be the major risk bearer on a construction project. At the request of the owner he must provide an assortment of bonds which are issued solely to protect the owner. In addition, the contract documents tell him specifically what insurance to carry in addition to that required under the law. Finally, when the contractor begins to bill the owner for services provided, his payments are subject to retainage of as much as 10 percent and they are often late.

Bonding. "Bondability equals capability" was once a guide to owners seeking qualified contractors for their construction projects. However, there have been periods when this statement was of dubious value. In the past there were surety companies who moved into the construction bond market on the assumption that it was a place to pick up some easy money. The result, due to lack of diligence on the part of some sureties, was that unqualified contractors found it easy to obtain bonding. As we move into the 1990s, it would appear that the reverse may be true. Sureties willing to provide bonding are limited in number, and their standards are so rigid that some capable contractors find it difficult to obtain bonds. This seems to be particularly true of subcontractors.

In late 1988 there were over 100 companies underwriting surety bonds in the United States. Major companies operated in all 50 states, but there were a few regional carriers located primarily in the midwest. Projects involving public funds almost universally require bid and performance bonds, and they are being used increasingly on private projects. Where required from the general contractor, it is natural that any subcontractors on the job will be asked to provide similar protection to the general. To the contractor whose financial house is in order, bonding is probably not a serious problem. But, as use of bonds increases, some contractors are finding it difficult to obtain acceptance by a surety company. This has led to the use of individual or personal sureties, letters of credit, certificates of deposit, and occasionally cash. The bonding industry, which had not made a profit from 1983 to 1989, appeared to be moving into a stronger position in 1989, and there is some indication that it will be better able to meet the needs of both small and large contractors in the 1990s.

Unlike insurance, which sets premiums based on statistical analysis of potential losses, bonds are issued on the assumption that the surety can draw on unexpended owner funds and the assets of the contractor should it be called into action. In effect, the bond is a three-party contract between the owner, the contractor, and the surety. Thus, bond costs have been quite reasonable in the past. However, bonding went through some serious troubles in the late 1980s, and prices have begun to rise. Contractors who historically have obtained bonding easily are going to find it more difficult if they suddenly seek bonding for jobs that are larger than they typically handle or in fields where their experience is limited.

The performance bond is the owner's basic protection against contractor failure to perform in accordance with the contract documents. When it goes into effect, the surety takes over the project and seeks to complete it using unexpended owner funds and any contractor assets it can recover. While this might mean the award of a new contract to a new firm, there are occasions when the surety may wish to keep the original contractor on the job when his difficulties are the result of forces beyond his control. However, if the contractor is incompetent or dishonest, it is the surety's responsibility to seek out all his assets and apply them to the project as necessary to bring it to a successful conclusion.

In addition to the performance bond, most surety companies provide bid bonds for their contractor clients at a nominal fee in addition to the performance bond fee. The bid bond is usually written for a specified amount and is designed to compensate the owner for the difference between the low bid and the next-to-low bidder in the event that the low-bid contractor refuses to sign. In lieu of the bid bond, a certified check or other security may be acceptable to the owner in the range of 2 to 20 percent of the anticipated cost of construction. The bid bond or deposit is obviously voided when the low bidder signs a contract.

The subcontractor bond, under which the surety company protects the general contractor against default by the various subcontractors, is also a typical part of most single contract construction projects. In addition, material and labor bonds are often required to protect the project from liens filed by unpaid suppliers or workers. There are also a number of special-purpose bonds to meet a variety of problems encountered in the industry.

Construction Insurance. The contractor's insurance requirements are both mandatory and optional. First, he must comply with the law which requires that he provide worker's compensation and other types of insurance. Second, he must comply with the requirements of the contract for a particular project. Finally, he must decide on further insurance needs as the result of a thorough risk analysis of his position on each project. Legal insurance requirements serve to protect the construction worker; contractual requirements protect the owner; and contractor-determined ones fill the gaps left by the other two. As with bonds, contractors faced serious increases in insurance costs in the early 1980s. However, with the exception of worker's compensation, costs appeared to be stabilizing in early 1989.

In the early 1900s an employee injured on the job was at the mercy of his employer. Often, the employer invoked the well-established doctrines of "assumed risk," "contributory negligence," and the "fellow servant rule" to avoid financial responsibility. Workers were expected to understand and assume the risks of the workplace, were assumed to have contributed to their injury because of negligence, and, all else failing, the fault for accidents was attributed to fellow workers. With the coming of worker's compensation laws, that picture changed rapidly. Now the construction worker is covered both on and off the job, on the scaffold or at the company picnic. However, some states are comparatively stingy when compared to others where benefits are extremely generous.

There is wide variety in the administration of the various state laws covering worker's compensation. Some are entirely state operated, while others offer the use of private sureties and sometimes self-insurance. Most of these programs include an experience-rating approach that allows the contractor with a good safety record to reduce his premiums. All are based on a classification system that sets premiums per $100 of payroll based on the risk assigned to each construction job. Thus, while worker's compensation forces the employer to take care of the injured workman, it also provides incentive for establishing good on-the-job safety practice and careful classification of workers by risk.

In addition to worker's compensation and employer's liability, contractors are required to carry insurance that covers premises and operations, products and completed operations, property damage, automobiles, and a variety of other risks as part of their contractual obligation to the owner. What was once known as the comprehensive general liability policy is less common, and risks tend to be individually identified with specific premiums assigned. Among the newer approaches to construction insurance is the formation of risk-retention groups (RRGs), which self-insure. This approach may wane as insurance rates stabilize, but some of these groups have been financially successful. Another approach is the use of risk-purchasing groups (RPGs), which are in effect insurance purchasing coops seeking lower rates through group action. A third approach is the coordinated insurance package required for a specific construction project.

Whatever their approach to insurance, it behooves contractors to keep good records, both to aid the surety in providing claim defense and to reduce insurance costs to a minimum. Faster incident reporting, well-kept job logs, and awareness of insurance company information needs are all important. Safety and loss prevention services provided by the insurer are vitally important to the smaller contractor and should play an integral role in selection of an insurance provider.

INTERNAL BUSINESS CLIMATE

Ease of entry and initial low capital requirements lead to a large number of construction firms, with over three-quarters operating as sole proprietorships. Partnerships account for less than 5 percent and corporations about 20 percent of all firms. While the changing economic climate has an impact on corporations and partnerships, its biggest impact is felt by the many small proprietorships in the industry. A recession will often wipe out the smaller firms, not because they are proprietorships, but rather because they have failed to set up a good financial system to warn them of impending cash flow problems. There is more truth than humor in the comment, "Look at old Charlie smile. He's been broke for 6 months and doesn't even know it!" With the passage of the Tax Reform Act of 1986, a few contractors have made use of the "S Corporation." Under this form of business organization a small number of shareholders pay taxes earned by the corporation rather than have both corporate and dividend income taxed. However, contractors should be wary of the "S Corporation" because it is not always advantageous.

Accounting

Since loss of financial control is a major factor in contractor failures, a good accounting system is mandatory. If the size of the firm does not warrant the full-time employment of a competent accountant, it is advisable to retain a consulting firm to handle the chore on a weekly or monthly basis. Since contractors are almost continuously spending money well in advance of expected income from a project, they must have a current picture of their financial position in order to determine whether an additional project can be financed. More work, even though profitably priced, may ultimately create a fatal cash flow weakness due to delays in payment from other projects or changes in the planned pace of work on existing or new projects. Finally, the contractor must be able to present his financial statement to surety companies, banks, and frequently owners to obtain necessary bonds, loans, or prequalification for bidding a new project.

Many small contractors find that they can live with cash or accrual methods of accounting. However, these methods may not present a true and current picture of the firm's financial position so they must be used with caution. Larger contractors tend to use the completed contract or percentage-of-completion of contract approaches. Since these contractors often work on projects with a duration of a year or more, other methods of accounting are unsatisfactory. The Internal Revenue Service has often complained that some contractors manipulate the completed contract accounting system, and the 1988 Tax Act reflects this concern. While contractor accounting methods are still being debated in the Congress, indications are that contractors' taxes will rise and that their costs for accounting costs may well double or triple unless new legislation eases the burden.

The most important consideration in setting up a construction firm's accounting system is its ability to provide immediate availability of cost data that accurately reflect events on the construction site. The second most important consideration is that the system must present current information in a format that lends itself to the preparation of cash flow plans. Finally, the cost accounting system must be able to present the contractor's financial position in a format easily understood by those who have a legitimate need to evaluate the firm's financial position.

With the rapid developments in the computer industry, particularly the microcomputer, there has come a rapid rise in the number of contractors who use computerized accounting systems. Most of these, even for smaller firms, are capable of handling payroll and purchasing as well as the broad range of other accounting functions. This has led some firms to integrate, via the computer, their entire gamut of activities—estimating, scheduling, field cost accounting, and others—with their central accounting system.

Cost Engineering

Owners and designers tend to think of cost engineering as the private domain of the constructor. Only recently have they begun to realize that they too play an important role in the game of cost containment. The owner who is slow to make decisions and quick to make changes can destroy the best efforts of the contractor to control project costs. Similarly, the designer who creates an impossible detail or specifies a product no longer on the market can have the same effect. Thus, while the contractor is an unlikely candidate for contributions to the esthetics of a church or school, most designers and some owners are beginning to seek out his advice on design details and cost. Unfortunately, in the competitive bid situation, this is seldom possible and an adversary relationship is often created.

Whatever his problems with the owner and designer in terms of their understanding of cost engineering, it is the responsibility of the contractor to view jointly the topics of cost planning and cost control—to cost engineer the project! First, based on his estimate, the constructor must distribute his costs across the life of the project, thus establishing the budget. Then, using a well-planned system of field cost accounting codes, he must compare cost data from the site with the budget in a timely manner. It is vital that these comparisons occur frequently enough to ensure that no project activity is allowed to run over budget so long that there is no time left to seek correction. It is important to remember that the job cost control system is an information tool that helps the manager control the project. If the system does not get the needed information to him soon enough, it becomes nothing more than another history of project failure.

At the heart of cost engineering is a well-designed field cost accounting code. If it is too complex, information will be misplaced, distorted, or never supplied. If it is too simple, micro problems may be concealed by macro data. For the small firm, codes should be simple enough that most workers can become comfortable with them and regularly assign their work time to a specific code. For larger firms, the same rule should generally apply, but the availability of job site payroll staff to check worker input may allow a more complex code.

Cost engineering is based on a project budget, which, in turn, is based on the project estimate; thus it is important that cost engineering perform another function besides project control. Good cost engineering should be a constant source of current information about field costs and this information should be fed back to the estimating department. Changes in field cost may reflect changes in methodology, crew makeup, or use of new equipment or materials. The system should thus be designed to contribute to more accurate estimating on a continuing basis.

Some of the difficulty with cost engineering in the past can probably be laid at the door of union labor. Management had, in essence, negotiated away its right to manage in the area of methodology, crew size, and crew composition. Thus, too often, mediocrity has been the norm. Now, with the rise of the open-shop movement, there appears to be a renewed interest in cost engineering and accompanying scientific production studies in an effort to set more realistic productivity goals. At least at the national level, and in some locals in economically distressed areas, the unions seem willing to cooperate.

Taxes

The Internal Revenue Service (IRS) is an intimate acquaintance of most construction firms. It exercises some degree of control over the contractor's accounting methods and at the same time has much to say about his depreciation programs for fixed assets and machinery. For the contractor using the completed contract method of accounting, there have been numerous "zigs and zags," both in terms of the tax laws and the way the IRS interpreted them during the 1980s. The investment tax credit has also become a thing of the past and no longer provides an incentive for contractors to purchase new equipment.

While the IRS exerts similar control over all industries, the construction industry becomes a special case because of its inability to exercise close control over the flow of money, both in and out. It is also subject to the vagaries of weather and widely varying site conditions. Thus, it is only on completion of the contract that a firm begins to calculate project profits. Percentage-of-completion accounting is beset by problems. For example, although a project may be half completed physically, the contractor has almost certainly not been paid half of the bid price because of retainage, slow pay, and disputes over change orders.

On the state and local level, the contractor is often the victim of taxation in the guise of registration fees and a variety of charges which are basically discriminatory because they do not apply to other industries. While potential clients might appreciate a professional contractor licensing law, few states offer such a program, and many that do are more interested in collecting fees than in establishing contractor competence. Companies must also deal with the problems of sales tax on construction materials, fuel, and utility services. These vary widely, and exemptions for public projects need to be determined.

Overhead

For some contractors, overhead is a nebulous item that is often felt but seldom seen and measured. This should not be so because combined job and company overhead can represent as much as 20 percent of sales volume. The prudent contractor can reduce this figure, sometimes to as little as 5 percent, but if it is not included in the contract price, reduced profits are the result. One of the most elusive of overhead costs is the cost of money invested in a particular project. Whatever method of financing a firm chooses to use—bank loan, line of credit, or company capital—the cost of the money required to meet payroll and materials costs not covered by owner payments must be calculated and charged to the job.

Job overhead, as defined by the Associated General Contractors (AGC) of

America's "Job Overhead Summary," is represented by a lengthy list, the contents of which are obviously influenced by the particular character of each project. In fact, the AGC list implies a sophistication in the assignment of overhead items to each specific job that is seldom displayed by the small contractor. However, it is logical to assume that small projects often require more overhead than large on a percentage basis, that high-rise projects demand more expenditure on safety than one-story jobs, that a job 500 miles from home will entail higher phone bills and travel costs than one across town, and that winter work will necessitate weather protection costs that may be nonexistent for summer work. Thus, job overhead needs to be carefully analyzed for each particular project and cannot be charged as a constant percent of total bid costs.

General office overhead is another area where contractors need to exercise good judgment. A cost plus contract under which the client has access to the contractor's records will consume a larger volume of office staff time than will a typical fixed price contract. Similarly, negotiated contracts need to be evaluated in terms of the time key personnel will have to spend in bringing them to fruition. Finally, each competitive bid contract that is won must bear its fair share of the costs for those lost.

While the benefits of overhead costs are often difficult to analyze, it is obvious that the stingy firm may be hurting itself as much as the spendthrift firm. On the job site there is a minimum level of spending on safety below which insurance and lost time costs will mushroom—not to mention loss of reputation. In the office there is a similar minimum in terms of furniture, business machines, and decor. A bright and cheerful office with adequate equipment creates a climate of success that is as impressive to visitors as it is to employees. It is a wise contractor who recognizes that it is often better to subcontract work which requires a heavy capital investment and which will burden the firm's overhead account for years. Also, the retention of an accounting service might avoid a major investment in business machines.

Profit

Too often in the construction industry, profit is what is left when all the bills are paid. Unfortunately, the busy contractor is in the position of never having all the bills paid and thus is subject to "delayed-action" failure that may come when his work volumes give him every indication of being highly successful. The notoriously low profit margin under which most contractors work is probably more often due to the failure to set profit goals than to the obviously rigorous competition in the marketplace.

The real measure of a company's success is return on investment (ROI) (see Fig. 1.1). A good ROI can be achieved at one extreme by doing a relatively small amount of work at very high profit on sales. At the other extreme the contractor can rely on capital turnover as a multiplier for relatively low profit on sales. Neither strategy is without risk in what is already a risky business. The contractor seeking high profit on sales is unlikely to be the low bidder in competitive bid situations, and unless he has an outstanding performance record, he is likely to be out-negotiated in a negotiated bidding situation. Similarly, the firm that undertakes projects at a low profit on sales may find that it requires so much work to achieve a desirable ROI that it is in danger of losing control.

Return on Investment Flow Chart

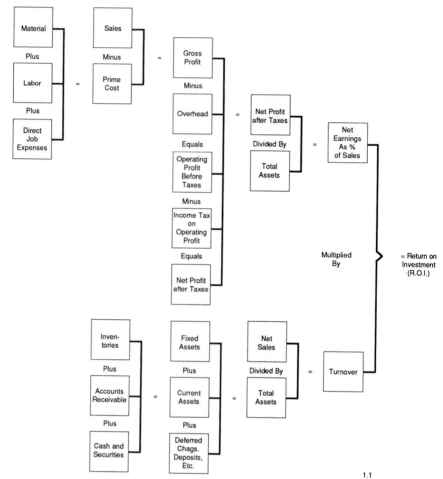

FIGURE 1.1   Flowchart for calculating return on investment (ROI). (*National Electrical Contractors Association.*)

In the early 1980s a Dun & Bradstreet, Inc., report showed a median profit on sales of 2.66 percent for a group of over 1000 contractors (Table 1.4). The median sales to net worth (turnover of equity) ratio for this same group was 6.63, and the median profit on net worth was 18.89. The middle 50 percent of this group had a range of net profit on sales from 5.44 to 1.25, sales to net worth from 11.23 to 3.18, and profit on net worth from 31.67 to 9.20. In the 1984–1985 period, Dun & Bradstreet (Table 1.5) reported a gross margin of 43.19 percent for all industry as a whole. This compares to the following figures for the construction industry:

	Corporations	Partnerships	Proprietorships
All contractors	21.33	25.89	51.32
General building contractors	15.24	17.60	45.37
Heavy contractors	21.58	—	—
Specialty contractors	28.24	43.12	55.38

TABLE 1.4 Range of Selected Business Ratios for a Large Sample of Contractors in 1980

Ratios	Upper quartile	Median	Low quartile
Net profits over sales (net margin)*	5.44	2.66	1.25
Sales over net worth (turns of equity)*	11.33	6.63	3.18
Profits over net worth (return on equity)*	31.97	18.89	9.2
Profit over working capital	48.49	27.28	11.88
Sales over working capital	17.84	9.4	4.81
Current assets over current liabilities*	2.53	1.58	1.28
Fixed assets over net worth	40.8	19	8.6
Current debt over net worth	214.5	101.8	39.7
Funded debt over working capital*	67.9	26.6	8.5
Total debt over net worth	241.1	119.3	52.2

*Indicates vital ratios.
Source: The Dun & Bradstreet Corporation.

While these figures do not readily translate to profit on sales or return on net worth, they do give some credibility to the assumption that smaller contractors, i.e., partnerships and proprietorships, expect larger profits than those common to corporations (Table 1.5). A 1987 study of 255 member firms of the Sheet Metal and Air Conditioning Contractors' National Association produced average net profits before taxes of 3.88 percent on sales and net profit to net worth of 22.9 percent. Contractors wishing to set viable profit goals would be well advised to study data available from their trade organizations, industry consultants, and accounting firms.

Construction industry profits should include a reasonable markup on labor and material plus other normal overhead costs of doing business plus a markup determined by the specific risks the contractor must take to complete the project. In simple terms, a bridge across the Mississippi should return a greater percentage of profit than a conventional residence. Contractors must set realistic profit goals and attempt to achieve them if the industry is to live down the widely held belief that "by its nature" construction is a low-profit operation. Owners, architects, and engineers must recognize that the contractor working on a project priced to give a reasonable profit is the contractor most likely to deliver a quality project on the scheduled completion date.

Business Failure

Because it is a business that is easy to enter, the construction industry is plagued with operators who, while technically qualified, do not have the management

TABLE 1.5 Selected Costs and Operating Expenses for Contractors Operating as Partnerships, Proprietorships, and Corporations (Fiscal Year July 1984–June 1985)

Partnerships[a]

Industry	Number of returns filed	Selected costs					Selected operating expenses							
		Cost of goods sold, %	Profits on business receipts, %	Merchandise purchased, %	Labor and supplies, %	Gross margin, %	Salaries and wages, %	Payments to partners, %	Rent, %	Interest, %	Taxes, %	Bad debts, %	Repairs, %	Depreciation and depletion, %
All industries	1,643,581	56.81	31.53	24.65	43.19	8.96	2.36	2.37	7.99	2.10	0.21	0.72	0.09	(1.10)
Construction	64,607	74.11	23.15	50.76	25.89	3.61	1.75	0.51	2.05	0.96	0.05	0.43	0.00	9.45
General contractors	25,574	82.40	19.47	61.56	17.60	2.04	1.59	0.42	2.37	0.74	0.04	0.22	0.00	7.07
Special trade contractors	39,001	56.88	31.07	28.07	43.12	6.96	2.09	0.72	1.38	1.44	0.06	0.87	0.00	14.22

Proprietorships[a]

Industry	Number of returns filed	Selected costs				Selected operating expenses					
		Cost of goods sold, %	Other business deductions, %	Labor, %	Gross margin, %	Salaries and wages, %	Rent, %	Interest, %	Bad debts, %	Depreciation and depletion, %	Profits on business receipts, %
All industries	11,262,390	44.55	20.72	2.52	55.45	6.72	2.77	2.14	0.10	4.82	13.71
Construction	1,386,099	48.68	16.58	7.64	51.32	7.62	0.97	1.73	0.05	3.97	15.27
General contractors and operative builders	388,944	54.63	16.57	7.19	45.37	5.75	0.59	2.48	0.08	3.79	12.57
Special trade contractors	992,092	44.62	16.58	7.96	55.38	8.93	1.22	1.21	0.03	4.10	17.09
Plumbing, heating, and air conditioning	95,466	59.49	12.33	7.02	40.51	7.15	0.67	0.86	0.05	3.13	11.20
Painting, paperhanging, and decorating	180,209	39.44	16.40	7.66	60.56	9.13	1.21	0.70	0.04	3.14	22.50
Electrical work	93,695	51.07	15.06	4.22	48.93	8.72	0.75	1.38	0.01	3.75	12.85
Masonry, stonework, tile setting, and plastering	71,408	40.21	13.42	8.74	59.79	19.37	1.95	1.24	0.01	3.46	15.14
Carpentering & flooring	312,842	38.43	15.73	8.52	61.57	3.00	1.15	0.97	0.00	3.95	29.25

Corporations[†]

Industry	Number of returns filed	Cost of sales, %	Gross margin, %	Compensation of officers, %	Rent paid on business property, %	Selected operating expenses						
						Repairs, %	Bad debts, %	Interest paid, %	Taxes paid, %	Amortization, depreciation and depletion, %	Advertising, %	Pension and other employee benefit plans, %
All industries	3,170,743	67.53	32.47	2.26	1.72	1.10	0.49	7.71	2.76	4.00	1.18	1.69
Contract construction	306,906	78.67	21.33	3.47	0.85	0.53	0.23	1.83	2.24	2.22	0.30	1.07
General building contractors and operative builders	126,870	84.76	15.24	2.75	0.60	0.31	0.17	2.37	1.49	1.49	0.33	0.68
Heavy construction contractors	19,021	78.42	21.58	2.36	1.16	1.07	0.21	2.15	2.22	4.24	0.11	1.44
Special trade contractors	161,015	71.76	28.24	4.76	1.02	0.56	0.31	1.08	3.10	2.22	0.35	1.37

*The data are average operating ratios for 108 lines of business. The ratio represents a percentage of business receipts (sales). All figures were derived from representative samples of the total of all federal income tax returns filed for 1984–1985 by partnerships and proprietorships.

[†]The operating ratios for 191 lines of business have been derived to provide a guide as to the average amount spent by corporations for these items. They represent a percentage of business receipts as reported by a representative sample of the total of all federal income tax returns filed for 1984.

Source: The Dun & Bradstreet Corporation.

skills required to keep them in business through downturns in the economic cycle. And even well-managed companies may founder as a result of an unanticipated spell of bad weather, an unanticipated strike, poor soil conditions discovered after the job begins, or any one of hundreds of other risk factors that are part and parcel of this unique business. Thus, it is not surprising that the construction industry has a very high failure rate. However, it is interesting to note that between 1978 and 1986, the construction industry failure rate (number of failures per 10,000 firms) exceeded the average rate for all businesses only in 1984. Still, in the mid 1980s, construction failure rates were the highest since the depression in the 1930s (see Figs 1.2 to 1.4).

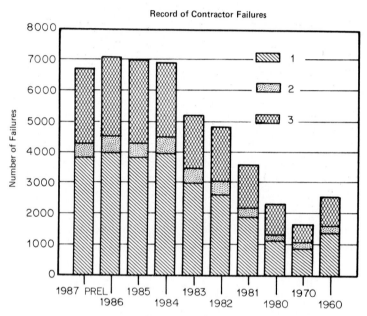

FIGURE 1.2 Number of construction company failures in selected years. (1) General contractors and operative builders; (2) contractors other than building; (3) specialty trade contractors. (*Dun & Bradstreet.*)

According to Dun & Bradstreet, construction failures peaked out at 7109 in 1986 with a failure rate of 108 per 10,000 firms. Total liabilities were $1.783 billion, less than the $2.003 billion for 1985 when the failure rate was 109. In terms of the number of failures, 1984 was the peak year at 112, but liabilities were only $1.651 billion. There are many factors contributing to this sorry record, but these facts clearly point out that the construction industry has a delayed response to economic downturns, in this case the recession starting in late 1980. Failure figures in 1987 and 1988 appeared to be trending down, leading optimists to predict that the industry was returning to "normal." Others point out that changes in the bankruptcy laws may have had some impact on the industry failure record, making it easier for firms to close down and reopen as a new venture. According to Dun & Bradstreet 33,079 new firms appeared on the scene in 1987. This number

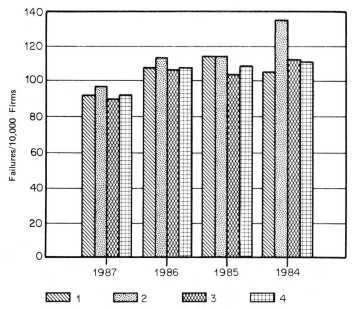

FIGURE 1.3 Construction company failure rate per 10,000 firms. (1) General contractors and operative builders; (2) contractors other than building; (3) specialty trade contractors; (4) all contractors. (*Dun & Bradstreet.*)

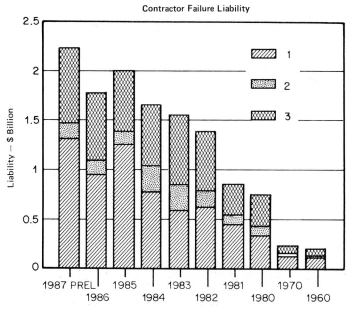

FIGURE 1.4 Contractor failure in billions of dollars. (1) General contractors and operative builders; (2) contractors other than building; (3) specialty trade contractors. (*Dun & Bradstreet.*)

declined to 31,246 in 1988. In both years specialty contractors constituted more than half of the new firms.

The reasons for construction company failures are many, but, contrary to the "bad guy" image portrayed by television, fraud and negligence are generally not as prevalent in construction as in many other businesses (see Table 1.6). In fact, just over half of all failures appear to be caused by poor profits. Other important causes for failure include lack of management skill, attempts to build volume in new areas of construction without the necessary technical competence, and slow pay on the part of clients.

CLIENT INTERFACE

Many construction companies are formed as the result of close personal relationships developed between clients and practitioners on a specific project. However, once a company is formed, the press of daily business tends to loosen these bonds as the firm seeks new avenues for growth. Although some contractors have shown a natural talent for marketing their services, it is only in recent years that the industry has begun to pay attention to the subject of marketing in a formal way. The four elements of a marketing program include planning, promotion (sales), pricing, and successful execution of the procured project. The benefits of a well-planned market program include the ability to

1. Control peaks and valleys in the firm's work load
2. Direct growth in the most profitable types of work
3. Reduce competition by being placed on limited bid lists or negotiating contracts
4. Develop a reputation for performance over price
5. Provide challenges and opportunities for employees
6. Diversify to promote growth or maintain a stable volume of work
7. Attract capable new employees as needed

Successful marketing demands a strong commitment backed by a willingness to spend the necessary time and money to make it work. Elements of the marketing program will range from personal contact and letters to a complete range of brochures, newsletters, regular phone calls, and visits to targeted contacts that can either be considered potential customers or can lead to customers. Contacts with the local press and participation in related civic activities are also important in helping the company draw attention to itself.

Project Procurement

The fixed price competitive bid has been the traditional approach to project procurement, both in public and private work. Working from a detailed estimate of costs based on a complete set of working drawings and specifications provided by the client, the contractor must decide to add either a fair profit or a profit he thinks will make him low bidder on a specific project with a known group of competitors. When there are few projects coming on the market, the list of

TABLE 1.6 Causes of Business Failures

	Agriculture, forestry, and fishing	Mining	Construction	Manufacturing	Transportation and public utilities	Wholesale trade	Retail trade	Finance, insurance, and real estate	Services	Total
Neglect causes	2.2%	0.8%	1.9%	1.9%	1.6%	2.0%	2.0%	1.1%	1.1%	1.6%
Bad habits	19.0	20.0	27.4	33.0	29.8	33.6	19.8	21.4	25.9	25.4
Business conflicts	3.6	60.0	10.7	18.3	21.6	25.6	15.0	28.7	13.6	15.1
Family problems	7.1	0.0	9.2	7.3	10.8	4.7	8.5	10.7	10.9	8.8
Lack of interest	52.4	0.0	19.8	24.4	16.2	11.6	22.3	14.3	14.3	21.0
Marital problems	4.8	0.0	11.5	6.1	8.1	10.5	10.9	7.1	9.7	9.4
Occupational conflicts	3.6	0.0	2.3	2.4	2.7	3.5	8.5	7.1	8.5	5.9
Poor health	9.5	20.0	19.1	8.5	10.8	10.5	15.0	10.7	17.1	14.4
Disaster causes	0.2%	0.2%	0.4%	0.6%	0.3%	0.6%	0.6%	0.2%	0.2%	0.4%
Act of God	50.0	0.0	11.5	14.3	42.8	4.2	8.2	0.0	20.9	13.9
Burglary	0.0	0.0	0.0	0.0	0.0	4.2	5.5	0.0	2.3	2.8
Employee fraud	0.0	0.0	7.7	3.6	14.3	0.0	4.1	0.0	2.3	3.7
Fire	25.0	0.0	11.5	28.6	14.3	29.2	50.7	16.7	42.0	35.6
Death of owner	25.0	100.0	69.3	53.5	28.6	58.2	31.5	83.3	30.2	43.1
Strike	0.0	0.0	0.0	0.0	0.0	4.2	0.0	0.0	2.3	0.9
Fraud causes	0.1%	0.5%	0.2%	0.6%	0.4%	0.5%	0.4%	1.0%	0.1%	0.3%
Embezzlement	0.0	33.4	27.4	15.4	30.0	22.7	13.5	28.0	21.4	20.0
False agreement	0.0	33.3	0.0	19.2	10.0	4.5	11.5	8.0	10.7	10.6
False statement	0.0	33.3	9.1	11.5	10.0	0.0	5.8	4.0	10.7	7.2
Irregular disposal of assets	100.0	-	27.3	30.9	40.0	31.9	30.8	44.0	35.8	33.9
Misleading name	0.0	0.0	27.3	11.5	10.0	13.6	5.8	8.0	10.7	10.0
Premeditated overbuy	0.0	0.0	9.1	11.5	0.0	27.3	32.6	8.0	10.7	18.3
Economic factors causes	83.3%	85.0%	72.8%	67.7%	70.2%	70.7%	71.2%	68.1%	71.4%	71.7%
Insufficient profits	71.1	76.2	73.5	74.2	71.7	72.1	71.1	73.1	79.9	75.2
High interest rates	4.7	0.2	0.4	0.2	0.4	0.2	0.1	0.5	1.3	1.0
Loss of market	2.8	11.9	7.4	7.8	5.9	7.8	5.9	9.3	4.0	5.5
No consumer spending	11.1	4.3	9.7	5.2	12.0	6.0	13.3	9.7	7.6	9.3
No future	10.3	7.4	9.0	12.6	10.0	13.9	9.6	7.4	7.2	9.0

TABLE 1.6 Causes of Business Failures (*Continued*)

	Agriculture, forestry, and fishing	Mining	Construction	Manufacturing	Transportation and public utilities	Wholesale trade	Retail trade	Finance, insurance, and real estate	Services	Total
Experience causes	12.6%	10.5%	19.4%	18.4%	19.8%	17.1%	20.1%	14.6%	23.0%	20.3%
Incompetence	63.0	32.3	47.1	46.1	50.6	41.8	44.6	41.5	33.1	39.7
Lack of line experience	3.0	12.3	6.7	11.2	10.1	12.0	14.2	14.2	13.3	11.8
Lack of managerial experience	14.8	33.9	18.8	12.3	17.1	12.3	16.6	12.9	9.3	12.6
Unbalanced experience	19.2	21.5	27.4	30.4	22.2	33.9	24.6	31.4	44.3	35.9
Sales causes	5.5%	6.6%	11.9%	10.4%	12.1%	10.2%	13.0%	8.3%	11.6%	11.1%
Competitively weak	8.6	2.4	20.4	15.8	26.1	17.8	24.5	17.5	12.4	17.3
Economic decline	49.8	73.2	33.3	21.8	29.8	26.2	23.6	30.3	28.2	28.2
Inadequate sales	41.6	24.4	46.0	60.0	42.2	53.2	47.8	52.2	58.8	52.9
Inventory difficulties	0.0	0.0	0.0	2.2	1.5	2.3	1.6	0.0	0.2	0.8
Poor location	0.0	0.0	0.3	0.2	0.4	0.5	2.5	0.0	0.4	0.8
Expenses causes	5.3%	3.5%	6.0%	6.4%	6.3%	5.6%	5.8%	5.5%	10.6%	8.1%
Burdensome institutional debt	78.0	31.8	34.4	53.3	35.5	46.9	47.5	46.8	49.8	46.4
Heavy operating expenses	22.0	68.2	65.6	46.7	64.5	53.1	52.5	53.2	50.2	53.6
Customer causes	0.1%	0.0%	0.8%	0.8%	0.7%	0.7%	0.3%	0.2%	0.4%	0.4%
Receivables difficulties	25.0	0.0	80.8	66.7	53.3	89.7	28.2	75.0	28.2	52.7
Too few customers	75.0	0.0	19.2	33.3	46.7	10.3	71.8	25.0	71.8	47.3
Assets causes	1.2%	0.0%	0.2%	0.2%	0.2%	0.2%	0.3%	0.2%	0.1%	0.2%
Excessive fixed assets	6.7	0.0	8.3	33.3	25.0	25.0	8.8	60.0	7.4	12.5
Overexpansion	93.3	0.0	91.7	66.7	75.0	75.0	91.2	40.0	92.6	87.5
Capital causes	0.4%	0.3%	0.6%	0.6%	0.6%	0.5%	0.7%	0.5%	0.2%	0.5%
Burdensome contracts	12.5	50.0	33.3	22.2	15.4	8.7	14.0	50.0	8.5	17.6
Excessive withdrawals	68.7	0.0	25.6	22.2	15.4	39.1	34.9	25.0	39.0	33.8
Inadequate start capacity	18.8	50.0	41.1	55.6	69.2	52.2	51.1	25.0	52.5	48.6

*Due to the fact that some failures are attributed to a combination of causes, the total of the major categories exceeds 100.0%. The individual major category total was used to achieve the percents in the minor categories.

Source: The Dun & Bradstreet Corporation.

bidders tend to become long. In the recession of the early 1980s, it was not un-common to find a list of 30 or more bidders seeking a half million dollar job. In these situations the low bidder was either the one who had made the biggest mis-take in his estimate or the owner who was most desperately trying to keep the company active while waiting for better times to come. Conversely, when too many competitive bid projects are on the market in a limited area, contractors will be tempted to bid with high profit margins because competition will be lim-ited to the capacity of local firms. To avoid these situations, owners of private projects often limit bidding to a selected group, and in public work pre-qualification of bidders is often required to ensure that firms have the technical competence and the financial stability to handle the work.

While the fixed price competitive bid approach is still widely used, there has been a proliferation of different approaches. They range from direct negotiation between owner and contractor to the use by the owner of a construction man-agement firm that oversees both design and construction as the direct represen-tative of the owner and that has the responsibility for delivering a project on bud-get and on time. The design/build concept had its beginnings in the United States around the turn of the century. It continues to flourish and usually involves a single firm with both design and construction talent working with an owner to establish a budget-constrained design under which construction can begin as spe-cific design packages are completed. Often known as fast-track construction, the system can shorten project delivery time and is particularly effective in periods of high inflation or when quick project completion is required to meet competitive market requirements. Construction is usually on a cost plus basis and sometimes includes shared savings when the design and build firm can produce a quality project below the estimated budget.

The project management system of project delivery was espoused by the Gen-eral Services Administration in the 1960s and continues to be used even though the GSA for a time abandoned it. Essentially, the project management firm func-tions as the owner's representative and in its broadest application is retained be-fore design firms are selected. The construction manager (CM) then controls de-sign to ensure conformity to an established budget and to ready design segments that can be put out for competitive bid as soon as they are completed. This es-sentially puts the CM in the role of the general contractor as far as construction is concerned and allows for fast tracking.

In recent years more sophisticated owners have been actively seeking project delivery systems which will ensure them the best quality for the least dollar ex-pended. Contractors will, in these circumstances, be negotiating with the owner under the owner's ground rules rather than the traditional ground rules of the past. In fact, some owners are tending toward bringing greater responsibility for construction execution to their architectural and engineering firms. Overall, today's contractor will find the project procurement process becoming much more complex than in the past, and it behooves him to study new concepts as they appear in the literature.

Contract Administration

Once a contract has been signed, the construction firm must set basic goals and policies for the execution of the work in accordance with the contract documents. This implies full understanding and agreement from top management down to the lowest management level in the field. If the management team in the field is not in full accord with the administrative goals and policies established to meet contract conditions, a dissatisfied client is the inevitable result. The field superintendent who is not fully briefed cannot be expected to communicate properly with his project chief in the home office and may, unknowingly, get a project so thoroughly fouled up that no amount of remedial action can bring it back on budget and schedule.

There is growing evidence that the mechanical details of project administration can be far less important than the integration of involved personnel into a smoothly working team with common goals that are clear to all. This means that regular meetings with home office personnel, field personnel, and owner representatives need to be scheduled frequently enough so that good personal relationships are developed and minor problems do not fester and create adversarial relationships. The computer has made the mechanical administration of the contract easier, but it can never replace the give and take of face-to-face contact between project participants who must resolve their understandable differences in an equitable manner.

Changes in Contract Conditions

The perfect set of construction documents has yet to be prepared, and the owner whose mind is completely made up is yet to be discovered. Similarly, the construction firm that can develop a perfect production plan and schedule in spite of the vagaries inherent in a unique project remains unknown. Thus, it is inevitable that there will be change orders and schedule adjustments during the course of the project that will result in claims from both the owner and the contractor. For the contractor who has priced his work based on a careful and complete estimate and plans the work on a prudent schedule, these problems can usually be resolved in a reasonable manner. For the contractor living with a careless bid and an unrealistic schedule, there is the danger that changes will result in a further erosion of potential profit.

Adding to the normal incidence of unavoidable problems are the owner and his design team who go into the project with unreasonable expectations. It is no secret that some owners commit themselves to contracts with which they cannot comfortably live and are forced to seek a way out at another party's expense. Similarly, the architect whose plans and specifications are inadequate will seek to place blame on the contractor. The prudent contractor cannot ignore these possibilities and must be prepared to face them.

Needless to say, the majority of construction projects are handled by men of good will who can usually arrive at reasonable agreements via mutual concessions when changes are introduced. However, the contractor should never rely on word-of-mouth agreements and the time-worn phrase "we'll work it out at the end of the project." Claims for extra cost or time extension that result from change orders should be presented by the contractor in writing and backed up by detailed documentation. Further, he should not do work which he believes was not included in the original contract without written agreement from the owner and/or his project representative.

Unfortunately, construction contracts tend to favor the owner or his designers over the contractor, so it is the contractor who is often forced to give in to what he sees as unfair demands. Obviously, where onerous contracts are involved, the prudent contractor must price the job accordingly. When contract documents are unclear on how change orders are to be handled, the contractor may be well advised to send the owner a written statement which clearly indicates that he is not giving a waiver of claims for extra work. This leaves the door for legal action at least partly ajar should future problems lead to litigation.

RISK FACTORS IN CONSTRUCTION

Every construction project is unique. It follows that there are unique risks which the constructor must face in the execution of those projects. The list of risks is long, but three that have drawn critical attention from outside the industry are safety, seasonality, and technological innovation. The constructor has been faulted for failure to progress in all three areas, and although much of the criticism is overblown, there is a thread of legitimacy running through it.

Safety

According to the Business Roundtable summary report of the Construction Industry Cost Effectiveness Project, "Construction is one of the nation's most hazardous occupations. Work-related injuries and illnesses—including fatalities—occur at a rate 54 percent higher than the average rate for all U.S. industries. With six percent of the nation's work force, construction accounts for 10 percent of all occupational injuries and 20 percent of work-related fatalities." From 1980 to 1984, for every 100,000 construction workers there were 23.1 fatalities according to the National Institute of Occupational Safety and Health (NIOSH). This annual death toll of around 1000 (including about 100 due to trenching accidents) is estimated to be 50 percent too low by the AFL-CIO. Tables 1.7, 1.8, and 1.9 present data from the National Bureau of Labor Statistics concerning accidents and occupational illness in the construction industry. Figure 1.5 presents causes of construction fatalities occurring in 1986.

In addition to the human toll, the price tag for poor safety performance in construction may run as high as $9 billion per year according to the Construction Industry Institute. This figure includes both direct (insured) and indirect costs. Direct costs include medical expenses and premiums for worker's compensation benefits, liability, and property losses. Uninsured indirect costs make up the bulk of the total and include reduced productivity, delays in project schedules, admin-

TABLE 1.7 Construction Accidents and Lost Workdays in 1986

	Cases* per 100 workers	Lost workdays per 100 workers
Masonry, stonework, plaster	17.2	176.0
All construction	15.2	134.5
All private industry nationwide	7.9	65.8

*Cases are reported incidents in which injuries or death occurred.

Source: National Bureau of Labor Statistics, 911 Walnut, Suite 1604, Kansas City, Missouri 64106.

TABLE 1.8 Construction Accidents and Lost Workdays
from 1980–1986 for Masonry, Stonework, and Plastering

Year	Cases* per 100 workers	Lost workdays per 100 workers
1980	16.2	137.5
1981	15.8	138.6
1982	15.0	120.0
1983	15.8	124.7
1984	17.3	154.2
1985	16.6	150.9
1986	17.2	176.0
7-year average	16.3	143.1

*Cases are reported incidents in which injuries or death occurred.
Source: National Bureau of Labor Statistics.

TABLE 1.9 Occupational Injury and Illness Incidence Rates for the Construction
Industry

	Incidence rates per 100 full-time workers*								
	1979	1980	1981	1982	1983	1984	1985	1986	1987
Total cases	16.2	15.7	15.1	14.6	14.8	15.5	15.2	15.2	14.7
Lost workday cases	6.8	6.5	6.3	6.0	6.3	6.9	6.8	6.9	6.8
Lost workdays	120.4	117.0	113.1	115.7	118.2	128.1	129.9	134.5	135.8
General building contractors									
Total cases	16.3	15.5	15.1	14.1	14.4	15.4	15.2	14.9	14.2
Lost workday cases	6.8	6.5	6.1	5.9	6.2	6.9	6.8	6.6	6.5
Lost workdays	111.2	113.0	107.1	112.0	113.0	121.3	120.4	122.7	134.0
Heavy construction contractors									
Total cases	16.6	16.3	14.9	15.1	15.4	14.9	14.5	14.7	14.5
Lost workday cases	6.7	6.3	6.0	5.8	6.2	6.4	6.3	6.3	6.4
Lost workdays	123.1	117.6	106.0	113.1	122.4	131.7	127.3	132.9	139.1
Special trade contractors									
Total cases	16.0	15.5	15.2	14.7	14.8	15.8	15.4	15.6	15.0
Lost workday cases	6.9	6.7	6.6	6.2	6.4	7.1	7.0	7.2	7.1
Lost workdays	124.3	118.9	119.3	118.6	119.0	130.1	133.3	140.4	135.7

*Incidence rate equals $(N/EH) \times 200,000$, where N = number of injuries, illnesses, or lost work
days, EH = total hours worked by all employees in calendar year, and 200,000 = total hours for 100
workers putting in a 40-hour week, 50 weeks per year.
Source: U.S. Department of Labor, Bureau of Labor Statistics.

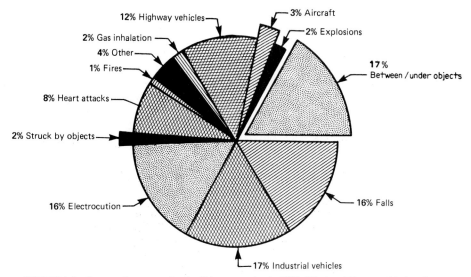

FIGURE 1.5 Causes of construction fatalities occurring in 1986. (*National Bureau of Labor Statistics.*)

istrative time and expense, as well as damage to equipment and the facility under construction. Not included in the $9 billion is the potential cost of damage awards from lawsuits.

While unsafe conditions undeniably exist on construction projects, it is estimated that 50 percent of all accidents are caused by unsafe acts on the part of workers themselves and that these activities contribute to as much as 85 percent of all accidents. However, there is enough research—much of it done at Stanford University—to indicate that construction management can take measures to reduce the accident toll. In fact, because a poor safety record can increase a contractor's labor costs to the point where competitive position is lost, the industry has a vested interest in safety beyond the obvious humanitarian aspects of the problem. It has been estimated that a contractor can reduce his average labor costs by reducing his insurance premiums through good safety practices at least 2 percent and perhaps by as much as 4 percent on excavation work.

The passage of the Occupational Safety and Health Act (OSHA) in 1970 placed responsibility for safety with management, and construction was selected as a "target" industry when it went into force in 1971. However, the problem in construction is complicated by the worker's lack of allegiance to a particular employer. Since workers may move from job to job and contractor to contractor, it is difficult for management to exercise the continuous control necessary to keep its employees alert to poor safety practices. Indeed, there is a growing opinion that OSHA should be amended to place more responsibility on the individual worker. The unions counter with the argument that OSHA penalties are mere slaps on the wrist for most safety violations and that inspectors have been lax in enforcement.

There is strong evidence to back the assertion that safety is a state of mind. Certainly there is no lack of technology to serve the interests of those who are trying to promote construction safety. Successful contractors with good safety records report that they can maintain a good record only with constant vigilance. Their approach begins with top management and runs all the way down through the superintendent and foreman to the lowest hourly rate group on the job. Key personnel regularly attend safety programs and short courses, and carry the word back to field personnel. Detailed records are kept for each project, and safety dinners and awards are used extensively. In addition, good programs use time off from the job to run toolbox safety sessions for crews and explain in detail the functioning of new equipment in relation to good safety practice. Violators of safety rules are dealt with fairly but firmly, and a hard-headed attitude toward enforcement tends to make everyone on the job aware of inherent danger and the personal value of good safety practices.

Seasonality

Because it is labor intensive and many materials are weather sensitive, the construction industry tends to be seasonal. Work slows or stops when the weather is too cold or too hot. Thus, in spite of the existence of technological solutions to seasonality problems, efforts to stabilize construction employment throughout the calendar year have been sporadic because of the assumption that bad weather construction is too costly. But there are many measures of cost, and too often the public pays the price for unemployment compensation and slow delivery of needed construction projects. As early as 1924, President Herbert Hoover expressed this national concern when he said, "Bad weather is not the principal cause of seasonal idleness [in the construction industry]." Customs which became fixed when builders had not yet learned how to cope with adverse weather conditions have not been changed to meet improvement in building materials, the development of new equipment, and innovations in management methods.

Interestingly enough, 1924 is also the year cited by many researchers who have studied the history of construction seasonality. They point out that the contractor on a major project in St. Louis continued to place reinforced concrete through the winter of 1924–1925 at temperatures averaging between 10° and 20°F with lows of 0°F. Even though similar projects were carried out in even colder regions of the United States in succeeding years, the problem was significant enough to gain the attention of the Congress in 1968. An extensive study of seasonal unemployment in the construction industry was carried out and resulted in a bill (H.R. 15990) that said, "The Congress finds that seasonal unemployment represents a substantial portion of the unemployment in the construction industry; and a significant portion of all unemployment; that seasonal unemployment results in economic hardship for construction employees, employers, and for the consumers of construction services; that such unemployment constitutes unnecessary and wasteful misuse of the Nation's manpower resources; that stabilization of construction operations may be expected to have a correspondingly stabilizing effect on construction employment and costs; and that it is highly desirable from the standpoint of the economy as a whole, and manpower policy in particular that positive and expeditious action be taken by public authorities and private groups to stabilize construction employment."

Meanwhile, progress was being made in other countries through government-sponsored incentives, and many U.S. contractors were recognizing that they could benefit from year-round construction via higher rates of capital turnover. With the completion of the Alaska pipeline from the North Slope oil fields to the Port of Valdez, the viability of winter construction was given a significant boost. Research by the Army Corps' Cold Region Research and Engineering Laboratory provided valuable data, and many industry associations began research projects to determine the effects of weather on both workers and construction quality. Still, there is a stigma against winter construction, as much on the part of the public and construction clients as on the part of the industry itself.

While numerous studies have been made of winter construction, the results vary from claims of significant economic benefit to no benefit at all and the risk of increased safety hazards for workers. As reported in *Civil Engineering,* a Purdue University study of Ohio contractors clearly illustrates the variation in contractors' estimates of the increased cost of working at various temperatures as a percentage increase over normal costs.

Temperature	Winter working contractors	Nonwinter working contractors
40°F and above	0	0
30°–39°F	8	40
20°–29°F	17	44
10°–19°F	32	60
Below 10°F	58	—

Whether these contractors considered the social effects of seasonality is left unsaid, but in 1977 about 175,000 Ohioans worked construction in summer and only about 150,000 in winter. The Purdue study concluded that the cost of working in winter versus not working was a trade-off but that safety was adversely affected by winter construction. At almost the same time, the Chicago Construction Coordinating Committee came to the conclusion that significant savings could be achieved by winter work, the largest part being contributed by reduced unemployment benefits.

While the discussion continues, there is a growing arsenal of technology available to overcome the problems of seasonality. From innovative design to enclosure of all or portions of a construction project within heated-air-supported structures or framed panels to fast-setting cements, the tools are available and many contractors are using them successfully. With predictions of manpower shortages in construction as early as the 1990s, there will be strong pressure on contractors to stabilize employment in an effort to stem the tide of workers defecting to other work opportunities.

Technology

Construction technology is basically concerned with the relationship between the men and machines necessary to get materials and equipment in place in a completed project. It is interesting to note that the work of F. W. Taylor in the late 1800s was quickly adopted and improved on by Frank Gilbreth, a construction contractor. What was then known as "scientific management" is now the growing field of industrial engineering. Ironically, the extensive work done by Gilbreth in the fields of concrete and masonry construction still stands as classic, even though Gilbreth's role as a contractor doing industrial engineering has largely been forgotten.

In its summary report of the Construction Industry Cost Effectiveness Report, the Business Roundtable states:

The disinterest of owners, contractors, architect-engineer firms...in university research is all of a piece with their diffidence toward unfamiliar new technology. The construction industry adopts technological innovations far more slowly than it could—and probably should. Some promising new technology goes unused for many years due to 'institutional barriers' to wide dissemination. And that torpid pace of change is one more reason why construction costs have been rising so rapidly in recent years.

The organization of the industry, splintered as it is into myriad segments each more concerned with its own preservation than overall advances, may well account more than any other single reason for this inertia. Moreover, an array of institutional barriers blocks the spread of new technology from where it originates to places where it might be used to cut building costs and increase productivity. A CICE study team identifies the major impediments as these: restrictive building codes and technical standards, some labor agreements and craft jurisdictional issues, liability and legal considerations, lack of profit motive or other compelling incentives, counter productive contractual relationships and government regulations, industrial inertia, and communication difficulties. The list, long familiar to construction executives, typifies the intertwining problems that tend to tether construction to the past.

Even among the sectors of construction studies by the CICE project, there are considerable differences in the rate of technological progress. Commercial construction appears to be well in the lead over the past two decades, despite the absence of any visible research and development structure. Intense competition has prompted developers, designers and owners to work together to cut costs...

In contrast, the spread of new construction technology has been comparatively modest in general industrial construction, process-industry (refineries, chemical and cement plants, etc.) and power plants. Buyers of factories are usually more interested in a trouble-free facility than one made less costly by a new technology that has not yet become standard practice. Companies that own process plants focus on improving the technology of the process or the product, rather than on better ways to erect the maze of equipment and controls that form a plant. Electric utilities have a jointly funded research institute, but so far it spends only about 2½ percent of its $200 million a year budget on ideas applicable to construction.

Despite this gloomy scenario, the construction industry had had some success with technological innovation. In particular, from 1950 to 1974 the index

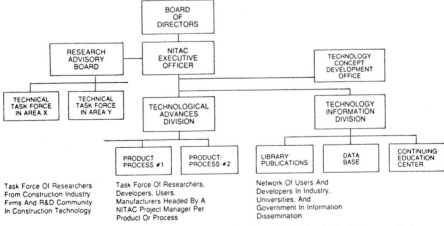

FIGURE 1.6 Suggested organization for a National Institute for Technological Advances in Construction. (*From the Business Roundtable, "Construction Industry Cost Effectiveness Report."*)

(1950 = 100) for wages of workers in highway construction jumped from 100 to 340 while the composite contract bid price index rose to only 200. Meanwhile, the labor factor, measured in man-hours used per $1000 of construction adjusted to 1954 constant dollars, fell from 160 to only 70 during the 1950–1974 period. Thus, in a rapidly expanding market for highway construction, there obviously was technological innovation in the form of new and better methods and equipment for earthwork and paving. Other examples could be cited, yet the fact remains that these bursts of innovation are sporadic and often short lived.

The CICE study indicates that there is an organizational structure in place for construction research including nonprofit groups, universities, federal government agencies, professional and trade associations, and private companies (see Fig. 1.6). These groups are growing and have done some effective work, but there is no existing organization to identify industry needs and to facilitate the transfer of technology from one place or segment to another in the splintered construction industry. It is therefore recommended by CICE that a National Institute for Technological Advances in Construction be established. It cannot come too soon!

CHAPTER 2
CONSTRUCTION ASSOCIATIONS

George B. Roscoe
6609 Rosecroft Place
Falls Church, Virginia

THE ROLE OF ASSOCIATIONS

The construction industry, a vast service operation accounting for approximately a fifth of the gross national product of the United States, is perhaps the most diverse of all industries. To meet the problems of this diversity, a complex network of organizations to perform the functions of coordination, research, communication, and planning has been developed.

This provision of the design, engineering, installation, guarantee, service, and maintenance for buildings and facilities for every conceivable occupancy and use has made the construction industry the largest single unit in the nation's economy. Accordingly, the number and size of the organizations servicing the construction industry is likewise the largest servicing any industry. The number exceeds 500 and includes trade associations, professional societies, labor unions, and research and development organizations representing architects, engineers, general and specialty contractors, speculative and investment builders, labor, building-material manufacturers and distributors, and real estate, insurance, surety, and financial and credit interests.

The combined memberships of these organizations are estimated conservatively to approximate 5 million (the building-trades unions alone account for 3.5 million), and through them flows annually some ½ of 1 percent of the construction industry's gross sales. These sums are used for research in product, method, and management improvement; labor and management training; consolidation of labor and job stability through collective bargaining; industry promotion and communications; and public and governmental relations.

The construction industry is perhaps the greatest assembly of uncoordinated elements in modern society. In this respect it has the precedent of diversity and fragmentation established in the building of the Tower of Babel in biblical days. Yet it has an uncanny capacity to come together to perform almost miraculously. This is made possible by the sharing of technology and information through this network of trade associations, professional societies, and labor unions. Sharing is a uniquely American way of doing things in the industrial, commercial, and professional world. It is in contrast to the practices in most foreign countries, that adhere to the cartel-system philosophy which guards trade and professional "secrets" tightly. The American business and professional man, while having a healthy respect for trade secrets, has been inclined to let the U.S. Patent Office guard them and is rather liberal in his methods and policies. He has been receptive to the argument that an informed competitor is a better and safer competitor, so he is inclined to share methods and experiences, which he does through the apparatus of the trade association and professional society. Just when this practice started is not clearly recorded, but some of the transactions of the American Philosophical Society, founded in 1789 by Benjamin Franklin, provide the rationale and inspiration for such thinking.

This sharing movement made its first appearance in the United States construction industry in 1852 with the formation of the American Society of Civil Engineers. The American Institute of Architects followed in 1857. Of the contractor organizations, the oldest is the National Association of Plumbing-Heating-Cooling Contractors, which was established in 1882. Next was the Painting and Decorating Contractors of America in 1884. The National Roofing Contractors was formed in 1886 and the Mechanical Contractors Association in 1889. The National Electrical Contractors Association was founded in 1901. The general contractors did not form an organization until 1919. Many of these organizations have undergone name changes since their founding.

Labor organizations preceded their counterpart contractor organizations by many years. Although there have been numerous name changes for the organizations that go back to the historic struggle between Samuel Gompers and the Knights of Labor, the records show the Operative Plasterers & Cement Masons International Association to be the oldest union, having been founded in 1864. The Bricklayers, Masons & Plasterers International Union followed in 1865. The United Brotherhood of Carpenters and Joiners was established in 1881.

Building-material manufacturers, industry product groups, and support organizations came along considerably later, with two exceptions. In the insurance field the Factory Mutual System goes back to 1835. The American Bankers Association was founded in 1875. The first product groups to organize were the American Concrete Institute in 1906 and the American Concrete Pipe Association in 1907, followed by the American Iron & Steel Institute in 1908.

CATEGORIES AND SERVICES

Construction-industry organizations generally fall into these categories:

1. Design
2. Construction and building
3. Suppliers-manufacturers, distributors, product research, and promotion
4. Labor unions
5. Support-finance, credit, insurance, surety, real estate

The types of services rendered by construction-industry organizations include:

1. Industry information and communications

2. Development and maintenance of standards of safety, adequacy, and quality
3. Interindustry coordination
4. Collective bargaining
5. Statistics (market and industry)
6. Meetings and conventions
7. Public relations
8. Joint industry promotions
9. Management education
10. Market development
11. Apprenticeship and training
12. Legislative (local, state, federal)
13. Relations with government (local, state, federal)
14. Product research

Industry Information and Communications

Most organizations in the construction industry were formed to provide a means of transmitting information to members and to the industry branch involved. This continues to be a major part of their function, and national, regional, and local groups publish more than 150 magazines and hundreds of newsletters for this purpose. All issue periodic bulletins, reports, and studies.

Standards

The development and maintenance of standards and codes of safety, adequacy, and quality are activities reflecting the construction industry's sensitivity and regard for the public interest. Such standards as the many structural codes and the National Electrical Code were developed as minimum safety standards. The development of and adherence to standardization and uniform specification standards are the work of trade associations and societies, and they have taken much of the "Babel"—the impractical, uneconomical diversity of product and method—out of modern construction. The present-day awareness of consumer interest places increasing emphasis on quality and adequacy.

Interindustry Coordination

Essentially, the construction industry is a conglomerate of autonomous units, each fiercely jealous of its scope and jurisdiction. There have been numerous attempts to bring about coordination, but so far they have not been too successful on an overall basis. What progress that has been made has been by ad hoc groups or by formal groups operating in an ad hoc manner.

The Chamber of Commerce of the United States has since World War II sought to coordinate the construction interest through its construction department, headed by a director elected from the industry. This department includes the broad-range interests in the industry, with the exception of the labor unions.

It has operated chiefly as an occasional forum for designers, contractors, builders, suppliers, and financial, credit, real estate, and insurance interests to express views, but it lacks the power or direction to undertake specific activities and programs.

A considerable degree of liaison in specific areas has been accomplished by committees of contractor, designer, and supplier groups. In 1950, the mechanical-specialty contracting associations formed a liaison committee which was incorporated in 1955 as the Council of Mechanical Specialty Contracting Industries. It maintains working contact with the Associated General Contractors and the American Institute of Architects and several other groups. An attempt to bridge the vital contact gap between construction management and labor was made in 1958 with the establishment of the Construction Industry Joint Conference. It was comprised of the contractor-association management and the 18 unions comprising the AFL-CIO Building and Construction Trades Department. One result was that for the first time construction labor and management combined to produce promotional and public relations literature in support of the industry.

The latest effort in interindustry coordination was for formation in mid-1979 of the Construction Industry Foundation, a direct-membership association drawn from the design professions; general and specialty contractors; builders and suppliers; and insurance, financial, credit, and real estate interests, to define specific industry problem areas and provide for research, study, recommendations, and action.

Collective Bargaining

Inasmuch as labor constitutes as much as 50 percent of the cost of building construction, harmonious and stable labor relations are vital in the construction industry. Consequently, the collective bargaining process is particularly important. In the construction industry collective bargaining is carried on locally, and the management apparatus for this purpose is the chapter or local association. In some of the contractor associations this activity has been the dominant operation.

Statistics

The association and society provide a logical and practical means of gathering statistics as to both the complexion of the industry and its marketing accomplishments and potential. Statistical information gathered and disseminated by associations and societies includes payroll, employment, sales volumes, shipments, inventory, and other items of marketing significance, and operating experiences, material-labor-financial ratios, and costs and overhead to assist in management decision making and planning.

Meetings and Conventions

From the individual members' standpoint the local, regional meetings and the national convention are the most popular. Meeting others in the same business from other areas affords an opportunity to compare and glean new ideas and methods.

The exposition, held in conjunction with the convention by many organizations, affords an opportunity for personal contact with suppliers.

Public Relations

Public relations is an activity construction-industry groups have paid only nominal attention to in the past. The vulnerability of the industry to criticism is placing greater emphasis on this activity.

Joint Industry Promotions

Most associations in the industry are involved in some type of industry promotion jointly with trade allies, and in some instances labor unions are prominently involved. Legislation has been before the last two Congresses to assure the legality of labor-management participation in financing such operations.

Management Education

Management education in business fundamentals, administration, and planning has proliferated as an association activity since 1950. This takes the form of correspondence courses, workshops, seminars, and sponsored courses and classes conducted by industry groups in colleges and universities.

Market Development

This is a fairly recent activity of associations in the contracting phase of the industry. It was the reason for being of most of the supplier product-development associations. The advent of the systems approach in the construction industry is giving impetus to this aspect of association activity.

Apprenticeship and Training

The on-job and indenture aspects of training initiated by the medieval guilds were adopted early by the construction industry as a means of assuring adequate skill. This was done first by the unions, but since World War II the trend has been to make this a joint labor-management responsibility. National standards and a comprehensive program of on-job training and related classroom instruction have been instituted in most branches and are a major association-union program.

Legislative

Involving as it does a major public interest, the construction industry is involved continuously with legislative matters at local, state, and national levels. Since government is the industry's largest single customer, there are many laws and proposed laws relating to public procurement of construction services. Although nationally this is a relatively small part of the association activity, it is a vital one. It becomes of greater proportional significance at state and local levels.

Relations with Government

Business and professional men have found that broad problems involving governmental regulations, laws, and procedures often can be handled more effectively through their organizations than by themselves acting individually. Accordingly, government relations have become a major activity of the association and society in the areas of procurement, regulation, standards, taxation, labor, and antitrust laws.

Product Research

Product research and development is the primary activity of several scores of associations and councils concerned with industry promotion. Mainly, these are in the areas of basic materials such as steel, concrete, and aluminum and energy forms such as electricity and gas. Another type of product research is concerned with safety and reliability and is carried on mostly by testing laboratories.

DIRECTORY OF ASSOCIATIONS SERVING THE CONSTRUCTION INDUSTRY

Following are lists of many of the organizations that can provide reference materials and information in regard to the construction process, in the following categories:

- Organizations of construction contractors
- Organizations of the design and management professions
- Construction-material and equipment suppliers and product research
- Construction labor organizations
- Coordination and arbitration
- Inspection, specifications, and cost

The year in which the organization was founded is included for many of them.

Organizations of Construction Contractors

American Road and Transportation Builders Association, ARTBA Bldg., 525 School St., S.W., Washington, DC 20024. (202) 488-2722.

American Subcontractors Association, 1004 Duke St., Alexandria, VA 22314. (703) 684-3450.

Associated Builders and Contractors, Inc., 729 15th St., N.W., Washington, DC 20005. (202) 637-8800.

Associated General Contractors of America, 1957 E. St., N.W., Washington,

DC 20006. (202) 393-2040.

Ceilings and Interior Systems Construction Association, 104 Wilmot Rd., Suite 201, Deerfield, IL 60015. (312) 940-8800.

Insulation Contractors Assoc. of America (1977), 15819 Crabbs Branch Way, Rockville, MD 20855. (301) 926 3083.

International Association of Lig;:ting Maintenance (1953), 2017 Walnut St., Philadelphia, PA 19103. (215) 569-3650.

Mason Contractors Association of America, Inc., 17 West 601 14th St., Oakbrook Terrace, IL 60181. (312) 620-6767.

Mechanical Contractors Association of America, Inc., Suite 750, 5330 Wisconsin Ave., N.W., Washington, DC 20016. (202) 654-7960.

National Acoustical Contractors Association of America, 5410 Grosvenor Ln., Suite 120, Bethesda, MD 20814. (301) 897-0770.

National Association of Dredging Contractors (1934), 1625 I St., N.W., #321, Washington, DC 20006. (202) 223-4820.

National Association of Elevator Contractors, 2964 Peachtree Rd., N.W., Suite 665, Atlanta, GA 30305. (404) 261-0166.

National Association of Home Builders of the United States, 15th and M Streets, Washington, DC 20005. (202) 822-0200.

National Association of Plumbing-Heating-Cooling Contractors, 180 S. Washington St., Box 6808, Falls Church, VA 22046. (703) 237-8100.

National Association of the Remodeling Industry, 1901 North Moore St., Suite 808, Arlington, VA 22209. (703) 276-7600.

National Constructors Association, 1101 15th St., N.W., Suite 1000, Washington, DC 20005. (202) 466-8880.

National Electrical Contractors Association, 7315 Wisconsin Ave., Bethesda, MD 20814. (301) 657-3110.

National Erectors Association (1969), 1501 Lee Highway, Suite 202, Arlington, VA 22209. (703) 524-3336.

National Roofing Contractors Association (1886), One O'Hare Centre, 6250 River Road, Des Plaines, IL 60018. (312) 318-6722.

Painting & Decorating Contractors of America (1884), 7223 Lee Highway, Falls Church, VA 22046. (703) 534-1201.

Pipe Line Contractors Association (1948), 4100 First City Center, 1700 Pacific Ave., Dallas, TX 75201. (214) 969-2700.

Sheet Metal and Air Conditioning Contractors National Association, Inc. (1943), 8224 Old Courthouse Road, Vienna, VA 22180. (703) 790-9890.

Tile Contractors Association of America, Inc. (1903), 112 N. Alfred, Alexandria, VA 22314. (703) 836-5995.

Organizations of the Design and Management Professions

American Association of Engineering Societies (1979), 415 Second St., N.E., Washington, DC 20002. (202) 546-2237.

American Association of Health Care Consultants, 1235 Jefferson Davis Highway, Suite 602, Arlington, VA 22202. (703) 979-3180.

American Consulting Engineers Council (1973), 1015 15th St., N.W., Washington, DC 20005. (202) 347-7474.

American Institute of Architects (1857), 1735 New York Ave., N.W., Washington, DC 20006. (202) 626-7300

American Society of Civil Engineers (1852), 345 E. 47th St., New York, NY 10017. (202) 705-7496

American Society of Golf Course Architects, 221 N. LaSalle St., Chicago, IL 60601. (312) 372-7090.

American Society of Heating, Refrigerating and Air-Conditioning Engineers, Inc., (1894), 1791 Tullie Circle, N.E., Atlanta, GA 30329. (404) 636-8400.

American Society of Landscape Architects (1899), 1733 Connecticut Ave., N.W., Washington, DC 20009. (202) 466-7730.

American Society of Mechanical Engineers (1880), 345 E. 47th St., New York, NY 10017. (212) 705-7722.

American Society of Professional Estimators, Inc., 6911 Richmond Highway, Suite 230, Alexandria, VA 22306. (703) 765-2700.

Construction Management Association of America, 12355 Sunrise Valley Drive, Suite 640, Reston, VA 22091. (703) 391-1200.

Illuminating Engineering Society of North America (1906), 345 E. 47th St., New York, NY 10017. (212) 705-7926.

Industrial Designers Society of America, Inc., 1142 E. Walker Rd., Great Falls, VA 22066. (703) 759-0100.

Institute of Electrical & Electronic Engineers (1884), 345 E. 47th St., New York, NY 10017. (212) 705-7900.

International Society of Interior Designers (1979), 433 S. Spring St., Suite 6D, Los Angeles, CA 90013. (212) 408-5100.

National Society of Professional Engineers (1934), 1420 King St., Alexandria, VA 22314. (703) 684-2800.

Project Management Institute (1969), Box 43, Drexel Hill, PA 19026. (215) 622-1796.

Society for Advancement of Management, 2331 Victory Parkway, Cincinnati, OH 45206. (513) 751-4566.

Construction-Material and Equipment Suppliers and Product Research

Adhesive & Sealant Council (1957), 1500 N. Wilson Blvd., Suite 515, Arlington, VA 22209. (703) 841-1112.

Air Conditioning and Refrigeration Institute (1953), 1501 Wilson Blvd., Suite 600, Arlington, VA 22209. (703) 524-8800.

Air Distributing Institute (1947), 4415 W. Harrison St., Suite 242C, Hillside, IL 60162. (312) 449-2933.

Air Pollution Control Association (1907), Box 2861, Pittsburgh, PA 15230. (412) 232-3444.

Air Movement and Control Association (1955), 30 W. University Drive, Arlington Heights, IL 60004. (312) 394-0150.

Aluminum Association (1933), 900 19th St., N.W., Suite 300, Washington, DC 20006. (202) 862-5100.

American Architectural Manufacturer's Association (1962), 2700 River Rd., Suite 118, Des Plaines, IL 60018. (312) 699-7310.

American Association of Nurserymen (1876), 1250 I St., N.W., Suite 500, Washington, DC 20005. (202) 789-2900.

American Concrete Institute (1906), P. O. Box 19150, Redford Station, Detroit, MI 48219. (313) 532-2600.

American Concrete Pavement Association, 2625 Clearbook Dr., Arlington Heights, IL 60005. (312) 640-1020.

American Concrete Pipe Association (1907), 8320 Old Courthouse Rd., Vienna, VA 22180. (703) 821-1990.

American Forest Council (1932), 1250 Connecticut Ave., N.W., Suite 320, Washington, DC 20036. (202) 463-2455.

American Gas Association (1919), 1515 Wilson Blvd., Arlington, VA 22209. (703) 841-8400.

American Hardboard Association (1976), 520 N. Hicks Rd., Palatine, IL 60067. (312) 934-8800.

American Home Lighting Institute (1945), 435 N. Michigan Ave., Suite 1717, Chicago, IL 60611. (312) 644-0828.

American Institute of Steel Construction (1921), 400 N. Michigan Ave., Chicago, IL 60611. (312) 670-2400.

American Institute of Timber Construction (1952), 333 W. Hampden Ave., Engelwood, CO 80110. (303) 761-3212.

American Iron & Steel Institute (1855), 1000 16th St., N.W., Washington, DC 20036. (202) 452-7100.

American National Standards Institute (1918) (formerly United States of America Standards Institute), 1430 Broadway, New York, NY 10018. (212) 354-3300.

American Nuclear Society (1954), 555 N. Kensington Ave., La Grange Park, IL 60525. (312) 352-6611.

American Pipe Fittings Association (1938), 8136 Old Keene Mill Rd., Suite B311, Springfield, VA 22152. (703) 644-0001.

American Plywood Association (1936), P. O. Box 11700, Tacoma, WA 98411. (206) 565-6600.

American Public Works Association (1894), 1313 E. 60th St., Chicago, IL 60637. (312) 667-2000.

American Society for Concrete Construction (1965), 3330 Dundee Rd., Suite N-4B, Northbrook, IL 60062. (312) 291-0270.

American Society for Metals (1913), Metals Park, OH 44073. (216) 338-5151.

American Waterworks Association, Inc. (1881), 6666 W. Quincy Ave., Denver, CO 80235. (303) 794-7711.

American Wood Preservers Association (1904), P. O. Box 849, Stevensville, MD 21666. (301) 643-4163.

Architectural Precast Association (1966), 825 E. 64th St., Indianapolis, IN 46220. (317) 251-1214.

Asphalt Institute (1919), Asphalt Institute Bldg., College Park, MD 20740. (301) 277-4258.

Asphalt Roofing Manufacturers Association (1919) 6288 Montrose Rd., Rockville, MD 20852. (301) 231-9052.

Asphalt Rubber Producers Group (1985), 5235 S. Kyrene Rd., No. 210, Tempe, Arizona 85281. (602) 267-8806.

Builders Hardware Manufacturers Association (1925), 60 E. 42nd St., Suite 511, New York, NY 10165. (212) 682-8142.

Building Stone Institute (1919), 420 Lexington Avenue, New York, NY 10017. (212) 490-2530.

Certified Ballast Manufacturers Association (1939), 772 Hanna Bldg., Cleveland, OH 44115. (216) 241-0711.

Concrete Pipe Institute (1907), 8320 Old Courthouse Road, Suite 201, Vienna, VA 22180. (703) 821-1990.

Concrete Reinforcing Steel Institute (1924), 933 N. Plum Grove Rd., Schaumburg, IL 60195. (312) 490-1700.

Construction Industry Manufacturers Association (1909), Marine Plaza 1700, 111 E. Wisconsin Ave., Milwaukee, WI 53202. (414) 272-0943.

Copper Development Association (1963), 2 Greenwich Office Park, Box 1840, Greenwich, CT 06836. (203) 625-8210.

Door and Hardware Institute (1975), 7711 Old Springhouse Rd., McLean, VA 22102. (703) 556-3990.

Edison Electric Institute (1933), 1111 19th St., N.W., Washington, DC 20036. (202) 828-7400.

Expanded Shale, Clay and Slate Institute (1952), 6218 Montrose Rd., Rockville, MD 20852. (301) 231-9497.

Fine Hardwoods Association (1971), 5603 W. Raymond St., Suite 0, Indianapolis, IN 46241. (317) 244-3311.

Flexicore Manufacturers Association (1952), Box 1807, Dayton, OH 45401. (513) 226-8849.

Forest Products Research Society (1947), 2801 Marshall Ct., Madison, WI 53705. (608) 231-1361.

Gas Appliance Manufacturers Association, Inc. (1935), Box 9245, Arlington, VA 22209. (703) 525-9565.

Gypsum Association (1930), 1603 Orrington Ave., Evanston, IL 60201. (312) 491-1744.

Hardwood Plywood Manufacturers Association (1921), Box 2789, Reston, VA 22090. (703) 435-2900.

Home Manufacturers Council of NAHB (1943), 15th & M Streets, N.W., Washington, DC 20005. (202) 822-0576.

Indiana Limestone Institute of America (1928), Stone City Bank Bldg., Suite 400, Bedford, IN 47421. (812) 275-4426.

Industrial Fasteners Institute (1950), 1505 East Ohio Building, 1717 E. 9th St., Cleveland, OH 44414. (216) 241-1482.

Instrument Society of America (1945), 67 Alexander Dr., Box 12277, Research Triangle Park, NC 27709. (919) 549-8411.

International Institute for Lath & Plaster (1985), 25332 Narbonne Ave., No. 170, Lomita, CA 90717. (213) 539-6080.

International Masonry Institute (1970), 825 15th St., N.W., Suite 1001, Washington, DC 20005. (202) 783-3908.

Lead Industries Association, Inc. (1928), 292 Madison Ave., New York, NY 10017. (212) 578-4750.

Lightning Protection Institute (1955), 48 N. Ayer St., Harvard, IL 60033. (815) 943-7211.

Manufacturers Standardization Society of Valve and Fitting Industry (1924), 127 Park St., N.E., Vienna, VA 22180. (703) 281-6613.

Maple Flooring Manufacturers Association (1897), 60 Revere Dr., Suite 500, Northbrook, IL 60062. (312) 480-9138.

Marble Institute of America (1944), 33505 State St., Farmington, MI 48024. (313) 476-5558.

Metal Buildings Manufacturers Association (1956), 1230 Keith Bldg., Cleveland, OH 44115. (216) 241-7333.

Metal Lath/Steel Framing Association (1910), 600 S. Federal St., #400, Chicago, IL 60605. (312) 346-1600.

National Apartment Association, Inc. (1939), 1111 14th St., N.W., #900, Washington, DC 20005. (202) 842-4050.

National Asphalt Pavement Association (1955), 6811 Kenilworth Ave., Riverdale, MD 20737. (301) 779-4880.

National Association of Architectural Metal Manufacturers (1937), 600 S. Federal St. #400, Chicago, IL 60605. (312) 922-6222.

National Association of Decorative Architectural Finishes (1968), 112 N. Alfred St., Alexandria, VA 22314. (703) 836-7670.

National Association of Electrical Distributors (1908), 28 Cross St., Norwalk, CT 06851. (203) 846-6800.

National Association of Marble Dealers (1901), 219 E. Island Ave., Minneapolis, MN 55401.

National Association of Mirror Manufacturers (1957), 9005 Congressional Ct., Potomac, MD 20854. (301) 365-4080.

National Association of the Remodeling Industry, 1901 N. Moore St., Suite 808, Arlington, VA 22209. (703) 276-7600.

National Building Granite Quarries Association (1917), c/o John Swenson Granite Co., North State St., Concord, NH 03301. (603) 225-2783.

National Building Materials Distribution Association (1952), 1417 Lake Cook Rd., Suite 130, Dearfield, IL 60015. (312) 945-6940.

National Clay Pipe Institute (1942), 201 N. Fairfax Street, Suite 32, Alexandria, VA 22314. (703) 548-1463.

National Concrete Masonry Association (1920), Box 781, Herndon, VA 22070. (703) 435-4900.

National Corrugated Steel Pipe Association (1955), 2011 I St., N.W., Suite 500, Washington, DC 20006. (202) 223-2217.

National Decorating Products Association (1947), 1050 N. Lindbergh Blvd., St. Louis, MO 63132. (314) 991-3470.

National Electrical Manufacturers Association (1926), 2101 L Street, N.W., Washington, DC 20037. (202) 467-8400.

National Electric Sign Association (1944), 801 N. Fairfax St., Suite 205, Alexandria, VA 22314. (703) 836-4012.

National Elevator Industry (1934), 630 Third Ave., New York, NY 10016. (212) 986-1545.

National Forest Products Association (1902), 1250 Connecticut Ave., N.W., Washington, DC 20036. (202) 463-2700.

National Glass Dealers Association (1948), 8200 Greensboro Dr., McLean, VA 22102. (703) 442-4890.

National Hardwood Lumber Association (1898), Box 34518, Memphis, TN 38184. (901) 377-1818.

National Insulation Contractors Association (1954), 1025 Vermont Ave., N.W., Suite 410, Washington, DC 20005. (202) 783-6277.

National Kitchen Cabinet Association (1955), P. O. Box 6830, Falls Church, VA 22046. (703) 237-7580.

National Lime Association (1902), 3601 N. Fairfax Dr., Arlington, VA 22201. (703) 243-5463.

National Lumber & Building Materials Dealers Association (1916), 40 Ivy St., S.E., Washington, DC 20003. (202) 547-2230.

National Oak Flooring Manufacturers Association (1909), 8 N. Third, Suite 804, Sterick Building, Memphis, TN 38103. (901) 526-5016.

National Ornamental Metal and Miscellaneous Metals Association (1958), 2996 Grandview Ave., N.E., Suite 109, Atlanta, GA 30305. (404) 237-5334.

National Paint and Coatings Association (1933), 1500 Rhode Island Ave., N.W., Washington, D.C. 20005. (202) 462-6272.

National Particleboard Association (1960), 18928 Premiere Ct., Gaithersburg, MD 20879. (301) 670-0604.

National Ready Mixed Concrete Association (1930), 900 Spring St., Silver Spring, MD 20910. (301) 587-1400.

National Sand & Gravel Association (1916), 900 Spring St., Silver Spring, MD 20910. (301) 587-1400.

National Sash & Door Jobbers Association, 2300 E. Devon Ave. #358, Des Plaines, IL 60018. (312) 299-3400.

National Slag Association (1918), 300 S. Washington St., Alexandria, VA 22314. (703) 549-3111.

National Stone Association (1918), 1415 Elliot Place, N.W., Washington, DC 20007. (202) 342-1100.

National Terrazzo and Mosaic Association (1924), 3166 Des Plaines Ave., Suite 132, Des Plaines, IL 60018. (312) 635-7744.

National Wood Window and Door Association (1926), 1400 E. Touhy Ave., Des Plaines, IL 60018. (312) 299-5200.

Painting and Decorating Contractors of America (1884), 7223 Lee Hgwy., Falls Church, VA 22046. (703) 534-1201.

Perlite Institute, Inc. (1949), 6268 Jericho Turnpike, Commack, NY 11725. (516) 499-6384.

Plastic Pipe and Fittings Association, 800 Roosevelt Rd., Bldg. C, Suite 20, Glen Ellyn, IL 60137. (312) 858-6540.

Plastics and Metal Products Manufacturers Association (1937) 225 W. 34th St., New York, NY 10122. (212) 564-2500.

Plumbing-Heating-Cooling Information Bureau (1917), 800 Roosevelt Rd., Suite C-20, Glen Ellyn, IL 60137. (312) 858-9172.

Portland Cement Association (1916), 5420 Old Orchard Road, Skokie, IL 60077. (312) 966-6200.

Prestressed Concrete Institute (1954) 201 N. Wells St., Chicago, IL 60606. (312) 346-4071.

Red Cedar Shingle & Handsplit Shake Bureau (1915), 515 116th Ave., N.E., Suite 275, Bellevue, WA 98004. (206) 453-1323.

Reinforced Concrete Research Council (1948), 5420 Old Orchard Road, Skokie, IL 60077. (312) 966-6200.

Resilient Floor Covering Institute, 966 Hungerford Dr., Suite 12-B, Rockville, MD 20850. (301) 340-8580.

Rubber Manufacturers Association (1915), 1400 K St., N.W., Washington, DC 20005. (202) 682-4800.

Screen Manufacturers Association (1955) 655 Irving Park at Lake Shore Dr., Suite 201 Park Place, Chicago, IL 60613. (312) 525-2644.

Society of the Plastics Industry, Inc. (1937), 1025 Connecticut Ave., N.W. #409, Washington, DC 20036. (202) 822-6700.

Southern Forest Products Association (1915), P. O. Box 52468, New Orleans, LA 70152. (504) 443-4464.

Steel Deck Institute (1936), P.O. Box 9506, Canton, OH 44711. (216) 493-7886.

Steel Door Institute (1955), 712 Lakewood Center North, 14600 Detroit Ave., Cleveland, OH 44107. (216) 226-7700.

Steel Joist Institute (1928), 1205 48th Ave. North, Suite A, Myrtle Beach, SC 29577. (803) 449-0487.

Steel Plate Fabricators Association (1933), 1250 Executive Place, Suite 400, Geneva, IL 60134. (312) 232-8750.

Steel Service Center Institute (1907), 1600 Terminal Tower, Cleveland, OH 44113. (216) 694-3630.

Steel Structure Painting Council (1950), 4400 5th Ave., Pittsburgh, PA 15213. (412) 268-3327.

Steel Window Institute (1920), 1230 Keith Building, Cleveland, OH 44115. (216) 241-7330.

Stucco Manufacturers Association, 14006 Ventura Blvd., Suite 207, Sherman Oaks, CA 91423. (213) 789-8733.

Tile Council of America (1945) Box 326, Princeton, NJ 08542. (609) 921-7050.

Timber Products Manufacturers (1916) 951 E. Third Ave., Spokane, WA 99202. (509) 535-4646.

Vermiculite Institute (1950), 600 So. Federal St., Chicago, IL 60605. (312) 346-1600.

Water and Wastewater Equipment Manufacturers Association, Inc. (1908), Box 17402, Dulles International Airport, Washington, DC 20041. (703) 661-8011.

Water Pollution Control Federation (1928), 3900 Wisconsin Ave., N.W., Washington, DC 20041. (703) 661-8011.

Water Systems Council (1932), 600 S. Federal St., #400, Chicago, IL 60605. (312) 346-1600.

Western Wood Products Association (1964), 1500 Yeon Building, Portland, OR 97204. (503) 224-3930.

Wire Reinforcement Institute (1930), 8361A Greensboro Dr., McLean, VA 22102. (703) 790-9790.

Wood and Synthetic Flooring Institute, 4415 W. Harrison St., Suite 242C, Hillside, IL 60162. (312) 449-2933.

Zinc Institute, 292 Madison Avenue, New York, NY 10017. (212) 578-4750.

Construction Labor Organizations

Construction and Building Trades Department AFL-CIO (1908), 815 16th St., N.W., Washington, DC 20006. (202) 637-5000.

International Association of Bridge, Structural & Ornamental Iron Workers of America (1901), 1750 New York Ave., Suite 400, Washington, DC 20006. (202) 383-4800.

International Association of Heat & Frost Insulators & Asbestos Workers (1910), 1300 Connecticut Ave. N.W., Suite 505, Washington, DC 20036. (202) 785-2388.

International Brotherhood of Boilermakers, Iron Ship Builders, Blacksmiths, Forgers & Helpers (1881), 753 State Ave., 5th Floor, New Brotherhood Building, Kansas City, KS 66101. (913) 371-2640.

International Brotherhood of Electrical Workers (1891), 1125 15th St., N.W., Washington, DC 20005. (202) 833-7000.

International Brotherhood of Painters & Allied Trades (1887), United Unions Bldg., 1750 New York Ave. N.W., Washington, DC 20006. (202) 637-0720.

International Union of Bricklayers & Allied Craftsmen (1865), 815 15th St. N.W., Washington, DC 20005. (202) 783-3788.

International Union of Elevator Constructors (1901), Suite 530, Clarke Bldg., 5565 Sterrett Place, Columbia, MD 21044. (301) 997-9000.

International Union of Operating Engineers (1896), 1125 17th St., N.W., Washington, DC 20036. (202) 429-9100.

Laborers International Union of North America (1903), 905 16th St., N.W., Washington, DC 20006. (202) 737-8320.

Operative Plasterers & Cement Masons International Association of the U.S. and Canada (1864), 1125 17th St., N.W., Washington, DC 20036. (202 (393-6569.

Sheetmetal Workers International Association (1888), 1750 New York Ave., N.W., 6th Floor, Washington, DC 20006. (202) 783-5880.

Tile, Marble, Terrazzo, Finishers, Shop Workers & Granite Cutters International Union (1980), 801 N. Pitt St., Suite 116, Alexandria, VA 22314. (703) 549-3050.

United Association of Journeymen & Apprentices of the Plumbing & Pipe Fitting Industry of the U.S. and Canada (1889), 901 Massachusetts Ave., N.W., Washington, DC 20001. (202) 628-5823.

United Brotherhood of Carpenters and Joiners of America (1881), 101 Constitution Ave., N.W., Washington, DC 20001. (202) 546-6206.

Coordination and Arbitration

American Arbitration Association (1926), 140 W. 51st St., New York, NY 10020. (212) 484-4000.

Associated Specialty Contractors (1950), 7315 Wisconsin Ave., Bethesda, MD 20814. (301) 657-3110.

Building Officials and Code Administrators International (1915), 4051 W. Flossmoor Rd., Country Club Hills, IL 60477. (312) 799-2300.

Chamber of Commerce of the United States of America (1912), Construction and Community Development Department, 1615 H St., N.W., Washington, DC 20062. (202) 659-6000.

Construction Industry Management Board (1974), 1101 15th St., N.W., Suite 1040, Washington, DC 20005. (202) 223-1510.

Construction Writers Association, Box 259, Poolesville, MD 20837. (301) 972-7440.

International Conference of Building Officials (1922), 5360 So. Workman Mill Rd., Whittier, CA 90601. (213) 699-0541.

National Association of Women in Construction (1954), 327 So. Adams St., Ft. Worth, TX 76104. (817) 877-5551.

National Construction Industry Council (1974), 1919 Pennsylvania Ave. N.W., Suite 850, Washington, DC 20006. (202) 887-1494.

Inspection, Specifications, and Cost

American Association of Cost Engineers (1956), 308 Monongahela Bldg., Morgantown, W. VA 26505. (304) 296-8444.

American Council of Independent Laboratories (1937), 1725 K St., N.W., Suite 301, Washington, DC 20036. (202) 887-5872.

American National Standards Institute (1969) (formerly United States of America Standards Institute, the predecessor of which was the American Standards Association), 1430 Broadway, New York, NY 10018. (212) 354-3300.

American Society for Testing and Materials (1898), 1916 Race St., Philadelphia, PA 19103. (215) 354-3300.

Construction Specifications Institute (1948), 601 Madison St., Alexandria, VA 22314. (703) 684-0300.

International Association of Electrical Inspectors (1928), 930 Busse Hgwy., Park Ridge. IL 60068. (312) 696-1455.

National Fire Protection Association (1896), Batterymarch Park, Quincy, MA 02269. (617) 770-3000.

Society of Fire Protection Engineers (1950), 60 Batterymarch St., Boston, MA 02110. (617) 482-0686.

Underwriter's Laboratories, Inc., (1894), 333 Pfingsten Road, Northbrook, IL 60062. (312) 272-8800.

CHAPTER 3

CONSTRUCTION EDUCATION AND TRAINING

Dr. Harold D. Robertson, AIC, AIA
Associate Professor of Construction Management
University of Nebraska
Lincoln, Nebraska

INTRODUCTION

As the twentieth century draws to a close, the construction industry faces the major problem of recruiting and training new workers to maintain a pool of skilled craftspersons large enough to meet its needs. Disenchantment with the industry and the decline of union-sponsored apprenticeship programs are two factors contributing to the problem. Data from a study by the U.S. Department of Labor indicated that in January of 1986 construction accounted for 5 percent of the industrial labor force but was contributing 10 percent of the displaced workers in the total industrial work force. In 1986 the construction industry picked up about 68,000 workers displaced from other industries, but in 1987 this number had dropped to 37,000. While some major construction companies have been running their own training programs for many years, it is only recently that the industry as a whole has faced the problem and decided to do something about it.

On another front, the construction industry has long been criticized for poor management. However, the proliferation of universities offering construction management degrees appears to be on the way to solving this problem. In addition, industry associations, consulting firms, and in-house programs are providing continuing education in construction management for both old and new employees.

Meanwhile, the industry continues to draw lower-level management personnel from its pool of skilled craftspersons. The old adage "Good carpenter, bad foreman!" was never universally true, but there is evidence that such promotions are now being made only after careful evaluation and with provisions for on-the-job training and participation in continuing education programs.

Philosophically, the difference between education and training is difficult for the layman to define. According to Webster, to educate is "to develop mentally and morally by instruction," and to train is "to undergo instruction, discipline or drill." Implied is the idea that education is a long and broad process, training a shorter and narrower process. Because craftspersons in the construction industry are often employed by several companies in a single year, companies are faced with an economic dilemma. To offer financial support for worker "education" may not benefit the individual employer because the employee may not stay with the company long enough for it to benefit from its long-term investment. Thus, many companies opt for "training" in hopes that short-term benefits will be achieved by quickly improving a worker's productivity.

The development of industry association programs that can, as far as possible, combine education and training is therefore of great importance to the industry. As the twenty-first century approaches, the construction industry will probably become increasingly high-tech and require a larger number of "educated," as opposed to "trained," workers.

CRAFT TRAINING

Historically, the construction industry has relied on the apprenticeship system to provide it with a pool of skilled workers. The system had its origins in ancient Greece and Rome, but was formalized under the English guild system. As "masters" and their apprentices migrated to America, the system was often bastardized to provide a source of cheap labor. However, by the late 1830s the American unions began efforts to limit the number of apprentices and a few decades later were lobbying for state regulation of apprenticeship programs. Wisconsin was the first to do so in 1911. It was not until 1937 that the federal government moved in with passage of the National Apprenticeship Law. Better known as the Fitzgerald Act, this law brought into existence the Bureau of Apprenticeship and Training (BAT).

For the strongly union-oriented construction industry, the creation of BAT put training programs for new entrants to the construction trades in the hands of the unions. Programs were financed by union contractors who agreed to add a few cents to the hourly wages of their employees, which was diverted into an education fund jointly administered by management and the unions. Since the construction unions were strongly oriented to the concept of "one man, one skill," the apprenticeship programs were similarly oriented.

A typical apprentice could expect to spend three to four years in the program, gaining experience on the job under the direction of a skilled journeyman. At the same time, the apprentice would spend 40 to 44 hours each year in the classroom. While many programs worked well, contractors were restive because of their length and the fact that the unions often used them to restrict the flow of new workers into the industry, thus keeping craft wages high. It is also true that many apprenticeship programs suffered from high dropout rates, often as high as 80 percent. However, studies in the 1960s and 1970s indicated that more than 50 percent of the skilled construction workers in many trades were products of the apprenticeship system.

As the open-shop movement began to spread, the union-oriented apprenticeship programs began to decline. In the early 1980s, the Business Roundtable study of the construction industry indicated that while open-shop construction controlled 60 percent of the market, it contributed only 10 percent of the training funds expended (see Fig. 3.1). The same report predicted serious shortages of trained workers by 1990, with only 50,000 workers per year currently being

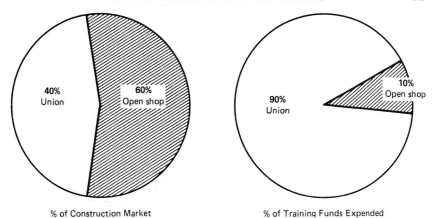

% of Construction Market   % of Training Funds Expended

FIGURE 3.1   A comparison between share of market and share of training funds expended between open shop and union contractors. (*The Business Roundtable.*)

trained (see Fig. 3.2). However, it should be noted that the Associated Builders and Constructors, an organization of open-shop contractors, was aware of the problem. Though somewhat belatedly, ABC began to seek acceptance of open-shop apprenticeship training programs by the Bureau of Apprenticeship and Training. Their efforts were finally rewarded in 1971 with the publication by BAT of the National Apprenticeship and Training Standards for Associated Builders and Contractors. Since then, ABC has aggressively attacked the training problem and has developed a building block approach known as Wheels of Learning (see Figs. 3.3 and 3.4).

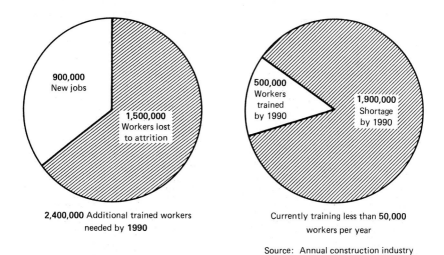

2,400,000 Additional trained workers   Currently training less than **50,000**
needed by **1990**   workers per year

Source: Annual construction industry
report dept of labor **1/80**

FIGURE 3.2   The need for new construction workers by 1990 will not be met if increasing efforts are not made to swell the ranks of trainees. (*The Business Roundtable.*)

HOW WHEELS OF LEARNING
Programs are Developed and Used

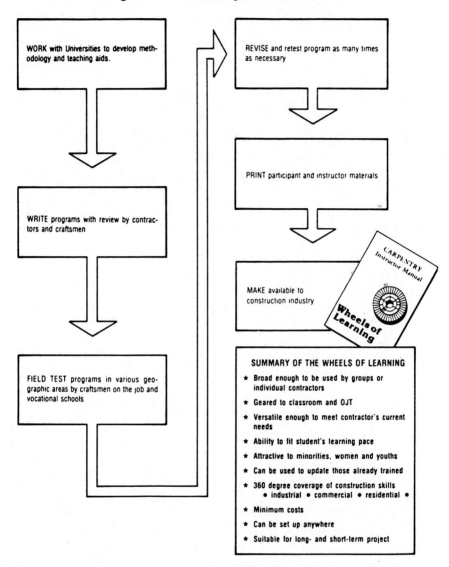

Source: Associated Builders and Contractors.

FIGURE 3.3 How the Wheels of Learning program was developed by the Associated Builders and Contractors.

Curriculum Options

Creating a Multiskilled Craftworker

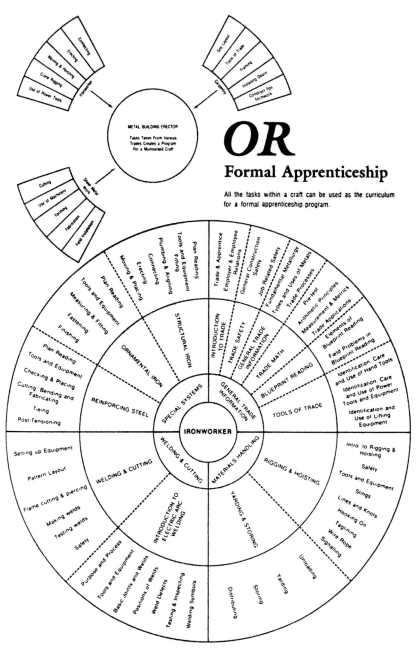

FIGURE 3.4 The Wheels of Learning program uses building blocks to create a multiskilled worker or, through formal apprenticeship, a skilled tradesman in a specific area. (*Associated Builders and Contractors.*)

Currently, in addition to the ABC program, open-shop training is offered by:

Associated General Contractors (AGC)—1980 BAT approval

National Association of Home Builders (NAHB)—some government funds

National Association of Plumbing, Heating, and Cooling Contractors (NAPHCC)

National Utility Contractors Association (NUCA)

Independent Electrical Contractors (IEC)

Carolina Construction Training Council (CCTC)

Painting and Decorating Contractors of America (PDCA)

National Insulation Contractors Association (NICA)

In addition to association training programs, it should be noted that many contractors have run their own programs. These programs range from smaller, informal programs at medium-size organizations to larger, more formal programs run by such industry giants as Brown & Root, Daniel International, and H. B. Zachry. There have also been a number of "bootleg" programs run by local groups of contractors with the cooperation of teachers from industry and educational institutions. There are also some workers coming into the industry from high school and 2-year college programs.

While progress in training skilled construction workers is evident, the industry must vigorously push for continued and accelerated action. It is appropriate to end this section with recommendations from the Business Roundtable study in three different areas:

RECOMMENDATIONS RELATING TO GOVERNMENT

The Construction Industry Cost Effectiveness Task Force makes these recommendations, most, if not all of which can be put into effect through administrative changes without need for new legislation.

1. Union contractor organizations in cooperation with the building trade unions through their joint-apprenticeship committees should

   • Modernize the traditional system of apprenticeship training within each craft, but retain this means of developing base cadres of broadly trained journeymen

   • Employ training techniques, course content, and schedules which promise advancement based on proven skills developed, not on length of training

   • Conduct such training off-site but with each apprentice utilizing on-site time to apply knowledge gained and get additional experience while performing productive work

2. The Department of Labor, Bureau of Apprenticeship and Training should

- Critically examine their current procedures for registering construction apprenticeship programs, giving due consideration to the changing technology and techniques used in modern-day construction practice
- Provide for task-oriented training to satisfy local market needs through the development of those skills needed for the job at hand, including helpers and subjourneymen as well as formal apprentices in the program
- Certify and register all apprenticeship and training programs meeting appropriate criteria without regard to sponsorship of the program

3. The Department of Labor and the several states having prevailing wage laws should

- Review their procedures to take cognizance of the fact that much of the work on today's construction projects does not require the full skills of a journeyman
- Provide means by which helpers or subjourneymen as well as apprentices can be an essential and substantial part of a cost-effective construction crew
- Recognize that such workmen often work independently with the tools of their trade, not necessarily under the direction of or assisting a journeyman

RECOMMENDATIONS RELATING TO OPEN-SHOP TRAINING

The responsibility for training in open-shop construction rests with contractors and their contractor associations. Since training costs are ultimately borne by owners, the recommendations of this report set forth actions recommended for individual contractors and outline the supportive role recommended for individual owners to improve open-shop craft training.

Contractors should consider

- Establishing open-shop construction training councils or centers in metropolitan areas similar to those which now exist in the Carolinas. Such councils will be most effective if they are only concerned with training of construction skills and are supported broadly by contractor associations in the area. It is essential that such councils use a well-developed, nationally recognized and accredited curriculum.
- Developing a broad funding mechanism to support open-shop craft training. It is legally possible to have individual labor arrangements which provide for payment of a cents-per-hour labor charge to be allocated to support a local construction training council or center providing a broad spectrum of craft training.
- Strengthening liaison relationships between open-shop contractor associations and vocational education directors and educators in their areas. This could be an essential part of the development of local construction training councils.

Owners should consider

- That it is in their self-interest to ensure that sufficient funding and effective programs for training craftsmen are provided to meet future needs

- Working through local users' groups to develop programs which increase owner awareness of craft training activities within both the union- and open-shop sectors of the construction industry
- Support of contractors in their area in the establishment of local construction training councils or centers
- Working with contractors in developing a broad funding mechanism to support open-shop craft training
- Including in bid solicitations a requirement that contractors outline their plans for assessing adequately trained workmen and the extent of their financial support to craft training programs
- Including a clause in their bid solicitations to the effect that each contractor shall include in his bid an amount equal to a certain number of cents per field man-hour worked to be used in a mutually agreed-upon craft training program
- Including in bid solicitations on cost-reimbursable work a willingness to accept contractor contributions to mutually agreed-upon training programs as a reimbursable expense
- Support and financial assistance to national construction craft curriculum development programs such as ABC's Wheels of Learning

RECOMMENDATIONS RELATING TO VOCATIONAL EDUCATION

An implementation team is needed to coordinate the efforts to expand vocational education for construction. Dealing with all aspects of the subject will require a large number of personnel with diverse areas of expertise. The formation of subgroups to concentrate on communications, secondary schools, and adult training appears desirable.

- Since improved communications is the most promising route to more and better construction training, especially in secondary schools, a communications improvement subgroup should be formed. It will require representation at the executive level from owners, construction trade associations, and various state and national vocational education groups. They should develop more specific information on the positions of all who have an impact on construction training. Resolution or accommodation of philosophical differences will be needed before broad-based national developments are possible. Over time, this group could be expanded to include more employers, union representatives, and educators as specific items to be treated at the national level are more sharply defined.
- Toward that end, contractor trade associations and other segments of the industry should present specific information to educators at national and state levels about the opportunities industrial construction can offer to young people entering the work force. There should be planned presentations at educators' conferences to state education representatives, government, and union groups. Educators, in turn, should inform industry representatives regarding their organizational and physical assets, including the possibilities of expansion.

- Educators and industry representatives should develop programs aimed at improving owners' understanding of the problems related to craft training.
- A secondary school subgroup should be formed to study and recommend ways to interest more young people in careers in construction. It should deal with such topics as:

  Social attitudes toward craft training
  Promotional programs aimed at teenagers
  Appropriate curriculum
  How the industry can develop reliable work force forecasts
  Ways of adapting existing vocational education programs to the needs of industrial construction

- Along with this effort, a special effort should be made to identify one or more local areas with significant long-range needs for more manpower. In those localities work should begin to expand vocational education training, giving priority to curriculum development, work force forecasting, and coordination among interests involved.
- An adult-age training subgroup should deal primarily with how specialized short courses, usable in all states, can be developed for skills most often in short supply. There is considerable training of this type now, but most of it appears to be local. This group is likely to be primarily concerned with specific logistics problems such as which states need quick development of short-term programs to relieve anticipated shortages of highly specialized skills in the major industrial construction trades. Adult training probably presents the best possibility for quick gains, especially in those localities where long-term manpower needs have been identified.

MANAGEMENT EDUCATION

The traditional path to a management position in construction was either "up from the ranks of skilled craftsmen" or via a civil engineering degree and experience in the field. However, as engineering education tended to become more science-oriented, civil engineers began to graduate without exposure to construction-oriented courses such as estimating, scheduling, specifications, and legal problems. As early as the 1940s, a few educators recognized this problem and began to develop construction-oriented curricula. Early programs were offered at the University of Florida and Michigan State University, the former oriented to heavy construction, the latter to residential construction. Meanwhile, the construction industry was encountering growing criticism for its poor management practices.

Industry response to this criticism took various forms. One was increasing use, either by individual firms or by local groups, of programs conducted by outside consultants such as the Fails Management Institute and several large accounting firms. Another was the encouragement of management employees to enroll in management classes at local colleges and universities. On another front, national contractor associations were at work developing their own programs such as the Supervisory Training Program (STP), developed under the sponsorship of AGC, and, later, Management Education the Merit Shop Way by ABC.

TABLE 3.1   Four-Year Undergraduate Programs in Construction and Project Management

	(1981 Roundtable survey)		
	Number of schools	Number of graduates	
University subdivision	1981 Roundtable survey	1980	1981
Construction	54	1182	1272
Civil engineering or civil engineering construction option	40	1140	1207
Other	17	214	243
Totals	111	2536	2722

But the major effort in many areas was the formation of committees to promote the development of construction programs as unique curricula in area universities.

By the late 1960s there were a substantial number of programs in place, but their location within the various universities gave some indication of the difficulty contractor groups were encountering. Some appeared in colleges of engineering, architecture, business administration, and a variety of others. In an effort to improve curriculum development for construction education, the Associated Schools of Construction was formed during this period. With the formation of the American Institute of Constructors in 1971, the movement toward an accreditation program for construction curricula was accelerated. With the support of ASC and AIC, as well as other contractor organizations, the American Council for Construction Education (ACCE) was formed in 1974. It was soon granted accreditation authority for construction curricula by the Council of Postsecondary Education (COPA) and the U.S. Department of Education. For engineering-oriented construction curricula, accreditation authority is vested in the Accreditation Board of Engineering and Technology (ABET).

TABLE 3.2   Subject Matter Breakdown in Four-Year Construction Programs

	(Expressed as a % of total course units)			
	1981 Roundtable survey			
General topic	Construction	Civil engineering	Other	ACCE guidelines
1. General education (socio-humanistic)	20.5	17.9	16.1	12.5
2. Mathematics and science	16.5	28.5	19.5	15.0
3. Construction design	12.3	20.4	20.4	17.5
4. Construction business	11.0	3.8	7.0	15.0
5. Construction technology	17.6	9.4	18.8	12.5
6. Management of construction	10.8	4.8	7.4	17.5
7. Other requirements (electives)	11.3	15.2	10.8	10.0
Total	100.0	100.00	100.0	100.0

TABLE 3.3 A Typical Management-oriented B.S. Program: University of Nebraska–Lincoln

First year			
Construction communications	2	Construction communications	2
Analytic geometry & calculus	5	Microcomputer applications & analysis	3
General physics	4	Introduction to construction management	3
English composition	3	Physical geology and laboratory	4
Environmental studies	3	Philosophy	3
	17		15
Second year			
Construction equipment & methods	3	Construction equipment & methods	3
Construction materials & specifications	2	Construction materials & specifications	2
Materials testing laboratory	1	Materials testing laboratory	1
Engineering surveying	3	Statistics and operations research math	3
Engineering statics	3	Strength of materials	3
Introduction to economics	5	Technical writing	3
	17	Survey of accounting	3
			18
Third year			
Mechanical systems and equipment	3	Electrical systems & equipment	3
Construction cost analysis	3	Construction cost analysis	2
Industrial engineering management	3	Work analysis and simplification	2
Business speaking	3	Structural design	3
Social/humanistic elective	3	Human resources management	3
	18	Social/humanistic elective	3
			16
Fourth year			
Structural design	3	Construction cost control	3
Human elements in construction	2	Contract administration	3
Project planning	3	Senior construction project	3
Business law	3	Construction technical elective	3
Professional practice	2	Technical electives	6
Social/humanistic or technical elective	3		18
	16		

Graduation requires 135 credit hours, including 18 elective hours. Note that electives must include a minimum of 6 credit hours in social/humanistic fields, and 6 credit hours in technical fields. Of the remaining 6 credit hours, 3 credit hours in construction management courses and 3 credit hours in either social/humanistic or technical fields are required. Social/humanistic electives as well as required courses in those areas are being used to meet the demand for general education at most American universities.

Tables 3.1 and 3.2 indicate the status of construction education as reported by the Business Roundtable study in 1981. The numbers in Table 3.1 are probably on the low side because of the survey limitations. Table 3.2 is important because it indicates the subject matter emphasis in three different types of programs. In its 1988 report, ACCE listed 22 accredited programs along with 13 which are in candidate status. There are also several programs accredited by ABET. Table 3.3 covers the curriculum for a B.S. degree in construction management at the University of Nebraska–Lincoln. It is typical of programs strongly oriented toward

TABLE 3.4 Annual Contribution to University Construction Programs as Reported in the Roundtable Survey

Purpose	Annual amounts (thousands of dollars)		
	Undergraduate programs	Graduate programs	Total
Scholarships	$379	$ 73	$ 452
Research	151	822	973*
Program support	293	126	419
Totals	$823	$1,021	$1,844

*Total support in 1980 for all university engineering research was $620 million, of which 80% came from governmental agencies.

management and requires 135 credit hours for graduation. Contractors are advised to study curricula carefully before interviewing graduates from accredited programs to be sure candidates have the type of background they need and want. It should be pointed out that there are several excellent construction programs operating at the graduate level in departments of civil engineering, such as those at Stanford and Texas. In addition, a number of universities are offering advanced degree programs in their construction departments.

Based on an AIC survey of 27 construction programs, 1988 graduates received an average starting salary of $26,624. Figures vary widely by geographic area and the average is inflated by the fact that 36 percent of the reporting graduates were from the West Coast and Hawaii. Fifty-five percent of the graduates were employed by commercial building contractors, 17 percent industrial, 14 percent highway-heavy, 9 percent developers, 3 percent residential, and 2 percent municipal-utility. Company health benefits were provided for 91 percent, pension programs 56 percent, profit sharing 62 percent, and vehicles 25 percent.

While advanced-degree holders are not much in demand by contractors (fewer than 10 percent of employees, according to the Business Roundtable study), they are important in terms of the nurture and preservation of current and future college programs. Faculty in most universities are now required to have the Ph.D. and the road to that degree is paved with published research. Thus, both owners and contractors have a vested interest in the development of strong graduate programs if they are to benefit from sound research and the continuation of collegiate construction programs. Currently, the construction industry is supporting teachers and researchers at a minimal level, as indicated by Table 3.4 from the 1982 Business Roundtable publication "Management Education and Academic Relations."

CHAPTER 4
THE LABOR FORCE AND INDUSTRIAL RELATIONS LAW

Paul P. Poppler
College of Business Administration
University of Nebraska
Lincoln, Nebraska

This chapter discusses several fundamental labor relations laws and presents a brief overview of the structure and character of the unionized labor force in the construction trades. More specific information can be garnered from trade associations or competent legal counsel.

THE LABOR FORCE

As contractors know, the volume of construction is strongly affected by fluctuations in the economy. Other factors such as seasonality, regional economic health, and government spending on large construction projects can also affect the volume of construction in progress. The inherent characteristics of construction can also affect the volume of work (e.g., size of project, duration, and requirements for labor types at different stages). Given these variables, the contractor wishes to remain as flexible as possible in the execution of operations. The ability of the contractor to hire at a predetermined wage scale is also critical (large wage changes after the negotiated bid price could nullify project profit). For their part, labor organizations attempt to moderate the effects of these sources of change through the collective bargaining process. It may be said that employment security for membership is a primary goal of construction unions.

A net effect of the economic conditions and employment characteristics is often a much more intimate relationship between employers and unions than in other industries. Mills[1] notes

Contractors and unions must negotiate not only wages and working conditions but also hiring and training practices. The responsible contractor realizes that in an unstable industry, the development and retention of a skilled labor force require that the employers and the unions agree to practices that preserve the job opportunities for craftsmen. The problem, of course, is to adopt policies that are effective in protecting employment opportunities without unduly restricting needed expansion of the labor force or promoting uneconomic practices.

DECLINING UNION DENSITY

The percent of a given labor market organized by unions is often referred to as union density. Union density in the construction industry has steadily declined in the past 25 years. Allen[2] constructed Table 4.1 (first two columns) from various sources (current population surveys, the U.S. Bureau of Census, Freeman and Medoff's[3] study, and the 1967 Survey of Economic Opportunity).

TABLE 4.1

Year	Percentage union members	Percentage change
1966	41.4	
1970	41.9	+1.2
1973	39.4	−5.9
1974	37.2	−5.6
1975	37.0	−0.5
1976	35.7	−3.5
1977	35.7	0.0
1978	31.9	−10.6
1979	31.6	−0.9
1980	30.8	−2.5
1981	32.8	+6.5
1982	28.2	−14.0
1983	27.5	−2.5
1984	23.5	−14.5
1985	22.3	−5.1
1986	22.0	−10.3

Troy and Sheflin report similar decline trends in their thorough handbook on union data.[4] Clearly, the percentage of union construction is on the decline. Extrapolating the mean of this downward trend through 1990 indicates that unions would represent less than 17.5 percent of construction labor. Similarly, the absolute number of union workers in construction is falling. Table 4.2 reports membership for major construction unions using Troy and Sheflin's *Union Sourcebook*[4] and Courtney Gifford's most recent *Directory of U.S. Labor Organizations.*[5]

Unfortunately, estimates of union membership in the construction industry are difficult to make with a high degree of accuracy. The industry has several fluctuations (seasonal, macroeconomic, and microeconomic) that cause the total number of workers to change constantly. National unions are more likely to inflate their membership numbers in order to portray strength, while locals may slightly underreport membership in order to pay lower per capita dues to the national. Moreover, many retired or inactive construction union members maintain union membership in order to retain eligibility for union-sponsored welfare or pension plans. Finally, union workers may temporarily work for a nonunion con-

TABLE 4.2   Membership of Selected Large Construction Unions (Thousands)

Union	1989	1987	1983	1979	1975	1971	1960
IBEW	790	791	869	922	909	836	690
Carpenters	609*	628	678	727	789	788	757
Laborers	371*	433	461	537	549	555	443
Plumbers and pipefitters	330	226	329	338	331	313	261
Painters	128	133	146	199	208	187	183
Sheet metal workers	150	108	141	158	159	142	106

*Figures from the AFL-CIO's report of average per capita membership paid by each of its affiliates during the period ending June 30, 1987.

tractor in the absence of union-referred work. These difficulties cannot be assumed to randomly cancel each other because they are errors of different sources and proportion. Even with this warning, the data do indicate a pronounced downward trend for the last 30 years.

Several hypotheses have been offered to explain the downward trend. Among the more prevalent in the literature have been:

1. Structural changes in the composition of construction workers (e.g., more women, minorities, and part-time workers) have occurred, and the new workers are less likely to identify with a union.

2. Right-to-work laws and open-shop practices have encouraged contractors to use less expensive and less qualified nonunion workers.

3. The productivity advantage union labor produced (which justified higher labor costs) has diminished to near zero as a result of new techniques and technologies.

4. Union workers often work for nonunion contractors when they are unable to secure union employment.

5. Traditional union regions of the country have been losing population, and therefore the amount of available construction work in these areas has not kept pace with construction work in nonunion regions.

6. Government construction (traditionally heavily unionized) has been declining relative to private construction (traditionally less unionized).

The debate on the virtues of these explanations goes on, but it is not within the scope of this chapter to analyze them. Despite the trends, it is important to remember that all contractors, union or nonunion, are influenced by the labor relations policies of the others. Wages in the union sector influence what nonunion contractors must pay. Traditionally, nonunion scales have been below union scales, with union personnel considered better mechanics. In the past 5 years, however, nonunion scales have often been made competitive with union scales. Union contractors and union leaders have therefore sought to make union work more competitive and attractive (see *Engineering News Report,* 2/16/84: pp. 46–57, and *Midwest Contractor,* 11/23/87: pp. 13–16). The trend toward competitive wage rates between the two sectors means that the contractor needs to keep an even closer eye on the productivity of the labor he or she hires. Other things being equal, it is advised that the contractor focus on total labor costs (including some measure of quality) per unit of output rather than wage scales explicitly in deciding his or her uses and types of labor.

THE BUILDING TRADES UNIONS AND CONTRACTORS' ASSOCIATIONS

Structure and Government of Building Trades Unions

The National. The national (sometimes referred to as the international) labor organization is essentially a confederation of chartered local unions. During the closing decades of the nineteenth century, groups of U.S. (and some Canadian) locals founded the structure of the national union. It was hoped that through such association, the organized portion of the trade might not be undercut by unorganized labor. The national was given power to charter and organize local unions and to combine or remove local unions from the association. In some cases, there were bitter struggles over the roles and relationships of the union entities, which have continued to date in one form or another.

The functions of the national union, the duties of its officers, and the relationship of the national to the affiliated locals are specified in a constitution of the national union. Conventions are held (usually in periods of 2 to 5 years) at which the national constitution may be amended, resolutions proposed for adoption, officers elected, strategies recommended, dues modified, operating budgets or program budgets modified or adopted, and other business conducted. The convention then is the supreme governing body of the union system.

The national or international union is managed by a general president and his or her staff. The general president runs the national with the approval of the general executive board. This board is usually composed of elected general vice presidents who represent various parts of the country. Although the general president usually has authority over the work jurisdiction of the union, he or she rarely has a direct involvement in the collective bargaining process except for the coordination of a national agreement. In cases where general union policy, jurisdiction, or direct decision of the convention is involved, there may be an exception. However, the general president is aware of the political dangers of alienating some locals or factions by a direct involvement in issues.

The larger national (or international) unions may have additional staff departmentalized and attached to the office of the general president. Such staff serve as "representatives" (from national to the local) and play intermediary roles in grievance handling, protection of craft jurisdiction among the locals, and assistance in the administration of the local. Such staff may also administer such things as strike funds, pension or welfare funds, legal assistance, or education programs.

In some national unions an intermediate governance level may exist, e.g., regional councils and regional vice presidents. The roles played by the regional councils and officers and their involvement with the local bodies varies. In general, the regional aids in the administration of local affairs, provides legal aid, and gives support and advice in collective bargaining matters.

The national union is financed by a "per capita" tax levied on each associated local. This amount is specified at the convention and entered into the current constitution. The amount can be stipulated as a dollar amount or as some percentage.

The Local. Of the three levels of unions (association, national, and local), it is the local which is the closest to the rank-and-file member. The typical member identifies with the local and exercises most activity through the local (meetings, grievances, strike activity, or the bringing of issues to the attention of local officers).

The local is a branch of the national; it receives its charter from the national, albeit some locals predate the national association to which they belong. As such, the local operates under the constitution and bylaws of the national. The degree and depth of influence on the daily operation of the locals by the national varies. Typically, however, local collective bargaining agreements must conform to some standards of a national agreement (if there is industrywide bargaining), certain financial and operational reports might be mandated by the national, and the national union may prescribe the numbers and types of officers of the local, their duties, limits of authority, and so forth.

Historically, local building trades craft unions have retained more autonomy in the conduct of their affairs than industrial unions. Craft unions in the building trades usually negotiate shorter agreements than industrial unions, and such agreements may be supplemented by special topics (such as safety or apprenticeship programs). The nature of construction work often causes employees to work for several different employers in the same year, working at several different jobs sites under the same labor agreement.

Large locals often have a business agent (and staff). This person is a full-time salaried official of the union who plays a significant external role. The business agent (as well as officers of the union) represents the union in the collective bargaining process, at the job site (such as enforcement of the contract, grievances, and preventing jurisdictional disputes), and in legislative or legal arenas (such as in lobbying, appearing before public officials, or assisting counsel in court). The business agent's job is essentially a political one: representation of the institution of the union. As such, he or she also may direct a strike, boycott, or other organized activities. Since the agent can be voted out of office, it is imperative that the agent stay attuned to the needs of his constituencies.

The business agent and other officers of the union perform vital institutional maintenance roles because they essentially police the trade. The continually shifting nature of the construction business and its natural dispersion of work (and sites) require individuals to maintain the agreement, clarify ambiguities that arise, maintain standards, and delineate jurisdiction.

Brief Description of Several Prominent Building Trade Unions

The International Brotherhood of Electrical Workers. The International Brotherhood of Electrical Workers (IBEW) is a multiindustry international union. Current membership is approximately 790,000. Electrical construction, electrical manufacturing, communications, and power utilities are among the industries within which the IBEW has membership. The international maintains jurisdiction over a broad range of activities concerning the production of electrical equipment including manufacturing, assembly, construction, installation, erection, maintenance, and repair.

The locals of the IBEW often bargain collectively with local chapters of the National Electrical Contractors Association. Moreover, the industry has a joint labor-management Council of Industrial Relations. Established in 1921, it has served to render final and binding decisions in grievance disputes and to minimize the occasion of strikes.

The United Brotherhood of Carpenters and Joiners of America.   The Carpenters is composed of many locals (many of them small). Current membership is approximately 609,000. The union maintains jurisdiction over most work operations involving wood, plastic, and metal used in substitution for wood (such as aluminum studs). Occupational elements of the union include general construction carpenters, millwrights, marine carpenters, lumber and sawmill workers, piledrivers, and furniture workers. The general construction carpenters are the largest of these elements.

Laborers International Union of North America.   The Laborers membership is largely composed of workers employed in large building projects, highways, and heavy construction. Current membership is approximately 371,000. The Laborers represent common laborers and helpers, but jurisdiction has expanded in recent years to more skilled elements such as tunnel work, drilling, blasting, and concrete placement. The membership turnover in this area is relatively high, and the union helps to stabilize some of the fluidity in this labor market.

The United Associations of Journeymen and Apprentices of the Plumbing and Pipe Fitting Industry.   Members of the plumbers and pipefitting union are primarily employed in new construction. Membership is approximately 330,000 currently. Membership and bargaining agreements extend into industrial maintenance, pipeline construction, gas distribution and utilities, panelboards, instrumentation and control manufacturing, refrigeration and air conditioning, naval and private shipyards, and building construction.

The Brotherhood of Painters and Allied Trades.   Members are involved in general construction painting, repainting, dry walling, glazing, sign painting, and paint manufacture and work for public agencies that employ men in their jurisdiction. Current membership is approximately 128,000. Local unions or district councils often negotiate contracts with local associations of the Painting and Decorating Contractors' Association.

The Sheet Metal Workers' International Association.   Current membership of the Sheet Metal Workers is approximately 150,000. The international asserts jurisdiction over handling, fabrication, assembly, and the erection of all sheet metal work (including such things as duct work and air conditioning or heating systems). The union represents employees of production companies in such areas as shipbuilding and railroads as well as building construction.

Other Unions.   Several other large unions deserve mention, although limitations of space prevent a thorough description of each. Among those relevant to the contractor are the following:

- The International Brotherhood of Boilermakers, Iron Ship Builders, Blacksmiths, Forgers, Helpers (current membership: 105,000)
- The International Association of Bridge, Structural and Ornamental Ironworkers (current membership: 135,000)
- The International Association of Heat and Frost Insulators and Asbestos Workers (current membership: 12,000)
- The International Brotherhood of Teamsters, Chauffeurs, Warehousemen and

Helpers of America (now affiliated with the AFL-CIO; current membership: 1,600,000)
- The Bricklayers, Masons and Plasterers International Union (current membership: 102,000)

Contractors' Associations

There are approximately 60 national associations of construction contractors in the United States. Some associations are made up of predominantly union-shop contractors; others are largely composed of open-shop contractors. Some have a mix of both.

National Association of Home Builders. The National Association of Home Builders (NAHB) is one of the largest associations. It is largely composed of home-building contractors and specialty contractors who service residential builders. Residential construction has become one of the most unorganized sectors of the industry. Northrup[6] notes

> Today only a few NAHB chapters have labor agreements with some or all of the building trades unions, and even in these jurisdictions, an increasing number of builders are conducting open shop operations outside the coverage of the contracts. There are also a few cases of individual builders with union contracts, but these instances are infrequent and dwindling. On the whole, the NAHB is an organization comprised of predominantly open shop employers, a direction in which the association has steadily moved for the past quarter century.

The NAHB has a national staff which is headquartered in Washington, D.C. The NAHB primarily provides advice and research concerning labor relations; it does not directly engage in any collective bargaining activities.

Associated Builders and Contractors. Associated Builders and Contractors (ABC) was founded in the early 1950s in Maryland. It has expanded considerably and now has chapters in nearly every state. The ABC is composed of both general and specialty contractors. Also headquartered in Washington, D.C., the ABC has staff functions in areas such as labor law, public relations, training, and employee benefits to render advice and do research for charter members. ABC has had considerable involvement in lobbying at the congressional and state legislative levels in issues relating to illegal union picketing and construction union violence. ABC is an open-shop association.

Associated General Contractors. Associated General Contractors (AGC) is composed of a mix of open- and union-shop contractors. In many states there are separate chapters for building contractors and for heavy or highway contractors. Moreover, the building construction chapters are usually located in several large metropolitan areas in the state, while the highway or heavy chapters are organized on a statewide basis. The building chapters are less likely to serve both a union and a nonunion constituency. Since the bylaws vary from chapter to chapter, contractors may or may not be bound by a contract negotiated by the chapter. If the bylaws give the power of attorney to the association, the contractor will be bound by any labor agreement negotiated by the chapter. If this power is optional, open shops can associate and capitalize on other services offered by the association.

At the national level the AGC participates in a variety of activities that have no direct relevance to the union or nonunion status of the contractor. For instance, the AGC has national committees on environmental issues, fuel and material supplies, equal employment opportunity, and manpower and training.

National Constructors Association. The National Constructors Association (NCA) is one of the largest associations for unionized contractors who specialize in large industrial and heavy projects (e.g., utilities, dams, and industrial complexes). The NCA negotiates labor agreements with the construction unions, represents members' political interests, and makes studies of such relevant matters as open-shop penetration in the industrial sector.[7]

Other Associations. Several specialty trade associations are worth noting. Several of these are split between union and open shop. Northrup[6] has an excellent discussion of the activities of such associations as well as the trend (by sector) of construction toward greater open shop. Some of the principal specialty trades associations are given in Table 4.3.

It can be seen that the construction industry is composed of a diverse set of institutional players, each created through a particular need. Construction embraces a wide variety of activities and work processes. Union-contractor negotiated agreements have a tendency to influence the wages and working conditions of similar nonunion construction. Generalization is difficult, however, because

TABLE 4.3 Principal Specialty Trade Association

Association	Bargaining unions	Comments
American Road and Transportation Builders	Operating Engineers, Teamsters, others	About 60% open-shop contractors
Independent Electrical Contractors	—	All open-shop contractors
International Association of Wall and Ceiling Industries	Plasterers	About 80% unionized contractors
Mason Contractors Association of America	Bricklayers	100% union contractors
Mechanical Contractors Association of America	Plumbers and pipefitters	100% union contractors
National Association of Heating and Cooling Contractors	Plumbers and pipefitters	About 60% open-shop contractors
National Roofing Contractors Association	Roofers	About 60% union contractors
Painting and Decorating Contractors Association	Painters	About 50% open-shop contractors

Source: Reference 6, p. 23.

(1) the degree of union density (and union strength) is variable among industry segments and (2) there are different trends within a given segment (see Ref. 6).

LABOR LAWS

The network of laws governing labor relations, personnel, pay, and employment practices in the United States is vast and complex. This section covers federal legislation, but the practitioner is advised to become conversant with state and local legislation affecting labor relations.

For conceptual purposes it is helpful to think of the laws as grouped into three sets.

1. *Labor relations laws:* Labor relation laws specify conditions and limitations to the actions which employers and employees (or unions) can take relative to their employment relations with each other. Specifically this means the "rights" which both the employer and the employee have in representing their respective interests in the collective bargaining process. The corpus of labor relations laws is made up of the National Labor Relations Act of 1935 (NLRA) and its amendments: the Labor Management Relations Act of 1947 (LMRA) and Labor Management Reporting and Disclosure Act of 1959 (LMRDA).

2. *Wages and hours laws:* Wages and hours laws specify conditions about the wages (e.g., minimum, overtime, and prevailing rates) and about the corresponding hours of work which would affect a condition of the law. Included in this grouping is the Fair Labor Standards Act of 1938, the Copeland Act 1934, the Davis-Bacon Act of 1936, the Equal Pay Act of 1963, and the various wage payment laws of individual states.

3. *Fair employment practices laws:* These laws (and executive orders, judicial decisions, and administrative rulings) enumerate and forbid conditions which are discriminatory, unsafe, or unfair to the employee or job applicant. Among this group is Title VII of the Civil Rights Act of 1964, the Age Discrimination Employment Act of 1968 (amended 1978), Executive Order 11246, and the Occupational Health and Safety Act (OSHA) of 1970.

Competent legal advice must be obtained if the employer runs afoul of these or other laws governing employment practices. In addition, information services such as the Bureau of National Affairs (BNA), Commerce Clearing House (CCH), and Prentice-Hall (PH) provide excellent loose-leaf binder services covering these and many other legal areas. An employer of sufficient size and staff would be well advised to add a staff member dedicated to the administration and monitoring of labor relations issues and requirements.

Labor Relations Laws

In the interests of industrial harmony and greater production, the National Labor Relations Act and its amendments (LMRA and LMRDA) were passed by Congress. The composite purpose of the acts is to define and protect the rights of employees and employers, to encourage collective bargaining, and to eliminate certain practices on the part of labor and management which are harmful to the employee or the general public. It was apparently felt that the effect of employee representation in the decisions of their welfare would facilitate commerce and reduce industrial strife.

The rights of employees are principally set forth in Section 7 of the act which guarantees the "right to self-organization, to form, join, or assist labor organizations, to bargaining collectively through representatives of their own choosing," and the "right to refrain from any or all such activities," except where a union-shop agreement requires membership in a labor organization as an ongoing condition of employment. Examples of the rights protected by Section 7 are

- Forming or attempting to form a union among the employees
- Joining a union whether the union is recognized by the employer or not
- Going on strike in order to secure better working conditions
- Refraining from activity on behalf of the union

It is illegal for an employer or a union to interfere with the stipulated or implied rights of employees. Section 8(a) delineates unfair labor practices (UFLPs) from which the employer and management must refrain. Violation of 8(a) comprises violation of employee rights. Similarly, Section 8(b) stipulates unfair labor practices forbidden to unions and their representatives.

Examples of employer UFLPs are

- Interference, restraint, or coercion of employees
- Domination of unions
- Discrimination in hire, or in tenure, terms, or conditions of employment
- Refusal to bargain with the duly authorized union
- Spying or the pretense of spying on employees for union activities

Examples of union UFLPs are

- Restraint or coercion of employees
- Discriminatory or excessive dues or fees to members
- Causing or attempting to cause discrimination
- Engaging in prohibited strikes or boycotts as forbidden by the act
- Featherbedding

The LMRA established the National Labor Relations Board to administer the act. The NLRB is composed of five members with their respective staffs, a general counsel and staff, and regional, subregional, and residential offices for the purposes of investigation of charges and the issuance of complaints. The members of the NLRB and the general counsel are appointed by the president, with the consent of the senate. The Board has two main functions: (1) to conduct representation elections and to certify the results and (2) to prevent employers and unions from engaging in unfair labor practices. In either case, the NLRB's processes are initiated only when requested. A request for an election is called a "petition," and a request for the investigation of an UFLP is called a "charge."

The NLRB has the power to order either the employer or the union to "cease and desist" an illegal action. This order can be backed up by real civil and criminal jurisdiction if the order (or settlement agreement) is entered into court whereupon subsequent violations would give rise to contempt of court actions.

Among other important provisions of the NLRA and its amendments is the duty of both parties (the union and the employer) to "bargain in good faith" [these are stipulated in sections 8(a)5 and 8(b)3]. The act does not require that either party agree to any particular proposal or require any particular concession by either side; however, certain subjects are "mandatory" to negotiation if either party raises them. These mandatory subjects are those found by the board to be included in the general rules of "wages, hours, and conditions of work." A proposed pay raise and a retirement plan are mandatory subjects if either or both sides raise them. The board has ruled "that in negotiations a union or employer may refuse to execute a contract if an agreement is not reached on a mandatory subject of bargaining." When such an impasse occurs over a mandatory issue, "the union may strike or the employer may lockout in support of its bargaining position."[8]

Other issues are legal but not mandatory. Such issues are called "permissible" issues. Either party may request negotiations over permissible issues but may not carry the negotiations to an impasse over such an issue. If the union strikes or the employer locks-out over a failure to agree on a permissible issue, the strike or lockout is a UFLP.

Finally, certain topics are illegal and will be considered a UFLP regardless of initiation or intent. Hot cargo agreements, featherbedding, and union management agreements which purposely discriminate against certain employees are examples of illegal subjects.[9]

The NLRA as amended includes several provisions for the construction industry which differentiate it from other industries covered by the act. Section 8(f) allows an employer engaged primarily in the building or construction industry to sign a union-security agreement with a union without the union's prior designation as the representative of the employees as otherwise required by the act. Section 8(f) was added to the NLRA by the Labor Management Reporting Disclosure Act, November 13, 1959.

This provision in the act allows contractors to establish "prehire" agreements with unions. This allows the contractor to employ union people at predetermined wage scales and conditions of work *without* an NLRB determination of which union should represent the contractor's work force on each separate project. Section 8(f) also allows a 7-day union shop[10] to be negotiated (whereas the rest of covered industry is limited to a 30 day union shop). Other agreements in the construction and building trades industry can include

- A requirement that the employer notify the union concerning job openings
- A provision that gives the union an opportunity to refer qualified applicants for such jobs
- Job qualification standards based on training or experience
- A provision for priority in hiring based on length of service with the employer, the industry, or the particular geographic area

Wages and Hours Laws

A brief synopsis of the major wage and hour laws will help the practitioner appreciate the scope of federal influence in construction. It is also important to remember that the vast majority of states have passed laws regulating the method and frequency of wage payments and often the method of collecting unpaid wage claims. These laws might well specify such things as the minimum frequency of payment, type of payment, and conditions in the cases of quitting, discharge, strikes, absences on payday, and so forth. While many collectively bargained contracts will spell out such detail, it is important for the contractor to be aware of the relevant state laws. It is vitally important that the contractor keep accurate and timely records of the hours worked and the wages paid to employees.

The Fair Labor Standards Act, 1938.   The principal law regulating wages and hours is the Fair Labor Standards Act (FLSA). The intent of the law is to prevent the payment of substandard wages and to increase the number of persons employed. The FLSA requires all private employers (above a certain minimum size) subject to federal law to pay at least a minimum hourly wage to "nonexempt" personnel as specified by the law. In addition, nonexempt personnel are to be paid time and a half of the worker's regular hourly wage for work beyond 40 hours in a week. There are many specific employer exemptions to the act. It is advised that the contractor become fully aware of these provisions.

The Copeland Act (1934).   Often referred to as the "anti-kickback" law, the Copeland Act makes it illegal for an employer to require workers to return part of their wages as part of the employment condition. While the Copeland Act pertains only to federally assisted contracts (projects), states have similar legislation.

The Davis-Bacon Act (1936).   Also known as the Prevailing Wages Law, the Davis-Bacon Act requires that wages and benefits paid be of a certain minimum amount as found by the secretary of labor to be prevailing in the geographic area. The requirement, however, is pertinent only to federal and federally assisted construction projects above a certain minimum size.

The Equal Pay Act (1963).   The Equal Pay Act is an amendment to the FLSA. Simply put, it requires equal pay for equal work regardless of the sex of the employee. Aimed at eliminating discriminatory practices toward women in the workplace, the Equal Pay Act defines equal work as work performed by men and women requiring equal skill, effort, and responsibility performed under similar working conditions. Wage differentials can be justified on the basis of seniority, merit, or measures of quality or quantity of performance. It is critically important to have valid and objective measures of these criteria, however!

Fair Employment Practices Laws

In addition to the above conditions the contractor needs to be aware of several laws which have a say about the terms and conditions of the employment relationship. The following are prominent laws affecting the practices of employment.

The Civil Rights Act (Title VII, 1964).   The Civil Rights Act has an influence on the establishment and operation of employment conditions. Employers are prohibited from discriminating against any individual with respect to compensation, terms, conditions, or privileges of employment because of an individual's race, color, religion, sex, or national origin.

In addition, labor organizations cannot discriminate. Some prohibitions the union faces are:

- The union cannot exclude or expel individuals from membership because of the aforementioned conditions.

- The union cannot cause an employer to discriminate against an individual.
- The union cannot utilize discriminatory practices with respect to admission or employment in apprenticeship programs.

The coverage of Title VII of the Civil Rights Act is based on the phrase "industry affecting commerce," and except for exemptions related to small size and a few others, the coverage is extremely extensive. The term "commerce" is defined in Title VII to mean trade, traffic, commerce, transportation, transmission, or communication among the several states; or between a state and any place outside thereof; or within the District of Columbia, or a possession of the United States; or between points in the same state but through a point outside thereof. The Title VII equal opportunity employment obligations extend to all government contracts of $10,000 or more.

Executive Order 11246.   Executive Order 11246 was issued by President Johnson in September 1965. This order required "affirmative action" (by federal government contractors) in the recruitment, treatment, and retention of minority employees. Basically, the affirmative action concept requires that an employer seeking to do business with the federal government do more than refrain from discriminatory practices and policies and go beyond the maintenance of current passive discriminatory conditions of employment. Affirmative action requires specific results and positive steps oriented toward the elimination of employment barriers to minorities and women.

The Office of Federal Contract Compliance (OFCC) was created in the Department of Labor to carry out the enforcement of 11246. In June of 1975, the OFCC was merged with two other equal employment programs to create the Office of Federal Contract Compliance Programs (OFCCP), which currently monitors employment practices of federal government contractors with respect to women and minorities.

In the early years, the OFCC concentrated much of its effort on the construction industry. It encouraged contractors, associations, unions, minority organizations, and other groups to develop "hometown plans" that include annual minority employment goals for individual trades.

In 1978 extensive revisions were issued by the OFCCP concerning the affirmative action regulations as they apply to the construction industry. Affirmative action requirements apply to all contractors and subcontractors holding a federal government contract in excess of $50,000 and who employ 50 or more employees. Contractors who pass this threshold of size are required to develop affirmative action plans and to take positive steps to eliminate discrimination in their organization. Such contractors will not be considered in compliance until affirmative action plans are developed and approved by the government. The Labor Department has broad authority in the administration of contracts and sanctions of noncompliance.

Moreover, the regulations generally apply to all employees of the contractor, not just those working on a federal or federally assisted project. Individual states have their respective addenda to the laws. It is advised that the contractor consult legal aid in the event that he or she is in doubt about the coverage, intentions, or specific requirements of Civil Rights Act and Equal Employment Opportunity.

Age Discrimination Employment Act of 1967.   The Age Discrimination Employment Act is a federal statute which prohibits discrimination in employment against workers over 40 years of age. ADEA's authority largely parallels that of

Title VII and previous legislation mentioned. ADEA applies to all private employers with 20 or more employees, all state and local governments, employment agencies servicing covered employers, and labor unions with 25 or more members.

Several amendments have been made to ADEA. In 1974 the coverage of the law was extended to federal government employees. In 1978 ADEA was amended to raise the upper age limit on coverage from 65 to 70. Additionally, it prohibited the forced age-based retirement of employees younger than 70. The Older Americans Act amendments, effective October 9, 1984, granted ADEA coverage to any U.S. citizen employed by a U.S. employer in a workplace in a foreign country. In 1986 the Act was amended to remove the mandatory retirement age of 70 for most of the nation's private sector workers.

It is unlawful under the ADEA for employers of 20 or more persons

- To fail or refuse to hire, discharge, or otherwise discriminate against any individual with respect to compensation, terms, conditions, or privileges of employment because of age
- To limit, segregate, or classify employees in any way which would deprive any individual of employment opportunities or otherwise adversely affect his status as an employee
- To reduce the wage rate of any employee in order to comply with this act
- To indicate any "preference, limitation, specification, or discrimination" based on age in any notices or advertisements for employment
- To operate a bona fide seniority system or employee benefit plan that requires or permits the involuntary retirement of an employee because of his age

Exceptions for certain age-based conduct of the employer or covered institution exist, however. Among these are

- Where age is a bona fide occupational qualification reasonably necessary to the normal operation of the business
- Where the differentiation is based on a reasonable factor other than age
- Under the terms of a bona fide seniority system or any bona fide employee benefit plan . . . which is not a subterfuge to evade the purposes of the act
- Where the discharge or discipline of an individual is for good cause

As one can see, the law is full of obligatory actions for the employer to prevent discrimination of all types. The construction manager needs to develop careful plans and actions in the compliance to these obligations lest he or she run the risk of loss of federal government contracts, disbarment, or even a possible civil suit alleging discrimination. Unfortunately, there are no universal definitions to some of the terms and requirements of the laws. "Affirmative action," "positive steps," "bona fide seniority systems," and the like are largely a matter of court or Department of Labor interpretive precedence. In case of doubt, the contractor should contact the appropriate government regional office (e.g., Department of Labor or EEOC) or trade association for advice and consultation regarding design or implementation questions.[11]

Occupational Safety and Health Act.   Although not considered a fair employment practice law, the Occupational Safety and Health Act should be of concern to the employer. This law gives the secretary of labor the authority to promulgate mandatory health and safety standards applicable to every private employer in a business that affects interstate commerce. Inspections to determine compliance to the standards are conducted by OSHA inspectors operating out of offices throughout the United States. OSHA inspectors are authorized to issue citations in the event of noncompliance. An employer can contest a citation by appealing the citation to an Occupational Safety and Health Review Commission within 15 days of the citation, as specified by the act.

It is the function of the Commission to review and adjudicate such contested cases. Section 5(a)1 of OSHA imposes a duty on employers to provide their employees with an employment environment which is free from recognized hazards likely to cause injury or death. In order to prove a Section 5(a) violation the secretary of labor must prove that

1. A cited condition is "recognized" as a hazard by the employer, or its industry, or that an ordinary, reasonable person familiar with the industry would recognize the condition as presenting a hazard.
2. The hazard is "likely to cause" death or serious physical injury.

Among the many other provisions of the act worth noting is its prohibition of employer retaliation against any employee who files a health-related complaint to an OSHA field unit. Specifically, employers are forbidden to "discharge or in any manner discriminate" against any employee who has

1. Filed a complaint under or related to the act
2. Instituted or caused to be instituted any proceeding under or related to the act
3. Testified or is about to testify in any proceeding under or related to the act
4. Exercised on his own, or on another's behalf, any right afforded by the act

Any employee who feels that he or she has been discriminated against may, within 30 days after such a violation occurs, file a complaint with the secretary of labor. If the secretary finds merit to the complaint, he has the power to initiate a civil action in a federal district court for "appropriate relief."

This brief survey of industrial relations law demonstrates only the main federal legislated obligations. Many states and local ordinances also may need to be considered in the execution of a given project or in ordinary operations.

OTHER COLLECTIVE BARGAINING ASPECTS

Collective bargaining agreements in construction are often negotiated between local unions (representing different crafts) and the employers of that craft represented by an association. Contractor associations vary widely in their composition and related bargaining structure; moreover, the structure of bargaining (between locals and associations) varies widely in the various regions of the country. Very typically, however, negotiations with each craft are conducted by a committee which includes contractors and/or association representatives and representatives of the germane building trades unions. Either side (labor or management) may be consulted by a national arm. For instance, the national contractor's association may represent the local chapters to the international union and may provide information and assistance to the local association.

If the employer is included in a multiemployer bargaining unit (e.g., through an association), that employer may be unequivocally bound by the joint action of the bargaining unit if such a condition is a requirement for membership or if such a condition is authorized to the unit by the contractor. If, on joining the association, the contractor clearly states that he or she will not be bound by the joint negotiation, he or she cannot be bound. Generally, the contractor can withdraw from a multiemployer bargaining unit at any time given appropriate notice to the unit. An exception to this is that the contractor cannot usually withdraw from the unit once negotiations have begun (except by the joint consent of the other employer and union bargaining parties to the negotiations). In this case, the former employer member will still be legally bound by the association's agreement. The employer cannot make his participation in the bargaining unit contingent on the outcome of the negotiations. In the event that other contractors withdraw from the unit during the negotiations with union consent, the remaining members of the bargaining unit remain bound by the agreement reached by the association.

CONTENT OF THE COLLECTIVE BARGAINING AGREEMENT

The collective bargaining agreement in construction is often a relatively short document printed in booklet form. Copies are often distributed to workmen. Since business agents and union stewards will generally carry a copy of the agreement (and be very familiar with it), it is advised that the contractor become very knowledgeable about it as well. A typical contract will include:

1. The jurisdiction of the craft union[12]
2. The scope of the agreement (geographic area and type of work covered)
3. A union security provision
4. The hours of work (including overtime or holiday provisions)
5. Any provisions for shift work
6. The frequency and method of payment
7. Wage rates (including any specified time before increases, fringe benefits, and different scales for different tasks)
8. Travel provisions (if the employee travels any unusual distances to work, related expenses may be negotiated as part of compensation)
9. Holidays (including specification for holiday work or holiday pay if any)
10. Working conditions (including such things as work rules, responsibility for tools, liability for loss of personal property, and storage of tools)
11. Prohibition of piecework (many agreements prohibit payment of any type of compensation to employees other than hourly wage rates, fringes, and premiums for overtime)
12. Reporting pay
13. Designation of foremen when a specific number of journeymen are on a job
14. Safety provisions
15. Subcontractor provisions

16. Dispute settlement procedures (e.g., grievance procedures and arbitration avenues to be taken)
17. Contractor's liability (if the contractor is required to put up cash bonds for performance of its obligations under the collective bargaining contract)
18. Picket line conditions (often providing that the contractor will not penalize or discharge in any manner any work person who refuses to cross valid picket lines of any trade in order to report to work)
19. Clean-up time
20. Contract enforcement (The business agent is often granted access to construction sites in order to perform his or her duty to police the work. He or she cannot interfere with the progress of the work, however.)

The contract will contain an expiration date. When either side wishes to terminate or modify the contract, it must notify the other party of its desire to do so at least 60 days in advance of the termination date of the contract, and such party must be available for negotiations. When 30 days have expired from the notification to reopen contract talks, the party desiring to change conditions must notify the Federal Mediation and Conciliation Service (or a similar state agency) as to the existence of the dispute.

CONCLUSION

This chapter has introduced the fundamental labor law and characteristics of unions and employer associations. It is recommended that concerned contractors keep abreast of the frequent changes in this field and their commensurate responsibilities. Other recommended sources are

Bureau of National Affairs, *Construction Labor Report* (a private weekly newsletter service for construction), Washington, D.C.

Bureau of Labor Statistics, *Employment and Earnings* (monthly), Washington, D.C.

Benjamin Taylor and Fred Whitney, *Labor Relations Law,* 5th ed., Englewood Cliffs, N.J.: Prentice-Hall, 1987.

REFERENCES

1. Dan Q. Mills, "The Labor Force and Industrial Relations," in James O'Brien and Robert Zilly, eds., *Constructors Management Handbook,* New York, New York: McGraw-Hill, 1971, p. 9.3.
2. Steven Allen, "Declining Unionization in Construction: The Facts and the Reasons," *Industrial and Labor Relations Review,* vol. 41, 1979, p. 345.
3. Richard Freeman and James Medoff "New Estimates of Private Sector Unionism in the United States," *Industrial and Labor Relations Review,* vol. 32, 1979, pp. 143–174.
4. Leo Troy and Neil Sheflin, *Union Sourcebook,* West Orange, New Jersey: Industrial Relations Data Information Systems, 1985.

5. Courtney Gifford, *Directory Of U.S. Labor Organizations,* Washington D.C.: Bureau of National Affairs, 1986–1987 and 1988–1989.

6. Herbert Northrup, *Open Shop Construction Revisited:* Philadelphia, Pennsylvania: Wharton School, Industrial Research Unit, 1984, p. 19.

7. Reference 6, p. 22.

8. Dan Q. Mills, *Labor Management Relations,* 2d ed., New York, New York: McGraw-Hill, 1986, pp. 147–148.

9. For an excellent synopsis of federal labor relations law consult *A Guide to Basic Law and Procedures under the National Labor Relations Act* Washington, D.C.: Office of the General Counsel, 1987. It is available through the Superintendent of Documents, U.S. Government Printing Office, 20402.

10. There are different kinds of union security terms allowed by the NLRA as amended. A *closed-shop* contract is one which *requires* union membership as a condition of hire or continued employment. Under the original NLRA of 1935, closed-shop agreements were permitted. The 1947 LMRA amendments to national labor law *prohibits* closed-shop contracts. A *union-shop* contract requires union membership as a condition of retaining employment. Union membership is not required as a condition of hiring; however, employees must join the union within a specified time after they are hired or after execution of the contract (usually 30 days, but in construction such time may be as short as 7 days). A *maintenance of membership* contract is one which requires all employees who are union members at the time the contract is executed or at a specified time after its execution, and all employees who become members thereafter, to retain union membership as a condition of continued employment. This type of contract imposes no membership obligation on employees who do not join the union or who resign from the union before the contract takes effect or during a contractual "escape" period (a period often 15 to 30 days after the contract's effective date). An *agency shop* contract requires all employees covered by the agreement to pay the union amounts equivalent to regular dues and fees (or some percentage of such) required of union members.

11. The Bureau of National Affairs, *Labor Relations Expeditor,* Washington, D.C., 1989, pp. LRX 410:103.

12. For a good source on jurisdiction, see *Construction Craft Jurisdiction Agreements,* Washington, D.C.: Bureau of National Affairs, 1987.

CHAPTER 5

MARKETING CONSTRUCTION SERVICES

Verner M. Meyers Architect

Associate Professor of Construction Management
Emeritus
University of Nebraska
Lincoln, Nebraska

The successful marketing of construction services is the prime factor in the life of a construction firm. Elementary as that may be, the simple requirement that business must be acquired under highly competitive conditions often leads to the quite unintentional acquisition of business resulting in a loss. Doing business at cost is only an illusion. It must be done at a profit or at a loss!

This primacy of business acquisition easily leads toward its isolation. However, it cannot remain isolated, for its strength or weakness is really the summation of the strengths and weaknesses of all the elements that go together to form the business entity. It is as if marketing were the apex of a broad-based pyramid built upon a many-faceted base of necessary talents required to bring a construction project from contract document stage to physical completion. A weakness in any of these facets will ultimately result in a weakness at the apex—the marketing function.

For example, bidding, negotiating, and bonding are all important facets in the pyramid structure and cannot be treated as isolated management functions. To do so is to bid or negotiate emotionally rather than logically—an indication of incompetence, which is the primary cause of failure in the construction industry. It does not follow, however, that excellence in all the facets that make up the firm will automatically lead to business acquisition. There are other forces at work in the marketplace, many of which are beyond the control of the individual firm. Failure to recognize these forces and their destructive power is failure to face reality. Marketing, then, involves using the total strength of the firm in the best way possible under existing external limits within which a firm must live.

MARKET LIMITATIONS

Not all construction work can be considered a part of the available market for a specific firm's services. Limitations are imposed by the qualifications of the firm

5.1

to perform specific types of work. To successfully compete for work a firm must recognize and evaluate its limitations before beginning attempts at market penetration.

Market limitations can be quickly recognized by comparing a firm's available capabilities with the requirements of a specific construction project. For example, a firm with excellent qualifications for handling projects involving cast-in-place reinforced concrete may not have the ability to perform well on projects involving structural steel assembly. Thus, a firm's ability to penetrate a specific market is determined by its ability to perform in accordance with the construction documents.

Every phase of the market under consideration must be evaluated after careful analysis by management from the standpoint of its ability to meet contract performance requirements. Inaccurate analysis at this point is a clear indication of incompetence, not only because of possible failure to perform, but more seriously because of the underlying inability, refusal, or failure to objectively assess the firm's capabilities.

Serious problems sometimes result with the construction process when careless marketing puts a company on a project that is foreign to its inherent capabilities. Most contractors, especially in the beginning stages of their existence, are wise enough to seek projects with which they are familiar. Those who do not may suddenly discover the limitations of their firms and gain a reputation of incompetence.

Marketing efforts must be limited to those areas with which the contractor is familiar. This is often difficult, for construction firms are generally aggressive and strive to expand their range of market capability and volume. This is, of course, desirable if it is done carefully and with a full understanding of the problems to be encountered in recruiting employees with necessary skills and establishing good working relationships with a new group of specialty contractors.

Incompetence in marketing can be disastrous. Dun and Bradstreet reports that over half of all construction failures result from incompetence, much of it in the marketing area. An executive of a major surety company concurs: "I would agree that the selection of work acquired and the price at which it is acquired is an indication of management competence or a lack of it." Successful marketing, then, depends on the ability of management to thoroughly understand the firm's capabilities and capacity.

MAJOR MARKET AREAS

The Private Sector

Construction work in the private sector includes that which is financed by private funds under the control of an individual, a partnership, or a corporation. The expenditure of private funds is usually not controlled by statute but rather by the owner acting in his own best interest. Within the private sector construction work may be acquired by competitive bidding directly with the owner or his representative or by negotiation.

Competitive Bidding. Under this system the owner will normally award a contract to the low bidder from a selected list of contractors or, occasionally, from a group of contractors who have volunteered to bid. Marketing efforts under this approach may be difficult, but in the private sector contract awards do not always go to the lowest bidder. Project documents may include such statements as:

"The owner reserves the right to reject any or all bids."

"In awarding the contract for the work involved, the owner will take into consideration that bidder's proposal which is in the best interest of the owner."

These clauses are included in the bidding documents to prevent the owner from being put in the position of agreeing to a contract with an unknown or unsatisfactory bidder. However, they also imply that the owner may select the successful bidder from the list of submittals whether or not the selected bidder is low. Thus, under these conditions, it is evident that marketing efforts may be effective in securing work for a firm even under competitive bidding.

Successful marketing under these conditions requires more than the mere submittal of a brochure or a brief letter. To influence the owner's decision it is necessary for the contractor to have provided detailed information about the firm's capabilities and its management personnel long before the bid date. This process may require a year of lead time to have any significant impact on the owner, implying that the contractor must be constantly on the alert to identify potential projects.

Negotiated Contract. There are several forms of negotiated contracts used in the industry and their procurement can often be achieved through an effective marketing program. In the early stages of project development, the owner may not have decided on an approach to signing a final project contract. At this point, the alert contractor is in an excellent position to orient the owner toward a negotiated contract through timely marketing.

Since all owners are not familiar with the negotiated contract, it may be feasible for the contractor to arrange a series of educational meetings to sell the owner on the idea. Under this form of contract the relationship between owner and contractor is quite sensitive and the most successful negotiated contracts are those under which the two parties achieve a clear understanding of their roles before the contract is signed.

Of course, the contractor may not succeed in selling the owner on the negotiated contract concept. However, time has not been wasted if the owner has been left with a good image of the construction firm. Even if the project goes out for competitive bidding, the aggressive contractor will almost surely be placed on an invitation-to-bid list and may still be selected even though he is not the low bidder.

Construction Management. The construction manager approach to project delivery has been in existence for over 20 years and takes a variety of forms. Essentially, the owner retains a construction management firm which may or may not do any of the actual construction work. In effect, the construction manager (CM) is retained by the owner as his representative and usually guarantees a maximum project price via control of both the design and the construction function. Generally, the CM utilizes the "fast track" approach, under which bid packages are prepared as soon as portions of the design are completed. These packages then go out for competitive bids and work on the project gets under way before the total design is completed.

For contractors seeking work under this system, their marketing program may well involve an approach to both the owner and the CM. However, care must be exercised to avoid challenging the leadership role of the CM even though the owner may be actively involved in the process. Often the CM has sole responsibility for putting together a list of contractors invited to bid on specific packages and may on occasion actually negotiate contracts when time and quality are dominant factors.

The Public Sector

Nearly all public work is awarded on the basis of competitive bidding. Since public work is funded through either taxation or assessment, opportunity to secure construction work so funded must generally, by statute, be given to all qualified contractors. Bidding procedures on public work are similar to those for private work except for the following:

1. Technicalities in bidding are more closely observed. Since the work involves public funds, all procedures are vulnerable to attack from any taxpayer. This necessitates rigid control on the part of the public officials.

2. Public work may require a certified check or cashier's check as security in lieu of a bid bond. The submission of such checks may significantly affect the contractor's cash flow until canceled.

3. The low bidder may be required to submit to the governing body complete details of company operations and finances to prove the firm's competence and financial stability.

4. Prequalification may be required before a contractor is allowed to bid. This is usually a formal process involving filling out detailed forms and participating in interviews.

While this set of conditions appears to leave little room for marketing efforts, it must be noted that the clauses quoted under private competitive bidding are also found frequently in the documents for public projects. Thus, work does not necessarily always go to the low bidder. And, there are often situations resolved by judgment calls on the part of public officials. Thus, it behooves the prudent contractor to extend his marketing efforts to each and every public official who might be involved in contract decisions.

IMPORTANT FACTORS IN MARKETING

Business Reputation

The reputation of a construction firm is largely determined by the owner(s). People in leadership positions tend to surround themselves with people who conform to their own set of standards. Thus, reputation is built by company managers who deal with the client, and their values are more often than not the values of their superiors. The prime qualifications for building a sound company reputation include the ability to make timely decisions with the competence to see that these decisions are delegated and executed at all levels throughout the firm.

Every contact made between the company and the public adds or detracts from its reputation. Much like the reputation of an individual, company reputation is formed slowly over a period of time through the accumulated weight of its individual contacts with people outside the firm. But reputation is a many-faceted thing; to some clients a construction firm's reputation for low-cost construction may be paramount; to others a reputation for superb craftsmanship may be of prime importance. Obviously, a firm cannot be all things to all clients, so in the long run any firm's reputation has the effect of limiting its market. Thus, in the final analysis, it is essential that company reputation is formed as the deliberate result of the owner's efforts.

Since the activities of constructors are so openly concerned with the general public—a 40-story building or an interstate highway is hard to hide—they are often judged and labeled. Job progress, housekeeping, noise levels, concern for the public, and a host of other details all add bits of color to the collage called reputation. Whether that collage is pleasing or irritating depends entirely on the contractors and the care with which they build.

Skill, integrity, and responsibility are the hallmarks of most successful construction companies. That this is so is a tribute to those who provide the leadership in their firms. Of course, business reputations must finally be based on the ability to perform all phases of the work required by the contract. This is essential both in times of stress and when things are going well. The reputable contractor earns his reputation in periods of real difficulty: surviving strikes, overcoming inclement weather, solving errors and omissions by the designer, and working around delayed materials shipments to keep the project on schedule.

The nature of the construction business is unique in the fact that daily operations are carried out on the basis of trust and faith between the parties involved. Even new, small firms expend large sums of money on a daily basis. The rapid flow of funds implies the need for a first-class accounting system complete with foolproof checks and balances. However, errors in recording fund transfers may still occur even with the best accounting system. If such errors can be quickly explained to the client he will probably understand, but if they occur too often and are detected too late, the contractor's reputation may quickly be destroyed!

Financial Status

Success in marketing is difficult to achieve unless the company being marketed is strong both managerially and financially. Any prospective client will require assurance, before signing a contract, that the construction firm being dealt with is financially able to provide required services without encountering financial difficulty. An attractive four-color brochure cannot conceal a weak financial position.

Undercapitalization imposes a serious penalty on the contractor because operating costs are increased to the point where competitively priced cost estimates are impossible. At current charges for financial service, these additional overhead costs become substantial. Few businesses can operate without short-term loans, often at regular intervals, and the cost of such financing must be considered in determining project costs. Inadequate financing, which results in failure or inability to discount payables, unnecessarily penalizes the firm financially. This in turn leads to a weak credit rating, adding further penalties in the form of higher interest rates proportionate to the higher risk assumed by the lender.

Intelligent financing is an important key to the success of any construction venture, large or small. The maximum bonding provided by a surety is dependent on the contractor's financial position, thus setting an upper limit on the amount of work that can be undertaken. As a rule of thumb, the average maximum bond that will be written for an otherwise acceptable construction company ranges from 5 to 10 times the net quick assets—current assets minus current liabilities. This, of course, assumes that receivables are good, that the statement is normal both above and below the line, and that steady progress is being made.

To operate successfully, the contractor must maintain a complete and continuing relationship with banking and bonding companies. To establish such a relationship, the contractor must involve both in every detail of the business, whether requested or not. Further, to withhold information at any time, even though it appears to be private and may be discouraging, can only serve to breach the mutual confidence that must exist. A review of financial status with both banker and bonding company should occur at regular intervals, certainly once a year. For more aggressive construction firms this interval could be shortened to every three to six months, and under rapidly fluctuating conditions even shorter intervals should be considered.

Credit rating of both individuals and companies are of utmost importance in the operation of a business. The client's final selection of a contractor may well be determined by credit rating, financial condition, and bonding capacity. Net worth cannot be a sole measure of financial acumen and competence. A financial statement showing a large net worth may, because of heavy short-term liabilities or questionable receivables, reflect only a moderate quick position. Pending litigation may also render the statement worthless.

Financing encompasses all phases of a contractor's operation including such areas as purchasing, invoicing, review and authorization of invoices for payment, actual payment of those invoices, submission of statements for work done, and actual collection of accounts receivable. To permit collection of receivables to lag is to seriously injure the contractor's financial position, both in day-to-day operation as well as in the acquisition of new business. It is not in the best interest of either the contractor or the client to permit accounts to become delinquent.

Experience

Even though there is no past construction record to report for a new firm, a marketing program should be an integral part of the firm's formation. A carefully planned brochure containing a brief but complete history of the firm's principals should be prepared, not only for use with potential clients but also to acquaint specialty contractors, material suppliers, and financial organizations with the new firm. The brochure should acquaint all of these contacts with projects on which the principals have played a significant role and emphasize their construction management capabilities learned while employed by other firms.

Personal contact is important in the early stages of a firm's growth and few projects can be unworthy of consideration. Experience is the measure of a firm's capability and that can only be obtained by taking on any project that can be efficiently handled. The accumulation of a good track record on many small projects is the best route to consideration for larger ones. Along the way, errors and omissions on projects may occur and even the best marketing program will fail if these are not disposed of quickly. A reputation for following up on architects' punch lists, resolution of disputes over the meaning of specifications, and prompt response to change orders is invaluable in promoting future work for a contractor. This does not mean that the contractor must capitulate to every demand of the architect, engineer, or owner, but a reputation for fair and prompt response to those demands can be a strong plus.

MARKETING INFORMATION SOURCES

Trade Magazines

The many trade magazines serving the construction industry provide an invaluable source of information for the contractor's long- and short-term marketing program. In addition to providing coverage of new products, methods, and management techniques, trade publications provide data on market trends that can be useful in charting the direction of a firm's future growth. Reading detailed project reports may also give the discerning contractor insights on how other firms have acquired work and how they deal with their clients to maintain successful long-term relationships. While most of these publications also carry invitations to bid for public—and sometimes private—work, it is generally true that this information comes too late to be of great value. Aggressive contractors are aware of and actively seeking these projects long before the print invitation appears.

Since the list of trade magazines is long and varied, construction firms should study them carefully and select only those that are pertinent to their own specialized areas of interest. Once this selection has been made it is wise to appoint one or more people to be responsible for reading the magazines as they are issued and alerting other personnel to read articles that will be useful to them in their particular area of responsibility. The importance of forming regular reading habits for publications important to the firm cannot be overemphasized.

Public Advertisements

Statutes generally require that invitations to bid be published for projects sponsored by government agencies at all levels from local to national. These are usually placed in newspapers and magazines and often are posted in public areas of government buildings. The purpose of these published invitations is to alert the public to the proposed expenditure of funds. Notification is also often made directly to a list of qualified contractors. The bid notices are assumed to provide sufficient information if bid date and time, place of letting, and a brief description of the work are included. Quite often, additional information is provided such as name of the designer(s), location where documents may be inspected, bonding requirements, and an estimate of project cost.

Architects and Engineers

In developing a mailing list for marketing efforts it is important for the contractor to include the names of architects and engineers practicing in the area in which the firm wishes to find work. However, marketing efforts with design firms should include more than mail contact. Personal contact is extremely important because these firms hope the owner will receive several competitive bids from well-qualified contractors. They welcome the contractor who is able to convince them that the work will be produced by a competent and financially qualified organization.

When the designers' documents are ready for bidding, oral or written notice is given to qualified contractors. Established firms with a strong estimating staff may elect to bid all jobs about which they are advised by a selected group of design firms. Assuming that this approach can be used consistently, there is no better way for the contractor to develop strong ties with design firms as they are assured that a responsible bid will be made to the owner for all their projects.

It is important to point out that acceptance and retention of plans and specifications from the designer is an indication that a bid will be submitted. Failure to bid under these circumstances results in a hardship for the owner and an embarrassment for the designer if sufficient bids from qualified firms are not presented. When the contractor procures documents and decides not to bid it is good practice to notify the owner and the design firm and return the documents.

Governmental Agency Bid Lists

Marketing efforts should also be directed to all agencies such as those at city, county, state, and federal government levels. These agencies, like the design firms, depend on current lists of active contractors who can translate plans and specifications into useful structures.

At the time the bidding documents are complete, but prior to their distribution, the formal notice to bidders is presented to those contractors currently on the agency list. Interested contractors may then formally request that the bidding documents be forwarded to them. To be included on an agency bid list requires that the contractor be prequalified. This may involve anything from filling out a simple form to a lengthy process involving extensive paperwork and personal interviews with contractor key personnel.

Plan Services

During the comparatively short period between the publication of bidding documents and the actual receipt of bids it is important that the documents be made available to the greatest number of specialty contractors and material suppliers possible. The cost of supplying each of these with a complete set of documents soon becomes prohibitive, even for relatively small projects. To assist the designer in covering these parties and as a service to general contractors, plan service centers have been set up in many cities. Membership in these centers is available at a relatively low cost and they usually publish a list of projects for which documents are available in the center's plan room.

The use of documents in these centers is generally by specialty contractors and material suppliers whose estimating work can be completed in a relatively short time. Prime contractors are normally issued a complete set of documents for their own use by the owner or his design firm. However, many general contractors use documents from the plan room to determine whether or not they wish to seriously pursue the project. General contractors also benefit from the plan service center's publication of parties using the plans, thus assuring them that they get prices from all specialty contractors and material suppliers who have prepared quotations for their portions of the work.

In addition to the above plan service centers there are a number of commercial ventures at the national and regional level designed to serve the construction industry. The best-known national service is provided by Dodge Reports, a subsidiary of McGraw-Hill. Participants in the construction process can order reports based on project type, location, size, and other options. Also available is complete project documentation on microfilm with a viewing table to project the information on a flat reading surface to original scale. Similar, but less sophisticated, services are provided by a number of companies operating on a regional basis.

Promotional Media

Advertising. Paid advertising in print, radio, or television is generally not a viable option for contractors because of the poor cost/benefit ratio. However, a few very large firms have run effective campaigns in such publications as *Fortune, The Wall Street Journal,* and *Engineering News-Record (ENR)*. Help wanted advertising in specialized trade journals can also be used effectively as a marketing tool. While the main goal may be recruitment of personnel, the company can be presented in a manner that is appealing both to potential employees and to potential clients.

It must also be pointed out that some advertising in local newspapers or publications with localized circulation may be a necessity. Typically this involves a contribution to a congratulatory ad run at the completion of a project which is important to the immediate community. It might also involve a contribution to public service ads such as those supporting the local police, charitable fund drives, or church attendance. While these contributions individually are inexpensive, a firm may reach the point where cumulative costs are prohibitive. However, used discreetly, such advertising can help to create a good image of the company and contribute to its marketing campaign.

Brochures. A well-designed, four-color brochure can be a very expensive promotional tool. However, it is also an effective tool for providing a potential client with basic information about the firm's capabilities and may be a door opener for personal contact. For general distribution, a brochure should offer a quick overview of the construction firms's capabilities, personnel, and project experience. But, as a construction company becomes more sophisticated in its marketing effort it may wish to present more carefully targeted information in pursuit of a particular project. For this purpose a colorful binder and a collection of individual personnel résumés, project pictures, and other information sheets can be prepared. By carefully selecting the right collection of single sheets, tailor-made brochures may be bound for use with a specific client and a specific project.

Newsletters. For the new or small company, a newsletter might well serve the dual role of communicating with employees and promoting the firm with potential clients. There are many areas of company activity which are of interest to employees as well as clients and a cleverly prepared bulletin may pique the interest of both. However, as a firm grows it might prove more effective to prepare a separate newsletter for promotional use with clients. Whatever the choice, newsletters should be published at scheduled intervals so that they have a cumulative effect on their intended audience.

PUBLIC RELATIONS

Maintaining an Image

Image, whether corporate or individual, is the conception of the corporation or individual as it is seen by the public and the firm's clients. It differs from reputation because, to some extent, it is possible to deliberately create and maintain an image. Image is developed with every contact between a firm, the public, and the firm's clients. Individuals react differently to those contacts; what appears to be high-pressure selling to one client may simply appear to be aggressive marketing to another. Therefore, the development of the company image requires constant watchfulness on the part of management. Written policies are essential and must be rigidly enforced and constantly restated. Employees are rightly most concerned with their own areas of responsibility, so it is up to management to ensure that they contribute to the overall image the company wishes to present. Important elements that create company image include letterheads and other company stationery, external communications, and community relations.

Letterheads and Other Company Stationery.   While it is important to maintain an established standard, stationary styles are subject to change. Thus it is important to review the appearance of all company paperwork and redesign it when necessary. Essential elements such as the company logotype should be retained, but even these should be subject to change when they no longer create the desired company image.

External Communications.   The image formed by a well-designed letterhead may be quickly destroyed by sloppy typing and poor writing. The business letter cannot be anything less than clear, concise, and neatly typed with the addressee's name properly spelled. Similarly, phone contacts should be initiated by contractor personnel only after they have given careful thought to what they have to say and how they want to say it. The construction industry's public image is often that of the rough-and-ready "bull of the woods" management approach and every firm should be contributing to the disappearance of this negative image.

Community Relations.   Involvement by company personnel in community affairs is one of the best ways for a company to enhance its image. However, such involvement must be sincere because phonies are quickly detected and written off as opportunists. Thus, firms should limit the involvement of key personnel and support their efforts on behalf of the community only in those areas where a genuine interest is apparent. Boy Scouts of America, American Red Cross, churches, service organizations, and a host of other local groups are in need of assistance and sincere effort by volunteers is usually given due notice in the local press and by word of mouth.

Responsibility for Public Relations

Every person in the employ of the construction firm has a direct impact on its public relations effort. The surly craftsman on the job site may do as much damage to a firm's reputation as a thoughtless vice president. Thus, it is important for a company to have a well-planned public relations approach and to make it known throughout the company. Construction is inherently fascinating to the general public as evidenced by the well-worn term "sidewalk superintendent." However, it can also be an irritant. The unscheduled arrival of a foreman, two carpenters, and a laborer at a retail store remodeling project can cost the client loss of customers. The congestion on a downtown project created by poor signing can irritate the public to such a degree that the contractor's reputation is marred for years. Working with the client to schedule arrival of crews, placing prominent signs to route traffic around construction sites, and a variety of other techniques can be used to make the client and the public aware of the fact that the contractor is concerned about their problems and willing to try to minimize them.

Telephone Procedure

Unless management carefully establishes and maintains basic rules governing telephone communication, it can become an irritant instead of a convenient tool for marketing in addition to its basic communication function. The following items are important in establishing phone procedures:

1. An approach to the handling of incoming calls must be established, particularly for phone operators, receptionists, and secretaries.
2. At crucial times, such as during the few hours prior to bid submittal and opening, phone lines must be kept clear by careful and courteous screening of incoming calls.
3. During a client visit, incoming calls must be deflected to avoid offending the client and, perhaps, interrupting a train of conversation that could lead to signing of a contract.
4. Return calls must be handled promptly. Clients and potential clients expect and deserve immediate response.
5. To be effective, business telephones must be available. This means that nonbusiness calls must be discouraged except in cases of emergency.

Client Contact

The transition from potential to actual client is dependent on the contractor's ability to develop a close relationship based on mutual understanding. Personal contact is mandatory and the contractor must use every possible approach to establish frequent contact with potential customers. This contact may be in the formal setting of either party's office, but there are opportunities for contact at social gatherings, community activities, and other informal occasions.

Entertainment is a valuable tool for business development because it allows the contractor to better understand the nonbusiness facets of a client's character and personality. However, before it can be used successfully the contractor must know something about the client's attitudes. For some individuals a pleasant business lunch is routine, for others it is tantamount to a bribe. Thus, the contractor must gear the cost level of entertainment to the client's concept of ethical conduct.

Of course, the Internal Revenue Service has something to say about the deductibility of business entertainment expense and the contractor should be aware of its rules. These have become more restrictive in recent years and it behooves the prudent host to consult with his advisers about the tax deductibility for more expensive forms of entertainment. Finally, however, for the contractor who has become familiar with clients' outside interests and hobbies, an afternoon at the ballpark may well be worth a dozen office visits in developing a solid business relationship.

Maintaining Client Contact

At regularly scheduled intervals, management should review its list of prospective clients and the projects they have in the development stages. These meetings have three principal objectives:

1. Eliminate the possibility that a potential client has been overlooked or neglected.
2. Provide the opportunity for management to review the current workload potential and to select key client projects to be pursued.
3. Analyze available marketing tools and select those best applicable to the development of selected projects.

It should be the responsibility of each individual on the marketing team to provide a current status report on each of the client projects he is attempting to develop. A sample form for this report is shown in Fig. 5.1. Suggestions for developing the project may be offered by the review group and priorities established for each project on the active list. The personal computer is an effective tool for keeping this information up to date.

Of course, the client list must include those clients who have no projects in the development stage as well as those for whom previous marketing efforts have been unsuccessful. For the latter group it is important to analyze all actual bids and proposals presented to them to seek out the basic reason for the failure to make a sale. Figure 5.2 is a simple form that can be helpful in this analysis. The infor-

```
CURRENT STATUS REPORT          Date_____Project Number _____

Name of Project_____

Location_____

Name of Client_____

Name of Architect/Engineer_____

Current status of project _____

_____

Client contacts since last report_____

_____

Client contacts Satisfactory _____  Unsatisfactory _____

Explain _____

_____

Tentative date of bid or construction start _____

Name of Sponsor _____

Comments by review committee _____

_____
```

FIGURE 5.1 Current status report for active projects.

```
BID OR PROPOSAL ANALYSIS                   Date _____

Name and Description of Project _____

_____

Location _____

Architect/Engineer_____

Owner _____

Total square feet _____   Total cubic feet _____

Cost per SF _____   Cost per CF _____

Tabulation of bids submitted _____

_____

Our bid was _____% high _____% low   Explain _____

_____

Unusual conditions affecting cost _____

_____

Name of Sponsor _____

Committee comment and analysis _____

_____
```

FIGURE 5.2 Bid analysis form.

mation can be collected from company files and presented to a review committee at regularly planned meetings.

Client Contact via Letter

Letter writing sometimes appears to be on the road to extinction in the conduct of daily business. However, there are many occasions when a letter from a construction executive to a client or potential client can give the marketing process a significant boost. Well-written letters may not only improve the company's image but also create the opportunity for personal contact. Letters expressing appreciation for contracts awarded, clarifying proposals, or even offering best wishes on a project awarded to a competitor can be effective in maintaining contractor-client contact.

Sample form letters are provided in Figs. 5.3, 5.4, and 5.5. If carefully used they can make a contribution to the marketing program. However, since letters should reflect the personality, character, and ability of the writer, it is probably best that they be written individually and tailored to cover specific aspects of each unique contractor-client relationship. Such letters are not easy to write and they must be mechanically perfect in spelling and grammar.

Mr. Alfred _____, President
_____
_____

Dear Al:

Thank you for your telephone call this morning asking that we
proceed with your office addition. We appreciate your confidence
in our firm and we intend to complete the work to your entire
satisfaction.

Your project is important to us and we recognize that it will be
a vital addition to our city's business center. We are,
therefore, especially pleased to have been selected as your
general contractor.

Within the next few days we will submit a suggested construction
schedule along with procedural details for your review. At that
time we would also like to have you meet with the project manager
who will be in charge.

Again, our sincere thanks for your confidence in our firm.

Cordially,

William _____, President
_____
_____

FIGURE 5.3   Sample client follow-up letter on award of contract.

Mr. William _____, President
_____
_____

Dear Bill:

Just a few minutes ago we finished reviewing our monthly list of
receivables and again found your company listed in the current
column. As you can guess, Bill, we spend a great deal of time on
delinquent accounts but often forget to thank those who are
always in the current column. We want to correct that with this
letter, so please accept our sincere thanks for your prompt
response to our requests for payment.

Your confidence in our firm is sincerely appreciated and we will
continue to do everything possible to maintain it.

Sincerely,

John _____, President
_____

FIGURE 5.4   Sample letter of appreciation for prompt payment.

Mr. Joseph H. Collington, Vice President

_____
_____

Dear Mr. Collington:

Bill Johnson advised me of your visit to our office yesterday to discuss your proposed warehouse addition. I am sorry that I was out of the office and I want you to know that we are eager to work with you.

Since we have not previously done any work for your firm I am enclosing a brochure prepared especially for you to demonstrate our capability for handling the type of project you have in mind. If you wish to have any additional information, please feel free to contact me or Bill.

As your requirements develop, we would be pleased to explore your project in more detail and help to solve any problems you may encounter.

Sincerely,

Peter _____, President

_____
_____

FIGURE 5.5   Sample follow-up letter after potential client's office visit.

CHAPTER 6
ESTIMATING

First Edition

Robert B. Hemphill
Barclay White
Philadelphia, Pennsylvania

Second Edition

Lillian Watson, CPE
O'Brien-Kreitzberg & Associates
Pennsauken, New Jersey

PHILOSOPHY OF ESTIMATES

What is an estimate? According to the dictionary, to estimate is "to judge tentatively or approximately the value, or to produce a statement of the approximate cost." This is truly the interpretation of an estimate in the broadest sense. For the construction industry, an estimate encompasses many things, but in every case it involves an approximation of the value of a project, not the exact cost that will be encountered. This is true whether the estimate is prepared for budget purposes or for a firm-price contract in a competitive situation. A construction-cost estimate is prepared by evaluating the various component elements that make up the project. Theoretically, the finer the detail, or the larger the number of elements used in estimating a project, the more accurate the total estimate should be. This can be proved mathematically. However, it does not always work out in practice.

PURPOSE OF ESTIMATE

A construction-cost estimate is used for different purposes by different people. Those primarily involved in its preparation and use are the owner of the facility, the architect or engineer, and the building contractor. The owner uses the estimate to determine capital-investment costs, to assist in financial arrangements, or to determine the economic feasibility of a project, as well as for taxation, insurance, and evaluation purposes. The engineer uses the cost estimate to aid in site selection, to determine the design of a facility, or to choose between alternate designs. The contractor relies on a cost estimate for the submission of a competitive bid for a lump-sum contract or the preparation of a definitive estimate for a negotiated contract.

SCHEMATIC ESTIMATES

Contractors are finding that they need to do estimates early in the project cycle. These early estimates are necessary to facilitate fast-track projects with a guaranteed maximum price (GMP). Other reasons can include the role of construction manager or participation in a development team.

The schematic cost estimate is an estimate done early in the design of a project. Unlike the traditional detailed estimate done by subcontractors or general contractors, the schematic estimate is prepared within a short time frame and is not considered to be a hard bid (although it can be the basis for a GMP).

During the first phase of a project, the architect prepares single-line drawings that show the tentative layout and relationship of the project's programmed components as required by the owner. These drawings can be either freehand or performed by a draftsman. They are not always to scale but are usually in reasonable proportion to the intent of the project. Complete construction documents will not be available at this early stage. In prior meetings, the architect and owner should have discussed and made decisions regarding the level of quality versus costs, building size, location, etc. At this time, the estimate or statement of probable construction costs, known as a schematic cost estimate, is useful in feasibility studies and in creating general budget allowances.

TYPES OF SCHEMATIC COST ESTIMATES

In contrast to a general contractor who submits a bid that incorporates quotes or bids worked up by subcontractors' estimators for various disciplines, the schematic cost estimate is done completely by an estimator knowledgeable in many trades or by estimators from each of three prime disciplines—general trades, mechanical, and electrical. The depth of detail is the same as if each subcontractor had prepared his own bid.

There are four ways to prepare a schematic cost estimate: on a cubic foot basis, on a square foot basis, by assemblies, and by using an abbreviated CSI format method. It has been said that an estimate can be prepared on a postage stamp when the first two methods are used.

   Cubic foot basis: It isn't often that you will find an estimate done on a cubic foot basis. Cost files for such estimates are limited. As the name implies, you must calculate the number of cubic feet in the building before applying the appropriate costs per cubic foot.

   Square foot basis: To prepare a schematic cost estimate on a square foot basis, first calculate the gross square footage of the building. Organize the takeoff by floor from the basement to the roof. Also, measure the perimeter of the footprint of the building and note the floor-to-floor heights. Application of this information to the information found in reference books for square foot costs allows project costs to be estimated.

Assemblies: To estimate by the assemblies method, group the construction information by function—foundations, skins, roof, finishes, etc.—instead of separating the data by individual line items. For example, a skin assembly would consist of face brick, rigid insulation, and 8-in block backup. In a detailed estimate it would be broken down into three line items. Assemblies are sometimes referred to as systems. The optimum is to combine assemblies with the abbreviated Construction Specification Institute (CSI) format.

Abbreviated CSI format: CSI format is a method of organizing construction information according to a system of classifications and numbering that is widely accepted as a standard in the industry. (Refer to Figure 6.1.) It was developed by the Construction Specifications Institute. A detailed estimate

---

CONSTRUCTION SPECIFICATIONS INSTITUTE
DIVISIONS 1–16

Division 1   General Requirements

Division 2   Sitework

Division 3   Concrete
              03100   Concrete Formwork
              03200   Concrete Reinforcement
              03300   Cast-in-Place Concrete
              03400   Precast Concrete

Division 4   Masonry
              042100 Brick Masonry
              042200 Concrete Unit Masonry
              044000 Stone

Division 5   Metals

Division 6   Wood and Plastics

Division 7   Thermal and Moisture Protection

Division 8   Doors and Windows

Division 9   Finishes

Division 10 Specialties

Division 11 Equipment

Division 12 Furnishings

Division 13 Special Construction

Division 14 Conveying Systems

Division 15 Mechanical
              15300   Fire Protection
              15400   Plumbing
              15500   Heating, Ventilating & Air Conditioning

Division 16 Electrical

FIGURE 6.1 Construction Specifications Institute divisions. This is not a complete list of the CSI Divisions with corresponding subdivisions. It is shown to illustrate a portion of the intended format.

uses each division and subdivision that applies to the project being bid, involving as many line items as necessary to make sure that "all bases have been covered" and that no portion of the project has been overlooked. Since a minimum of drawings, details, and specifications are available at the schematic cost estimate level, you cannot create a "nuts and bolts" estimate using the complete CSI system. Hence, the abbreviated CSI format.

DATABASE AND COST FILES

Reference material is usually sorted by type of project—residential, commercial, and industrial. These are further subdivided by the specific type of project. Construction magazines publish project costs each month. Over a period of time you can create your own cost file. It is possible to subscribe to one magazine that will photocopy four looseleaf notebooks containing all costs in CSI format from past publications.

At this early phase, it is necessary to use short cuts and one way is to estimate some trades on a square foot basis. Fire protection, HVAC, and electrical information is limited to the types of systems to be used. Specialty books and database files are available from which can be selected the appropriate costs for the type of project or system. In-house cost files can be even more valuable, especially if they apply to the project in hand. An architect whose projects lean heavily toward education facilities would have costs for schools that could be converted to present-day costs using historical cost indexes.

Historical Cost Index

An historical cost index is a table of figures that allows adjustments to known construction costs to be made forward (or even backward) from one year to another.

City Cost Index

It may also be necessary to use a city cost index (CCI) to adjust known construction costs from one geographic area to another. Most suppliers of database systems provide a CCI for their costs and instructions for its use.

PREESTIMATE MEETING

Before a schematic cost estimate is started, a meeting should be held to discuss the intent of the construction. Along with the architect and designer, the representatives from the consultants selected for mechanical, electrical, structural, and landscaping should be present. At this meeting each describes the guidelines on which the intent of the development was based. If outline specifications are not available, take notes regarding information or guidelines on which to base the schematic cost estimate. Do not hesitate to ask questions regarding finishes, the skin, the roof, level of quality, special systems, etc.

With copies of the single line drawings, which could be anything from one drawing to perhaps as many as three dozen, along with the outline specifications or notes, there should be enough information to prepare a schematic cost estimate. The use of the abbreviated CSI format will be expanded in this chapter along with selected use of assemblies.

FORMAT—QUANTITY TAKEOFFS

In addressing format for quantity takeoffs, there is no totally correct or incorrect method. Keep it simple and easy to follow. The best test for an acceptable format is to ask another estimator to follow the steps taken and continue the estimate. There are preprinted estimating sheets that can be purchased or specifics can be developed. Most experienced estimators don't use the preprinted forms for schematic cost estimating. Each project is so individual with respect to the information and documents available that most prefer using graph paper for quantity takeoffs. The importance of keeping the estimate organized, consistent, and concise can't be emphasized enough. (Refer to Fig. 6.2.)

One point of great significance is the use of columns. Areas have been taken off but not included in totals because the column system was not followed. For this reason, math extensions should not be performed until after the graph sheet has been partially used up, and, therefore, it dictates where the columns should be located.

Unless a digitizer or other computer program is used to perform mathematical extensions, the use of a calculator with a tape is recommended. A small, hand-held machine is too small, too time-consuming, and too inconvenient if more than a couple of extensions are needed. The keys just don't seem to fit adult-sized fingers. A full-size calculator or adding machine is to the estimator what the typewriter keyboard is to a secretary-typist. It is another tool for the estimator. Fingertips are sensitive to touch and can feel the raised bump on the middle key, so you can easily locate the keys without looking at the keyboard.

Another critical point which needs to be mentioned is legibility. Simply keep it readable. On the other hand, don't go to the opposite extreme and use one block on the graph paper for each letter. It is tedious to read. (Refer to Fig. 6.2.)

Assumptions

Since details and specifications are rarely available during this phase, make assumptions based on standard practices in the industry. For example, gymnasiums would be expected to have a special wood floor; most bathrooms would have a ceramic tile finish; executive areas receive upgraded finishes; frames, doors, and hardware in stair towers should be fire-rated and include panic hardware and closers; folding partitions require a support pocket above; and tempered glass is required in certain areas. Other considerations are perimeter foundation insulation, use of pressure-treated wood, and depth of footings in particular geographic areas. For future reference keep a list of assumptions that were made.

Direction for Measurements

When performing quantity takeoffs—specifically measurements—be consistent and go horizontally and then vertically. This may sound insignificant, but if you

JOB ASPE PROJECT

SHEET NO. _____ OF _____

CALCULATED BY _____ DATE 11/89

CHECKED BY _____ DATE _____

SCALE _____

	GROSS#	PERIM	F-F HT	SKIN
B $44 \times 65 - 14 \times 14^6$	2,657	218	15	3,270
1 " " $+150^6 \times 57 + 21^6 \times 35^6 - 17^9 \times 6$				
$+ \frac{1}{4} \pi r^2 \, r = 21^6 + 77^3 \times 51 + 70 \times 21^6 - 3^6 \times 10$				
$+ 92 \times 62$	23,369	885	15	13,275
2 $44 \times 65 - 14 \times 14^6 + 150^6 \times 57 + 21^6 \times 35^6 - 17^9 \times 6$				
$+ \frac{1}{4} \pi r^2 \, r = 21^6 + 77^3 \times 51 + 70 \times 24^6 - 16 \times 14$				
$- 4 \times 13$	17,634	716	13	9,308
3 $30^6 \times 65 - 10 \times 37 + 152 \times 51^6 + 20^3 \times 12 - 20^3 \times 6$				
$+ 70^6 \times 54^9 + 71 \times 12^3 - 20 \times 28^9$	13,717	671	12	8,052
4 SAME AS 3RD	13,717	671	12	8,052
5 $20 \times 59 + 75^6 \times 26^6 + 26^6 \times 45^6 + 20 \times 51^6$				
$+ 30 \times 113 + 20^6 \times 13^3$	9,078	676	12	8,112
	80,172#			46,799#

B Areaway 44×14

ROOF

	GROSS#	LF PERIM	ROOF HT
Lectures $92 \times 62 + 16 \times 11 - 49 \times 3$	5,733	336	21'H
Mech $49^9 \times 13^3$	660	126	28'6 H
Above 2ND Flr areas: $24^3 \times 50^3 - 10 \times 14$	1,079	149	28'6 H
20×28^9	575	97'6	28'6 H
$94^6 \times 5^6 + 7^8 \times 56$	949	316'4	28'6 H
$19^6 \times 11^3 + 20^3 \times 7^8 + 1^3 \times 6 + 0^9 \times 2^3$	-		
$+ \frac{1}{4} \pi r^2 \, r = 21^6 - 1^3 \times 5^6$	737	103'6	28'6 H
Above 4TH Flr areas:	-		
20×50^3	1,005	140'6	52'H
$10^3 \times 28^3 + 152 \times 6$	1,202	381	52'H
Mech at 5TH Flr:	-		
76×19^6	1,482	191	52'H
20×48	960	136	52'H
Above 5TH Flr:	-		
$20 \times 59 + 75^6 \times 26^6 + 26^6 \times 45^6 + 20 \times 51^6$	-		
$+ 30 \times 113 + 20^6 \times 13^3$	9,078	676	64'H
	23,460#	2,652'10 LF	

FIGURE 6.2   Quantity takeoff.

get into this habit, you will be able to tell at a glance where each measurement came from. This expedites figuring perimeters and perimeter-related quantities. Also, go clockwise or counterclockwise and always start at the same place on the drawings. Be consistent!

Beginning the Takeoff

If the single-line drawings are to scale, begin by taking off the gross square feet by floor, by wing, and by building. These figures provide a readily available tool for checking the work. For example, the total square footage of all the floor finishes or ceiling finishes should be close in value to the gross square footage. This also applies to the quantities used for the floor slabs, metal deck, and other horizontal materials. It won't be exact because there are openings for elevators, stairs, and shafts, plus allowances for wall thicknesses. Another example is that the area of the total roof coverings must at least equal the total of the largest floor area. Keep the areas of each floor, wing, and building separate and only total them on a summary sheet. During this phase, design changes are not uncommon, so if changes must be made, redoing the estimate is much easier.

Use of Highlighter Markers

Use highlighter colors for marking areas taken off. Never use ink or colored pencils. Once a drawing has been colored with solid markers, you can't read what was below. A black felt tip pen is an estimator's nightmare. Develop a consistent pattern of using certain colors to represent certain items. This is a tremendous help in spotting a specific item at a later date.

Continuing the Takeoff

In conjunction with the gross square feet, the next step is to take off the lineal feet of the building perimeter at each floor level. This information is used for footings, foundation walls, exterior walls, parapets, and roof-related items such as coping and flashing. Also list floor-to-floor heights at each level. The product of the lineal feet of perimeter and the floor height at each level equals the square foot of the skin, which is broken down into exterior doors, windows, precast, storefront system, or whatever the project requires.

On a separate sheet(s) of graph paper, take off the room areas by function. (Refer to Fig. 6.3.) Keep the areas to the left (also known as left-justified) so that the right-hand portion can be used to calculate doors, interior glass, interior finishes, etc. Using photocopies of the original sheet(s), develop columns on the copies to record the information needed. Figure 6.2 demonstrates a staggered-column technique, which was purposely used to separate dissimilar finishes. The extreme right is used to summarize and total the finishes. One set of copies can be used for miscellaneous information such as stairs—risers, treads, landings, and handrails; chalkboards and tackboards; count of toilet room fixtures, etc. Gather the quantities using as many sets of copies as needed. On some sets you will not use all the lines. Although it seems like a waste of paper, the time saved (labor) warrants this procedure.

Keep in mind that quantities are interrelated. Some quantities should be

JOB **ASPE PROJECT**

SHEET NO. **1** OF **4**

CALCULATED BY _____ DATE **11/89**

CHECKED BY _____ DATE _____

SCALE _____

			CLGS	FLRS
24 *Classrooms:*			2×4 14,712	VCT
32 seat (27×27)2	1458		7,370	14,712
50 " (27×27)2	1458		12,140	12,139
45 " (26×27)2	1404		9,648	2,124
45 " (25×27)4	2700		2,124	28,975 ✓
32 " (29×27)2	1566		45,994 ✓	
35 " (25×19)6	2850			CARPET 7,370
35 " (26×19)2	988		2×2 13,260 ✓	9,648
35 " (22×26)4	2288			13,259
4 *Lecture Halls:*	14,712 VCT, 2×4 A/c, INSUL.		2×2 M/R 2,940 ✓	30,277
100 seat (42×29)2	2436			3,364 ˢ
200 " (39×51+½[39×6+7×21])	2180		2×4 F/R 896 ✓	+1%=3398 ✓
275 " (51×53+3×17)	2754		STD D/W	
14 *Toilet Rooms:*	7,370 carpet, 2×4 A/c, INSUL.		536 ✓	PTD 188
(9×17)2	306	98	360	F/R D/W
9×24−2×2	212	63	236	9,420 ✓	9,406
(21×13)3	819	222	924	INSUL	9,594 ✓
13×17	221	57	252	14,712	CT FLOORS
21×11	231	71	264	7,370	2,605 ✓
(11×14−3×5)4	556	188	640	1,535	BASE
(10×14−2×5)2	260	90	264	23,617 ✓	789 LF
3 *Stairs:*	2,605 CT 789 LF ×4"=3,156 CT	2,940 2×2 M/R		WALLS
14×23 (1−5)	336			3,156
26×11 (1−2) 15°	24			
24×11 (2−3) 15°	60			
19×11 (3−5) 12°	72			
25×11 (5ᵀᴴ) 12+R	312			
4×22 (1−B) 15°	80			
7×14 (B) −	892 # F/R			
Grand stair incl. w/ Corrs & Lobbies				
5 *Jan Clo:*				
(7×6)2	84			
(8×5−3×1)2	74			
(6×5)	30			
	188 pts			

FIGURE 6.3 Takeoff by room areas.

worked together to expedite the completion of the estimate: for example, windows and blinds, and footings, foundations, and waterproofing.

No two projects are identical. Mentally build the project from the ground up to avoid missing anything. Be alert to an exceptionally small quantity that utilizes only one trade. This will affect pricing.

Once all the data are accumulated, transfer this information onto the computer final estimate form.

FORMAT—FINAL ESTIMATE

The format of the final estimate to be presented to the architect and client is also very important. (Refer to Fig. 6.4.) The descriptions need to be more than just a few words, although it is acceptable to use standard construction abbreviations. If a particular item is located in a single area, call this out: HM doors/HM frames/ hardware, fire-rated, 3070, w/panic hardware—*Fire Stairs*. The client knows assumptions made or codes followed by locating the item or group. It isn't neces-

SCHEMATIC COST ESTIMATE

ASPE PROJECT
CLASSROOM & OFFICE BUILDING

JOB NO: 077220-20
DATE: NOV. 4, 1989

ITEM	QUANTITY	COST	UNIT COST	TOTAL
9. FINISHES				
VCT - Classrooms, corrs.	28,975	SF	2.28	$66,063
Carpet: seating area, teaching platforms & offices	3,398	SY	28.00	95,144
Ceramic tile floors (T)	2,605	SF	6.80	17,714
Ceramic tile base	789	LF	7.35	5,799
Ceramic tile walls 4'H	3,156	SF	7.65	24,143
Ceilings:				
Exposed painted	188	SF	.50	94
Fire-rated drywall-Mech.	9,420	SF	2.11	19,876
Standard drywall	536	SF	1.48	793
Suspended acoustical:				
2'x2' M/R Toilets	2,940	SF	2.10	6,174
2'x2' SE Office flrs	13,260	SF	1.75	23,205
2'x4' F/R Stairs	896	SF	1.90	1,702
2'x4' Std. Clsrm flrs	45,994	SF	1.55	71,291
6" ceiling sound insul.	23,617	SF	.56	13,266
Ceiling verticals	1,516	LF	1.70	2,577
Acoustical wall treatment: 1-5/8" metal studs 16" O.C.; 1/2" gypsum drywall T&S; 1-1/2" polystyrene rigid insulation R8.1	34,914	SF	2.74	95,664
Painting:				
Doors (paint or stain)	222	EA	45.00	9,990
Drywall ceilings	9,956	SF	.40	3,982
Drywall walls	75,134	SF	.35	26,297
Drywall walls (epoxy)	34,914	SF	1.25	43,643
CMU walls (epoxy)	23,936	SF	1.67	39,973
Floors, epoxy Mech area	9,594	SF	2.10	20,147
Exterior soffits at entrances	160	SF	4.21	674
Drywall partitions - Off.	16,758	SF	2.37	39,716
Drywall partitions F/R or demising - Corridors	18,312	SF	3.69	67,571
TOTAL				$ 695,458
COST PER SQUARE FOOT				$8.67

FIGURE 6.4 Final estimate.

sary to have multiple line items for each part. Instead items are grouped into one unit. This is known as grouping by assemblies. For example, a suspended acoustical ceiling can be one line item. However, the acoustical subcontractor would have individual line items for the grid system, the lay-in ceiling panels, hanging wire, and wall angle or wall molding.

Simplicity and clarity are positive steps toward a finished estimate that doesn't appear busy. It is this estimator's opinion that upper and lower case letters are easier to read than all caps. Items such as CMU, VCT, and EWC stand out in all caps, as do headings, subtotals, and totals—creating a visual aid. The use of the dollar sign ($) should be used only at the extension on the first line and at the total line(s). Used at every extension, it becomes an interference.

The use of commas is of utmost importance. Make it a habit. When the "eleventh hour" type situation is at hand, it helps to eliminate possible errors. Reading 100000 as 10,000 or 1000000 as 100,000 is a large mistake that could have been prevented by the use of a comma.

In contrast to the subcontractor's estimate, the separation of material and labor costs in corresponding columns is not required. One unit price is all that is needed. It is too early in the design phase to go to such great detail. Since this is not a hard bid, it is also premature to assume that the unit costs can be given in less than even cents. To use $2.762 as a unit cost would be inconsistent with the approach that a schematic cost estimate is not a hard bid. Use prices from your own data first followed by costs from available costs files in printed or computer form.

The total cost column can be extended in full dollars instead of dollars and cents. It is acceptable to round off extensions to increments of tens, fifties, or hundreds. But it must be consistent. Or extensions can be made in full dollars and then rounded off the CSI division total to increments of tens, fifties, or hundreds. This estimator does not round off in the higher increments, but prefers to use dollars and cents or full dollars on the individual sheets but rounds them off on a summary sheet.

To create a summary sheet (refer to Fig. 6.5), set up the page in column form. There are several ways to do this. The simplest is to show only CSI divisions and total cost for that division. Figure 6.5 illustrates an expanded summary that also includes project gross square feet, unit cost, and percent of subtotal. After listing all the applicable CSI divisions and corresponding costs, draw a line, add the column, and create a subtotal.

To this subtotal add an amount for contingencies and general conditions. A contingency is a figure added to the estimated costs to cover unknowns—unforeseen or unpredictable work. Lack of specifications and details at this early stage warrants a higher percentage to be added to the estimate than at a stage of further development. It can be as low as 10 percent and as high as 20 percent. Even these extremes are not absolute. There may be a project with enough information to go below 10 percent or one so vague that it requires more than a 20 percent contingency. This requires a judgment call on the estimator's part.

General conditions can be included on a percentage basis or can be estimated according to the number of months allocated for the construction schedule. If calculated according to time, include this with CSI Division 1 "General Requirements." A percentage basis approach can be obtained from actual jobs with known costs. Once again, in-house database files would come into use.

Subtotal the accumulated costs so far. Overhead and profit is calculated on the new subtotal. This is done on a percentage basis and is determined by past experience, the construction market at the time, and geographic location.

SCHEMATIC COST ESTIMATE

```
ASPE PROJECT                              JOB NO: 077220-20
CLASSROOM & OFFICE BUILDING               DATE:   Nov. 4, 1989
```

DIVISION	QUANTITY		UNIT COST	TOTAL COST	% S/T
2. Site Work	80,172	SF	2.09	$ 167,560	2.37%
3. Concrete	80,172	SF	3.94	315,880	4.48%
4. Masonry	80,172	SF	13.21	1,059,070	15.00%
5. Metals	80,172	SF	15.09	1,209,800	17.14%
6. Wood & Plastics	80,172	SF	.26	20,840	.30%
7. Thermal Moist. Prot.	80,172	SF	1.26	101,020	1.43%
8. Doors & Windows	80,172	SF	8.18	655,810	9.29%
9. Finishes	80,172	SF	8.67	695,090	9.85%
10. Specialties	80,172	SF	2.15	172,370	2.44%
11. Equipment	80,172	SF	.10	8,020	.11%
12. Furnishings	80,172	SF	2.16	173,170	2.45%
14. Conveying Systems	80,172	SF	1.99	159,540	2.26%
15A. Plumbing & Site Util	80,172	SF	4.35	348,750	4.94%
15B. Fire Protection	80,172	SF	1.08	86,590	1.23%
15C. HVAC	80,172	SF	13.90	1,114,390	15.79%
16. Electrical	80,172	SF	9.61	770,450	10.92%
			88.04	$7,058,350	
Contingencies 10%				705,840	
General Conditions 6.5%				458,790	
				$8,222,980	
Overhead & Profit 10%				822,300	
				$9,045,280	
Escalation 7.5%				678,400	
				$9,723,680	
Bond 1%				97,240	
TOTAL PROJECT COSTS				$9,820,920	

FIGURE 6.5 Expanded summary.

Subtotal again. Since the project is still in the design stages, an escalation factor must be added. Escalation is a figure added to cover increases in construction costs. The amount is often calculated to the midpoint of construction. It is determined by current interest rates and increases in the cost of living. Add this amount to the previous subtotal.

Subtotal again. If the project is to be bonded, a ½ to 1 percent (1989 percentages) amount must be added to cover the cost of the bonding agent.

The last line is the total project cost.

TYPE OF ESTIMATE

The type of estimate required will be dictated by the purpose for which it is to be used. Estimates range all the way from an initial feasibility "guestimate" to a de-

TABLE 6.1 Types of Building Estimates

B1	Detailed quantity survey and application of unit prices for material and labor for all building components
B2	Preliminary quantity survey with application of installed unit prices. Some items may be approximated as a percentage of the building
B3	All building components priced on a unit cost basis, that is, cost per square foot of floor area, roof area, or wall area. Special items may be estimated on a lump-sum basis
B4	Entire building cost estimated on a total cost per square foot of floor area
B5	Building cost estimated as a function of occupancy, for example, cost per pupil for school buildings

TABLE 6.2 Types of Process-Plant Estimates

1. Detailed quantity survey and unit prices based on quotations or experience for all items of equipment, material, labor, and indirect charges
2. Price quotations for equipment and preliminary quantity survey with material and labor unit prices based on experience for all other items
3. Equipment prices based on budget quotations or published data, all other items based on a "flowsheet and layout" takeoff with installed unit prices from published data
4. Estimated cost of purchased equipment and multiplying factors applied to purchased-equipment cost for all other items
5. Estimated purchased cost of each item of equipment multiplied by an installed-cost factor
6. Total estimated cost of equipment multiplied by an overall factor
7. Actual cost of a similar plant of different capacity adjusted by a scale-up factor and a current-cost index
8. Average plant cost per unit of plant capacity

tailed lump-sum bid. A breakdown of the most common types of estimates for process plants and buildings is shown in Tables 6.1 and 6.2.

The feasibility, order-of-magnitude, or budget estimates are usually prepared by an architect-engineer or possibly by the owner himself. A contractor may be asked to prepare this type of estimate if he has had previous experience in building a similar facility.

This chapter concentrates on the preparation of lump-sum competitive-bid estimates and several types of factor estimates.

LUMP-SUM COMPETITIVE-BID ESTIMATE PREPARATION

In order for a contractor to prepare bid proposals successfully, the estimating group must be organized to handle estimate preparation efficiently. The following are suggestions for organizing and implementing the procedure for preparing a lump-sum competitive-bid estimate.

Decision to Bid or Not to Bid

Once a contractor has received an inquiry to bid a project, obtain the bidding documents and review the project in order to make an intelligent decision as to whether to bid the job. In reaching this decision, consider the following:

1. *Competition:* Who else is likely to bid this job? How many bidders will there be? Are the bidders equal, or are they smaller contractors with a lower overhead?
2. *Nature of the job:* Is our firm capable of building this project? Have we done any similar work? Do we have superintendents and project managers with the right kind of experience?
3. *Market conditions:* Is the job extended over a long period? Will there be many unknown factors such as labor rates, material prices, or other prevailing economic conditions which may upset the project?
4. *Firm's previous experience with this owner or architect:* Have we done work with them in the past? Has our relationship been satisfactory? Do we consider them a good client or a good architect? Would we like to work for them again? Are we obliged to submit a bid because of our past relationship?
5. *Cost to prepare a proposal:* Does the probability of getting the job warrant the cost of preparing the proposal? What are the chances of winning the job at a reasonable profit?

All these and other factors should be considered in a logical way in order to reach a decision to bid or not to bid. The contractor must pursue this thinking as early as possible and reach a firm decision in order to provide the estimating staff with as much time as possible to prepare the bid.

Record of Jobs Being Bid

For an active firm, it is essential that all involved personnel know which jobs are being bid and when each one is due. Someone should be responsible for maintaining a readily visible record of all jobs currently being bid, with pertinent information such as the client, date, architect, and project description and location. As soon as a decision is made to prepare a proposal for a project, the new job should be added to the list. Such a record is essential so that all personnel, including secretarial and clerical help, can offer intelligent answers to all inquiries made by vendors and subcontractors.

Organization of Estimate Team

For each project, management should organize a team to prepare the estimate and bid proposal. The chief estimator should assign a lead estimator to head up the estimate preparation. Takeoff assistants and personnel to contact subcontractors and material suppliers should be available. A survey of the needed takeoff requirements should be made, and then the project should be adequately staffed to assure that all takeoffs will be completed before the bid due date. On the day of the bid submittal, it will be necessary to have additional personnel assigned to call subcontractors, to take telephone quotations, to price extensions, and to check calculations. If the firm is going to estimate its own mechanical or electrical work, it will be necessary to have trade estimators assigned to prepare these estimates.

Breakdown of Trade Items of All Direct Work

After the estimate team is organized, its first task is to review the drawings and specifications and break down all elements by trade item for listing on the cost-summary sheet. Most building projects today have the specifications organized by trade sections in accordance with the Construction Specifications Institute (CSI) format.

The lead estimator should review the specifications in their entirety and list all items of work, identifying which items will be done by the firm's own forces and which will be subcontracted. Look for peculiar items in each section that may not be taken by the particular subtrade and be prepared to estimate the cost of these items. For example, the water stops for concrete work may be specified under the roofing and sheet-metal section. However, it is likely that the roofing and sheet-metal subcontractor will not include this item in his bid; thus, it must be picked up by the general contractor.

The list should combine all specification sections that will be worked on by the same subcontractor. For example, roofing, sheet-metal work, and dampproofing may each appear in different specification sections, but it is likely that all three items will be quoted by one subcontractor. Likewise, brickwork, stonework, and precast-concrete work may all be quoted by a masonry subcontractor even though each item is in a different specification section.

Preparing this breakdown early will provide the estimator with an overall format for organizing the estimate. Using this list as an overall guide, make assignments to subordinates for takeoff of certain trade items. The list will also serve as a guide for obtaining subcontractor and material quotations. Finally, the list will also serve as a direct-cost tabulation sheet on the day the bid is to be assembled. Figure 6.6 is an example of a direct-cost tabulation sheet.

Request for Quotations from Subcontractors and Material Suppliers

Once the estimator has prepared the work breakdown of trade items, the next step is to request quotations from subcontractors and material suppliers. This can be done in several ways, but one of the most efficient and least time-consuming is to prepare a mailing of form letters or postcards. Most subcontractors are used to receiving written requests for quotations and will respond accordingly. The letter or postcard should contain the following information:

1. Project identification
2. Owner's name
3. Project location
4. Architect's or engineer's name

DIRECT COST TABULATION SHEET

No.	Work item	Materials	Labor	Sub-contracts
1	Excavation & backfill			
2	Concrete			
3	Reinforcing steel			
4	Masonry			
5	Landscaping			
6	Misc. iron & structural steel			
7	Carpentry			
8	Roofing & sheet metal			
9	Insulation			
10	Lath and plaster			
11	Millwork			
12	Ceramic tile & Marble			
13	Terrazzo			
14	V. A. T.			
15	Hardware			
16	Misc. specials			
17	Painting			
18	Glazing & bulk aluminum			
19	HVAC & plumbing			
20	Electrical			
	TOTAL DIRECT COST			

FIGURE 6.6 Direct-cost tabulation sheet.

5. Date bid is due

6. Name of person receiving the bid

7. Item of work for which a quotation is required

It should also indicate where the subcontractor can obtain the drawings and specifications information. Figure 6.7 is an example of a postcard used to obtain subcontractor quotations. An important but time-consuming task in preparing requests for quotations is the maintenance of an accurate file of available suppliers by trade, with addresses, telephone numbers, and contact names. For contractors who have access to data-processing equipment, this file as well as the prep-

WE REQUEST YOUR QUOTATION FOR

Masonry Work

ON THE FOLLOWING PROJECT:

FACILITY: **Classroom Building, Wm Jones, Architect**

OWNER: **University of Penn.**

LOCATION: **Phila., Pa.**

BIDS ARE DUE IN OUR OFFICE NOT LATER THAN   **Sept. 1, 1990**
AND SHOULD BE DIRECTED TO

Mr. John Smith

PLANS AND SPEC ARE AVAILABLE IN OUR OFFICE FOR YOUR USE. PLEASE
ADVISE BY PHONE IF YOU CANNOT BID.

O'BRIEN-KREITZBERG & ASSOCIATES, INC.   **CONSTRUCTION MANAGEMENT**
4350 HADDONFIELD ROAD
PENNSAUKEN, NEW JERSEY 8109

FIGURE 6.7   Quotation request.

aration of the requests for quotations can be prepared and maintained by data
processing.

Quantity Takeoffs

Direct Work.   It is general practice for an estimator to take off the work directly
performed by the firm in sufficient detail to provide price extensions for all items
of material and labor. It is not the intent of this handbook to show how to prepare
a quantity takeoff for each trade item. Good manuals are available which describe
takeoff procedures for each trade. Those interested can refer to the bibliography
under Estimating Information Sources, which lists some of the available manuals.

Work should be taken off by trade item so that all like items can be tabulated
for both material and labor. Work sheets should be organized so that all similar
material items, such as framing lumber, can be subtabulated and then tabulated
on one sheet. Work performed by the same trade should be organized so that the
total man-hours can be tabulated for the trade and then multiplied by the appropriate rate. An estimator will soon learn to develop work sheets in preparing
takeoffs, although work sheets for each trade are available from a number of
sources. An example of an estimate work sheet which can be used for pricing and
labor extensions is shown in Figure 6.8.

Subcontract Work.   While it is necessary for the estimator to take off direct work
in complete detail, it is not necessary for subcontracted items. However, it is desirable to make an approximate takeoff in order to review the subcontract quo-

O'BRIEN-KREITZBERG & ASSOC., INC. 4350 HADDONFIELD ROAD PENNSAUKEN, NEW JERSEY 08109	ESTIMATE WORK SHEET

COMPANY _____ P.O. NO. _____

LOCATION _____ SHEET NO. ____ OF ____

SUBJECT _____

COMPUTED BY _____ CHECKED BY _____

ACCT. NO.	DESCRIPTION	QUANTITY	UNIT	LABOR UNITS	TOTAL LABOR MANHOURS	MAT'L UNIT	TOTAL MATERIAL COST	MAT'L CODE
	PAGE TOTAL_____				X$ /HR.			

MATERIAL CODES: Q = QUOTATION   SQ = SUBCONTRACTED QUOTATION INCL. MARKUP
                 E = ESTIMATE   SE = SUBCONTRACTED ESTIMATE INCL. MARKUP

FIGURE 6.8 Estimate work sheet.

tations intelligently and to be sure that the proper scope of work is covered. The subcontracted items should be taken off in a gross fashion. For example, masonry would be taken off by square feet of brick or block without consideration being given to subtracting openings or figuring all the special materials. Roofing would likewise be taken off by figuring the squares of roof and possibly the lineal feet of perimeter flashing and number of roof penetrations to be flashed. Flooring would be taken off by the square feet. Although this is not the way the subtrade estimator would take off his work, it is sufficiently accurate to provide the general contractor's estimator with an approximate quantity and price which he can use in checking the subcontract quotations.

Shortcuts to Quantity Takeoffs.   We have already mentioned the shortcuts that should be taken in computing quantities for subcontract work. Consideration should also be given to shortcuts in taking off direct work. Before embarking on a detailed takeoff, consider possible shortcuts and approximations that will not seriously affect the accuracy of the answers. Study the floor plans to see if they are repeated from one floor to another and whether a typical quantity on one floor can be taken off and multiplied by the number of similar floors. You may find that the same basic dimensional calculations can be used to compute the quantities for many different items. The square feet of floor area, the lineal feet of building perimeter, and the lineal feet of partitioning can often be used to compute many items such as top and base molding, grade beams, wall, floor, and ceiling finishing, and painting.

Checking Quantity Takeoffs.   A vital step in preparing an estimate is to check adequately that all quantity takeoffs and calculations have been made. If time does not allow for checking of every figure, the estimator should at least review the quantities and look for gross errors and omissions. An experienced estimator can compare quantities on a relative basis from one trade to another to determine where a gross error has been made. Spot checking of certain quantity tabulations is also helpful, but the calculations should be checked by someone other than the person who made them initially.

Job-Site Visits

An essential part of estimate preparation is a job-site visit by the lead estimator along with representatives from the contractor's management team. The construction superintendent should also make the visit to contribute information concerning the planning of the work. Certain preparations should be made prior to the job-site visit. The topographic-survey plan and the soil borings should be studied if these data are available to the bidding contractors. The extent of required demolition and sitework including excavation, underground utilities, and paving should be well noted. The estimator should make notes on the drawings of items to be checked firsthand in the field. A dictating device, a camera, a measuring tape, and a hand level would be helpful. Pictures should be taken of important features that may not be easily remembered. Accurate notes, sketches, and measurements should be taken as necessary.

During the site inspection note carefully the extent of demolition work, particularly any difficulties that might be encountered in performing it. Where possible, inspect the subsurface conditions by observing any excavated holes on the site or any rock outcropping that indicates where rock might exist. Also try to get an idea of groundwater conditions, again noting the condition of the soil and level of water in any excavations. Determine if the soil is the type that will drain well after a heavy rain, such as a granular soil, or if it is a heavy clay that will stay muddy for a long time. This will determine the amount of money allowed for temporary stone ballast to maintain the site. It is helpful to talk to local people familiar with the site or people who may have had previous experience working on an adjacent site.

Note where the access roads will be and where temporary facilities such as trailers, shops, and storage areas can be located. Determine where temporary construction power can be run and the extent of temporary service that will be required from the existing source. Also note the source of temporary water and whether project fences will be required if not clearly specified in the documents.

Often it is necessary to make a second job-site visit just prior to completing the bid to review conditions that may have been missed during the first visit.

Labor and Economic Surveys

An important part of bid preparation is the collection of data regarding the labor and economic situation in the area. If a job is located within a contractor's normal work area, it is a routine matter of projecting the known conditions for the project period. However, if a job is located outside the normal area of work, it is necessary to obtain accurate labor rates based on contract agreements with all the trade unions involved. The date of expiration of current agreements should be noted and an allowance made for the anticipated increase after the expired date. In recent years, it has been a difficult task to predict increases in wage rates accurately, since they have escalated far beyond the norm of previous years. Information can be obtained as to the projected wage-rate increase by talking to contractor associations and union business managers to obtain their opinion of what the new rates will be during the next period. The labor survey should also include information regarding the available number of men by trade so that this information can be correlated to the job requirements. Determine if there are any very large projects in the area that will be working concurrently and that may tie up all the available manpower. This condition may require the job to work with fewer people than necessary, thereby extending the schedule, or it may require an overtime schedule to attract the required labor.

It is also important to obtain any information that relates to the general economic situation in the area and that may affect the operation of the project.

Pricing

Pricing the Contractor's Own Work. First, price direct work. These items have been taken off and listed by trade section and have been tabulated on a pricing sheet that provides for the application of material and labor prices. Figure 6.8, the estimate work sheet, can also be used as a typical pricing sheet. Material prices for all direct work will be obtained from quotations of potential suppliers on major items such as form lumber, ready-mix concrete, and reinforcing steel. A contractor who continually uses a certain type of material may not bother to obtain a special quotation but rather will use the current price.

Next price out the cost of labor by using man-hour units based on your experience with the same items of work on past projects. Man-hour units should be used instead of actual dollar units since they are not affected by varying labor rates. It is extremely important that a contractor establish a cost-data system to know what labor costs are from each job and use this information in estimating future jobs. For special work items with no previous experience history, you must use judgment as to the amount of labor required. You may want to consult with the material supplier to get some assistance in pricing the installation cost. An example of this would be a special door system which the contractor has not installed previously, but for which the supplier would have reliable installation-cost data. Most equipment items would also be handled this way.

Once the direct work has been priced, check each category and compare the labor with the material to see if the balance looks right. With experience, each trade item should show a remarkably similar balance between material and labor, and any glaring errors will show up in this check.

Pricing Subcontracted Work.   The next step is to establish approximate prices for all subcontracted work. Based on the rough takeoffs described above under Subcontract Work, an estimator can apply unit prices for all subcontracted items based on a history of past experience with these trade items. Estimating manuals can also be very helpful. Some contractors take the view that taking off and pricing subcontracted items is a complete waste of time, and they rely solely on the subcontractor's quotations. However, there are several reasons why taking off and pricing subcontractor's work is beneficial. In many cases, the contractor will be able to obtain only one bid for a subtrade item, or occasionally not obtain any—a situation that may occur when the need for the subtrade is not recognized until just before the bid is due. In this event, if the subtrade item has not been estimated, the choice is to withdraw and not bid the project or make a wild guess at the last minute as to what the subtrade item is worth. In this case having a reasonably accurate subtrade estimate would be very helpful. Another benefit is derived when one subcontract bid among several from the same trade is extremely low. The estimator with a reasonably accurate takeoff available is in a better position to discuss intelligently the bid with the prospective subcontractor. A review may indicate that the subcontractor's quantities are substantially different from those of the estimator or that the subcontractor has a different view of the scope of work. With a reasonably accurate estimate by the general contractor, differences can be resolved prior to bid time. Estimating each subtrade item also provides the estimator with much more knowledge of the subtrade items and will help ferret out omissions as well as duplications among subtrade bids. When the subtrade items have been priced out, the estimator can make a rough tabulation of the total direct cost. This can be done well ahead of final bid preparation and will provide the estimator and management with a good approximation of the total bid price.

Receiving and Analyzing Subcontract Bids.   Receiving and analyzing subcontract bids is probably the most important, and the most difficult, task in preparing a lump-sum bid estimate. Although practice varies with contractors, it is likely that most of the subcontract quotations will be received just prior to the general contractor's deadline for submitting the bid. In many cases, telephone subcontract quotes will be received just minutes before the bid is due. This makes the task of intelligently analyzing subcontract quotes extremely difficult. Therefore, it is important that sound procedures be adopted in handling this difficult and delicate task.

There are several schools of thought as to how subcontract bids should be handled. One theory assumes that all subbids should be required at least 24 hours prior to the general contractor's due date. Many contractors operate this way and are very successful. The subcontractors who work with these contractors understand that this is their policy, realize that they are being fair and aboveboard in their dealings, and are willing to comply with the 24-hour requirement. However, the majority of general contractors go along with the practice of taking subbids right up to the last minute. This allows them to use the lowest possible subcontract bid offered just prior to the bid deadline. Whichever policy is adopted, the contractor should be consistent, so that his subcontractors understand how the contractor operates.

If most bids will be received by telephone on the due day, several people must be involved in taking these bids. Therefore, it is important that the bid-taking procedure be as standardized as possible. A standard form should be adopted which can be filled in by any person who takes a subcontract bid. A sample of a typical telephone bid form is shown in Fig. 6.9. Note that this form identifies the project, the subcontract bidder, the item of work, the name of the person calling for the subcontractor, the telephone number, the day and hour that the bid was received, and the person receiving the bid. All these data should be recorded in the event that it is necessary to pursue some specific detail at a later date. Note also that the form provides for certain questions to be asked by the bid taker, such as: "Is sales tax included?" "What delivery time is required?" "Is installation included?" "Are there any exceptions to the specifications and drawings?" "What is the specification trade section that the work covers?" "What addenda are included?" It is important that this form be filled out as completely as possible in spite of the limited time available for getting all the bids tabulated.

Another important step in analyzing subcontract bids is the establishment of a scope of work for each trade item and specific notations as to items that may be excluded from the bid by subcontractors. This scope of work should be in the form of a checklist. There should also be a listing of potential subbidders, which would be the same firms that were sent requests for quotations. This list can be used as a bid-tabulation sheet to record the prices so as to equate the scope of work from one bidder to another. An example of a subtrade bid-tabulation sheet is shown in Fig. 6.10.

Pricing Indirect Costs. Indirect costs can be estimated from a checklist type of work sheet. An example of an indirect-cost work sheet is shown in Fig. 6.11. In addition to figuring the cost of items on this sheet, carefully review the general and special conditions to determine what special requirements may add to the indirect costs. These include job photographs, rodent control, professional-engineering inspections, or unusual guarantees and warranties.

Some of the indirect-cost items can be figured on a monthly basis. Others can be figured as a percent of direct labor or a percent of job cost. Still others may be estimated only as an allowance. The indirect costs, often referred to as "the general conditions," often add up to a percentage of direct costs that will be fairly constant from project to project. Based on a contractor's experience, the estimator can soon learn to check the total estimate for indirect costs as a percentage of direct cost.

Proposal Preparation

Analysis of Invitation to Bid. At the start of the estimate preparation, the chief estimator or the contract administrator should make an analysis of the invitation to bid and the other bidding documents. The invitation should be reviewed to determine insurance and bond requirements, affidavits, certificates, guarantees, qualification statements, financial statements, and any other paper work that may be required to be submitted with the bid. It is extremely important that all this "boilerplate" be prepared well ahead of time so that no omissions are made in the haste of submitting a bid at the last moment.

O'BRIEN-KREITZBERG & ASSOC., INC.
4350 HADDONFIELD ROAD
PENNSAUKEN, NEW JERSEY 08109

TELEPHONE BID PROPOSAL

JOB _____   JOB NO. _____

FIRM NAME _____   DATE _____

ADDRESS _____   TIME _____

_____   BY _____

CONTACT _____   PHONE NO. _____

CLASS OF WORK _____

SPEC. SECTIONS: _____

AS PER PLANS & SPECS. _____ YES _____ NO.

INCLUDING ADDENDUMS NO. _____

DELIVERY TIME _____

DELIVERY TERMS _____

MATERIAL ONLY _____ INSTALLATION INCLUDED _____

INCLUDES:	PRICE
EXCLUDES:	
CHECK LIST:	

FIGURE 6.9   Telephone bid proposal.

Insurance and Bond Data.   The bidding documents should be screened to determine insurance requirements, including all-risk and fire insurance as well as public liability, property damage, and worker's compensation insurance. The requirements for bid bonds, performance bonds, material and labor bonds, and maintenance bonds should also be scrutinized. This information should be passed

CONSTRUCTION DIVISION		BID TABULATION
		BID DUE 4/ 7/90
==		
990 PAINTING		D&Z ESTIMATE
--------------		---------------
C O N T R A C T O R		QUOTE
-------------------------------------		---------------
0280 C.M. ROGERS COMPANY		
ONE MEADOWBROOK ROAD		
LAWNCREST, PA.		
456 3210		
ERIC COLLINS		---------------
0281 ANTHONY PIZZELLINI & SONS		
4309 S. 32ND STREET		
PHILADELPHIA, PA.		
333-4466		
MR. LORENZO PICOLLI		---------------
0282 J. BURTON JONES COMPANY		
100 SILVER LANE		
FELTONVILLE, PA.		
KU 3 2243		
BURTON R. JONES		---------------
0283 W. T. ROVNER COMPANY		
5000 WOODLAND AVENUE		
SOMERTON, NEW JERSEY		
221 5532		
DANIEL SMITH		---------------
0284 JOHN BURKE AND SONS		
853 PENN STREET		
CAMDEN, NEW JERSEY		
441 5536		
R. D. CANFIELD		---------------
REMARKS	PRICE USED	---------------

FIGURE 6.10 Bid-tabulation sheet.

on to the agent or broker responsible for handling the bond and insurance work for the contractor. Consideration should be given to the forms required. For example, is the bid bond to be furnished on the standard AIA form or some government agency form, or can it be on the insurance company's own form? The amount of the bid bond should be noted to see if it is a fixed dollar amount or a percentage amount. If a percentage of the base bid price is stipulated, it is sufficient to write this percentage on the bid bond and not worry at the last minute

ESTIMATE DETAILS

O'BRIEN-KREITZBERG & ASSOC., INC.
4350 HADDONFIELD ROAD
PENNSAUKEN, NEW JERSEY 08109

PLANT _____
SECTION _____
CLIENT _____

Page ____ of ____
Date _____
P.O. No. _____

INDIRECT CHARGES

Acct. No.	Description	Equip. No. or Unit	Unit Costs	Quantity	Estimated Cost Material	Labor	Total
10	Home Office Salaries & O.H.						
15	Home Office Expenses						
20	Field Office Salaries & O.H.						
22	Subsistence & Travel						
25	Photographs						
51	Temp. Trailers & Buildings						
23	Field Office Equipment & Supplies						
24	Field Office Telephone						
55	Temp. Electrical						
56	Temp. Heat						
58	Temp. Water Service						
54	Temp. Toilets						
52	Temp. Roads & Parking						
53	Drinking Water						
90	General Clean Up						
57	Barriers & Protection and Fences						
59	Job Sign						
41	Sales Tax						
31	Bonds						
34	Builder's Risk Insurance						
60	Permits & Licenses						
26	Tests & Inspections						
72	Major Equipment Rentals						
96	Premium Time Labor						
43	Payroll Taxes - Field Labor						
32	Liability Insurance						
33	W/C Insurance						
71	Small Tools & Consumable Supplies						
95	Unproductive Labor						
	TOTAL INDIRECT CHARGES						

FIGURE 6.11   Estimate details—indirect charges.

about converting the percentage to an actual dollar amount. Many times mistakes have been made in computation which have resulted in a bid bond lower than the specified amount. The result is a rejected bid.

Addendum Acknowledgment.   It is general practice during the bid period for the architect to issue addenda to the bidding documents. These are usually presented in the form of item changes to the original documents. It is usually necessary in the form of bid to acknowledge receipt of each addendum with the issue date.

Read these addenda carefully and pass on any changes to material suppliers and subcontract bidders. They, in turn, should acknowledge all addenda that affect their work.

Unit Prices—Add and Deduct.   Many bid forms require that unit prices for work added to or deleted from the project be supplied with the bid. Some contractor associations and many large contractors are currently resisting this practice, as it is often inequitable for both the contractor and the owner. However, it is often necessary to supply unit prices, and the contractor should take extreme care in preparing these prices. Make sure to understand what the work includes. For example, if a price for concrete is called for, does it include the formwork and reinforcement, or does it merely include the material and labor to place the concrete? The contractor should know if the concrete is to be placed in a footing in the ground or in the slab of an elevated structure. If no definition is given in the documents, the contractor should question the architect for clarification.

It is normal practice to provide different prices for work added and work deducted or deleted. The difference in price will usually be the cost of the contractor's overhead, profit, and indirect expenses. This may vary from as little as 10 percent to as much as 40 or 50 percent, depending on the item of work. In some situations the architect will ask for the add and deduct price to be the same. If this occurs, the contractor should question the validity of this approach and suggest to the architect that it is inequitable.

Scheduled Alternates.   Many bid forms will call for alternates to be quoted by the bidding contractors. The alternates are usually specified in detail and noted accordingly on the drawings and in the trade sections of the specifications. Carefully review the scope of each alternate to understand which trades will be affected. When taking subcontract and material quotations, ask for the alternate prices for those trades which are involved. At bid-closing time have a tabulation prepared for each alternate with the cost listed for each trade involved and the percentage markup added or deducted. It is difficult at the last minute to prepare an accurate price for alternates, and if this is the situation, the contractor should take a conservative approach rather than risk making a gross mistake.

CHAPTER 7
CONSTRUCTION COMPANY ORGANIZATION

Robert G. Zilly, P.E., M.A.S.C.E., A.I.C
Professor of Construction Management
Emeritus
University of Nebraska
Lincoln, Nebraska

The unique demands on the construction company organization are well described in a 1907 article from *Business World:*

> The manufacturer as a rule groups his men, machines, and facilities at one location, possibly under one roof, in any case in one plant. His forces, under effective direction, may work as a unit; one branch of the industry is within sound of the whir of machinery incident to the next step in the process of manufacture. Such contact makes for unity, and system may more nearly follow the points of least resistance. A contractor has no such grouping of his forces by location to aid him. One structure is erected in one state and another perhaps a thousand miles distant. The one building may be a factory, the other a city sky-scraper. Both are structures, but further than this the analogy may cease. Such conditions, peculiar as they are to the industry, must be met by a completeness of organization, and by an effectiveness and comprehensiveness of systematization, which will make for results in the strenuous competition which obtains in the building trade.

The article goes on to describe management techniques for the Frank B. Gilbreth construction firm which were widely acclaimed at the time. From what was written by and about Gilbreth in the early 1900s, it is evident that his company was organized as a tightly knit unit with every employee in his place and fully aware of what that place demanded of him. In short, Gilbreth took the time to establish goals and objectives for his firm and provided them in written form to make sure that every employee knew and accepted them.

Writing just over 50 years later, in his book *Construction Company Organization and Management,* George E. Deatherage said:

> At last contractors as a whole are realizing that organizing and managing a construction business differ only in detail from managing any other profit-making enterprise. It follows that the same degree of basic education, specialized training, and sound judgment are as essential in one as in the other. Violation of sound practice brings as heavy penalties in one as it does in the other.
> Because serious consideration of sound modern business practice has been so

much neglected by contractors in the past, many are still confused as to just what is meant by the term "construction organization." To many, "organization" means creating the means of orderly direction and control of only the functions having to do with the "on-the-job skills;" to others it also encompasses job, office, or administrative organization, all or some of which may include engineering functions.

In the broad sense organization means setting up the machinery to implement all the functions of a business, and that of construction differs from others only in detail. Fundamentally, the most common overall functions in the construction business are that of the executive, estimating, contracts, personnel, engineering, purchasing, accounting, payroll, and field construction....

Fundamentally these functions are not limited to areas within the contractor's organization itself but must of necessity include the interwoven relationships with architects, engineers, general contractors, subcontractors, manufacturers, material dealers, equipment distributors, labor, and finally, the general public.

Regardless of the special needs of the construction company organization, the traditional pyramid of management (Fig. 7.1), with its attendant personnel and functions, is still a valid guide for the construction company whether it is a one-man operation or a huge corporate entity. The version shown places strong emphasis on communication, verifying the need for a written document that can present a portrait of the company to everyone from chief executive down to foreman on the job site.

FIGURE 7.1 The traditional "pyramid of management" emphasizes the roles of various levels of management. Good communication up and down the scale creates an open environment under which the various levels of management can cross their boundaries to make contributions above and beyond their assigned areas.

Another way to look at the management levels is via the conceptual, human, and technical skills required (Fig. 7.2). At the top of the organization there must be strong conceptual skills, at the lower level strong technical skills. But, the chart does not do ample justice to the fact that human relations skills must be present at all levels of management—probably in equal quantities. This is evident in the field where the work is labor-intensive, but it is equally necessary at all other levels of management.

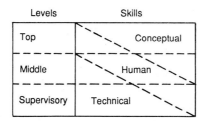

FIGURE 7.2 Human relations is the bridge between the conceptual and technical levels of management. It is the area in which most good managers must excel if their conceptual and technical skills are to be effectively applied.

ESTABLISHING GOALS AND OBJECTIVES

Few construction firms come into existence with a written set of goals and objectives. More often than not, construction firms are created to take advantage of an imbalance in local markets where there is more work than available firms to handle it or where old, dominant firms have gone into decline. For these new firms, the goal is survival by obtaining a series of projects that will be profitable enough to create financial stability. If work is plentiful and the firm survives, the entrepreneur may be able to pass along his goals and objectives to members of his firm by informal methods as long as it remains small enough for him to have personal contact with all of his employees. This situation is exemplified by a small contractor who was overheard to complain, "When I stick to an annual volume of about $2,500,000 my company runs smoothly. At $5,000,000 I get nothing but trouble and a decline in profit." After some subtle questioning on the part of his listener, the contractor was led to talk about his "span of control." Ultimately he came to recognize that doubling his volume mandated an increase in staff and that he had trouble with new people because, unlike his long-term employees, the newcomers could not "read him like a book." They simply could not absorb his unwritten goals and objectives quickly enough to perform effectively within the existing organization.

Thus, it behooves those planning to form a construction firm or those already in business to take the time to establish a written set of goals and objectives. The best outline for this undertaking is the traditional news reporter's set of questions: *who, what, where, when, why,* and *how?* The questions are obviously interrelated, but if each is explored thoroughly a clear picture of the prospective or existing company can be drawn.

Who?

The emphasis here is on defining the kind of people who will have leadership roles in the company. If the principal is a domineering personality he will work best with people willing to take orders, for his will be a military type of organization. If the principal prefers to let people do their thing he must be willing to let the firm develop by reaching consensus, for this firm will be democratic in the extreme. Finally, "who's" must share common ethical values, be compatible personalities, and meet a specific level of intelligence.

What?

What is the company going to do, right now and in the future? Will it serve governmental agencies, large corporations, small businesses, individuals? Will it build homes, high-rise office buildings, industrial plants, water and sewage treatment plants? Will it build large projects or small? Will it be primarily a builder of projects or a manager of projects? Will it be a general contractor or a specialty contractor or a construction manager? Will it specialize in reinforced concrete construction, steel, or timber? Low-rise or high?

When?

When should the new company begin operation? When should the existing company implement its new goals and objectives? If expansion is a goal, is it to begin now or in 5 or 10 years? If carving out a new market segment is in the works, when should the effort begin?

Where?

Where will the company seek projects? Intra or inter- city? Intra- or interstate? If a corporation, where should it incorporate to get the best tax treatment? In its early stages of development, how far away from home base should the company seek work?

Why?

The obvious reason for a firm to exist is to make money, both for the benefit of its principals and for the job security of its employees. However, over the long haul, providing satisfactory client service is the best reason for a construction firm to exist. This will establish long-term relationships with new customers and develop the firm's reputation to the point where it may even gain an edge over its competitors in competitive bid situations.

How?

Should the new or young company operate as a proprietorship (sole owner), a partnership, a corporation, or an "S" corporation? Should all activity be controlled from a single office or should there be branch offices or divisions operating as independent profit centers?

Having gone through this exercise conscientiously, the principal(s) of a construction firm should have drawn a verbal picture of goals and objectives that should be quickly put in written form. The written version is necessary because this is not a one-time exercise. It should be performed at planned intervals, both to determine whether the firm is living up to its goals and objectives and to decide whether changes in direction are necessary to meet changing market needs.

THE LEGAL BUSINESS ENTITY

Construction has long been hailed as the "last bastion of free enterprise." Hence it is no surprise to find that about 75 percent of all firms operate as proprietorships (sole owners). Only about 5 percent operate as partnerships, 20 percent as corporations, and a handful as "S" corporations. There are pros and cons for each of these types of legal entities, but for principals planning to establish a new company the proprietorship is the easiest route.

Proprietorship

On the positive side, this approach offers easy entry and easy exit. The sole owner has full control and is free to make decisions based on personal judgment. The owner reaps all the benefits and can maintain complete privacy in the conduct of the business. On the negative side, the owner is solely responsible for all business obligations and may find it difficult to raise capital when needed for expansion or large projects. It is also difficult to recruit talented executive personnel because avenues for advancement and ownership are limited. Finally, the death or serious disability of the owner may wipe out the business or at least force it to face a difficult transition period.

Partnership

Again, on the positive side, a partnership is easy to establish, by either verbal or written agreement. Indeed, under some legal jurisdictions, if two or more people give the impression that they are partners they may be legally considered a partnership. Thus, it is advisable to draw up a partnership agreement clearly stating the role of each member. For example, the silent partner may be a source of capital and may share in profits, but have no responsibility for day-to-day operations and be limited to the loss of his investment should the venture fail. The chief advantage of the partnership is to bring together people with complementary talents that meet the demands of a complex industry. Additionally, talented employees may be recruited because there is the potential for their being included in the partnership structure. On the negative side, it must be remembered that obligations taken on by one partner are the obligations of all. And, despite excellent balance in talent between the partners, personality conflicts may destroy the firm. Finally, capital beyond that the partners themselves can raise may be hard to obtain and the decision of a partner to sell out or the death of a partner may create financial stress that could collapse the firm.

Corporation

Since the corporation is a legal entity that can sue and be sued, it relieves management and stockholders of personal liability except under some fairly rare conditions. It can raise capital in a variety of ways that allow greater potential for expansion, and its shares can be readily bought and sold. Talent can be recruited via stock options and other incentives that give new management members a strong incentive to succeed. The major disadvantage is that earnings are subject to taxation as corporate profit and again as personal income via dividends to stockholders. It is also relatively expensive for a new firm to invest in necessary legal fees to set up the corporation and incorporation may limit the scope of the firm's operation. Finally, information about the business can no longer be private and there is an increased burden of report filing and government control.

"S" Corporation

The Tax Reform Act of 1986 may have created an advantage for this form of business because of the fact that individual tax rate limits are now below those for corporations. With 35 shareholders or less and conformance with several other rules, earnings are taxed directly to the shareholders and the corporate "double" taxation is eliminated. Thus this format may offer advantages for some companies, but a tax expert's advice is recommended.

THE ORGANIZATION CHART

Regardless of the legal business entity selected by the principal(s) of an emerging construction firm, it is wise to go through the exercise of preparing an organization chart. Construction company personnel can be broadly categorized as belonging to either "the blue serge suit" office group or the "muddy shoes" field group. While the responsibility and authority of these two groups may sometimes overlap, particularly in the small firm, the role they play in the organization needs to be clearly established. There are two common structures for handling construction projects in larger firms, and both are difficult to define via the organization chart. Project teams are sometimes set up on a permanent or temporary basis, with a project manager who is responsible for the project from the estimating stage all the way to project completion. Thus, this team includes both office and field functions. Another approach, sometimes known as *matrix management,* sets up a project manager who must seek out necessary services from various departments such as estimating, purchasing, and construction. Each specialist department is headed by an individual who retains control over personnel in his department and is responsible for keeping them in tune with the latest and best practices in their specialized area. Obviously, these kinds of relationships are difficult to display in the traditional organization chart.

The major benefit for the principal(s) working on an organization chart may come from the preliminary activity of preparing a list of functions necessary to keep the firm afloat. Obviously, in the small firm, one person may be responsible for many of these functions and the process of listing them will quickly bring to light personal weaknesses of the principal(s) that will need to be strengthened as the firm develops. The main functions are discussed briefly below.

Executive

These functions require leadership and administrative talent devoted to forecasting, planning, and organizing. They include such items as finance, legal problems, marketing, labor negotiations, wage and salary policy, contract negotiation and execution, and more.

Accounting and Payroll

Billing and collection are two vital functions in this area as contractors notoriously suffer from serious cash flow problems. The list goes on to include personnel and payroll records, tax returns, payment of invoices, and so on.

Purchasing

While primary functions include requisitions and purchase orders for job-related materials and equipment, insurance and bond purchases are often vitally necessary before the company can even embark on a project. Another important function for the general contractor is the purchase of specialty subcontracts. Other functions include inventory control, obtaining building permits, and the verification of supplier order fulfillment. While contractors owning extensive fleets of equipment may establish a separate unit for equipment selection, assignment, and maintenance, the final purchase order may be issued by the purchasing department. Also, the purchasing department may be responsible for the purchase of "expendables" such as those used in concrete forming.

Estimating

The procurement and analysis of bid documents is often a preliminary to the process of making and pricing a quantity takeoff. Sometimes the decision to bid or not to bid is the sole responsibility of the estimating group, but more often this decision would be made at a higher management level after briefing from an estimator. While estimating would normally also include preparation of a proposal, this would again involve a final decision a step or two up the management ladder.

Technical Support

Sometimes labeled "engineering," this group of functions is usually project-oriented. Engineering functions include site layout, reinforced-concrete form design, and such areas as shop-drawing processing. Planning and scheduling, project cost control, and safety policy are areas requiring technical competence in fields not necessarily demanding engineering input. Also under this heading in some firms are on-site labor relations and owner and architect-engineer relations.

Construction

Here we find the functions of supervision for both labor and subcontractors along with data gathering for cost and accident reports. Here too lie the functions of providing planned storage for materials on site and preparing equipment requirement schedules.

Storage, Maintenance, and Repair

Many firms prefer to own their own construction equipment and therefore need a storage yard and accompanying repair and maintenance structures. This involves the function of equipment management, usually with a manager and staff, including mechanics and parts controllers. In addition, some firms purchase expendables for use on construction projects, and this requires warehousing and inventory functions apart from those necessary for materials and equipment actually becoming a part of the finished project.

Having completed a list of necessary functions and a description of the qualifications of the people who are to provide them, the company principal(s) can prepare an organization chart. Some of the reasons for publishing a formal organization chart are as follows:

1. It serves as a reminder of how principals view the firm and provides a visual record of the original planning process if and when changes are proposed.

2. It is a public relations tool indicating to clients that the company is well organized and manned with capable personnel.

3. It shows new employees where they fit in the internal structure and reminds old employees of the limits on their areas of authority and responsibility.

4. It can nip wrangling over who is boss in certain situations before the problem becomes harmful to the firm.

Figures 7.3*a, b,* and *c* illustrate some typical organization charts, one each for a small, medium, and general building contractor firm. These skeletal organization charts display traditional approaches and are actually composites of charts prepared by a number of firms. Figure 7.3*a* fits a small company, probably a proprietorship (one owner) with a full-time payroll of perhaps three or four people, all of whom must wear many hats to meet the functional demands of the business. Figure 7.3*b* fits a medium-size firm which could be a proprietorship, partnership, or corporation. If a corporation, a board of directors would normally function from a position above the owner or president. Figure 7.3*c* is appropriate for a general building-construction firm and might operate under any of the three types of business entities. Many construction firms in this size range are closely held family operations. Though skeletal in detail, these charts clearly show the status of functions and the people manning those functions. The lower the box in the chart, the less the authority and responsibility involved. A greater elaboration of detail for each of the boxes in the chart is desirable, but to avoid clutter, this is best done in a printed document covering policies and procedures.

In view of the dire predictions that the industry faces severe personnel shortages in the not too distant future, all of the charts shown can be faulted for neglecting to show a box labeled "Personnel," or as is becoming the vogue, "Human Resources." If predictions are accurate, construction firms may well be forced to increase their spending on in-house training programs for personnel at all levels in the organization chart as well as for laborers and craftsmen working on the project site. Another box in two of the charts might also deserve more attention. The term *business solicitor* might well be replaced by *marketing* and include a number of people specializing in direct sales as well as public relations.

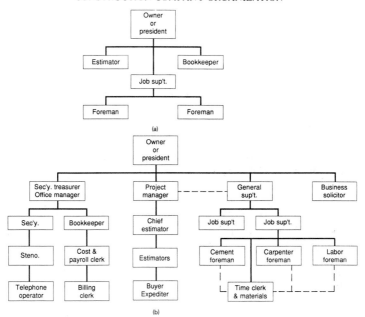

(a)

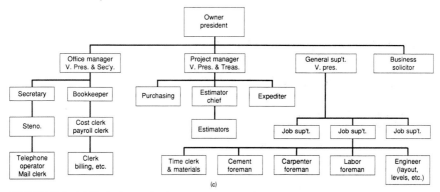

SUGGESTED ORGANIZATION STRUCTURE FOR A GENERAL BUILDING CONTRACTOR

(c)

FIGURE 7.3 (*a*) Typical organization chart—small company. (*b*) Typical organization chart—medium-size company. (*c*) Suggested organizational structure for a general building contractor.

POLICIES AND PROCEDURE MANUALS

Frank Gilbreth may well have been the first U.S. contractor to prepare detailed manuals covering policies and procedures applicable within his company. His manuals ranged from coverage of the job cost accounting system his people were required to use down to the number of bricks a bricklayer was required to lay in a day. These manuals were so admired by his competitors that they went to great lengths to obtain copies, and for a time Gilbreth exacted a bond from employees entrusted with these documents. Eventually, he went public with his management system and details were published in the trade press of the time.

Since Gilbreth's time many companies have used his approach and developed their own manual of policies and procedures. Some read like "vanity" books published to satisfy the author's ego, but more often than not they serve the purpose of binding the employee into a tightly knit organization that knows from whence it came and where it plans to go. They begin with a history of the company, describe the various positions within the company management structure, display a detailed organization chart, and then lay out the company's approach to marketing, client service, management employment policies, and proper procedures for handling the "normal" process of taking a project from procurement to delivery to the client. Other documents are less complete and some are segmented so that pieces can be put together to provide only enough detail to meet the needs of an individual at a particular management level.

It is interesting to note that the passage of the Occupational Safety and Health Act (1970) stimulated the preparation of safety manuals provided to workers at the construction site. A fallout from this activity was increased use of policy and procedure manuals covering construction companies' general labor policy. New concerns with drugs in the workplace and the introduction of drug testing may further stimulate the production of employee manuals covering these new problems but also including general company policy toward employees. A clear statement of company policy toward its craftsmen and laborers is a major first step in improving the recruiting climate for new construction workers.

CHAPTER 8
BUSINESS STRATEGY

William R. Park, P.E.
Consulting Engineer–Economist
Overland Park, Kansas

ELEMENTS OF BUSINESS STRATEGY

Role of Strategy

Strategy involves making competitive decisions; the more competitive an industry, the greater the need for making sound strategic decisions. Nowhere is this need greater than in construction contracting, where competitive pressures are probably more intense than in any other industry.

Competitive bidding, especially, offers abundant opportunities for the application of strategy. In competitive bidding, the contractor is faced with two seemingly incompatible and contradictory objectives: to bid high enough to make a profit, yet low enough to get a job—both at the same time!

Most contractors are able to estimate, at least with reasonable accuracy, what their direct costs on a job will be. And taking a single job, most of the competing contractors can also be expected to encounter roughly the same costs of performing the work: they are all subject to the same costs of operation, have access to the same labor supply, use the same types of equipment, obtain supplies and materials from the same sources, and have somewhat comparable, if not equal, supervisory capabilities.

Still, some contractors are able to operate successful, profit-making businesses, while other go broke or are, at best, barely able to survive. This is in spite of the fact that most are technically competent and are capable of actually performing the required quality of work.

What, then, makes the difference between success and failure in the contracting business? Most of the difference can be found in management's ability to make the strategic decision at the strategic time. Strategy is an essential ingredient for success in every competitive situation. The strategy of successful contracting depends more on management judgment than on any other single factor. More business failures are caused by poor judgment than by a lack of knowledge or technical competence. And despite the cries of unsuccessful businessmen, the causes of business failure can seldom be attributed to bad luck—just to bad business practices and poor business strategy.

Meaning of Strategy

Strategy can be defined in a number of different ways. For example, by various definitions, strategy is

- Skillful management in getting the better of an adversary
- The means by which a company uses its financial and physical resources to accomplish its objectives
- The science and art of meeting competition under the most advantageous conditions possible
- A careful plan or method
- The art of devising or employing plans toward a goal
- Management's ideas regarding its firm's objectives, the means by which these objectives will be accomplished, and the reasons for pursuing them

In all cases, strategy involves management's decisions in the face of uncertain competition. A strategy is primarily concerned with attempting to meet this uncertain competition under favorable terms, ideally, in matching one's major strengths against the competitor's major weaknesses.

The contractor's overall strategy in competitive bidding is to secure the combination of elements which will, in the long run, enable him to achieve certain desired objectives. Almost any sales volume can be generated by a contractor if bids are placed low enough, even though the jobs won are unlikely to result in a profit. Conversely, markup can be raised to any level desired, but the ultimate result will be a sales volume reduced to a point so low that there will be no profit. Somewhere between these unpleasant extremes of a high markup and no volume and a huge profitless volume with no markup, the contractor must find a markup which is compatible with the firm's objectives and which will allow the maximum profit possible under the existing competitive conditions.

Profit-Making Area

In contracting, the area where profits must be made is the area between the estimated direct cost of doing a job and the amount bid for the job. The lower limit of a job's price—the actual, out-of-pocket direct cost of the work—is more or less fixed, since there are few contractors who will willingly take a job at less than their direct cost. The upper limit of a job's price, on the other hand, may be established by several important factors, including

1. What the contractor considers a fair return on invested time and capital based on an appraisal of the risks associated with the particular job and on what could be earned elsewhere on the available capital
2. How badly the work is needed to keep men and machines occupied, thereby providing a larger base over which overhead and indirect cost can be spread
3. How much the traffic will bear, i.e., how much of a markup can be added to the direct job costs and still have some chance of getting the job

The first two factors depend primarily on the individual contractor's own business operation; the third factor depends chiefly on the actions of competitors, which can be anticipated but not controlled.

The profit-making area between the estimated direct cost and the bid price is also the area where most losses are incurred, either through management's failure to include sufficient markup or through its failure to attain sufficient volume to recover indirect costs. Probably the most important single responsibility of construction management is to make decisions within this area, and the success or failure of nearly every construction firm can be traced directly to these management decisions.

Strategic Decisions

In order to be able to make effective decisions, the executive must have alternatives to choose from, information on which to base decisions, and the authority to act on decisions once they are made.

Every important management decision involves a process of selection between alternative courses of action. In making the best possible decision under the existing, known circumstances, several well-defined steps should be followed:

1. Define the objectives: What is hoped to be accomplished by the decision?
2. Identify different approaches that might be used to attain the desired objectives.
3. Analyze and compare these alternatives to see which offer the best possibilities.
4. Choose the approach that is best suited to the firm's capabilities and objectives.

The first step in developing a suitable competitive strategy is to determine the firm's objectives. These objectives can be expressed and measured in a number of different ways. Profit, probably the most common business objective, such as gross sales volume or a specified share-of-market percentage, might also be used.

A single objective can frequently be achieved in several different ways. For example, a profit objective might be attained by means of a low markup on a large volume of work; this approach, however, might fail to meet a minimum return-on-invested-capital requirement. At the other extreme, a low volume of work taken with a high markup might yield a high rate of return on capital but fail to capture the desired share of the total market.

Careful and objective analyses of the possible outcome of each of the alternative means of reaching the desired objectives in the light of existing and expected competitive conditions allows the effect of each course of action on the company to be estimated. Can the large volume of work necessary with a low markup be achieved, even with the low markup, in view of the policies and pricing tactics of competitors? Or will it be more feasible to obtain the relatively small volume of work required to meet profit objectives with a higher markup?

Usually, the best answer will lie somewhere between the two extremes. The important thing for the executive to recognize is that for every competitive situation there is some decision that will, over the long haul, enable more success, as measured by internal standards or definitions of success, than will any other.

The most difficult types of management decisions that must be made are those which involve a high degree of uncertainty, especially when the uncertainty is in regard to the possible actions of competitors. These are strategic decisions and often must be made solely on the basis of management's informed judgment.

ESTABLISHING OBJECTIVES

Importance of Having Objectives

Effective business planning requires that appropriate objectives be established and pursued. Without well thought out, clearly defined goals, the contractor will only know past history and not be able to predict the future.

Good objectives will help the contractor in a number of ways:

1. Planning personnel requirements
2. Improving equipment utilization
3. Controlling inventories
4. Allocating overhead costs
5. Anticipating financial requirements
6. Forecasting profits
7. Increasing awareness of the firm's operations
8. Guiding company pricing policies

Personnel Requirements.   Most construction workers can be hired on a job-by-job basis, for there is generally a pool of available labor large enough to fill whatever needs might develop. Foremen and other supervisory personnel, as well as estimators and office employees, must be retained on a full-time basis, however, if the top-quality people necessary to assure efficient operations are to be available when needed. By establishing specific, attainable goals, the firm can anticipate the requirements for permanent office and field personnel and justify keeping them on the payroll.

Equipment Utilization.   Idle equipment is expensive. By planning ahead, the demands on major equipment items can be estimated, thus making possible the identification and allocation of their costs on a more realistic basis. Objectives, so long as the chances of attainment are good, are also invaluable in making economically sound decisions regarding the relative merits of equipment purchase, rental, or leasing.

Inventory Control.   Having more capital tied up in inventories than is absolutely essential means that less working capital will be available for other necessary purposes. Forward planning can identify the need for both the amount and type of inventory to be carried as well as for the most economical timing of purchases.

Overhead Cost Allocation.   Overhead costs are easy enough to identify in total but extremely difficult to spread among a company's various jobs. These costs can be realistically allocated to specific jobs only if a fairly accurate estimate of total sales volume can be made. If a company's annual volume can be projected within reasonably narrow limits, overhead costs can be charged to projects with almost the same accuracy as direct job costs.

Financial Requirements.   Becoming financially overextended is a major cause of business failure. By having specific objectives toward which to work, the firm minimizes the dangers of financial overextension. And by continually monitoring its progress toward these goals, the company recognizes any changes in financial requirements early on, perhaps resulting in substantial savings in interest charges and almost invariably bringing about better utilization of available capital.

Forecasting Profits.   The firm's growth depends primarily upon the ability of management to employ profits effectively. During prosperous times, increased capacity brought about by reinvesting profits in the business can lead to increased profits. During lean times, however, increasing the firm's capacity has little merit, and profits can be withdrawn and used elsewhere to better advantage.

Increasing Management Awareness.   The thought processes involved in establishing and analyzing a firm's objectives result in a keener awareness of the firm's overall operations and potential on the part of management and supervisory personnel. Further, the assignment of responsibilities to individuals for certain performance goals increases the probability that these will be reached.

Pricing Policies.   Different objectives can be achieved in different ways, and a primary consideration in most approaches is the firm's pricing philosophy. Increased sales, for example, can be achieved most easily by lowering prices. Increased profits, however, usually require that price levels be raised. And if the objective is to earn a certain return on invested capital, the optimum price may be higher than if a specific return on sales is desired. In any event, objectives will largely determine the company's pricing policies.

Types of Objectives

Different firms are motivated by different purposes, and management's initial task in setting goals is to decide exactly what tasks are to be accomplished and when. Many managements are satisfied simply to "make a living"; others are primarily interested in providing employment or in offering high-quality workmanship. Most, however, are concerned with making a profit, and various forms of the profit objective are most frequently used as business goals. The most commonly pursued objectives of construction management are directed toward

1. Sales volume
2. Gross profit
3. Percentage return on sales
4. Percentage return on investment
5. Percentage return on total assets
6. Improvement of performance
7. Share of market
8. Quality of performance
9. Employment security
10. Continuity of operations

Sales Volume.   The sales-volume objective, while a common goal of construction firms, is a dangerous one to pursue without carefully considering its effect on profits. Almost any sales volume can be achieved in competitive bidding simply by setting prices low enough. With sufficient working capital to support a profit-less operation, a contractor could conceivably capture almost an entire market—until funds were exhausted. Sales volume as an objective in itself, then, is economically unsound and should be discouraged. However, while sales volume cannot reasonably be pursued just for its own sake, neither can it be ignored, for only through sales can profits be generated. Sales volume should be looked on, therefore, as a means to an end—the end being profit—rather than as an end in itself.

Gross Profit. Gross profit is a function of the contractor's total sales volume, the fixed or overhead cost structure, and the percentage markups on direct job costs. Gross profits, while of primary importance, do not make as practical an objective as do profits related to other aspects of the firm's operations, for they measure neither the firm's earning capacity nor the efficiency with which profits have been generated.

Return on Sales. The percentage return on sales, also referred to as the "profit margin," is a frequently used profit objective since it can be taken directly from the profit-and-loss statement and provides a good indication of how the company fared over the past year. An added advantage of using the return on sales as an objective is that both the profit and the sales are measured in dollars having the same value, whereas either the net worth or total assets have probably been acquired over a period of years at varying price levels. The main disadvantage of using return on sales as an objective is that this measure does not show directly how effectively the firm's capital has been employed. For example, one company might require twice the capital investment to attain the same return on sales as another company that puts its capital to better use (see Table 8.1).

TABLE 8.1 Return on Sales Example

	Company A	Company B
Total sales	$100,000	$100,000
Total invested capital	20,000	40,000
Net profit before taxes	5,000	5,000
As percent of sales	5.0%	5.0%
As percent of invested capital	25.0%	12.5%

In this example, to infer that the two companies were operating with comparable efficiency would obviously be misleading even though their profit-sales relationships were the same. Company A is actually using its capital twice as effectively as Company B, as measured by its net profit per dollar of invested capital.

Return on Investment. The percentage return on invested capital is probably the best indicator of a company's financial performance and for that reason is usually the best way to set the company's objectives. The return on invested capital is a direct function of the profit return on sales and the rate of capital turnover (the sales to net worth ratio) and can be expressed as follows:

$$\frac{\text{Profit}}{\text{Sales}} \times \frac{\text{sales}}{\text{net worth}} = \frac{\text{profit}}{\text{net worth}}$$

A possible drawback to the use of net worth lies in the fact that the use of outside funds can exaggerate the firm's profitability, as long as these funds earn a return higher than the rate of interest paid on them. For example, by borrowing $100,000 at 6 percent interest and subsequently reinvesting it at only 8 percent, a firm with a net worth of $50,000 could increase the apparent rate of return on net worth by 4 percentage points by earning the additional $2000. If the firm was earning 16 percent on its $50,000 net worth, the borrowed capital would increase the return on net worth to 20 percent, even though these outside funds were earning only half the return shown by the rest of the firm's capital. Even so, this type of approach is often justified; whenever borrowed funds can be used to increase profits, their use may be warranted.

Return on Total Assets.   The percentage return on total assets is another way of measuring profit in relation to investment and, as such, shares some of the merits of the return–on–net–worth method. The reason for using total assets instead of the owners' equity in the business is the theory that all funds, whether supplied internally or externally, should be employed profitably. The return on total assets has the virtue of providing an incentive to increase sales and reduce costs as well as the exercise of extreme caution in adding assets which do not earn at a rate at least equal to the company's present return. This sometimes leads to overly cautious investment policies, however, since it tends to discourage the use of borrowed capital that might add to profits, even though it earns at a lower rate than the firm's own capital.

Improving Performance.   Many firms set their objectives simply "to do better than last year." This, in fact, may be an adequate objective in many cases so long as an attempt is made to define exactly which measures of performance are to be improved. However, if this is done, there is no reason to be so vague and the objectives should be expressed in more concrete terms.

Share of Market.   Attaining a specified share of the total market is a popular objective in many industries (such as automobile manufacturing) but has little justification in contracting. As pointed out previously, a contractor can obtain virtually any volume of sales, or any desired portion of the total construction market, simply by lowering prices sufficiently. As an objective, then, share of market is not feasible; it is, however, an important consideration in estimating a company's potential sales volume for industry totals, as a factor in determining the attainability of other, worthwhile goals.

Quality of Performance.   Some contractors desire nothing more than to be known for their high-quality work. And in some fields, such as in light commercial, residential, and highly specialized work, there is a place for this type of operation. However, so much emphasis has been placed on the low-priced job in most construction programs that the contractor who stresses the quality of work had best stay away from competitive bidding and concentrate on negotiated contracts.

Employment Security.   There are many small contractors whose operations are aimed solely at providing employment for the owners and their men. In these operations there is little incentive to expand and little need for profits beyond what constitutes a secure and comfortable living. Essentially, the owner is working for journeyman wages, with an added feeling of independence from operating a business.

Continuity of Operations. The sole purpose of many contracting firms is one of self-preservation. Often, a father will want only to keep his business running until his child is capable of taking over the operation. This sometimes goes on for generation after generation, with the business neither gaining nor losing but merely perpetuating itself.

General Procedures in Establishing Objectives

The attainability of a company's objectives will be influenced both by the effectiveness of its operations and by the external environment in which it must operate. Objectives, therefore, must be geared to a combination of these elements—what the company can hope to achieve within its own market.

The future events that influence the company's success in attaining its objectives cannot be predicted with certainty. Fortunately, a high degree of certainty is not required, since most future events are brought about by presently operating causes. Anticipating the future effects of what is presently happening, or what has already happened, is usually adequate for planning purposes. The general procedure to be followed in defining the firm's potential in view of the overall market situation requires that four major factors be considered:

1. The general economy
2. The industry
3. The company's position in the industry
4. Timing

The General Economy. A study of the general economy provides a picture of the overall framework in which the industry and the firm must operate. The economy as a whole will determine, to a large extent, total expenditures for new construction. Abundant data are regularly compiled and are available from a number of government sources, industry groups, trade associations, private research organizations, and banks. From these data, sufficiently reliable estimates can usually be made of the total construction volume during the next year or so for a given area. Breakdowns can also be obtained showing the general types of construction expected, based on building permits; work authorized by public agencies; and work already on the drawings boards.

Industry Volume. From the general economic data, estimates can be made of the portion of the work falling within the contractor's own field or specialty. For example, a projection of 10,000 single-family housing units for the following year might result in $4 million worth of residential heating and sheet metal work, $1 million in air conditioning equipment sales and installation, etc. Similarly, the estimated volume of commercial construction can be broken down into general construction work; electrical, mechanical, plumbing, and heating; and all its other component parts. Again, substantial amounts of data are, or should be, available from local trade associations and industry groups.

The Company's Position. The place to begin in estimating the company's share of its industry's total market is with the share of market that the company has already attained in the past. From this point, management should attempt to determine why the company has achieved this share of market, based on an analysis of competitive factors, the company's strengths and weaknesses, sales relationships, financial condition, quality of workmanship, and other factors. Then, management must critically examine each of these factors to decide which competitive advantages can be maintained and which shortcomings can be overcome. Considering this information in conjunction with recent trends in the company's share-of-market position should give realistic and workable estimates of what the company can reasonably hope to achieve in the near future.

Timing. Objectives are of little use unless specific time limitations are set for their accomplishment. The type and size of the contracting operation will dictate the actual time requirements for establishing objectives and forecasting sales. Many successful companies work with monthly goals, forecasts, and performance reviews for the following 1-year period, plus annual goals and forecasts for the next 5 years. Even the smallest firm should attempt to look at least 1, and preferably 2, years ahead.

Measuring Progress toward Objectives

Setting the company's objectives involves making estimates of a large number of variable factors, and changes in any of these factors can materially affect the firm's chances of accomplishing its objectives. Provisions must therefore be made to review periodically the firm's progress toward its goals. Developing a system for measuring performance is a necessary step once management has firmly committed itself to pursuing specific goals.

Preplanned checkpoints should be established for monitoring progress. Many companies have found monthly reviews to be of considerable value. Then, if the company's performance has not met expectations, the causes for variance can be determined and corrected before any permanent damage is incurred.

There are two general causes for a company's failure to meet its goals: internal and external. Internal causes mean that the company itself is at fault, and changes in operating procedures are necessary to improve performance. External causes, on the other hand, are a result of the environment in which the firm operates and may mean that changes in the firm's objectives will be necessary.

In both cases, whenever any broad discrepancies develop between planned and actual accomplishments, provisions should be made for taking prompt corrective action to bring either operations in line with objectives or objectives in line with operations. Only through constant monitoring can objectives exert the strong, constructive influence on the company's future that they should.

BREAK-EVEN ANALYSIS

Role of Break-Even Analysis

Identification of the firm's break-even point is essential, for there can be no profit until this point has been reached, and failure to attain the necessary break-even volume will result in a loss.

Break-even analysis is a useful tool for the contractor in running the business and in planning for profits; many management decisions require that the effect of changing sales volumes, markups, and overheads on the company's overall profit position be appraised. The major problem encountered by management in making these types of decisions is being able to visualize correctly the interactions among all the different elements that must be considered.

Break-even analysis can clearly illustrate the essential relationships among such profits. By clearly defining these relationships, management can objectively evaluate the impact of varying the different elements and can thus select appropriate strategies for working toward the firm's objectives.

Terminology of Break-Even Analysis

In break-even analysis, costs must be broken down into their fixed, semivariable, and variable elements.

Fixed costs remain constant over time, regardless of the amount of work performed by the firm. Fixed costs include many of the general-overhead items.

Semivariable costs may be fixed within certain ranges of sales volumes but will increase generally in some relation to sales. Semivariable costs include some of the capacity-related general-overhead items, plus any additional administrative expenses necessary to handle heavy workloads. If semivariable costs vary directly with the volume of work, they can be included with variable (or direct) costs; if they are stable over well-defined ranges, they may be handled in the same manner as fixed costs.

Variable costs are those that vary directly with the amount of work undertaken. They include both direct job costs and job-related overheads.

Total income and *total sales* are used synonymously, referring to the total amount of money generated by the contracts received.

Total costs are made up of the sum of all fixed, semivariable, and variable costs incurred over a specified period of time.

Profit refers to the difference between total income and total cost when income is greater than cost. Unless otherwise specified, profit is computed before income taxes.

Loss refers to the difference between total cost and total income when cost is greater than income.

The *break-even point* is the sales volume at which there is neither profit nor loss, or where total income is exactly equal to total cost. The break-even point may also be expressed as a percent of capacity rather than as volume of sales.

The *markup* is the percentage added to estimated direct costs—both job costs and job overheads—to recover all other costs of running the business and to return to the owners a profit on their invested time and capital.

Information Sources

Cost data provide the basis for break-even analysis. These basic cost data should be compiled, analyzed, and related to different levels of sales volume.

Historical accounting records usually provide the best source of information to be used in break-even analysis, although in the absence of such records, good estimates may be equally satisfactory for planning purposes.

Table 8.2 shows a summary operating statement (or profit-and-loss statement) for the Aardvark Bidding Company. From these data, plus an intimate knowledge of the firm's operations, sufficient information can be obtained or inferred to perform the break-even analysis.

TABLE 8.2   Aardvark Bidding Company
Operating statement for year ending December 31

Total sales		$500,000
Cost of operations		
Direct job costs	$407,000	
General expenses	76,000	
Total costs		483,000
Net profit before income taxes		$ 17,000

Basic Break-Even Arithmetic

Assuming that the "general expenses" of $76,000 shown in the operating statement of Table 8.2 refer to the firm's fixed costs and that the "direct job costs" figure of $407,000 includes all variable costs, the firm's break-even point can be quickly determined.

The break-even point, by definition, is the point at which total income equals total cost. Total cost, in turn, includes both fixed and variable costs. To find the break-even point for the Aardvark Bidding Company, then, calculate the amount of variable costs which when added to the $76,000 in fixed costs will equal total income at that point. In making this calculation, the total variable cost of $407,000 is assumed to have been accumulated at a constant rate over the $500,000 sales volume; therefore, for each dollar of sales, $407,000/$500,000, or $0.814, in variable costs is incurred. Or, stated another way, variable costs are equal to 81.4 percent of the sales volume.

Having accumulated the necessary information, the following basic formula can be used to calculate the break-even point:

$$V = F + D$$

where V = volume of sales required to break even
$\quad F$ = total amount of fixed cost
$\quad D$ = total amount of direct costs at the break-even point, expressed as a percentage of the sales volume.

Substituting the data for the Aardvark Bidding Company in the above formula

$$V = \$76,000 + 0.814V$$

$$0.186V = \$76,000$$

$$V = \$409,000$$

The break-even point for the Aardvark Bidding Company, then, occurs at a sales volume of $409,000. Should the company fail to achieve this volume, a loss would result, and the firm can begin realizing a profit only after a sales volume of $409,000 has been reached. The break-even calculation can be easily checked by working backward from the break-even point, as follows:

Sales volume at break-even point	$409,000
Less variable expenses at 81.4% of sales	333,000
Amount remaining to cover fixed costs	$ 76,000
Less fixed costs	76,000
Net profit or loss	$0

Break-Even Chart

While the arithmetic calculations involved in break-even analysis are simple and should be thoroughly understood, the use of a break-even chart provides a more vivid picture of exactly where the firm stands with respect to its break-even point. Also, the relationships among the various factors which influence the break-even point can best be expressed graphically.

The conventional break-even chart assumes that fixed costs remain stable regardless of the level of sales and that variable costs change in direct proportion to sales. Basically the same type of information is required to construct a break-even chart as is used in the arithmetic treatment: Cost data must be accumulated and summarized by varying levels of sales.

Figure 8.1 shows the essential features of a break-even chart, using again the operations of the Aardvark Bidding Company (whose operating statement was summarized in Table 8.2).

In Fig. 8.1, the vertical axis represents both income and cost, and the hori-

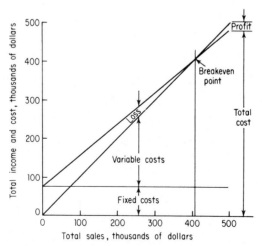

FIGURE 8.1 Conventional break-even chart. (*From The Strategy of Contracting for Profit, Prentice-Hall*)

zontal axis shows total sales volume. The units of measurement on both scales are dollars.

At zero sales, income would also be zero. Therefore, the "total income" line is a straight line passing through the origin (or zero point), representing the income increasing as sales increase. Since Aardvark Bidding Company's income is derived solely from sales, the total income shown on the vertical axis will always be equal to the total sales volume shown on the horizontal axis.

Next, the total amount of fixed costs is plotted on the graph. Fixed costs in Aardvark's case total $76,000 and are assumed to remain constant, at least throughout the range of sales shown on the break-even chart. The fixed-cost line, therefore, will be parallel to the horizontal axis. If some of the fixed costs are expected to increase with a larger volume of work, this fact should be reflected in the plot of fixed costs; situations involving such complications are treated later.

Variable costs are then added to fixed costs to arrive at total costs. The slope of the variable-cost line depends on the rate at which the variable costs are accrued. Variable costs are most conveniently plotted as a certain amount per dollar of sales; in this example, variable costs average $0.814 per sales dollar ($407,000 in variable costs for $500,000 in sales).

The variable costs are plotted above the fixed-cost line, thereby giving the total cost of operations for any given level of sales. The total-cost line—the sum of fixed and variable costs—indicates the total cumulative amount spent at a specific point.

The point at which the total-cost line intersects the total-income line—$409,000 in this example—is the break-even point. To the left of this point the vertical distance between the total-income and total-cost lines indicates a net loss. To the right, the corresponding vertical distance between the two lines represents a net profit. Any change in sales from the break-even point, however slight, will result in either a profit or a loss.

The break-even point of the Aardvark Bidding Company occurs at a sales volume of $409,000. At this point the $409,000 in sales revenues is exactly matched by the $409,000 in costs, made up of $76,000 in fixed costs and $333,000 in variable costs. At sales volumes of less than $409,000, losses will be suffered; at higher volumes, profits will be earned.

The break-even point could be described equally well in terms of the firm's operating capacity, instead of as a dollar sales volume, although dollars are more easily defined than capacity. For example, if the firm's annual capacity were $800,000, the break-even point would have occurred at 51 percent of capacity.

To earn net profits of $17,000, operations would have to be conducted at 62.5 percent of capacity. The procedure for calculating the break-even point is exactly the same as when sales volume is used; only the units of measurement along the horizontal axis of the graph would be different.

Effect of Overhead Costs on the Break-Even Point

The preceding example assumed that fixed costs remained constant regardless of the firm's sales volume. While this assumption may be valid for a limited number of firms, such a condition is unlikely to exist in most contractors' operations. As the capacity to do business increases, the overhead or fixed costs usually increase.

Figure 8.2 illustrates the effect on the firm's break-even point of varying fixed costs. The vertical axis still represents income and cost, and the horizontal axis

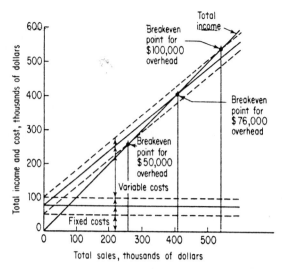

FIGURE 8.2   Effect of fixed costs on the break-even point.
(*From The Strategy of Contracting for Profit, Prentice-Hall*)

total sales volume. The total-income line remains the same: one dollar of total income resulting from each dollar of sales. Also, the slope of the variable-cost line is assumed to remain constant, rising $0.814 for each sales dollar.

As indicated by Fig. 8.2, the effect of lowering the level of fixed costs is to cause the total-cost line to intersect the total-income line more quickly, representing a lower break-even point. In the example, lowering the fixed costs from $76,000 to $50,000 reduces the break-even point from $409,000 to $269,000. In other words, a reduction of $26,000 in fixed costs results in a reduction of $10,000 in the break-even point. By reducing fixed costs by any given percentage, then, the break-even point can be reduced by that same percentage.

The same relationship holds true when fixed charges increase. An increase from $76,000 to $100,000 moves the break-even point farther away. In the example, the break-even point increases from $409,000 to $539,000—meaning that $130,000 in additional sales will have to be achieved to make up for the additional $24,000 in fixed-cost obligations. Again, the same percentage increase must be made in sales as in fixed costs to retain the same position of economic equilibrium.

Figure 8.3 shows how the Aardvark Bidding Company's operation might look if all three of these levels of fixed costs—$50,000, $76,000, and $100,000—were incurred over certain ranges of sales volume.

In Fig. 8.3, fixed costs of $50,000 are associated with sales volumes of 0 to $200,000; $76,000 in fixed costs will be incurred at sales volumes between $200,000 and $500,000; and $100,000 in fixed charges will be necessary to support sales between $500,000 and $1 million.

As is evident from Fig. 8.3, the firm will be unable to break even under the specified conditions with fixed costs of $50,000 chargeable against the first $200,000 sales volume, for the break-even point would not be reached until a

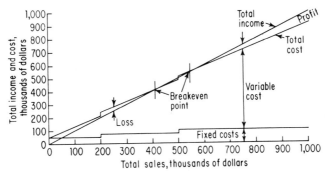

FIGURE 8.3   Break-even chart with varying levels of fixed costs. (*From The Strategy of Contracting for Profit, Prentice-Hall.*)

sales volume of $269,000 had been achieved—and any volume above $200,000 requires taking on additional fixed costs.

Over the second range of sales volumes—$200,000 to $500,000—the break-even point will occur at $409,000, with $76,000 in fixed costs. The net profit will rise to $17,000 at $500,000 in sales, made up of the difference between the $500,000 income and the $76,000 in fixed costs and $407,000 in variable costs.

At any point over $500,000 volume, however, fixed costs increase to $100,000 and the break-even point rises to $539,000. To break even, then, requires $130,000 more volume than before, and to make the same amount of profit as was made at $500,000 sales volume ($17,000) would now require sales of $630,000, also $130,000 more than before.

Effect of Markups on the Break-Even Point

The markup—or percentage added to direct job costs to cover overhead and profit—has an important effect on the volume of work required to break even. The higher the markup, the lower the break-even point; and the lower the markup, the higher the break-even point.

Figure 8.4 shows how the break-even point varies with the markup. In Fig. 8.4, the firm has annual fixed costs of $50,000. With a 10 percent markup, the break-even point occurs at a sales volume of $550,000. This volume is matched by total costs of $550,000, made up of $500,000 in direct (or variable) costs plus the 10 percent markup which covers the $50,000 in fixed costs. The variable-cost line has a slope of $500,000 in $550,000, or $0.909 per dollar of sales.

A higher markup decreases the slope of the variable-cost line, causing it to intersect the total-cost line more quickly. A 20 percent markup results in a break-even point of $300,000, representing a slope of $250,000 in $300,000, or $0.833 per sales dollar.

Similarly, a lower markup, by raising the slope of the variable-cost line, causes its intersection with the total-income line to come later. For a 5 percent markup the break-even point is at $1,050,000, made up of $1 million in direct costs and $50,000 in fixed costs. Variable costs in this case are incurred at a rate of $0.952 per dollar of sales.

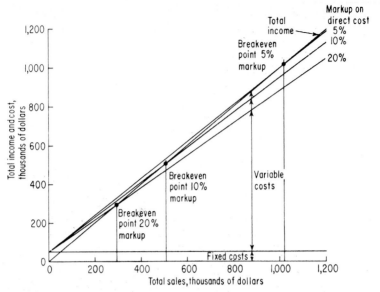

FIGURE 8.4 Break-even chart with varying markups. (*From The Strategy of Contracting for Profit, Prentice-Hall.*)

Contractor's Break-Even Formula

The mathematical relationships among fixed charges, percentage markups on direct job costs, and the volume of work required to break even, can be easily derived.

By definition the break-even volume V occurs at the point at which the sales volume, or total income, equals the total cost. The total cost consists of the sum of direct or variable costs D and indirect or fixed costs F. Thus,

$$V = D + F$$

Since fixed charges are recovered by applying some percentage markup M to the direct costs, the following relationship must exist at the break-even point:

$$F = \frac{M \times D}{100} \quad or \quad D = \frac{100F}{M}$$

Substituting for D in the first equation, the break-even volume is found to occur at

$$V = \frac{100F}{M} + F = F\frac{100}{M} + 1 = F\frac{100 + M}{M}$$

The ratio of the break-even volume to the fixed charges is therefore

TABLE 8.3 Sales Required per Dollar of Overhead at Various Markups

Percentage markup on direct cost	Sales required per dollar of overhead	Percentage markup on direct cost	Sales required per dollar of overhead
1	$101.00	12	$9.33
2	51.00	15	7.67
3	34.33	20	6.00
4	26.00	25	5.00
5	21.00	30	4.33
6	17.67	35	3.86
7	15.29	40	3.50
8	13.50	45	3.22
9	12.11	50	3.00
10	11.00	100	2.00

$$\frac{V}{F} = \frac{100 + M}{M} = \frac{100}{M} + 1$$

where M is expressed as a percent.

For example, using this formula, a 10 percent markup will require a sales-fixed charges ratio of 100/10 + 1, or 11.0. Similarly, a 20 percent markup will require a total sales volume of 100/20 + 1, or 6.0 times the fixed charges. Table 8.3 shows the sales dollars required per dollar of overhead for various markups. The same relationships are pictured graphically in Fig. 8.5.

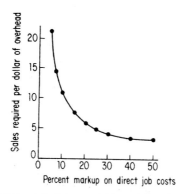

FIGURE 8.5 Sales required per dollar of overhead at various markups. (*From The Strategy of Contracting for Profit, Prentice-Hall.*)

Relationships among Factors Affecting the Break-Even Point

The break-even point depends on both the fixed costs and the percentage markups on direct job costs, and any change in either fixed costs or markups will be greatly amplified in the volume of work required to break even. If the markup is 10 percent, each dollar of overhead must be matched by $11 of sales. This relationship means that if an additional $1000 of overhead expense is taken on, an additional sales volume of $11,000 must be earned just to stay in the same position with respect to profits.

On the other hand, if overheads can be reduced by $1000 without changing the markup, the break-even volume will be $11,000 less. If, at the same time, the sales volume could be maintained, the $1000 reduction in overheads would result in an additional $1000 in profits.

Similar effects could be brought about by varying the percentage markup while keeping overheads and sales constant or by varying the sales volume with a fixed markup and overhead. One contractor may be able to reduce his overhead without difficulty, while another will find it easier to raise his volume slightly or to increase his markup by a percent or two.

In any event, only a small change in the contractor's markup, overhead cost, or sales volume makes a tremendous difference both in the volume of work he must obtain to break even and in his ultimate profit position.

The relationships among these factors explain to some extent how certain contractors are able to run more profitable businesses on $100,000 sales volume than others are able to manage with million-dollar volumes. A good markup on a small volume is apt to be far more profitable, and far less risky, than a large volume accumulated by means of low markups; no amount of volume can compensate for the lack of profit. The small-volume contractor with a large profit is working on either a high markup or a low overhead; the end result is the same in either case.

PROFIT ANALYSIS

Nature of Profits

Profits are easy enough to define, even though their adequacy is hard to measure. *Profits,* simply stated, represent the net difference between total income and total cost. Profits are the result of a firm's operations and a measure of the economic success of its operation.

Profits are influenced by a number of different factors, both internal and external. Internal factors refer to the company's operations, external factors to the industry in which the company operates and to the nature of the competition that is encountered.

The contracting industry probably comes closer to having "perfect competition" than any other modern industry—competition in which each seller has little or no control over prices. In such a profit-and-loss system (not just a "profit system"), the contractor is forced to get the most from his available resources.

The primary requirements for profitable operations in the contracting business are selecting jobs on the basis of their profit potential and then conducting operations with the greatest possible economy of performance.

Profits should be looked on as a kind of cost. At a bare minimum, profits must cover the cost of supplying capital for the business. Additionally, profits should cover the earnings of personally contributed resources; offer a reward for entrepreneurship; reimburse the risk taker for the chances he takes; and, in some cases, offer extra returns for some type of monopoly position.

Measuring Profits and Profitability

A distinction should be made between profits and profitability. *Profits* refer to the difference between total income and total cost and is therefore expressed in terms of dollars. Net profit, as used throughout this chapter, refers to the profit before income taxes but after all other deductions.

Profitability is a measure of the desirability of risking additional capital and expense in undertaking new projects and is also a measure of the efficiency with which the firm's resources have been employed. Return on investment is the most important measure of profitability.

Again, profits always refer to the difference between total income and total cost. There is a tendency on the part of some companies (and some labor unions) to define profits in terms of "cash flow"—after-tax profits plus depreciation and amortization allowances. Cash flow is undeniably an important measure of a company's ability to invest in new equipment and to expand its operation, since cash flow represents the actual amount of money generated by the business and available to it. But depreciation is equally undeniably a cost, and costs are the direct enemies of profits. Cash flow is not profit.

Probably the only valid generalization regarding a firm's profits is that profits are not as high as they should or could be. But the chances for raising profits to their optimum level are better if they are planned and measured as a percentage of the capital employed in the business.

What constitutes a satisfactory percentage return on invested capital has never been, and probably never will be, answered, for the adequacy of profits is not a measurable quantity and can be judged as satisfactory or unsatisfactory only by comparison with others. Some of the major considerations in determining the adequacy of profits are the profit levels of all other companies, the profit levels within the industry and similar industries, and the company's position and experience within its own industry.

According to Dun & Bradstreet, the minimum level of profitability sufficient to ensure continued company growth is 10 percent of the firm's net worth. But most contractors should be able to double this return, for by the very nature of the contracting business net worth is generally low in relation to the volume of business conducted.

Profit Analysis Techniques

The techniques of profit analysis are similar to the techniques of break-even analysis. Break-even analysis is, in effect, a special case of profit analysis in which the objective is to identify the point at which profits are zero. In profit analysis, relationships between profits and sales volumes are sought. As is the case with break-even analysis, the most meaningful and useful information can be obtained in profit analysis by presenting the data in graphical form, where relationships between different variables can be easily visualized.

Figure 8.6 shows a profit-volume chart for the Aardvark Bidding Company, based on the operating statement shown in Table 8.2.

In the profit-volume chart, the vertical axis is divided into two parts: the top part representing a net profit and the lower segment representing a net loss. The horizontal axis is drawn through the zero-profit point on the vertical axis, repre-

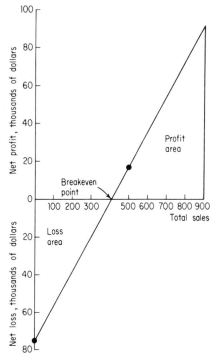

FIGURE 8.6   Profit-volume chart. (*From The Strategy of Contracting for Profit, Prentice-Hall.*)

senting the break-even point. Units along the horizontal axis measure the company's total sales volume.

The profit-volume chart (or the P-V chart), as its name implies, indicates the net profit or net loss associated with any given level of sales. At zero sales, the net loss will be equal to the amount of fixed expense. The P-V line, then, intersects the vertical axis at a net loss of $76,000, corresponding to zero sales volume. Aardvark's net profit at a sales volume of $500,000 was $17,000; this $17,000 can be plotted above the $500,000 point on the horizontal axis.

A straight line connecting these two points will, presumably, give the amount of net profit or net loss corresponding to any chosen level of sales, assuming that all other factors—such as the level of markups, the amount of variable cost per dollar of sales, and the amount of fixed costs—remain the same. The point at which the P-V line intersects the horizontal axis—at $409,000 in this case—is the break-even point. The area encompassed by the P-V line and the two axes to the left of the break-even point represent net losses; and the area bounded by the P-V line and the axes to the right of the break-even point represent the firm's profits.

Profits, then, can be easily projected for any desired or anticipated sales volume, again assuming that the relationships between all the different factors stay the same. For the Aardvark Bidding Company, sales of $500,000 brought in net profits of $17,000. A sales volume of $600,000 should therefore yield $35,000 in profits; further increases in sales to $700,000 will result in $19,000 additional profits, totaling $54,000.

As is apparent from the P-V chart, an increase of any given amount in sales will bring about a uniform increase in net profits. For Aardvark, each $100,000 change in sales volume results in approximately $19,000 change in profits.

The profit-volume ratio also provides a convenient means of measuring the firm's profit margin—the difference between sales and variable expenses. In the preceding example, each $100,000 in sales was accompanied by a marginal income of $18,600. The P-V ratio, equal to incremental (or marginal, or additional) income divided by incremental sales, is therefore 18.6 percent.

Having established the P-V ratio, several additional calculations can be made from it.

Break-even point: The break-even point can be found by dividing total fixed costs by the P-V ratio. For example,

$$\text{Break-even point} = \frac{\$76,000}{0.186} = \$409,000$$

Fixed expenses: Fixed expenses, expressed as a percentage of sales, can be found for any given sales volume by subtracting the P-V ratio from the net profit–net sales ratio.

$$\text{Fixed expenses} = \frac{17,000}{500,000} - 0.186 = 0.340 - 0.186 = 0.154$$

$$= 15.4\% \text{ of sales of } \$500,000$$

Variable expenses: Variable expenses, as a percentage of sales, are equal to 100 percent minus the P-V ratio:

$$\text{Variable expenses} = 100.00 - 18.6 = 81.4\% \text{ of sales}$$

Net profit: The profit at any given sales volume can be found by multiplying the sales by the P-V ratio and deducting fixed expenses:

$$\text{Net profit at } \$500,000 \text{ sales} = (500,000 \times 0.186) - 76,000$$

$$= 93,000 - 76,000 = \$17,000$$

Factors Affecting Profits

The preceding analyses are valid as long as the relationships between fixed costs, variable costs, and markups remain constant. But when the contractor's percentage markups on direct job costs change, the entire profit situation also changes.

When the level of fixed costs and markups is known, or can be estimated with reasonable accuracy, the amount of profit associated with any given sales volume can be quickly and easily determined.

The total sales volume S represents simply the sum of direct costs D and the percentage markup M added to these direct costs. Or, stated algebraically,

$$S = D + DM = D(100 + M)$$

Solving for D in this equation gives

$$D = \frac{S}{100 + M}$$

And since total costs C consist of the sum of fixed costs F and direct costs D,

$$C = F + D = F + \frac{S}{100 + M}$$

Profits P, the difference between total sales S and total costs C, are therefore,

$$P = S - C = S - \left(F + \frac{S}{100 + M}\right) = S\frac{M}{100 + M} - F$$

This formula is extremely useful to the contractor in identifying the effect of changes in the average percent markup on the firm's profit potential at any given sales volume. The factor $M/(100 + M)$ is referred to as the "profit factor." Table 8.4 gives the profit factors for selected markups ranging between 1.0 and 100 percent. This profit factor, multiplied by the company's anticipated sales volume, and less overhead or fixed costs, gives the net profit to be achieved at any combination of sales volume and markup.

Laws of Profits

Some general observations and conclusions can be drawn from the relationships among profits, sales, fixed costs, variable costs, and markups. These can be summarized as follows, representing the "laws of profits" for contractors.

- The first law of profits is that all costs—not just out-of-pocket costs—must be included when determining the firm's profits.
- Any change in fixed costs will change the net profit by a like amount, if all other cost relationships remain constant. Each dollar increase in fixed costs results in a dollar's decrease in profits; each dollar decrease in fixed costs increases profits by a dollar.
- Any percentage change in fixed costs will change the firm's break-even point

TABLE 8.4 Profit Factors for Various Markups

Percentage markup on direct cost	Profit factor	Percentage markup on direct cost	Profit factor
1	0.0099	12	0.1071
2	0.0196	15	0.1304
3	0.0291	20	0.1667
4	0.0385	25	0.2000
5	0.0476	30	0.2308
6	0.0566	35	0.2593
7	0.0654	40	0.2857
8	0.0741	45	0.3103
9	0.0826	50	0.3333
10	0.0909	100	0.5000

by the same percentage, and in the same direction, assuming other cost relationships hold steady.

- A change in the rate at which variable costs are incurred will change both the break-even point and the net profit earned at any specified sales volume for a constant level of fixed costs. An increase in the variable expense rate will raise the break-even point and lower profits; decreasing the rate will lower the break-even point and increase profits.

- An increase in the percentage markup on direct job costs will lower the break-even point and increase the net profit earned at any volume. A decrease in the markup will raise the break-even point and lower the profit realization at any sales volume.

- A change in both fixed costs and variable costs will have a significant effect on profits if they both change in the same direction, but a less noticeable effect if they move in opposite directions.

ANALYZING COMPETITIVE INFORMATION

Types and Availability of Information

The purpose of bid analysis is to identify significant relationships among the many variable factors involved in competitive bidding so that these relationships can be used to predict the course of future events. Many of these relationships are recognized intuitively by experienced contractors, but other relationships that are generally believed or assumed to be correct may actually have no basis in fact. Bid analysis can quickly separate truth from fiction.

Many significant relationships can be determined through analysis. The following are particularly important:

1. Number of bidders per job
2. Distribution of competitors' bids
3. Distribution of low bids
4. Effect of the number of bidders on the low bid
5. The spread

The information requirements for bid analysis are simple and straightforward, although obtaining some of the information is sometimes difficult.

1. General information concerning specific jobs, including the type of job, location, date, unusual conditions, etc.
2. The company's estimate of the direct costs associated with each job; this figure should include job overheads but not general overheads.
3. Tabulations of competitors' bids on all jobs, especially those for which estimates were prepared.

The first two items—job characteristics and estimated job costs—can be obtained from the company's own records. Only the third item—competitors' names and bids—is likely to cause trouble.

On public-works projects, and on many jobs carried out by private owners, public bid openings are common. In these cases the names and bids of all competitors are made known and no information problems arise. Bid tabulations are also published in construction trade journals such as *Dodge Reports* (McGraw-Hill) and by organizations.

Some private owners, however, are reluctant to reveal the bids submitted on their projects, perhaps feeling that such disclosure would decrease their subsequent bargaining power. Even so, most contractors are able to compare notes with their associates, and "secret" bids do not generally remain secret for long.

The contractor should carefully compile and retain all such information. Every competitor's bid on every job for which a detailed cost estimate is available will be extremely valuable.

Effect of Job Size on Number of Bidders

The average number of bidders on a job will depend upon both the job characteristics and the general competitive situation within the industry.

Logically, large jobs, offering a potentially greater profit opportunity, should attract more bidders than small jobs. However, as the size of the job increases, the number of contractors qualified for the work is likely to decrease, as bonding or credit requirements eliminate some of the marginal operators.

A sample of 100 jobs, ranging in size from about $10,000 up to $70 million, was drawn from published sources. Overall, an average of seven bids was submitted on each job. The average number of bidders varied with the job size as shown in Table 8.5.

TABLE 8.5   Variation in Number of Bidders with Job Size

Size of job	Average no. of bidders
Under $50,000	4.8
$50,000–$100,000	7.1
$100,000–$500,000	5.5
$500,000–$1,000,000	7.3
$1,000,000–$5,000,000	8.3
$5,000,000–$10,000,000	9.2
Over $10,000,000	7.9

On jobs over $100,000, the number of bidders increases as the job size increases, up to about $10 million; then the number of bidders tapers off. These jobs cover a wide range of project types, distributed geographically throughout the United States.

Analysis of this type—relating the number of bidders to the size of job (or other important job characteristics)—is useful to the contractor in developing an appropriate bidding strategy for situations in which the exact number and identity of competitors is not known. By anticipating just the approximate amount and type of competition to be encountered, the contractor can eliminate many jobs from further consideration—at a great saving in cost and with no sacrifice of potential profits.

The contractor should always try to predict, by any available means, the number (and identity) of competitors likely to be encountered on each prospective job.

The Spread

The spread—the difference between the low bid and the second low bid—is significant for several reasons.

1. The spread indicates, to some extent, the intensity of competition for a job.
2. The spread measures the amount of money left "on the table," and tells how much higher the low bidder could have been and still taken the job.
3. An unusually wide spread is probably indicative of an estimating error on the low bidder's part, especially if the second and higher bids are grouped closely together. The low bidder in such a case might well weigh the economic consequences of taking the job against the alternative of forfeiting his bid bond.

Based on a sample of 60 jobs ranging in size from $23,000 to $123 million and attracting anywhere from 4 to 15 bidders each, we can make several general observations. On jobs having from 4 to 6 bidders, the average spread was 8.0 percent; 7 to 9 bidders resulted in a spread averaging 5.8 percent; for 10 to 12 bidders, the spread averaged 3.8 percent; and jobs attracting 13 to 15 bidders had only a 2.0 percent spread.

Approximately 90 percent of all jobs have a spread of 1.0 percent or more; 77 percent have at least a 2.0 percent spread; and 42 percent of all jobs have a spread of 5.0 percent or more.

Since half of all jobs have a spread of 4 percent or more, there is an even chance that the contractor, by increasing the bid by 4 percent, will not affect his chances of being low bidder. The economic significance of this fact can be illustrated on a job having estimated direct costs of $90,000. If the contractor would normally bid the job at $100,000, it is easy to calculate the probable results of increasing the bid.

If the bid were increased by 1.0 percent to $101,000, there would still be 91 percent of the jobs on which the contractor would have been low bidder with a bid of $100,000. Instead of making $10,000, the contractor would have an opportunity 91 percent as many times of making $11,000, an average of $10,010. Raising the bid to $102,000 would yield a gross profit of $12,000 on 77 percent as many jobs as before, an average of $9,240. And a bid of $105,000 would yield $15,000 on 42 percent as many jobs as the $100,000 bid, or $6,300.

The obvious conclusion to be drawn from these calculations, then, is not to worry about leaving a percent or two on the table. Trying to decrease the amount in this situation will result only in getting fewer jobs. While an additional 1 percent may be justified, any more would be dangerous.

Again, these inferences apply only to the selected job sample. But a similar analysis, based on the contractor's personal experience, could provide much interesting and useful information.

Distribution of Bids

A common occurrence—one that has amazed outsiders and frustrated many contractors—is the fact that many of the bids submitted on all types of projects appear to be below cost.

Nearly 80 percent of all major jobs are let at less than the engineer's estimate; some jobs are even let at less than half the engineer's estimate. And these peculiar circumstances cannot be entirely attributed to the conservative nature of the engineer's estimates.

According to an analysis conducted for a large general contractor, covering competitors' bids submitted over a 2-year period, 35 percent of all competitors' bids were below the estimated direct out-of-pocket costs of performing the work. Some bids—nearly 3 percent of the total encountered—were placed at more than 30 percent below cost.

Figure 8.7 shows how the competitors' bids were distributed, expressed as a percentage of this contractor's estimated direct job costs. This figure vividly illustrates the contractors' problems in competitive bidding. To be 100 percent certain of getting a job would require bidding at about 50 percent of cost; if every job were bid at cost, the contractor would still be underbid by about a third of the competitors; and if all jobs were bid with a 15 percent markup, this bid would beat only a third of the competitors. Approximately two-thirds of all bids submitted by the competitors fell between 91 and 120 percent of estimated cost.

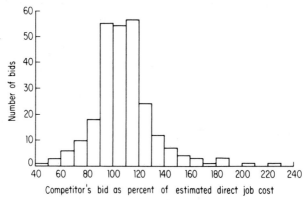

FIGURE 8.7 Typical distribution of competitors' bids. (*From The Strategy of Contracting for Profit, Prentice-Hall.*)

Distribution of Low Bids

Analyzing the distribution of low bids is even more depressing than analyzing the distribution of bids. Based on the same contractor's experience, the average low bid encountered on 73 jobs ranged from less than half the estimated job cost to approximately 25 percent above, with most falling on the low side. The low bids were distributed as shown in Table 8.6.

As would be expected, the low bid was found to vary generally according to the number of bidders encountered on the job. As the number of bidders increased, the low bid decreased.

TABLE 8.6 Distribution of Low Bids

Ratio of low bid to estimated cost	No. of jobs	Percent of jobs
Less than 0.80	8	11
0.80–0.90	13	18
0.90–1.00	24	33
1.00–1.10	16	22
1.10–1.20	10	13
1.20–1.30	2	3
Total	73	100

Causes of Variations in Bids

Some of the major causes of estimating errors include the omission of items, undermeasurement of quantities, underestimation of labor requirements, and a failure to recognize all elements of cost, such as overheads.

A cost estimate is never 100 percent accurate. The actual job costs will, instead, be distributed about the estimated cost. Estimating accuracy can be defined by the degree to which actual costs vary from the estimated costs, as well as by the relationships between average estimated costs and average actual costs.

A good detailed estimate should generally be accurate within 5 percent. Even so, on the average, actual costs may vary by as much as 20 percent from the estimated costs because of unforeseen job conditions. If the possibility of unusual job conditions is recognized by some contractors and not by others, those who failed to investigate the job thoroughly are apt to be the low bidders.

Even the best estimators will make outright mistakes, however, that may cause an estimate to be low by as much as 15 to 25 percent. And even if the chance of such an error is only 1 in 100, when a dozen different firms compete for the same job, the chances of errors are greatly magnified. In fact, if each of a dozen estimators has a 99 percent chance of being accurate within 5 percent, there will still be an estimate that falls outside the 5 percent range on more than 10 percent of the jobs. Few estimators can count on being within 5 percent on 99 jobs in 100.

Seasonal considerations may cause further fluctuations in bid levels. For some reason, many contractors feel that after they have reached a certain volume, "everything is profit from now on." This sometimes results in a complete disregard for overhead and equipment costs, thereby lowering bids to a dangerously low level.

And frequently this situation will lead to still another: desperation. Desperation—the feeling that any volume, regardless of profit, is better than no volume at all—is by no means uncommon. Once a financial position has been reached where money is urgently needed this month to pay last month's bills, money from any source is acceptable—even if the source is this month's jobs, taken at cost or below. By keeping enough jobs coming in, even at a direct out-of-pocket loss, a contractor can stay in business long enough to disrupt completely the profitability of an entire industry. This is a variation on the Ponzi or pyramiding scam.

COMPETITIVE STRATEGY

Basic Concepts

Disregarding errors, the lower limit of bids is generally set by the estimated direct cost of a given project. The relationship between the bid price and the estimated cost depends on several factors, such as the contractor's need for work, the minimum acceptable markup, and the amount of work available in the marketplace.

Every contractor realizes that the chances of being low bidder have a direct relationship to the bid. The higher the bid, the lower the chances of its being successful; the lower the bid the better the chances of getting a job. In extreme cases the contractor could either

1. Bid low enough to be sure of getting the job, even though there would be no profit.
2. Bid so high that a large profit is assured, even though the chances of getting the job would be nil.

The basic concept underlying the competitive-bidding strategy consists simply in recognizing that there is some one bid which results in the best possible combination.

1. The profit resulting from obtaining a contract at a specified bid price
2. The probability of getting the job by bidding that amount

Bidding against a Single Competitor

Figure 8.8 illustrates the effect of the bid price on the chances of being low bidder when bidding against a single competitor. In Fig. 8.8, the contractor can be certain of being low bidder only if bidding the job at cost. By bidding at 10 percent above cost, the contractor can expect to be low bidder on 60 percent of the jobs; a 20 percent markup will be low on 20 percent of the jobs: and a 25 percent markup will result in no jobs at all.

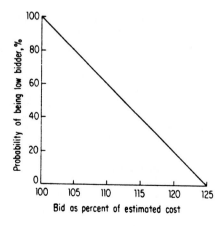

FIGURE 8.8 Effect of bid on chances of being low bidder against a single competitor. (*From The Strategy of Contracting for Profit, Prentice-Hall.*)

A few of the possible alternatives and their results, then, are

1. Bid at cost and get all the jobs but no profits.
2. Bid 5 percent above cost and get 80 percent of the jobs bid. The average profit per job bid—the "expected" profit—would then be 80 percent of 5 percent or 4.0 percent.
3. Bid 10 percent above cost and get 60 percent of the jobs bid for an expected profit of 6.0 percent per job bid.
4. Bid 12.5 percent above cost and get half the jobs for an expected profit of 6.25 percent.
5. Bid 15 percent above cost and get 40 percent of the jobs with an expected profit of 6.0 percent.
6. Bid 20 percent above cost and get 20 percent of the jobs giving an expected profit of 4.0 percent.
7. Bid 25 percent above cost and get no jobs and no profit.

Figure 8.9 shows the expected profit associated with each combination of markup and the probability of being low bidder when bidding against this one competitor. In this example the contractor will, in the long run, make more money by bidding at 12.5 percent above cost than could be made either by taking more jobs at a lower markup or by taking fewer jobs at a higher markup. A markup of 12.5 percent above cost, then, represents the "optimum"—or best possible—bid.

In this example the expected profit resulting from a bid that is above the optimum point—above 12.5 percent, in this case—will be the same as a bid placed the same amount below the optimum bid. In other words, exactly the same profit would result for getting 60 percent of the jobs at a 10 percent markup as would be realized from getting 40 percent of the jobs at a 15 percent markup. But the higher markup on fewer jobs would be far less risky and far more desirable.

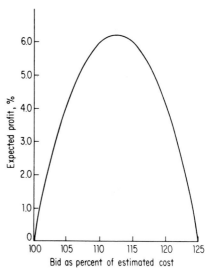

FIGURE 8.9 Effect of bid on expected profit against a single competitor. (*From The Strategy of Contracting for Profit, Prentice-Hall.*)

Bidding against More than One Competitor

The preceding example assumed that only one competitor was involved in the bidding and that the probability of underbidding this one competitor varied inversely with the bid price as shown in Fig. 8.8. If several similar competitors are involved in the bidding, however, the picture changes considerably.

One of the basic rules of probability states that "the probability that two or more independent events will occur simultaneously is equal to the product of their individual probabilities.'' In bidding, all competitors must be underbid at the same time; therefore, the probability of underbidding several competitors at the same time is equal to the probabilities of underbidding each one separately, all multiplied together.

Figure 8.10 illustrates how the probability of being low bidder varies according to the number of competitors involved in the bidding, assuming the probability of underbidding a single competitor is still as indicated in Fig. 8.8.

In Fig. 8.10 the top line is the same as in Fig. 8.8, representing the probability of underbidding a single competitor; this line indicates that a bid of 112.5 percent of cost—a 12.5 percent markup—will underbid the single competitor 50 percent of the time.

If two competitors are involved, the probability of underbidding both at the same time will be only 50 percent of 50 percent, or 25 percent. Similarly, the chances of underbidding three competitors will again be reduced by half— $0.50 \times 0.50 \times 0.50$—to 12.5 percent. Four competitors give only a 6.25 percent chance of being low bidder with a 12.5 percent markup, and five competitors reduce the chances to only 3.25 percent.

The other points on the curves in Fig. 8.10 are calculated in the same way. A 5.0 percent markup, for example, gives an 80 percent chance against one competitor, a 64 percent chance against two (0.80×0.80), a 51.2 percent chance against three $(0.80 \times 0.80 \times 0.80)$, a 40.96 percent chance against four $(0.80 \times 0.80 \times 0.80 \times 0.80)$, and a 32.768 percent chance against five competitors $(0.80 \times 0.80 \times 0.80 \times 0.80 \times 0.80)$.

Figure 8.11 shows the effect of these decreased probabilities of being low bidder on the job's profit expectations. With a 12.5 percent markup, the contractor could get half the jobs against a single competitor for an expected profit of 6.25

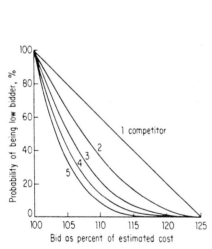

FIGURE 8.10 Effect of number of competitors on probability of being low bidder. (*From The Strategy of Contracting for Profit, Prentice-Hall.*)

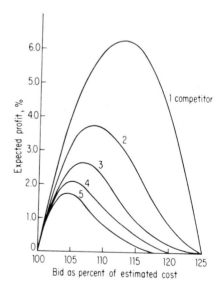

FIGURE 8.11 Effect of number of competitors on expected profit. (*From The Strategy of Contracting for Profit, Prentice-Hall.*)

percent. Against two competitors, however, he can expect to get only 25 percent of the jobs at this markup, reducing his profit expectation to 25 percent of 12.5 percent, or only 3.125 percent.

Similar effects are felt at each markup. As the number of bidders increases, the probability of getting the job with any given bid decreases, and the expected profit associated with any special markup also decreases. Also, the bid which will result in the highest possible long-run profits—the optimum bid—will decrease as the number of bidders increases. Figure 8.11 indicates that, in this example, the optimum bid against one competitor is 12.5 percent, with an expected profit of 6.25 percent. Against two competitors, the optimum bid drops to about 8.0 percent, with an expected profit of 3.8 percent. Against three competitors a markup of 7.0 percent will yield the highest possible expected profit, 2.6 percent. Against four competitors the optimum bid is 5.0 percent, giving an expected profit of 2.1 percent. And against five competitors a markup of 4.0 percent will result in the maximum expected profit of 1.7 percent.

Determining the Probability of Being Low Bidder

One of the key steps in developing a successful competitive-bidding strategy consists of identifying the probabilities of underbidding competitors.

The probability curve of Fig. 8.8 was a straight line, ranging from a 100 percent chance of being low bidder with a bid placed at cost, to a zero percent chance of getting the job at a 25 percent markup. Although this type of probability distribution is entirely possible, few competitors are likely to follow so regular a pattern. Most competitor's bidding patterns will more nearly resemble the distribution shown in Fig. 8.12.

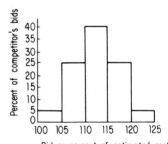

FIGURE 8.12 Normal distribution of competitors' bids. (*From The Strategy of Contracting for Profit, Prentice-Hall.*)

Figure 8.12 represents a "normal" distribution of a competitor's bids, as related to the contractor's own estimated direct costs of performing the work. In this example, the competitor was found to bid at between 100 and 105 percent of estimated direct cost on 5 percent of the jobs, between 105 and 110 percent of cost on 25 percent of the jobs, between 100 and 115 percent of cost on 40 percent of the jobs, and between 115 and 120 percent of cost on 25 percent of the jobs, and between 120 and 125 percent of cost on 5 percent of the jobs.

The bidding distribution pattern of this competitor could have been found simply by tabulating his bids on all jobs for which cost estimates were made, in each case relating the competitor's bids to the estimated job costs. Wide variations will be found in the bidding characteristics exhibited by different competitors; competitor's bids may range from less than half to more than double the estimated job cost, with the extreme variations most likely caused by errors or oversights on the low side and by a complete lack of interest in getting the job on the high side (perhaps a "complimentary" bid).

From the frequency distribution of the competitor's past bids, a probability

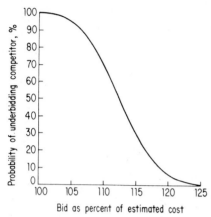

FIGURE 8.13 Probability curves based on a normal distribution of competitors' bids. (*From The Strategy of Contracting for Profit, Prentice-Hall.*)

curve can be constructed, giving the chances of underbidding this competitor with any given bid. Figure 8.13 shows how the probability curve looks for the frequency distribution of Fig. 8.12.

Figure 8.13 indicates that a bid placed at cost will result in underbidding this competitor on every job; in other words, on 100 percent of all past jobs involving this competitor, this competitor bid above the estimated job cost.

If a bid were placed at 5 percent above cost, the bid would have been lower than 95 percent of the competitor's bids on past jobs, for only 5 percent of the contractor's bids fell within the 100 to 105 percent of cost range. Similarly, a markup of 10 percent would have been higher than 30 percent of this competitor's bids—the 5 percent falling in the 100 to 105 percent range and the 25 percent falling in the 105 to 110 percent range—and lower than the remaining 70 percent of this competitor's bids. Thus the probability of underbidding this competitor by bidding at 10 percent above cost would be 70 percent. The remaining points on the probability curve of Fig. 8.13 are determined the same way, with each point defining the percentage of the competitor's bids which experience has shown to fall above that level.

Determining the Expected Profit

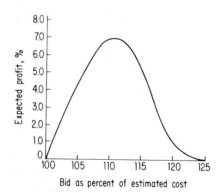

FIGURE 8.14 Expected-profit curve based on a normal distribution of competitors' bids. (*From The Strategy of Contracting for Profit, Prentice-Hall.*)

A profit-expectation curve can easily be developed from the probability curve. The expectation curve—shown in Fig. 8.14—gives the average long-run profit resulting from any given level of markup when bidding against a competitor having these bidding characteristics.

Figure 8.14 indicates that a markup of about 10 percent against this competitor would have yielded the highest possible profits; such a markup would have captured 70 percent of the jobs, giving an average profit per job bid of 70 percent of 10 percent, or 7.0 percent. A lower bid would have captured more jobs, and a higher bid would have resulted in higher profits on the jobs won; but neither a higher nor a lower bid would have equaled the total profit associated with a 10 percent markup in this case. A 5 percent markup would have taken 95 percent of the jobs, but the profit would have been only 4.75 percent per job bid; a 15 percent markup would have taken 30 percent of the jobs, for an average 4.5 percent profit.

Combinations of Competitors

Every competitor will exhibit different bidding characteristics; some bid consistently high, some bid consistently low, some spread their bids uniformly over a wide range, and some may bid within fairly well defined and narrow limits. The strategy to be employed against each must therefore vary to take maximum advantage of each one's individual characteristics and weaknesses.

Figure 8.15 shows three different bidding-distribution patterns, representing three different competitors. Competitor A (Fig. 8.15a) has the same characteris-

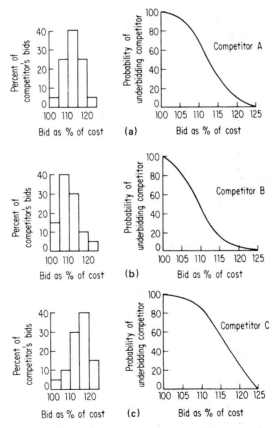

FIGURE 8.15 Bid-distribution and probability curves for competitors having different characteristics. (*From The Strategy of Contracting for Profit, Prentice-Hall.*)

tics as used in the preceding example. Competitor B (Fig. 8.15b) tends to group bids lower than competitor A, with 40 percent of bids falling in the 105 to 110 percent range. Competitor C (Fig. 8.15c) generally bids higher than the other two, with 40 percent of bids grouped in the 115 to 120 percent cost range.

When bidding against these three competitors, a given markup will offer different chances of underbidding each one. For example, a 10 percent markup gives a 70 percent chance of underbidding competitor A, a 45 percent chance of underbidding competitor B, and an 85 percent chance of underbidding competitor C. And since the probability of underbidding combinations of competitors is equal to their individual probabilities multiplied together, the chances of getting a job at any given markup are sharply reduced when more than one competitor is involved.

Since the probability of underbidding A with a 10 percent markup is 70 percent and the corresponding probability of underbidding competitor B with the same markup is 45 percent, the probability of underbidding both A and B at the same time is 0.70×0.45, or only 31.5 percent. The probability of underbidding both A and B with any specified bid can be found by identifying the probability of underbidding each one separately, then multiplying these probabilities together.

The probabilities associated with other combinations of competitors can be found the same way. For example, a 10 percent markup gives a 31.5 percent chance of underbidding A and B, a 59.5 percent chance of underbidding A and C (0.70×0.85), a 38.25 percent chance of underbidding B and C (0.45×0.85), and a 26.775 percent chance of underbidding all three competitors ($0.70 \times 0.45 \times 0.85$).

In each case, the optimum bid can be found by calculating the expected profit at various markups. Against all three competitors, for example, the optimum bid is at about a 7.0 percent markup, where a 60 percent chance of being low will yield an expected profit of 4.2 percent.

Typical Competitor

When individual competitors and their bidding characteristics can be identified in advance, the best results can usually be obtained by considering them individually as in the previous examples. However, there are apt to be relatively few jobs on which all competitors can be identified, or where sufficient data are available to determine properly the bidding characteristics of all participants. In such cases the concept of the "typical"—or average—competitor can be used to advantage.

The typical competitor is simply a composite made up of all bids of all competitors. As such, the typical competitor refers to no one competitor in particular, but to all competitors in general. The concept of a typical competitor is especially valuable when bidding against numerous unknown competitors. The use of this concept allows the general level of bids likely to result in maximum profits to be identified and used as a guide in setting an exact price or in identifying the most potentially profitable jobs.

The probability of being low bidder when bidding against different numbers of typical competitors can be calculated in the same manner as when the specific competitors are known. The probability of underbidding any given number of typical competitors can be found by first taking the probability of underbidding a single typical competitor, then multiplying this number by itself that same number of times. In other words, the probability P of underbidding n typical competitors is

$$P = C^n$$

where C is the probability of underbidding one typical competitor with a specific markup. The optimum bid against any number of typical competitors can then be found by the same trial-and-error approach as when the competitors are known.

THE BIDDING MODEL

Concept of a Mathematical Model

For every job, there is an optimum markup that will result in the best possible combination of a contractor's chances of getting the job and receiving a decent profit after winning the job. This optimum figure is not necessarily a good one or even a fair one. It represents the best he can hope to get on a particular job at a particular time. If the contractor were to bid every single job at its optimum markup, there still might not be a net profit at year's end. However, there would be either the greatest possible profit or the smallest loss.

A competitive-bidding strategy should help identify the optimum markup for each job to be bid. It should help

- Determine the chances of getting a job by bidding with a given markup
- Identify the markup that will result in the greatest possible profit on a specific job in view of the prevailing competitive situation surrounding that job
- Select from a number of different projects the jobs offering the highest profit potential

The only data needed for developing a bidding strategy can usually be found in files of past jobs over the past year or two. Needed will be a record of all the jobs bid, estimated costs on each job, who the competitors were on each job, and how much they bid. From this, the competitive-bidding model can be developed.

The details of a competitive-bidding model will vary from year to year, field to field, area to area, and contractor to contractor. But in all cases, two characteristics stand out: the more bidders on a job, the lower the optimum markup, and the larger the job, the lower the optimum markup.

Effect of Number of Bidders

For a job of given size, the optimum markup varies approximately inversely with the 0.7 power of the ratio of the number of bidders.

Figure 8.16 shows how the number of competitors on a job affects the optimum bid. Assuming the best markup against a single competitor to be 30 percent, the best markup against two competitors on the same job would be 18.5 percent; against four, 11.4 percent; against eight, 7 percent. Or, if the best markup against the single competitor were 20 percent, the best markups against two, four, and eight competitors would be 12.3, 7.6, and 4.7 percent, respectively.

Mathematically, the relationship can be expressed:

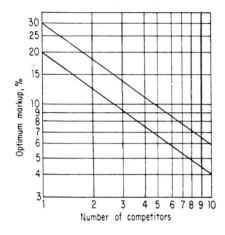

FIGURE 8.16   Effect of number of competitors on optimum markup. (*Engineering News-Record.*)

$$\left(\frac{N_1}{N_2}\right)^x = \frac{M_2}{M_1}$$

where N_1 and N_2 = number of competitors bidding on jobs 1 and 2
$\quad\quad\; M_1$ and M_2 = optimum markups on these two jobs
$\quad\quad\quad\quad x$ = appropriate exponent (which establishes the slope of line on graph), ranging generally between 0.50 and 0.80

For example, if the best markup on a $50,000 job against two competitors is known to be 20 percent, then the best markup against six competitors on the same job could be found as follows:

$$\left(\frac{6}{2}\right)^{0.7} = \frac{20\%}{M} \quad M = 20\% \div 2.16 = 9.2\%$$

Effect of Job Size

Job size has a significant effect on the optimum markup, although its impact is far less than that of the number of bidders.

For jobs with a specified number of bidders, the optimum markup varies inversely with approximately the 0.2 power of the ratio of the direct job costs. Figure 8.17 illustrates this relationship graphically, using 20 and 30 percent markups on a $10,000 job as starting points. Increasing the size of the job to $100,000 will

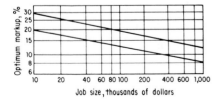

FIGURE 8.17   Effect of job size on optimum markup. (*Engineering News-Record.*)

bring the optimum markups down to 12.7 and 19 percent on the two curves. For a \$1 million job, optimum markups drop to 8 and 12 percent.

The mathematical model is

$$\left(\frac{C_1}{C_2}\right)^x = \frac{M_2}{M_1}$$

where C_1 and C_2 refer to the estimated direct job costs and M_1, M_2, and x carry the same designations as before. Here, though, the x will probably be in the 0.15 to 0.30 range. As another example, suppose that the best markup against three typical competitors on a \$20,000 job is 15 percent. Then the best markup against the same three competitors on a \$100,000 job would be calculated as follows:

$$\left(\frac{100,000}{20,000}\right)^{0.2} = \frac{15\%}{M} \qquad M = 15\% \div 1.38 = 10.9\%$$

Combined Effects of Competition and Job Size

Once the right numbers have been developed to plug into the two preceding mathematical expressions, the optimum markup for any job of any size, against any number of competitors, can be quickly approximated by applying the exponent values in Table 8.7 to the ratios of job sizes and number of competitors, in a simple two-part solution.

TABLE 8.7 Exponential Factors for Bidding Models

Ratio of job sizes or no. of bidders	Exponential factor	
	Job size (0.2 exponent)	No. of bidders (0.7 exponent)
2	1.15	1.62
3	1.25	2.16
4	1.32	2.64
5	1.38	3.17
6	1.43	3.51
7	1.48	3.91
8	1.52	4.28
9	1.55	4.66
10	1.58	5.01

Table 8.7 indicates that doubling the size of the job will reduce the optimum markup to 1/1.15, or 87 percent of its previous level, while doubling the number of bidders will reduce the markup to 1/1.62, or 62 percent of its former value.

The following example shows how these factors are used to apply a known set of job characteristics to another, unknown, situation.

Problem. If the optimum markup against one competitor on a \$10,000 job is 30 percent, what is the optimum markup against six competitors on a \$100,000 job?

Solution. First, find the optimum markup against one competitor on a $100,000 job:

$$\left(\frac{100,000}{10,000}\right)^{0.2} = \frac{30\%}{M} \qquad M = \frac{30}{1.58} = 18.9\%$$

Next, using the 18.9 percent markup as a new base figure for a $100,000 job against one competitor, find the markup to be used against six competitors on the same job:

$$\left(\frac{6}{1}\right)^{0.7} = \frac{18.9\%}{M} \qquad M = \frac{18.9}{3.51} = 5.4\%$$

Once a single situation is known, any other problem can be solved. In the example above, the optimum markup against four competitors on a $50,000 job would turn out to be 8.2 percent. Against two competitors on a $20,000 job, a 16.1 percent markup should be used.

Table 8.8 shows how the optimum markups associated with different combinations of competitors and job sizes vary for the situation described in Figs. 8.16 and 8.17.

TABLE 8.8 Relative Optimum Markups (percent) for Various Jobs

Job size	Number of competitors					
	1	2	3	4	5	6
$ 10,000	30.0	18.5	13.9	11.4	9.5	8.5
20,000	26.1	16.1	12.1	9.9	8.2	7.4
50,000	21.7	13.4	10.0	8.2	6.8	6.2
100,000	18.9	11.7	8.8	7.2	6.0	5.4
200,000	16.4	10.1	7.6	6.2	5.2	4.7
500,000	13.7	8.5	6.3	5.2	4.3	3.9
1,000,000	12.0	7.4	5.6	4.5	3.8	3.4

Table 8.8 assumes an optimum markup of 30 percent against one competitor on a $10,000 job and goes from there using the 0.2 and 0.7 exponential factors. While the general relationships are probably valid for many contractors, the specific figures are not. They are presented here as an example only to illustrate the general relationships between job sizes, the intensity of competition, and the optimum markups.

SUMMARY AND CONCLUSIONS

Evaluating the Strategy's Effectiveness

There is but one real measure of the effectiveness of any competitive strategy: profits. If the profits resulting from using a particular strategy are higher than can be achieved by any other available means, then it is a good strategy; if not, the strategy is worthless.

The procedures for finding the optimum bid that were discussed in the preceding sections were aimed at maximizing profits; other possible objectives might include:

1. Minimizing the possibility of loss
2. Maintaining some prescribed level of return on investment
3. Achieving a specified share of the total market
4. Increasing the likelihood of obtaining a particular job

Regardless of the specific objective, the competitive data that have been developed will prove helpful to the contractor in attaining desired objectives. Simply recognizing the probability of success associated with any bid on any job and the amount of profit associated with each bid, the contractor not only can identify the optimum bid in terms of gross profits but can also evaluate the expected outcome of any other bid and its compatibility with any chosen objectives.

Since no changes in estimating or operating procedures are required in applying a competitive-bidding strategy, the strategy can be implemented as soon as sufficient data are available and after management is completely convinced of the strategy's value and usefulness, and is aware of its limitations.

However, the strategy can—and should—be tested without risk prior to its actual use in competition. This can be done simply by bidding jobs in the usual way, but at the same time determining the optimum bid for the job as indicated by statistical means. By thus comparing the profits actually realized with those which would have resulted had the strategy been employed, the contractor can obtain an objective and realistic measure of the proposed strategy's effectiveness.

After this comparison between actual and potential profits has been made for a sufficient period, some indication will have been gained of the proposed strategy's probable effect on the company's overall operations, including its impact both on profits and on the volume of work obtained.

The sales volume resulting from using a bidding strategy can change in either direction. If the previous level of markups has been too low, using a higher markup will most likely result in a lower sales volume, accompanied by higher profits. If markups have been too high, the volume will probably increase when markups are lowered to an optimum level, again with an increase in profits.

In either case, then—whether more jobs are taken at a lower markup or fewer jobs at a higher markup—profits will increase when a properly designed competitive-bidding strategy is implemented.

Results of Strategic Bidding

Whether a firm can benefit from a competitive-bidding strategy depends primarily upon how successful it already is. The results of putting these strategic principles into practice can be predicted only in very general terms, based on the experience of other contractors.

Contractors applying these principles have been able to achieve bidding efficiencies in the 40 to 60 percent range—their total profits have amounted to between 40 and 60 percent of the amount they could have made if they knew their

TABLE 8.9 Results of Strategic Bidding

Specialty	Jobs bid	Jobs won	Actual gross profit	Maximum profit potential	Bidding efficiency, %
General contractor (heavy)	36	16	$1,014,000	$1,808,000	55.8
General contractor (buildings)	32	16	68,400	151,700	45.1
Subcontractor (building trade)	107	44	162,200	386,600	42.0

competitors' bids in advance and if they took every job at the lowest competitor's price, disregarding all jobs let at cost or below.

Table 8.9 shows the results achieved by three contractors operating in different fields and in different geographic areas.

In retrospect, it is easy to see how these three contractors could have improved their performance by being selective in the jobs they chose to bid. However, since everything is obvious in retrospect, perhaps 50 percent bidding efficiency is not an unrealistic goal for the contractor.

A contractor already operating above the 50 percent efficiency mark obviously can expect little in the way of improvement. But any firm operating at below 40 percent of its profit potential should realize that it could do better. Certainly, the cost to the contractor in terms of time, money, and effort can be amortized quickly through improved bidding efficiency. The mental exercise required to develop the competitive-bidding models will sharpen a contractor's intuitive sense and force a more objective look at business.

Results must always be considered in view of the contractor's objectives. Using the theoretically correct markups, while resulting in the highest possible gross profits, might not necessarily be the best course to follow in every case.

If no substantial increase in overhead or capital costs were required to support an additional volume associated with the optimum bids, over the costs of operating at, say, half that total volume, then the use of the optimum bids is well justified—so long as the contractor's objective is to maximize profits.

If, however, additional costs are likely to be incurred in handling a larger volume associated with optimum markups, then some intermediate solution is warranted. Probably the most satisfactory solution would be to set a minimum markup based on the firm's operating and financial requirements and objectives and to look for jobs offering at least the minimum potential.

By doing this, a substantial level of profits might be achieved by bidding many fewer jobs—all of which are easily identifiable for some time prior to the letting. And, by devoting more attention to identifying other jobs offering potentially greater profits, the results would probably be far better.

Using a well-thought-out competitive-bidding strategy in conjunction with management's own goals and requirements cannot help but improve a company's position, regardless of what the goals and requirements are.

Variable vs. Fixed Markups

Unless the contractor bids only one type of job against a fixed number of competitors in a completely stable market—a situation few contractors face—it will be much better in the long run to vary markups according to competition. If a relatively small number of competitors are faced on any given job—perhaps six or fewer—and if the same competitors are frequently encountered, profits can probably be raised substantially by considering both the number and the individual characteristics of these competitors. Beyond a half-dozen competitors on a single job, however, individual characteristics are apt to be obscured, and equally satisfactory results can usually be achieved by assuming that all competitors have the characteristics of the "typical" or average competitor.

The variable markup based on the existing competitive situation is likely to show a marked effect both on the contractor's sales volume and on his profits. Sales volume will decrease as the markup increases; profits, meanwhile, will begin at zero, rise to some maximum value, then decline to zero again as the markup increases. The amount to be gained by using a variable markup will almost invariably be much higher than could have been achieved by any fixed level of markups.

Thus a substantial argument is presented in favor of a variable markup, even if the markup is based upon nothing more than the number of competitors to be encountered on the project.

Management Review and Revision

A competitive-bidding strategy cannot just be implemented and forgotten but must be continually reviewed by top management to ensure the strategy's compatibility with the firm's objectives. If the strategy fails to accomplish the firm's objectives, then the strategy should be carefully reviewed. If it still fails to meet the firm's requirements, then the objective should be reviewed. One or the other must be changed.

In theory at least, the competitive-bidding strategy should change as each additional bit of competitive information becomes available. In practice, this would mean developing a new strategy each time another job is let on which the competitor's bids become known. Such continual revision is neither necessary nor desirable.

The strategy should be revised periodically, however. The elapsed time between revisions will depend largely upon the amount of new data that becomes available. For most contractors, annual or semiannual revisions should be adequate unless the competitive situation becomes significantly altered.

A complete revision of competitive-bidding strategy will require the addition of new data to existing data, thus changing the frequency distribution of competitors' bids and subsequently leading to the construction of new probability curves.

In most cases, one, or at most two, years of competitive data are sufficient. As the data from the most recent year's operations are added, the oldest year's data can be dropped. This practice keeps the strategy current.

Effect of Strategic Bidding on Industry Profits

One of the main points that rapidly becomes apparent in developing and applying a competitive-bidding strategy is the need for selectivity in bidding. By picking jobs with the greatest profit potential and concentrating on these jobs, all thinking contractors come around to seeing the idea of "volume for the sake of volume"

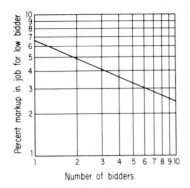

FIGURE 8.18 General relationship between markups and number of bidders. (*From The Strategy of Contracting for Profit, Prentice-Hall, 1966.*)

as distasteful. The effect in the long run will be to make the contracting industry profit-oriented, rather than—as is largely the present case—volume-oriented.

As shown both in theory and in practice, the number of bidders per job has a direct effect on the profits realized by the lower bidder. And the numerous contractors who feel obliged to bid every job that is offered are chiefly responsible for driving away the industry's profits. Figure 8.18 show the general relationship between the number of bidders on a job and the amount of profit in the job for the successful bidder. Based on these relationships between the profit on a job and the number of bidders for the job, it is apparent that reducing the number of bidders on each job will result in increased profits for everyone.

For example, assume that there are 10 general contractors competing for 100 jobs, each job having an estimated direct cost of $100,000. If each of the 10 contractors bids all the 100 jobs, the average job will, at best, go at about 2.4 percent above cost. Total profit on the $10 million worth of work will amount to $240,000, or $24,000 per contractor. But if each contractor bid only 50 of the jobs, then there would be an average of only five bidders per job. The average net should be approximately 3.3 percent per job, amounting to $330,000 total, or $33,000 per contractor. This is in spite of the fact that each contractor is bidding only half as many jobs as before and the total amount of available work remains unchanged.

The intensity of competition—the main cause of low profit margins—is not simply a function of the amount of work available and the number of firms in the business; it is just as much a function of the number of bids submitted by each contractor. There can be tougher competition, and lower profits, with half as many contractors in the business competing for the same volume if each contractor insists on bidding twice as many jobs. Profits depend more upon the number of bidders per job than on any other single factor.

More bidders per job means lower profits to the low bidder; lower profits in each job means that a higher volume must be obtained to break even; a higher volume requires that more jobs be bid; and bidding more jobs means that profit margins will become lower.

The construction industry can be a profitable business for all contractors provided that all contractors demand a reasonable profit from every job they bid.

FURTHER READING

Park, W. R. *Construction Bidding for Profit,* New York, N.Y.: John Wiley & Sons, 1979.

Park, W. R. *The Strategy of Contracting for Profit,* Englewood Cliffs, N.J.: Prentice-Hall, Inc., 1966.

CHAPTER 9
PURCHASING

James J. O'Brien, P.E.
Chairman of the Board
O'Brien-Kreitzberg & Associates, Inc.
Pennsauken, New Jersey

Since the cost of materials ranges from 30 to 60 percent of the average construction contract, purchasing is an important function in the contractor's organization. It has a direct impact on profitability and individual job profits. Any gain through savings in purchasing results in direct increase in profits.

Unfortunately, the importance of purchasing is most recognized when it becomes a problem. As the construction industry has matured, there has been less opportunity for the purchasing department to perform heroically. The improvement in definition of design specifications and a broad range of competitive trademarked material both operate to narrow the field of choice for a specific material required on a construction project. Although these factors have precluded many inappropriate purchases of inexpensive material, they do not operate to offer coordination and timing of purchases, so broad opportunity remains for failure or costly purchases.

Following Bernard Baruch's famous advice, it would appear that the function of the purchasing department is to "buy cheap . . ."

WHAT IS CHEAP?

The term "cheap" implies shoddiness, or lack of quality. The goal of the purchasing department, then, should be to avoid cheap purchases—but to look for optimum purchases. Traditionally, owners' inspectors view contractors' materials as though they were, in fact, cheap. In most cases, shaving specifications by purchasing below-standard material is a poor way to save. An apparently inexpensive purchase can result in rejections of the actual unit in place. This can result in a high labor cost to remove and replace the unit. Other apparently inexpensive purchases may require additional field labor and may tremendously escalate the total cost of the item in place.

Sometimes good material can be purchased at lower unit cost through large-order-size purchases. However, holding items for a long period of time, perhaps even never using them, can result in a higher true cost per unit. The cost of inventory and extra field handling is a factor in the true installed unit cost of an item.

PURCHASING ORGANIZATION

In large organizations, the purchasing group may include purchasing analysts, traffic experts, and expediters, as well as management. The general trend is toward a central purchasing control, rather than project-oriented purchasing.

In some cases, purchasing is expanded to include everything involved in the moving, handling, and storing of materials. In addition, there is a close rapport between the estimating and purchasing departments, which are often—in smaller organizations—interchangeable. In larger organizations, specialty areas are developed, particularly in heavy equipment, commodity purchases, and other specialized items.

Although usually a relatively small department, the purchasing department is quite important in terms of profit impact. Accordingly, it is usually organized on a par with other major line departments. In some cases, it may become part of the staff organization but continue to wield significant authority.

THE PURCHASE ORDER

The requirement for a purchase is usually presented to the purchasing department in the form of a requisition, with duly authorized signatures according to company procedures. The various items to be acquired by the purchasing department include items such as:

Subcontracts

Specific materials

Contract services and commodities

Fixed assets such as office equipment

Heavy equipment

The requisition establishes the amount and specifications of the item to be acquired. It is up to the purchasing department to select the vendor through its organized procedures and then to determine method of shipping, receiving instructions, and definite schedules. In addition, the purchasing department often is responsible for the handling of warehousing and inter- and intracompany deliveries.

The method of originating a requisition is a function of the type of item to be purchased. These items fall into two general categories, project and nonproject. Examples of nonproject acquisitions are general fuels, fixed equipment, and general overhead support, such as job trailers, utilities, and office housekeeping.

Project equipment falls into three major classifications:

Subcontracts to be performed in total

Materials to be warehoused on the job site

Materials to be delivered direct to the job site and utilized there.

While the purchasing agent may initiate requisitions, they are usually developed by the project team as a result of analysis of the specifications and drawings or scope and requirements. The order and quantity must be exact but are a function of the number of items required and their relative cost. Generally, major items are more easily identified in terms of exact quantities.

When the requisition has been received, the purchasing department orders from either existing purchase orders or directly from vendors for certain categories of equipment or materials. The majority of materials required by a contractor are ordered on bid. These bids may be requested on a job-by-job basis or may be for block quantities that are to be delivered over a period of time—as in the case of fairly standard valves, piping, lumber, and other stock materials.

The requisition may be computer-generated, particularly if the estimating phase has been computerized. Computerization may be initiated in the purchasing department at the requisition level.

After the requisition has been processed and a determination made as to whether it is to be handled by direct purchase, blanket purchase, or quotation, a request for bid is made in appropriate cases. When the cost information is available, a selection is made. This may involve technical assistance from the project team to determine compliance of specifications—particularly where additions or exceptions are mentioned.

The purchasing department then issues a purchase order to the successful vendor. If electronic data processing is utilized, the information is automatically transferred to the purchase-order format and a receiving report is generated at the same time.

VENDORS

The purchasing department should have preselected most of its vendors or potential vendors. Again, rapport is important. If the contractor follows a policy of buying cheap through all seasons, he will be unable to purchase materials in a timely fashion during peak activities. Conversely, he may pay somewhat more for the services of the vendor during the off season.

Vendors compete not only on a cost-for-material basis but also by furnishing a broad range of services which can be of direct assistance to the purchasing department. Catalogs and other descriptive material are readily available. Sales personnel are willing to furnish technical representatives for on-site evaluation and will even provide demonstrations as required. Other inducements may not be as technical. A personal relationship can be useful but must be kept scrupulously on proper ground. Nevertheless, the vendor can control supply and can offer price assistance by viewing scattered purchases in the aggregate. In many cases, he may carry popular items in his warehouse—shipping direct to the job site when required (i.e., drop shipping).

The purchasing department should keep a vendor file, including rating of prior vendor performance. Rating characteristics should include reliability, price history, delivery record, and technical assistance.

PURCHASING DOCUMENT

In addition to the internal purchasing document, the purchasing department requires a standard series of purchasing documents, including invitation to bid, bidder information forms, and binding contractual agreements for price and delivery. In addition, subcontractors are bound to the same project conditions as the general contractors to preclude nonliability on the part of subcontractors.

Forms should include

Requisition

Purchase order

Request for bid

Subbid form

Purchase-order commodities

Letter of intent

Subcontract form

Contract form

Contract-amendment forms

The basic contract includes type of items covered, length of contract, prices and discounts, delivery times, terms of payment, shipping points, method of transportation, methods for altering or revising contracts, receiving conditions, and special conditions.

SCHEDULING OF ITEMS

The usual method of establishing the delivery date is through the intuitive but arbitrary assignment of date by the project group. These field-need dates frequently shift during the progress of the project, and more advanced project purchasing departments keep apprised of these changes through scheduling techniques such as the critical-path method (CPM). Of course, if the overall project is not being scheduled by CPM, it is not feasible for the purchasing department to key into the CPM approach. Fortunately, many progressive contractors are utilizing such organized scheduling techniques. The participation of the purchasing department is vital to the success of an overall project-scheduling system. The delivery of materials at an early time will not necessarily expedite or speed up the overall project because progress of other activities, as described by the CPM, actually controls the earliest possible starting time. However, failure to deliver key materials for various activities may delay a project indefinitely. Unfortunately, the purchasing agent faces a difficult enigma; if he delivers late, he delays the project—if he delivers early, the field team complains about extra handling and storage requirements. The problem reaches its most acute stage in urban areas where project supervisors may have to lift materials directly from truck or railcar right to the final location.

Figure 9.1 is a small CPM network for a site-preparation activity. Figure 9.2 is the same network with a reasonable spread of materials superimposed. This poses a question in terms of which materials should be shown as part of a CPM network. Basically, materials fall into two categories: those which can be ordered out of stock for short-term delivery and can be classified as commodities, and those with relatively long delivery times and which require specific orders. The CPM networks should generally include only long-lead items.

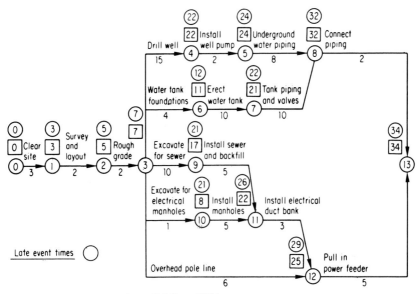

FIGURE 9.1 Late-event times. (*McGraw-Hill.*)

In Fig. 9.2, the materials listed are shown with a zero delivery time so that the early and late start dates relate only to the requirements of the project. The late dates (for instance, the twenty-second day for the well pump which is delivered to event 4 prior to installation) are the latest times in which the pump can be delivered and not delay the 34-day duration of the overall project. The CPM calculation for the materials shown would be as follows:

Activity	Delivery
0–4	Well pump
0–5	Underground water pipe
0–6	Water-tank parts
0–7	Tank valves and piping
0–9	Sewer pipe
0–10	Manhole frame and cover
0–11	Conduit
0–12	Power cable
0–101	Poles, crossbars, guys, insulators

Accordingly, the float value in this case represents the time allowable for delivery. Keep in mind that these times are in project days, so that 24 would represent almost 5 weeks, 26 would be 5 weeks, etc. If we now look at the materials placed on this network and assign reasonable delivery times, we could have a schedule such as the following:

I–J	Duration	Description	ES	EF	LS	LF	Float
0–4	0	Well pump	0	0	22	22	22
0–5	0	Underground pipe	0	0	24	24	24
0–6	0	Water tank	0	0	12	12	12
0–7	0	Tank valves	0	0	22	22	22
0–9	0	Sewer pipe	0	0	21	21	21
0–10	0	Manhole frame and cover	0	0	21	21	21
0–11	0	Conduit	0	0	26	26	26
0–12	0	Power feeder	0	0	29	29	29
0–101	0	Pole-line materials	0	0	23	23	23

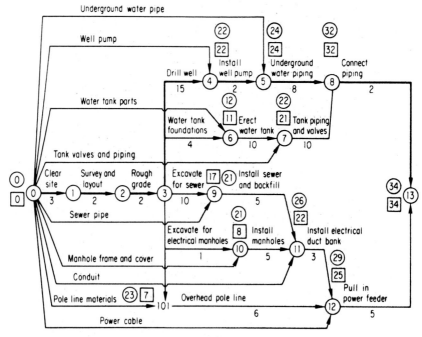

FIGURE 9.2   Delivery activities, network. (*McGraw-Hill.*)

Figure 9.3 then shows the Joe Doe site network with the same deliveries but now with reasonable delivery times assigned. Note that the project duration is increased from 34 to 52, as materials actually enter the critical path. The overall event-time calculations have changed as follows:

Early event times		Event	Late event times	
Old	New		Old	New
3	3	1	3	21
5	5	2	5	23
7	7	3	7	25
22	22	4	22	40
24	30	5	24	42
11	30	6	12	30
21	40	7	22	40
32	50	8	32	50
17	17	9	21	39
8	8	10	21	39
22	22	11	26	44
25	40	12	29	47
34	52	13	34	52
	10	101		41
Changes	7			14

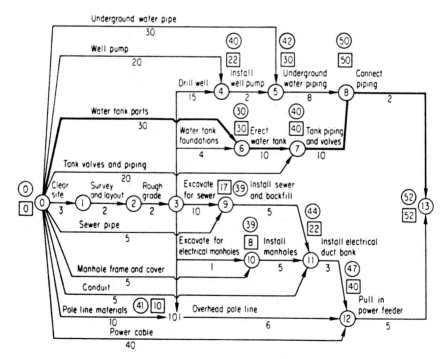

FIGURE 9.3 Delivery-time estimates, network. (*McGraw-Hill.*)

Note that 21 event times out of a possible 28 have changed. Using this new late-start information, the purchasing department would tend to delivery materials in the following order:

Activity	Description	Late start
0–6	Water tank	0
0–12	Power feeder	7
0–5	Underground water pipe	12
0–4	Well pump	20
0–7	Tank valves	20
0–101	Pole material	31
0–9	Sewer pipe	34
0–10	Manhole cover	34
0–11	Conduit	39

While this list gives the order in which materials should be requisitioned, it has two distinct weaknesses. First, although the late-start dates for ordering are important, they are extremes. If the order is placed this late, all activities following the delivery will be critical. Second, the early-start times have very little value. In this example, the purchasing department could initiate nine orders the first day of the project. What, for instance, if an enthusiastic buyer orders the sewer pipes and conduit on the first project day? The conduit would arrive on site about 8 weeks before it was needed; the sewer pipe would be 7 weeks early. The field group would have a storage problem and a poor opinion of the purchasing department. In practice, this has often happened. The purchasing department, enthusiastically participating in a new technique, where for the first time they have relatively good information, has ordered according to early-start dates—resulting in job-site bedlam. This has often discouraged the use of CPM for coordination of material procurement. The real defect is the lack of relation of the early-start time to the field work. Leaving the delivery arrows to represent delivery time, just as they were, add another set of arrows to represent actual movement of the material from storage to the jobsite. Figure 9.4 shows these "on-site material" arrows, which have the same late-finish times as the delivery arrows did. However, the activity now has an early-start time directly related to the requirements of the job. The calculation for Fig. 9.4 has the following values:

Activity	Description	ES	LF	Float
4–104	Well pump at site	22	40	18
5–105	Underground pipe at site	30	42	12
6–106	Water tank at site	30	30	0
7–107	Tank valves at site	40	40	0
9–109	Sewer pipe at site	17	39	22
10–110	Manhole cover at site	8	39	31
11–111	Conduit at site	22	44	22
12–112	Power feeder at site	40	47	7
101–102	Pole material at site	10	41	31

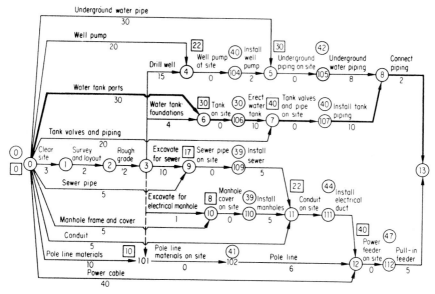

FIGURE 9.4 On-site delivery times. (*McGraw-Hill.*)

Note that the late-finish times for these activities are the same as the late-finish times for the delivery arrows. However, early and float times are now related to field progress. Using this as a basis, the priority of ordering would be

Priority	Position on first order list	Delivery as early as (days)	Delivery no later than (days)	Float
1. Water tank	1	30	30	0
2 Tank valves	5	40	40	0
3. Power feeder	2	40	47	7
4. Underground pipe	3	30	42	12
5. Well pump	4	22	40	18
6. Sewer pipe	7	17	39	22
7. Conduit	9	22	44	22
8. Manhole cover at site	8	8	39	31
9. Pole material	6	10	41	31

Note that all but two of the items are in a different position in terms of priority on the second list.

Thus far it has been assumed that required delivery time for materials is easily ascertained. However, there may be a number of steps in the material procurement which are time-consuming, and these should not be neglected. These steps can include shop-drawing approval, vendor time for shop-drawing preparation, resubmittal time for shop-drawing revisions, agency review by cognizant groups, engineering review, and other factors. These steps can sometimes be accelerated for critical activities, but there is a tendency to minimize the impact of routine processing. For instance, the purchasing department should have a complete shop-drawing record logging all transmittals to and from the owner, the vendor, and reviewing agencies. This can have substantial impact on claims for delay—but only if the delay can be quantified through a disciplined means such as a CPM diagram.

Figure 9.5 shows the interrelationship between two material orders (hardware and door bucks) before either reaches the job site. In this example, the door buck delivery has 5 days' float because of the additional time required to prepare hardware templates. Larger equipment may require additional time for the submission of formal bids. In Fig. 9.2, the addition of nine simple delivery arrows almost doubled the network size. In Fig. 9.6, the arrows showing the total materials-procurement situation more than doubled the number of activities relating to field work. While this is not the usual situation, it should be obvious that the purchasing department can have a very meaningful impact upon the project-scheduling activities.

The purchasing department should keep a current list of typical delivery times to be furnished to the planning-scheduling department for inclusion in schedules. Following is a typical listing:

	Building	
	Approval of drawings, weeks	Anticipated delivery (after approval and release), weeks
Enclosure		
Structural steel	4–6	8–13
Steel joists	2–4	8–10
Siding	3–4	13–26
Mechanical		
HVAC-fans	2–4	13–18
HVAC-chillers	4–6	18–26
Agitators and mixers	6–8	26–32
Centrifugal blowers	4–6	26–32
Compressors (packaged centrifugal)	8–10	20–26
Compressors (packaged reciprocating)	6–89	26–39
Electrical equipment		
Motor control centers	8–10	26–40
Switch gear (low voltage)	8–10	36–40
Switch gear (high voltage)	8–10	40–52
Transformers (low voltage)	6–8	30–39
Transformers (high voltage)	6–8	40–52
Motors (to 150 h)	6–8	16–26
Motors (over 150 h)	6–8	26–39 (dependent on horsepower)
Turbines	8–10	40–50
Power cable (600 V)	N/R	30–52 (dependent on quantity)
Bus duct	6–8	26–36
Cable tray	6–8	18–26
Conduit (rigid alum.)	N/R	Stock-28

Conduit (E.M.T.)	N/R	Stock-26
Emergency generators	10–12	26–30
Architectural		
Hollow metal frames	8–10	12–18
Hardware	10–12	18–26

Process equipment		
Pressure vessels (carbon steel)		
Small (noncode)	4–6	18–26*
Small (code—under 20,000 lb)	4–6	26–36*
Large (code—over 20,000 lb)	6–8	36–40
Towers (w/o internals or trays)	6–8	46–50
Towers (with internals or trays)	8–10	52–60
Jacketed vessels or tanks	8–10	52–60
		*Add 4 weeks for stainless
Field-erected tanks	8–10	40–52 (includes erection)
Heat exchangers		
Shell and tube (small)	4–6	18–20
Shell and tube (large)	6–8	36–46
Fintube	4–6	18–26
Plate type	4–6	36–40
Air-cooled	4–6	6–36
Conveyors		
Pneumatic	6–8	26–30
Screw	6–8	24–30
Live roller and drag	6–8	24–28
Vibrating	6–8	26–30
Bucket elevators	6–8	26–30
Belt	6–8	30–34
Pumps		
Centrifugal	4–6	20–26
Centrifugal (horizontal)	6–8	26–32
Centrifugal (turbine)	6–8	24–30
Metering	4–6	20–34
Positive displacement	4–6	20–24
Vacuum	6–8	26–30
Reciprocating	6–8	26–30
Dryers, filters, scrubbers		
Instrument air dryers	8–10	24–30
Filters	6–8	20–26
Dust collectors	6–8	30–40
Fume scrubbers	6–8	20–30
Control valves	3–4	20–24
Instrumentation		
Displacement-type flow meters	3–4	18–26
D.P. transmitters	4–5	16–22
Liquid level gauges	3–4	18–20

Building		
	Approval of drawings, weeks	Anticipated delivery
Transducers	3–4	14–28

Level switches	3–4	12–16
Pressure switches	3–4	16–18
Controllers	4–5	18–20
Recorders	4–5	18–20
Thermometers	3–4	14–16
Pressure gauges	3–4	16–20
Pipe, valves, flanges and fittings	N/A	
		Stock to 52 weeks

Materials handling equipment		
Monorail hoists	4–6	18–26 (dependent on capacity)
Traveling or trolley cranes	4–6	30–42 (dependent on capacity)
Fork lift trucks	4–6	26–30

Figure 9.5 shows a CPM output sorted by specification section. This permits purchasing specialists to identify items in their purchasing specialty area.

Figure 9.6 is a CPM output listing showing procurement items including shop drawings (S/D); submittal and approval; and fabricate and deliver (FAB/DEL). The items are listed in late start order, which can also function as a check list for procurement. (See Figs. 9.7 and 9.8 on p. 9.16.)

EXPEDITING AND RECEIVING

After material has been ordered, the purchasing department must maintain contact with the vendor to ensure delivery. Many things occur in the course of the delivery cycle, particularly when there are great demands generally for material. Telephone expediting can be very effective, but periodic job visits to the production shop must be made. The purpose of these visits is not only to check quality and view testing but to demonstrate contractor interest in the material itself.

The expediter should be scheduled automatically or keyed semiautomatically from the CPM schedule or other project requirements, however they are stated. Electronic data processing can reduce the paperwork involved in setting up a tickler file for periodic expediting by providing a list of material by category and by furnishing preprepared expediting reports. All data can be introduced into the report, leaving the expediter to input only a brief report on the actual contact made. This can be returned to a purchasing-department data bank and will be recycled for review or introduced into appropriate management reports. Where deliveries become critical, it is sometimes possible—if project management is forewarned—to rearrange work sequences or introduce work-arounds.

Receiving reports can be generated in the same manner and are most important to the maintenance of a useful materials file. The receiving report should also trigger the beginning of the project inventory-information file and reporting system. Receiving responsibilities should also be a purchasing department function, and the basic receiving report should indicate condition as well as quantity. Quality inspection should be cursory, as long as the items specified can be properly identified. In bulk materials, test samples should be taken as required by job specifications. Where any missing item or damage is noted, the receiving reportshould be structured so that information is recycled properly into the project-scheduling flow, again to bring the proper management attention to any problem areas.

JOHN DOE HASELINE CPM SCHEDULE
PREPARED BY O'BRIEN-KREITZBERG & ASSOC., INC.

I NODE	J NODE	ACTIVITY DESCRIPTION	ORG DUR	REM DUR	CNTP TYPE	WORK CAT.	SPEC SEC.	EARLY START	EARLY *FINISH	LATE START	LATE *FINISH	TOTAL FLOAT
		TILE-0930										
44	48	CERAMIC FILE	10.0	10.0	GC	3-7	0930	05FEB88	19FEB88	03MAR88	16MAR88	18.0
69	73	CERAMIC TILE OFFICE	10.0	10.0	GC	4-7	0930	23JUN88	07JUL88	29JUL88	11AUG88	25.0
72	80	FLOOR TILE OFFICE	10.0	10.0	GC	4-7	0930	05AUG88	18AUG88	05AUG88	18AUG88	0.0
		ACOUSTICAL-0950										
78	80	ACOUSTIC TILE OFFICE	10.0	10.0	GC	4-7	0950	05AUG88	18AUG88	05AUG88	18AUG88	0.0
		SUSPENSION SYSTEMS-0954										
77	78	INSTALL CEILING GRID OFFICE	5.0	5.0	GC	4-8	0954	08jul88	14JUL88	29JUL88	04AUG88	15.0
		RESILIENT FLOOR'G-0965										
53	57	FLOOR TILE P-W	10.0	10.0	GC	3-7	0965	11MAR88	11MAR88	2MAR88	06APR88	10.0
		PAINTING-0990										
48	53	PAINT ROOMS P-W	5.0	5.0	GC	3-7	0990	22FEB88	26FEB88	17MAR88	23MAR88	18.0
63	80	PAINT OFFICE EXTERIOR	5.0	5.0	GC	4-7	0990	01JUN88	07JUN88	12AUG88	18AUG88	51.0
71	72	PAINT EXTERIOR OFFICE	10.0	10.0	GC	4-7	0990	22JUL88	04AUG88	22JUL88	04AUG88	0.0
		FLAGPOLES-1035										
58	80	ERECT FLAGPOLE	5.0	5.0	GC	5-7	1035	21APR88	27APR88	12AUG88	18AUG88	79.0
		FURNISHING—1200										
57	58	INSTALL FURNISHING P-W	10.0	10.0	GC	3-7	1200	14MAR88	25MAR88	07APR88	20APR88	10.0
		HOISTS & CRANES-1430										
0	214	SUBMIT S/D CRANE	20.0	20.0	—	—	1430	01JUL87	29JUL87	06AUG87	02SEP87	25.0

FIGURE 9.5 Network report by specification section.

JOHN DOE HASELINE CPM
PREPARED BY O'BRIEN—KREITZBERG & ASSOC., INC.

PAGE
DATA DATE 01JUL87

I NODE	J NODE	ACTIVITY DESCRIPTION	ORG DUR	REM DUR	CNTP TYPE	WORK CAT.	SPEC SEC.	EARLY START	EARLY *FINISH	LATE START	LATE *FINISH	TOTAL FLOAT
0	212	SUBMIT S/D STRUCT STEEL	20.0	20.0	—	—	0510	01JUL87	29JUL87	01JUL87	29JUL87	0.0
0	220	SUB S/D PLANT ELEC LOAD CTR	20.0	20.0	—	—	1640	01JUL87	29JUL87	10JUL87	06AUG87	6.0
0	224	SUBMIT S/D EXTERIOR DOORS	20.0	20.0	—	—	0810	01JUL87	29JUL87	24JUL87	20AUG87	16.0
0	225	SUB S/D PLANT ELECT FIXIS	30.0	30.0	—	—	1640	01JUL87	12AUG87	24JUL87	03SEP87	16.0
212	213	APPROVE S/D STRUCT STEEL	10.0	10.0	—	—		03JUL87	12AUG87	30JUL87	12AUG87	0.0
0	222	SUBMIT S/D PWR PNLS-PLANT	20.0	20.0	—	—	1640	01JUL87	29JUL87	31JUL87	27AUG87	21.0
0	227	SUB S/D PLANT HTG VENT FANS	20.0	20.0	—	—	1580	01JUL87	29JUL87	31JUL87	27AUG87	21.0
0	210	SUBMIT S/D FOUNDATION REBAR	10.0	10.0	—	—	0230	01JUL87	15JUL87	03AUG87	14AUG87	22.0
0	214	SUBMIT S/D CRANE	20.0	20.0	—	—	1430	01JUL87	29JUL87	06AUG87	02SEP87	25.0
220	221	APPR S/D PL ELECT LOAD CTR	10.0	10.0	—	—		30JUL87	12AUG87	07AUG87	20AUG87	6.0
213	23	FAB/DEL STRUCTURAL STEEL	40.0	40.0	—	—		13AUG87	08OCT87	13AUG87	08OCT87	0.0
210	211	APPROVE S/D FDN REBAR	10.0	10.0	—	—		16JUL87	29JUL87	17AUG87	28AUG87	22.0
221	37	FAR/DEL PLANT EL LOAD CTR	90.0	90.0	—	—		13AUG87	21DEC87	21AUG87	30DEC87	6.0
224	225	APPROVE S/D EXTERIOR DOORS	10.0	10.0	—	—		30JUL87	12AUG87	21AUG87	03SEP87	16.0
0	229	SUB S/D BOILER	20.0	20.0	—	—	1560	01JUL87	29JUL87	21AUG87	18SEP87	36.0
222	223	APPROVE S/D PWR PNLS-PLANT	10.0	10.0	—	—		30JUL87	12AUG87	28AUG87	11SEP87	21.0
227	228	APPR S/D PLNT HTG VENT FANS	10.0	10.0	—	—		30AUG87	12AUG87	28AUG87	11SEP87	21.0
211	16	FAB/DEL FOUNDATION REBAR	10.0	10.0	—	—		30JUL87	12AUG87	31AUG87	14SEP87	22.0
214	215	APPROVE S/D CRANE	10.0	10.0	—	—		30JUL87	12AUG87	03SEP7	17SEP87	25.0
225	37	FAB/DEL EXTERIOR DOORS	80.0	80.0	—	—		13AUG87	07DEC87	04SEP87	30DEC87	16.0
0	218	SUBMIT S/D SIDING	20.0	20.	—	—	0740	01JUL87	29JUL87	04SEP87	02OCT87	46.0
0	231·	SUBMIT S/D OIL TANK	20.0	20.0	—	—	1560	01JUL87	29JUL87	04SEP87	02OCT87	46.0
0	216	SUBMIT S/D BAR JOISTS	20.0	20.0	—	—	0520	01JUL87	11SEP87	08OCT87	50.0	
223	37	GAB/DEL POWER PANELS-PLANT	75.0	75.0	—	—		13AUG87	30NOV87	14SEP87	30OCT87	21.0
228	37	FAB/DEL PLANT HTG VENT FANS	75.0	75.0	—	—		13AUG87	30NOV87	14SEP87	30DEC87	21.0

FIGURE 9.6 Materials by late start, computer-run.

NETWORK REPORT
SORT BY PROCUREMENT /02

JOHN DOE HASELINE CPM
PREPARED BY O'BRIEN—KREITZBERG & ASSOC., INC.

PAGE
DATA DATE 01JUL87

I NODE	J NODE	ACTIVITY DESCRIPTION	ORG DUR	REM DUR	CNTP TYPE	WORK CAT.	SPEC SEC.	EARLY START	EARLY *FINISH	LATE START	LATE *FINISH	TOTAL FLOAT
215	31	FAB/DEL CRANE	50.0	50.0		—		13AUG87	22OCT87	18SEP87	30NOV87	25.0
229	230	APPROVE S/D BOILER	10.0	10.0		—		30JUL87	12AUG87	21SEP87	02OCT87	36.0
230	37	FAB/DEL BOILER	60.0	60.0		—		13AUG87	05NOV87	05OCT87	30DEC87	36.0
218	219	APPROVE S/D SIDING	10.0	10.0		—		30JUL87	12AUG87	05OCT87	16OCT87	46.0
231	232	APPROVE S/D OIL TANK	10.0	10.0		—		30JUL87	12AUG87	05OCT87	16OCT87	46.0
216	217	APPROVE S/D BAR JOISTS	10.0	10.0		—		30JUL87	12AUG87	09OCT87	22OCT87	50.0
219	35	FAB/DEL SIDING	40.0	40.0		—		13AUG87	08OCT87	19OCT87	15DEC87	46.0
232	35	FAB/DEL OIL TANK	50.0	50.0		—		13AUG87	22OCT87	19OCT87	30DEC87	46.0
217	33	FAB/DEL BAR JOISTS	30.0	30.0		—		13AUG87	24SEP87	23OCT87	07DEC87	50.0
0	235	SUBMIT S/D PACKAGING A/C	30.0	30.0		—	1580	01JUL87	12AUG87	29OCT87	11DEC87	84.0
225	226	APPR S/D PLANT ELECT FIXTS	15.0	15.0		—		13AUG87	02SEP87	27NOV87	17DEC87	73.0
235	236	APPROVE S/D PACKAGING A/C	10.0	10.0		—		13AUG87	26AUG87	14DEC87	28DEC87	84.0
226	51	FAB/DEL PLANT ELECT FIXTURES	75.0	75.0		—		03SEP87	21DEC87	18DEC87	05APR87	73.0
236	60	FAB/DEL PACKAGING A/C	90.0	90.0		—		27AUG87	06JAN88	29DEC87	04MAY88	84.0
0	233	SUBMIT S/D PRECAST	40.0	40.0		—	0340	01JUL87	25AUG87	29DEC87	24FEB88	124.0
233	234	APPROVE S/D PRECAST	10.0	10.0		—		27AUG87	10SEP87	25FEB88	09MAR88	124.0
234	28	FAB/DEL PRECAST	30.0	30.0		—		11SEP87	22OCT87	10MAR88	20APR88	124.0

FIGURE 9.6 (*Continued*) Materials by late start, computer-run.

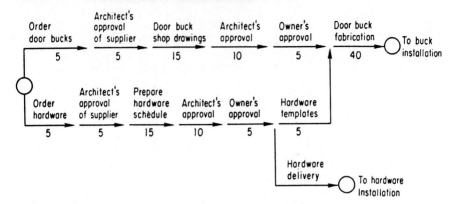

FIGURE 9.7 Typical material-procurement cycle. (*McGraw-Hill.*)

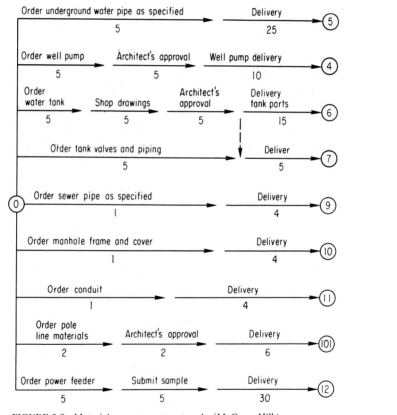

FIGURE 9.8 Material-procurement network. (*McGraw-Hill.*)

INVENTORY

In commerce and production, inventory has similar characteristics and management has similar goals. The principle is to operate at the lowest practical level of inventory in order to minimize capital investment in inventory, while having material on hand as required and holding material outages at the lowest practical level. (Statistically, the occurrence of no outages requires an infinite amount of material and is an impractical utilization of resources.) The contractor's problem is similar in terms of material ordered for installation on the job site. Major items are, ideally, delivered directly to the job site at the instant needed. Practically, certain latitude must be allowed, and if material is delivered late, careful attention must be paid to the potential costs of tying up field craft labor, the most expensive single category in the total project. The availability of commodity-type materials is exactly analogous to the industrial-production problem. Materials must be there to support the work and must be reordered when the available supply falls to a reasonably low point.

The availability of computers has vastly changed inventory techniques. In theory, there have been no changes, but computerization permits much closer approximation. Basic program packages are available from organizations such as IBM (IMPACT-Inventory Management Program and Control Technique). The principal characteristics of an inventory, regardless of type, involve the number of items held in inventory and the distribution of those items. The contractor should develop, through the purchasing department, a list of items held in inventory. This listing should be in machine-readable form and can be sorted by project, category of material, value, and other parameters. For basic inventory analysis, the item records are arranged in descending sequence by annual dollar utilization. In typical inventories, the top 1 or 2 percent of the items account for almost 20 percent of the usage range. Obviously, greater attention would be given to these areas, and on a cost-effectiveness basis, decreasing attention would be paid to lower use or lower cost items.

The standard ratio is a measure of the relationship between the number of items in an inventory and the cost of these items. This ratio is calculated by plotting the annual value of the inventory vs. cost value per item. The plot results in a straight line, as illustrated in Fig. 9.9. The standard ratio is utilized in calculations which lead to comparison values for inventory. Figure 9.10 shows types of characteristic inventory curves. They are plotted by value against the percentage of cumulative annual use. The shape of the individual curve is a function of the industry represented. In research work, the curve is a sharp one—almost a right angle, because a large part of the inventory is subject to obsolescence. Also, a few large components such as x-ray machines, microscopes, and special electronic equipment may have a high cost and appreciable volume. Conversely, a wholesale house would have a flat curve with a ratio in the range of 4:7. Retailers tend to have the lowest standard curve ratio of about 2:3.

Inventory information can be utilized in determining inventory order points, i.e., the time at which an order should be placed and the quantity of the order. In establishing the order point, two opposing considerations must be determined: the cost of lost production time vs. the cost of carrying more inventory than is currently required. Figure 9.11 shows a typical order-strategy curve which correlates the two costs. In addition to order time, lead time for delivery and other items such as review must be included.

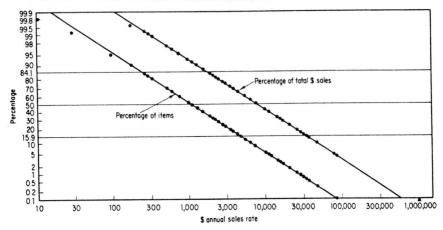

FIGURE 9.9 Standard inventory ratio. (*Used with permission of IBM.*)

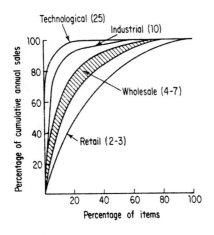

FIGURE 9.10 Typical distributions. (*Used with permission of IBM.*)

SHIPPING

The purchasing department also designates, in most cases, the method of shipping to the warehouse or job site. In certain cases, the project management team will place priorities on certain items, requesting special shipments such as air freight. (Again, in many cases, this can be precluded by careful preplanning that utilizes a scheduling system such as CPM.) The purchasing department must do cost evaluations between kinds of shipment and storage charges such as rail demurrage. In certain cases, it is advantageous to hold railcars at the job site rather than utilize a more expensive warehousing situation.

The purchasing department must also be cognizant of varying rates or different types of freight—less than carload (LCL) vs. carload lots, and other such factors. In a larger purchasing department, often there is a transportation department specializing in this type of information.

The purchasing department should build a data bank, either card file or computerized, which combines the departments' own experience with basic information regarding delivery methods and rates.

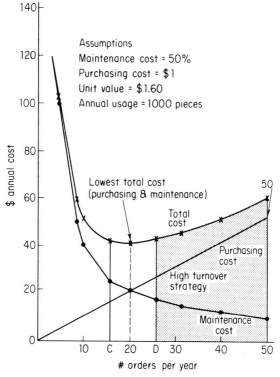

FIGURE 9.11 Purchasing-strategy curve. (*Used with permission of IBM.*)

SUMMARY

Purchasing is an important job that can make or break the profit situation on a specific contract and for the company as a whole. The best purchasing agent is not a wheeler-dealer but a competent businessman who recognizes that there are many more facets to his responsibilities than the basic establishment of purchase price. A single-minded old-fashioned purchasing group that fails to recognize this broad, comprehensive scope of responsibilities can go on buying trees and never find the right forest.

CHAPTER 10
SCHEDULES

James J. O'Brien, P.E.
Chairman of the Board
O'Brien-Kreitzberg & Associates, Inc.
Pennsauken, New Jersey

Schedules are one of the most important factors in the success (or failure) of a construction project. From 1910 to 1958, the principal tool for construction planning and scheduling was the Gantt chart, more commonly called the bar graph.

GANTT BAR GRAPHS

Although this technique was originally aimed at production scheduling, it was readily accepted for planning construction and recording its progress. The bar graph was, and is, an excellent graphical representation of activity. It is easily read and understood by all levels of management and supervision.

If the bar graph is so well suited to construction activity, why look for another planning aid? The reason is that the bar graph is limited in what it can contain. In the preparation of a bar chart, the scheduler is almost necessarily influenced by desired completion dates. The resultant mixture of planning and scheduling is often no better than wishful thinking.

The bar graph cannot show (or record) the interrelationships and interdependencies which control the progress of the project. At a later date, even the originator is often hard-pressed to explain the plan using the bar graph. Figure 10.1 is a simplified bar chart for the construction of a small one-story office building. Suppose that after this 10-month schedule has been prepared, the owner asks for a 6-month schedule. By using the same time for each activity, the bar chart can be changed as shown in Fig. 10.2. Although this looks fine, it is not based on logical planning; it is merely a juggling of the original bar graph.

The overall construction plan is usually prepared by the general contractor. This is sensible since the schedules of the other major contractors depend on the general contractor's schedule. Note that in Figs. 10.1 and 10.2, the general contractor's work is broken down in some detail, while the mechanical and electrical work are each shown as a continuous line starting early and ending late. In conformance with the bar graph "Schedule," the general contractor often pushes the subcontractors to staff the project as early as possible with as many mechanics as

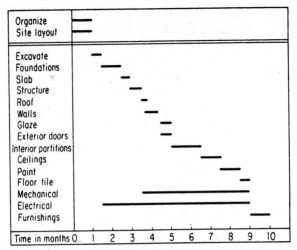

FIGURE 10.1   Bar chart, small office building.

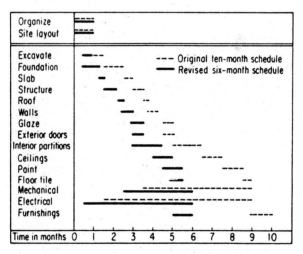

FIGURE 10.2   Revised bar chart, small office building.

possible, while the subcontractors would like to come on the project as late as possible with as few mechanics as possible. At the same time, the subcontractor often complains that the general contractor is not turning work areas over to him or her and that he or she, the sub, will have to go into a crash effort to save the schedule. As in most things, the truth of the matter is somewhere between the extremes.

The bar chart often suffers from a morning-glory complex: It blooms early in the project but is nowhere to be found later on. We can suppose some general reasons for this disappearing act: Prior to the construction phase, the architect, the engineer, the owner, or all of them are trying to visualize the project schedule in order to set realistic completion dates. Most specifications require the submission of a schedule in bar-graph form by the contractor soon after the award of the contract. When the project begins to take shape in the field, the early bar-chart plans become as useful as last year's calendar because the bar graph does not lend itself to planning revisions.

Although progress can be plotted directly on the schedule bar chart, the S curve has become popular for measuring progress. The usual S curve consists of two plots (see Fig. 10.3): scheduled dollar expenditures vs. time and actual expenditures vs. time. Similar S curves can be prepared for worker-hours, equipment and material acquisitions, concrete yardage, etc.

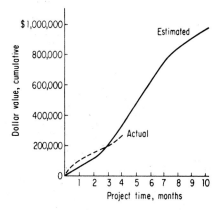

FIGURE 10.3   Typical S curve.

NETWORK SCHEDULING

From 1956 to 1958, a scheduling task force at the E. I. DuPont de Nemours Company successfully developed a computerized construction planning and scheduling system. The result was called *critical path method* (CPM). This creation became the state-of-the-art in construction scheduling in the 1960s. Now, over 30 years old, it is broadly accepted as a mature component in management of construction.

The initial purpose of CPM was to find a way to apply the relatively new electronic computer to construction. The team (James E. Kelley, Jr., of UNIVAC and Morgan Walker of DuPont) had to find a mathematical method of expressing construction sequence as an algorithm. Kelley has explained that the team then used graphical logic networks to explain the algorithm to DuPont management. In practice, the network "arrow" diagram has become the cornerstone of the CPM scheduling system.

Although some contractors were in the early "evangelistic" group of CPM supporters, the greater majority of early contractor contact with CPM was through mandated usage. Starting as early as 1962, the U.S. Army Corps of Engineers included a comprehensive requirement that the successful contractor utilize CPM (described as a Network Analysis System, to permit use of the DOD-sponsored PERT system).

SP-4. CONTRACTOR-PREPARED NETWORK ANALYSIS SYSTEM: The progress chart to be prepared by the contractor pursuant to the General Provisions entitled "Progress Charts and Requirements for Overtime Work" shall consist of a network analysis system as described below. In preparing this system the scheduling of construction is the responsibility of the contractor. The requirement for the system is included to assure adequate planning and execution of the work and to assure adequate planning and execution of the work and to assist the Contracting Officer in appraising the reasonableness of the proposed schedule and evaluating progress of the work.

a. An example of one of the numerous acceptable types of network analysis systems is shown in Appendix I of Corps of Engineers Regulation ER-1-1-11 entitled "Network Analysis System," single copies of which are available to bona fide bidders on request. Other systems which are designed to serve the same purpose and employ the same basic principles as are illustrated in Appendix I will be accepted subject to the approval of the Contracting Officer.

b. The system shall consist of diagrams and accompanying mathematical analyses. The diagrams shall show elements of the project in detail and the entire project in summary.

(1). Diagrams shall show the order and interdependence of activities and the sequence in which the work is to be accomplished as planned by the contractor. The basic concept of a network analysis diagram will be followed to show how the start of a given activity is dependent on the completion of preceding activities and its completion restricts the start of following activities.

(2). Detailed network activities shown on a detailed or sub-network diagram shall include, in addition to construction activities, the submittal and approval of samples or materials and shop drawings, the procurement of critical material and equipment, fabrication of special materials and equipment and their installation and testing, and delivery of Government Furnished Property primary priority by scheduled late delivery and secondary priority by scheduled early delivery. The network diagrams shall contain a priority by scheduled early delivery. The network diagrams shall contain a minimum of one activity showing scheduled dates (early and late) for each delivery of major elements of Government Furnished Property (GFP) listed in Section 1B of these specifications, properly located to reflect the logical restraints to on-site activities. The description of each GFP delivery activity shall include the drawing reference, quantity of GFP items required for the activity and an adequate word description. All activities of the Government that affect progress, and contract required dates for completion, shall be such that duration times of activities will range from 3 to 30 days with not over 2 percent of the activities exceeding these limits. The selection and number of activities shall be subject to the Contracting Officer's approval. Detailed networks, when summary networks are also furnished, need not be time scaled but shall be drafted to show a continuous flow from left to right with no arrows from right to left. The following information shall be shown on the diagrams for each activity: Preceding and following event numbers, description of the activity, cost, and activity duration. *The critical path shall be determined and shall be clearly indicated on the diagram.*

(3). Summary Network: If the project is of such size that the entire network cannot be readily shown on a single sheet, a summary network diagram shall be provided. The summary network diagram shall consist of a minimum of fifty activities and a maximum of one hundred. Related activities shall be grouped on the network. The critical path shall be plotted generally along the center of the sheet with channels with increasing float placed toward the top or bottom. The summary network shall be time scaled using units of approximately one half inch equals one week or other suitable scale approved by the Contracting Officer. Weekends and holidays shall be indicated. Where slack exists, the activities shall be shown at the time when they are scheduled to be accomplished.

(4). The mathematical analysis of the network diagram shall include a tabulation of each activity shown on the detailed network diagrams. The following information will be furnished as a minimum for each activity:

(a). Preceding and following event numbers. (Numbers will be selected and assigned so as to permit identification of the activities with bid items.)

(b). Activity description

(c). Estimated duration of activities (being the best estimate available at time of computation.)

(d). Earliest start date (by calendar date).

(e). Earliest finish date (by calendar date).

(f). Scheduled or actual start date (by calendar date).

(g). Scheduled or actual finish date (by calendar date).

(h). Latest start date (by calendar date).

(i). Latest finish date (by calendar date).

(j). Slack or float.

(k). Monetary value of activity.

(l). Responsibility for activity (prime contractor, subcontractors, suppliers, Government, etc.)

(m). Manpower required.

(n). Percentage of activity completed.

(o). Contractor's earnings based on portion of activity completed.

(p). Bid item of which activity is a part.

(5). The program or means used in making the mathematical computation shall be capable of compiling the total value of completed and partially completed activities.

(6). In addition to the tabulation of activities the computation will include the following data:

(a). Identification of activities which are planned to be expedited by use of overtime or double shifts to be worked including Saturdays, Sundays and holidays.

(b). On-site manpower loading schedule.

(c). A description of the major items of construction equipment planned for operations of the project. The description shall include the type, number of units and unit capacities. A schedule showing proposed time equipment will be on the job keyed to activities on which equipment will be used and will be provided.

(d). Where portions of the work are to be paid by unit costs, the estimated number of units in an activity which was used in developing the total activity cost.

(7). The analysis shall list the activities in sorts of groups as follows:

(a). By the preceding event number from lowest to highest and then in order of the following event number.

(b). By the amount of slack, then in order of preceding event number.

(c). By responsibility in order of earliest allowable start dates.

(d). In order of latest allowable start dates and then in order of preceding event numbers and then in order of succeeding event numbers.

c. Submission and approval of the system shall be as follows:

(1). A preliminary network defining the contractor's planned operations during the first 60 calendar days after Notice to Proceed shall be submitted within 10 days. The contractor's general approach for the balance of the project shall be indicated. Cost of activities expected to be completed or partially completed before submission and approval of the whole schedule shall be included.

(2). The complete network analysis consisting of the detailed network mathematical analysis (on-site manpower loading schedule, equipment schedule) and network diagrams shall be submitted within 40 calendar days after receipt of Notice to Proceed.

d. The contractor shall participate in a review and evaluation of the proposed network diagrams and analysis by the Contracting Officer. Any revisions necessary as a result of this review shall be resubmitted for approval of the Contracting Officer within 10 calendar days after the conference. The approved schedules shall then be the schedule to be used by the contractor for planning, organizing and directing the work and for reporting progress. If the contractor thereafter desires to make changes in his method of operating and scheduling he shall notify the Contracting Officer in writing stating the reasons for the change. If the Contracting Officer considers these changes to be of a major nature he may require the contractor to revise and submit for approval without additional cost to the Government, all of the affected portions of the detailed diagrams and mathematical analysis and the summary diagram to show the effect on the entire project. A change may be considered of a major nature if the time estimated to be required or actually used for an activity or the logic of sequence of activities is varied from the original plan to a degree that there is reasonable doubt as to the effect on the contract completion date or dates. Changes which affect activities with adequate slack time shall be considered as minor changes, except that an accumulation of minor changes may be considered as a major change when their cumulative effect might affect the contract completion date.

e. The contractor shall submit at intervals of 30 calendar days a report of the actual construction progress by updating the mathematical analysis. Revisions causing changes in the detailed network shall be noted on the summary network, or revised issue of affected portions of the detailed network furnished. The summary network shall be revised as necessary for the sake of clarity. However, only the initial submission or complete revisions need be time scaled. Subsequent minor revisions need not be time scaled.

f. The report shall show the activities or portions of activities completed during the reporting period and their total value as basis for the contractor's periodic request for payment. Payment made pursuant to the General Provisions entitled "Payments to Contractor" will be based on the total value of such activities completed or partially completed after verification by the Contracting Officer. The report will state the percentage of the work actually completed and schedule as of the report date and the progress along the critical path in terms of the days ahead or behind the allowable dates. If the project is behind schedule, progress along other paths with negative slack shall also be reported. The contractor shall also submit a narrative report with the updated analysis which shall include but not be limited to a description of the problem areas, current and anticipated, delaying factors of their impact, and an explanation of corrective action taken or proposed.

g. Sheet size of diagrams shall be 30" by 42". Each updated copy shall show a date of the late revisions.

h. Initial submittal and complete revisions shall be submitted in 6 copies.

i. Periodic reports shall be submitted in 4 copies.

j. The contractor shall maintain on the job site as part of his organization, a staff trained in the use and application of scheduling systems whose sole responsibility will be the monitoring of progress and providing computer input for updating the mathematic analysis and revising logic diagrams when necessary. The size of this staff will be subject to the approval of the Contracting Officer and will be supplemented at no additional cost to the Government, if additional personnel are required by directive of the Contracting Officer.

k. When modifications in the work are found to be necessary, and Notice to Proceed with the changes must be issued prior to settlement of price and/or time to avoid delay and additional expense, the Contracting Officer will furnish the contractor, promptly thereafter, suggested changes in the network logic and/or duration time of all activities affected by the modifications. The contractor shall use the suggested logic and/or duration change in updating network diagrams and machine printouts in subsequent required submittals; provided, however, that if the contractor has objections to any of the suggested logic and/or activity duration time changes he shall advise the Contracting Officer promptly, in writing, of such objections fully supported by his own counterplan, and provided further, that if the contractor does not submit such written objection and counterplan within thirty (30) days after the date of the Notice to Proceed with the modifications, the contractor will be deemed to have concurred in the Contracting Officer's suggested logic/duration time changes, which changes then will be the basis of any required equitable adjustment of the time for performance of the work.

l. Float or slack is defined as the amount of time between the early start date, and the late start date, or the early finish date, and the late finish date, of any of the activities in the NAS schedule. Float or slack is not time for the exclusive use or benefit of either the Government or the contractor. Extensions of time for performance required under the contract General Provisions entitled, "CHANGES," "DIFFERING SITE CONDITIONS," "TERMINATION FOR DEFAULT—DAMAGES FOR DELAY—TIME EXTENSIONS" or "SUSPENSION OF WORK" will be granted only to the extent that equitable time adjustments for the activity or activities affected exceed the total float or slack along the channels involved.

m. In order to provide specific information for planning purposes, network analysis systems will clearly indicate the scheduled completion dates for the items of work listed below:
(At this point, the specification goes on to list project milestones.)

CPM DIAGRAM—EXAMPLE

The site (see Fig. 10.4) is in a low area overgrown with scrub timber and bushes; the soil is a sand and gravel mixture overlaid by clay. Cast-in-place piles will be driven to about 30 feet for the plant and warehouse foundations. The office building will be on spread footings. Since there is no water supply available, a well and 50,000-gal elevated water tower will be installed. Sewage and power trunk lines are 2000 feet away. Power connections will be by an overhead pile line up to 200 feet from the building; from that point on, the power line will run underground (see Fig. 10.5). The sewer will pass under part of the power line. The activities representing the above site work are

Survey and layout	Drill well
Clear site	Install well pump
Rough grade	Install underground water supply

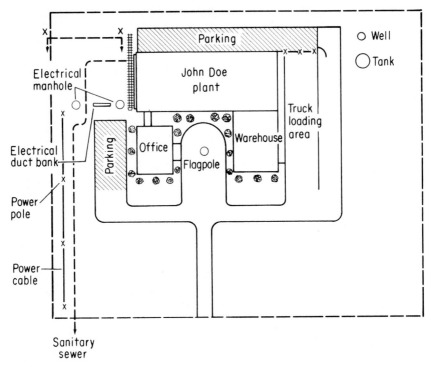

FIGURE 10.4   Site plan, John Doe project.

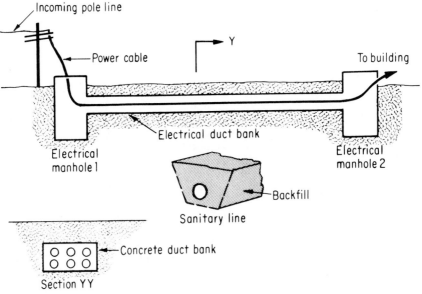

FIGURE 10.5   Electrical duct bank section XX.

Drive and pour piles

Excavate plant and warehouse

Pour pile caps

Excavate office building

Pour spread footings

Pour grade beams

Install power feeder

Excavate for sewer

Install sewer

Set pole line

Excavate for electrical manholes

Install electrical manholes

Energize power feeder

The first rough arrow diagram usually becomes the activity list. For a number of reasons, this owner elects to proceed in a definite fashion. In order to expedite the project, site preparation and utilities work (see Fig. 10.6) are put out as a separate package which is to be accomplished before the foundation contractor moves on the site.

	Event
0	Project start
0–1	Clear site: Necessary before any survey work can start.
1–2	Survey and layout: Cannot start before the site is clear; otherwise, many of the survey stakes would be lost in the clearing operation.
2–3	Rough grade: Cannot start until the area has been laid out. This activity ties up the whole site with earth-moving equipment.
3–4	Drill well: Cannot start until the rough-grading operation is completed.
4–5	Install well pump: Cannot be done until well is completed and cased.
5–8	Underground water piping: Although this work might be started earlier, the site contractor prefers to work from the pump toward the building site.
3–6	Water tank foundations: After the rough grading, these simple foundations can be installed.
6–7	Erect water tank: Obviously the water tank cannot be erected until its foundations are poured.
7–8	Tank piping and valves: Cannot be fabricated and erected until the tank is completed.
8–13	Connect piping: The water piping cannot be linked up until both sections are completed.
3–9	Excavate for sewer: Can be started after rough grading.
9–11	Install sewer and backfill: Immediately follows the sewer excavation, working from the low point uphill.
3–10	Excavate for electrical manholes: Can start after rough grading.
10–11	Install electrical manholes: Cannot start until the excavation is completed.
11–12	Install electrical duct bank: Is started after the electrical manholes are complete. The start of this also depends on the completion of the sewer line since that line is deeper than the duct bank.
3–12	Overhead pole line: Can be started after the site is rough-graded.
12–13	Pull in power feeder: Can start after both the duct bank and the overhead pole line are ready to receive the cable.
13	Site preparation and utilities work are complete.

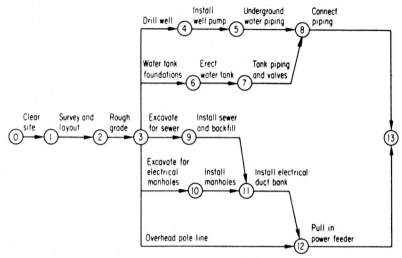

FIGURE 10.6 CPM network, site preparation and utilities.

MATHEMATICAL ANALYSIS

Analysis of the logic diagram is very straightforward. It is based on simple arithmetic and can be done manually. (This, ironically, was not readily recognized for some time by the founders. In fact, the discovery of "the obvious" has no specific author.) All CPM programs follow the general approach described in this section.

The addition of time to the arrow does *not* make it a vector, and the arrow is *not* drawn to scale. (There are certain uses of time-scaled networks, but these should not be drawn for the initial network.)

From the network showing the site preparation for the John Doe project (Fig. 10.6), the first nine activities are

0–1	Clear site
1–2	Survey and layout
2–3	Rough grade
3–9	Excavate for sewer
9–11	Install sewer and backfill
3–10	Excavate for electrical manholes
10–11	Install electrical manholes
11–12	Install electrical duct bank
3–12	Overhead pole line

An estimate of the time required for these activities, based on materials and takeoffs, is shown in Tables 10.1 and 10.2.

TABLE 10.1 Estimation of Time Durations

	Activity	Quantity	Project time, days
0–1	Clear site	Four acres at 2 dozer days per acre by four dozers	2
1–2	Survey and layout	Set control traverse—1½ days; layout, grade, and line—½ day	2
2–3	Rough grade	One acre, move 1000 yards, two dozers at 250 cubic yards per day	2
3–9	Excavate for sewer	Approximate cross section at deep end (10-foot depth) is 12 square yards by 667 yards in length. Averaging, approximately 4000 cubic yards, clamshell with 2-yard bucket at 100 cubic yards per hour.	5
9–11	Install sewer and backfill	2000 feet at 60 feet per hour—33 hours.	4
3–10	Excavate for two electrical manholes	At 2 hours per manhole, say.	1
10–11	Install two electrical manholes	800 square feet forms total at 100 square feet per team-hour—8 hours. Crew setup time—4 hours; pour concrete—4 hours; strip—8 hours.	4
11–12	Install electrical duct	800-foot conduit at 2 feet per hour—400 worker-hours per 10-person crew. Concrete follows by 1 day.	6
3–12	Overhead line	1800 feet, set 24 poles—one crew, 3 days; string wire—3 days.	6

TABLE 10.2 Informal Time Estimates for These Activities

	Activity	Brief description	Assumed crew size	Project time, days
0–1	Clear site	Four acres, four bulldozers	5	3
1–2	Survey and layout	Four acres, benchmarks available	3	2
2–3	Rough grade	One acre, two dozers	3	2
3–9	Excavate for sewer	Average depth 5 feet, 2000 feet long	5	10
9–11	Install sewer and backfill		5	5
3–10	Excavate for electrical manholes	Two manholes, 5 feet deep	2	1
10–11	Install electrical manholes	Poured in place	4	5
11–12	Install electrical duct	200-feet-long by 5-feet-deep 4-inch conduit, straight run	7	3
3–12	Overhead line	1800 feet	4	6

EARLY EVENT TIMES (T_E)

The network provides the order in which each activity must be performed. Clearly, the earliest time at which an activity can logically start (i.e., early event time = T_E) is the sum of all preceding activity times. Figure 10.7 shows the entire site preparation network with times assigned and early event times noted. The T_E at event 12 is the choice of the time along path 11–12 (22 + 3 = 25) or along path 3–12 (7 + 6 = 13). The T_E at event 12 is the longer time, or 25. The early event time at event 13 along this lower path is 25 + 5, or 30.

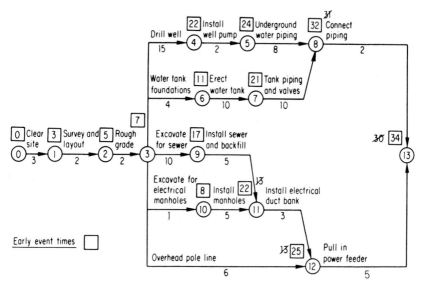

FIGURE 10.7 Early event times, site preparation.

Now observe the two upper paths. The path through events 3–4–5–8 totals 25 days. This, added to the T_E at event 3, gives an early time along this path to event 8 of 7 + 25, or 32. Along the path through events 3–6–7–8, the activities total 24 days. This 24 + 7 is 31 days, which is less than 32. Thus, the T_E at event 8 is 32. The early time to event 13 along this upper path is 34 days. Since this is longer than 30 days, the T_E for this network is 34.

The result is 34 days, but what is the significance of this figure? Based on our logical sequence and time estimates, the shortest time in which this work could be completed is 34 working days, or about 7 weeks.

LATE EVENT TIMES (T_L)

The late event time (T_L) for an event is defined as the latest time at which an event may be reached without delaying the computed project duration.

Keep in mind that "late" in this context is late in terms of this computed completion time rather than a desired or prescribed completion time. To determine late event times, work backward through the network. From Fig. 10.7 the final event 13 has two activities (8–13 and 12–13) leading into it (see Table 10.1).

By definition, the late event time at event 13 is 34 days, since the late event time for the terminal event equals the early event time for the event. If event 13 is to be reached by time 34, event 8 must start no later than 34 less the duration of activity 8–13 (34 − 2). Thus, the late event time for event 8 is 32. The late event time for event 12 is 34 − 5, or 29.

To show the late event times T_L on the diagram, put them in circles to differentiate them from the T_E values. Figure 10.8 shows the late event times for this network. In determining T_L values, there is a choice between values when two or more arrow tails converge.

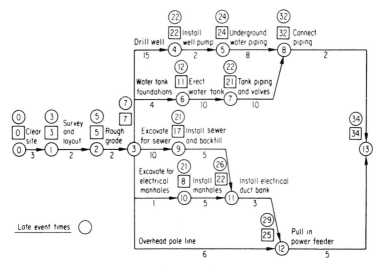

FIGURE 10.8   Late event times, site preparation.

The choices for T_L at event 3 (see Fig. 10.9) are, as shown in Figure 10.8, are given in Table 10.3.

ACTIVITY TIMES

The event times, early and late, are fundamental information. Nonetheless, the network events are not too descriptive. Certain key events, or milestones, are easily identified and are of interest. Among them would be complete foundations, start steel erection, start lath, complete plaster, start piping, etc. However, construction is work-oriented, and activity descriptions better define the CPM plan. Accordingly, activity time information is the more useful format.

The source of this information is the event time calculations. Look at the typical activities in Tables 10.1 and 10.2. Each activity must be bounded by two

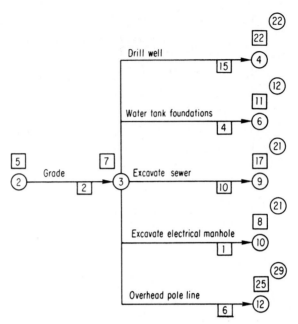

FIGURE 10.9 Network at event 3.

TABLE 10.3 Selection of Late Event Times

Activity	T_L, last event*	–	Duration	=	Possible T_L
3–4	22	–	15	=	7
3–6	12	–	4	=	8
3–9	21	–	10	=	11
3–10	21	–	1	=	20
3–12	29	–	6	=	23

*The T_L is the *smallest* of the values or 7.

events. What is the earliest time that an activity can start? It can start when the T_E for its start (or i) event has been reached. That is,

$$\text{Early start} = \text{ES} = T_E \text{ (event } i)$$

If the early start (ES) is known, what is the earliest time that this activity can be completed? The answer is the start time plus the job duration D:

$$\text{Early finish} = \text{EF} = \text{ES} + \text{duration} = \text{ES} + D$$

After determining the early times for an activity, what are the late times? The late finish is, of course, the T_L for the finishing (or j) event; that is,

$$\text{Late finish} = \text{LF} = T_L \text{ (event } j)$$

After late finish, the late start is obviously

$$\text{Late start} = \text{LS} = \text{LF-}D$$

Certain information about activities can be summarized before any calculations are made. For instance, from Fig. 10.7, the first nine activities offer the information in Table 10.4. After the event times are computed, the following additional information from Fig. 10.8 can be listed as shown in Table 10.5. Now, adding duration to the ES column and subtracting it from the LF gives the results shown Table 10.6.

TABLE 10.4 Basic Computer Input

Activity	Duration, days	Description
0–1	3	Clear site
1–2	2	Survey and layout
2–3	2	Rough grade
3–4	15	Drill well
3–6	4	Water tank foundations
3–9	10	Excavate sewer
3–10	1	Excavate electrical manholes
3–12	6	Pole line
4–5	2	Well pump

TABLE 10.5 Calculations Directly from Diagram

Activity	Duration, days	Description	ES	LF
0–1	3	Clear site	0	3
1–2	2	Survey and layout	3	5
2–3	2	Rough grade	5	7
3–4	15	Drill well	7	22
3–6	4	Water tank foundations	7	12
3–9	10	Excavate sewer	7	21
3–10	1	Excavate electrical manholes	7	21
3–12	6	Pole line	7	29
4–5	2	Well pump	22	24

TABLE 10.6 Event Times by Adding and Subtracting Duration

Activity	Duration, days	Description	ES	EF	LS	LF
0–1	3	Clear site	0	3	0	3
1–2	2	Survey and layout	3	5	3	5
2–3	2	Rough grade	5	7	5	7
3–4	15	Drill well	7	22	7	22
3–6	4	Water tank foundations	7	11	8	12
3–9	10	Excavate sewer	7	17	11	21
3–10	1	Excavate electrical manholes	7	8	20	21
3–12	6	Pole line	7	13	23	29
4–5	2	Well pump	22	24	22	24

The early CPM team referred to the critical path as the "main chain." This term was dropped in favor of "critical path," which was used by the early PERT group. The critical path determines the length of the project. This is the longest path into the last event, since it establishes the latest T_E for the last event. Accordingly, the longest chain or path of activities through the network is the critical path.

The critical path is not always obvious. You might guess at the critical path based on experience, but without a project time estimate for each activity, you cannot identify it (see Fig. 10.10).

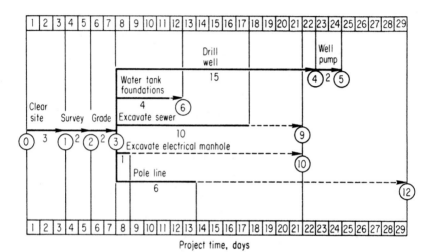

FIGURE 10.10   Activity times to time scale.

FLOAT

$$\text{Float} = F = (\text{LF} - \text{ES}) - D$$

Since EF = ES + D, then

$$\text{Float} = (\text{LF} - \text{ES}) - D = \text{LF} - (\text{ES} + D) = \text{LF} - \text{EF}$$

Also, since LF = LS + D and EF = ES + D, then

$$\text{Float} = \text{LF} - \text{EF} = (\text{LS} + D) - (\text{ES} + D) = \text{LS} - \text{ES}$$

Getting away from formulas, it is reasonable that the difference between the early and late starts should equal the scheduling flexibility, or float. Also, the differences between the late and early finishes furnish the same values.

Again in the network shown in Fig. 10.7, the total float for all activities, by using each of the previously mentioned formulas, is given in Table 10.7.

$$F = \text{LF} - \text{ES} - D$$

TABLE 10.7 Float Times

Activity	LF	–	ES	–	Duration	=	Float
0–1	3		0		3		0
1–2	5		3		2		0
2–3	7		5		2		0
3–4	22		7	15		0	
3–6	12		7		4		1

TIME-SCALE NETWORK

Figure 10.10, which demonstrates the critical activities, was the front end of a plot of the site work activities plotted according to a time scale. If all the activities are plotted according to the time scale, the result is a graphical calculation of the network (see Fig. 10.7 for a time-scale network of the John Doe project). The activities are plotted in solid lines to scale, with dotted connections to the event connection point. The dotted section is equal to the float in the chain of activities.

In plotting a network where a computer or manual calculation has not been made, all activities are plotted by early start. Float will appear as dotted lines following the last activity in a series. If the network has been calculated, either manually or by computer, the preferred plot is by late start. The early-start plot gives the CPM calculation, but experience confirms that activities do not start at the earliest point. Accordingly, an early-start plot will be patently incorrect at each update. And if the network is to be updated correctly, each review will require a time-consuming redraft.

SCHEDULE PREPARATION

How is the actual network preparation initiated? There is no one correct method. Sometimes the *conference approach,* where key persons involved in the project take part, is most effective. However, the conference approach is not suitable for all projects. There are situations where there are too many key people to make it manageable. There are others where there are too few for a full-blown conference. In both situations, an *executive approach* is required. The planning group is limited to two or three people. A typical group would be the general contractor's superintendent and the project manager plus the staff CPM engineer or CPM consultant. With such a small group, the diagram preparation can go more quickly; of course, there is a commensurate loss in communication among key people (see Fig. 10.11).

The diagram is prepared as the project is talked through. A blackboard can be used for drawing the rough diagram; however, with the smaller group a long sheet of reproducible paper with a blue-line disappearing grid can also be used. This saves the step of transferring the information from the blackboard to the paper. There is rarely an initial network which would not be much improved if it were redrawn. Also, the rough diagram can be drawn two to three times as quickly as a finished network. This minimizes the time demands on the group.

There is an inherent danger in committing the plan to paper, i.e., the tendency to make the project suit the network, rather than to have the network suit the

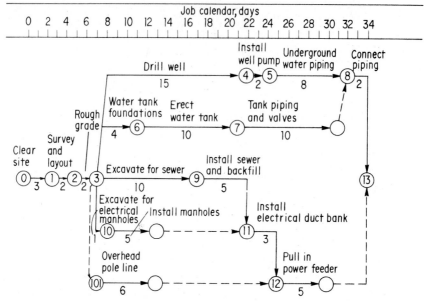

FIGURE 10.11 John Doe to time scale, plotted early times.

best planning. A network must be flexible; don't allow it to lock in your thinking. The network should be altered if better ideas are offered after the network has been prepared. This is, in fact, one of the prime advantages of CPM. Most people, understanding something clearly, assume that everyone else views it with the same clarity. The CPM plan is the communication medium which can demonstrate this clarity, or the lack of it, to the various planners of a project.

On a recent hospital project, the contractor's project superintendent (an up-through-the-ranks type), the project engineer, and the author prepared the first rough arrow diagram at the job site. It took us about 4 days to talk the project through. When we finished, the superintendent said, "Well, now I've built the job." He had been able to think the project through the completion in unaccustomed detail. The diagram had 1500 arrows, so that no activity described more than 1 percent of the project value and the average arrow covered about one-tenth of 1 percent.

A modified version of the executive approach is the *consultant approach*. It involves a CPM consultant or staff engineer talking the project through with the general contractor's superintendent and key people and then preparing the diagram. This method is the least demanding on the time of the people involved in the project. It can be effective but it must be applied with care. The primary problem is that project people do not accept the diagram as their plan as readily as a diagram which they helped to prepare.

A large diagram can be more than a little overwhelming (even to an experienced CPM planner). The project people must be properly oriented in CPM fundamentals if this approach is used. But it can be very effective when the project people have participated in at least one previous CPM-planned project and have developed confidence in CPM itself.

Large contractors and industrial firms who use CPM often set up staff planning groups. Some cautions are in order here: A group of this type has a tendency to be out of touch with the needs of the project group, particularly the field portion of that group. It is not unusual to find field people servicing the planning group rather than the planning group fulfilling its mission of servicing the project group.

The work of some subcontractors is independent of the work of the general contractor after the site has been prepared for them. This subcontracting category would include operations such as structural steel erection, cooling tower erection, and tank erection. All these are essentially package units. However, major subcontract operations such as electrical, mechanical, heating, and plumbing work are entirely dependent on the progress of the general contractor's work. It is not usually practical to prepare a separate network to show the subcontractors' work (except for the package units). Experiments in this regard have resulted in disjointed, disconnected failures unless the general work is also indicated on the diagram. But when the general work is so indicated, the subcontract network is no longer separate. Even if it were practical to draw the subcontractors' work on a separate network, the result would be self-defeating since the purpose of the CPM is to show a coordinated plan of the work that all the contractors are doing.

During the later stages of a project, the subcontracts often include much of the critical work. If the conference approach is used in planning the network, key subcontractor personnel can be included in the conference group. If the executive approach is used, the general contractor assumes a sequence of work and time estimates for the subcontractors' work. These assumptions are then reviewed with the applicable subcontractors and revised as necessary. It is quite important that subcontractors point out those areas where they need special consideration. For instance, a school kitchen equipment subcontractor might need complete control of the kitchen area to install the equipment. The kitchen work being done by other subcontractors (electrical, plumbing, plaster, painting, quarry tile, etc.) would have to be coordinated to recognize this requirement for space. The general contractor often does not allot sufficient time for the subcontractors' work because he or she is necessarily preoccupied with his or her own responsibilities. But through the use of a network, proper work sequences and time estimates can be made before the coordination problems ever get to the field. The diagram can be used to demonstrate to the general contractor that the subcontractor does not need workers on the job at certain times and could not use them effectively if they were there. Of course, this is a two-way street: The diagram may show the subcontractor that his or her work is critical during certain phases and must be staffed accordingly.

PRECEDENCE NETWORKS

An increasingly popular alternate form of CPM is the precedent diagram method (PDM). The form for precedence networks was originally termed "activity on node." The activity description is shown in a box or oval, with the sequence or flow still shown by interconnecting lines. In some cases, arrowheads are not used, although this leaves more opportunity for ambiguous network situations.

Figure 10.12 shows the John Doe network in precedence form. There are 17 precedence activities shown, the same number as the regular activity-oriented CPM network. However, simplicity of form is purported to be one of the advantages of precedence networks. In situations where activities have been subdi-

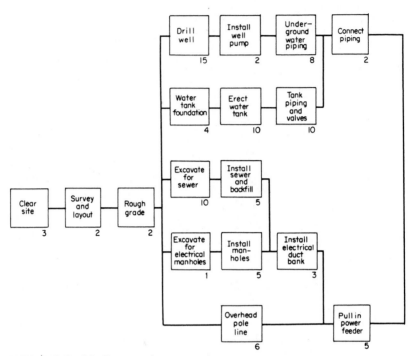

FIGURE 10.12   John Doe precedence network.

vided to show phased progress, the precedence network may result in fewer notations. In some cases, the reduction can be more than 50 percent, so the precedence network can have the advantage of a simple appearance. To those utilizing
precedence networks continually, their interpretation can be straightforward.
However, the ability to interpret them is not as easily acquired by someone used
to CPM.

One reason for the apparent simplicity of precedence networks is that a work
item can be connected from either its start or its finish. This allows a start-finish
logic presentation with no need to break down the work item.

The translation of the John Doe network into the precedence form shown in
Fig. 10.12 consists of only one type of connection: end to start. Figure 10.13 illustrates the three basic precedence relations: start to start, end to end, and end
to start. Although precedence networks are simpler in appearance than regular
CPM diagrams, greater thought must be given to reading and interpreting them.

Another characteristic of PDM is the use of lead and lag factors. In CPM, lead
activities can be introduced which logically delay the start of a particular activity
or group of activities (see Fig. 10.14). Assignment of a duration to the lead activity imposes a delaying factor in the CPM calculation. (This effect can be achieved
in many CPM computer programs by locking in an event date to occur "not earlier than.") Similarly, a lag activity can be imposed to direct the completion of an
activity to occur some time after either the start or completion of another activity
(see Fig. 10.15.)

The lead-lag factors assigned to work packages in PDM can replace the mul-

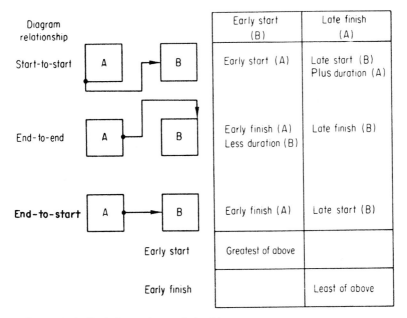

FIGURE 10.13 Typical precedence relationships.

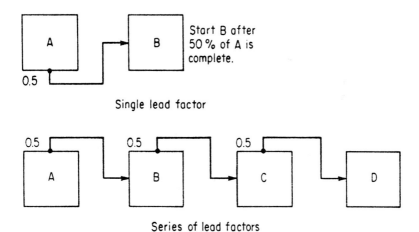

FIGURE 10.14 Precedence interrelationships: lead factors.

tiple activities required in CPM to reflect "start-complete" or "start-continue-complete," that is, they can replace the multiple activities required in CPM to create an interim event or events, at which point(s) other activities start or conclude.

The result can be a network diagram which is apparently simpler than a regular CPM network, since it takes fewer work package "boxes" to describe the

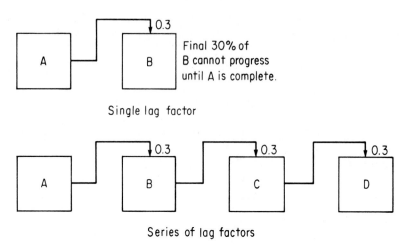

FIGURE 10.15   Precedence interrelationships: lag factors.

same set of circumstances. While the depiction appears simpler, however, it is necessary for the user of PDM diagrams to think harder to understand the logic depicted. Perhaps the greatest strength of the CPM network diagram is its ability, first, to record the logical sequence of a plan and, second, to communicate that logic. PDM, in its sophistication, takes a step backward on communications capability.

There is no doubt that PDM can be a powerful scheduling tool. Experienced schedulers using PDM on a regular basis have stated that they can fine-tune and change schedules more readily with computerized PDM. At the same time, the leads and lags make the hand calculation of PDM less practical, if not impractical. Further, time scaling of PDM is much more difficult than time scaling of CPM. And since time scaling is, in itself, a calculation, the difficulty in doing it confirms two things: First, manual calculation of PDM is impractical, and, second, PDM obfuscates the use of a network as a means of communicating information. This is a significant loss.

PDM has the paradoxical characteristics of apparent simplicity and built-in sophistication. The result can make the PDM scheduler into the project guru rather than a project team participator.

COMPUTER CALCULATIONS

Today, the major network calculation programs can handle either precedence or CPM. Ironically, the initial programs were a translation of PDM into a CPM format (internally in the computer program), calculation by CPM algorithm, and a retranslation back into the PDM format.

One problem with inputting the PDM diagram is the lack of event numbers. If all the activities were end-to-start, the work package numbers could be used similarly to i–j numbers. However, the complexity introduced by start-to-start, start-to-end, and end-to-end relationships requires a cumbersome cataloging of predecessor and successor work items.

In terms of whether the systems are arrow diagram or precedence, the results of Table 10.8 were obtained. The size and detail of the projects that are being planned, scheduled, and controlled with the aid of networks are given in Table 10.9.

TABLE 10.8 Arrow Diagrams vs. Precedence

	Number of programs	Percentage of total
Arrow diagram	35	87.5
Precedence	32	80.0
Both	26	65.0

TABLE 10.9 Activity Size vs. Programs Available

Activities per network	Number of programs	Percentage of total
0–10,000	12	30
10,001–20,000	2	5
20,001–30,000	3	7.5
30,001–40,000	8	20
40,001–50,000	0	0
Over 50,000	15	37.5
Total	40	100

Fifteen (37.5 percent) of the 40 best-known programs have the capability of handling over 50,000 activities per network. Several programs indicate that there is no upper bound on the size of the networks they can handle.

All 40 programs surveyed have some form of internal calendar that allows the user to select from a shop calendar, a fiscal calendar, or some combination of both. Their flexibilities range from a standard fiscal calendar to customized project calendars containing holidays, nonworking days, standard work weeks that range from 1 to 7 days, etc.

Of the 40 programs, 39 provide a graphical representation by activity or work versus time. Some depict, using various notations, critical activities, free float, total float, activities in progress, activities completed, etc.

One of the options that can be valuable to a user is a program's ability to specify the type and format of reports. These include management summary reports, time-related reports, cost-related reports, and resource-related reports. Of the 40 programs, 34 indicate various degrees of report generator flexibility.

Projects vary in their degree of required cost control, from a simple comparison of actual costs versus budgeted costs to more complex plots of cash flow, cumulative cash flow, budgeted cost of work scheduled (BCWS), actual cost of work performed (ACWP), budgeted cost of work performed (BCWP), monies committed, etc. Of the 40 programs, 39 claimed to be able to handle some form of cost control.

All programs allowed the development of a plan and cost resource program with the constraint of meeting predefined milestones and completion dates.

One of the options many project managers require is the ability to sort activities according to such user specifications, such as cost accounts, responsibility, active jobs, finish jobs, late jobs, amount of float, etc. Most of the programs surveyed provided at least a limited amount of this type of flexibility.

The technique of resource allocation, leveling, and balancing is an important option, especially in a multiproject environment. It is the most important technique available when attempting to prioritize the allocation of resources. In its simplest form it allows the user to see a histogram of resources required and to make changes accordingly. In its most useful format, resource allocation balances resources and simultaneously adjusts the schedule. In the survey, 34 programs indicated they had some capability of allocating resources.

Once the logic has been developed and the interrelationships of activities evaluated, it may be beneficial to have the network plotted. Because of the development in plotting techniques and graphics, there has been an increase in availability of this type of option.

UPDATING

The period review of the CPM plan to both demonstrate and review the logic is termed "updating." The object in updating the network (either with a computer or manually) is to introduce the project status as well as any logical revisions into a new computation of the completion date. To do this, all completed activities are given a duration of zero. Activities in progress are assigned the duration required to complete them. Activities are removed, added, or assigned new event numbers to recognize any logical revisions. The first few updatings may have extensive revisions as plans are influenced by job conditions. However, after the project gets into full swing, there will be perhaps only five or ten revisions per update. The exact extent of logic revisions to be expected is, of course, unpredictable.

When the updating information has been entered in the network, a new computation is made from the present date (calendar or project day). This new run must be checked, just as the first ones were; an update is not immune to error. After the run has been established as valid, the results are analyzed. The critical path may shift, and often does. Float activities may become near critical and must be monitored regularly.

Typical updating frequency is monthly. The updated package should include

- Revised network sheets
- Mathematical analysis (printout)
- i–j "directional" sort
- Total float (at least for critical and low float paths)
- Narrative discussion

Although completed work is "zeroed out," it is good practice to use a computer program that accepts actual start and completion dates for activities so that as-built information is collected on a current basis.

OTHER SCHEDULING USES

Other chapters demonstrate the use of scheduling in Purchasing (Chap. 9) and Claims and Litigation (Chap. 25).

CHAPTER 11
INSURANCE AND BONDS

Second Edition

Walter T. Derk, V.P.
Fred S. James & Co.
Chicago, Illinois

First Edition

Stephen Beinfest, CPA
O'Brien-Kreitzberg & Associates, Inc.
San Francisco, California

INTRODUCTION

The prime function of insurance is to protect against loss, and it must first be thought of in that light rather than as a fixed overhead cost, which it is not.

Convincing contractors that the subject of insurance is worthy of the most serious consideration has never been much of a chore. Just dividing the total number of dollars expended for all forms of coverage by the square feet of work will get the proper attention; indeed, it is a most effective method of making job superintendents and foremen aware of the need to minimize accidents.

Any insurance company is going to need more than a dollar of premium for every dollar of routine loss it pays in the contractor's behalf. The concern of a contractor must always be protection against catastrophe.

The contract specifications will usually require specific coverages and limits, but since each one is different (and some woefully deficient), the contractor really has no course but to preselect an insurance program. One purpose of this chapter is to help make this complicated subject more understandable, and to assist in making a selection of what should be insured by an insurance company rather than the assets of the business.

CONTRACT AND OTHER BONDS

A necessary part of administration of a contractor's insurance program is the performance of services with regard to contract-bond requirements. Close working knowledge of work in progress and projects being bid or completed helps to enhance the close relationship which ideally exists between the contractor and the insurance/bond counselor. Obviously this is a relationship that depends on confidence; in many respects it parallels a good banking connection.

As a minimum, your broker will need

1. The latest fiscal financial statement, preferably prepared by a certified public accountant in accordance with generally accepted accounting principles (GAAP) for contractors. In lieu of this, any unaudited statement should be accompanied by a complete schedule of accounts receivable and accounts payable. There should be an explanation of any material liabilities appearing on the statement, such as long-term debts.
2. The work experience and history of the construction firm and the individuals who operate it.
3. The name of the commercial bank and the individual to contact for reference and confirmation of any outstanding lines of credit.
4. A schedule of work previously performed by the firm, and a schedule of uncompleted contracts on hand and estimated dollar cost to complete.
5. A list of material suppliers where the contractor has established credit or normally buys material.

With this information, and answers to specific questions, a broker can make an intelligent appraisal of the contractor's liabilities and either secure a reasonable line of surety credit or predetermine the amount of liability a surety company would assume. An experienced bond broker will lend a sympathetic ear to the contractor's specific problems and help translate them into language a surety company can understand.

All too often the submission of insufficient information leads the surety company to decline a bond simply because someone went to the bonding company ill-prepared, making it all the harder for the next effort to be successful.

Briefly, this is what the commonly required bond forms do:

Bid bonds: Given by the contractor to the owner, guaranteeing that if awarded, the contract will be accepted and final performance or payment bonds will be furnished as required.

Completion bonds: Given by the contractor to the owner and/or lending institution, guaranteeing that the work will be completed and that funds will be provided for that purpose.

Labor- and material-payment bonds: Given by the contractor to the owner, guaranteeing that all labor and material bills arising out of the contract will be paid.

License or permit bonds: Given by the contractor/licensee to a public body, guaranteeing compliance with statutes or ordinances, sometimes holding the public body harmless.

Maintenance bonds: Given by the contractor to the owner, guaranteeing to rectify defects in workmanship or materials for a specified time following completion. A one-year maintenance bond is normally included in the performance bond without additional charge.

Performance bonds: Given by the contractor to the owner, guaranteeing the contract will be completed as specified.

Self-insurers' worker's compensation bonds: Given by a self-insured employer to the state, guaranteeing payment of statutory benefits to injured employees.

Subdivision bonds: Given by the developer to a public body, guaranteeing construction of all necessary improvements and utilities; similar to a completion bond.

Subcontractor bonds: Given by a subcontractor to the contractor, guaranteeing performance of the subcontract and payment of all labor and material bills.

Supply bonds: Given by the manufacturer or supply distributor to the owner, guaranteeing that the materials contracted for will be delivered as specified in the contract.

Union-wage bonds: Given by the contractor to a union, guaranteeing that the contractor will pay union-scale wages to employees and remit to the union any welfare funds withheld.

WORKER'S COMPENSATION AND EMPLOYERS' LIABILITY

As a contract, the standard worker's compensation and employers' liability policy does little more than agree to provide benefits to injured employees in accordance with the provisions of the applicable worker's compensation law. The variations and technicalities arise from differences in the worker's compensation statutes of the various states, not from the policy itself.

The policy provides coverage A, worker's compensation, which agrees to "pay promptly when due all compensation and other benefits required of the insured by the Worker's Compensation Law"; and coverage B, employers' liability, which gives common-law defense of the employer for employee injuries, subject to a basic limit of liability of $100,000, "for all damages because of bodily injury by accident, including death at any time resulting therefrom, sustained by one or more employees in any one accident."

Policy Extensions

Increased Limits—Employers' Liability. It is permissible to increase the basic limit of coverage B from $100,000 per accident to $500,000 for approximately 1 percent additional premium, subject to a $50 minimum charge per year; an increase to $1,000,000 averages 2 percent additional premium subject to a $75 minimum charge per year. The increase is recommended, unless higher limits are provided via a separate umbrella excess-liability policy.

Additional Medical Benefits. Some states limit by statute the amount of medical benefits payable to an injured employee, in terms of either dollars or period of time. In most cases, all reasonable medical expenses are payable without specific limitation.

Several of those states which do limit medical benefits permit a voluntary extension, either $10,000 or $100,000 per employee beyond legal requirements, for payment of additional premium. Where desired, it is best first to determine whether the states in which the contractor operates include such limitation and then establish the additional cost for voluntary extension by endorsement.

Where the amount of additional premium so developed is small, a modest minimum charge may be applicable per state. This additional charge is recommended.

All-States Endorsement. Your insurance carrier can endorse the policy without charge to provide coverage A automatically in any state except those monopolistic-fund states which do not permit private insurance. These are Nevada, North Dakota, Ohio, Washington, West Virginia, and Wyoming.

Coverage B is applicable in the United States of America, its territories and possessions, or Canada, to injury sustained "by any employee of the insured arising out of and in the course of his employment by the insured, either in operations in a state designated in the policy declarations or in operations necessary or incidental thereto." The endorsement is recommended.

Longshoremen's and Harbor Workers' Act Coverage; Maritime and Federal Employers' Liability Act. If any work involving maritime or railroad exposures is contemplated, it is important to endorse the policy to provide coverage under these acts, which may prove applicable in lieu of a state's worker's compensation act.

COMPREHENSIVE GENERAL LIABILITY

General-liability exposures and available insurance remedies are probably the least understood and most likely to produce a loss of consequence to a contractor.

Comments will refer to the standard comprehensive general-liability policy form, commonly called ISO forms, used by member companies of the Insurance Rating Board.

The important insuring agreement simply commits the insurance company to pay all sums (including defense costs) which the insured becomes legally obligated to pay as damages because of bodily injury or property damage "to which this insurance applies, caused by an occurrence . . ." and is followed by a statement about what will be defended. Five distinct divisions of coverage are involved.

Division I: Operations-Premises

Covers legal liability for bodily injury or property damage caused by an occurrence (as defined) and arising from (1) buildings or premises owned or leased by the insured and (2) business operations in progress anywhere in the United States, its territories or possessions, or Canada (including international waters or airspace as defined earlier).

Rating basis, usually per $100 of payroll.

Example 1—Premises Liability. A boy, attracted to a piece of equipment in the contractor's supply yard, fell and was injured. The insured's premises coverage provided for defense and settlement of the ensuing claim.

Example 2—Premises Liability. In getting rid of some boxes along with other building materials, the contractor set them afire in the building's incinerator over a period of three weeks. Something in the materials being burned caused gradual damage to the paint on the house next door. It was repaired by virtue of the contractor's premises coverage.

Example 3—Operations Liability. A painter working on a scaffold at a job site, dropped a bucket of paint on the head of someone playing below. The employing contractor's operations coverage similarly defended and paid the claim.

Example 4—Operations Liability. A roof-deck contractor's employee allowed a light spray of gypsum-like material to drift onto several cars over a period of days. The damage was paid for by the contractor's operations coverage.

Division II: Elevator Liability

Automatically covers the insured's legal liability for bodily injury caused by an occurrence and arising from ownership, maintenance, and use of elevators owned, controlled, or operated by the insured. Property damage is not compensable unless separate elevator collision coverage is purchased. Note: Elevator liability is an implied, rather than an expressed, coverage under the bodily injury provisions of the insurance contract. The definition of elevator does not include a hod or material hoist used in construction operations; these are covered under Division I.

Rating basis, usually number and kind of elevators.

Example. A defective elevator on premises owned and occupied by a contractor for office and warehouse purposes fell several stories, causing serious injury to two occupants, one a visitor and the other an employee. Elevator liability coverage took care of the former, worker's compensation insurance the latter.

Division III: Contractor's Protective Liability; Owner's Protective Liability

Covers the named insured's legal liability for bodily injury and property damage caused by an occurrence and arising out of operations performed for him by an independent contractor, including that arising from the insured's general supervision of such work.

When a comprehensive general-liability policy is issued to a contractor, automatic insurance is provided for the contingent (or secondary) liability which may result from sublet operations. Issued to the property owner, the same contingent coverage is called owner's protective liability, providing protection from injury or damage claims caused by a general contractor or any of his subcontractors. This latter form is discussed in connection with hold-harmless agreements.

This division is becoming more and more important. It is commonplace to sue the owner, general contractor, architect, or engineer when an employee of a subcontractor is injured.

It is also common practice to jot down names off the sign out front and sue everybody in sight; so owners and contractors may expect to be drawn into litigation for accidents allegedly caused by someone else. Even assuming that the negligent party has adequate insurance to cover the ultimate loss, defense fees for the others could be costly indeed. Thus defense is often the most advantageous and practical feature of the coverage granted under this division.

Where the work to be performed is inherently dangerous or the damage proves to be a necessary consequence of following contract specifications, more than mere defense may be involved. In such cases, judgments may be awarded against the owner or general contractor even though the work has been sublet to someone else. This coverage becomes applicable, too, where the subcontractor's primary insurance limits may be inadequate or his coverage entirely void.

Rating basis, usually per $100 of sublet contract cost.

Example 1.   The owner of a new building under construction required that the general contractor furnish him with an owner's protective policy, while the general contractor had a comprehensive-liability policy which automatically covered him for sublet operations. An employee of the subcontractor, a roofer, dropped a tool onto someone below, causing injury.

A suit was filed naming all three in complaint. Defense of the owner was provided by the owners' protective policy, and the general contractor's comprehensive-liability policy, in turn, assured him of legal representation, while the subcontractor's basic operations-premises insurance took care of his defense and ultimately paid the loss.

Example 2.   An acoustical-tile contractor sublet a rush portion of his job to a lather, whose certificate of insurance was delayed for several days. When it did arrive, after an accident had occurred because of the lather's negligence, it revealed bodily-injury limits of $50,000 each person and $100,000 each occurrence. Both contractors were named in a suit resulting in an eventual judgment of $83,500 to one person. The tile contractor's protective liability coverage provided for his defense and payment of the $33,500 in excess of the subcontractor's policy limit.

Division IV: Completed Operations and Products Liability

Optional under the comprehensive general-liability policy form, this division covers the insured's legal liability for bodily injury or property damage arising out of: (1) completed or abandoned operations, if caused by an occurrence (as defined) away from premises owned by or rented to the insured, and (2) the insured's products, if caused by an occurrence away from the insured's premises and after physical possession of the product has been relinquished to others.

The standard policy form, however, calls operations completed: (1) when all operations to be performed by or on behalf of the insured contractor under the contract have been completed, or (2) when all operations to be performed by or on behalf of the insured contractor at the job site have been completed, or (3) when the portion of the work out of which the bodily injury or property damage arises has been put to its intended use.

In general terms, then, completion of work rather than acceptance is usually the determining factor. It is important to note, too, that operations which may involve later service or maintenance work are completed insofar as coverage is concerned. This also applies to further repair or replacement work because of a defect or deficiency; if the work is otherwise completed, the policy calls the operation completed.

Fortunately, if both coverages, operations-premises (Division I) and completed operations-products (Division IV), are written by the same insurance company at identical limits of liability, the question of which policy applies becomes academic. One or the other will cover insured losses without gap or overlap.

Although listed as an optional coverage under the comprehensive general-liability policy form, the protection provided by Division IV is no luxury. Anyone operating a business without completed-operations coverage has every right to feel apprehensive about it; this is particularly true of contractors. The relatively high liability premium developed in certain contracting trades has tended to delay unanimous acceptance, but those premium rates are a sure measure of exposure to loss. In short, the coverage is urgently recommended.

A contractor buying this insurance for the first time today can be protected, in the absence of an exclusion to the contrary, for injury or damage occurring anytime thereafter during the policy period, regardless of the completion date or when the defect or faulty workmanship took place. The date of the occurrence causing injury or damage is the important factor; it must fall within the policy period, and coverage ceases at expiration unless renewed (when policy is written on a "claims-made" basis). Occurrence form coverage remains in force and effective and subject to being triggered by claims lodged subsequent to the policy effective dates, but arising out of workmanship performed during the policy period. The completion date may have some bearing on the extent of a contractor's legal liability of injury or damage, but not on the question of coverage.

Several important limitations specifically applicable to this section are referred to in the list of policy exclusions and limitations.

Rating basis, usually per $1,000 of gross receipts.

Example 1. A manufacturer of building materials sold and delivered a proprietary product to a contractor, learning some 6 months later that those materials proved to be defective after installation by the contractor. Not only did they have to be replaced, but they permitted damage to property stored in the finished structure. The manufacturer's product-liability insurance, while excluding replacement of the proprietary material (see exclusions), paid for damage to the stored property.

Example 2. As some children sat in a new movie theater, they were struck on the head by falling ceiling tiles, work completed by a tile contractor 30 days previously. The insurance carrier settled the claims under a completed-operations rider added just 10 days before the accident.

Example 3. A plumbing contractor was charged with the expense of replacing defective piping, replastering of ceiling and walls, as well as interior furnishings on several floors of a high-rise apartment building, the damage being gradually noticed rather than happening all at one time. Completed-operations insurance paid for replastering and interior damage. The cost of piping replacement was not insured (see Exclusions).

Division V: Contractual Liability

Covers the named insured's liability for bodily injury or property damage assumed under written contract with another party. It is important to understand the distinction here; this is someone else's legal liability which the insured contractually agrees to assume.

There is very little contractual coverage automatically provided by standard comprehensive general-liability policies. They define a covered incidental contract as a written "lease of premises, easement agreement, indemnification of a municipality required by ordinance, sidetrack agreement, or elevator maintenance agreement."

Nothing is said about other hold-harmless agreements arising out of construction contracts, and even some of those listed above have strings on them. It is still necessary, therefore, to endorse specific agreements onto the policy or buy blanket contractual-liability coverage before coverage applies.

Rating basis, usually per $100 of contract cost.

Purchase Order Agreements. The fine print on the bottom or reverse of routine purchase orders often includes something to the effect of the following:

> Seller agrees that seller shall be responsible for any injuries to persons (including death) and damages to property, including buyer's employees and buyer's property,

that occur in the performance of this purchase order, and that seller shall save harm-less and indemnify buyer from and against any liability or costs arising from such injuries and/or damages.

In the absence of specific or blanket contractual-liability insurance via endorse-ment, no coverage is provided by the standard policy.

Since there is nothing uniform about indemnifying or hold-harmless clauses, they are difficult to classify. To decide how much premium is required, insurance companies generally try to group them into one of the following categories.

Limited-Form Indemnification—Contractor's Negligence. A limited form holds someone harmless against claims due to the contractor's operations, negligence, or that of any subcontractors. For example:

> The Contractor agrees to indemnify and save harmless the Owner, Architect and En-gineer, their agents and employees, from and against all loss or expense (including costs and attorneys' fees) by reason of liability imposed by law upon the Owner, Architect or Engineer for damages because of bodily injury, including death at any time resulting therefrom, sustained by any person or persons or on account of dam-age to property, including loss of use thereof, arising out of or in consequence of the performance of this work, provided such injury to persons or damage to property is due or claimed to be due to negligence of the Contractor, or his Subcontractors, em-ployees or agents.

This is not giving them much; you were already responsible for your own negli-gent acts or omissions, as well as those of your subcontractors. Essentially, a limited-form contract agrees to defend others if they are sued or incur expense because of something you did or should have done. If both you and your subcon-tractors are adequately insured, this means payment of legal fees.

Intermediate-Form Indemnification—Joint Negligence. An intermediate form adds agreement to defend and pay where both parties to the contract may be contributorily negligent and therefore legally liable for a loss. For example:

> The Contractor agrees to indemnify and save harmless the Owner, Architect and En-gineer, their agents or employees, from and against all loss or expense (including costs and attorneys' fees) by reason of liability imposed by law upon the Owner, Architect or Engineer for damages because of bodily injury, including death at any time resulting therefrom sustained by any person or persons or on consequence of the performance of this work, whether such injuries to person or damage to property is due or claimed to be due to the negligence of the Contractor, his Subcontractors, the Owner, Architect, or Engineer, their agents or employees, except only such in-jury or damage as shall have been occasioned by the sole negligence of the Owner, Architect or Engineer.

Here, instead of splitting the bill for jointly caused injury or damage, the contrac-tor agrees to waive the defense of contributory negligence and pay as if the only responsible party.

Broad-Form Indemnification—Sole Negligence of Indemnitee. A broad form in-demnifies the other party even where he is solely responsible for a loss. For example:

> The Contractor agrees to indemnify and save harmless the Owner, Architect and Engineer, their agents and employees, from and against all loss or expense (including costs and attorneys' fees) by reason of liability imposed by law upon the Owner, Architect or Engineer for damages because of bodily injury, including death at any time resulting therefrom, sustained by any person or persons or on account of damage to property, including loss of use thereof, whether caused by or contributed to by said Owner, Architect or Engineer, their agents, employees or others.

Broad-form contracts are not rare. They crop up every day, agreeing in any number of ways to defend everybody against everything, with the shortest, most innocent-looking clause often being the most dangerous.

Certain clauses which make no reference to negligence at all have been interpreted in the same manner as one which spells out its intent to include sole negligence of the indemnitee, and most companies base their premiums accordingly.

Insertion of the phrase "except that caused by sole negligence of the indemnitee" at the proper place in a contract before accepting it for signature may cut the contractor's specific contractual premium—and exposure to loss—approximately in half. However, it is most important to keep in mind, even where coverage does exist either on a blanket basis or by specific endorsement, that it is still another's liability which is assumed. If there is a loss, it will be charged against the contractor's claim-experience record, and it is not at all unusual to be charged for the same loss twice.

Example. A contractor, working under specifications which included a broad hold-harmless agreement, learned that an employee was accidently killed on the job solely because of the owner's negligence. The deceased's dependents first collected worker's compensation benefits from the employer, then filed suit against the owner, whose liability-insurance company defended the suit and settled with the estate. That company then secured a judgment for the full amount against the contractor because of his agreement to hold the owner harmless.

Many states do not ordinarily permit an injured employee (or the estate) to sue the employer at common law if the injury arose out of and in the course of employment. Yet, by signing a hold-harmless agreement, a contractor may be in the position of (1) paying full worker's compensation benefits, (2) paying a common-law judgment to the same employee, and (3) losing the right of subrogation, that is, the right to be reimbursed by the responsible party for compensation benefits paid (although the amount of worker's compensation benefits paid may be credited back as part of the liability settlement).

Limits of Liability

The comprehensive general-liability policy provides for one bodily injury limit per person, another per occurrence, and a third limit as an aggregate for all completed operations-products bodily-injury claims arising during the policy period, per year if the policy is written for three years.

Thus, 100/300/300,000 contemplates a bodily-injury limit of $100,000 per person injured, $300,000 per occurrence regardless of number of persons involved, and a total limit of $300,000 for all completed operations-products bodily-injury claims during a single policy year.

Property-damage liability lists one limit per occurrence, and another as an aggregate limit individually applicable to each of the five separate hazards contemplated by the comprehensive policy form, except elevator liability, which has no aggregate limit.

Thus, 50/100,000 means a property damage limit of:

- $50,000 each occurrence
- $100,000 aggregate independent contractors protective
- $100,000 aggregate completed operations
- $100,000 aggregate contractual

Unlike bodily injury, however, the property-damage limits for operations, protective, and contractual apply separately to each project with respect to operations being performed away from premises owned by or rented to the named insured. The completed operations-products aggregate limit continues to apply to all claims within a single policy year.

Coverage Extensions

Blanket Contractual Liability.   This coverage extension heads the list in importance to anyone in the construction industry.

Blanket contractual-liability insurance to cover automatically all written agreements is available from most insurance companies, although some still call for submission of contracts for examination of the degree of liability assumed by the insured and the premium developed to cover it. Occasionally, an agreement is so dangerous that immediate reinsurance is required.

Beware of so-called blanket contractual-liability endorsements, which provide automatic coverage but exclude broad-form agreements. This practice employed by some insurance companies may lull the insured into relying on "automatic" coverage, only to leave the contractor uninsured when the protection is needed most (i.e., when it is agreed to assume sole negligence of the indemnitee). Who decides whether a contract is limited, intermediate, or broad is anybody's guess.

The trick now is to negotiate the lowest possible premium rates per $100 of contract cost based upon the number of agreements the contractor signs and what is in them. Because there is no uniformity in these indemnifying clauses, as well as a wide divergence of opinion about their seriousness, depending on which side of the fence you are on, this is a job for the insurance representative, whether the coverage is blanket or specific. Left to their own devices, some underwriters are prone to interpret them from a pessimistic point of view, often coming up with a premium which reflects that pessimism unless rates are negotiated in the contractor's behalf.

It is important to point out that even blanket contractual-liability coverage is subject to certain exclusions:

1. Professional liability for plans, specifications, design, etc., if the insured or the indemnitee is an architect, engineer, or surveyor
2. Supervisory, inspection, or engineering services if the insured or the indemnitee is an architect, engineer, or surveyor
3. Liquor liability
4. Liability to a third-party beneficiary under a contract with a public authority
5. Damage to property in the insured's care, custody, or control
6. Damage to the insured's premises following transfer of ownership to someone else
7. Injury or damage caused by failure of the product or work to perform as intended (in the absence of an active malfunction) as a result of design, specification, or similar error
8. Damage to the insured's product itself

9. Damage to the insured's work or materials or equipment

10. Expense of recall or replacement of insured's work or product

11. Explosion, collapse, and/or underground damage (x, c, u) as respects specific classifications of work

These exclusions closely parallel exclusions appearing in the standard comprehensive general-liability coverage part, the point being that one cannot pick up excluded hazards merely by signing a contract to be responsible for them. It requires more than a contractual agreement to achieve x,c,u, completed operations, products, fire legal liability, or similar coverage. The contractual-liability endorsement will not cover automatically, regardless of what the agreement itself might say.

Broad-form Property Damage. This endorsement is designed to help answer at least one major question concerning the care, custody, or control exclusion: Just how much of the property being worked on is subject to the exclusion? Its reception has been good.

Intended primarily for contractors, the rider somewhat modifies this troublesome exclusion. It still excludes coverage in many of the situations excluded by the basic policy, but it uses different and more specific language to do so, thereby covering without question some damage situations. For example, while continuing to exclude liability for damage to property being worked on, the endorsement deletes coverage only for that particular part, provided the accident occurs away from the insured's premises. Too, if a general contractor damages the property of a subcontractor at the site of operations, no work being performed on it at the time, there may be no coverage under the basic policy, but there is under the broad-form property-damage endorsement. The rider specifically excludes

1. Damage to property owned by the insured

2. Damage to property occupied by the insured

3. Damage to property rented by the insured

4. Damage to property given to the insured for storage or safekeeping

5. Damage to property to be worked on at the insured's premises

6. Damage to tools or equipment while being used in performing the work

7. Damage to property in the insured's custody for installation, erection, or use in construction by the insured

8. Damage to property transported by the insured via motor vehicle or team

9. Damage to property during the loading or unloading of such vehicle

10. Damage to that particular part of any property away from the insured's premises being worked on at the time of loss

11. Damage to that particular part of any property away from the insured's premises out of which the injury or destruction arises

12. Repair or replacement of damage to that particular part of any property away from the insured's premises made necessary because of faulty workmanship

13. Damage to products manufactured, sold, or handled by the insured or work completed by or for the insured, out of which the accident arises

This extension without doubt covers more claims without the necessity of going to court for a decision. Additional premiums required are subject to negotiation. The coverage is recommended if the price is right, so long as the contractor understands that it does not completely eliminate the care, custody, or control exclusion itself.

Personal Injury.   The first insuring agreement in the policy refers to bodily injury, which implies tangible physical injury. An extension is available to include personal-injury liability, that is, intangible harm. Usually written in three divisions, these include

I   False arrest
    Malicious prosecution
    Willful detention or imprisonment
II Libel
    Slander
    Defamation of character
III Wrongful eviction
    Invasion of privacy
    Wrongful entry

The endorsement commonly excludes claims brought by employees, advertising activities, and such liability assumed under contract. The additional premium required is variable, being much more expensive to a hotel or store owner than to someone having no apparent exposure. It is recommended where exposure to such claims may exist and, again, if the price is right.

Fire Legal Liability.   This endorsement bypasses the exclusion of property in the care, custody, or control of the insured only as respects buildings or portions thereof rented to or occupied by the insured and designated in the endorsement, covering the insured's legal liability for such property if accidentally damaged by fire. The practical purpose here is to insure the tenant against subrogation claims brought by the owner or the fire insurance carrier for fire damage caused by the tenant's negligence.

The same thing can be accomplished under fire forms by eliminating the subrogation clause as respects the tenant or by issuing a fire policy in his name. The usual charge for this endorsement is 25 percent of the building fire rate per $100 of insurance purchased.

Vendor's Liability.   The manufacturer of a material or product may purchase products-liability insurance to protect against bodily-injury or property-damage claims resulting from its use after sale. The policy may also be endorsed to protect those who sell the manufactured product, either individually or on a blanket basis, from contingent liability claims arising from such sale. Although final responsibility may accrue to the maker, this optional vendor's endorsement assures the seller of legal representation and defense. The usual premium charge is 15 to 25 percent of the products-liability premium otherwise developed, less than would be charged under a separate policy issued to the vendor.

Policy Exclusions and Limitations

The comprehensive general-liability policy form, while providing broad coverage, is still subject to basic exclusions and limitations. The fine print is there to eliminate (1) hazards better insured elsewhere, (2) employee injuries covered by worker's compensation statutes, (3) certain special risks that would be prohibitively expensive to include on a blanket basis, and (4) hazards considered completely uninsurable. They include, but are not limited to:

1. Contractual liability, except for incidental contracts
2. Automobiles
3. Aircraft
4. Watercraft
5. War, civil war, insurrection, rebellion, or revolution
6. Liquor liability arising from its sale, manufacture, distribution, or the use of premises for such purposes
7. Employee injuries
8. Damage to property owned by the insured
9. Damage to property occupied by the insured
10. Damage to property rented to the insured
11. Damage to property used by the insured
12. Damage to property in the care, custody, or (not and) control of the insured
13. Damage to property over which the insured has physical control
14. Damage to the insured's premises following transfer of ownership to someone else
15. Injury or damage caused by failure of the product or work to perform as intended (in the absence of an active malfunction) as a result of design, specification, or similar error
16. Damage to the insured's product itself
17. Damage to the insured's work or materials or equipment
18. Expense of recall and replacement of insured's work or materials or equipment
19. Nuclear-facility hazards
20. Water damage (now a nonstandard exclusion applicable only in certain areas of the country; listed here as a precaution)
21. Explosion, collapse, and/or underground damage as respects specific classifications of work

Explosion, Collapse, or Underground Damage. The basic general-liability policy excludes property damage arising out of explosion, collapse, or underground damage, but the exclusions (any one, two, or all three of them) apply only to specific classifications of contracting (and other) work identified in the policy by the letters *x*, *c*, and/or *u* after the usual four-digit classification code number. Unfortunately, some policies are none too clear in this respect, so it will pay a contractor to become familiar with these exclusions and then carefully examine company policies to determine if any apply to company operations.

Exclusion x. Excludes property damage arising out of blasting or explosion other than the explosion of air or steam vessels, piping under pressure, prime movers, machinery, or power-transmitting equipment.

Exclusion c. Excludes property damage arising out of collapse of or structural injury to any building or structure due to grading of land, excavating, borrowing, filling, backfilling, tunneling, pile driving, cofferdam or caisson work, or the moving shoring, underpinning, raising, or demolition of any building or structure, or removal or rebuilding of structural supports.

Exclusion u. Excludes property damage to wires, conduits, pipes, mains, sewers, tanks, tunnels, any similar property, and any apparatus in connection therewith beneath the surface of the ground or water, caused by and occurring during the use of mechanical equipment for the purpose of grading land, paving, excavating, drilling, burrowing, filling, backfilling, or pile driving.

In most states, the classes of contracting work listed in Fig. 11.1 are commonly subject to exclusions as indicated.

This is not a complete list; there are more affecting other industries, including

Classification of work	Applicable exclusions
Building raising or moving	x, c
Caisson work	x, c, u
Clay or shale digging	x
Cofferdam work	x, c, u
Conduit construction	x, c, u
Contractors' equipment rented to others with operators	x, c, u
Dam construction	x, c, u
Electric-light or power-line construction	x, c, u
Excavation	x, c, u
Gas mains or connections construction	x, c, u
Gas pipeline construction	x, c, u
Geophysical exploration---seismic	x
Grading of land	x, c, u
Iron or steel erection---subway construction	x, c, u
Irrigation or drainage-system construction	x, u
Landscape gardening	x, c, u
Oil or gas pipeline construction	x, c, u
Pile driving	x, c, u
Pulmbing	u
Quarries	x, c, u
Railroad construction	x, c, u
Salvage operations	x, c, u
Sand or gravel digging	x
Septic-tank systems installation	x, c, u
Sewer construction	x, c, u
Shaft sinking	x, c, u
Steam mains or connections construction	x, c, u
Stone crushing	x, c, u
Street or road paving or repaving	x, c, u
Subway construction	x, c, u
Telephone, telegraph, or fire-alarm line construction	x, c
Tunneling	x, c, u
Underpinning buildings or structures	x
Water mains or connections construction	x, c, u
Welding or cutting	x
Wrecking operations	x, c

FIGURE 11.1 Classification of work.

manufacturers, oil- and gas-well operators, etc. These exclusions do not ordinarily apply to owners' or contractors' protective liability (work sublet to others) or to completed operations.

COMPREHENSIVE AUTOMOBILE LIABILITY

This discussion will similarly refer to the Insurance Rating Board's standard comprehensive automobile liability policy form, which parallels the general-liability policy. The automobile form provides three distinct coverages, discussed next.

Division I: Owned Automobiles: Automobiles under Long-Term Lease

Covers legal liability for bodily injury or property damage caused by an occurrence (as defined) and arising from the ownership, maintenance, or use of owned automobiles anywhere in the United States, its territories or possessions, or Canada. This same section permits coverage for vehicles operated by the named insured under long-term lease, where the lessee provides primary insurance and the lessor is named as additional insured; there is no added charge for the latter.

Rating basis, usually per vehicle insured.

Example. A truck owned by the named insured damages a parked car in making a delivery. Though the truck was acquired after the policy was written and is not included in the schedule of owned vehicles, coverage is automatic, usually for a period between 30 to 60 days following the insured's acquisition of the vehicle, under the comprehensive policy form. However, the insured should contact the carrier and schedule the vehicle prior to this time elapsing. Only if the policy is written on a "composite basis" would the resultant property damage claim be fully covered and additional premium be picked up at final audit.

Division II: Hired Automobiles

Covers the named insured—and in this case not the lessor—for bodily injury or property damage caused by an occurrence and arising from use of a hired vehicle. Vehicles operated by the named insured under long-term lease may be insured just as if they were owned in consideration of a specified car premium charge. Optionally, the insured may instead pay a premium charge per $100 cost of hire, subject to adjustment at final audit. The latter method does not permit naming the owner as additional insured. Short-term lease agreements automatically come under this division.

Example. The insured hired a truck to deliver building materials during a peak rush, and driven by an employee, it damaged a parked car. The claim was settled under hired-automobile liability, the insurance carrier making a premium charge based on the cost of hire at the time of final audit, again assuming that coverage is written on a composite basis.

The premium rates per $100 cost of hire may be markedly reduced upon presentation of a certificate of insurance from the lessor as evidence of primary insurance applying also to the lessee. These should be given to the auditor along with the cost-of-hire figures to permit calculation of the reduced rates.

Division III: Employers' Nonownership Liability

Covers the named insured (only) for business use of automobiles individually owned by employees or firm members, but not partners, resulting in bodily injury or property damage caused by an occurrence. This insurance, which is purely excess over any applicable primary coverage the owner may have, protects the employer if the employee has no insurance on his car, or where limits prove to be inadequate. Note that it affords no protection at all to the owner of the automobile.

For premium-determination purposes, all employees of the insured are grouped into two classes: (1) those whose duties involve regular use of personally owned automobiles for business purposes and who receive some sort of reimbursement for such use, and (2) all other employees. Class I premiums amount to several dollars per employee; class II premiums are several cents per employee.

Purchase of nonownership coverage does not mean that certificates of insurance are unnecessary, but rather that such evidence of coverage from the employee-owner is not required before the employer is protected. So far as practical, continuing efforts should be made to confirm that all class I employees are adequately insured and stay insured.

In the event of an accident involving one of these cars, the employee will be held first responsible for any injury or damage, and if the family-policy insuring agreement is broad enough to provide primary protection for the employer as well. But, with 10/20,000 or 25/50,000 limits, it would not be difficult to run into a demand or judgment in excess of those amounts, which means direct involvement of the employer in such loss.

Personal automobile limits should be high enough to (1) protect the employee, (2) keep the employer's insurance costs down, and (3) avoid unpleasant subrogation action against the employee, technically permitted by policy conditions.

Example. A contractor at a job site, finding his supply of materials getting low, sent his foreman out to pick up more. The employee took his own car and on the way struck a pedestrian, both he and his employer being named in the subsequent suit. It then became apparent that the employee had no liability insurance.

Employers' nonownership liability coverage defended the employer and settled the loss. A happy ending, but the claim cost went into the contractor's overall premium-loss record with his insurance carrier and inevitably resulted in somewhat higher premiums over the next few years.

Limits of Liability

The comprehensive automobile liability policy provides for one bodily-injury limit per person, another per occurrence. Property-damage liability is subject to one limit per occurrence.

Definition of Automobile. Although the comprehensive automobile liability policy form is broad enough to cover all the named insured's automobile exposures, whether owned, hired, or nonowned, there is some limitation in defining exactly what kind of mobile equipment is an automobile. This is of particular importance to contractors.

For example, aside from passenger cars, trucks, truck-type tractors, trailers, semitrailers, and similar land motor vehicles designed for travel on public roads, the new automobile policy excludes "mobile equipment" defined as land motor vehicles, whether or not self-propelled, that meet at least one of the following criteria:

1. Not subject to motor-vehicle registration
2. Maintained for use exclusively on the insured's premises, including ways immediately adjoining
3. Designed for use principally off public roads
4. Designed or maintained for the sole purpose of affording mobility to equipment of the following types forming an integral part of or permanently attached to such vehicle:

pumps	power cranes
generators	concrete mixers
shovels	road-construction equipment
loaders	road-repair equipment
diggers	air compressors
drills	spraying equipment
graders	building-cleaning equipment
scrapers	geophysical-exploration equipment
rollers	well-servicing equipment
	welding equipment

Use of such mobile equipment is covered without gap under the insured's comprehensive general-liability policy. Deciding exactly where to draw the line is often difficult; to eliminate possible disagreement between automobile and general-liability carriers at the time of loss, both coverages should be written together wherever possible and at identical limits of liability. In that case, any question of which policy applies is purely academic and of no concern to the insured.

Loading and Unloading.   The standard automobile policy form includes bodily injury and/or property damage resulting from loading or unloading of automobiles as defined. We list it as a limitation here because at some stage of loading and unloading operations, automobile coverage ceases to apply and general-liability coverage takes over. When?

The only way to be free of arguments between insurance carriers is to purchase both forms of insurance together and at identical limits of liability.

Contractual Liability.   Such agreements are normally covered under the general-liability policy's contractual division, although some provision may be made in the automobile format for a separate contractual liability "coverage part" in consideration of an additional premium charge.

Care, Custody, or Control.   The policy excludes damage to property owned or transported by the insured, or property rented to or in charge of the insured.

Policy Extensions

Medical-Payments Coverage.   This endorsement calls for reimbursement of reasonable medical expenses incurred by occupants of an insured automobile. Not applicable to employees eligible for worker's compensation benefits. Recommended.

Uninsured Motorists.   Now compulsory in many states, this extension is sometimes called *family-protection coverage.* With it the contractor's own insurance company agrees to pay occupants of the insured automobile for injury sustained as a result of an accident with an uninsured motorist. The amount collected approximates what the contractor might have recovered from the other driver if there was insurance. Employees eligible for worker's compensation benefits may present claims under uninsured motorist coverage, then reimburse the compensation carrier for any amounts paid.

Use of Other Automobiles.   Specific individuals may be named by endorsement to protect against bodily injury, property damage, and medical payment losses arising from use of a nonowned automobile, whether for business or pleasure purposes. It is ordinarily not required where that individual has in force a family automobile policy. There is enough variance in personal automobile liability policies, however, to make close examination of this subject mandatory. It is recommended where needed.

Foreign Coverage.   Use of any automobile outside the United States, its territories or possessions, or Canada requires special foreign coverage.

AUTOMOBILE PHYSICAL DAMAGE

Physical damage to owned vehicles, as well as those under long-term lease, may be covered either as part of the automobile liability contract or as an entirely separate policy form. Insured hazards may include the three categories discussed below.

Comprehensive Coverage.   For a single premium the hazards of fire, theft, glass breakage, malicious mischief, vandalism, and accidental damage to the vehicle, other than that caused by collision, may be insured on an actual-cash-value or stated-amount-of-insurance basis. In either case, the amount recovered in the event of total loss is the current market value of the vehicle at the time of loss. In most cases, however, less premium will be developed by carrying insurance on a stated-amount basis, particularly when a fleet of five or more units is covered. The coverage may be written with a deductible.

Fire, Theft, and Combined Additional Coverage.   Alternatively, the specific perils of fire, theft, windstorm, hail, earthquake, explosion, flood or rising waters, riot, civil commotion, malicious mischief, and vandalism may be insured at a premium saving over comprehensive coverage, particularly where the omitted glass-breakage exposure is negligible. It may be written with a deductible.

Collision.   Damage to owned or long-term-leased automobiles is available at deductibles ranging from $50 to $1,000 or more. The premium saving at a higher deductible is often enough to justify its purchase in lieu of a more conservative amount. Some of this advantage is offset at high deductible levels by the insurance carrier's inability to seek reimbursement from responsible third parties without an express monetary interest in the transaction. That is, if the contractor's collision damage should be $225 and the deductible is $250, the company cannot help to recover the loss. It may do so when the amount of damage exceeds the deductible, of course. Occasionally an insured's brokerage claims department will pursue the subrogation against the third-party on a "client-assist" basis.

Coverage Extensions

Fleet Automatic Coverage.   A fleet consists of five or more insured units, and if automatic coverage is desired, a fleet automatic endorsement is available without additional charge to pick up changes and additions to the schedule without the need to endorse midterm.

UMBRELLA EXCESS LIABILITY

It would be difficult to exaggerate the importance of this broad liability policy to any contractor. Available through Lloyd's of London, various foreign companies, and many domestic insurance carriers under various names, it can provide high enough limits to eliminate, for all practical purposes, the question of adequacy in the amount of insurance carried.

There is little standard about these forms, and only a specific quotation can provide a complete explanation of hazards insured and exclusions or limitations applicable. In general, these policies operate in two ways: as excess over primary insurance and as excess over self-insured hazards.

As Excess over Existing Primary Insurance

Existing liability insurance policies are not eliminated with the purchase of umbrella coverage. Rather, they become the underlying layer, above which umbrella provides excess limits for the same hazards insured under primary policies, subject to a high limit per occurrence.

As Excess over Self-Insured Hazards

For hazards not insured in existing liability insurance policies, umbrella provides coverage in excess of a self-insured retention or deductible. Such exposures may (but do not always) include

Damage to property of others in your "care, custody, or control"

Blanket contractual liability

Worldwide coverage

Completed-operations liability

Product liability

Personal-injury liability

Automobile liability

Professional or malpractice liability

Liquor-law liability

Advertisers' liability

Nonowned-aircraft liability

Nonowned-watercraft liability

Employers' liability

Example: Excess over Existing Primary Insurance. A masonry contractor carried a comprehensive general-liability providing a property-damage limit of $100,000 each occurrence and, fortunately, a $1,000,000 umbrella excess policy. In effect, this increased his total property-damage limit to $1,100,000 each occurrence. In using a bulldozer, one of his employees struck an underground utility, causing $29,000 damage.

His primary general-liability policy did not cover the loss in view of the x,c,u exclusion applicable to underground damage caused by excavation. Since the loss was otherwise uninsured, the contractor's umbrella policy paid $19,000 in excess of the applicable $10,000 self-insured retention or deductible.

Even small contracting firms should secure a quotation for this broad coverage. It is sometimes available for less cost than would be charged for higher limits under policies providing far less protection. Because so much is automatically included, albeit subject to a substantial deductible, it serves to close unforeseen gaps in coverage, thereby becoming the nearest thing to an insurance buyer's errors and omissions policy.

Policy Exclusions

Exclusions appearing in umbrella policies are relatively simple, most being confined to

1. Assault and battery committed by or at the direction of the insured
2. Intentional property damage
3. Damage to property owned by the insured
4. Worker's compensation, unemployment, or similar benefits-law liability
5. Damage to the insured's product and/or work arising out of the product or work itself
6. Loss of use of any such defective products or work
7. Improper or inadequate performance, design, or specification in the absence of personal injuries or tangible damage to the property of others
8. Advertising claims from
   a. Failure of performance of contract
   b. Trademark or trade-name infringement
   c. Incorrect description of an article or commodity
   d. Mistake in advertised price
9. Nuclear-facility hazards
10. Liability as a consequence of war, invasion, hostilities, civil war, rebellion, insurrection, etc.

Maintenance of Underlying Insurance

Umbrella policies normally schedule underlying primary liability-insurance coverage maintained by the insured, and the insured warrants to keep such insurance in force during the umbrella-policy term. Failure to comply with this condition does not necessarily invalidate the policy, but the insurance company's responsibility then applies only to the same extent as it would if the insured had maintained such coverage. Such underlying policies should not be dropped or reduced without approval of the umbrella carrier.

Following-Form Excess Liability

By way of specific policy conditions or endorsement, umbrella underwriters commonly restrict their policies so that umbrella coverage applies to certain hazards only to the same extent that they are covered by underlying primary insurance. That is, if covered in the underlying policies, umbrella will cover too; otherwise not.

This is pure following-form excess-liability insurance as respects such enumerated hazards.

Such restrictions are most often concerned with (1) contractual liability, (2) damage to property of others in the insured's care, custody, or control, and/or (3) explosion, collapse, or underground damage. Where such restrictions are in force, the broadest possible underlying comprehensive general-liability insurance should be secured.

EXPERIENCE RATING

Contractors, when their premium level at normal manual rates reaches a practical level, become eligible for experience rating, that is, credits or debits applied to manual rates, based upon the ratio of premiums to losses over a given number of years. These rating plans vary a good deal with the kind of coverage involved. In principle, they are similar, however; all are supervised by state insurance departments, intrastate and interstate rating authorities, and independent rating organizations.

Manual rates contemplate a certain average level of losses, and by mathematical formula, a comparison is made annually of actual losses reported over roughly three years compared with expected levels. Weights are allowed to minimize the effect of large losses so that the small operator who has one serious case does not pay an astronomical premium for eternity. In general, a frequency of claims will count more in experience rating than will severity, but this effect decreases as premium volume increases.

COMPOSITE RATING

Instead of paying general-liability premiums based upon payroll, number of elevators, amount of work sublet, gross receipts, and total contract cost, some contractors are billed a composite rate for all five divisions of general-liability coverage combined. Some medium-sized and most large contracting firms are covered this way. There really is no mystery about this basically simple technique, but it is often misundertood.

At least in theory, the insurance carrier will first arrive at a premium quotation by individually rating each division of coverage, using payrolls, receipts, etc., as measures of exposure, to arrive at the dollars of premium they require to write the coverage (see Table 11.1). This dollar quotation remains constant, but if the contractor prefers to simplify bookkeeping and gear the policy cost to payroll or receipts, it can be arranged as shown in the following example.

Example of Composite Rating

Desired total premium quoted: $4,525

Total payroll expected: $500,000

Composite rate = $4,525 divided by 500,000, or $0.905 per $100 of payroll

Or alternatively:

Desired premium quoted: $4,525

Total receipts expected: $1,500,000

Composite rate = $4,525 divided by 1,500,000, or $3.016 per $1,000 of receipts

The policy can then be issued without the usual myriad of schedules and rates; the insurance company's auditor makes a final computation based upon total payroll or total receipts reported for the policy year. Actually, it does not make a great deal of difference what the measure of exposure is, so long as the insurance company ends up with approximately $4,525 for the amount of work contemplated. The intent of composite rating is to arrive at the same premium level as before, not to achieve a price advantage.

This procedure can also be followed in insuring a large number of automobiles and trucks; the composite rate can be geared to the total number of automotive units, number of power units (omitting trailers), payroll, or gross receipts, so long as the insurance company collects so many dollars for the exposure.

Obviously, this method will appeal most to large contractors and those whose exposures are relatively stable or predictable and not to those who report widely fluctuating payrolls or receipts each year. If completely accurate premium allo-

TABLE 11.1 Example of Usual Rating Method

Coverage	Anticipated premium bases	Annual premium quoted	
		B.I.	P.D.
I. Operations—premises*	$500,000 payroll	$2,000	$1,000
II. Elevator	One owned elevator	100	10
III. Protective	$75,000 sublet work	40	10
IV. Completed operations	$1,500,000 receipts	525	240
V. Blanket contractual	$1,500,000 contracts	500	100
	Total	$4,525	

*Normally broken down into a number of work classifications and differing rates.

cation between subsidiaries or divisions of a company is vital for internal reasons, the advantages of composite rating (clarity, elimination of paperwork, ease in arriving at insurance costs for bidding purposes) may be somewhat offset by new clerical problems.

RETROSPECTIVE RATING

Guaranteed-cost experience-rating plans take into account the insured's premium-loss record over the past several years to arrive at a fixed renewal rate. Retrospective rating plans do exactly the same thing, then go one step further to determine the final premium for policies subject to the plan, after they expire.

By adjusting the standard premium in direct relation to losses reported under those very same policies, retrospective rating reflects more promptly and more closely the effect of the loss experience, whether it is good or bad. In short, it is true cost-plus insurance.

Available as an option to guaranteed-cost plans, retrospective-rating premiums are popular with contractors developing sufficient premium under normal rating methods to make costs fairly stable and predictable. Some contractors engaged in extra-hazardous work may find it difficult to buy insurance any other way, because there is a degree of protection for the insurance company built into most of these plans, specifically, the difference between standard and maximum premium. To illustrate how they work, we must first define some terms:

Manual premium: The premium developed by manual rates applied to units of exposure, that is payroll, contract cost, gross receipts, or number of vehicles.

Standard premium: Manual premiums plus credit or debit factors produced by experience-rating plans. In theory, the same as premium developed under guaranteed-cost policies.

Basic premium: A percentage of the standard premium retained by the company to cover acquisition costs, general administration, safety engineering, audit expenses, company profit, loss-limitation charges, etc.

Incurred losses: Amounts paid and held in reserve by the insurance company, sometimes limited to maximum amounts chargeable because of any one claim or accident.

Loss-conversion factor: A percentage loading added to incurred losses to cover claim investigation and adjustment expenses.

Tax multiplier: A fixed-percentage factor designed to cover premium taxes regulated by the individual states involved.

Minimum premium: A percentage of the standard premium designed to fix the lowest possible premium under retrospective rating.

Maximum premium: Conversely, the highest premium possible under retrospective rating, regardless of losses, expressed as a percentage of the standard premium.

Loss limitation: The maximum amount chargeable under the plan (not available to pay a given loss) because of any one claim or accident, where such limitation applies. The charge for limiting losses is sometimes indicated separately, sometimes included in the basic premium factor.

Making use of these terms, we can state the formula for determining the final retrospective premium after expiration of such policies:

Basic premium + incurred losses × loss-conversion factor × tax multiplier
= retrospective premium

Most plans call for evaluation of losses and adjustment of premium 6 months after expiration of the policy and annually thereafter. Final premium determination may be delayed by agreement for years until all claims have been closed.

Example 1: One-Year Plan

Manual premium	$15,000
Experience modification (20% credit)	0.80
Standard premium	$12,000
Basic premium	20% of $12,000, or $2,400
Minimum premium	50% of $12,000, or $6,000
Maximum premium	135% of $12,000, or $16,200
Loss-conversion factor	1.14 × losses
Tax multiplier	1.03

Repeating our formula, then, the losses shown in Table 11.2 would produce retrospective premiums as indicated.

Retrospective plans may also be written for a period of 3 years or for the duration of one particular project, as in the case of a joint venture.

In general, 3-year plans provide a greater degree of protection to the insurance company than 1-year plans and in return offer more attractive basic, minimum, and maximum premium factors to the insured (see Table 11.3). In the long run, they often provide insurance protection at the lowest cost possible, but it is impossible to state flatly which is better for everybody; too much depends upon the amount of losses incurred by policy year.

Example 2: Three-Year Plan. Before accepting coverage under a retrospective-rating plan, a contractor should be certain that it has been negotiated with his interests in mind by someone professionally competent in whom he has supreme confidence.

The premium penalty for cancellation of a 3-year plan by the insured before expiration is prohibitively severe, a necessary inducement to continue the agreement once made, regardless of loss experience, as shown in Table 11.4.

TABLE 11.2 One-Year Plan: Loss-Generated Retrospective Premiums

Basic premium	+	Incurred losses	×	Loss-conversion factor	×	Tax multiplier	=	Retrospective premium
$2,400		$ 8,114		1.14		1.03		$12,000
$2,400		$ 3,004		1.14		1.03		$ 6,000
$2,400		$11,691		1.14		1.03		$16,200

TABLE 11.3 Example 2: Three-Year Plan

	First year	Second year	Third year
Manual premium	$15,000	$14,000	$15,600
Experience modification	×0.80	×0.75	×0.82
Standard premium	$12,000	$10,500	$12,792 third year
		+12,000	+10,500 second year
			+12,000 first year
		$22,500	$35,292
Basic premium*	18%, or	18%, or	18%, or
	$2,160	$4,050	$6,353
Minimum premium	45%, or	45%, or	45%, or
	$5,400	$10,125	$15,881
Maximum premium	130%, or	130%, or	130%, or
	$15,600	$29,250	$45,880
Loss-conversion factor	1.14	1.14	1.14
Tax multiplier	1.03	1.03	1.03
Actual losses incurred	$5,000	$11,500	$2,000

*Variable each year under some plans.

"WRAP-UP" INSURANCE PROGRAMS

The past several years have seen a tremendous increase in the number of major construction projects insured under wrap-up insurance programs, wherein the owner, architect, engineer, general contractor, and subcontractors are protected under a single insurance package applicable to all. The New York World's Fair, UN Building, Lincoln Center, Seattle World's Fair, San Francisco Bay Area Rapid Transit Project, Boston Prudential Building, Chicago John Hancock, First National Bank, and Continental Center Buildings are representative of such undertakings.

When applied with skill and professional competence to the right job, this approach can benefit the owner by reducing overall insurance costs through mass purchasing power and elimination of coverage duplications inherent in separately purchased insurance policies.

The best advice we can give any general contractor or subcontractor when bidding such jobs is to have an insurance representative review the specifications in advance. The representative can advise exactly how they affect the contractor's normal insurance program, which hazards are not included in the wrap-up package, and the degree of protection they do afford. Once the contract is awarded, there should be an arrangement for an endorsement to the contractor's policies to delete the coverages otherwise duplicated—but only those coverages—to make certain the contractor is not charged for them when the policies are finally audited. The contractor will probably find it necessary to prepare a certificate of automobile liability insurance for the general contractor, owner, or architect. Policies or certificates attesting to the insurance supplied by the wrap-up carrier will be prepared for the contractor.

Particular attention must be paid to the degree of completed operations-products liability and contractual liability afforded, since the contractor will not want to do with less protection on a large project.

TABLE 11.4 Three-Year Plan: Loss-Generated Retrospective Premiums and Results

Basic premium	+	Incurred losses	×	Loss-conversion factor	×	Tax multiplier	=	Retrospective premium	Paid to date	Result
First retrospective adjustment (first year)										
$2,160		$5,000		1.14		1.03		$8,096	$12,000	$3,904 refund
Second retrospective adjustment (first and second years)										
$4,050		$16,500		1.14		1.03		$23,546	$18,596	$4,950 additional
Third retrospective adjustment (all three years)										
$6,353		$18,500		1.14		1.03		$28,266	$36,338	$8,072 refund

JOINT VENTURES

Joint ventures, wherein two or more contractors team together to perform a specific job, call for specialized treatment in establishing an insurance program.

Some of the premium-rating and policy-writing methods discussed earlier continue to apply, but others are disregarded in recognition of the individual exposures involved in that particular project. In this case, the insurance carrier weighs the relative loss experience of each contractor forming the venture, performance records, interest in accident prevention, size and duration of the contract, and so on. Premiums are largely negotiated, either on a guaranteed-cost or retrospective basis.

The controlling contractor should call in an insurance representative before bidding such a project to determine in advance how much premium may be involved. It is important at this point to make available as much information as possible about the work to be performed and physical hazards or good points of the job site. This is one place where insurance firms' engineers will be overjoyed to get an advance look at work and insurance specifications, blueprints, and plans; making them available will do much to hold insurance costs down to a minimum, thereby increasing the likelihood of presenting a successful bid.

Underwriters tend to be apprehensive over what they do not know, and they often make some allowance for unanswered questions when determining how much premium to charge. By answering those queries as fully as possible, the contractor will convey a feeling of confidence in knowing everything important there is to know, thereby enhancing chances of securing a favorable quotation.

CERTIFICATES OF INSURANCE

While a contractor is most often in the position of providing someone else with a certificate of insurance as evidence of adequate protection, it is equally important that there be certificates from the subcontractors and suppliers. Most insurance carriers have their own version of the printed form, and most require close examination to determine exactly what is provided.

In general, a contractor should look to the subcontractors and suppliers for the same coverage required of him under contract specifications. To give the greatest degree of protection, the existence of the same worker's compensation, comprehensive general liability, and comprehensive automobile liability policy forms should be verified by certificates issued. All should allow for at least 10 or 15 days' advance written notice of any cancellation or material change. Completed operations-products liability coverage should be included.

Where the contractor requires a hold-harmless agreement from a subcontractor or anyone else, proof of insurance for that contract should be supplied by a certificate. Mere mention of a comprehensive policy form is not sufficient, since there is nothing automatic about the contractual coverage provided by most such policies. Where any doubt exists about the matter, the insurance representative should be consulted and the certificates sent for examination and comment.

PAYROLL-AUDIT PROCEDURES

Worker's compensation, general liability, automobile, and sometimes umbrella excess-liability policies, along with certain others, are subject to periodic audit adjustment by the insurance company. The frequency of such adjustment and the corresponding amount of deposit premiums payable under each of these policies are largely within the contractor's control as well as of that of the insurance carrier.

It is not uncommon to have contractor's payrolls, gross receipts, amount of work sublet, and related exposures calculated semiannually, quarterly, or monthly. Depending upon the size of risk and the amount of work involved, this need not require a physical audit but only submission of a voluntary and simple report from the contractor's own accounting department, commonly subject to one physical audit annually.

The contractor should take care to exclude from such reports and figures any projects insured by someone else via "wrap-up" or direct insurance programs handled entirely by the owner or general contractor. Separately insured joint ventures might also involve some payroll which should not be reported again to the company under normal insurance policies. At times such breakdown will require a certain amount of guesswork, but if the total amount of payroll the contractor reports each year represents 100 percent of amounts actually paid, no objection should be raised by any insurance carrier.

The contractor can save time, and perhaps premium, by arranging in advance the specific records which must be maintained for examination by insurance company auditors.

For example, an up-to-date list of maximum payroll limitations which apply under worker's compensation and general-liability policies should be made available and adhered to.

BUILDERS' RISK INSURANCE, INSTALLATION FLOATERS, AND CONTRACTORS' EQUIPMENT FLOATERS

Property insurance during the course of construction is dealt with by builders' risk policy forms designed for that purpose. A good many variables tend to surround the subject, including not only the degree of coverage contemplated by several different policy forms, but also who is covered and even what the coverage is called. The recommended completed-value builders' risk policy and its inland marine counterpart, the installation floater, may be written in the name of both the owner and the general contractor, either of them, or any one of several variations; coverage may also apply to the work of subcontractors. The prudent contractor, therefore, should review contract specifications to determine obligations for this form of coverage.

Equipment and machinery, including electrical, plumbing, heating, and air-conditioning systems, should be insured as required, while in transit from manufacturer to job site and during the period of actual installation or testing until fully released.

Coverage generally terminates when the insured's interest in the property terminates, when it is accepted, or when it is occupied by the owner. Covered building materials, such as bricks, steel, and lumber, are normally insured until actual installation into the real structure or until the insured's interest terminates, whichever happens first.

In some states, similar coverage is afforded the contractor under special builders' risk form, contractors' automatic builders' risk, or contractors'/builders' risk completed-value policies. What is available in a contractor's area is best determined by an insurance representative, who should make known what options are available and then determine which policy is recommended.

Even the perils covered by builders' risk and installation floater policies vary; they may insure against fire, lightning, the perils of extended coverage (windstorm, hail, explosion, riot, civil commotion, aircraft, vehicles, smoke), vandalism, and malicious mischief or be so-called all-risk floaters designed to include still other risks. The latter are subject to variable deductible amounts, normally not applicable to the basic fire policy perils.

The inland marine policy applicable to contractors' equipment, other than vehicles designed for use on public highways, is called an equipment floater because it applies to things of a mobile or "floating" nature. Almost anything movable can be insured, whether a large crane, power shovel, Caterpiller tractor, lift truck, or small tool. Most large units carrying high values are specifically scheduled on such policies, while a blanket amount takes care of smaller items. Coverage can be made to apply automatically to new or replacement equipment. Automatic coverage for leased equipment usually requires a specific policy statement or endorsement to that effect.

Coverage is largely tailor-made to suit the exposure. It may apply to named perils or be written "all-risk," sometimes a combination of the two. To provide protection against meaningful losses at a reasonable premium level, the insurance representative must arrive at a suitable deductible amount. If the exposures can be clearly separated, there is no reason why differing deductibles cannot be selected.

Premium rates are largely negotiated but based upon loss history; in general, elimination of petty pilferage claims is preferred to ground-up coverage. The small ones are best chalked up as a business expense.

COVERAGE CHECKLIST

Without implying that any contractor, large or small, should necessarily buy all the following basic coverages and optional extensions or that doing so will guarantee a good insurance program, we offer here a checklist that includes most of the commonly available coverages. The contractor or insurance representative should periodically examine current and renewal policies to determine which of these are presently in effect, how much additional premium needed extensions would cost, and which, if any, to buy.

General-Liability

1. Comprehensive rather than "schedule" policy form
2. Property-damage liability coverage
3. Elevator liability coverage
4. Independent contractors' protective liability coverage
5. Contractual liability-blanket coverage with few limitations

6. Completed operations-products liability coverage
7. Limits of liability consistent with automobile policy
8. Property damage—explosion, collapse, or underground damage coverage
9. Broad-form property-damage liability coverage
10. Host liquor-liability coverage
11. Employee benefit liability coverage
12. Personal-injury liability coverage including employees' claims
13. Fire legal liability coverage or waiver of subrogation for leased premises
14. Vendors' liability coverage, if required
15. Professional liability coverage for maps, plans, designs, specifications
16. Worldwide coverage
17. Owned or nonowned watercraft liability coverage
18. Owned or nonowned aircraft liability coverage

Automobile Liability

1. Comprehensive rather than "schedule" policy form
2. Medical-payments coverage
3. Uninsured-motorist coverage
4. Use-of-other-automobiles endorsement
5. Foreign coverage
6. Limits of liability consistent with general-liability policy
7. Complete and accurate schedule of vehicles

Automobile Physical Damage

1. Fleet automatic coverage (composite rate form)
2. Fire
3. Theft
4. Combined additional coverage
5. Malicious mischief and vandalism
6. Comprehensive coverage
7. Collision
8. Towing
9. Foreign coverage, if required
10. Leased-equipment coverage, avoidance of duplication
11. Complete and accurate schedule of vehicles

Worker's Compensation and Employers' Liability

1. Increased limits—employers' liability

2. All states endorsement
3. Separate coverage as required in monopolistic-fund states
4. Status of executive officers or partners
5. Longshoremen's and Harbor Workers', Jones Act, or Federal Employers' Liability coverage
6. Additional medical-coverage endorsement
7. Voluntary compensation coverage endorsement
8. Status of domestic employees sent outside the United States
9. Foreign coverage

Umbrella Excess Liability

1. Accurate schedule of underlying primary policies
2. Underlying policy limit requirements
3. Employee benefit liability coverage
4. Status of following-form excess limitations, if any

Contractors' Equipment Floater

1. "All-risk" perils
2. On contractor's premises coverage
3. Material in transit
4. On-site coverage
5. Rented equipment
6. Deductible features
7. Report of insurance values requirements

Installation Floater

1. "All-risks" perils
2. Deductible features
3. Excess of builders' risk coverage applicable under other policies covering job

General

1. Complete and accurate list of entities to be insured
2. Up-to-date list of locations covered

CHAPTER 12
SEASONALITY

Robert G. Zilly, P.E., M.A.S.C.E., A.I.C.

Professor of Construction Management
Emeritus
University of Nebraska
Lincoln, Nebraska

All construction projects are weather-sensitive in the early stages and many remain so for the duration of the project. In addition, the construction industry is relatively labor-intensive and its workers are subject to both physiological and psychological stress as a result of their exposure to the vagaries of the weather. Construction materials, too, are weather-sensitive; concrete, for example, cannot be placed when it is too hot or too cold or too wet or too dry. These factors have led to the acceptance of seasonality in the industry by both contractors and their clients. Projects are abandoned with the onset of winter in the north, sometimes for several months, and the rainy season or hot season may cause shutdowns for periods ranging from a few days to several weeks. However, there is some evidence that contractors are gradually extending the construction season by using a variety of techniques to reduce the impact of inclement weather.

Despite its broad and often in-depth study of the construction industry, the Business Roundtable's Construction Industry Cost Effectiveness Project pays scant attention to the problem of seasonality. Yet, as early as 1924, seasonality was a concern of President Herbert Hoover's. In 1968 the U.S. Congress embarked on a major study of the problem. As early as the 1950s in Europe and during the 1960s and 1970s in the United States, a steady stream of research reports and studies flowed from various sources.

Meanwhile, the Army Corps of Engineers continues to study facets of the problem at its Construction Engineering Laboratory in Illinois and its Cold Region Research and Engineering Laboratory in New Hampshire. Yet, today the subject of seasonality appears to be low on the construction industry's list. If the industry were using all the information available to stabilize the year-round level of construction activity, this would be understandable. Progress has been made, but for many reasons—some not the fault of the industry—seasonality still takes its toll on the efficiency of the construction process.

MAGNITUDE OF THE PROBLEM

Figure 12.1 covers the total employment in construction on a monthly basis from May 1988 to May 1989. The difference between the August 1988 peak and the

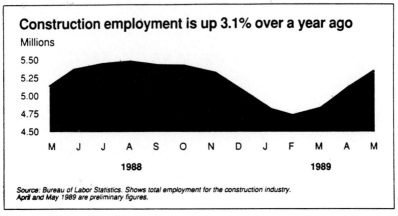

FIGURE 12.1   Construction employment drops significantly in the winter months. The 14 percent drop for the winter of 1988–1989 is typical and based on figures from the Bureau of Labor Statistics.

February low is about 750,000 workers. Although this difference may not be caused entirely by seasonality, similar data for the state of Ohio indicate the same relative figure—construction employment appears to drop by about 14 percent from summer peak to winter low. In areas subject to severe climate the figure is higher. For example, construction employment in Alaska appears to drop by about 45 percent. Of course, the impact of seasonality is not equal on all of the construction trades or all of the different types of projects. But, the average number of hours worked per week in the industry tends to remain under 40, in spite of the fact that overtime is not uncommon during peak seasons.

Based on Department of Labor figures, the data in Table 12.1 indicate the annual average work hours for several groups of construction workers.

TABLE 12.1   Typical Average Annual Work Hours

Year	1977	1979	1980	1981
Carpenters	1665	1680	1591	1590
Others	1695	1748	1721	1730
Laborers	1298	1351	1335	1306
Average—all	1673	1720	1675	1674

Clearly, construction workers fall far short of the traditional 2000 hours of work per year based on 50 weeks of employment at 40 hours per week. Again, these figures cannot be solely attributed to seasonality, because the construction market is an extremely volatile one. For example, for several years following 1981 the industry was in recession and the figures for those years would be significantly lower than those shown. However, seasonality cannot be ignored and its impact on a trade such as bricklaying is a matter of real concern. A survey published by the International Masonry Institute of several years ago showed that bricklayers work an average of only 35 weeks per year. Bad weather costs the bricklayer 15 weeks of work annually. If the average work year were extended to only 45 weeks, it would add some 64 million man-hours of skilled craft labor to the economy. This would be the equivalent of 35,000 new trained bricklayers overnight.

Monthly output as a percentage of a contractor's total annual volume was studied in a limited survey of building, highway, and electrical contractors. The results, shown in Table 12.2, are interesting:

TABLE 12.2 Annual Workload in Percent of Total per Month

	Building	Highway	Electrical
January	7.3	4.6	7.7
February	7.3	5.2	7.7
March	7.6	5.9	7.7
April	7.8	7.3	7.8
May	8.2	8.9	8.1
June	8.7	10.2	8.4
July	9.1	10.5	8.7
August	9.2	10.7	8.8
September	9.0	10.5	8.8
October	8.9	10.1	8.9
November	8.7	8.9	8.7
December	8.2	7.2	8.7

Note that highway contractors did 52 percent of their annual volume in the 5 months from June through October, building contractors 44.9 percent, and electrical contractors 43.6 percent. Electrical contractors obviously maintained the most stable production level, but their peak month lags behind the building contractors' by about 2 months. This probably indicates some correlation between electrical and general building work, for the electrical work in buildings sometimes cannot proceed full tilt until the structure is closed in.

Seasonality varies in its impact on project types, as indicated in Fig. 12.2. Water and sewage treatment plants appear to be the least affected, highways the most. Building construction activity peaks in November, probably as the result of contractors trying to get structures enclosed so that interior finish work can proceed during the coldest part of the year. Since much of the construction work on sewage and water treatment plants is below grade, weather protection is probably more easily provided for both workers and materials.

Winter construction has, of course, been done by many contractors for many years and there are major projects dating as far back as the 1970s to prove its feasibility. However, there has been no strong promotion for the elimination of seasonality since the late 1960s when federal concern peaked. Thus, though the technology for cold- and hot-weather construction has been steadily developing, the tradition of seasonality still hangs heavily over the construction industry. Although there has been a significant recovery from the industry's early 1980s recession, that period probably helped to maintain the tradition because there is little incentive to avoid shutdowns of construction projects if there are no new ones coming on the market. Thus, the problem remains in need of an industry-wide effort to find a solution.

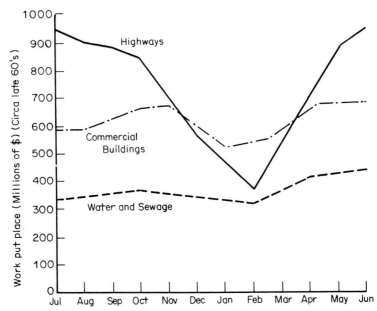

FIGURE 12.2 The winter drop in construction employment is confirmed by monthly value of work put in place. Data for highway, water, and sewage plant and commercial building contractors is from the Department of Commerce (circa late 1960s).

SOCIAL COSTS OF SEASONALITY

The largest social cost of long-term shutdowns in the construction industry is created by unemployment compensation. A 1976 study by the Chicago Construction Coordinating Committee projected a 20 to 1 benefit-to-cost ratio for winter construction, with 90 percent of the benefit created by reduced unemployment compensation. An early 1980s study in Ohio contradicts this conclusion and raises the question of increased chance for injury in winter construction. This study indicated that lost working days on winter work because of injury was twice as high as the summer figure. If true, this would be a negative factor in winter work via a rise in cost of worker's compensation. However, many contractors have claimed significant cost/benefit ratios on specific winter projects and there is a need for detailed comparative studies of accident rates for the period when contractors are pushing their workers into overtime schedules during good weather versus normal hours worked during winter.

Society also pays a price for delays in the completion of construction projects because of the significant amount of capital that is tied up without any return until the job is finished. Apartment rentals are higher because the developer ties up nonearning capital and the price of "widgets" remains high because the new, more efficient plant takes too long to get into production. In fact, the cost of capital tied up in unfinished construction projects is a significant burden on the overall economy that is too seldom recognized and calculated.

Another hidden social cost of seasonality in construction is the impact of unemployment on construction workers who lose their skills and incentive through long lay-offs. How productive is the 35-week-per-year bricklayer when he returns to work after a winter layoff? And what is the ripple effect on a community when well-paid construction workers are forced to adjust family budgets to live within unemployment compensation income?

As the Business Roundtable Report makes very clear, many customers of the construction industry feel that it is pricing itself out of the market. The high cost of new manufacturing facilities inhibits companies from building because they feel that cost reductions created by modern facilities will be offset by the high cost of the facilities themselves. Indeed, the U.S. construction industry has lost its dominance of overseas markets and is being forced to compete with contractors from overseas in its home territory. There are obviously many factors at play in this phenomenon, but seasonality is surely a contributing factor.

CONSTRUCTION CLIENT COSTS

The traditional belief that construction in unseasonable weather cannot be of high quality is strongly rooted in the minds of many construction clients, whether private or government. Thus, with rare exceptions, they are willing to accept long delivery schedules and are reluctant to pay the contractor a bonus for early project delivery. Yet, these same clients are often eager to engage in litigation because the contractor did not deliver their project on schedule. In the late 1960s there was strong pressure on government agencies at the federal level to encourage winter construction in an effort to help level employment and achieve more effective use of capital. However, recent studies show that these same agencies display little in the way of uniform and intelligible rules for what constitutes a legitimate weather delay on a project. They are also unwilling to accept slight cost increases to give the contractor an incentive to use available technology to overcome adverse weather.

A long construction schedule marked by at least one winter shutdown can cause the construction client significant financial loss. First, capital is tied up for long periods in an unfinished project. Second, there may be a loss of income because apartments come onto the market at a time when renters are not willing to move, schools are not available for the opening fall semester, or, worst of all, a new product may not be able to go into production ahead of the competition. It is difficult to measure these losses, but they are nevertheless real. Some contractors have pointed up these losses in their sales approach to potential clients and successfully negotiated contracts based on rapid project delivery through minimizing delays due to weather by using the available technology. The slight additional cost to the client can be shown to be more than offset by early beneficial occupancy.

CONSTRUCTION WORKER LOSSES

Seasonality affects the construction worker adversely in many ways:

1. Annual income is uncertain, making family financial planning extremely difficult.

2. Acceptance of unemployment compensation is demeaning to many workers. The alternative is to find temporary employment, usually unrelated to construction.

3. Even relatively short layoffs result in a loss of skill that requires a relearning process when the worker is called back to the job.

4. Crews which have shaken down into a smoothly functioning team are broken up and seldom reassembled with original personnel intact.

5. It is difficult to maintain an enthusiastic work ethic when a seasonal layoff is imminent.

There are so many uncertainties for construction workers inherent in the business that it behooves employers to eliminate or minimize as many of them as possible. A heavy construction craftsman may work 5 miles from home one week and be forced to live in a motel hundreds of miles from home the next. Workers may learn the ropes with one company only to be laid off and forced to learn a new set of rules with a new company. Seasonality adds to the confusion and uncertainty and its elimination or minimization could help to make the industry more attractive to quality craftsmen.

CONTRACTOR COSTS

With the exception of a few unusual circumstances, carrying on production of a project during adverse weather conditions is going to cost money. The question is, how much? Obviously, heating or cooling work areas is an energy-consuming process which probably accounts for the major cost of minimizing seasonality. Surprisingly, however, the literature on seasonality indicates little difference in the overall cost of winter construction before and after the oil embargo which jolted petroleum prices around the world.

In 1969 the Canadian Construction Association estimated an increase in cost for winter construction ranging from 0.75 to 1.5 percent. A report by David Morris of the University of Virginia published in the A.S.C.E. *Journal of the Construction Division* in 1976 indicated cost increases in the range of 2.0 percent exclusive of mechanical, electrical and plumbing work; 1.25 percent for the total project. However, a report by Enno Koehn and Dennis Meilhede of Purdue University published in the same journal in 1981 tells a different story. Based on 119 usable responses to a survey of Ohio contractors, the 106 firms reporting that they worked in the winter indicated cost increases of 12 percent in the 30 to 39°F temperature range and 58 percent at temperatures below 10°F. The authors attempted to evaluate the safety aspects of winter work in Ohio and concluded that the cost of more frequent accidents was about 76 percent of the cost of unemployment. Overall, they concluded that the cost of continuing construction in winter was about equal to the losses created by shutting down. Obviously, there is a need for definitive studies of the increase in construction costs caused by working during adverse weather. They will have to be done both by geographic area and type of project.

Whatever the cost of reducing seasonality, there is a need to recognize and evaluate the cost of traditional shutdowns. Disregarding inflation and possible increases in interest rates, significant problems in the 1970s, there are many other costs the contractor must accept as the price of shutting down his projects for extended periods:

1. Protecting incomplete construction against weather damage.
2. Keeping key personnel on the payroll in spite of the fact that there is little or nothing for them to do.
3. Potential loss of productive craftsmen who can probably find other employment and may not be available when work is resumed.
4. Cash flow interruption and delayed receipt of retainage.
5. Reduced capital turnover, which impacts on return on investment. Remember that ROI equals number of times capital is turned over times percent profit on jobs.
6. Inability to bid new work because key people are committed to the interrupted project.
7. Extended payment for project insurance.
8. Low utilization for owned construction equipment.
9. Forced use of overtime during peak season to meet schedule or to "button up" the project before shutdown.
10. Forced peaks in job materials purchases that can cause cash flow problems.
11. Possible higher subcontractor costs because subs are forced into overtime operation to meet tight peak-season schedules.

Whether or not these costs are applicable to a particular firm should be carefully analyzed by management and costs should be assigned where they apply. Many of the items appear to be qualitative rather than quantitative, but an effort should be made to put a number on everything. Only after this is done can a contractor evaluate the gains or losses that can be expected from reducing seasonality. Even if the balance works out in the contractor's favor, his innate caution may lead him to continue to avoid work during bad weather. For, if the schedule is built on the basis of "beating" the weather, there is always the chance that the weather will turn abnormally foul and make work impossible. Further, the decision is not left to the contractor alone. Often the client may be more conservative than the contractor and simply refuse to accept the notion that modern technology can be used to produce quality construction during inclement weather. Finally, not too many clients are willing to measure their own benefits from a minimization of seasonality and early project delivery. In fact, they might strenuously object to even the 2 percent markup that many researchers have reported.

It must also be noted that producers of construction materials and equipment going into a project tend to be rather rigid in their pricing to contractors. In fact, the contractor who buys on a leveled purchasing plan throughout the year may end up paying more than the contractor who makes a single, large-quantity purchase. This is sometimes based on a manufacturer's true production costs, but often is not. Thus, there is little incentive for the contractor to aid in the stabilization of the production process.

Without belaboring the point, what seems to be indicated is the fact that if year-round construction is ever to become the norm, it will be because contractors can individually profit from it. It is a truly generous firm that will take a cut in profits to benefit society in general. However, it is worth pointing out that in the late 1960s a group of architects, engineers, contractors, and owners in Chicago did make an attempt to stabilize the industry. This private-sector effort tried to organize owners so that many large projects were not dumped on the market at the same time. This obviously entailed some emphasis on reducing seasonality. Though not overly successful, the idea is worthy of renewed study in areas where construction is booming.

SHOULD GOVERNMENT INTERVENE?

By 1970, after several years of hearings and commission studies, reams of reports were issued by the U.S. government dealing with the problem of seasonality. On May 17, 1979, President Nixon, in his message concerning the various problems of the construction sector, announced several steps to implement the recommendations of the Joint Labor Commerce report. A report by David D. Martin of Indiana University published by the Department of Commerce in *Construction Review* included the following items from the President's message:

A. Stabilizing Industry Operations
   The intermittent and seasonal nature of the construction industry has always been a problem in the full utilization of construction resources—especially human resources. The Departments of Commerce and Labor recently completed a joint study of seasonal unemployment in the construction industry. I am directing that the following recommendations of this study be carried out:
   1. Counter-seasonal contract award procedures shall be used whenever practical so that peak on-site employment coincides with peak construction unemployment.
   2. Experimental pilot projects in off-season construction shall be conducted by Federal agencies and departments.
   3. Interior construction activities such as repair, rehabilitation, and painting shall be performed during winter months unless specific permission for performing these activities at other times during the year is obtained from the agency head.
   4. Within the next 3 months, agencies responsible for Federal construction shall identify those programs that can best use off-season labor without substantial extra direct costs.
   5. Each agency or department of the Federal Government shall report to the Cabinet Committee on Construction by July 1 of each year on the steps it has taken during the fiscal year to lessen seasonality and intermittency in its construction projects.

    Among the President's additional recommendations was a directive to the secretary of labor to develop a pilot construction labor market information system. Interestingly enough, this same idea is highlighted in the Business Roundtable Report published 10 years later. This is just one indicator of the fact that all of the studies and presidential directives had only minor impact on the construction industry. Whether this was due to Nixon's flawed presidency or the inertia of the bureaucratic system is a moot question.
    Though government influence on the seasonality problem in the U.S. does not

yet seem to be effective, the same report quoted above goes on to point out successes by the governments of Canada and Europe:

Nearly all industrialized countries have been forced to find ways to lengthen the construction season in order to meet construction needs.

Among the policies and programs on winter work relevant to the American enterprise economy are (1) seasonal programming or ordinary public work; (2) compensatory public works to take up seasonal slack; and (3) governmental measures to encourage the private construction subsector to do winter work.

~~The net result of these programs and policies has been a reduction in unworked days~~ and an increase in construction output. This increased output has contributed to economic growth and is deemed to offset the additional expense of winter construction.

Seasonal Programming of Regular Public Works Program

In Austria and the Federal Republic of Germany, the government strives to lay aside 30 percent of building funds for winter work.

In Canada and Denmark, government financed maintenance and repair work is earmarked for the winter.

In Norway, Sweden, and the United Kingdom, the various government agencies concerned with construction coordinate their activities and policies by a variety of measures to maximize winter employment.

Compensatory Public Works

Usually, we think of such programs as counter-cyclical in intent (e.g., the Works Progress Administration). Other countries now use a variety of techniques to achieve a counter-seasonal emphasis.

In Austria a payroll grant system is used; in Finland a flexible, decentralized system tailored to local conditions and finance is used; the Norwegian National Labor Board has authority to subsidize public works to combat seasonality.

Assistance to Private Construction

Information and educational programs to stimulate winter work are now common in most industrial countries...[see Fig. 12.3]. In addition, several countries, specifically Denmark, Germany, and the United Kingdom, provide consultants and other technical assistance to contractors.

Financial incentive programs such as loans, grants, rebates on social insurance contributions, and government loans at low interest to purchase machinery and equipment also are used to stimulate winter work.

Compensatory Income Support and Other Assistance to Workers

In theory, foreign unemployment compensation insurance plans are similar to those in the United States. But in practice, foreign plans stress prevention of unemployment in construction by variations in premiums, rebates of premiums, and the use of reserve funds to provide financial incentive to entrepreneurs.

Some countries give grants and loans for the purchase of winter clothing. The Swedish Government has developed a more effective construction uniform. Lastly, special training programs have been developed to utilize time lost due to bad weather to upgrade the skills of the seasonally unemployed.

FIGURE 12.3 *Winter Building* is a brochure which was published in the United Kingdom by the Department of the Environment in 1971. It includes information on climate, along with descriptions of a variety of methods and equipment useful for overcoming winter conditions. A more limited area is covered by the brochure *Recommended Practices & Guide Specificaitons for Cold Weather Masonry Construction*, published in 1973 by the International Masonry Industry All-Weather Council.

PHYSIOLOGICAL FACTORS

Human beings display a wide variation in their reaction to abnormal temperatures, both high and low. As anyone who has played or watched the "thermostat game" in an air-conditioned office can testify, it is a rare occasion when the majority of the workers find the temperature "just right." Whether it is winter or summer, some are always too hot, some too cold. There are both physiological and psychological reasons for this disparity in opinion, and sorting the two is no simple task. However, for purposes of this discussion Department of the Army studies are useful in setting the limits for conditions under which construction work can proceed. It appears that at temperatures above 110°F and below 10°F, with relative humidity above 50 percent, useful work can simply not be done. Outside the given extremes workers become irritable, the quality and quantity of work goes into rapid decline, errors increase, and work stoppage is frequent.

Within the limits stated, there is some evidence that, given the proper incentives and training, many workers can be productive close to the top and bottom of the range.

The metabolic process which creates the energy workers use to perform their tasks and sustain life can at best convert about 25 percent of the energy contained in the food the worker ingests. Workers therefore vary in their ability to perform. Whatever the demands of the job, the human body temperature must be maintained within a very narrow temperature range. Since heat is generated in the metabolic process, the excess in summer must be dissipated whereas in winter heat must be carefully conserved. In general the body's mechanism for thermoregulation seems better able to function in hot weather than in cold. The heat transfer process involves conduction, convection, radiation, and evaporation. All of these factors are influenced by weather: hot or cold, humid or dry, sunny or cloudy, and windy or still.

Unfortunately, it is difficult to combine all these elements in a single chart to provide definitive information on the overall impact of a given set of conditions on the work force. Figure 12.4 provides guidance for the combined factors of wind and temperature—wind chill. This is a popular feature of radio and TV weather forecasts and should be useful to contractors attempting to work in adverse weather. Figure 12.5 deals with temperature alone, but introduces the concept of efficiency of both manual tasks and those tasks involving use of equipment. It is based on research by the U.S. Army Cold Region Research and Engineering Laboratory. Another study by Enno Koehn of Lamar University and Gerald Brown of the U.S. Construction Engineering Laboratory indicates that workers should be at about 100 percent efficiency in a temperature range from 40° to 80°F across a broad range of relative humidity. At temperatures

WIND-CHILL CHART											
Estimated Wind Speed			ACTUAL THERMOMETER READING °F.								
MPH	50	40	30	20	10	0	—10	—20	—30	—40	—50	—60
			Equivalent Temperature °F.									
Calm	50	40	30	20	10	0	—10	—20	—30	—40	—50	—60
5	48	37	27	16	6	—5	—15	—26	—36	—47	—57	—68
10	40	28	16	4	—9	—21	—33	—46	—58	—70	—83	—95
15	36	22	9	—5	—18	—36	—45	—58	—72	—85	—99	—112
20	32	18	4	—10	—25	—39	—53	—67	—82	—96	—110	—124
25	30	16	0	—15	—29	—44	—59	—74	—88	—104	—118	—133
30	28	13	—2	—18	—33	—48	—63	—79	—94	—109	—125	—140
35	27	11	—4	—20	—35	—49	—67	—82	—98	—113	—129	—145
40	26	10	—6	—21	—37	—53	—69	—85	—100	—116	—132	—148
Wind speeds greater than 40 MPH have little additional effect	Little danger for properly clothed person		Increasing danger				Great danger				
				Danger from freezing of exposed flesh							

To use the chart, find the estimated or actual wind speed in the left-hand column and the actual temperature in Degree F. in the top row. The equivalent temperature is found where these two intersect. For example, with a wind speed of 10 MPH and a temperature of —10° F., the equivalent temperature is —33 F. This lies within the zone of increasing danger of frostbite, and protective measures should be taken.

FIGURE 12.4 Wind-chill chart which was published by many construction magazines in the early 1970s. It is a good guide, but does not take humidity into consideration.

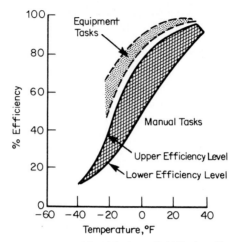

FIGURE 12.5 The U.S. Army Cold Regions Research and Engineering Laboratory produced this graphical presentation, which indicates the percent production efficiency at various temperatures for both manual and machine tasks.

approaching − 20°F and + 120°F productivity sinks rapidly from around 25 percent as relative humidity rises from 5 percent to 75 percent.

Hot-weather site conditions can put workers at risk of suffering heat stroke or heat exhaustion. In heat exhaustion, the internal body or core temperature may be normal or only slightly elevated. There is usually heavy sweating, a rapid heart rate, extreme weakness, and dizziness. Nausea, vomiting, and fainting are also possible. More serious is a heat stroke which classifies as a medical emergency. Here the body temperature is elevated to 105° or 106°F. The skin is hot and dry, pulse rate is rapid and shallow, and breathing is rapid. Confusion and sometimes a deep coma can occur along with the possibility of seizures. Nausea, vomiting, and diarrhea may also be involved. Contractor personnel should be aware of these symptoms; work stoppage is advised if several workers seem to be affected. Supplying ample water, providing shady areas for rest breaks or shade at the workplace, and even using fans to create air movement can help to reduce risk.

Cold-weather site conditions can lower body temperatures and cause frostbite either locally on exposed body parts or more generally over larger body areas. While workers may initially experience discomfort due to cold, it is unfortunate that in extreme cases this may be replaced by a feeling of euphoria and lethargy that seriously affects individual judgment. Providing thermal protection with proper clothing, wind breaks, and heated rest areas, and enclosing and heating the work area are all effective in keeping workers productive in winter.

TECHNICAL SOLUTIONS

Whatever the adverse weather conditions that affect construction activity, there is a technical "fix" that will allow work to proceed. The question is, at what cost? A review of the literature indicates a wide range of opinion and figures are often quoted without reference to geographic area or detailed information on the type of project. For example, estimates of 1.5 to 2.0 percent of job cost have been previously mentioned. However, a 1988 article in *Midwest Contractor* quotes William Quinn, chief of the Geotechnical Research Branch of the Army Corps' Cold Region Laboratory, as stating that the cost of heating a winter job site alone can range from 1 to 2 percent of the bid price. Thus, in using modern technology to reduce seasonality, it behooves the contractor to do his own detailed analysis of increased cost based on the techniques he feels are appropriate for a specific project in a specific geographic area.

The following is a brief summary of a variety of technical "fixes":

Long-Term Weather Forecasting

While this still appears to be more art than science, a number of contractors are using commercial weather forecasting services to provide weather information used in project scheduling. Based on long-term forecasts, contractors can make the decision of whether to work "around" bad weather or use special techniques to work "through" it.

Industrialized Building

Quoting from a 1969 report of the National Swedish Institute for Building Research, "Industrialized building methods greatly facilitate winter work. The utilization of prefabricated components eliminates many of the most expensive winter measures. Such building methods also facilitate the employment of older workers since many heavy and tiresome operations are removed. All efforts to promote industrialized building will, therefore, contribute to the seasonal stabilization of the construction industry." This prediction has proven accurate, for many observers report steel and precast concrete erection being carried out in the 0°F temperature range. Huge oil platforms have also been successfully prefabricated ashore and floated to their final destination. And, large dormitories for Alaskan oil workers have been fabricated in the northwest and barged to their final destination.

Construction Materials

Quick-setting cements and mortars have been on the market for some time and can be effectively used when there is a short break in low winter temperatures. Heating of water, aggregate and sand in concrete and mortars is also effective in allowing workers to place the material in cold weather, although insulation may be required to allow the material to cure satisfactorily.

Total or Partial Enclosure

Reports on winter projects dating back to the 1920s involved jerry-built enclosure systems of wood and canvas that enclosed all or parts of the projects. Today there are a number of manufacturers making use of synthetic fabrics and panels that, because of their translucence, may eliminate the need for special lighting and can take advantage of solar heating on sunny days. Figure 12.6 is a sketch of an air-supported structure being used to totally enclose a manufacturing plant addition. Figure 12.7 illustrates a rigid plastic panel system used to form partial or complete enclosure systems.

FIGURE 12.6 The sketch illustrates the use of an air-supported structure for completely enclosing a project. Access is provided through the air-lock tunnel at left. (*Illustration courtesy of Sheltair.*)

Temporary Heat

Modern space-heating units are available for purchase or rental in a wide range of sizes and using a variety of fuels as well as electricity. Manufacturers are able to provide information on sizing and provision of proper fresh air mix to protect workers in the area from danger of asphyxiation. Some contractors are also taking advantage of the structure's own HVAC system by ensuring that ductwork proceeds along with the general structural work so that the system is ready to provide heat to enclosed areas ready for interior finish.

Insulated Forms for CIPC

Cast-in-place concrete generates heat as it cures and this makes it possible to insulate forms for columns, beams, and girders—and sometimes slabs—to ensure that temperature of the concrete does not fall below the specified limit.

Cold-Weather Clothing

Spin-offs from the sporting goods industry now provide workers with thermally effective clothing that allows freedom of movement that was impossible with older, bulkier cold-weather gear.

Worker Training

With a growing body of medical knowledge about the physical effects of heat and cold on the human body and a better understanding of the psychological reactions of people working in adverse weather, training programs can prepare workers to produce effectively in spite of heat or cold.

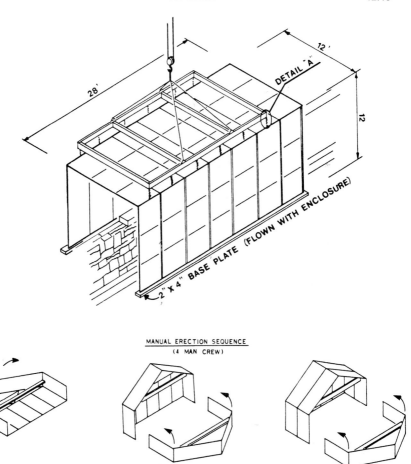

MANUAL ERECTION SEQUENCE
(4 MAN CREW)

ENDWALL SECTION ASSEMBLED
ON THE GROUND & ROLLED
INTO PLACE.

4' SECTION ASSEMBLED
& ROLLED INTO PLACE.

REPEAT

NOTE: BOTTOM CORDS INSTALLED PRIOR TO RAISING EACH SECTION

FIGURE 12.7 The Kelly Klosure system of rigid panels can be used for masonry wall work as a partial enclosure or to form a total enclosure for the entire work site. Panels are easy to assemble and knock down.

CHAPTER 13
EQUIPMENT MANAGEMENT

Terry D. Peters
Equipment Consultant
Elkhorn, Nebraska

INTRODUCTION

Cost information for specific equipment operations will vary from one location to another and from one contractor to another. There are certain factors, however, which affect equipment cost regardless of geography or ownership. Equipment management is a total consideration of these factors.

With the bigger and more specialized equipment available today, the contractor's equipment advantage lies in a good equipment-management program. Equipment management, like operations management, must incorporate a carefully planned and well-executed program where all personnel understand and accept their responsibility.

Good equipment management begins with proper equipment selection. This means selecting the equipment that matches job conditions and gives the lowest total cost. Lowest total cost is a combination of highest production, lowest operating cost, and lowest investment cost. Buying equipment based entirely on purchase price or production seldom results in lowest total cost.

To assure lowest cost, the question of rental vs. purchase must first be analyzed. If the decision is to purchase, then a choice between new and used equipment must be made. Finally, procurement must be based on the profit potential of the equipment, not on quick delivery, emotional attachment to a brand, or friendship with the equipment dealer.

Proper financing must be arranged for purchase. If cash is available, it can be used. However, elimination of interest cost may be offset by the value of cash kept on hand for emergencies. Financing can be arranged through commercial banks, commercial and dealer financing, or leasing. There is no one way that is best for all circumstances.

To yield maximum profit, equipment must be properly operated by keeping it on the job and eliminating abuse and misuse. Proper service and maintenance keeps equipment working at peak efficiency; so service and maintenance should not be looked at as a drain on income. Rather, they should be considered a contribution to output. The key to a good service and maintenance program is preventive maintenance. Preventive maintenance is the mechanical adjusting and tune-up of equipment and the detection and correction of small problems before they become major problems.

Records must be kept to provide information for planning maintenance and replacement activities so that they occur at the proper time. Records clearly establish the equipment's productivity, problem areas, and repair costs. The equipment cost must be related to specific cost items to provide good background information for future use.

A contractor who is going to continue to be successful in getting new jobs must have a well-planned equipment-replacement policy. As equipment ages, production falls because of increasing downtime. More downtime means more repairs and expense. And more efficient new machines may be introduced by manufacturers so older models may become obsolete long before they are worn out.

Good equipment management requires that everyone share the responsibility. The equipment department must make the best equipment selection and follow up on the problems encountered. The purchasing department must procure the equipment at the best price. The field operators and mechanics must make sure the equipment is properly operated and cared for.

SELECTION

Since the cost of owning and operating equipment runs between 20 and 30 percent of the job cost on some construction projects such as highways, the selection of the proper size and type of equipment is of prime importance. Looking at it another way, every dollar saved by proper equipment selection goes directly into the profit column.

All equipment should be checked out thoroughly before purchase. However, evaluation can be carried too far, particularly on less expensive equipment. Thus, it is wise to establish some dollar figure, say $2000, above which level a purchase would be considered major, below minor. The $2000 level puts all important production equipment in the "major" category.

Major Equipment

There are many factors to consider in the selection of equipment. The lowest purchase price will not necessarily be the most economical. The best buy is the piece of equipment which will give the lowest total cost.

To achieve this economic goal requires the use of a concept called value engineering, sometimes referred to as value analysis. The basis for value analysis is comparison. This involves considering the following factors for the best equipment selection:

1. Application
2. Lowest total cost
   a. Highest production
   b. Lowest operating cost
   c. Lowest investment cost
3. Standardization
4. Follow-up

Once a requirement has been established, it must be determined which piece of equipment best fits the job conditions. This question can best be answered by past experience. Lack of this experience will necessitate the gathering of equipment information from such sources as salesmen, manufacturers and distributors, catalogs, and professional publications. This information must be related to job conditions and support equipment to evaluate the application fully. The best machine in the wrong application is expensive. The equipment should be utilized to its designed capacity and the number of units balanced to the work load. If the equipment is being selected for general work and not a major project, the equipment should be sized to meet average job requirements.

It has been shown that even the most carefully selected equipment can be uneconomical when forced on job personnel. It is vital that job supervisors have a role in the selection and be kept informed of what is being purchased. They need to know the reasons for the selection and be familiar with the equipment's capabilities and limitations.

Equipment selected must meet both owner and union safety requirements. The new safety standards in force in some areas can mean spending considerable time and money to modify equipment to make it acceptable.

After the list of manufacturers whose product can satisfy the application has been established, it is time to make the final selection, after a careful analysis of total cost. Total cost can be expressed per unit of time or per unit of production. Since most jobs are bid on the basis of yards of dirt moved, pounds of steel erected, or yards of concrete placed, the most meaningful cost for the selection is based on production units.

Maximum production must be evaluated in the context of job conditions. For example, a 10-yard loader will outproduce a 5-yard loader, but if the job conditions call for a 5-yard capacity, the 10-yard machine should not be considered.

The best source of information about a machine's production capability comes from past experience. Of course, this experience must have been recorded under similar job conditions. If no past experience records are available, or a new machine is involved, most dealers will be happy to demonstrate their machine's performance. This demonstration is best conducted under job conditions, where the machine's power and maneuverability can be evaluated and its production capacity measured.

Head-to-head demonstrations prove very little. The machines in this type of demonstration are not operated at the best pace but are highballed to beat competition.

Demonstrations are and should be considered a courtesy offered by the dealer. Abuse of this courtesy by asking for or accepting demonstrations on units not really being considered can only waste time and may ultimately force dealers to discontinue the service.

High-production machines are of little value if they are not designed to stand the pace. Again, it is past experience that will provide the best information on operating costs, including maintenance, fuel, oil, grease, normal replacement items; transportation; and erection. As with production records, operating-cost records must be compared on the basis of similar job conditions. Machines working on different applications or with different attachments will have a wide variation in operating costs. The same wide variation is evident from one contractor to the next, depending a great deal on individual maintenance programs.

A new machine must be evaluated as to ease of servicing to ensure that service downtime will not reduce available time for productive use. Important factors include the number of grease fittings and sealed bearings, the location of filters, and replacement of cutting edges and other wear items. Also important is the ability to remove a major component and replace it with a new or rebuilt component, so the machine can continue to operate with minimum downtime.

When considering new models of equipment currently in use, or used in the past, it is important to note whether the manufacturer has improved the design to eliminate problems previously encountered. Since it is important to keep on-the-job spare-parts stock at a minimum level, it would be wise to check on dealer availability.

Since most purchases are made f.o.b. factory, the cost of transportation and erection must be figured. These are repetitive cost items which the contractor must consider on every new job. The machine that can be roaded or easily dismantled has a definite advantage.

Once the production rate and operating cost have been investigated, economic life, purchase price, and resale value should be considered. This sequence of investigation is important because too often production rate and operation costs are ignored when a low price is quoted.

The greatest influence on total cost of equipment is its economic life. This varies widely from one job to another, one application to another, and one owner to another. The Internal Revenue Service of the U.S. Treasury Department has established guidelines for equipment life in its depreciation rules according to various specific activities, e.g., general-contract construction, 5 years; mining, 10 years; and logging, 6 years. These life figures apply to all equipment regardless of use. For example, the same life is assigned to a crane handling light loads as to a crawler tractor ripping rock.

These guidelines were established for depreciation allowances which must be consistent with the owner's replacement practices and do not attempt to establish true economic life. Economic life cannot be evaluated by any rule of thumb but must be established on the basis of past experience. Economic life certainly varies with single-, double-, or three-shift operation as well as application, climate, and other job conditions. A realistic work schedule must be established to determine the economic life of the equipment in years.

Difference in purchase price between two different manufacturers in most cases makes a very small difference in the total cost per unit of production. The price paid is always lower than list and will depend on the dollar volume of business which a firm generates. However, it should be noted that price cutting is sometimes accompanied by cuts in dealer service or warranties.

The total expenditure for a piece of equipment is determined by subtracting resale price from purchase price. Thus, a $60,000 piece of equipment with a $10,000 resale value after 5 years is a better buy than a $57,000 piece of equipment with a $4000 resale value after the same 5 years, all other factors being equal.

At the time of purchase, the resale value is, of course, an unknown. It is influenced by the introduction of new and improved equipment or techniques which may make existing equipment obsolete. Name-brand equipment is usually influenced to a lesser degree.

When all acquisition costs have been collected, it is time to estimate the cost per unit of production. The life of the equipment multiplied by the operating hours per season equals the total production hours. Dividing the total expenditure by total production hours provides cost per hour. Previous experience or demonstrations can be used to establish production units per hour. Dividing production units per hour into costs per hour furnishes cost per unit of production.

Adding the operation cost per unit of production yields total cost per unit of production. The best machine is that machine which gives the lowest cost per unit of production when all factors have been considered.

Once the best equipment has been selected, it is wise to standardize. Further requirements should be anticipated so that the same type of equipment can be purchased to fulfill future needs. It is unwise to delay buying until the requirement is so great that the first available unit is purchased, regardless of manufacturer. Poor selections are the usual result of haste.

No value analysis would be complete without follow-up to make certain that the best selection has been made. This also aids in future selections because it provides a continuing equipment evaluation.

Minor Equipment

All the factors used to select major equipment apply to minor equipment. However, two factors have a stronger influence than lowest total cost. These are:

1. Standardization on first-line items
2. Local dealers

Standardization is more important in minor equipment because usually there are more minor-equipment units. The contractor that does not standardize must deal with numerous dealers and manufacturers. By standardizing, a contractor can expect better prices and service.

First-line items provide the contractor with equipment which was designed to stand up to rough construction applications. If the work is in many geographic locations and equipment is transferred, the contractor can expect better service in all areas by selecting name-brand items.

There are numerous types of minor equipment such as pumps, light plants, and generators, and contractors cannot afford to stock all the parts required for minor-equipment repair. The contractor must rely on local dealers for service and may have to pay a higher initial cost for the unit to get this service. In the long run, however, this may result in lower job cost, because failure of a piece of minor equipment can cause production to cease. If local dealer service is unavailable, the contractor must have a standby unit or remain idle while awaiting repairs.

PURCHASING

After the best equipment is selected, it must be purchased at the right price. The decision must be made whether to rent, lease, or purchase and, when purchasing, whether to buy new or used. Procurement must be based on what the equipment can develop in terms of profit and must not be based on emotion, friendship, or haste.

Rental

Rental of equipment can be beneficial, particularly for short periods, but the rental period must be determined beforehand. Renting equipment also allows evaluation of different manufacturers. If, in the value analysis, two or more manufacturers rate very closely, short-term rental will allow first-hand evaluation of production and establish actual operation costs. This information is beneficial in later purchase selection of equipment.

Most dealers will offer a rental option, which permits verification of dealer claims and establishes operating costs on a longer-time basis than dealer demonstrations. If the equipment can produce as claimed, the amount of rental paid is subtracted from the purchase price. If it does not produce, if operation costs are excessive, or if it is not compatible with the rest of the equipment or job conditions, cost is limited to the rental paid.

Equipment should be selected just as carefully under a rental option as for outright purchase. It is possible to get to the point where rental payments become so large that the contractor feels compelled to exercise the purchase option, only to find that the machine is no longer being used. This may be because it is an off-brand and does not fit with the rest of the fleet, there is no further need for it, or there is no current job on which conditions are similar.

Leasing

Leasing is similar to rentals but less flexible. Since leasing is longer term, more favorable fees are usually available.

Used Equipment

Many factors must be weighed before used equipment is purchased. The advantage of purchasing used equipment is lower initial investment, and therefore lower hourly depreciation for the new owner, because new equipment depreciates most rapidly on the first few thousand hours of operation. However, with used equipment, more repairs will be required and more downtime should be expected. Used equipment may also become obsolete rather quickly because of major improvements.

The size and type of job are the most important factors in considering used equipment. Used equipment may prove economical for support work, such as cleanup or backfill, but should never be considered for major production equipment or for a large job. For example, where a loader is being used to service a fleet of trucks, the trucks must be shut down during any loader repairs. The loader in this case must be the best available. That means selecting the best and purchasing a new unit.

Used equipment may also prove economical in standby service on larger jobs, where it will then be required only when a productive new unit is down for repairs.

Before used equipment is purchased for any application, it should be thoroughly inspected. Just because a unit has a new paint job does not mean it is ready to work. Remember, the previous owner wanted to sell it for some reason.

The best buys usually can be made from reliable dealers. These dealers have the facilities to put the equipment in the best condition. In some cases, the dealer will warranty the purchase for a short time.

Used purchases from other sources sometimes save additional money. Many contractors sell their own equipment, and good buys can be found from this source. It is sold as is and where it is; so the new owner assumes all the risks.

New Equipment

When new equipment is purchased, quotes from various dealers will help to assure a competitive price. Whenever possible, it is best to purchase the equipment from a local dealer. This is particularly true if the dealer is able to provide the parts and service required during use. Cost of this maintenance service is significant, so it may be profitable to buy from a local dealer even though the purchase price may be a few percentage points higher. The amount paid for dealer service will vary with the requirements and complexity of the machine but may go as high as 5 percent of the purchase price.

OPERATION

Proper scheduling of available equipment is essential in obtaining maximum profits. The investment value of equipment makes idle time just as costly as tying up a job because too few equipment units are available. A schedule must be established before startup and the proper number of units procured. As the schedule changes, there must be enough lead time to anticipate equipment needs so the most efficient number and type of units can be made available.

Regardless of how carefully the equipment is selected, misuse will still be expensive. Operation supervision must accept the responsibility for preventing equipment abuse. Before operations personnel can eliminate misuse or abuse of equipment, they must be aware of what constitutes abusive action or misuse of equipment. Thus, they must become familiar with the equipment's capabilities and limitations. The more familiar supervisors are with the equipment, the easier it is for them to communicate with the operators. Most abuse is a result of using the equipment in ways for which it was not designed or intended. Equipment is becoming more complex and more specialized in the work it is designed to do. There is no longer one unit that can be considered the "jack-of-all-trades." Instead, there are a multitude of units, each one designed for one job and only one job. Using a piece of equipment for a job for which it was not designed results in downtime and may lead to unsafe operation.

Another form of abuse is exceeding the equipment's designed limits. This type of abuse may not lead to immediate downtime, but the continual severe strain on the equipment will eventually cause a failure. Exceeding the machine's design limits leads to a serious safety violation, particularly in the case of cranes.

The best source of operating information is the manufacturer's brochures. Many times the delivering dealer, particularly a local dealer, will have service people who can instruct operators and supervisors on proper operating procedures. This introduces operators to the machine so they understand how to operate safely at maximum production. This also introduces the dealer's personnel should their help be needed later.

Most operators come from the local unions. This does not allow direct selection of operators and requires an introductory period during which the operator can become familiar with each machine and its mode of operation. The supervisors should be concerned about the machine. Where union rules permit and there are numerous similar units, such as a fleet of trucks, consideration should be given to having a lead or training operator. This individual would be a union member and would train new operators, orienting them to a particular operation.

Inexperienced operators should be given the easier jobs and allowed time to gain experience with the equipment before being given a difficult task. Operating procedures should not encourage the hot-rod operator. This type of operator is hard on equipment and is prone to commit serious safety violations. Although it may appear that the hot-rod operator is outproducing the constant-pace operator, this will not prove to be so over a reasonable period.

MAINTENANCE AND SERVICE

With the increase in size of equipment, proper maintenance and service are becoming more important. With a large number of small units in operation, each failure causes production to drop, but not as significantly as a failure of one of only a few larger units. Also, as equipment becomes larger, it becomes more complex. These facts, combined with the demand for more qualified mechanics, present the contractor with a problem of how to maintain his equipment properly.

Materials and manufacturing procedures are being improved to provide better equipment, but this equipment is expected to do more and more. And, since it is still being operated by humans, it will continue to be abused.

Equipment maintenance and service on any job begin with the organization of the equipment department. This includes establishing policies and procedures, setting up an effective shop and yard layout, scheduling maintenance and service personnel to fit around the working shifts and the needs of equipment, and finally, establishing an effective system of equipment record keeping.

When setting up the maintenance and service department, advantage should be taken of the expert outside help which is available. Manufacturers of equipment will provide the information required to get maximum production out of each unit. Tire manufacturers have excellent service people to help solve tire problems. Petroleum companies will help to select lubricants designed to minimize service problems.

Total equipment availability should not be sought because it would be too expensive to achieve. There must be proper balance between equipment availability and equipment maintenance costs. An availability of 85 to 95 percent could be acceptable for most machines, depending on their age and job conditions. Crash repair programs must be avoided because they are not only costly but usually haphazard and ineffective.

Preventive Maintenance

In the past, repairs and service were considered a drain on income. They were handled using unsophisticated tools. Typically the equipment was not maintained but simply repaired when it broke down. This method cannot be used to properly maintain today's complex equipment. The key to today's maintenance is preventive maintenance, or PM, which is a positive approach. No longer can repairs and service be considered a drain on income; they must be considered as a direct contribution to output. Some people feel that PM should stand for "productive maintenance," because it is more descriptive of what is being achieved.

Preventive maintenance is the mechanical adjustment and tune-up required to keep equipment operating at peak efficiency. It involves seeking out and repairing minor defects before they become major problems. Reducing downtime increases production time; therefore, it is productive maintenance. It involves work such as repairing a leaking radiator before the engine fails from overheating; adjusting a bearing before it becomes so loose as to lose the shaft, gears, and housing; and replacing the cutting edges before the bucket is ruined.

Preventive maintenance, in practice, involves daily visual inspections. These inspections must be made by every individual who is working with or around the equipment. They are directed at finding obvious signs of possible trouble, for example, oil or coolant leaks, tire and track wear, structural cracks, cutting-edge wear, and excessive engine smoking. Items requiring attention should be reported. Repairs which are required must be scheduled first on the basis of the nature of the repair and then on their compatibility with operating requirements. For example, a leaky radiator must be repaired immediately, while an engine using too much oil can continue to work until it can be scheduled compatibly with operations.

Where repairs are made will depend on previous arrangements, the nature of the repair, and the location of the job. Repairs can be accomplished in either the dealer's or the contractor's shop. There are advantages and disadvantages to both.

Dealer Service

Most dealers are equipped with the specialized tools and trained mechanics for extensive repair work. Dealers equipped to provide this service can probably save the contractor money whether the equipment is repaired in the dealer's shop, on the job, or via a component-exchange program.

In some areas union requirements demand that all repair work be done on the job. Before making any arrangement with dealers, be sure that union working agreements are not violated.

Many contractors feel that dealer service costs more money than staffing their own shop. However, when all costs are considered—including overhead, extra downtime, spare-part inventory, mechanic's idle time, and all shop costs—the actual cost per repair hour is about the same whether handled in house or by the dealer.

Dealer service offers the additional advantages of specific experience, special equipment, and guaranteed work. Dealers are equipped with the instrumentation that determines whether the equipment meets the manufacturer's specifications, and they can confirm their own analysis. Contractor mechanics working under job conditions are more likely to repair the unit but not correct the cause of the problem. This may result in another failure, all at the contractor's expense. Also, staff mechanics tied up making emergency repairs cannot provide the preventive-maintenance checks which are required to reduce major failures. Preventive maintenance is essential to proper equipment maintenance of modern equipment.

Some dealers are now providing off-season servicing, which provides the owner with two types of service for a flat fee:

1. A detailed report of the condition of the machine showing items requiring attention to provide better service or prevent major failures

2. The mechanical tune-up and adjustments which are required to return the machine to the manufacturer's rated performance

This offers a definite advantage to a contractor who is between jobs or does not have a maintenance staff and facility to accomplish this servicing. Off-season is a slack period for the dealer so service can be provided faster and cheaper than during a peak working season. In this way, the owner gets equipment in tip-top shape before putting it back to work.

Dealers are offering maintenance and service contracts, either combined or individual. In these contracts, they will also provide the job shop. These contracts offer a real advantage because the equipment receives expert maintenance, and the contractor's personnel do not have to become involved. If the contractor does not have qualified maintenance personnel, this would be a good approach for large jobs with standardized equipment. If the majority of the equipment is not made by the same manufacturer or sold by the servicing dealer, the maintenance and service contract will not be as effective. The contractor must still have someone oversee and schedule the maintenance to be sure it is accomplished in a way that is compatible with operation requirements and at a reasonable cost.

Manufacturers are making it easier to maintain their units via component exchange, based on designs which permit rapid change for such items as engines, pumps, and transmissions. Dealers are stocking the replacements and will repair the field components.

There are two main advantages to component exchange:

1. By exchanging components and making repairs later, downtime is cut to a minimum. For example, instead of opening the transmission, determining the problem, and making repairs at a high cost, the entire unit is replaced.

2. Better repairs, in most cases guaranteed, preclude the expense of a second repair should the first one fail immediately.

Both these advantages spell profit. Component exchange should be used wherever availability is of prime importance on a job.

Contractor's Shop

The type of organization and facilities the contractor must have will depend on the amount of maintenance work expected. To repair and/or service all of the equipment will require staffing a maintenance organization, and building and outfitting the facilities accordingly. If relying on dealer service, the contractor must have someone oversee this service and provide the preventive-maintenance checks. In this case, the facilities would be needed only to handle minor repairs and adjustments.

Personnel required to staff the maintenance department will vary with the size and nature of the job. The mechanics in almost all cases will have to be union members, hired from the local hall. The union, in some cases, will require a union foreman. It is to the contractor's advantage to also have a company foreman, since 25 percent of the total job expenditure may go to maintenance.

It must be impressed on job supervisors that the maintenance force is to look after the equipment and not be turned into job fabricators. Too often when maintenance costs become excessive, it will be found that mechanics have been building jigs, forms, and fixtures which operation people felt they needed. Most often these field-fabricated items are more expensive than those built by an outside shop. Even more discouraging is the discovery that after these items are built in the field, they do not work and are not really needed. Not only does this increase obvious maintenance costs, but in many cases other equipment is not getting properly maintained.

There is no such thing as a typical or universal shop. However, there are certain items which must be considered. The shop and yard must be of adequate size to accomplish the work which will be required. Its location should be convenient to the work area, but out of the traffic pattern. The area should be clear and as free as possible of overhead obstructions. It should be well lighted. In certain areas, it should be fenced to prevent vandalism. Fuel and oil should be stored in this area but away from the shop.

The shop itself must be sized to the equipment. If the shop is permanent, it should probably be larger than necessary for existing equipment since there seems to be a definite trend toward larger equipment. The doors must be wide enough and high enough to handle the largest unit. Drive-through bays are necessary so failed equipment can be pulled in. A cleaning and washing area will be required. This area must have good drainage, and access must be well planned. Good maintenance requires a clean area. This means the shop should have a concrete floor embedded with rails so that heavy equipment will not crack it. The shop must be well lighted and properly ventilated. Some type of overhead crane must be provided, its size depending on the equipment maintained. If extensive cutting and welding are anticipated, the area for this purpose should be separated from the general repair area. Some place must be provided to store spare parts and servicing supplies. This area must be clean and dry and kept locked to minimize pilferage.

Spare Parts and Service Supplies

It is often necessary to stock certain expendable repair and replacement parts to avoid excessive equipment downtime. The extent of parts to be stocked will depend on availability of supply, the importance of the unit to job progress, and the amount of equipment of a given type on the job.

When moving into a new area, a contractor should establish a working relationship with the area dealers, providing them with information on the number, condition, and models of equipment to be maintained. As realistic a picture as possible of expected parts and service requirements should be given to the dealers, and which items should be stocked and in what quantity should be determined. The contractor should stock only expendable and maintenance items required in day-to-day service and operation, or parts with a known failure rate. Internal parts for engines, transmissions, or other gear cases should not be stocked unless experience has shown that specific parts are subject to failure without damaging other parts. Complete major components can be obtained from dealers on an exchange basis. In some cases, where the project is remote or the quantity of equipment is large enough, it may be desirable to stock spare engines or transmissions.

Spare-parts control should include inventorying a shipment as it arrives on the job, making notations as parts are used, and reordering to keep stock up to required levels.

When purchasing parts for an overhaul or major repair, the contractor should purchase with the understanding that surplus parts will be returned. This is important because parts are often ordered before the unit is completely disassembled. All dealers will accept these terms provided parts are returned to them in their original containers.

Service

Servicing must be the foundation for an effective preventive-maintenance program. Petroleum companies are the best source of information for selection of lubricants and solution of service problems.

A contractor should use products of reputable suppliers and try to avoid the use of special lubricants. It is not necessary to use additives since the proper additives have been added by the refinery and special additives are expensive. Manufacturers' recommendations should be followed as closely as possible, but to reduce cost, the minimum of different lubricants that will meet the needs of the equipment should be used.

A list of fuels, lubricants, and supplies required should be prepared and minimum stock maintained. The lubrication specialist should never be caught with inadequate amounts of lubricants and supplies. The supplier should warehouse enough for current needs and set up a supply schedule. Where possible, lubricants should be delivered in bulk because they are sold on a volume discount.

Storage areas must be in a clean and protected location, and proper storage techniques should be used. Most petroleum companies will provide storage tanks at no cost or at a minimum rental. Cleanliness in the handling of lubricants is of the utmost importance.

The lubrication people are generally responsible for fueling, checking and changing crankcase and gear-case oils, maintaining coolant level, servicing air cleaners and breathers, changing filters, general greasing, and caring for batteries. Equipment manufacturers provide information pertaining to the service requirements of their units.

The work should be scheduled so the lubrication people can make the best use of their time. Equipment should be parked so the lubrication people can reach all necessary points easily. Units should also be parked together to minimize service travel time. Oil changes should be scheduled so service for the various units is staggered to balance the work load.

Tires

Today much construction equipment rides on $10,000 or more worth of rubber. Therefore, every contractor benefits from on-the-job tire care.

Tire service can be purchased from major tire companies. These companies will contract for tire service and provide manpower, service truck, and know-how. This service will be tailored to the job. The cost will vary with the equipment and job conditions, but in most cases will keep tire maintenance costs in line.

Safety

No discussion of equipment maintenance and service would be complete without mentioning safety. Construction does not produce the safest working conditions, and maintenance and service are among the most hazardous operations. To make maintenance operations safer, the contractor should provide safe working conditions and proper tools, and make sure safe work rules are enforced. Remember, accidents reduce profit.

RECORDS AND COST DISTRIBUTION

The importance of good record keeping cannot be overemphasized. Records provide maintenance costs and information needed to distribute equipment cost to job items so that correct job costs are included in future bids. Analysis of these records also helps in planning and controlling maintenance costs and will indicate abusive equipment operation, maintenance errors, equipment flaws, or equipment misapplication.

The hardest task in record keeping is to impress people with the importance of good, properly kept records. Records must be brief yet complete. Incomplete records are as worthless as no records at all, but if they are made too comprehensive there will not be enough time to fill them out. Examples of important records are given in Figs. 13.1 to 13.5.

Equipment Identification Card

Proper management of equipment requires a detailed inventory of all major items. This should include the manufacturer, model, year and number, attachments, and a list of the major components and parts required for normal service. This record should also provide a place to list major repairs. The card must be made up as soon as the equipment is purchased and must be transferred as the equipment is transferred. This record is useful when buying attachments and replacements or repair parts. It is useful in the future when purchasing new equipment to review experience and to help determine when to replace equipment (Figure 13.1).

This record should be filed even after the equipment is disposed of because it provides important cost information on its operation. (Once the equipment has been disposed of and has been obsoleted, the record itself becomes of little value.)

Equipment Rental

One reason for bankruptcy is the contractor's failure to charge rental on equipment owned. If this cost is not charged to the proper job items, later bids based on past experience will be inaccurate. In addition, when it comes time for equipment replacement, no money is available.

The rental rate is determined by establishing the total cost, i.e., cost of the original equipment plus the additional cost for increased price of replacement units, obsolescence, and possible idle time. Specialized equipment may have to be written off on one job. If so, the rental rate must be such that when it is multiplied by the hours worked, it will equal the total cost of the unit. There are various rental rates established by rental agencies and distributors. One such rate is

EQUIPMENT IDENTIFICATION	COMPONENT	MAKE	MODEL	SERIAL NO.
	Engine			
	Auxiliary Engine			
	Transmission			
	Auxiliary Trans.			
	Power Take Off			
	Final Drive			
	Starter			
	Generator			
	Battery			
	Compressor			
	Steering Pump			
	Hyd. Pump			
	Tires: Front			
	Tires: Center			
	Tires: Rear			
	Filters: Fuel			
	Filters: Lube Oil			
	Filters: Trans.			
	Filters: Final Drive			
	Filters: Air			
	V-Belts: Fan			
	V-Belts: Alternator			
	V-Belts: Water Pump			
	V-Belts: Steering			
	Spark Plugs			
	Other Attachments			
	Overall Length			
	Overall Width			
	Overall Height			
	Total Weight			

(Left margin labels: MODEL YEAR, PURCHASED FROM, NAME, DATE ACQUIRED, MODEL, SERIAL NO., MAKE)

FIGURE 13.1 Table of equipment identification.

compiled by AED (Associated Equipment Distributors). This is a statistical average and is not intended for establishing definite rental rates.

In order to assure that rental is being paid by the jobs, the equipment should be permanently assigned and a definite rental rate established. The rate may be hourly, daily, weekly, or monthly.

Once the job rate is established, the job must pay to a central fund the rental on the equipment assigned to it. The only exceptions occur when the equipment is being repaired, awaits transfer, is in dead storage, or is idle because of bad weather. The job must have an equipment time card so that the rental cost can be distributed to the appropriate job items. This could be a separate card, but in order to keep the amount of paper work to a minimum, the equipment time card could be on the back of the employee time card (Fig. 13.2).

DAILY EQUIPMENT TIME REPORT			
DATE_____ SHIFT_____ FOREMAN_____			
EQUIPMENT NO.	TYPE OF EQUIPMENT	HOURS	COST ITEM

FIGURE 13.2   Daily equipment time report.

Equipment Utilization Report

To document the equipment rental report, there must be some way to identify inactive equipment. This can be done by using an equipment utilization report which is filled out monthly by the job personnel or whenever equipment is put in dead storage or is available for transfer. The report should be sent to the person responsible for managing equipment. In this way, the rental rates can be verified and equipment available for transfer identified. If the equipment is transferred, a copy of the utilization report and the equipment identification card should be forwarded to the receiving job (Fig. 13.3).

Maintenance Records

Significant equipment repairs are kept on the back of the equipment identification card. Any other maintenance records are primarily for job use. It is these records which inform the mechanic when work or lubrication is required. The key to proper maintenance, again, is preventive maintenance. It is everyone's responsibility to be alert for minor problems and to report them immediately. Reports must be written and turned over to the equipment supervisor for proper handling. Although reports do not have to be lengthy, they should be uniform in format. If written on a scrap of paper, they will probably be overlooked or discarded. Labeled "gripe sheet" or "repair request," these reports should identify the equipment requiring attention and state the problem clearly. When they are signed by the reporter, the mechanic can check for any additional information and inform the originator of the outcome of the repairs (Fig. 13.4).

The lubrication specialist must have a schedule of the lubrication required. This should be a chart listing all the equipment on the job. As the equipment is lubricated, it should be so noted. The amount of makeup oil between changes

EQUIPMENT UTILIZATION REPORT						
DATE_____				JOB NO._____		
EQUIP. NO.	TYPE OF EQUIPMENT	HOURS WK'D	HOURS IDLE	ARRIVED	MOVED	AVAILABLE

Reasons for idle hours:

  W - Weather

  R - Repair

  D - Dead Storage

EXAMPLE: 8-W means "8 hours down because of weather".

FIGURE 13.3 Equipment utilization report.

DATE	HOURS OR MILEAGE	REPAIRS

FIGURE 13.4 Repair log.

should also be noted to provide a check on component condition. The chart will also help the lubrication specialist determine which supplies to keep on hand.

Tire Records

The amount of money spent on off-highway tires justifies records to ensure maximum service life. Tires are listed on the equipment identification card, and when changes are made, they should be noted as significant repairs. The contractor should make sure that hours of service from the tire are noted. If the tire change is made because of a failure, another report should be made stating the condition and reasons for the failure. This record will help determine adjustments from the manufacturer.

Computer Records

Many contractors are developing computer programs to help with their record keeping. This can be done by buying a computer, leasing time, or sending the work to a data center for processing. There are many computer consultants who have devised equipment programs to keep a record of significant events. The practical facts about such a program can be learned from the business-equipment manufacturer, a data-processing center, or a consulting firm. However, it is important to note that the output can be no better than the input, and the input is the contractor's responsibility.

REPLACEMENT

A planned equipment-replacement program can save unnecessary expense. Machines should be traded when the accumulated cost per hour becomes progressively higher. Operating a machine after it has passed its point of economic operation or trading in the equipment while accumulative cost is becoming lower will reduce profits.

Determining replacement time is difficult, and all too often equipment is replaced on a hit-or-miss basis. Some owners replace their equipment when it requires a major overhaul. Some trade as they begin a major project; others wait until they have sufficient capital. With the cost of equipment constantly rising, a contractor cannot afford this hit-or-miss replacement program.

In order to establish replacement timing, the contractor must make a thorough study of the six factors which influence the replacement time. They are depreciation costs, ownership costs, replacement costs, downtime costs, maintenance costs, and the cost of obsolescence.

These factors are influenced by job conditions, maintenance care, and operation. There is a wide variation in these factors from one contractor to another. Therefore, any replacement program must be based on in-house records and repair costs. The following example shows the effect of these various factors and is not based on actual data.

Assume a piece of equipment with a purchase price of $100,000 that has worked 2000 hours per year (assuming 95 percent availability). All six factors will be considered separately, showing their effect on cumulative costs per hour.

Depreciation Costs

For replacement purposes, consider the true or actual depreciation. Actual depreciation is the dollar difference between purchase price and selling or trading price.

With more frequent model improvements, a greater percentage of depreciation costs occurs during the equipment's first few years. Frequent model changes and

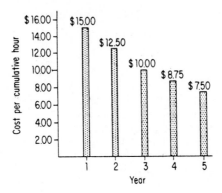

TABLE 13.1 Depreciation Costs at $100,000 Initial Price with 2000 Working Hours per Year

	Year				
Item	1	2	3	4	5
Trade-in value, % of delivered price	70	50	40	30	25
Trade-in value	$70,000	$50,000	$40,000	$30,000	$25,000
Yearly depreciation	$30,000	$20,000	$10,000	$10,000	$ 5,000
Cumulative depreciation	$30,000	$50,000	$60,000	$70,000	$75,000
Cumulative equipment hours	2,000	4,000	6,000	8,000	10,000
Depreciation cost per hour	$15.00	$12.50	$10.00	$8.75	$7.50

innovations have a definite effect on resale or trade-in value, and thus a greater depreciation cost must be paid by the initial owner.

The resale value of a piece of equipment will vary widely depending on its condition, its state of obsolescence, and the general market. Depreciation rate varies for different types of equipment just as economic life varies. For example, a crane may have an economic life of 10 years while a tractor and ripper operation may have an economic life of 4 years.

Although future resale value of equipment cannot be assured by studying current used prices, a reasonable value can be estimated. For example, assume the values in Table 13.1. If depreciation alone is considered, the machine will be retained indefinitely.

Ownership Costs

Ownership costs are usually estimated as a percent of the average investment cost and can vary greatly from one area and one owner to another. The following items are part of ownership costs (Table 13.2):

1. *Interest and finance charge:* Regardless of whether a unit is purchased with borrowed or capital funds, interest must be charged. If the unit is bought with capital funds, interest must be charged equal to that which could have been earned if the capital funds had been invested. When all factors are considered, 10 percent is not unrealistic for interest and finance charges.

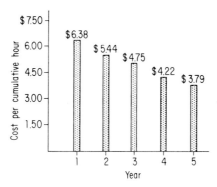

TABLE 13.2 Ownership Cost

Item	Year				
	1	2	3	4	5
Investment (first of year)	$100,000	$70,000	$50,000	$10,000	$30,000
Less depreciation	$ 30,000	$20,000	$10,000	$10,000	$ 5,000
Investment (end year)	$ 70,000	$50,000	$40,000	$30,000	$25,000
Avg. yearly investment	$ 85,000	$60,000	$45,000	$35,000	$27,500
Ownership cost, 15%	$ 12,750	$ 9,000	$ 6,750	$ 5,250	$ 4,125
Cumulative ownership cost	$ 12,750	$21,750	$28,500	$33,750	$37,875
Cumulative equipment hours	2,000	4,000	6,000	8,000	10,000
Ownership cost per cumulative hour	$6.38	$5.44	$4.75	$4.22	$3.79

2. *Property tax:* Although there may be a few areas where there is no property tax, the average rate is approximately 2 percent.

3. *Insurance:* Although many owners carry their own insurance, money must still be set aside for fire, theft, and damage to the equipment. This will vary from 2 to 4 percent.

For example, use 15 percent of the average yearly investment for ownership costs. Ownership costs favor retaining the machine indefinitely.

Replacement Costs

The price of equipment is increasing every year. Some prices increased as much as 8 percent in the last few years. The average increase for all equipment was 4.3 percent. For the last 10 years, the increase has been approximately 5 percent. For the purpose of this example, assume that this 5 percent per year increase will continue.

The purchasing power of the dollar is decreasing by 2 percent every year. The example assumes that this trend will continue. Combining the increased purchase price with the decrease in the purchasing power of the dollar, we can arrive at the replacement cost (see Table 13.3). Replacement costs favor retention. However, this item has a much smaller influence on cumulative cost.

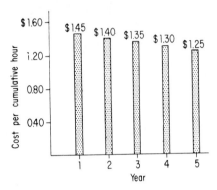

TABLE 13.3 Replacement Costs

Item	Year				
	1	2	3	4	5
Price replacement	$105,000	$110,000	$115,000	$120,000	$125,000
5% increase per year price adjustment;	$102,900	$105,600	$108,100	$110,400	$112,500
2% decrease purchasing power of dollar					
Less original cost	$100,000	$100,000	$100,000	$100,000	$100,000
Loss on replacement	$ 2,900	$ 5,600	$ 8,100	$ 10,400	$ 12,500
Cumulative equipment hours	2,000	4,000	6,000	8,000	10,000
Loss replacement per cumulative hour	$1.45	$1.40	$1.35	$1.30	$1.25

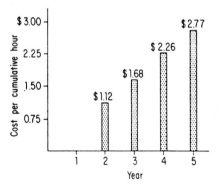

TABLE 13.4 Downtime Costs

Item	Year				
	1	2	3	4	5
Availability	95	93	91	87	85
Hours available	2000	1953	1,911	1,827	1,785
Hours lost	0	147	189	273	315
Cost at $30 per hour	0	$4410	$ 5,670	$ 8,190	$ 9,450
Cumulative downtime cost	0	$4410	$10,080	$18,270	$27,720
Cumulative equipment hours	2000	4000	6,000	8,000	10,000
Cumulative downtime cost per hour	0	$1.12	$1.68	$2.26	$2.77

Downtime Costs

Normal wear and tear will increase downtime as a machine becomes older. Downtime is a loss of profit. To maintain the 2000 hours of production time would require rental of another unit for the downtime period. Availability must be maintained as required for the job. This will vary with the age of the machine and operating conditions.

For the example, availability figures shown in Table 13.4 are used. Since 2000 hours was already based on 95 percent availability, this will be the figure for the first year. For cost, outside rental is estimated to be $30 per hour.

Downtime costs favor replacing the machine every year. With a trend toward bigger and faster machines, this factor plays an increasing role in equipment replacement.

Maintenance Costs

With more downtime, maintenance costs increase. These costs will vary greatly from one machine to another in the same fleet. The figures used should be based on actual experience. However, some contractors estimate these costs as percentage of depreciation, which varies a great deal. In some instances, it is 50 percent of the total depreciation for the life of the machine, while in others it may be as great as 100 percent of the total depreciation during a 3-year period. This estimate must be backed by experience to be valid. Individual machine-repair costs may show an irregular pattern. This is the result of major overhauls or expensive replacements. Figure 13.5 shows the actual repair costs on one unit.

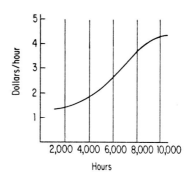

FIGURE 13.5   Repair costs, one unit.

For this example, we use the average actual repair cost for the fleet, which will closely parallel the costs shown in Fig. 13.5. The effect of maintenance costs on a replacement program is shown in Table 13.5.

Price of Obsolescence

With the increase in size and speed of equipment, another factor of replacement costs must be the cost of obsolescence. This is the cost of owning a piece of equipment which has been superseded by a more efficient or higher production machine.

Past history indicates that change in models or introduction of new models occurs every 2 to 3 years. These improvements have increased production by approximately 10 percent per year. This means that for every year that a piece of equipment has been superseded by a new model, it must operate an additional 10 percent more hours to achieve the same production. Table 13.6 shows the effect of obsolescence on replacements. For this example, $30 per hour is used to determine the cost of obsolescence.

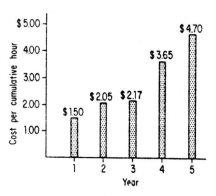

TABLE 13.5 Maintenance Costs

	Year				
Item	1	2	3	4	5
Maintenance cost	$3000	$5200	$ 7,820	$13,180	$17,850
Cumulative maintenance	$3000	$8200	$16,020	$29,200	$47,050
Cumulative availability	2000	4000	6,000	8,000	10,000
Cumulative maintenance cost per hour	$1.50	$2.05	$2.17	$3.65	$4.70

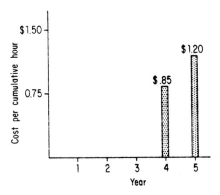

TABLE 13.6 Cost of Obsolescence

	Year				
Item	1	2	3	4	5
Obsolescence factor, %				10	10
Additional hours to match production of new model			200		200
Cost at $30 per hour			$6000	$ 6,000	
Cumulative cost			$6000	$12,000	
Cumulative equipment hours	2000	4000	6000	8000	10,000
Obsolescence cost per cumulative hour			$0.85	$1.20	

If only obsolescence is considered, the equipment would be replaced with each model change.

Summary

When considered separately, some of the factors favored retaining indefinitely, while others indicated a trade each year. The total effect, rather than the individual, shows the most economical time to replace. Table 13.7 is a summary of all the factors which influence the equipment-replacement program and their total cost per cumulative hour.

TABLE 13.7 Summary of Costs

Factor	Year				
	1	2	3	4	5
Depreciation	$15.00	$12.50	$10.00	$ 8.75	$ 7.50
Ownership	$ 6.38	$ 5.44	$ 4.75	$ 4.22	$ 3.79
Replacement	$ 1.45	$ 1.40	$ 1.35	$ 1.30	$ 1.25
Downtime	0	$ 1.12	$ 1.68	$ 2.26	$ 2.77
Maintenance	$ 1.50	$ 2.05	$ 2.67	$ 3.65	$ 4.70
Obsolescence	0	0	0	$ 0.75	$ 1.20
Total cumulative cost per hour	$24.33	$22.51	$20.45	$20.93	$21.21

The time to replace a piece of equipment is when the cost per cumulative hour begins to rise. In this example, this would occur at the end of 3 years. Certain situations require a special review of these factors. Getting a long-term job which requires new equipment may be sufficient reason to trade before the normal economical replacement time. Equipment requiring major overhauls may be traded instead of repaired. The completion of a job may also be a reason for replacement. However, all these reasons must be backed up by records and an analysis of cost before they can be justified.

Just as selecting and buying the right equipment can save the contractor money, so can the proper replacement program. To have equipment which is too new or too old is costly. There is only one ideal time to replace, and this must be based on experience.

Trading or Selling of Used Equipment

The contractor must make a decision whether to trade in or to sell the used equipment. There is a good market for certain name-brand used equipment, and a contractor can probably make money selling directly. Table 13.8 takes the $100,000 piece of equipment used in the example and shows what might be expected.

This is not $10,000 profit, because the unit will have to be cleaned and painted as well as advertised and sold. The cost to sell will vary, and some items that are specialized may end up creating a loss.

TABLE 13.8 Final Summary

Cost of new machine	$115,000
Cash discount	15,000
Cash price	$100,000
Trade-in of old unit	$ 35,000
Less cash	15,000
Cash value of old unit	$ 20,000
Sale price of old unit	$ 30,000
Less trade cash value	20,000
Difference between trade-in and selling	$ 10,000

ADMINISTRATION

The method used to administer this program will depend upon the size of the company and the type of work it does. The most important thing, regardless of size, is designation of one individual who has the responsibility for making all major purchases based on a study of field information.

In a small company this will probably be handled by one individual who selects and purchases the equipment and follows up to make sure the equipment is working at a profit. This individual is usually given the title of purchasing agent (PA). By the nature of this job, the equipment PA must have mechanical aptitude as well as an understanding of equipment operations.

In larger companies there should be all or combinations of the following departments:

1. Equipment
2. Purchasing
3. Field

Equipment Department

This department must be charged with the responsibility of coordinating all phases of equipment management. This is the department that ensures that equipment is operating profitably. It requires personnel that have mechanical aptitude and an understanding of equipment operations.

The department should have equipment-cost figures available to help estimators determine the method used to build a project when they are submitting bids. Once the method is established, the department should provide operational cost, purchase price, and production information on equipment and plants to incorporate into bids. If bid successfully, the equipment department, the estimators, and the project personnel should take another look at the method to be used and the equipment selected.

After the equipment is put to work, this department should be certain that adequate records are being kept to determine production rates and costs. It also should provide guidelines for the operation and maintenance of the equipment, and when problems occur, the equipment department should provide solutions.

After the project is completed, the equipment department must compile the field reports and data. This will provide the information in one centralized location so that it will be readily available to the rest of the organization. This will avoid duplication and give a more complete and adequate record of equipment operations.

The equipment department must continually evaluate new equipment and developments. This will require reviewing technical publications and manufacturers' literature as well as visiting manufacturers' representatives and plants. The manufacturer contacts are also valuable in arriving at solutions to equipment problems which develop.

Purchasing Department

This is the department which does the actual purchasing. Once the type and manufacturer of equipment have been selected, the purchasing department should be called on to procure it. This requires contacting the various suppliers and asking for quotes on the units desired. Once the quotes are received, they must be analyzed to determine which supplier can provide the best service at the best price and meet the delivery schedule required. On equipment where delivery schedule is critical because of poor planning, scheduling, or some other reason, the purchasing department should be provided with two or three different manufacturers listed in order of preference.

One person who has the responsibility for major purchases is in a position to analyze quotes and determine which is a good price and which is not. This also helps to standardize both the equipment and the attachments on the equipment, making it more compatible with the rest of the fleet.

Field

At the project level there will be both operations and maintenance personnel responsible for the equipment. These two groups must coordinate their efforts and cooperate with each other.

The operations personnel must first make themselves aware of the design capabilities and limitations of the equipment and make sure it is operated within these limits. They should also study the equipment so they know when maintenance and service are required. Most engines require coolant, but many operators would run an engine with coolant leaks, which will do the same damage as running with no coolant. Supervision must understand the advantage of preventive maintenance and enforce its use to give maximum production.

Operation supervision must see to it that competent operators are hired and properly trained. They should make use of dealer's or manufacturer's training programs where appropriate. Operators who do not respond to training must be eliminated.

Schedules must be established to eliminate both excessive equipment idle time and overload periods. Equipment needs should be determined with proper lead time to allow procurement of the best equipment for the job.

Operation and maintenance personnel must work together to establish a proper balance between equipment availability and maintenance cost. Crash repair programs must be eliminated. Scheduled maintenance must be compatible with both operation and maintenance. Field personnel must establish a favorable working relationship with dealers. A determination must be made as to which spare parts will have to be stocked. Once stocked, they must be properly administered.

Equipment maintenance and service are the maintenance personnel's responsibility. They must keep supervision advised as to the equipment status.

Equipment management can mean the difference between job profit and loss. In the future, as equipment costs rise and mechanics become more scarce, equipment management will have an increasing effect on job profits.

CHAPTER 14
CONSTRUCTION SAFETY

Paul E. Harmon, P.E., N.S.P.E., A.S.C.E., A.C.I.
Associate Professor of Construction Management
University of Nebraska
Lincoln, Nebraska

INTRODUCTION

The construction industry has long recognized the demand for a safe work environment on all of its projects. Everyone associated with the construction process has a responsibility to act in a manner that will not endanger the lives and property of others. By definition, an accident is "an event occurring by chance from an unknown cause," but data have shown that the majority of accidents result from negligence. With proper training and guidance the number and severity of the accidents recorded can be substantially reduced.

A contractor must be concerned about safety not only for humanitarian reasons, but also because of the economic and legal impacts accidents may have on the firm. A good safety record can also improve the public image of the company. The humanitarian basis for safety is quite apparent. If a fellow employee is killed or disabled as a result of an accident, everyone understandably is distressed. Reducing human pain and suffering resulting from accidents and illnesses is the prime objective of safety based solely on humanitarian concerns. However, many contractors fail to realize the financial consequences of accidents. Worker's compensation premiums, public liability, property damage, and equipment insurance rates are based on a company's historic accident record. Incentives include not only reducing direct costs for insurance premiums, but minimizing many indirect costs as a result of accidents.

IMPORTANCE OF SAFETY

The construction industry, employing nearly 5 percent of the total labor force in this country, accounts for nearly 11 percent of all occupational injuries and 20 percent of all deaths resulting from occupational accidents (see Table 14.1). This equates to nearly $9 billion in losses per year, for both direct and indirect costs of accidents. Many of these accidents, as represented by Fig. 14.1, could be elimi-

TABLE 14.1 Employment and Occupational Injury and Illness Fatalities

For employers with 11 employees or more by industry division 1985 and 1986

Industry division	Annual average employment				Fatalities			
	1985		1986		1985		1986	
	Number (thousands)	Percent	Number (thousands)	Percent	Number	Percent	Number	Percent
Private sector*	70,263	100	71,739	100	3,750	100	3,610	100
Agriculture, forestry, and fishing	807	1	804	1	100	3	110	3
Mining	829	1	681	1	260	7	200	6
Construction	3,603	5	3,745	5	980	26	670	19
Manufacturing	18,690	27	18,358	26	820	22	770	21
Transportation and public utilities	4,836	7	4,841	7	730	20	800	22
Wholesale and retail trade	18,851	27	19,423	27	440	12	510	14
Finance, insurance, and real estate	4,932	7	5,267	7	70	2	190	5
Services	17,715	25	18,617	26	340	9	370	10

*Employment data are derived primarily from the BLS-State Current Employment Statistics program. Employment and fatality estimates have been adjusted to exclude establishments with fewer than 11 employees as obtained from the Annual Survey of Occupational Injuries and Illnesses. *Note:* Because of rounding, components may not add to totals.

Source: Bureau of Labor Statistics.

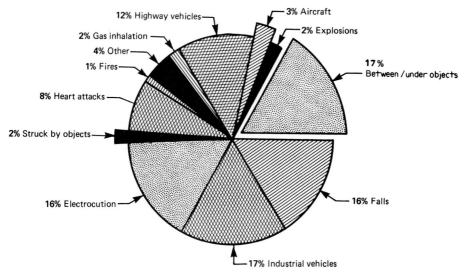

FIGURE 14.1 Causes of construction fatalities: 1986.

nated or greatly reduced, thereby reducing the overall costs of the construction industry. As stated earlier the reasons for considering safety include

1. *Humanitarian concern:* The suffering as a result of an accident both to injured parties and their families cannot be measured in economic terms. The contractor should never disregard this, even when the injured parties have been adequately compensated by insurance.
2. *Economic considerations:* The contractor must realize that even with adequate insurance coverage, accidents will reduce company profits through the increased costs of future insurance premiums. Direct and indirect costs or hidden costs of accidents have been identified as (see Fig. 14.2):
    a. Direct costs:
       (1) medical
       (2) compensation
    b. Indirect or hidden costs:
       (1) time lost from work by injured
       (2) loss in earning power
       (3) economic loss to injured's family
       (4) lost time by fellow workers
       (5) loss of efficiency by breaking up crew
       (6) cost to train new employee
       (7) damage to equipment and tools
       (8) loss of production
       (9) failure to fill orders
       (10) overhead costs (while work was disrupted)
3. *Legal considerations:* The Occupational Safety and Health Act of 1970 (OSHA) is a comprehensive set of safety and health regulations, inspection procedures, and record keeping requirements. OSHA requires that each employer provide to each of his employees a place of employment that is free

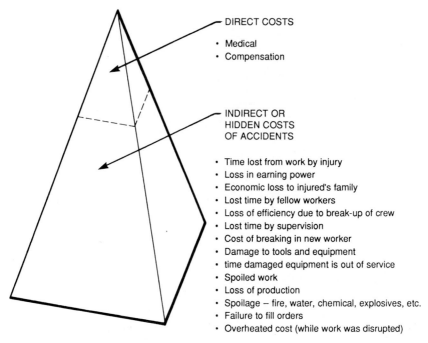

DIRECT COSTS

• Medical
• Compensation

INDIRECT OR
HIDDEN COSTS
OF ACCIDENTS

• Time lost from work by injury
• Loss in earning power
• Economic loss to injured's family
• Lost time by fellow workers
• Loss of efficiency due to break-up of crew
• Lost time by supervision
• Cost of breaking in new worker
• Damage to tools and equipment
• time damaged equipment is out of service
• Spoiled work
• Loss of production
• Spoilage – fire, water, chemical, explosives, etc.
• Failure to fill orders
• Overheated cost (while work was disrupted)

FIGURE 14.2   Hidden costs of accidents.

the employee. The law also established both civil and criminal penalties for violation of OSHA regulations.
4. *Company image:* A good safety record is a proven means of increasing worker morale and productivity. This in turn improves the company's public image, and therefore improves the company's bargaining position for negotiating future jobs.

BASIC ELEMENTS OF A SAFETY PROGRAM

The key to any successful safety program is organization. The method by which management assigns responsibilities for accident prevention and assures performance under these responsibilities is paramount to a safety program.

The National Safety Council has identified seven basic elements of successful safety programs as gathered from surveys of all sizes and types of organizations:

1. Declaration of management policy and leadership
2. Assignment of responsibility, authority, and accountability
3. Maintenance of safe working conditions
4. Establishment of safety training
5. Establishment of an accident reporting and analysis system
6. Creation of medical and first aid programs
7. Acceptance of personal accountability by employees

Management Policy

A critical task in developing a viable safety program is to define management's policy. Most programs fail due to the lack of sincere interest by top management. If top-level management is not authentically interested in safety procedures, most likely no one else in the company will be. The policy established should contain only what can be supported by intentions and resources available (see Fig. 14.3). The safety program goals (see Fig. 14.4) should be achievable, but demanding and measurable, so that accomplishments can be monitored and measured. When setting safety goals, it is important to develop a plan by which the goal can be achieved (see Fig. 14.5).

ANY COMPANY CONSTRUCTION, INC.

SAFETY POLICY STATEMENT

It is the policy of the management of ANY CONSTRUCTION COMPANY, INC. that all reachable and practical efforts will be made to provide a safe and healthful place of employment for all employees and to do everything reasonable to protect equipment and other properties from accidental losses.

Accidents interfere with the orderly progress of our work and are indications of an inefficient operation. All necessary action will be taken to prevent losses at the lowest operating level consistent with the operating policy of this firm.

It is the intent of this firm to comply with all local, state, and federal safety standards, codes, and regulations. We expect every employee of the firm to perform their job in a safe manner and in accordance with the procedures outlined in the company safety program.

SIGNED: _____

TITLE: _____

FIRM: _____   DATE:_____

FIGURE 14.3   Sample safety policy statement.

SAFETY PROGRAM GOALS

It is the policy of the firm that both long- and short-term goals be set to be accomplished within our safety program. The goals established will be based on the need to improve safety performance and to reduce the operating expenses associated with accidents.

At the beginning of each year major objectives to be accomplished for the year will be established. Short-term or specific goals will be established as the need arises. Goals will be documented on the SAFETY PROGRAM GOALS form and filed for use on all projects.

Recognition of the problem and the establishment of a goal to overcome the problem are primary steps; determining the solution to the problem is the challenge. The goals must be realistic and obtainable to make the plan workable.

FIGURE 14.4   Sample statement of safety program goals.

```
┌─────────────────────────────────────────────────────────────────┐
│                     SAFETY PROGRAM GOALS                          │
│   START DATE:_____        COMPLETION DATE:_____    │
│                                                                   │
│   GOALS:                                                          │
│     A.  _____       │
│         _____       │
│         _____       │
│                                                                   │
│     B.  _____       │
│         _____       │
│         _____       │
│                                                                   │
│     C.  _____       │
│         _____       │
│         _____       │
│         _____       │
│                                                                   │
│   PLAN FOR ACCOMPLISHING GOALS:                                   │
│     A.  _____       │
│         _____       │
│         _____       │
│                                                                   │
│     B.  _____       │
│         _____       │
│         _____       │
│                                                                   │
│     C.  _____       │
│         _____       │
│         _____       │
│                                                                   │
│   SIGNED: _____                         │
│   TITLE: _____                         │
│   FIRM: _____                         │
│   DATE: _____                         │
└─────────────────────────────────────────────────────────────────┘
```

FIGURE 14.5 Sample evaluation form for monitoring safety policy goals.

Safety Responsibilities

Once the safety program has been established, assignment of responsibilities, authority, and accountability must be made. To be effective, the safety program will require the effort and attention of each member of the firm. Active management and control of a safety program may be vested in the top executive, the general manager, or a qualified supervisor with both authority and status.

Company managers generally assume the responsibilities of program implementation, measurement of performance, budget and expenditures for safety, and approval of policies, to name a few. Most important, since management has full responsibility for the safety program and the results that are achieved, it must set a proper example in safety for all employees.

The supervisors become a key element in any safety program due to their direct contact with the workers. To the employees the supervisor is management. General duties of the supervisor include inspection of the workplace for compliance with work rules and safety standards, instruction of employees on safety procedures, maintenance of a safe and healthful workplace, treatment of injuries, investigation of accidents and injuries, and compilation of accident and injury reports as required (see Fig. 14.6).

REPORT OF INJURY

Project _____

Name of injured _____

Date injured _____ time _____ craft _____

Lost time injury   yes _____   no _____   not known _____

Nature of task at time of injury _____

How long has injured been employed by company?_____

Was employee instructed in assigned task? _____

Describe how accident occurred _____

_____

_____

Nature of injury _____

_____

_____

Witnesses _____

_____

_____

What was the cause of the accident? _____

_____

_____

How could this accident have been prevented? _____

_____

Has this accident been discussed at the job site safety meetings? _____

Yes _____   no _____   date _____

Supervisor's comments_____

_____

_____

_____

_____

_____   _____

Foreman's/supervisor's signature   Date

FIGURE 14.6   Sample injury report for job-site accident.

The employees' responsibilities are to work in accordance with safe job practices and comply with the company's safety rules, to use personal protective equipment, to report unsafe conditions, to perform only jobs that they have been trained or checked out on, and to take an active part in safety meetings.

Working Conditions

Hazards in the workplace must be identified before any preventive maintenance program can be implemented. Minimum guidelines should be defined based on federal, state, and voluntary safety and health standards. Inspections by qualified personnel should be made to identify the immediate hazards for specific projects. Planned inspections should go beyond routine site checks. These inspections should be used to identify areas of safety deficiencies and to establish goals for improvement on future projects. Areas for such inspections should include but not be limited to processing and storage of materials; general housekeeping methods; compliance with electrical, lighting, and heating and ventilation standards; use and maintenance of hand and power tools; and fire prevention techniques.

Safety Training

Safety training has been shown to be most effective when provided during the employees' initial production training. It is important to influence the voluntary acts of employees by education and motivation. Good safety practice depends to a large part on the employees' own actions and conduct. It is management's responsibility to instruct employees in recognizing and avoiding unsafe and hazardous conditions associated with particular job assignments, and to ensure that they understand the safety regulations that may apply to particular work assignments. These instructional efforts are important to the loss-control concept. In addition, regular safety meetings and training sessions are a visible measure of the company's commitment to the safety program.

Safety Records

Accident records are an important tool of the safety program, serving a variety of purposes. By accurately recording accidents and their causes, identification of strengths and weaknesses can be easily tracked by management, making the task of improving the safety program easier. Records are also required by insurance carriers and many state and federal agencies for establishing industry guidelines and costs. Because of the varied uses of these data, the method of keeping records should be consistent with external requirements as well as the needs of the company. The Occupational Safety and Health Act (OSHA) requires a written report of each illness or injury (OSHA Form 101; see Fig. 14.7) as well as a log and annual summary of all injuries and illnesses (OSHA Form 200; see Fig. 14.8).

First Aid Programs

Medical and first aid programs should include elements and services designed to maintain the health and welfare of the work force by controlling or preventing occupational and nonoccupational diseases and accidents. The purpose of a first aid program is to treat minor injuries and to provide basic treatment to employees with more serious injuries until professional medical assistance can be administered. Training should be equivalent to those courses offered by the American Red Cross. A responsible and willing employee should be trained to handle the first aid on every job site. However, training of all employees has the advantage of not only ensuring adequate first aid staff on the job, but helping all employees to see the effects of accidents, providing them with an awareness that may make them more cautious and less likely to have an accident on the job.

Preplacement medical and physical exams are also an important aspect of safety evaluation and training. Once an employee's physical condition has been evaluated, a job can be assigned based on the worker's mental ability or physical capacity. A worker's disability (hearing, sight) may place the worker or fellow employees in a hazardous situation. Periodic follow-up exams are recommended for employees regularly exposed to processes or materials that are known health hazards.

Personal Accountability

The passing of laws, the development of safety and health regulations, and the threat of penalties for violations will not of themselves assure safety at the

Bureau of Labor Statistics
Supplementary Record of
Occupational Injuries and Illnesses

U.S. Department of Labor

This form is required by Public Law 91-596 and must be kept in the establishment for 5 years. Failure to maintain can result in the issuance of citations and assessment of penalties.	Case or File No.	Form Approved O.M.B. No. 1220-0029

Employer

1. Name

2. Mail address *(No. and street, city or town, State, and zip code)*

3. Location, if different from mail address

Injured or Ill Employee

4. Name *(First, middle, and last)* — Social Security No.

5. Home address *(No. and street, city or town, State, and zip code)*

6. Age

7. Sex *(Check one)* — Male ☐ Female ☐

8. Occupation *(Enter regular job title, not the specific activity he was performing at time of injury.)*

9. Department *(Enter name of department or division in which the injured person is regularly employed, even though he may have been temporarily working in another department at the time of injury.)*

The Accident or Exposure to Occupational Illness

If accident or exposure occurred on employer's premises, give address of plant or establishment in which it occurred. Do not indicate department or division within the plant or establishment. If accident occurred outside employer's premises at an identifiable address, give that address. If it occurred on a public highway or at any other place which cannot be identified by number and street, please provide place references locating the place of injury as accurately as possible.

10. Place of accident or exposure *(No. and street, city or town, State, and zip code)*

11. Was place of accident or exposure on employer's premises? Yes ☐ No ☐

12. What was the employee doing when injured? *(Be specific. If he was using tools or equipment or handling material, name them and tell what he was doing with them.)*

13. How did the accident occur? *(Describe fully the events which resulted in the injury or occupational illness. Tell what happened and how it happened. Name any objects or substances involved and tell how they were involved. Give full details on all factors which led or contributed to the accident. Use separate sheet for additional space.)*

Occupational Injury or Occupational Illness

14. Describe the injury or illness in detail and indicate the part of body affected. *(E.g., amputation of right index finger at second joint; fracture of ribs; lead poisoning; dermatitis of left hand, etc.)*

15. Name the object or substance which directly injured the employee. *(For example, the machine or thing he struck against or which struck him; the vapor or poison he inhaled or swallowed; the chemical or radiation which irritated his skin; or in cases of strains, hernias, etc., the thing he was lifting, pulling, etc.)*

16. Date of injury or initial diagnosis of occupational illness

17. Did employee die? *(Check one)* Yes ☐ No ☐

Other

18. Name and address of physician

19. If hospitalized, name and address of hospital

Date of report	Prepared by	Official position

OSHA No. 101 (Feb. 1981)

FIGURE 14.7 OSHA form 101.

Bureau of Labor Statistics
Log and Summary of Occupational
Injuries and Illnesses

U.S. Department of Labor

Page ___ of ___

For Calendar Year 19 ___

Form Approved
O.M.B. No. 44R 1453

NOTE: This form is required by Public Law 91-596 and must be kept in the establishment for 5 years. Failure to maintain and post can result in the issuance of citations and assessment of penalties. (See posting requirements on the other side of form.)

RECORDABLE CASES: You are required to record information about every occupational death, every nonfatal occupational illness, and those nonfatal occupational injuries which involve one or more of the following: loss of consciousness, restriction of work or motion, transfer to another job, or medical treatment (other than first aid). (See definitions on the other side of form.)

Company Name ___
Establishment Name ___
Establishment Address ___

Case or File Number	Date of Injury or Onset of Illness	Employee's Name	Occupation	Department	Description of Injury or Illness
Enter a nonduplicating number which will facilitate comparisons with supplementary records.	Enter Mo./day.	Enter first name or initial, middle initial, last name.	Enter regular job title, not activity employee was performing when injured or at onset of illness. In the absence of a formal title, enter a brief description of the employee's duties.	Enter department in which the employee is regularly employed or a description of normal workplace to which employee is assigned, even though temporarily working in another department at the time of injury or illness.	Enter a brief description of the injury or illness and indicate the part or parts of body affected. Typical entries for this column might be: Amputation of 1st joint right forefinger; Strain of lower back; Contact dermatitis on both hands; Electrocution—body.
(A)	(B)	(C)	(D)	(E)	(F)

Extent of and Outcome of INJURY

Fatalities	Nonfatal Injuries			Injuries Without Lost Workdays
Injury Related	Injuries With Lost Workdays			
Enter DATE of death. Mo./day/yr.	Enter a CHECK if injury involves days away from work, or days of restricted work activity, or both.	Enter a CHECK if injury involves days away from work.	Enter number of DAYS away from work.	Enter number of DAYS of restricted work activity.	Enter a CHECK if no entry was made in columns 1 or 2 but the injury is recordable as defined above.
(1)	(2)	(3)	(4)	(5)	(6)

Type, Extent of, and Outcome of ILLNESS

Type of Illness — CHECK Only One Column for Each Illness (See other side of form for terminations or permanent transfers.)

(a) Occupational skin diseases or disorders	(b) Dust diseases of the lungs	(c) Respiratory conditions due to toxic agents	(d) Poisoning (systemic effects of toxic materials)	(e) Disorders due to physical agents	(f) Disorders associated with repeated trauma	(g) All other occupational illnesses

Fatalities
Illness Related
Enter DATE of death. Mo./day/yr.
(8)

Nonfatal Illnesses
Illnesses With Lost Workdays
Enter a CHECK if illness involves days away from work, or days of restricted work activity, or both. (9)
Enter a CHECK if illness involves days away from work. (10)
Enter number of DAYS away from work. (11)
Enter number of DAYS of restricted work activity. (12)

Illnesses Without Lost Workdays
Enter a CHECK if no entry was made in columns 8 or 9. (13)

PREVIOUS PAGE TOTALS →

TOTALS (Instructions on other side of form.)

Certification of Annual Summary Totals By ___ Title ___ Date ___

POST ONLY THIS PORTION OF THE LAST PAGE NO LATER THAN FEBRUARY 1.

OSHA No. 200

OSHA No. 200

ILLNESSES

INJURIES

FIGURE 14.8 OSHA form 200. Log and summary of occupational injuries and illnesses.

workplace. Employees' safety will depend largely upon their own conduct and concern coupled with the interest and leadership shown by management.

To make sure that employees take the responsibility for personal accountability, management must provide leadership by:

1. Conforming to the policies and guidelines established for the workers on the job site, thus setting a leadership example
2. Attending the safety meetings along with the employees
3. Making sure that safety is emphasized as a tool for increasing efficiency and productivity
4. Reviewing and acting upon the safety records (good and bad) of the individual employees and production units
5. Posting notices, bulletins, and other public announcements for all employees to see

Safety Procedures

Numerous studies have shown that most construction accidents directly involve construction equipment, excavation and trenching failures, collapse of structures (including temporary structures and formwork), and falls from elevated work stations. OSHA regulations regarding these and many other types of hazards are quite explicit. The complete list of construction safety rules compiled by OSHA is voluminous, and a complete listing is not feasible in this chapter. However, a listing of some of the major safety precautions is included here as a general guide to OSHA requirements.

CONCRETE, CONCRETE FORMS AND SHORING (1926-700-701)

a. All equipment and material used shall comply with ANSI A10.9-1970, "Safety Requirements for Concrete Construction and Masonry Work."
b. Employees shall not be permitted to work above vertically protruding reinforcing steel, unless it has been protected to eliminate the hazard of impalement.
c. Powered and rotating-type concrete troweling machines that are manually guided shall be equipped with a deadman-type operating control.
d. Formwork and shoring shall safely support all loads imposed during concrete placement. Drawings or plans of formwork and shoring systems shall be available at the jobsite.
e. Wear gloves, face shields or goggles during stripping operations.
f. Employees are not to work under the pour when concreting.
g. Install plywood walkways so employees do not have to walk on 4 × 4's.
h. Lay stringers, shores, runners and other material on the floor. Do not lean such material on columns, beams, shores or walls.
i. Clean and remove nails from form material while it is being stripped.
j. Rope off stripping areas.
k. When standing and working in concrete rubber boots shall be worn.
l. Concrete finishers should wear knee pads.

EXCAVATING AND TRENCHING (1926-650-652)

a. Before opening any excavation, efforts shall be made to determine if there are underground utilities in the area, and they shall be located and protected during the excavation operations.

b. The walls and faces of all excavations, and trenches more than five feet deep, in which employees are exposed to danger from moving ground shall be guarded by a shoring system, sloping of the ground, or some other equivalent means.

c. In excavations in which employees may be required to enter, excavated or other material shall be effectively stored and retained at least 2 feet or more from the edge of the excavation.

d. Daily inspections of excavation shall be made by a competent person. If evidence of possible cave-ins or slides is apparent, all work in the excavation shall cease until the necessary precautions have been taken to safe guard the employees.

e. Trenches more than 4 feet deep shall have ladders or steps located so as to require no more than 25 feet of lateral travel.

HOISTS MATERIAL AND PERSONAL (1926-552)

a. The employer shall comply with the manufacturer's specifications and limitations.

b. Rated load capacities, recommended operating speeds, and special hazard warnings or instructions shall be posted on cars and platforms.

c. Hoisting entrances of material hoists shall be protected by substantial full width gates or bars.

d. Hoisting doors or gates of personal hoists shall be not less than 6 feet 6 inches high, and be protected with mechanical locks which cannot be operated from the landing side and are accessible only to persons on the car.

e. Overhead protective coverings shall be provided on the top of the hoist cage or platform.

f. Only passenger elevators or hoists may be used for personnel.

g. The construction site safety program contains the hand signals in the safety manual for maintenance and general construction.

MOTOR VEHICLES AND MECHANIZED EQUIPMENT (1926-600-601-602)

a. All vehicles in use shall be checked at the beginning of each shift to assure that all parts, equipment, and accessories that affect safe operation are in proper operting condition and free from defects. All defects shall be corrected before the vehicle is placed in service.

b. No employer shall use any motor vehicle, earthmoving, or compacting equipment having an obstructed view to the rear unless:

- the vehicle has a reverse signal alarm distinguishable from the surrounding noise level, or
- the vehicle is backed up only when an observer signals that it is safe to do so.

c. Heavy machinery, equipment, or parts thereof shall be substantially blocked to prevent falling or shifting before employees are permitted to work under or between them.

d. Crawler tractor, bulldozer, etc. must be resting on ground or blocked when not in use—set the parking brake, remove the keys, and substantially lock.

e. All equipment not in use must have motor turned off and key removed.

f. When parking vehicle at end of day:

1. Allow engine to cool.

2. Park on level firm ground.

3. Place transmission in neutral and lock, if possible.

4. Block tracks, wheels, etc.

5. Bleed air tank.

g. All construction vehicles SHOULD have back-up alarms.

h. Check for morning start-up procedures. Every operator should have a list to check for:

1. Broken parts—hoses, gaskets, safety equipment, etc.

2. Low, cut, bulging tires.

3. Dirty windows and mirrors.

4. Broken linkage, gears.

SCAFFOLDS (1926-451)

a. Scaffolds shall be erected on sound, rigid footing, capable of carrying the maximum intended load.

b. Scaffolds and their components shall be capable of supporting without failure, at least 4 times the maximum intended load.

c. Guardrails and toeboards shall be installed on all open sides and ends of platforms more than 10 feet above the ground or floor, except needle beam scaffolds and floats. Scaffolds 4 feet to 10 feet in height, having a minimum dimension in either direction of less than 45 inches, shall have standard guardrails installed on all open sides and ends of the platform.

d. There shall be a screen with maximum ½-inch openings between the toeboard and midrail, where persons are required to work or pass under scaffold.

e. All planking shall be Scaffold Grade as recognized by grading rules for the species of wood used. The maximum permissible spans for 2 × 9 inches or wider planks are shown in the following table:

	Material				
	Full thickness undressed lumber			Nominal thickness lumber	
Working load (psf)	25	50	75	25	50
Permissible span (ft)	10	8	6	8	6

The maximum permissible span for 1¼- × 9-inch or wider plank of full thickness is 4 feet, with maximum loading of 50 psf.

f. Scaffold planking shall be overlapped a minimum of 12 inches or secured from movement.

g. Scaffold planks shall extend over their end supports not less than 6 inches nor more than 12 inches.

h. All scaffolding and accessories shall have any defective parts immediately replaced or repaired.

i. Look for rusted parts which indicates abuse or neglect. Check for damaged welds.

    j. All members and components must be straight. No kinks, bends or dents in metal parts.

    k. Know the maximum load and make sure that it is not being violated.

    l. Locking devices must be operable.

    m. Make sure there is adequate support under EVERY LEG.

    n. Swinging scaffolding must also contain adequate guard railing and be suspended properly. Each employee working on the scaffold must have a safety harness and line tied to the structure being worked on.

    o. Unless the legs are on concrete or similar rigid material, the leg shall rest on a base plate. Where there are conditions of unlevel elevations, this base plate shall be of the adjustable type. Furthermore, if the legs are to be set on non-compacted soil material, a mud sill shall be provided. In addition, the base plate shall be nailed or otherwise secured to the mud sill.

    p. Many scaffolds have built-in ladders. These ladders are on a 90° angle and therefore more hazardous than portable ladders placed properly. When the man reaches the platform the ladders stops and he does not have the three foot continued railing as prescribed in a portable ladder. It is recommended that a portable ladder be utilized and not the built-in ladder.

ENVIRONMENTAL HEALTH CONSIDERATIONS

With the increased concern for occupational safety there has been an increased awareness of occupational health hazards and protection of the environment. The major environmental health problems related to construction typically are dust, noise, heat and cold, toxic materials, and radiation. Methods of appropriate control of these hazards are addressed by OSHA as outlined in the following paragraphs.

Dust

Dust not only is a hazard reducing visibility, but also may cause respiratory ailments to workers subject to the dust. Asbestos dust and silica dust are of particular concern, and specific regulations have been enacted to address these materials. All employees subject to unacceptable levels of dust and airborne particles must be furnished respiratory devices appropriate to the material and instruction in the use of the equipment.

Noise

By its nature, construction often is a source of high noise levels. This has prompted the public to register complaints about disturbing the environment, and the government to question the health and safety of the employees. Noise is a primary concern of OSHA and some other public concerns, as evidenced by the rules and regulations set forth to monitor and control it.

    OSHA regulations prescribe a maximum noise level to which workers may be exposed, based on the duration of exposure and the range. Permissible noise levels range from 90 dBA (decibels measured on the A-scale of a sound meter) for a period of 8 hours to 140 dBA for impulse or impact noise. When engineering the noise to a satisfactory level cannot be obtained, personal ear protection must be provided to the workers involved. Noise controls have also resulted in the increased use of equipment cab enclosures to protect the operators from equipment noise. Although the equipment noted is intended to protect the worker, the equipment may pose added hazards by reducing the ability of the worker to effectively communicate while wearing or working it.

Heat and Cold

Construction workers are often required to work in varying temperature conditions, ranging from high-temperature conditions to extreme cold. The human body is able to adapt to high-temperature conditions within a period of 7 to 10 days; however, when a person is not properly acclimated or protected serious illness due to the heat can occur. The severity of illness can range from minor heat fatigue to fatal heatstroke. The effect of heat, humidity, and physical activity can be measured as the "heat stress index." By maintaining body fluids and salt intake one can reduce the risks of heat illness. The effect of heat stress can also be greatly reduced or eliminated by scheduling hot work for the cooler part of the day, relying on the use of equipment to reduce physical labor, and providing sheltered or cooled rest areas.

Extreme cold-weather conditions are not as common due to the general nature of the construction business. The body takes longer to acclimatize to cold conditions than to high temperatures. Protected clothing and reduced exposure to the cold conditions are the most effective measures to protect the worker.

Radiation

Advances in measuring and testing equipment have increased the awareness of radiation safety procedures on the construction site. Laser equipment used for surveying and alignment of structures and tunnels utilize non-ionizing radiation to operate. OSHA regulations limit the exposure to workers and also recommend operating and safety procedures. Ionizing radiation, produced by x-ray equipment and radioactive material, is encountered when measuring soil density, x-raying welds, and on some nondestructive material tests. Use of this equipment is restricted to personnel trained in accordance with the regulations of the Nuclear Regulatory Commission.

ECONOMICS OF CONSTRUCTION SAFETY

Cost Savings

Many contractors can tell you their expenses to the penny, yet the cost of safety, which can exceed many thousands of dollars, escapes them completely. Worker's compensation insurance, a major expense on any job, is usually assumed by many contractors to be a set fee over which they have little or no influence. In actuality the contractor plays the major role in determining these costs, thus providing an edge in the overall cost of a project in this highly competitive market.

The contractor who has an understanding of worker's compensation and how these costs are calculated will be on the way to improving profits for his company.

The cost of worker's compensation insurance is determined by two components. The first component, the manual rate, is based on the average medical costs and benefits paid out in the previous year for each designated type of work. The second component, the experience modification rating (EMR), is based on the employer's accident costs compared to the set average.

Manual Rates

Contractors must buy insurance to cover their worker's compensation exposure, unless covered by some other means. The cost of the insurance will vary from state to state since the rates and claims for accidents are set in accordance with state law. Manual rates are established for about 450 work classifications (e.g., painters, masons) based on medical costs and benefits paid for accidents in each classification plus administrative costs. The rates for each year reflect the costs of the previous year expressed in dollars per $100 dollars of payroll. The comparative accident costs of different trades can be seen in looking at the "WC rates" illustrated in Table 14.2.

TABLE 14.2 Worker's Compensation (WC) Premium Rate for an Average Construction Project

Classification	Payroll*	WC rate†	Insurance cost
Laborers	$1,800,000	8.40	$151,200
Carpenters	$ 900,000	5.66	$ 50,940
Masons	$ 200,000	7.63	$ 15,260
Painters	$ 200,000	6.30	$ 12,600
Steel erection	$ 600,000	9.92	$ 59,520
Roofers	$ 600,000	13.55	$ 81,300
Pipefitters	$3,300,000	3.24	$106,920
Electricians	$1,500,000	3.17	$ 47,550
Concrete finishers	$ 400,000	5.22	$ 20,880
Total	$9,500,000		$546,170

*Base salary, excluding overtime and fringe benefits.
†Dollars per $100 of insured payroll, using the Nebraska 1988 rates.

To show how the manual costs are calculated, an example of a project with a $9.5 million-dollar payroll, utilizing mixed trades, is illustrated in Table 14.2. A contractor working in the state of Nebraska would have a manual insurance cost of 5.7 dollars per $100 dollars of payroll, based on the 1988 rates. Without the second component (EMR) all contractors working with the same payroll work classification would pay the same amount, regardless of their past accident record. Instead, contractors experiencing higher claims than the average will pay a premium rate, while those with a lower average will receive a discount. The experience modification rating is based on the accident claims record of the contractor. The actual formula is complex, but the basic meaning is not. The EMR is a modifier of the manual rate based on a contractor's past accident claims record.

The impact of EMRs on the premium cost is illustrated in Table 14.3, in which the manual rates of Table 14.2 were used.

TABLE 14.3 EMR Impact on Cost of Worker's Compensation Insurance for Typical Construction Project

EMR	Cost of WC insurance
50	$273,085
75	$409,628
100	$546,170
120	$655,404
165	$901,181

Hidden Costs

Typical costs, including worker's compensation and liability and property insurance, are easy to identify as a specific cost of doing business. However, when an accident occurs, not only direct but indirect or hidden costs are involved. Hidden costs may include

- Loss of productivity as a result of decreased morale or the addition of a new or untrained employee to an established crew
- Wages paid to the injured for time not worked
- Costs for cleanup and repair
- Costs incurred by delays as a result of the accident
- Administrative costs of investigations and reports
- Cost of fines
- Loss of future projects due to adverse publicity

Estimates of the ratio between hidden costs and direct costs vary from 4 to 1 to 17 to 1. The ratio will vary with the magnitude of accidents; however, it is not necessarily linked to the severity of the injuries. A serious and costly accident may occur without any person sustaining injury. The indirect cost ratio is influenced by a great many variables, among which are type of project, diligence of the investigation, severity of accident, and impact on the contractor's clients. Since so many variables are present, a single multiplier cannot be applied to all construction-industry accidents.

COST OF SAFETY PROGRAMS

Based on figures accumulated for the Business Roundtable Construction Industry Cost Effectiveness Project in 1979–1980, the cost of construction accidents is a critical financial concern.

1. Construction was estimated to be a $300 billion-per-year industry in the United States alone.
2. Builder's risk and liability insurance averaged about 1 percent of direct labor payroll.
3. Worker's compensation insurance averaged about 7 percent of direct labor payroll.
4. Direct labor payroll was estimated to be about 25 percent of total project costs.

Based on the factors given above, insurance represents 2 percent of the total project costs, or $6 billion. Of this total an estimated 65 percent ($3.9 billion) is paid for accident losses; the remaining 35 percent represents administrative costs of the insurance industry. Using a conservative ratio of 4 as the indirect to direct costs multiplier, the construction industry absorbs an additional cost of $15.6 billion (4 × $3.9 billion). The total minimum cost to owners as a result of direct and indirect cost, in 1979 dollars, approaches $19.5 billion annually.

Costs can also be calculated by adding up the average costs of accidents to contractors as a percentage of direct labor costs:

- Insurance costs average about 8 percent of direct labor cost, assuming 7 percent of worker's compensation and 1 percent liability insurance.
- Accident claims costs are assumed to be 5.2 percent of direct labor costs (65 percent times 8 percent).
- Hidden costs will be approximately 20.8 percent of direct labor (5.2 percent times 4).
- Average claims costs will be 26 percent of direct labor costs (5.2 percent plus 20.8 percent).

These high costs can be reduced by the implementation of a viable safety program.

Accidents by their very nature can be controlled, and substantial cost savings can be made by reducing accidents. Effective safety programs are a means of meeting the goals of accident cost reduction. The study completed for the Business Roundtable Construction Industry Cost Effectiveness Project Report A-3 (1982) states

Insurance costs, costs of injuries, and the expense of liability suits are easily documented and rather readily available. The cost of establishing and administering a construction safety and health program is somewhat less tangible, but can be estimated with reasonable accuracy. Data collected from a significant sample of contractors working at various construction sites in 1980 indicate that the cost of administering a construction safety and health program usually amounts to about 2.5% of direct labor costs. These costs include

- Salaries for safety, medical, and clerical personnel
- Safety meetings
- Inspections of tools and equipment
- Orientation sessions
- Site inspections
- Personal protective equipment
- Health programs such as respirator-fit tests
- Miscellaneous supplies

Some of the costs above are items mandated by law and thus are an expense that would be paid by any contractor adhering to the laws of the construction industry. Thus the actual estimated cost of a safety program would be less than the 2.5 percent indicated. An investment of 2.5 percent or less in a safety program should decrease claims cost by a minimum of 25 percent. Applying this savings to the costs previously determined, insurance claims cost will be 3.9 percent of direct labor, hidden costs 15.6 percent of direct labor, or a total cost of 19.5 percent as compared to 26 percent. The net savings assuming 2.5 percent costs for a safety program will be conservatively 4 percent (6.5 percent savings minus 2.5 percent for safety program).

CHAPTER 15
COST ENGINEERING

First Edition

Joseph Alcabes, C.C.E.

483 Steven Avenue
West Hempstead, New York

Second Edition

Wesley F. Mikes

Senior Vice President
O'Brien-Kreitzberg & Associates, Inc.
Pennsauken, New Jersey

INTRODUCTION

Everyone associated with a project will have an inherent interest in the cost for implementation and completion of construction. The interest will vary depending on each individual's association with the project. The owner will have an established budget to implement his plan and provide a finished project to meet his criteria and needs. The contractor, if working on a fixed price contract, has a similar goal to complete the project within his bid price and to cover all costs of material and labor and ultimately make a profit. The more accurately cost records are maintained, the better the chances for a financial success of the project.

To assist in meeting these objectives, this chapter contains information for reporting and analyzing project costs. It describes an effective recording and reporting system that will give a measure of performance for the project's budget and will allow a reasonably accurate estimate of the cost to complete the project. Upon completion, accurately maintained records can be utilized for future bidding, insurance, or tax purposes.

This chapter contains descriptions and samples of forms for recording and reporting project costs, along with notes describing the purpose and use of each. It is divided into eight sections which are convenient for describing the cost of the project.

1. Introduction
2. Definitions and objectives
3. Classification of accounts
4. Materials and equipment
5. Subcontracts

6. Field labor
7. Distributable accounts
8. Revised estimate and job cost report

These divisions allow the cost accounting system to be easily adapted and suited to various sizes and types of projects which may have different reporting needs. Reports may be prepared in the home office prior to mobilization and later in the field when job-site conditions allow. When the general contractor is essentially the broker, the amount of cost control reporting and analysis can be greatly reduced. Each project must be carefully analyzed in advance and a cost reporting system to specifically meet the project's needs must be established. There is no need to overdo a cost reporting system which may later become a burden for site or office personnel.

Cost can be viewed from the position of the engineering contractor, who must deal with few self-managed subcontracts and a great deal of construction engineering design. In this type of an operation, a heavy burden is placed on the management skills of the project manager who has to coordinate the activities of the engineering and construction specialists who make up the project team. Costs may also be viewed from the vantage point of the construction contractor, who deals with many self-managed subcontracts and little construction engineering design. In this situation, architectural and engineering services are provided by others and the large engineering force is not required. Here, each subcontractor has to provide his own management skills, thus reducing the need for those skills on the part of the general contractor. The general contractor and the subcontractors can concentrate their efforts on the construction work rather than on the problems associated with engineering and design. From either of these positions, or from the third-party viewpoint of the owner, owner-operator, or construction manager, reporting and recording costs for cost control purposes are extremely important. The system provided in this chapter allows for this variation of viewpoints.

DEFINITIONS AND OBJECTIVES

Definition of Cost Engineering

Cost engineering is defined as the application of procedures to minimize cost in relation to the budget estimate prepared for any specific project. The budget estimate together with all documents defining the scope of work (and approved or finalized in a signed contract with a client) will be the control document for any specific project. In order to have effective cost control, any deviation from the scope of the budget estimate must be defined, evaluated, and presented to the client or to management for approval as a change in the scope of work.

Objectives and Responsibilities

The objective of the cost engineering function is to keep management advised of the current cost status of the project. This function can be accomplished by analyzing and controlling costs, maintaining an orderly system of records and reports, measuring the progress or work accomplished, and forecasting the total cost to complete the project in comparison with the budget or control estimate of the project.

The cost engineer is responsible for cost control through the preparation of cost engineering procedures or computerized programs, or revised estimates and project cost reports; classification of accounts; cost coding and distribution; cost control documents and reports; and evaluation and incorporation of scope changes and deviations into the revised budget.

Such a system provides feedback of cost statistics for evaluation of the project, for use in the preparation of a final project cost analysis report, and for use by the estimating department on future projects. On smaller projects, this may be the responsibility of a single individual, whereas for larger projects, it can be the responsibility of an entire department.

Principles of Effective Cost Control

1. When the original budget estimate is established, all elements of the project should be adequately defined. If a number of items are lumped together in a single line item for cost, notations should be made as to specifically what the line item contains to avoid future confusion.

2. Every item in the budget estimate must be measured in relationship to the status of the completion of the line item and its expenditure. If the item did not appear in the budget estimate, that is a strong indication that it was not in the initial scope of work. In order to have effective cost control, the cost trends must be established as soon as possible and measured against physical progress of the project so that remedial action by management can be taken in a timely fashion, if required.

3. A good definitive cost estimate and a realistic and tight master project schedule will provide excellent control documents from which the cost engineer can provide a measure of progress of the project for management's use.

4. When the initial engineering is managed effectively, both engineering and design are on schedule, and material deliveries are held on schedule for construction, management is achieving the end of reducing the final costs of the work.

5. Field cost engineering (after briefing by the home office as to the scope of work in the budget and instructions as to the reports expected on a monthly basis or other predetermined intervals) is the keystone to forecasting cost performance of the project. The construction manager should be alerted immediately when unit costs and quantities are overrunning the budget estimate. Likewise, he should also be notified when unit costs are running substantially lower than anticipated. This ultimately can assist both the construction manager and the owner with respect to future change orders on the contract.

6. It is the responsibility of the project manager and the construction superintendent to specifically define in sufficient detail the scope of changes in work that depart from the contract documents so that an evaluation of the effects and cost of changes can be made for presentation to the client or management. It is also advantageous at this time to review the specific impact of a change order with respect to completion of the project. When properly evaluated, it may be to everyone's benefit when preparing a change order cost estimate to include acceleration or buying-back time impact of the change.

7. In order for the cost engineer to provide management with an accurate, unbiased forecast of the anticipated project costs in comparison with the budget estimate, basic reports must be prepared and analyzed. These reports must be accurate, current, and measured against the progress of the project in order

for them to work effectively. Proper cost control necessitates getting a "fix" on the trend of the cost as soon as possible so that action can be taken if necessary. Cost reports that are running 2 or 3 months behind the actual project become historical documentation. The cost engineer's reports will sound a warning of any unfavorable cost trends in order to alert management to initiate corrective measures. Cost reports that are not current tend to reduce or eliminate the chances of timely reactions.

CLASSIFICATION OF ACCOUNTS

General

The backbone of the estimates and cost control system is the classification of accounts which is initially established for the project. As soon as a project has been authorized, a preliminary classification of accounts or an outline is prepared to cover the items of work included in the scope for the specific project. No one classification of accounts has been developed that can adequately cover every project. While various projects do have a number of similarities, they also have their own unique features. Hence, for each new project, it is essential that the project team prepare such a code of accounts from a master classification to cover the specifics of the project. There are various master systems which are utilized for different types of facilities. These include

1. Nuclear projects
2. Water and wastewater treatment facilities
3. High-rise construction
4. Paper or pulp mills
5. Hydroelectric projects
6. Dams and locks
7. Refineries
8. Industrial plants

Classification of accounts is the method of allocating actual expenditures and commitments for proper cost control. All estimates and material contract commitments are coded in accordance with the established classification breakdown. The classification code should be placed on all documents, including purchase orders, receiving records, requisitions, and payments. It is the cost engineer's responsibility to maintain proper classification coding for all documents and to see that costs are properly allocated. The cost engineer must work closely with the field accountant, purchasing agents, craft supervisors, foremen, and project engineers. This requires close personal contacts with foremen and craft supervisors during each working day to be certain that craft labor costs are being properly classified. The results from the cost accounting system are only as reliable as the data which are entered. Every effort must be made to properly allocate both labor and materials. Preprinted time cards with descriptions of various accounts can substantially aid proper allocation. This eliminates the need for craft labor to make decisions based on limited information in the construction field. The cost engineer and the timekeeper must also be alert and knowledgeable as to the actual work being performed in the field so as to eliminate obviously miscoded accounts.

The actual responsibility for preparation of cost ledgers in the field office rests with the field accountants. This frees the cost engineer to perform duties with respect to the cost analysis. Along with posting the cost ledgers, the field accountant with the assistance of the chief timekeeper will ascertain that the time cards are properly coded and prepare the necessary journal entries. The cost engineer will be provided with this information and other pertinent documents as required for the cost control function.

As noted, the classification of accounts is used throughout the project for identification purposes on all documents including requisitions, purchase orders, cost reports, and payments. The cost coding system also becomes the basis for historical retrieval of information for estimating purposes on future projects. Many times the cost engineer is faced with the realities of having to live with a coding system that is preestablished by the client or a regulatory agency. These could include the Federal Energy Regulatory Commission, the Nuclear Regulatory Commission, or simply the client's in-house system. In order to maintain historical records, a construction manager or contractor may elect to maintain a dual system of coding for a specific project, one system for the client or the regulatory agency and a second system that is compatible with his own company's procedures. Through the use of on-site PCs, a cross-referencing system can readily be established.

Sample Classifications

As previously outlined, there are a number of established classification coding systems available for the cost engineer. Experienced cost engineers will most likely have their own preferred system based on previous applications. If the experience is on a nonrelated type of project, it may be necessary for them to utilize a coding system which is more applicable to their current project assignment.

Appendix A contains the most common coding system for typical building construction type projects. This is the Construction Specification Institute (CSI) MASTERFORMAT. This system is very compatible with computer application on site. Appendix B contains an alphabetical system utilized by some firms. Appendixes C and D contain numerical systems, which are more applicable to industrial and power-generation projects.

MATERIALS AND EQUIPMENT

General

Effective cost control for materials and equipment depends on the efforts of both home office and field office. Extremely close cooperation is required with both offices. If either party fails to maintain complete control, it will tend to mitigate the efforts of the other party. Material costs must be controlled by constant review of both quantities and unit costs.

Quantities are controlled first during the design stage by the production of economic and cost-efficient designs, which are a measure of the skill and experience of the design team. During the construction phase, costs are controlled by the economical use of materials (e.g., control of breakages, losses, theft, and wastage of materials, and in the judicious reuse of materials such as form lumber).

Initial cost savings are first controlled by the choice of the most economical types of material and equipment which are capable of performing the required task and then by adherence to up-to-date and competitive purchasing practices (such as competitive bidding and bulk purchasing when practical).

Budget

When the budget estimate is prepared, it is most important that all material quantities be calculated carefully and unit or lump sum costs established on a subaccount basis. The budget estimate must include all costs associated with material deliveries such as taxes, freight, duty, and escalation where applicable. The worksheets and records that are prepared during the preparation of the budget estimate should be maintained for future comparison. These records will show the scope of work at the time that the budget estimate was prepared. Deviations during and after construction can then be established and substantiated.

Ordering of Materials

As soon as a notice of award is received, the purchasing agent should meet with the project management and construction management teams to determine which items are to be purchased by the home office and which items will be obtained locally by the field office. Responsibilities thus are indicated with respect to each item on the control budget, which is prepared as soon as the budget estimate becomes available.

An equipment list showing all equipment ultimately required for the project and a materials list itemizing all required materials are prepared. As drawings are completed, bills of material should be prepared that list all items of equipment and materials covered by the drawings. In order to obtain materials or equipment, a requisition is then completed describing in appropriate detail the items required. It is extremely important that adequate descriptions, catalog numbers, finishes, etc., be provided for purchasing's use. Many times, individuals in the purchasing group will not fully understand the material or products which are being purchased. Incomplete information can result in incorrect equipment and poor quotations.

Coding Purchase Requisitions

The purchase requisition is implemented by engineering or construction for the purchasing department to procure the necessary materials and equipment for the project. The requisition is routed through the cost section for assignment of a proper cost code. Each item of the requisition must be individually coded if more than one item is contained therein. As soon as the code has been added, the requisition is then returned to the purchasing department for review and issuance to the proper vendor.

Each requisition must have the proper cost account code to allow for proper allocation into the system. Purchases made through the home office should be approved by the project engineer or manager and purchases made through the field office should be approved by the superintendent of construction. Each purchase order should show clearly the price of the item and other applicable costs including duty, freight, and taxes that may be applicable.

One definition should be made here which will apply throughout the chapter. *Commitment* is used to denote the sum of money that the company has obligated itself to pay. This includes the value of purchase orders placed and contracts signed and also payments for labor for which there may be no formal signed contract. Accurate records must be kept for unit price work which is a measure of work completed rather than a purchase order or invoice. *Commitment* should not be confused with *records of payments,* which are generally kept by the accounting group. The completion of a purchase order constitutes a commitment of funds. For proper control to be exercised at the appropriate time, when the project engineer or manager or the construction superintendent is asked to approve a purchase order, they must be provided with the proper data showing the budgeted allowance for the items involved. (When possible, this check should be carried out when the requisition is prepared.)

The Cost Engineer and Purchasing Function

The purchasing agent or purchasing department is generally responsible for all purchases required to support the project team. No purchases or commitments should be made without going through the proper channels. Unauthorized purchases can result in duplication of materials and equipment or unallocated costs. The cost engineer has a definitive role to play in the implementation of the purchasing functions. The engineer or construction superintendent initiates the purchase request, which is then prepared by the purchasing department or purchasing agent. The individual requesting the purchase order is responsible for properly describing the item to be purchased and including the cost account number and the budget evaluation for the items as indicated in the authorized budget. As the purchase order is routed through the cost engineer, it is his responsibility to check that the proper cost code and budget have been entered onto the requisition. It is also the cost engineer's responsibility to alert the project manager when a requested item deviates from the control budget or does not exist in the control budget. Prior to the authorization for purchasing such items, a complete evaluation must be made to ascertain and verify the necessity for the specific item. This authorization becomes the responsibility of the project manager, who ultimately will be responsible for cost overruns. The budget allowance and delivery schedule of the item become two of the prime factors in evaluating and reviewing bids received by the purchasing department.

The purchasing department is responsible for the evaluation of *commercial aspects*: the estimated costs of transportation, escalation, payment terms, and other applicable conditions. The purchasing department should also participate with the project manager in the preparation of variance requests to use foreign material when the "Buy American Act" may be applicable to the contract. This requires an analysis of cost variations and delivery schedules. Upon receipt of bids, the purchasing agent should forward to the requesting engineer copies of the bids for review and recommendation. The engineer or construction superintendent is the individual who is responsible for the technical evaluation of the materials or equipment for specification compliance. The purchasing department should not issue purchase orders for technical equipment and materials without approval from either engineering or the construction superintendent. Compliance with these requirements is essential.

After a comparison of bids has been initiated by the purchasing department and reviewed by the engineers, and a recommendation of bidders to be selected has been made, the cost engineer will be issued a complete breakdown of bids received. This will allow the cost engineer to do a complete cost analysis with respect to the current budget allowed for the item. As soon as this analysis has been completed, authorization to issue the purchase order can proceed.

When quotations are received which are not in conformance with the current budget and delivery schedule, the cost engineer is responsible for notifying the project manager accordingly. Once given this information, the project manager can then determine what course of action may be required.

The cost engineer is the individual who can best perform this analysis because of his association with the estimators and his participation in the preparation of the original bid estimate. Every item of the budget represents a cost center that has a definite meaning and scope of work to be performed. The bids received through the purchasing group must be compared against the applicable cost center prior to issuing a purchase order. What the cost engineer must determine is what else must be added to this cost center that was included in the budget estimate. An example of this would be the procurement of a major piece of equipment. The cost center that was included in the budget may represent a total package and not just the major piece of equipment. The cost engineer will then have to incorporate the cost for piping, valves, etc., that will be required for systems operation. Many times a vendor will only provide the equipment and piping and other utility connections remain to be completed. These may or may not be included as part of the specific cost center. In light of this, the actual bid prices received may only be a small part of the cost center, thus the purchasing department is not in a position to fully evaluate the best prices. If the cost engineer is capable of providing this type of specific information, he will have provided the means for control of purchased items prior to the issuance of a purchase order and not after the fact.

Purchase Order Register

Purpose. To record in numerical sequence of purchase order number each commitment of materials and equipment as it is made. The log is utilized for the preparation of the cost report.

Prepared By. The register should be prepared by the prime individual in charge of purchasing. If this is being done through a home office, the register should be prepared by them. If purchasing is being done both by the home office and the field office, a consolidated log should be maintained. When the field office is purchasing materials and equipment, the effort must be coordinated. With this in mind, it is an assignment that can readily be maintained by the cost engineer.

Frequency. Continuously updated as purchase orders are issued.

Preparation. The purchase order register should be established immediately upon project authorization. Any and all material and acquisitions for the project should be included in the register.

As soon as site work begins, a single party, whether it be at the home office or the field office, should then have the responsibility of maintaining the coordinated log. From a convenience standpoint, whichever office is doing the primary purchasing should also maintain the register. If not being maintained by the cost engineer, this information should be provided to him on at least a weekly basis. A sample purchase order register is shown in Fig. 15.1.

Commitment Record

Purpose. To record by subaccount all commitments for material and equipment. The commitment record is utilized for the preparation of the cost report and further delineates information which is similarly shown in the purchase order register.

Prepared By. This document should be maintained by the same individual that maintains the purchase order register. This is also a task which can be as-

PURCHASE ORDER REGISTER

CLIENT ABC CHEMICAL CO.   JOB ORDER NO.   SHEET   OF

P. O. NO.	VENDOR AND DESCRIPTION	QUANTITY	UNIT PRICE	AMOUNT	OTHER EST. CHARGES INCL. OR TO BE ADDED TO P.O. FREIGHT	ESCALATION	OTHER	ESTIMATED P.O. TOTAL	ACCOUNT	REMARKS
EC-1	Delta Southern									
	Quench Tower T-1001	1	40,100	40,100	500	200	–	40,800	A1.11	
	Amine Scrubber T-1002	1	43,500	43,500	600	200	–	44,300	A2,11	
	Caustic Scrubber T-1003	1	45,000	45,000	600	200	–	45,800	A3.11	
	Total – EC-1			128,600	1,700	600	–	130,900		
EC-2	Fritz W. Glitsh & Sons Inc.									
	Ripple Trays - Quench Tower	5	1,200	6,000	Incl.	Firm	–	6,000	A1.12	
	Valve Trays - Amine Scrubber	34	250	8,500	Incl.	Firm	–	8,500	A2.12	
	Valve Trays - Caustic Scrubber	28	250	7,000	Incl.	Firm	–	7,000	A3.12	
	Total – EC-2			21,500				21,500		
EC-3	Industrial Steel Products Co. Inc.									
	Galvanized Steel - Pipe Racks	400 tons	340 ton	136,000	Incl.	Firm	–	136,000	D3.11	
	Galvanized Steel - Fractionation Structure	190 tons	360 ton	68,400	Incl.	Firm	–	68,400	D1.11	
	Total – EC-3			204,400				204,400		
EC-4	Samuel Moore & Co.									
	12 Tube Multiple Tube Instrument Cable	14,000 ft	2.26 ft	31,640	Incl.	Firm	–	31,640	K70.1	
	4 Tube Multiple Tube Instrument Cable	6,000 ft	.895 ft	5,370	Incl.	Firm	–	5,370	K70.1	
	Total – EC-4			37,010				37,101		
EC-5	Chamman Division - Crane Co.									
	24" 125 Lb C.I. Tilting Disc Check Valves	3	2,600	7,800	Incl.	Firm	–	7,800	C2.71	
EC-6	Barton Instrument Corp.									
	Model 200 Flow Indicators	68	190	12,920	100	Firm	–	13,020	K10.1	
EC-7	General Electric Company									
	2,300 V Substation	1		52,500	Incl.	Firm		52,500	E1.1	
	480 V Substation No. 1	1		14,800	Incl.	Firm		14,800	E1.1	
	480 V Substation No. 2	1		14,800	Incl.	Firm		14,800	E1.1	
	Total – EC-7			82,100				82,100		
EC-8	Byron Jackson Pumps Inc.									
	Condensate Pumps									
	P2001 Centrifugal Pump			1,500	Incl.	Firm		1,500	P1.11	
	P2002 Centrifugal Pump			1,800	Incl.	Firm		1,800	P2.11	
	P2003 Centrifugal Pump			1,500	Incl.	Firm		1,500	P3.11	
	P2004 Centrifugal Pump			1,800	Incl.	Firm		1,800	P4.11	
	Total – EC-8			6,600				6,600		

FIGURE 15.1 Purchase order register.

signed to the cost engineer. This report also requires a coordinated effort between the home office and the field office when purchasing is a dual role.

Frequency.   The commitment record should be maintained on a continuous basis as information is received.

Preparation.   The project accountant should prepare the commitment record transparency sheet, filling in each appropriate subaccount immediately upon project authorization. Typical subaccounts are as follows:

Estimated home office purchase—quantity

Estimated field office purchase—quantity

Budget—net amount

Budget, taxes, etc. (if applicable to the subaccount)

Budget—total

As soon as a purchase order or an amendment to a purchase order is received, it should be immediately recorded by the project accountant in the appropriate column. When authorized changes are approved which affect the subaccount, appropriate entries showing quantity, amount, etc., should be made in the line marked "authorized change number." The next line in each case may be used to show the current approved budget for the account (original budget amount plus the value of all authorized changes to date).

From the project authorization, until the start of field operations, the commitment record (Fig. 15.2) should be maintained in the home office. Then, the maintenance of the commitment record should be assigned to a single individual, regardless of whether this individual is in the home office or in the field. This will require coordination between the two offices on a regular basis.

Cost Report—Materials and Equipment

On a regular basis, a cost report—materials and equipment is prepared to show the quantity and amount of commitments to date, forecasts to complete, current estimated completion costs, and current approved budget allowances (see Fig. 15.3) Variations between the current estimated completion cost and the current approved budget allowances are shown in the last two columns.

The information for the preparation of this report is obtained from commitment records with appropriate references to the purchase order register, approved change orders, and pending engineering changes.

Purpose.   This report will show by subaccount for material and equipment items, quantities and costs committed to date with forecasts to complete and to provide a comparison between committed estimated completion costs and current approved budget allowances.

Prepared By.   This report requires a joint effort between the project accountant and the cost engineer. Ideally, this report is maintained in the field.

Frequency.   The material and equipment report should be maintained on at least a monthly basis. At certain times throughout the project when major groups of purchases are being made, the report should be updated more frequently. With the use of a PC at the job site, this report may be kept current on a weekly basis.

Preparation.   As soon as the control budget has been completed, the cost engineer should prepare the master transparency sheets showing for each material and equipment subaccount:

LABOR AND MATERIAL COMMITMENT RECORD

DESCRIPTION OF ACCOUNT
Ripple Trays - Quench Tower T-1001

JOB ORDER NO.   PAGE NO.   ACCOUNT NO.

| ESTIMATE NUMBER | DATE | MATERIAL | | LABOR | | SUBCONTRACTORS | | | TOTAL LABOR | | TOTAL | |
		HOME OFFICE	FIELD	MAN-HOURS	AMOUNT	MAN-HOURS	LABOR AMT.	MATERIAL	MAN-HOURS	AMOUNT	MATERIAL	TOTAL
BUDGET		6.200				280	1.400		280	1.400	6.200	7.600
AUTH. CHANGES												
TOTAL												
REV. EST.–1												
REV. EST.–2												
REV. EST.–3												
REV. EST.–4												
REV. EST.–5												
REV. EST.–6												
REV. EST.–7												

DETAIL OF COMMITMENTS

| | MATERIAL | | | | LABOR | | | | | SUBCONTRACTORS | | | |
REF. P.O.	DESCRIPTION	HOME OFFICE	FIELD	REF.	MAN-HOURS	AMOUNT	ACCUM. MAN-HOURS	ACCUM. AMOUNT	REF.	DESCRIPTION	MAN-HOURS	LABOR AMT.	MATERIAL
FC-2	Ripple Trays-Quench Tower	6.000											

ACCOUNT NO.   A1.12

FIGURE 15.2 Commitment records.

Account number

Description

Unit

Original budget—quantity

Original budget—amount

These reports should be maintained in a single location, which is most logically the site office. When purchasing is being done at the home office, the information must be coordinated on a regular basis between the office accountant and the site accountant. When the report is being prepared, the project accountant or field accountant uses the commitment records and fills in the quantity and amounts committed to date. From the change order records, the cost engineer is then able to fill in the quantity and amounts of authorized changes.

After checking the pending engineering change record, making appropriate references to the purchase order register, and commitment records, and, if nec-

COST REPORT _____

MONTH ENDING _____

JO. NO. _____

PROJECT _____

REPORT NO. _____
SHEET ____ OF ____
DATE PREPARED _____
PREPARED BY _____

ACCT. NO.	DESCRIPTION	UNIT	COMMITTED 1 FOR PERIOD			COMMITTED 2 TO DATE			FORECAST TO COMPLETE 3			CURRENT EST. TOTAL 4 = (2 + 3)			APPROVED BUDGET ORIGINAL BUDGET 5			AUTHORIZED CHANGES 6			CURRENT BUDGET (INCL. AUTHORIZED CHANGES) 7 = (5 + 6)			OVERS + UNDERS − 8 = (4 − 7)
			QUANTITY	UNIT COST	AMOUNT	QUANTITY	UNIT COST	AMOUNT	QUANTITY	UNIT COST	AMOUNT	QUANTITY	UNIT COST	AMOUNT	QUANTITY	UNIT COST	AMOUNT	QUANTITY	UNIT COST	AMOUNT	QUANTITY	UNIT COST	AMOUNT	DIFFERENCE BETWEEN CURRENT ESTIMATED TOTAL COSTS AND CURRENT BUDGET

FIGURE 15.3 Cost report form.

essary, talking to the project manager and other site personnel, the cost engineer then completes the quantity and amount of forecast to complete. With this information, the project accountant is then able to complete a report and return it to the cost engineer. The cost engineer must then review the complete report, explaining briefly any discrepancies, large overruns, or large underruns.

SUBCONTRACTS

Lump Sum Price Contracts

Subcontracts issued on a lump sum basis are treated as a commitment from the time the contract is executed. From a cost control standpoint, very little is achieved by the monthly or routine reporting of a contract broken into its component subaccounts. Unless the client insists on such a detailed regular report, the preferred method would be percentage complete of the subcontract agreement.

At the end of the project, each contract can then be broken down into appropriate subaccounts in the completion cost report. The subcontract agreements should contain a requirement that the subcontractor submit subaccount information at the completion of the subcontracted work.

Unit Price Contracts

With unit price contracts, the company's commitment at any time is usually the equivalent value of the work completed or in place by the subcontractor. When utilizing such contracts, it is necessary that a suitable procedure be established and followed whereby the completed work to date is measured or calculated at regular intervals and the appropriate details and backup information are forwarded to the project accountant for entry into the commitment records.

Progress Payments

For both lump sum and unit price subcontracts, progress payments based on work in place are generally made on prestipulated intervals—most commonly monthly. When such payments are submitted by a subcontractor, it is necessary for the project superintendent or the project manager to review construction progress and verify that the work has been satisfactorily completed. It is, therefore, necessary that a suitable procedure be followed for reporting progress.

Reports

Subcontractor Register

Purpose. To record in numerical sequence by contract number each subcontract agreement entered into. The subcontract register is used for reference in preparation of the cost report—subcontracts.

Prepared By. This report should be prepared by the purchasing agent in the home office initially and may ultimately be maintained on-site.

Frequency. The register should be updated continuously each time a new subcontract agreement has been entered into.

Preparation. The register should be started when project authorization is granted. The form should be established prior to the issuance of any subcontract agreement, and updates should be recorded as soon as the first subcontract agreements are entered into. Ultimately, this report should be transferred to the site when site operations begin. Change orders will necessitate revisions or additions to the subcontract register based on the scope of work contained in the change orders. The field engineer who is handling change orders can generally maintain this register.

For a sample of the subcontract register form, see Fig. 15.1, which is the purchase order register; it serves the same purpose as the subcontract register.

Commitment Records.

Purpose. To record by account or subaccount the total value of lump sum contracts, including contract changes, and the value of the work done on unit price contracts. This report is used in the preparation of the cost report—subcontracts.

Prepared By. These records should be initially prepared by the project accountant and maintained in the home office. When the field work begins, these records should be transferred to the site project accountant to maintain. (In some firms, the commitment record is maintained on site by the cost engineer.)

Frequency. These records must be maintained on a continuous basis.

Preparation. As soon as the control budget is completed and available, the project accountant should prepare the commitment record transparency sheets, filling in the budget allowances for each subaccount as follows:

Quantity

Man-hours (if required)

Labor—amount

Materials—amount

Total—amount

Immediately upon receipt of each contract or contract change, the individual maintaining the commitment records should enter the following:

Lump sum price contracts

Reference contract number

Quantity (if available)

Labor amount (if available)

Material amount (if available)

Total amount (if available)

Unit price contracts

Reference contract number

Unit rate—in accordance with details of contract

When site operations commence, the project accountant should forward to the field accountant an up-to-date set of commitment records showing all home office commitments. From that time forward, the field accountant should maintain detailed records for all commitments made by both the home office and the field office.

Lump Sum Price Contract. See preceding list under this heading. Similar details are entered each time a field order is issued or a copy of a contract change is received. It should be noted that a contract change can result from an engineering change originating in the home office or from a field order. The authorization of a field order constitutes a commitment, although the value of the commitment may be unknown at the time. Ultimately, a contract change is issued to formalize each field order or group of field orders; care should be taken not to duplicate the entry of any commitment.

UNIT PRICE CONTRACTS: See the preceding list under this heading. At a predetermined period monthly, the field accountant records the number of units completed and the value of the work in place. For a sample unit price commitment record, see Fig. 15.4.

Cost Report—Subcontracts

Purpose. To record subcontracted items, quantities, and costs committed to date with forecasts to complete and to provide a comparison between current estimated completion costs and current approved budget allowances.

LABOR AND MATERIAL COMMITMENT RECORD

DESCRIPTION OF ACCOUNT	JOB ORDER NO.	PAGE NO.	ACCOUNT NO.
Pipe Racks - Galvanized Steel			D3.11

ESTIMATE NUMBER	DATE	MATERIAL		LABOR		SUBCONTRACTORS			TOTAL LABOR		TOTAL	
		HOME OFFICE	FIELD	MAN-HOURS	AMOUNT	MAN-HOURS	LABOR AMT.	MATERIAL	MAN-HOURS	AMOUNT	MATERIAL	TOTAL
BUDGET		*141,450	2,000	15,800	58,000				15,800	58,000	143,450	201,450
AUTH. CHANGES												
TOTAL												
REV. EST.−1												
REV. EST.−2												
REV. EST.−3												
REV. EST.−4												
REV. EST.−5												
REV. EST.−6												
REV. EST.−7												

*410 tons - $345 per ton

DETAIL OF COMMITMENTS

	MATERIAL				LABOR					SUBCONTRACTORS			
REF.	DESCRIPTION	HOME OFFICE	FIELD	REF.	MAN-HOURS	AMOUNT	ACCUM. MAN-HOURS	ACCUM. AMOUNT	REF.	DESCRIPTION	MAN-HOURS	LABOR AMT.	MATERIAL
EC-3	Galvanized Steel	136,000											
	400 tons - $340 per ton												
											ACCOUNT NO.	D3.11	

FIGURE 15.4 Unit price commitment record.

Prepared By. These reports are prepared and maintained by the project accountant and the cost analyst before site work begins. Then the project accountant in cooperation with the cost engineer should maintain these records on-site, recording all subcontract activity for the project whether initiated in the home office or the field.

Preparation. As soon as the control budget is completed, the cost engineer should prepare the master transparency sheets showing for each subcontract account:

Account number

Description

Unit (if applicable)

Original budget—quantity

Original budget—amount

Sets of transparencies are sent to the project accountant for home office–prepared reports and to the field accountant for site-prepared reports. When preparing these reports, the project accountant and the field accountant utilize the commitment records and subcontract register to obtain the quantity and amount committed to date.

From the change order records, the cost engineer fills in the quantity and amount for authorized changes. After reviewing the pending engineering change records; making appropriate references to subcontract register, commitment records, contract changes, and field orders; and if necessary, speaking to the project manager and the project engineer or superintendent of construction, the cost engineer fills in the quantity and amount of forecast to complete.

The project accountant or field accountant finalizes the report and returns it to the cost engineer who uses the remarks column to briefly describe any discrepancies and differences from the previous reports. The cost report form (Fig. 15.3) can be utilized for this purpose.

FIELD LABOR

General

The field superintendent, in conjunction with his supervisory staff, is responsible for directing and controlling the efforts of the field forces to ensure that the work is performed in the most cost-efficient manner and within the project schedule. Inefficient labor performance is the most common cause of project overruns.

It is essential that an effective day-to-day reporting system be maintained to measure the performance of the field forces compared to either the budget estimate or productivity standards. The system described below utilizes the information on hours and cost available from the field accounting staff, supplements them by quantity reports, and analyzes them to produce a database which the superintendent of construction then uses to make key decisions.

Basic Accounting Data

1. The time clock card provides the accounting team with the detailed hours worked by each man and is used only in the preparation of the payroll journal.

2. The foreman's time card provides detailed daily totals of craft hours, which are coded by the proper cost account classification. The foreman's time cards are incorporated into the labor distribution schedule, which shows the daily hours expended by craft and identified by cost classification codes on a monthly basis.

3. The monthly analysis is used to record the weekly totals of man-hours and cost by craft. At the conclusion of each month, the monthly average hourly rates per craft may be calculated and used on the labor distribution schedule showing the month's total labor costs by account and craft. At the end of the month, the monthly totals of man-hours and labor costs per account are posted to the cost ledger sheets. These reports provide an accurate recording of craft hours and labor costs required for accounting purposes.

Cost Control

When combined with the accounting data, the methods described below for recording units of work performed provide the complete database for the analysis of productivity for craft labor control and reporting.

Foreman's Quantity Report.   The foreman's records should contain detailed records of completed work coded to specific cost accounts as work progresses. The reports should be maintained minimally on a weekly basis; for critical work and for areas where significant progress is being made, they should be maintained on a daily basis.

Man-Hour and Quantity Record.   The man-hour and quantity record is used to record the periodic and cumulative man-hours expended and units of work completed for each cost accounting classification. The information for these records is obtained from the foreman's time cards and the units of work from the foreman's quantity report. This form also provides space for showing the estimated quantities and man-hours in the approved budget. This provides a basis for review of performance and allows the user to immediately identify areas that may be overrunning the initial budget. There is also space provided for showing quantities and man-hours for revised estimates in the event that the specific area is affected by a change order.

As work is started on a new account, the cost engineer should closely monitor the unit rates of man-hours expended per unit quantity of work completed to ascertain progress in comparison with the budgeted rate. The cost engineer should observe the work in the field and discuss the productivity with the superintendent and his supervisory staff to assist them in forecasting the trend (e.g., will production rates increase or decrease as specific work progresses). The cost engineer must alert the superintendent and his supervisory staff at the earliest possible time so appropriate action may be implemented. The importance of this cannot be overemphasized: Prompt daily scrutiny of these records by the cost engineer may avoid costly overruns.

On at least a monthly basis, the field engineer should perform a physical progress survey in the field and check quantities in place utilizing contract drawings and bills of material. Discrepancies between his measurements and cumulative figures obtained from foreman's quantity reports must be adjusted in the cumulative column of the man-hour and quantity record and in the "units completed to date" column of the next foreman's quantity report.

Man-Hour Report. The man-hour report should be prepared weekly and will show in summary form man-hours worked during the week for each account by craft. The report will also show by account the total man-hours worked and the total labor cost for the week.

Cost Report—Field Labor. This report is prepared on a monthly basis and shows by account the quantities and unit labor costs for the period and to date with forecasts to complete in comparison with the budgeted amounts. Work completed and in place to date is posted from the man-hour and quantity records and cost data from the cost ledger sheets. The forecast to complete is provided by the cost engineer after discussions with the project superintendent and his supervisory staff.

Forms and Procedures

Basic Accounting Forms. The following forms are standard record-keeping documents which are in general use in the industry: time clock card, payroll journal, monthly analysis, foreman's time card, labor distribution schedule, and cost ledger.

Cost Control Forms. The preparation and use of the following forms are described in detail and are included below. It is essential that records of this nature be maintained if proper cost control is to be achieved on the project.

> Foreman's quantity report
>
> Man-hour and quantity report
>
> Cost report—site labor

The following form is mentioned and described briefly to show how it can be utilized within the system if required: man-hour report

Basic Accounting Forms

Time Clock Card
   Purpose. The time clock card records when each individual employee arrives and leaves the project site. The data collected are used for the preparation of the payroll journal.
   Prepared By. Project timekeeper.
   Frequency. Daily.
   Preparation. Each card generally documents one person for each week. New cards are provided on a weekly basis. Standard time and overtime work are recorded separately.

Payroll Journal
   Purpose. The journal is used daily to record the hours worked by the individual employee and weekly for calculation of payrolls. Each week total man-

hours and labor costs by craft are summarized for preparation of the monthly cost analysis.

Prepared By. The timekeeper.

Frequency. Weekly (man-hours worked recorded daily).

Preparation. On a daily basis, the time clock cards from the previous day are reviewed and utilized to record "days and hours" in the proper column of the payroll journal. Both standard time and overtime are recorded. At the conclusion of each week, the hours worked are totaled and entered into the "hours worked" column. The payroll is calculated, and a summary sheet showing the total man-hours and cost for each craft is then prepared.

Monthly Analysis

Purpose. To record during the month the weekly gross payroll costs by craft and to provide a method of determining the average wage rates for each craft during the reporting period.

Prepared By. The timekeeper.

Frequency. One set used per month for recording data weekly.

Preparation. The total man-hours and labor costs for each craft are transcribed weekly from the payroll journal summary sheets to the appropriate weekly portion of the monthly analysis sheet. At the conclusion of each month, the weekly man-hours and labor costs are totaled and the cost divided by the total man-hours to determine the average hourly labor cost per craft. These hourly rates will then be established and used on the appropriate labor distribution schedules to calculate the month's total labor cost for each subaccount.

Foreman's Time Card

Purpose. To record by subaccount the man-hours worked per man and per crew. The data collected are used to calculate unit labor costs.

Prepared By. Craft foreman.

Frequency. On a daily basis.

Preparation. Each day, the foreman enters the subaccount number and a brief description of work being performed by his crew. He must record the hours worked per man and the total number of man-hours for the crew for each subaccount. At the completion of his shift, the foreman should sign his cards and turn them over to the craft supervisor.

Approved By. The craft supervisor.

Routing. The craft supervisor then turns the cards over to the timekeeper who cross checks the hours shown with the time clock cards and records them on the payroll journal. The timekeeper is then responsible for recording the man-hours worked onto the appropriate labor distribution schedules. The foreman's time cards are then passed to the cost engineer who enters the man-hour data on the appropriate man-hour and quantity records.

Labor Distribution Schedule

Purpose. To segregate into subaccounts labor hours worked by craft during the month so that monthly labor costs per subaccount may be obtained.

Prepared By. The timekeeper.

Frequency. One set maintained daily and aggregated weekly is used throughout the monthly period.

Preparation.   A separate sheet is used monthly for each subaccount for the specific craft.

Each day the hours are recorded on the foreman's time cards and transferred to these sheets.

Each week the man-hours are totaled and balanced with those transferred from the payroll journal to the monthly analysis.

At the completion of each month, the man-hours are totaled and multiplied by the average craft rate (obtained from the monthly analysis) to determine the total labor cost for the subaccount during the month.

Routing.   The schedules are used by the field accountant for posting monthly labor costs to the appropriate cost classification at the completion of the month.

Cost Ledger

Purpose.   To record by subaccount all costs and man-hours expended. The data recorded are used to prepare of the cost report—field labor.

Prepared By.   The field accountant.

Frequency.   On a monthly basis.

Preparation.   At the completion of each month, the total man-hours and total labor costs per subaccount are recorded from the labor distribution schedules and entered into the appropriate cost ledger sheets. The man-hours expended and total labor costs to date are obtained by totaling the respective columns.

Cost Control Forms

Foreman's Quantity Report

Purpose.   To record each crew and by subaccount the units of work in place or completed on a daily basis and the foreman's estimate of units to complete. The data recorded are used to prepare the man-hour and quantity record.

Prepared By.   The craft foreman.

Frequency.   Should be maintained on a daily basis.

Preparation.   From the onset of construction, the cost engineer establishes the following items to be filled in on an appropriate number of forms for a monthly period to show each labor subaccount:

Account number

Craft

Unit of quantity

Description of work

Original budget quantity   (a)

When change orders are approved or revised estimates prepared, the cost engineer must then arrange for the following items to be filled in on future sheets:

Budget including authorized changes quantity   (b)
Current estimate completion quantity   (c)

At the start of each day, the craft supervisor must distribute appropriate report forms to his foreman to cover the items which their crews will be working on

FOREMAN'S QUANTITY REPORT   DATE _____

J. O. NO _____ UNIT _____ CRAFT _____ ACCOUNT NO _____

DESCRIPTION OF WORK _____

(a) Original Budget Quantity	
(b) Budget Incl. Auth. Changes No's____ to_____Quantity	
(c) Current Estimated Completion Quantity	
(d) Units Previously Reported	
(e) Units Completed Today	
(f) Units Completed to Date	
(g) Foreman's Estimated Units to Complete	
(h) Total Manhours Worked Today	Signed	Foreman	Supervisor
Field Engineer's Progress Measurement	
Field Engineer's Remarks	
	Field Engineer	Date

FIGURE 15.5 Foreman's quantity report.

that day. At the completion of the day's work and prior to returning the report to the supervisor, the foreman fills in:

Units completed today	(e)
Units completed to date	(f)
Foreman's estimated units to complete	(g)
Total man-hours worked today	(h)

Routing. The craft supervisor transcribes figure (f) from today's card onto the following day's card against item (d), "units previously reported." After signing the foreman's quantity cards, the craft supervisor then forwards them to the cost engineer. A sample foreman's quantity form is shown in Fig. 15.5.

Notes. This report is intended to be completed and submitted daily to correspond with the man-hours reported by the foreman or his foreman's time cards. In cases such as erection of a specific piece of equipment taking several days, the foreman's quantity report may be submitted instead on an event basis at the completion of the erection rather than daily. The craft supervisor should notify the cost engineer when reports are being accumulated to cover more than a one-day period.

Progress Measurement. On at least a monthly basis, it is necessary for the field engineer to physically check progress measurements in the field and compare them with quantities completed using the drawings and bills of material. Any discrepancy between these check measurements and cumulative figures from the foreman's quantity reports must be immediately adjusted by the cost engineer in the "cumulative" column of the man-hour and quantity record in the "units completed to date" column of the next day's foreman's quantity report.

Man-Hour and Quantity Record

Purpose. To record and accumulate by subaccount the man-hours expended and the units of work completed and in place so that a comparison with the budget allowance of man-hours per unit is available. The data recorded are used in the preparation of the cost report—field labor.

Prepared By. The cost engineer.

Frequency. On a daily basis.

Preparation. When construction begins, the cost engineer must arrange for sheets to be prepared for each labor subaccount showing

Account number

Craft

Unit

Description of work

Original budget—quantity

Original budget—total man-hours

Original budget—man-hours per unit

The cost engineer must on a daily basis obtain the previous day's foreman's quantity report and foreman's time cards and enter the day's quantities and man-hours into the "actual for period" columns of the appropriate man-hour and quantity record sheets (see Fig. 15.6). The cost engineer must also forward the cumulative total to date and calculate and enter the man-hours per unit both for the day and for the cumulative totals. At the completion of the month, man-hours recorded are checked against those on the labor distribution schedules and corrections or adjustments are made if necessary.

Progress Measurement. Periodically, but not more often than monthly, the field engineer should carry out a physical progress survey in the field and check quantities of work completed utilizing drawings and bills of material. The field engineer should also check the quantities to complete. Details of quantities are then established and forwarded to the cost engineer who enters these quantities in the "cumulative quantity" column and the "current established completion quantity" column on the next line of the appropriate man-hour and quantity record. The cost engineer then rules off data previously recorded above this line and henceforth uses this corrected quantity to establish future quantities. If measured quantities differ, he must reconcile the difference the cumulative obtained from the foreman's quantity report and make the necessary corrections against the "units previously reported" on the next day's foreman's time card.

Authorized Change Orders. Immediately upon receipt of an approved change order which affects a specific subaccount, the cost engineer must record the new budgeted quantities, man-hours, and man-hours per unit in the "current budget" column and rule out the entry above.

Current Estimated Completion. Periodically, but not more often than monthly, the cost engineer analyzes all other data recorded to date and after discussions with the superintendent, his supervisory staff, and the field engineer records into the "current estimated completion" columns the best estimate of

MAN-HOUR AND QUANTITY CONTROL ANALYSIS

PERIOD ENDING ___ SHEET ___ OF ___ J.O. NO. ___

ACCOUNT NUMBER	DESCRIPTION	MAN-HOUR DATA						BUDGET EST. & AUTH. CHANGES			ACTUAL			REVISED		
		BUDGET (1)	TO DATE (2)	PREVIOUS (3)	CURRENT (4)	% EXPEND (2) (5)	PHY. COMP. % (6)	QUANTITY	UNIT PRICE	AMOUNT	QUANTITY IN PLACE	UNIT PRICE	AMOUNT	QUANTITY	UNIT PRICE	AMOUNT

FIGURE 15.6   Man-hour and quantity control analysis.

15.23

(total) quantities, total man-hours, and man-hours per unit for each subaccount. As this is recorded, the line above is then ruled out.

Notes. There are some labor items for which it is not practical to submit daily quantity reports. In such cases, in lieu of a daily entry, an entry for the period covered by the foreman's quantity report is made and matched to the appropriate foreman's time cards for the same period.

The man-hour and quantity records give the earliest available information for comparing actual labor productivity with the productivity from the budget estimate. It is extremely important that in the early stages of each section of work, the cost engineer monitor closely the actual unit rate in comparison with the budgeted unit rate.

The cost engineer must observe the performance of the work in the field and discuss productivity with the project superintendent and his supervisory staff to assist in forecasting future trends and the project schedule. The cost engineer must also advise the superintendent of construction promptly of actual or suspected problem areas so that corrective action may be initiated.

Cost Report—Field Labor

Purpose. To record and show for each labor subaccount quantities, units, and total costs committed for the period, committed to date with forecasts to complete and to provide comparisons between current estimated completion costs and current approved budget allowances.

Prepared By. Field accountant in conjunction with the cost engineer.

Frequency. Monthly, or more frequently if required.

Preparation. When the control budget is established, the cost analyst prepares master transparency sheets showing for each labor subaccount:

Account number

Description

Unit

Original budget—quantity

Original budget—unit cost

Original budget—amount

Sufficient sets of the transparencies are sent to the cost engineer to cover the number of reports required for the duration of the project.

For each report, the field accountant uses the cost ledger sheets and man-hour and quantity records and fills in

Quantity for period	(a)
Quantity to date	(b)
Amount for the period	(c)
Amount to date	(d)

The field accountant must also fill in the unit costs:

Unit cost per period	(c)	(by calculation)
	(a)	
Unit cost to date	(d)	(by calculation)
	(b)	

Utilizing the change order records, the cost engineer must fill in the quantity, unit cost, and amount for all authorized changes.

After reviewing the pending engineering change records, making appropriate references to man-hour and quantity records, and talking to the superintendent and the field engineer, the cost engineer then fills in the quantities, unit costs, and amounts for forecast to complete.

The field accountant then completes and returns the cost report to the cost engineer who uses the remarks column to explain discrepancies from the previous report. The cost report form (Fig. 15.3) can be used for this purpose.

Man-Hour Report (Optional)

Purpose.   To show in summary form by subaccount the man-hours per craft, total man-hours, and total labor costs on a weekly basis.

Prepared By.   The timekeeper.

Frequency.   Weekly if required by the superintendent of construction.

Preparation.   The total weekly man-hours per craft per subaccount are transcribed from the labor distribution schedule, which may then be added to obtain the total man-hours per subaccount. Total costs may be calculated by* multiplying the man-hours per craft by the average rate per craft. For a sample man-hour report form, see Fig. 15.7.

DISTRIBUTABLE ACCOUNTS

General

Distributable accounts often constitute a significant portion of the total construction budget, and it is important that they be properly recorded and controlled. In order for actual costs to be compared with budgeted allowances, they must be distributed and recorded in the same fashion that they were in the project budget.

When a project is partially or completely subcontracted, many of the items described are distributed over direct accounts and may never be shown as individual items. An example of this is the rental of construction materials and equipment. On a subcontracted project, the subcontractor will generally prorate his distributable costs into the cost of his work. To the subcontractor, equipment rental would be distributable; to the general contractor, it would be considered part of direct costs he is paying to the subcontractor. When a field organization exists, costs for distributable items such as the cost of the field office are incurred and must be periodically reported. If these costs have been included in the budgetary allocations as a line item, record keeping during construction will be simplified.

---

*For weekly reports throughout the monthly period, the average craft rates obtained from the previous month's monthly analysis should be used. For the last weekly report of the month, the average rates may be obtained from the current monthly analysis.

MAN-HOUR REPORT

WEEK ENDING	SHEET OF	J. O. NO.

ACCOUNT NUMBERS	DESCRIPTION	TOTAL		NUMBER OF MAN-HOURS																
		MAN-HOURS	COST	BOILER-MAKERS	BRICK-LAYERS	CARPEN-TERS	CEMENT FINISHERS	ELEC-TRICIANS	IRON-WORKERS	LABORERS	MILL-WRIGHTS	OPERATING ENGINEERS	PAINTERS	STEAM-FITTERS & PLUMBERS	TEAMSTERS					MISCELLAN-EOUS

FIGURE 15.7 Man-hour report.

The distributable accounts are estimated and controlled under the following categories:

1. Field offices
2. Insurance—injuries and damages
3. Temporary construction
4. Construction equipment
5. Other distributables

Field Office

This account will be charged the expenditures of the field office staff which include, but should not be limited to, the following:

1. Construction supervision
2. Field office engineering staff
3. Accounting staff
4. Other staff
   a. Labor relations
   b. Purchasing
5. Quality control

These accounts will also be charged with the material expenses that are incurred for maintaining the field complex for the life of the project.

The field cost engineer should periodically (preferably on a monthly basis) update the personnel schedule and report summary, showing actual costs incurred as compared to what has been budgeted. Expenses are similarly collected and reported for comparison against the budgeted figures. For a sample nonmanual personnel schedule and report summary see Fig. 15.8.

Insurance—Injuries and Damages

This account will be charged for the expenditures for premiums of all classes of insurance protection for the project. In addition, costs for medical, hospital, and other services resulting from personal injuries not reimbursable by insurance carriers and payments to an injured person or to the owner or any other property which may be damaged will also be charged to this account. A partial listing of items included in this account are as follows:

Worker's Compensation Insurance and Employer's Liability Insurance

Bodily Injury and Property Damage Insurance

Property Insurance

State Insurance Funds

Miscellaneous insurance (employee's personal insurance, fidelity and surety bonds, etc.)

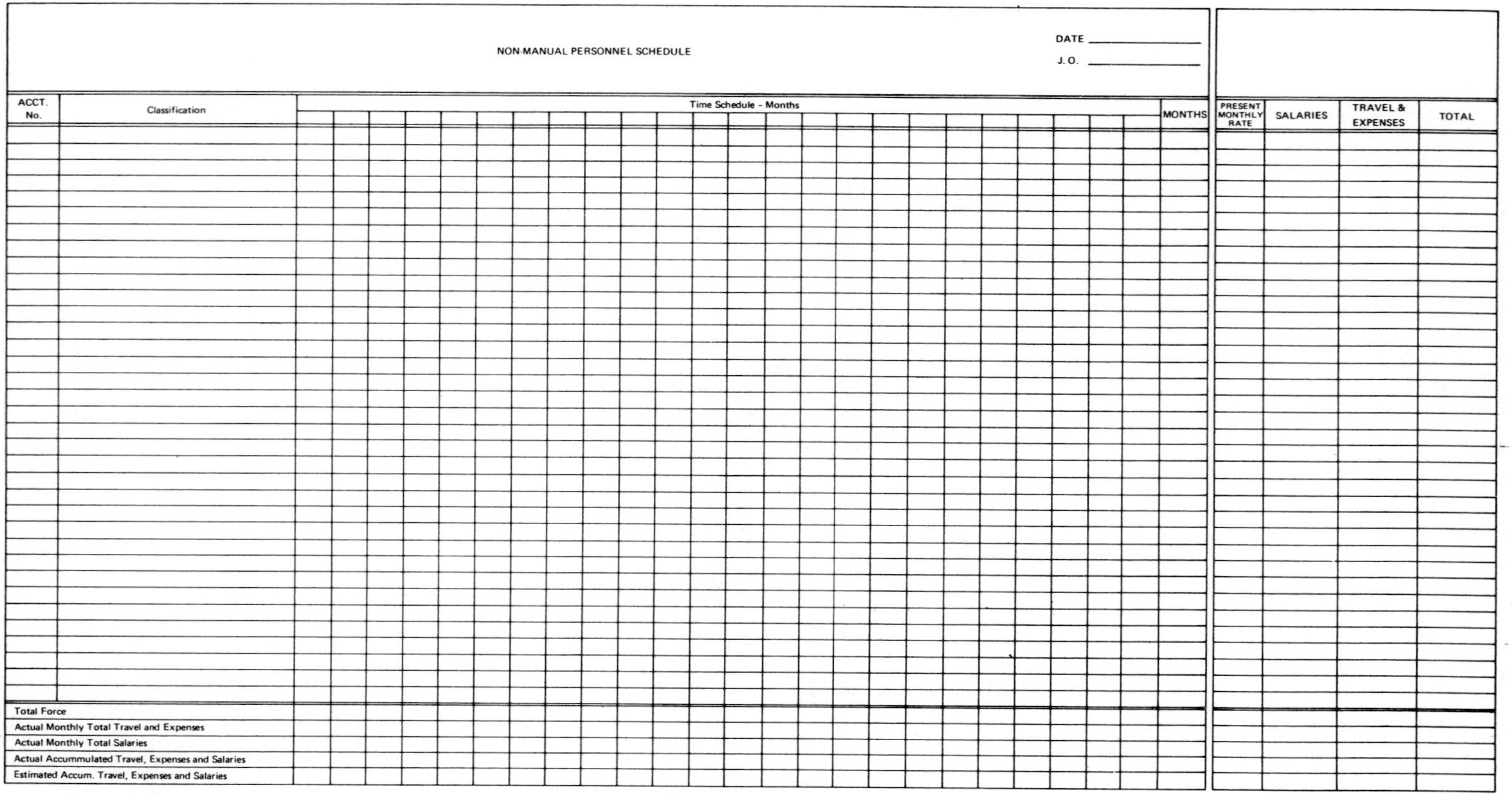

NON-MANUAL PERSONNEL SCHEDULE

DATE ______

J.O. ______

ACCT. No.	Classification	Time Schedule - Months	MONTHS	PRESENT MONTHLY RATE	SALARIES	TRAVEL & EXPENSES	TOTAL
Total Force							
Actual Monthly Total Travel and Expenses							
Actual Monthly Total Salaries							
Actual Accummulated Travel, Expenses and Salaries							
Estimated Accum. Travel, Expenses and Salaries							

FIGURE 15.8 Nonmanual personnel schedule.

Temporary Construction

This account is established to track the expenditures of all work of a temporary nature that is done solely for the purpose of construction, such as roads, storage facilities, job buildings, service systems and structures, supports and installation of equipment for construction plant, and construction equipment.

Temporary Roadways, Railroads, Parking Areas, etc.   Included in the account are all temporary transportation facilities necessary to get supervisory and craft personnel and material to and about the project. Associated items such as culverts for drainage should be included as part of the roadway work. Gin pole foundations and deadmen should be included in the account with crane mats.

Temporary Storage Facilities.   Included in this account should be material storage yards, and warehouses, including racks and other items for the storage of construction material. The account should also include ancillary costs associated with temporary warehouses such as plumbing, heating, and lighting installation, both within the building and in adjacent areas. Specific features of the building such as dimension and type should be recorded in the cost ledger for future bidding purposes.

Temporary Buildings.   Included in this account should be all temporary buildings and facilities necessary for the performance of contract work. This should include, but not be limited to, the office building, shops, and locker and shower rooms. Costs associated with these facilities such as plumbing, heating, lighting, and air conditioning should be included. The account should also include costs for necessary relocation of existing buildings that will be used for the project. The building dimensions, and type of construction, should be recorded in the cost ledger for future reference.

Temporary Service Facilities.   Included in this account are all costs for installing temporary services such as water lines, heating and gas lines, air lines, sewer and drains, culverts, and disposal equipment. Also included are light and power lines and equipment and oxygen, acetylene, and other piping manifolds. The costs for the installation start at the point of connection to the permanent service and the end at the point of connection to the temporary building or area. Also included is the cost of temporary services to permanent buildings or areas.

Miscellaneous.   All expenditures for operation and supplies, including utility charges, e.g., water and electricity, required for the temporary construction accounts above are included in this account. Expenditures for items such as removing snow from roads and work areas, temporary closures, temporary heat, and weather protection should also be included in the miscellaneous account. For some projects, it may be desirable to break out the miscellaneous account into subaccounts to identify such items such as temporary heat, winter protection, etc.

Construction Equipment

1. This account contains types of equipment, tools, and supplies as follows:
   a. Automotive equipment
   b. Heavy construction equipment
   c. Light construction equipment
   d. Craft tools (salvagable)
   e. Expendable tools and supplies
2. Rental rates for all heavy and light construction equipment should be established for estimating and control purposes regardless of whether such equipment is owned, purchased for the client's account, or rented or leased from an independent company.
3. The heavy construction equipment (listed as "b" above) account will be charged with the expenditures for major construction equipment procured through an outside firm or purchased with the anticipation of resale value at the completion of the project and charged to the project on a rental basis. Charges for assembling and dismantling equipment should also be included in this account. Costs incurred for putting second-hand equipment into operating condition or into saleable condition at the completion of the project should be considered as a decrease in salvage value when establishing the applicable rental rates.

Operators and operation costs (fuel, oil, etc.) should be charged to the "and use" accounts. This includes operators of equipment rented on a fully maintained and operated basis.

For a sample of the construction equipment rental form and the construction equipment purchase form, see Figs 15.9 and 15.10.

Other Distributables

Premium Pay. Costs should be included in the budget estimate if an extended work week is anticipated at the time that the estimate is prepared; covered by an authorized change if an extended work week is authorized in the change order; or accumulated from various daily premium overtime work.

Premium costs incurred for casual or incidental overtime labor should be charged to the appropriate account subdivisions. This will include the premium cost of day-to-day overtime other than scheduled for an extended work day or work shift in specific instances, such as concrete pouring or finishing.

The premium cost of overtime that is authorized over and above a standard work week or shift period should be charged to the appropriate account subdivisions.

The premium cost of scheduled overtime for one or more crafts over and above an authorized work week should be charged to the appropriate account subdivisions. Special scheduled overtime may be required and is advantageous when one or more crafts are working in confined areas or behind schedule.

Note. When overtime is scheduled for any period of time, there is a loss in productivity, and such costs must be taken into consideration when estimating the cost of work as well as the premium time portion. The project superintendent must participate in a decision to authorize overtime hours.

RENTED CONSTRUCTION EQUIPMENT

PROJECT CLIENT AND LOCATION

J.O. NO.

DATE ISSUED

| EQUIP. NO. | DESCRIPTION | P. O. REF. | RENTAL PERIOD | | | RENTAL RATE | ESTIMATED—ACTUAL | | | REMARKS |
			START	FINISH	TIME		RENTAL AMOUNT	TRANSP. CHARGES	TOTAL	

FIGURE 15.9 Rented construction equipment.

15.31

PURCHASED CONSTRUCTION EQUIPMENT

EQUIP. NO.	DESCRIPTION	P. O. REF.	NUMBER OF UNITS	TOTAL PURCHASE PRICE	NEW	USED	PERIOD OF USE ON JOB	ESTIMATED—ACTUAL		REMARKS
								SALVAGE CREDIT	COST TO JOB	

PROJECT, CLIENT AND LOCATION

J.O. NO.

DATE ISSUED

FIGURE 15.10 Purchased construction equipment.

Employer's Labor Expenses and Benefits (Except Taxes and Insurances). Included in these accounts are transportation and subsistence allowances paid to workers; nonproductive time (reporting time, stand-by time, generated work day or work week, treatment time for job-incurred injuries, and idle time of construction equipment operators); recruiting expenses; and employer's contributions to union health and welfare and other benefit funds as set forth in working agreements. Contributions for Social Security, income tax withholding, state medical aid, or group insurance and transportation (buses furnished by employer for employee transport) are included.

Survey Account. This account should include all expenditures for site layout, surveys, test pits, borings, test piles, river gauging, and the like that will be utilized for engineering studies and design.

Clen-Up Account. The clean-up account covers all charges for final clean-up and final disposal of construction debris prior to turning the project over to the owner. This account should also include the day-to-day clean-up charges for work performed by an assigned crew for the duration of the project.

When clean-up work is performed by company forces, day-to-day clean-up associated with specific craft work should be chargeable to the respective "and use" accounts.

Subcontracted work that requires the contractor to perform all clean-up associated with his work will be allocated to the "and use" accounts.

General Condition Accounts. The accounts cover costs of guards and watchmen, building permits, and licenses including inspection and other miscellaneous fees, operators of utility trucks, and automobiles used for general work whose wages cannot be allocated to direct accounts and wages of warehousemen.

Cost Report Form

1. Detailed cost reports similar to those prepared for material and labor must be maintained for each of the distributable accounts.
2. Each of the distributable accounts must be summarized for inclusion into the revised estimate and job cost report.

REVISED ESTIMATE AND JOB COST REPORT

General

Periodically, there should be a project oversight review performed in conjunction with a revised budget estimate and a job cost report prepared. The purpose of this is to control and forecast the total cost of the project through completion. Based on specific projects, this may be warranted quarterly or semiannually. It is even more important that this evaluation be performed for projects that have experienced a significant number of change orders or where work is being performed on a time-and-material basis. The overview should take into consideration any and all changed conditions that may have occurred during the life of the project. Obviously, the type of contract will dictate the requirements for the updated budget and its distribution. A typical sample of a revised estimate and job cost report is shown in Fig. 15.11.

This report should be updated periodically and presented. It will be noted that the report is summarized into the following constituent parts:

Account number and description

Commitments

   Present material commitments

   Present labor commitments

Estimate to complete

   Material estimate to complete

Labor estimate to complete

Revised estimate (material, labor, and total)

Budget estimate (material, labor, and total)

Differences—variations between revised estimate and budget estimate in terms of material, labor, and total

The preparation of the revised estimate should be consistent with the accounting system being used on a weekly and monthly basis for the project. All responsible groups involved in the project must submit this data to the cost engineer in the form of account code, present commitment, and projected estimate to complete.

The basis for reporting accurate cost projections is the standard working documents prepared by the various individuals on the project team. These include man-hour charts; nonmanual personnel schedules; purchased and rented construction equipment forms; time, labor, and commitment records; purchase order register; materials committed records; and specially designed forms for the reporting and control of structural, mechanical, and electrical work items. These are all incorporated into the overall job cost report and when put to their ultimate use, provide a successful means of reporting and controlling project costs.

Revised Estimate Totals

The revised estimate totals are ascertained by adding the commitments to the estimate to complete. The revised estimate may be summarized as in Fig. 15.11a and b. Items where a change is indicated from the budget estimate or the previous estimate should be verified, and if an increase or decrease is of significant value, it should be explained in a narrative form and submitted to the owner or client for review. It is essential that this report be provided at the earliest possible date to allow the maximum time to implement corrective measures.

Review of Job Cost Report

The cost engineer has a significant, important assignment on a project and must place particular emphasis on checking the proper preparation of the following items:

ABC Chemical Company

Process Unit

J.O. NO. 000
REPORT NO.   DATE

Account number	Description	Commitments Material	Commitments Labor	Estimate to complete Material	Estimate to complete Labor	Revised estimate Material	Revised estimate Labor	Revised estimate Total
	Process Equipment							
A	Towers	895,000	90,000	15,000	25,000	910,000	115,000	1,025,000
B	Boilers, steam superheaters	—	—	—	—	—	—	—
F	Process furnaces	1,050,000	53,000	160,000	62,000	1,210,000	115,000	1,325,000
G	General equipment	170,500	31,000	39,500	33,000	210,000	64,000	274,000
L	Reactors	75,000	4,000	5,000	1,000	80,000	5,000	85,000
M	Drums	306,000	12,000	12,000	6,000	318,000	18,000	336,000
Q	Storage tanks	204,000	8,000	8,000	4,000	212,000	12,000	224,000
P	Pumps and drivers	525,000	11,500	22,000	5,000	547,000	16,500	563,500
R	Compressors and drivers	1,225,000	26,500	53,000	17,000	1,278,000	43,500	1,321,500
S	Stacks	10,000	1,000	—	—	10,000	1,000	11,000
T	Heat exchangers	1,675,000	22,000	40,000	8,000	1,715,000	30,000	1,745,000
	Total—Process equipment	6,135,500	259,000	354,500	161,000	6,490,000	420,000	6,910,000
	Process Materials							
C	Piping	1,718,500	806,000	1,081,500	1,094,000	2,800,000	1,900,000	4,700,000
D	Structures	255,500	100,500	14,500	39,500	270,000	140,000	410,000
E	Electrical	287,500	327,500	102,500	272,500	390,000	600,000	990,000
H	Buildings	112,300	90,500	27,700	24,500	140,000	115,000	255,000
J	Civil	438,500	411,500	66,500	73,500	505,000	485,000	990,000
K	Instruments	377,500	25,500	172,500	64,500	550,000	90,000	640,000
N	Insulation and painting	485,000	636,000	95,000	94,000	580,000	730,000	1,310,000
	Total—Process materials	3,674,800	2,397,500	1,560,200	1,662,500	5,235,000	4,060,000	9,295,000
	Distributable Accounts							
V	Insurance and taxes	190,000	205,000	130,000	235,000	320,000	440,000	760,000
O	Other distributable items	57,000	35,000	163,000	245,000	220,000	280,000	500,000
X	Temporary construction facilities	55,000	60,000	15,000	20,000	70,000	80,000	150,000
Y	Field office	30,500	190,500	29,500	189,500	60,000	380,000	440,000
Z	Construction tools and equipment	450,000	150,000	130,000	40,000	580,000	190,000	770,000
	Total—Distributable accounts	782,500	640,500	467,500	729,500	1,250,000	1,370,000	2,620,000
	Indirect Accounts							
U	Headquarters office	70,500	709,700	34,500	135,300	105,000	845,000	950,000
	Total—Project costs	10,663,300	4,006,700	2,416,700	2,688,300	13,080,000	6,695,000	19,775,000

FIGURE 15.11 Revised estimate and job cost report.

JOB TITLE

ABC Chemical Company J.O. NO. 000 REPORT NO. DATE

Process Unit

Account number	Description	Commitments		Estimate to complete		Revised estimate		
		Material	Labor	Material	Labor	Material	Labor	Total
	Process Equipment							
A	Towers	930,000	125,000	1,055,000	-20,000	-10,000	-30,000	
B	Boilers, steam superheaters	—	—	—	—	—	—	
F	Process furnaces	1,190,000	110,000	1,300,000	+20,000	+5,000	+25,000	
G	General equipment	195,000	57,500	252,500	+15,000	+6,500	+21,500	
L	Reactors	85,000	6,000	91,000	-5,000	-1,000	-6,000	
M	Drums	330,000	20,000	350,000	-12,000	-2,000	-14,000	
Q	Storage tanks	220,000	15,000	235,000	-8,000	-3,000	-11,000	
P	Pumps and drivers	550,000	20,000	570,000	-3,000	-3,500	-6,500	
R	Compressors and drivers	1,270,000	50,000	1,320,000	+8,000	-6,500	+1,500	
S	Stacks	10,000	1,500	11,500	—	-500	-500	
T	Heat exchangers	1,710,000	30,000	1,740,000	+5,000	—	+5,000	
	Total—Process equipment	6,490,000	435,000	6,925,000	—	-15,000	-15,000	
	Process Materials							
C	Piping	2,895,000	1,980,000	4,875,000	-95,000	-80,000	-175,000	
D	Structures	290,000	150,000	440,000	-20,000	-10,000	-30,000	
E	Electrical	410,000	620,000	1,030,000	-20,000	-20,000	-40,000	
H	Buildings	135,000	125,000	260,000	+5,000	-10,000	-5,000	
J	Civil	500,000	490,000	990,000	+5,000	-5,000	—	
K	Instruments	575,000	110,000	685,000	-25,000	-20,000	-45,000	
N	Insulation and painting	585,000	730,000	1,315,000	-5,000	—	-5,000	
	Total—Process materials	5,390,000	4,205,000	9,595,000	-155,000	-145,000	-300,000	
	Distributable Accounts							
V	Insurance and taxes	315,000	450,000	765,000	+5,000	-10,000	-5,000	
O	Other distributable items	190,000	285,000	475,000	+30,000	-5,000	+25,000	
X	Temporary construction facilities	80,000	90,000	170,000	-10,000	-10,000	-20,000	
Y	Field office	60,000	390,000	450,000	—	-10,000	-10,000	
Z	Construction tools and equipment	590,000	210,000	800,000	-10,000	-20,000	-30,000	
	Total—Distributable accounts	1,235,000	1,425,000	2,660,000	+15,000	-55,000	-40,000	
	Indirect Accounts							
U	Headquarters office	100,000	870,000	970,000	+5,000	-25,000	-20,000	
	Total—Project costs	13,215,000	6,935,000	20,150,000	-135,000	-240,000	-375,000	

FIGURE 15.11 Revised estimate and job cost report. (*Continued*)

1. Changes in scope—authorization and pending
2. Manual manpower projections—rates and benefits used
3. Basis of calculation of insurance and taxes
4. Nonmanual projection
5. Projection of purchased and rented construction equipment including development of estimated salvage
6. Quantities, source, and use
7. Field order extras
8. Calculations of premium pay—manual and nonmanual (particularly if job is on an extended work week)
9. Check of estimated project schedules and completion date
10. Material and labor escalation
11. Contract terms regarding compensation and fee calculation

The results of the cost engineer's efforts will be a complete and comprehensive report with up-to-date information. The report should be reviewed by the project management and supervision prior to issuance to the client.

SUMMARY

With today's projects becoming more and more complex and costly, a major project cannot succeed without proper controls. Maintaining proper records requires excellent documentation, accurate cost estimating, up-to-date cost controls, and up-to-date scheduling. Each of these is interrelated and ultimately will affect the success or failure of a project from a financial standpoint. Figure 15.12 is a typical estimated and actual expenditures chart graphically representing these interrelationships in a summary fashion. When utilizing proper cost controls, a chart of this nature can be maintained on a monthly basis and will work as an early warning system for management.

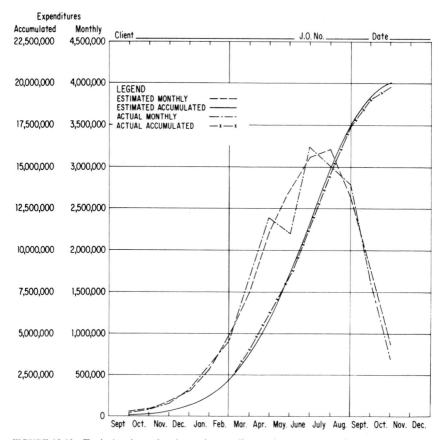

FIGURE 15.12 Typical estimated and actual expenditures chart: process unit-cost control.

APPENDIX A

02450   Railroad Work
02480   Marine Work
02500   Paving and Surfacing
02600   Utility Piping Materials
02660   Water Distribution
02680   Fuel and Steam Distribution
02700   Sewerage and Drainage
02760   Restoration of Underground Pipe
02770   Ponds and Reservoirs
02780   Power and Communications
02800   Site Improvements
02900   Landscaping

Division 3—Concrete

03100   Concrete Formwork
03200   Concrete Reinforcement
03250   Concrete Accessories
03300   Cast-in-Place Concrete
03370   Concrete Curing
03400   Precast Concrete
03500   Cementitous Decks and Toppings
03600   Grout
03700   Concrete Restoration and Cleaning
03800   Mass Concrete

Division 4—Masonry

04100   Mortar and Masonry Grout
04150   Masonry Accessories
04200   Unit Masonry
04400   Stone
04500   Masonry Restoration and Cleaning
04550   Refractories
04600   Corrosion-Resistant Masonry
04700   Simulated Masonry

Division 5—Metals

05010   Metal Materials
05030   Metal Coatings

05050   Metal Fastening
05100   Structural Metal Framing
05200   Metal Joists
05300   Metal Decking
05400   Cold-Formed Metal Framing
05500   Metal Fabrications
05580   Sheet Metal Fabrications
05700   Ornamental Metal
05800   Expansion Control
05900   Hydraulic Structures

Division 6—Wood and Plastics

06050   Fasteners and Adhesives
06100   Rough Carpentry
06130   Heavy Timber Construction
06150   Wood and Metal Systems
06170   Prefabricated Structural Wood
06300   Wood Treatment
06400   Architectural Woodwork
06500   Structural Plastics
06600   Plastic Fabrications
06650   Solid Polymer Fabrications

Division 7—Thermal and Moisture Protection

07100   Waterproofing
07150   Dampproofing
07180   Water Repellents
07190   Vapor Retarders
07195   Air Barriers
07200   Insulation
07240   Exterior Insulation and Finish Systems
07250   Fireproofing
07270   Firestopping
07300   Shingles and Roofing Tiles
07400   Manufactured Roofing and Siding
07480   Exterior Wall Assemblies
07500   Membrane Roofing
07570   Traffic Coatings
07600   Flashing and Sheet Metal

07700   Roof Specialties and Accessories
07800   Skylights
07900   Joint Sealers

Division 8—Doors and Windows

08100   Metal Doors and Frames
08200   Wood and Plastic Doors
08250   Door-Opening Assemblies
08300   Special Doors
08400   Entrances and Storefronts
08500   Metal Windows
08600   Wood and Plastic Windows
08650   Special Windows
08700   Hardware
08800   Glazing
08900   Glazed Curtain Walls

Division 9—Finishes

09100   Metal Support Systems
09200   Lath and Plaster
09250   Gypsum Board
09300   Tile
09400   Terrazzo
09450   Stone Facing
09500   Acoustical Treatment
09540   Special Wall Surfaces
09545   Special Ceiling Surfaces
09550   Wood Flooring
09600   Stone Flooring
09630   Unit Masonry Flooring
09650   Resilient Flooring
09680   Carpet
09700   Special Flooring
09780   Floor Treatment
09800   Special Coatings
09900   Painting
09950   Wall Coverings

Division 10—Specialties

10100	Visual Display Boards
10150	Compartments and Cubicles
10200	Louvers and Vents
10240	Grilles and Screens
10250	Service Wall Systems
10260	Wall and Corner Guards
10270	Access Flooring
10290	Pest Control
10300	Fireplaces and Stoves
10340	Manufactured Exterior Specialties
10350	Flagpoles
10400	Identifying Devices
10450	Pedestrian Control Devices
10500	Lockers
10520	Fire Protection Specialties
10530	Protective Covers
10550	Postal Specialties
10600	Partitions
10650	Operable Partitions
10670	Storage Shelving
10700	Exterior Protection Devices for Openings
10750	Telephone Specialties
10800	Toilet and Bath Accessories
10880	Scales
10900	Wardrobe and Closet Specialties

Division 11—Equipment

11010	Maintenance Equipment
11020	Security and Vault Equipment
11030	Teller and Service Equipment
11040	Ecclesiastical Equipment
11050	Library Equipment
11060	Theater and Stage Equipment
11070	Instrumental Equipment
11080	Registration Equipment
11090	Checkroom Equipment
11100	Mercantile Equipment
11110	Commercial Laundry and Dry Cleaning Equipment

11120   Vending Equipment
11130   Audio-Visual Equipment
11140   Vehicle Service Equipment
11150   Parking Control Equipment
11160   Loading Dock Equipment
11170   Solid Waste-Handling Equipment
11190   Detention Equipment
11200   Water Supply and Treatment Equipment
11280   Hydraulic Gates and Valves
11300   Fluid Waste Treatment and Disposal Equipment
11400   Food Service Equipment
11450   Residential Equipment
11460   Unit Kitchens
11470   Darkroom Equipment
11480   Athletic, Recreational, and Therapeutic Equipment
11500   Industrial and Process Equipment
11600   Laboratory Equipment

APPENDIX B

CLASSIFICATION OF ACCOUNTS, MAIN STEM ACCOUNT CODES

Direct Accounts

Code	Process Equipment
A	Towers
B	Boilers, Steam Superheaters
F	Process Furnaces
G	General Equipment
L	Reactors
M	Drums
Q	Storage Tanks
P	Pumps and Drives
R	Compressors and Drivers
S	Stacks
T	Heat Exchangers

Process Materials

C	Piping
D	Structures
E	Electrical
H	Buildings
J	Civil
K	Instruments
N	Insulation and Painting

Distributable Accounts

V	Insurance and Taxes
W	Overseas Shipping Costs
O	Other Distributable Items
X	Temporary Construction Facilities
Y	Field Office
Z	Construction Tools and Equipment

Indirect Accounts

U	Headquarters Office

APPENDIX C

CLASSIFICATION OF ACCOUNTS, MAIN STEM AND SUBSTEM ACCOUNT CODES

Land, Land Rights, and Yard Work

1000   Land and land rights

    .11 Negotiated Purchases
    .21 Easements and Permits
    .22 Acquisition Cost
    .23 Damages to Crops, etc.
    .24 Protection of Property
    .31 Miscellaneous Charges
    .32 Miscellaneous Credits

1100   Yard work

    .11 Clearing
    .12 Grading
    .13 Surfacing (Yard and Parking Area)
    .14 Landscaping

    .21 Roads
    .22 Walks
    .23 Fences

    .31 Water System
    .32 Sewer System
    .33 Storm-Sewer System
    .34 Fire-Protection Lines
    .35 Process Sewers
    .36 Steam Lines and Returns
    .37 Gas Fuel Lines
    .38 Oil Fuel Lines
    .39 Other Yard Services

    .41 Fire Pumps and Housing
    .42 Fire Hose and Housing
    .47 Fire Meters and Instruments

    .61 Trackwork—Subgrading
    .62 Trackwork—Ballast
    .66 Railroad Track
    .69 Trackwork—Miscellaneous

    .71 Yard Lighting—Duct Lines
    .72 Yard Lighting—Conduit
    .73 Yard Lighting—Supports for Overhead Lines
    .74 Yard Lighting—Fixtures and Supports
    .75 Yard Lighting—Transformers
    .76 Yard Lighting—Wire and Cable

    .81 Wharfs
    .82 Waterfront Improvements
    .83 Retaining Walls

.84 Bridges
.86 Earth Dikes
.99 Painting—Yard Services and Appurtenances

Nonprocess Buildings

1100	General Facilities Buildings

Includes all buildings outside the process areas, such as administrative, service, and auxiliary buildings.

Building numbers (third and fourth digits) will be used to segregate each building. Note: Building numbers assigned for process plants—general facilities buildings are compatible with those for similar buildings for generating stations.

Representative Building Numbers

1101	Main Powerhouse
1105	Administration Building
1107	Water-Treatment Plant
1108	Warehouse
1109	Machine Shop
1110	Sewage-Treatment Plant
1114*	Well Pump House
1115	Fire Pump House
1117*	Gatehouse
1119*	First-Aid Building
1123	Laboratory
1128*	Locker Rooms and Change House
1160*	Miscellaneous Structures (Other)

Note: *indicates costs will be accumulated by major subaccount only for low-cost buildings as follows:

.10 Substructure
.20 Superstructure
.30 Miscellaneous Construction
.40 Building Services (Mechanical)
.50 Building Services (Electrical)
.60 Building Appurtenances
.80 Nonprocess Equipment
.90 Painting

For large and/or high-cost buildings, detail cost breakdown will be as follows:

.11 Excavation and Backfill
.12 Pumping and Sheeting
.13 Bearing Piles
.14 Concrete (Substructure)
.16 Underpinning

.21   Structural Steel
.22   Siding
.23   Masonry Walls
.24   Concrete Superstructure
.25   Floors (Other than Concrete)
.26   Doors and Sash
.27   Roof Deck, Roofing, and Sheet Metalwork
.28   Interior Millwork and Finishing
.29   Miscellaneous (Canopies, etc.)

.31   Cutting and Patching
.33   Temporary Protection
.36   Shoring
.39   Temporary End Walls

.41   Plumbing
.42   Heating
.43   Ventilating and Air Conditioning
.46   Fire Protection
.47   Elevators and Service Equipment

.51   Lighting Conduit
.52   Wire and Cable
.54   Lighting Fixtures
.57   Distribution Cabinets
.58   Lighting Transformers
.59   Emergency Lighting System

.61   Stack
.62   Walkways (Overhead) between Buildings
.63   Tunnels between Buildings
.64   Signs

.91   Painting Substructure
.92   Painting Superstructure
.94   Painting Service Equipment
.96   Painting Building Appurtenances

1200–6900   These account numbers are used for identifying various major
process areas. These can be further subdivided as follows:

.1   Civil Work
.2   Equipment Structures
.3   Equipment
.4   Piping
.5   Electrical
.6   Services (Drains, etc.)
.7   Instrumentation
.8   Insulation and Fireproofing
.9   Painting

7100–7800   These account numbers are used for identifying support areas
such as waste-treatment facilities or electrical supply systems.
These areas can also be subdivided as shown above under major process areas (.1 through .9).

7900   This account grouping is used to identify suspense accounts which include stock, blanket orders, accruals, and receivables.

Distributable Costs

8030   Field Office (Complete)
- .10 Superintendent and Accountant
- .21 Construction Supervisors
- .22 Field Office Staff
- .23 Field Engineering Staff
- .31 Office Supplies
- .32 Office Furniture and Equipment
- .33 Medical and First Aid
- .81 Construction Drafting

8039   Overhead Allowance (Field Office)

8040   Other Construction Items
- .21   Insurance—Workmen's Compensation
- .22   Insurance—Construction Equipment
- .31   Temporary Roads
- .32   Temporary Storage Facilities
- .33   Temporary Buildings
- .34   Temporary Services
- .391 Temporary Facilities—Operating Supplies
- .393 Temporary Facilities—Maintenance and Repair
- .394 Temporary Facilities—Removal Cost
- .395 Temporary Facilities—Salvage (Credit)
- .399 Temporary Facilities—Winter Operation
- .421 Construction Equipment—Cost
- .423 Construction Equipment—Maintenance and Repair
- .424 Construction Equipment—Dismantle
- .425 Construction Equipment—Salvage
- .426 Construction Equipment—Operator Idle Time
- .427 Construction Equipment—Rental
- .428 Construction Equipment—Revenue
- .43   Auto Equipment—Cost (Detail as above)
- .44   Small Equipment and Durable Tools (Detail as above)
- .45   Scaffolding
- .47   Expendable Tools and Supplies
- .511 Premium Pay—Casual Overtime
- .512 Premium Pay—Extended Week
- .521 Premium Pay—Casual—Subcontractor
- .522 Premium Pay—Extended Week—Subcontractor
- .81   Labor Expense—Transportation
- .82   Labor Expense—Reporting Time
- .84   Labor Expense—Other Allowance
- .85   Transportation by Employer
- .88   Labor Expense—Benefit Funds
- .91   Preliminary Site Surveys
- .92   Cleanup and Housekeeping

.93 Guards and Watchmen
.94 Permits and Licenses
.95 Operators—Utility Trucks and Autos
.96 Warehousemen

Construction Taxes

8091   Field Payroll

.11 Field Payroll—Unemployment Insurance
.12 Field Payroll—Federal Insurance Contribution

8093   Taxes—Sales and Use

Headquarters Office

8100   Headquarters

.10 Engineering—Consulting and Administrative
.11 Engineering Divisions
.12 Design Divisions
.13 Engineering—Operational
.14 Engineering—Surveys and Reports
.15 Engineering—Computing Service
.16 Engineering—Purchased
.19 Engineering Design Travel Expense
.21 Inspecting and Expediting
.30 Communications and Reproductions
.40 Purchasing
.531 Construction Specialists
.532 Construction Computing Service
.54 Accounting—Auditing
.55 Clerical—General
.56 Construction and Project Managers
.71 Estimating
.72 Cost Division
.790 Computing Service—Estimating
.791 Computing Service—Cost
.81 Engineering—Preliminary Operation
.91 Premium Time—Headquarters Office

8190   Overhead—Headquarters

.11 Overhead—Engineering
.12 Overhead—Design
.13 Overhead—Other

8192   Federal and State Taxes

.21 Headquarters—Unemployment Insurance
.22 Headquarters—Federal Insurance Contributions

Other Costs

8300	Allowance for Indeterminates
	.11 Allowance for Indeterminates—Material
	.22 Allowance for Indeterminates—Labor
	.30 Allowance for Labor—Nonproductivity

8300   Allowance for Indeterminates
       .11 Allowance for Indeterminates—Material
       .22 Allowance for Indeterminates—Labor
       .30 Allowance for Labor—Nonproductivity

8400   Escalation
       .11 Estimated Escalation—Material
       .22 Estimated Escalation—Labor

8500   Fee
       .11 Fee

8600   Changes pending authorization
8700   Fee on pending changes

APPENDIX D

CLASSIFICATION OF ACCOUNTS, MAIN STEM ACCOUNT CODES

Class No.	Classification Title
0100	Fired Heaters and Boilers
0200	Stacks
0400	Reactors and Internals
0500	Towers and Internals
0600	Heat-Exchange Equipment
0700	Cooling Towers
0800	Vessels, Tanks, Drums, and Internals
0900	Pumps and Drivers
1000	Blowers and Compressors
1100	Elevators, Conveyors, Materials-Handling Equipment
1200	Miscellaneous Mechanical Equipment
1300	Piping
1400	Sewers
1500	Instrumentation
1600	Electrical
1700	Concrete
1800	Structural Steel
1900	Fireproofing
2000	Buildings
2100	Site Development
2200	Insulation
2300	Painting and Protective Coatings
2400	Field Testing
2500	Tankage
2600	Chemicals and Catalyst
2700	Piling
2800	Filters, Centrifuges, Separation Equipment
2900	Agitators and Mixers
3000	Scrubbers and Entrainment Separators
3100	Machine Tools and Machine-Shop Equipment
3200	Heating, Ventilation, Air Conditioning, Dust Control (process only)
3300	Fire Protection
3400	Package Units

3500	Miscellaneous Furniture
3700	Miscellaneous Direct Charges
3800	Storehouse Accounts
3900	Construction Supplies and Petty Tools
4000	Field Extra Work
5000	Insurance and Taxes
6000	Field Supervision and Field Office
6500	Construction Equipment and Tools
7000	Engineering Department
7300	Estimating and Project Cost Control
7400	Purchasing Department
7500	Construction Department Planning and Scheduling
7900	General Services and Expenses
8000	Main Office Expense
9000	Branch Office Expense

CHAPTER 16
CONTRACT ADMINISTRATION

Fred C. Kreitzberg P.E.
President and Chief Executive Officer
O'Brien-Kreitzberg & Associates, Inc.
San Francisco, California

The administration of the construction contract begins before it even exists. The record of preconstruction conference form (Fig. 16.1) provides a good agenda outline for the meeting and documents the items discussed.

After the contract is awarded, a meeting is conducted with the contractor, the architect-engineer, and the owner. The purpose of the meeting is to introduce key personnel and to review contract requirements and procedures. Normal items discussed include:

Functions and authority of personnel

Schedule for progress meetings

Submittals and shop drawings

Requests for information

Field instructions

Applications for payment

Progress schedules

Safety and job site security

Change order procedures

Subcontractors

Labor matters: Equal Employment Opportunity (EEO), Minority Business Enterprise (MBE), Woman-Owned Business Enterprise (WBE), Disadvantaged-Person Business Enterprise (DBE)

Disputes

Quality control

Site contractor coordination

Access and use of the site

The term *contract* is defined as "an agreement between two or more parties, sometimes written and enforceable by law." The term *administration* is defined as "the management of affairs." Just by their definitions alone, one is not aware of all the activities involved in proper *contract administration* nor is one aware of

RECORD OF
PRECONSTRUCTION CONFERENCE

Page 1 of 4

NAME OF OWNER	ADDRESS (Including Zip Code and Telephone Number)
NAME OF ARCHITECT/ENGINEER	ADDRESS (Including Zip Code and Telephone Number)
NAME OF CONTRACTOR (FIRM)	ADDRESS (Including Zip Code and Telephone Number)
LOCATION OF CONFERENCE	DATE

SUBJECTS TO BE DISCUSSED

1. Identification of Official Representatives of Owner, Engineer, Contractors and Other Interested Agency:

OWNER: _____   ENGINEER: _____

ADDRESS: _____   ADDRESS: _____

CONTRACTOR: _____   OTHER _____

ADDRESS: _____   ADDRESS: _____

2. Responsibilities of Engineers and Architect (Does not "supervise" the Contractor's employees, equipment or operations):

3. Responsibilities of Owner's Governing Body (Actual Contracting Organization):

4. Responsibilities of Contractor (Review Contract Terms):

5. Responsibilities of Any Other Agency Contributing to the Project:

FIGURE 16.1   Record of preconstruction conference.

the importance of contract administration in the day-to-day operation and the successful completion of a construction project. This chapter outlines the necessary steps to successfully manage the contractual elements of a construction contract.

The general contractor in today's construction world has a very difficult and important function: to execute satisfactorily all accepted contracts. The contractor must take an owner's ideas and turn them into reality. These ideas are usually in the form of drawings and specifications developed by a third-party architect-engineer. The basic construction contract between the owner and the contractor calls for the contractor to construct a building or facility in accordance with these plans and specifications. It is very important that both the contractor and the owner have the same understanding of these documents. Often an engineer is retained to interpret and clarify the contract plans in a fair, impartial manner.

In the past, the general contractor performed most of the work with in-house forces. As time passed, however, it became more economical to use subcontractors who were specialized in various areas. It is usually the general contractor's prerogative whether to use subcontractors. The general contractor will usually elect to subcontract if:

A subcontractor possesses specialized technical, engineering, or construction skills.

The general contractor's in-house abilities are limited in a particular area.

A subcontractor can augment the general contractor's labor force at a lower cost than maintaining an in-house capability.

The work represents a small fraction of the overall project.

Thus, when utilized, subcontractors become the responsibility of the general contractor and are not accountable to either the owner or the architect-engineer (AE). The proportion of work done by the general contractor versus that done by subcontractors on the project still varies. It depends largely on the type of project and the capabilities of the general contractor.

The chain of command in the design-and-construct contract depends on the job and the wants and needs of the owner. Often, the owner retains the architect-engineer to act as the owner's representative and supervise the work of the contractor. Other times the architect-engineer will have separate but equal status with the contractor, and still other times, the owner will hire a independent third-party or construction manager to oversee the work of the contractor and/or the AE. The AE will be there to answer any questions that arise that the owner himself cannot resolve. These relationships are represented in Fig. 16.2. In any case, the contractor always maintains control and supervision over the subcontractors.

For any of these relationships to be successful, well-defined agreements or contracts need to be in place. These contracts need to define the duties and responsibilities as well as the authority and accountability of each party. These contracts are usually administered by the owner or the owner's agent, who is responsible for ensuring that the performance of all parties involved is in accordance with the contract documents. The contractor must be concerned with:

- Performing all work in accordance with the owner's contract, drawings, and specifications, which are often defined by the architect-engineer.
- Overseeing the performance of his subcontractors to ensure that they are also in compliance with the owner's requirements. This requires technical as well as administrative skill.

There are two aspects to the relationship between the owner and contractor. The first and highest is the legal aspect of the relationship. The contractual agreement between the two parties must be fair and clearly understood by both. The second aspect involves the day-to-day working relationship of the parties. It should be close enough so that the owner is kept abreast of all aspects of the project and is able to respond quickly to the contractor's questions and yet far enough removed so as not to hinder or delay the contractor.

TYPES OF CONTRACTS

The type of contract administration required by the owner and general contractor depends largely on the type of contract in effect and whether the owner is a public agency, a public corporation, or a private developer. Most construction contracts today fall into one of these five broad categories:

1. Lump sum or fixed price contracts
2. Guaranteed price contracts
3. Cost plus construction contracts
4. Unit price contracts
5. Management contracts

Some contracts are combinations or variations of these five types. Each type is discussed in detail below.

Lump Sum Contract or Fixed Price Contracts

A lump sum contract specifies that the owner will pay the contractor a fixed sum of money for the completion of a definite described and fixed amount of work. This type of contract is used where the plans and specifications are complete and the scope of work is readily defined. The sum is usually based on the contractor's low bid, which was developed utilizing the plans and specifications. This type of contract provides little cost risk to the owner and shifts the risk of performance to the contractor. For this reason, public agencies tend to prefer the lump sum–type contract. It is extremely important that the plans and specifications given to the contractor by the owner be as complete as possible. The general contractor compiles and analyzes the estimates and subcontractor bids for the various aspects of the work with careful consideration to both quality and cost before the final estimate and proposal are prepared.

Lump sum construction contracts typically provide that the owner make partial payments of the contract amount to the contractor as the work progresses. In lump sum contracts, *progress payments* are usually determined by estimated percentage of completion of major job components. These estimates should be based on objective measures of performance (e.g. project milestones) and agreed upon by both owner and contractor at the beginning of the project. As each milestone is reached, a requisition for payment is submitted to the owner. This requisition should reflect the amount of work actually performed during a given period. It is important for the general contractor to prepare specific and accurate payment requests. To accomplish this, the contractor should have an individual on the job site capable of determining:

Which materials have been utilized or stored

How much labor has been expended

What other resources have been committed

This information should be compiled into an accurate record of the amount of work that is complete. The record should note the proportion of completed work to total contract costs.

The general contractor's requisition should incorporate the contents of a similar requisition from the subcontractor to the general contractor. The general contractor has the responsibility to analyze the subcontractor's submittal to ensure that the labor and cost reflected are accurate and representative of the work performed.

Guaranteed Price Contract

This type of contract, which is most commonly used by private owners, is the same as the lump sum contract, except that the contractor accepts the responsibility to complete the work for the estimated cost even if there are minor changes caused by errors and omissions, unless "extras" are requested by the owner. Significant in this type of contract is the contractor's guarantee of total cost. It provides the least risk to the owner and the greatest risk to the contractor because the contractor accepts part of the design responsibility for minor changes within a fixed price. In most cases, it is agreed that the contractor will share or participate in any savings at a percentage agreed upon between the parties during contract negotiations. Since the owner and the contractor both can benefit from a well-run project, it is advantageous for the contractor to continually monitor the efficiency of his operations to ensure that costs are being kept to a minimum without sacrificing quality.

Cost-Plus Construction Contracts

The "cost" element of the cost-plus construction contract refers to reimbursable labor, material, and other items. The *plus* element refers to the contractor fee for performing the work contracted for. This "fee" factor can take several forms. The fee factor can take the form of a fixed percentage fee of some portion or all of the costs, a sliding scale fee of some portion or all of the costs, a percentage of the above two types with ceilings or limitations, a fixed or lump sum fee, a target sharing or incentive fee, or a combination of any of the above types with ceilings and limitations.

Cost-plus contracts are especially effective when the scope of work is unknown or hard to define, such as when an owner requires that work be started very early without a full set of design documents and specifies that the timely completion of the project is critical. It is possible, under this type of contract, to start work with nothing more than a preliminary set of drawings and an outline of specifications and to develop a working budget in conjunction with the architect-engineer. Cost-plus contracts are usually used wherever competitive bids of lump sum or other types are impractical because of unpredictable physical conditions, unstable labor and material markets, or an undefined or very poorly defined project scope.

Because of the high dollar contingency associated with these unforeseen factors, the cost of a lump sum or unit price contract would be prohibitively high.

The following discussion describes some of the different types of cost-plus construction contracts.

Fixed Percentage Fee. The fixed percentage is based on all reimbursable costs or some portion of the costs. Therefore, the more the costs increase, the more the contractor's profit increases.

The fixed percentage does not lend itself well to any incentive for cost savings. Because all costs are reimbursable, any savings in costs would directly lower the fee received. In fact, the motivation with this type of contract is to maximize costs in order to maximize fees.

One major advantage to the fixed percentage fee is that the contractor is very willing to provide any service possible for the client. Cooperation will be at its peak.

One way to minimize the total cost would be to limit the fixed percentage fee to only a portion of the costs. Exclude such items as premium labor costs and overhead, subcontracted work, equipment rentals, and normal payroll overheads (e.g., taxes and insurance).

Sliding Scale Percentage. The intent of the sliding scale percentage fee construction contract is to keep the fee in line with the type and amount of work originally estimated at the date of the original contract by attempting to control the disadvantages of the fixed percentage fee contract. The sliding scale fee is used to provide for possible increases in the volume of work. If the volume of work increases beyond the scope that was originally estimated, the rate of the fee should become progressively smaller, especially on work that is repetitive and requires little or no reengineering, replanning, or layout by the contractor.

Percentage Fees with Ceilings or Limitations. As previously stated, cost-plus contracts do not provide an incentive for cost savings. Therefore, to place a certain amount of incentive back into this type of contract, a ceiling is placed on the total fee. Once the ceiling is reached, the contractor has an incentive to get the job done as there is no further profit to be made for his efforts.

Fixed or Lump Sum Fee. This type of fee provides a bit more incentive than the percentage fee with a ceiling in that the disadvantage of the contractor increasing profit at the expense of increasing cost is removed to a certain extent. While the contractor now has no incentive to increase costs, he also has no incentive to decrease the costs on which the fee had previously been based. The incentive of meeting the construction schedule is foremost. To maximize net return on the fee, the contractor is not going to spend any more time than necessary earning his fee. The disadvantage of the fixed fee is that in case of any great change in the scope of the work, a readjustment of fee is usually made. Such contingency should be provided for in the contract agreement relative to the formula to be used for arriving at this adjustment.

Target Sharing or Incentive Fee. The target sharing or incentive fee provides more contractor incentive than any of the aforementioned types. The amount of the contractor's profit is regulated by his performance.

Basically, this type of fee is based around a target or goal. If the contractor underruns the target, his profit increases and if the contractor overruns the target, his profit decreases. The target may be based on man-hours, dollar amounts, schedule, or a combination of these items.

The target sharing fee may contain "excludable" items. Any target excludable item needs to be carefully scrutinized from all perspectives to ascertain its legitimacy and applicability.

Incentive targets are difficult to arrive at for very large and expensive facilities. It requires an experienced estimating department to determine reasonable target incentive bases for both the contractor and owner.

Staying within the budget under a cost-plus contract depends on cooperation among the architect-engineer, the owner, and the contractor. It requires continual consideration and evaluation of cost alternatives throughout the project. Record keeping by the general contractor becomes extremely critical because records are the basis for reimbursement of costs to the contractor and because the owner often has the right to audit the project records. Specifically, the contractor must maintain very detailed records of all salaries paid, materials purchased, and equipment rented. The record-keeping requirements of this type of project make it prudent for the general contractor to have an experienced staff performing this function.

Unit Price Contract

This type of contract is used where certain operations or services are to be performed repetitively or definite units of physical items of certain quality are to be provided and can be measured in some manner of units but the final quantities to be provided are indefinite.

The unit price construction contract can be used when the total quantity is fixed or definite but is most useful when the total quantity is not readily defined.

The unit price is readily applicable to such construction work as excavation and associated work, dredging, concrete work, steel work, asphalt work, pipelines, transmission lines, road work, etc. Such work can be measured by units such as foot, yard, square foot, square yard, cubic foot, cubic yard, ton, gallon, etc. Units such as these are established standards of measurement. The variables that control the price per unit are the number of units to be furnished and how the units are to be furnished.

Management Contract

On certain large or complex projects, the owner may decide to contract with a nationally known contractor, construction manager, and/or consultant who, acting as the owner's agent, manages the overall project and provides coordination and representation for the owner in the field. The owner usually uses one of the previously mentioned contractual forms for actual performance of the project. This approach affords the owner the services of an experienced, well-established firm at a nominal cost and maintains all the advantages of a bid-type contract.

The basic services provided by the construction management consultant may include overall project and construction management, project schedule development and coordination, budgeting and cost control, review and approval of all subcontracting, preparation of progress reports and financial statements, and analysis and approval of change orders and extras. In many cases the construction management consultant can also approve all requisitions for payment, inspect the work in the field, and act as the liaison between the owner and architect.

With this type of contact, the construction management consultant must be assured of the confidence of the owner and, if possible, the major contractors. If this is not the case, record keeping and reporting could become redundant and the advantages of construction management could be lost. The real advantage of construction management for the owner is the reduction of owner responsibilities through trust that the consultant will maintain control of the entire project.

ORGANIZATION FOR CONTRACT ADMINISTRATION

In general, owners are not in the business of construction. At the project inception they often establish a project office which is charged with the task of controlling the project. From this office, the initial bidding, negotiation, and administrative and contractual follow-up are conducted. Depending on the size and complexity of the project and the sophistication of the owner, this may be a formal well-staffed office, or a less formal, satellite office. The owner may, alternatively, elect to use the services of an outside consultant or construction manager. In any case, it is vital that the individuals assigned by the owner to administer the construction contract be experienced and well-qualified in the areas of both contracts and construction.

Generally, the owner assigns a project manager, field representative, and clerical assistants to administer the general contract according to its requirements. These people interact with the various departments of the general contractor, including estimating, purchasing, accounting, and special services. The general contractor maintains a contract-administration office that performs many of the same functions but focuses on subcontracts. The typical owner–contractor–architect-engineer, or project, organization chart is shown in Fig. 16.2

In those situations where a construction manager (CM) is involved in the project, four of the most common owner–architect-engineer–CM organizational relationships are illustrated.

The general contractor's basic organization depends on the size of his firm. The central department within a contractor's organization is, of course, the construction department, which includes project managers and field superintendents along with their assistants and supporting staff. Supporting departments may include estimating, project engineering, purchasing, accounting, contracting, auditing, and equipment maintenance.

The general contractor's project manager is one of the keys to a successful organization, for this is where the overall project responsibility lies. The project manager must act as the liaison between the field staff, architect, and owner and at the same time control all cost, schedule, and contractual aspects of the project. In turn, the project manager places a great deal of dependence upon the field superintendent, who is responsible for all activities at the project site. The performance of these two individuals is essential to a successful project. The size of the rest of the project management staff depends largely on the size and complexity of the project. The project manager's staff usually includes a project engineer, field staff, and office engineers, as required, in addition to accounting and administrative specialists.

The project manager and his team are responsible for all the administrative functions necessary to support the field superintendent. This includes ensuring an adequate supply of labor, materials, subcontract services, equipment, and site services. In addition, the project manager is responsible for:

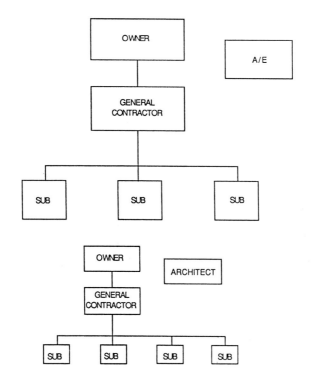

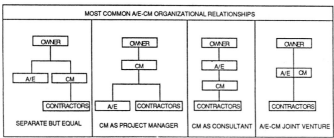

MOST COMMON A/E-CM ORGANIZATIONAL RELATIONSHIPS

A/E = ARCHITECT ENGINEER
CM = CONSTRUCTION MANAGER

FIGURE 16.2 Project organization chart.

Processing of all general correspondence

Assuming timely submittal of shop drawings

Obtaining clarification of project documents

Supervising subcontractor and major equipment buy-outs

Scheduling and attending meetings with the architect and owner

Checking and approving subcontractor requisitions

Making field purchases

Resolving disputes with the owner or subcontractors

Preparing and reviewing progress payment requests

Negotiating all cost and schedule matters with the owner, architect, and sub-contractors

Overseeing field document and cost control

Handling all matters relating to organized labor

In addition, the field superintendent must be kept current of any and all contract changes in order to ensure timely completion of the project in accordance with the plans and specifications.

The field superintendent's staff consists of assistant superintendents, general foreman, area foremen, and a large labor force made up of various building trades. His knowledge of construction is extremely important since he must ensure that the work performed in the field is in compliance with drawings and other project documents. He is primarily responsible for providing daily on-the-job field supervision of the building trades, coordination of subcontractors, and quality control. Included in his duties are

Providing field engineering and layout

Scheduling resources and labor

Working closely with owner and architect field personnel (inspector)

Maintaining daily logs of performance

Controlling the quality of construction

Reviewing schedules

Assisting the project manager in the preparation of various reports

The field superintendent is also responsible for identifying required materials and equipment to be purchased and monitoring the status of all leased equipment.

The project manager and accounting personnel, using information from the field superintendent, must be able to provide accurate reports to the general accounting, auditing, and financial departments in the general contractor's home office. In addition, field accounting personnel must prepare reports that are in compliance with the owner's contract-administration requirements in order to receive progress payments from the owner, as well as be able to establish the contractor's financial status as it relates to the overall project.

The project manager and the field superintendent rely on certain administrative tools to do their jobs. Although each contractor functions a little differently, the basic tools are comprehensive project records, accurate cost records, and realistic schedules. These are discussed in the next three sections.

PROJECT RECORDS

The project manager and staff should maintain a formal filing system of contemporaneous project documentation. Documentation systems can vary according to project requirements but should contain, at a minimum, the following:

Project Files

An organized central filing system is essential to any well-run project. The larger and more complex the project, the greater the need for an organized filing system. Project files can be divided into the following categories:

- Legal files consisting of contract documents, specifications, change orders, and related materials
- Chronological files for all correspondence, internal and external
- Subject-matter files for each subcontract, construction phase, or other readily identifiable unit of the project

Job-Site Logs

Some contractors require that field superintendents and other site personnel maintain daily logs. These logs are essentially daily diaries of the events of a given day or shift. The logs would record the date and time of any significant events (e.g., material deliveries, subcontractor start dates, when questions requiring answers were submitted to the owner or AE, etc.). Logs such as these are valuable provided that each individual religiously maintains his own log and that all information is recorded in a consistent manner.

In addition to the daily diary type of log, important project documents can be tracked using logs. Many of these logs can be maintained manually; however, with the widespread use of personal computers, these logs can include much more information in greater detail and be easier to maintain and use. Typical documents that can and should be tracked via log include

- Incoming and outgoing correspondence
- Submittals
- Requests for information (RFI)
- Replies to requests for information
- Change orders
- Records of change order negotiations
- Punchlists
- Telecons

Incoming Correspondence Logs.   Incoming correspondence logs help track letters and memos being received by the contractor (see Fig. 16.3). Each document is assigned a sequential numeric or alphanumeric code. At a minimum, the date, originating company, and subject matter of the letter are required. This provides the contractor with a sequential list of all correspondence received. It also allows the contractor to quickly identify and locate correspondence:

Received during a specific period or on a specific date

Sent by a particular company

Related to a particular subject

Logs can be maintained either manually or by computer. They can vary in degree of sophistication. A more sophisticated log will reference the specification or

INCOMING CORRESPONDENCE LOG

CORRESPONDENCE NUMBER	LETTER DATE	COMPANY NAME/ SYMBOL	SUBJECT OF CORRESPONDENCE	SUBJECT CODE
∨				
∨				
∨				
∨				
∨				
∨				
∨				
∨				
∨				
∨				
∨				
∨				
∨				
∨				
∨				
∨				
∨				
∨				
∨				
∨				

FIGURE 16.3 Incoming correspondence log.

contract, contain a response due date or actual response date, contain a response letter reference number or file number, etc.

Outgoing Correspondence Log. Outgoing correspondence logs are a method of tracking correspondence sent out by the contractor (see Fig. 16.4). Each document is assigned a sequential numerical or alphanumeric code. At a minimum, the date, receiving company, and subject matter of the letter are recorded. This provides the contractor with a sequential list of all correspondence sent out. It also allows the contractor to quickly locate and identify correspondence:

Sent out during a specific period or on a specific date

Transmitted to a particular company

Pertaining to a particular subject

Logs can be maintained either manually or by computer. They can vary in degree of sophistication. A more sophisticated log will reference the specification or contract, contain a response due date or actual response date, contain a response letter reference number or file number, etc.

Request for Information. The request for information form (see Fig. 16.5) is used by the contractor to document all requests for additional information necessary to provide either clarification or instructions and the related response by the architect-engineer or others. It can at times be the precursor to potential change orders and therefore is central to the contractor's contract administration system.

Request for Information Log. The request for information log is a tracking system for all requests for additional information by the contractor and subcontractors (see Fig. 16.6). It provides a summary of all RFIs and their status, making it easy for the contractor to identify any outstanding RFIs.

Request for Information Log (Computerized). The computerized request for information log (similar to the manual log) is a computerized tracking system for all requests for additional information by the contractor and subcontractors (see Fig. 16.7). It provides a summary of all RFIs and their status, making it easy for the contractor to identify any outstanding RFIs. On major projects where a large number of RFIs can be expected, a computerized system is most practical.

Change Order Log. A change order log is a method of tracking change orders or proposed change orders (see Fig. 16.8). It provides both current and historical data for each change order and is used to track all change orders for a project and quickly assess their status.

Record of Change Order Negotiations. This document provides a summary of any negotiations that have taken place regarding a given change order (see Fig. 16.9). It provides a single source identifying all pertinent documentation regarding the change, what initiated the change, and how any disputes concerning the change were resolved. It can be useful in justifying future progress payments.

Change Order Breakdown Form. The change order breakdown sheet, similar to the detailed breakdown sheet, provides the necessary detail to determine an equitable amount owed to the contractor for work performed to date (see Fig. 16.10).

OUTGOING CORRESPONDENCE LOG

CORRESPONDENCE NUMBER	LETTER DATE	COMPANY NAME/ SYMBOL	SUBJECT OF CORRESPONDENCE	SUBJECT CODE
O/ .LTR				
O/ .LTR				
O/ .LTR				
O/ .LTR				
O/ .LTR				
O/ .LTR				
O/ .LTR				
O/ .LTR				
O/ .LTR				
O/ .LTR				
O/ .LTR				
O/ .LTR				
O/ .LTR				
O/ .LTR				
O/ .LTR				
O/ .LTR				
O/ .LTR				
O/ .LTR				
O/ .LTR				
O/ .LTR				
O/ .LTR				
O/ .LTR				
O/ .LTR				

FIGURE 16.4 Outgoing correspondence log.

REQUEST FOR INFORMATION

RFI NO._____

TO:	TRANSMITTAL RECORD	ATTN/FIRM	DATE SENT	DATE REC'D	DATE DUE
INFORMATION REQUESTED BY:	CONTRACTOR to A/E				
SUBJECT:	A/E ☐ to CONSULTANT(S)				
DRAWING REF.:	CONSULTANT(S) to A/E				
SPEC. REF.:					
CONTRACT NO.	A/E to CONTRACTOR				

INFORMATION NEEDED:

DATE: _____ SIGNATURE: _____

REPLY:

DATE: _____ SIGNATURE: _____

You are authorized to proceed with the work identified in the reply to this RFI on the assumption that no change in the contract amount o completion date is required. If the RFI reply involves a change in the work affecting your contract amount or completion date, contact the Owner's Representative immediately.

FIGURE 16.5   Request for information.

Change orders are broken down by the following:

Change order description

Budget value of change order

Value of work completed up to the last report

Value of work completed since last report

Total value of work completed to date

O'Brien-Kreitzberg

ATTACHMENT

REQUEST FOR INFORMATION LOG

CONTRACT: ______________________ CONTRACT NO: __________ PAGE _____ OF_____

NO.	DESCRIPTION	SPEC./ DWG. REF.	DATES						REMARKS
			REC'D FR SUBCONTR	TO A/E	REQUESTED DUE DATE	REC'D FR A/E	TO SUB-CONTR.	DAYS	

OKA - REV. 2 3/90

1/20/89

FIGURE 16.6 Request for information log.

STATUS AS OF: 8/30/88

No.	DESCRIPTION	SPEC/ DRWG REF.	DATES					DAYS	REMARKS
			REC'D FR SUBCONTR	TO A/E	REQUESTED DUE DATE	REC'D FROM A/E	TO SUBCONTR		
1 – 3	NOT USED	—	—	—		—	—		
4	CENTERING HEADS IN CEILING TILES	15300	JUL 19, 88	JUL 20, 88	AUG 2, 88	JUL 25, 88	JUL 27, 88	8	
5	FIRE LINE SIZE	C–8	AUG 3, 88	AUG 4, 88	N/A	N/A	JUL 6, 88	—	ISSUE RETROACTIVELY
6	STORM DRAIN CL III V CL.	C–8	AUG 3, 88	AUG 4, 88	N/A	N/A	JUL 6, 88	—	ISSUE RETROACTIVELY
7	DRAWING DIMENSIONS	A4.1,A4.2	JUL 19, 88	JUL 20, 88	AUG 2, 88	JUL 25, 88	JUL 27, 88	8	
8	MECHANICAL	A4.4,A2.1	JUL 19, 88	JUL 20, 88	AUG 2, 88	JUL 25, 88	JUL 27, 88	8	
9	MECHANICAL	A4.5	JUL 19, 88	JUL 20, 88	AUG 2, 88	JUL 26, 88	JUL 27, 88	8	
10	MECHANICAL	A4.3	JUL 19, 88	JUL 20, 88	AUG 2, 88	JUL 27, 88	JUL 27, 88	8	
11	CHAIN LINK FENCE	02030	JUL 27, 88	JUL 27, 88	AUG 2, 88	AUG 1, 88	AUG 2, 88	6	
12	FIRE PROTECTION DOMESTIC VS FOREIGN PRODUCTS	10560	JUL 27, 88	JUL 27, 88	AUG 5, 88	AUG 1, 88	AUG 2, 88	6	
13	BECK STEEL TRENCH DRAIN & ELEVATOR BRACKET	05500	JUL 27, 88	JUL 27, 88	AUG 5, 88	AUG 1, 88	AUG 2, 88	6	
14	SECURITY METAL PRODUCTS	08110	JUL 27, 88	JUL 27, 88	AUG 11, 88	AUG 12, 88	AUG 12, 88	16	PARTIAL REPLY ISSUED 8/8/88
15	COORDINATE 252 STORM DRAIN DETAIL	02720	JUL 28, 88	JUL 28, 88	JUL 28, 88	JUL 28, 88	JUL 28, 88	0	PRELIM. REPLY VIA FI B–4 7/28/88
16	COORDINATE 253, 254 S.D. DETAILS	02720	JUL 28, 88	JUL 28, 88	JUL 28, 88	AUG 2, 88	AUG 3, 88	6	PARTIAL REPLY VIA FI B–4 7/28/88
17	BLDG. I SEWER CO. FALL & ALIGNMENT	P2.2	AUG 1, 88	AUG 2, 88	AUG 2, 88	AUG 2, 88	AUG 2, 88	1	
18	McCLENAHAN	15400	AUG 2, 88	AUG 2, 88	AUG 5, 88	AUG 5, 88	AUG 5, 88	3	
19	McCLENAHAN	15400	AUG 2, 88	AUG 2, 88	AUG 5, 88	AUG 5, 88	AUG 5, 88	3	
20	McCLENAHAN	15400	AUG 2, 88	AUG 2, 88	AUG 5, 88	AUG 8, 88	AUG 9, 88	7	
21	McCLENAHAN	15400	AUG 2, 88	AUG 2, 88	AUG 5, 88	AUG 3, 88	AUG 3, 88	1	
22	McCLENAHAN	15400	AUG 2, 88	AUG 2, 88	AUG 5, 88	AUG 3, 88	AUG 3, 88	1	
23	McCLENAHAN	15400	AUG 2, 88	AUG 2, 88	AUG 5, 88	AUG 5, 88	AUG 5, 88	3	
24	SEWER LINES ALONG I/C & I/F 5	P2.1,P2.2	AUG 3, 88	AUG 3, 88	AUG 4, 88	AUG 3, 88	AUG 3, 88	0	
25	OVERFLOW PIPE COORINDATE & ELEVATION	C–8	AUG 3, 88	AUG 4, 88	AUG 4, 88	AUG 8, 88	AUG 9, 88	6	
26	VOID – NOT USED	—	—	—					
27	BATHROOM PLUMBING WALLS	15060	AUG 8, 88	AUG 9, 88	AUG 10, 88	AUG 12, 88	AUG 12, 88	4	
28	HANDSINK VS L–1	K3.3/P2.18	AUG 12, 88	AUG 12, 88	SEP 1, 88	AUG 18, 88	AUG 18, 88	6	
29	TESTING U/G WASTE	02730	AUG 12, 88	AUG 12, 88	NOT GIVEN	AUG 18, 88	AUG 19, 88	7	OK WITH COUNTY
30	SEWERS IN ROOM 11014, 11018, BLDG. I	P2.2	AUG 4, 88	AUG 4, 88	NOT GIVEN	AUG 8, 88	AUG 9, 88	5	
31	SEWERS IN TYPICAL BUILDINGS	P2.10	AUG 4, 88	AUG 4, 88	AUG 8, 88	AUG 8, 88	AUG 9, 88	5	
32	COORDINATE 287 ELEVATION	C–8	AUG 4, 88	AUG 5, 88	NOT GIVEN	AUG 8, 88	AUG 9, 88	5	
33	DIMENSIONS AT STAIR S2.13	S2.10	AUG 4, 88	AUG 5, 88	AUG 8, 88	AUG 10, 88	AUG 10, 88	6	
34	SEWER ALONG I/9 – BLDG. I	P2.1	AUG 8, 88	AUG 8, 88	AUG 8, 88	AUG 8, 88	AUG 8, 88	0	
35	PG&E SERVICE POLE & WIRE	E1.4,E1.7	AUG 8, 88	AUG 9, 88	AUG 11, 88	AUG 11, 88	AUG 11, 88	3	UPDATE 8/17
36	MOVE SEWER MH & LINE	P2I./C8	AUG 9, 88	AUG 9, 88	AUG 11, 88	AUG 12, 88	AUG 12, 88	3	

FIGURE 16.7 Computerized request for information log.

16.17

CHANGE ORDER LOG

PROJECT_____

CONTRACT NO._____

CONTRACT AMOUNT_____

CONTINGENCY_____

SHEET_____OF_____

PCO NO.	RFI NO.	FI NO.	CO NO.	DATES						PRICING			CONTINGENCY BALANCE	REMARKS
				TO CONTR.	REC.	EST. COMP.	NEG. COMP	CO ISSUED	EST.	CONT. PRICE	CO AMT.			

FIGURE 16.8 Change order log.

 **O'Brien-Kreitzberg**

RECORD OF CHANGE ORDER NEGOTIATION

PROJECT LOCATION AND DESCRIPTION	CONTRACT NO.	
	PCO NO.	CO NO.
	RFI NO.	FI NO.

CONTRACTOR REPRESENTATIVES	OWNER REPRESENTATIVES
NAME AND TITLE	NAME AND TITLE
NAME AND TITLE	NAME AND TITLE
NAME AND TITLE	NAME AND TITLE

RESUME OF NEGOTIATION

ESTIMATE	NEGOTIATIONS WERE CONCLUDED WITH CONTRACTOR ON	
PROPOSAL	REVISED CONTRACT COMPLETION	
FINAL PRICE ACTUALLY AGREED TO	ADJUSTMENT IN TIME (ATTACH JUSTIFICATION)	
REVIEWING OFFICIAL SIGNATURE	TITLE	DATE

OKA - REV. 1 1/86   1/20/86

FIGURE 16.9 Record of change order negotiation.

CHANGE ORDER BREAKDOWN

PAGE_____ OF _____

REPORT NO.	DATE

CONTRACT NO.	PROJECT			

		VALUE OF WORK COMPLETED		(3)
CHANGE ORDER NO.	TOTAL VALUE OF WORK	TO LAST REPORT	SINCE LAST REPORT	TOTAL VALUE OF
(1)	(DOLLARS ONLY) (2)	(DOLLARS ONLY) (A)	(DOLLARS ONLY) (B)	COMPLETED WORK (4)

FIGURE 16.10 Change order breakdown.

Logs such as these provide a quick method of checking the status of important project documents and will aid in preparing or defending future claims and disputes.

Project Photographs. These are a list of the photographs taken on the job along with dates and a description of the subject of each photograph. While photographs are not documents in and of themselves, they can be useful to:

Accurately assess the progress of the work to date

Aid in the settlement of disputes

Mitigate future claims

Promote good public relations

Good judgment must be used in the selection of the subject and the timing of the photographs so that they will be useful for these purposes. Figure 16.11 shows a typical project photograph index.

The need for documentation on a project usually depends on the size of the project, its complexity, the reputation of the parties involved, and the contractor's personal preference. During the course of a project, the amount of paperwork can seem unduly burdensome and unnecessary; however, should disputes and claims arise, their value will be become apparent by the man-hours and dollars saved.

COST RECORDS

Cost Record Systems

The methods used to maintain cost records varies from contractor to contractor depending on how the particular corporate accounting system is structured. Project costs should be assembled and maintained in a manner that is compatible with the corporate system.

Cost records should show the continuous development of construction or project costs. Actual construction costs should be compared with the estimated amount prepared as part of the original budget estimate. The primary objective of any cost-accounting approach is to establish a timely, accurate picture of actual job expenditures versus estimated job expenditures as construction moves ahead. These data will allow the project manager to take appropriate corrective actions. The data will also be valuable in preparing future estimates and bids.

When a cost-accounting system is developed, the structure should be carefully considered and defined so that all project personnel who must use it will understand it. Data sources that provide regular, timely, and accurate information should be established. Cost data must be processed quickly and reviewed often so that potential problem areas can be identified and, if required, corrective action can be taken in a timely manner. The data usually include basic timekeeping information provided by the foreman, and material and equipment charges provided by the purchasing department.

One of the basic tools of cost control is the cost ledger. The cost ledger records all project costs, such as labor, materials, equipment operation, subcontracts, and overhead. The items can be divided into three major categories:

- Direct costs (to include subcontract costs)
- Indirect costs
- Overheads

A separate cost ledger should be maintained for each of these three cost categories. The way these three categories are subdivided depends on the project and how

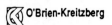 O'Brien-Kreitzberg   **ATTACHMENT**

PROJECT PHOTOGRAPH INDEX

CONTRACT NO. & TITLE: PAGE ____ OF ____

PHOTO NO.	DATE TAKEN	SUBJECT

OKA REV.1 1/89   1/20/89

FIGURE 16.11   Project photograph index.

it can be best broken into separate work items using the general contractor's estimating procedures as a guideline. The project accounts should closely resemble the work items developed in the original estimate. All classifications must be sufficiently detailed so that the data will be of practical use to the estimators, project manager, and field personnel. Once it is developed and implemented, the cost accounting system must be religiously followed by everyone. The overall effectiveness of the system will depend largely on how closely all parties adhere to the system and on the accuracy of the information supplied.

The breakdown of project accounts must be compatible with the project breakdown approved by the owner, since this breakdown will be the basis for payments. The project is usually broken down by milestones, which often correspond to activities on the project schedule: e.g., foundation, structural steel, framing, exterior walls, interior partitions, piping-HVAC, piping-water, and electrical systems. On larger projects these categories can be further subdivided by section, floor, service, and other physical parameters. Once a construction contract is initiated, the breakdown of the project accounts is reviewed and an appropriate combination of accounts is selected.

From the inception of the job, each time a cost is incurred, it should be posted to the appropriate account. Each expenditure should be recorded within each major category and work item. Field personnel can assist the accounting function by recording the appropriate account number on every financial document. This is really a key operation in the cost records system. Ideally the person performing this function, in addition to having a good understanding of the accounting system and its work item breakdown, should have a thorough knowledge and understanding of construction methods and should be familiar with the specifics of the project. The more accurately expenditures are posted, the more effective the entire system will be.

Under most contracts, all expenses can be assigned directly to some cost account. Sometimes on very large contracts and on unit price contracts, however, suspense accounts must be used for expenses associated with plant and equipment operation. These accounts accumulate those costs that cannot be readily identified to particular accounts on a daily basis. They collect certain costs for the purpose of future allocation. For example, a concrete-mixing plant may include mixers, batchers, hoppers, conveyors, loaders, screens, and similar items, and the plant may provide concrete for several different work items under a unit price contract. It will be necessary to collect all the concrete-plant operating and repair costs into a single suspense account and distribute these costs on a weekly or monthly basis to various work activities that required the use of the concrete plant. These costs are usually apportioned equitably on the basis of the quantities involved in each bid item.

Cost allocation is not an exact science nor a perfect way to account for costs. The contractor must decide how the cost data are to be used and then determine if allocation will give an accurate portrayal of expended costs. Uniformity and consistency in cost-accounting practices and procedures can contribute significantly to the success of the system. The need for care and accuracy in allocating costs, including making the proper distinction between overhead and other expenses, cannot be overemphasized.

Major Cost Items

One of the most significant parts of the cost records program is the establishment of labor costs. The accumulation of this information is extremely time-consuming but is a must for an effective system. The daily allocation of labor costs is usually performed by a timekeeper and, in some cases, junior engineers. If it is done by junior engineers, they also will measure quantities of work in place and they will perform some basic cost reviews. On many smaller jobs, the project manager or foreman can record labor costs. The field superintendent, or others depending on the type of job, completes the time report showing the hourly distribution of work by each of his men. He verifies the rate of pay and assigns the proper account number. The daily time reports are submitted to the payroll office after each shift. The project manager, since he has overall responsibility for cost, should review time sheets for accuracy. The hours worked by each worker along with rates and gross amounts are distributed to the appropriate cost account. This information, along with the value of work in place, is the basis for the running totals for each cost account. Figure 16.12 shows a typical example of a time report. This information can also be used to ensure that resources are being expended in accordance with the original work plan or schedule.

A daily force account report (Fig. 16.12) quantifies the labor, material, and equipment utilized by the contractor on a daily basis. This report is used when a time and material change order is necessary. This usually occurs when there is an emergency, a failure to negotiate, a failure to price, or an activity that cannot be readily defined and estimated. It allows work to continue without delay and gives a daily accounting of costs expended by the contractor. A not-to-exceed price can be agreed on in advance by the contractor and the owner. The contractor can then give the owner a daily update on percentage of cost expended to date or warn the owner when a certain percentage of the not-to-exceed price is expended (e.g., 80 percent).

A contractor's lost time accident report form provides the contractor with a method of documenting lost time accidents (see Fig. 16.13). While accidents are not pleasant matters, they should be documented and recorded for future reference in the event that legal actions arise. The properly filled out form will provide a starting point for any investigations. It will also serve to refresh the memories of those personnel involved.

Other major cost items involve materials, supplies, and subcontracts. These cost items are recorded in the appropriate work item accounts. The cost items are accumulated from bills, invoices, receipts, and requisitions. The recorded cost of these items, examined in conjunction with the recorded labor costs and measured against the budgets of each account, can be a valuable administrative tool for the contractor.

Principles of Cost Control

It is the responsibility of the project manager and his staff to determine how much money has been expended to date, the quantity of work performed for the expenditure, how the expenditure and amount of work performed compare to the original plan, and whether the expenditure was reasonable. Unfortunately, no amount of cost engineering can overcome losses due to adverse weather, a low bid, or unanticipated price rises, nor can cost control retrieve money already lost through inefficient management or poor supervision. Cost control does enable the contractor to analyze his field methods and measure the performance of labor and equipment and compare it to expected performance. It provides a basis for the contractor to make future decisions regarding manpower levels, equipment selection, and construction methods. It makes it possible for him to determine quantitatively the maximum rates of production he can expect from his workers and machines.

The reputable contractor exercises the same tight control over his costs for jobs with cost-plus contracts as he does on his jobs with other types of contracts. A contractor should make the cost-control system an important part of company

DAILY FORCE ACCOUNT REPORT

CONTRACTOR/CONTRACT NO. _____

PROJECT NO. _____ LOCATION _____

WORK PERFORMED BY _____

DESCRIPTION OF WORK _____

REPORT NO. _____

PCO NO. _____

FI NO. _____ AMOUNT AUTHORIZED $ _____

CO NO. _____ PREVIOUS EXPENDITURE $ _____

DATE PERFORMED _____ TODAY $ _____

TO DATE $ _____

EQUIP. NO.	EQUIPMENT	HOURS	HOURLY RATE	EXTENDED AMOUNTS	PAY R. NO.	LABOR (INCLUDED DAILY TIME SHEET)	HOURS	BURDENED HOURLY RATE	EXTENDED AMOUNTS
							O.T.		
							REG.		
							O.T.		
							REG.		
							O.T.		
							REG.		
							O.T.		
							REG.		
							O.T.		
							REG.		
							O.T.		
							REG.		

MATERIAL and/or WORK done by specialists (included invoices)

Description	No. Unit	Unit Cost	Extended Amount

TOTAL COST OF LABOR   A

TOTAL COST OF EQUIPMENT, MATERIALS AND WORK   B

_____ % ON LABOR COST   (A)

_____ % ON EQUIP., MAT'L AND WORK COST   (B)

TOTAL THIS REPORT

SUBMITTED - CONTRACTOR _____ DATE _____

RECOMMENDED - RES. PROJ. REPRESENTATIVE _____ DATE _____

FIGURE 16.12 Daily force account report.

16.25

CONTRACTOR'S LOST TIME
ACCIDENT REPORT

PROJECT _____ NO. _____

CONTRACTOR _____

SUBCONTRACTOR _____

CONDITIONS

DAY	S	M	T	W	TH	F	S
WEATHER	Brite Sun	Clear		Overcast	Rain		Snow
TEMP.	To 32°	32° to 60°	60° to 70°	70° to 85°	85° up
WIND	Still	Moderate	High		Report No.

NOTE: INFORMATION IN THIS REPORT IS TO BE USED FOR THE PREVENTION OF ACCIDENTS AND IS NOT INTENDED AS A BASIS FOR INJURY CLAIMS. IN COUNTING TIME LOST, START WITH THE FIRST FULL DAY OR SHIFT LOST AFTER DATE OF INJURY AND INCLUDE WEEKENDS AND HOLIDAYS.

TYPE OF ACCIDENT		LOCATION	
INJURED EMPLOYEE	NAME	AGE	OCCUPATION
	WAGE HOW LONG EMPLOYED	REMARKS (Previous Injuries, etc.)	
NATURE AND PLACE OF INJURY	DESCRIBE INJURY		
	EXACT PLACE WHERE INJURY OCCURRED		
TIME AND SEVERITY OF INJURY	DATE OF INJURY	TIME	
	STARTED LOSING TIME (Never Date of Injury)	DID INJURY RESULT IN DEATH OR PROBABLE PERMANENT DISABILITY?	
	RETURN TO WORK (Date)*	DATE OF DEATH	
	CALENDAR DAYS LOST TIME*	FIXED CHARGE FOR PERMANENT DISABILITY	
	* Estimate Date of Return to Duty to Avoid Delay in Submitting Report		
DESRIPTION OF ACCIDENT	DESCRIBE ACCIDENT (Not Injury)		
STATEMENT BY FORE-MAN OR IMMEDIATE SUPERVISOR	HOW COULD THIS HAVE BEEN PREVENTED?		
		FOREMAN or IMMEDIATE SUPERVISOR	

FIGURE 16.13   Contractor's lost time accident report.

policy and thoroughly indoctrinate his personnel into its use. The cost-control system should automatically become part of any project undertaken.

The control of costs during the construction phase of a project involves these four considerations:

1. Through advance planning, manpower levels, equipment type, and construction methods are selected that will allow the project to be completed within the required schedule and contractual requirements.

2. The actual work is accomplished in accordance with the planned procedures.

3. Actual project performance is continuously monitored and measured against projected expenditures.

4. If actual costs begin to exceed projected expenditures, the problem area is identified and isolated quickly so that the appropriate corrective actions can be implemented.

A final word about project cost control. The cost-control system and its results should never be viewed by field personnel as a negative comment or criticism of their work. Rather, it should be viewed as a tool for identifying problem areas that are not readily apparent to field personnel. It can also be used to measure overall project performance.

PROGRESS PAYMENTS

Schedule of Values

The schedule of values is essentially a listing of work elements and their estimated dollar value (see Fig. 16.14). It is used to provide an agreed-upon and equitable basis for future progress payments. The work elements usually correspond to activities on the accepted project critical path method (CPM) schedule. The sum of the dollar values of all the work activities corresponds to the contractor's bid price. Requests for progress payments by the contractor are based on the percentage completion of these work activities and their corresponding dollar values.

Request for Payment and Detailed Breakdown Sheet

These reports provide the contractor with a means of requesting payment for work performed to date and the detail that supports the dollar value of the payment request. Progress payments provide the contractor money to cover the cost of work performed to date. The request for payment form (see Fig. 16.15), when used in conjunction with the schedule of values, provides an efficient and equitable method of determining the value of the work completed to date and the fair amount owned to the contractor.

Detailed breakdown sheets (Fig. 16.16) provide the following:

Item of work description

Budget value of the work team

Value of work completed up to the last report

Value of work completed since last report

Total value of work completed to date

Request for Payment for Materials on Hand

When used with the request for payment form, this form (see Fig. 16.17) provides additional detail justifying contractor material expenditures to date. Contractors and subcontractors should use this form when requesting payment for materials purchased but not necessarily installed.

O'Brien-Kreitzberg

SCHEDULE OF VALUES
(Allocation of Total Contract Price)

PROJECT TITLE	PROJECT NO.	SPEC. OR CONTRACT NO.	PAGE OF
NAME OF CONTRACTOR	CONTRACT TYPE	CONTRACT DATE	

SCHEDULE & ITEM	DESCRIPTION OF COMPONENT PARTS	ALLOCATION*		TOTAL
		MATERIAL	LABOR	
		TOTAL		**

* Allocation shall be in percents of total contract price of the items allocated or in dollars and cents.
** This total shall be equal to the total contract price of all items allocated.

O-KA REV 1 1-89   1/2X/89

FIGURE 16.14 Schedule of values.

DETAILED BREAKDOWN

PAGE_____ OF _____

REPORT NO.	DATE

CONTRACT NO.   PROJECT

ITEM OF WORK	TOTAL VALUE OF WORK	VALUE OF WORK COMPLETED (3)		TOTAL VALUE OF
(1)	(DOLLARS ONLY) (2)	TO LAST REPORT (DOLLARS ONLY) (A)	SINCE LAST REPORT (DOLLARS ONLY) (B)	COMPLETED WORK (4)

FIGURE 16.15 Detailed breakdown.

SCHEDULES

Construction schedules are essential to ensure that all parties involved in the construction process—the contractor, subcontractors, construction manager, architect-engineer, and owner—complete their obligations within the time frame specified by contract requirements. In today's litigious society, schedules are vital for demonstrating how each party's actions affected the contract milestone dates. It is there-

REQUEST FOR PAYMENT

CONTRACTOR		
LOCATION	PAGE_____ OF _____	

PROJECT TITLE	REPORT NO.	DATE
CONTRACT NO.	PROJECT NO.	

WORK STATUS:

COMPLETION DATES

INITIAL CONTRACT	REVISED CONTRACT	ESTIMATED SUBSTANTIAL	ACTUAL SUBSTANTIAL	PERCENT COMPLETED	
				THROUGH THIS MONTH (Sum of Line 4 and Line 5 ÷ Line 3)	NORMAL TO DATE

AVERAGE WORK FORCE

NUMBER EMPLOYED

REPORT BELOW ANY CIRCUMSTANCES WHICH MAY HAVE ADVERSELY AFFECTED THE PROGRESS SUCH AS STRIKES, WEATHER, DELAYS BY THE OWNER, ETC. INCLUDING EXPLANATION OF ANY "NO" ANSWERS GIVEN IN THE BLOCKS ABOVE.

PROGRESS PAYMENT SUMMARY

1.	INITIAL CONTRACT AMOUNT	
2.	CHANGE ORDERS (Total of Column 2, Form 8-D)	
3.	TOTAL CONTRACT AMOUNT TO DATE (Line 1 plus Line 2)	
4.	VALUE OF WORK COMPLETED TO DATE (Total of Columns 3A and 3B of Form 8-C)	
5.	VALUE OF WORK COMPLETED UNDER CHANGE ORDERS (Total of Column 4, Form 8-D)	
6.	VALUE OF MATERIAL	
	A. MATERIAL ON SITE	
	B. MATERIAL IN STORAGE	
7.	TOTAL VALUE OF MATERIALS (Line 6A plus Line 6B)	
8.	TOTAL VALUE OF COMPLETED WORK AND MATERIALS (Sum of Lines 4, 5 & 7)	
9.	LESS RETAINAGE	
10.	SUB-TOTAL (Line 8 minus Line 9)	
11.	LESS PREVIOUS PAYMENTS	
12.	AMOUNT OF PAYMENT THIS REPORT (Line 10 minus Line 11)	

SIGNATURE	DATE	SIGNATURE	DATE
SIGNATURE	DATE	SIGNATURE	DATE

FIGURE 16.16 Request for payment.

fore extremely important that all parties ensure that the construction schedules are submitted on time and that they accurately reflect the sequence of work.

The detailed construction schedule should be a practical plan to complete the contract work. In addition to construction activities, it should include the sequence and scheduling for the following:

- Shop drawing preparation, submittals, and reviews
- Outside agency reviews, permitting, and approvals
- Fabrication and delivery, testing, and startup
- System testing and startup

REQUEST FOR PAYMENT FOR MATERIALS ON HAND

INSTRUCTIONS:

TO CONTRACTORS:
Forward original and one copy to Resident Project Representative. Attach evidence of purchase (and warehouse receipt when required) to the original.

TO RESIDENT PROJECT REPRESENTATIVE:
Retain original in your files with supporting documents for progress payments.

TO (Resident Project Representative)	DATE
	PROJECT NO.
FROM (Contractor)	CONTRACT NO.

In accordance with the provisions of the General Conditions of the Contract,
request is made for payment of materials on hand for the following materials:

ITEM NUMBER	QUANTITY	UNIT	MATERIAL DESCRIPTION	VALUE	WHERE STORED

AFFIDAVIT

The materials listed above have been purchased exclusively for use on the above referenced project. The material is separate from the other like materials and is physically identified as our property for use only on Contract No._____. The Owner may enter upon the premises for inspection, checking or auditing, or for any other purpose as you consider necessary. It is expressly understood and agreed that this information and affidavit is furnished to the Owner for the purpose of obtaining payment for the above materials before they are delivered to, or incorporated into, the project described above, and that the storage thereof at the location shown shall not relieve the Contractor of full responsibility for the security and protection of all such materials until acceptance by the Owner of the completed project.

CONTRACTOR: BY_____ TITLE_____DATE_____

FIGURE 16.17   Request for payment for materials on hand.

Submittal Schedule (Computerized)

A submittal schedule is a planning system for identifying individual submittals and required turnaround items (see Fig. 16.18).

Submittals are required in accordance with the contract to amplify the contract drawings and specifications to provide sufficient detail for actual construction. The primary responsibility for submittals lies with the contractor and the primary responsibility for review and approval rests with the architect-engineer.

SAMPLE SUBMITTAL SCHEDULE

CONTRACT SUBMITTAL SCHEDULE
SORTED BY DATE TO OWNER

SPEC SECTION	DATE TO OWNER	SUB NO	REVIEW/ RECORD	REQD FRM OWNER	REQUIRED ON SITE	SUBCONTR RESPONSIBL	REMARKS	CPM ACT #
14212	08/19/88	RFI	REVIEW	09/06/88	10/04/88	LODESTAR	ELEVATOR	P1500
05500	08/19/88	B-045	REVIEW	09/02/88	12/12/88	BECK	BUILDING 3 MASONRY EMBEDS	P1260
05500	08/19/88	B-051	REVIEW	09/02/88	12/12/88	BECK	BUILDING 4 MASONRY EMBEDS	P1260
14500	08/23/88	B-062	REVIEW	08/30/88	11/22/88	PNEUMATIC	PNEUMATIC TUBE SYSTEM	P1550
09510	08/23/88		REVIEW	09/26/88	03/17/89	CARLOS	ACOUSTICAL CEILING TILE	P1800
09520	08/23/88		REVIEW	09/26/88	04/17/89	CARLOS	ACOUSTICAL WALL TREATMENT	P1800
09542	08/23/88		REVIEW	09/26/88	04/17/89	CARLOS	REINFORCED PLASTIC PANELS	P1800
02810	08/26/88		REVIEW	09/02/88	09/13/88	BAUMAN	IRRIGATION SYSTEM	P1245
15000	08/26/88		REVIEW	09/16/88	04/03/89	MCCLENAHAN	MECHANICAL-HVAC ROUGH IN	P1050
16000	08/26/88	B-042	REVIEW	09/16/88	03/17/89	CON COSTA	FIXTURES	P1021
16000	08/26/88	B-040	REVIEW	09/16/88	05/10/89	CON COSTA	SWITCHGEAR-CONTACTORS AND RELAYS	P1022
15000	08/26/88	B-012	REVIEW	09/16/88	04/03/89	MCCLENAHAN	MECHANICAL-PIPING DRAINS ETC.	P1052
16000	08/26/88	B-034	REVIEW	09/16/88	03/17/89	CON COSTA	GROUNDING SYSTEM-MISC DATA	P1021
16000	08/26/88	B-054	REVIEW	09/16/88	03/17/89	CON COSTA	MISCELLANEOUS FITTINGS	P1021
02314	08/27/88	B-050	REVIEW	09/19/88	09/19/88	GALLETTI	SITE CONCRETE WORK - REBAR BLD 1 EAST,TUNNEL	NONE
11400	08/29/88		REVIEW	09/09/88	05/17/89	NORWALK	FOOD SERVICE EQUIPMENT	P4160
10200	08/31/88		REVIEW	04/03/89	05/01/89	MCCLENAHAN	LOUVERS AND VENTS	NONE
04232	08/31/88	B-057	REVIEW	09/19/88	09/19/88	MASONRY SV	CMU REBAR-ALL BUILDINGS	P1195
04232	08/31/88		REVIEW	09/19/88	09/19/88	MASONRY SV	CMU REBAR-OTHER	P1195
11400	09/02/88		REVIEW	09/23/88	05/17/89	NORWALK	FOOD SERVICE EQUIPMENT-ROUGH IN IN DRAWINGS	P4160
11191	09/05/88	B-050	REVIEW	09/19/88	11/28/88	UNIVERSAL	DETENTION EQUIPMENT DOORS AND FRAMES	NONE
11110	09/09/88	B-026	REVIEW	09/29/88	07/21/89	WESTERN	LAUNDRY EQUIPMENT	P3000
11191	09/12/88	B-050	REVIEW	09/26/88	11/01/88	UNIVERSAL	DETENTION EQUIPMENT DOORS AND FRAMES	P1180

FIGURE 16.18 Sample submittal schedule.

In order to avoid unnecessary delay, it is in the contractor's interest to plan for the orderly flow of submittals in order to ensure that reviews and approvals by the architect-engineer will support the overall construction schedule. The contractor should plan to make all submittals sufficiently in advance of the construction requirements to permit a reasonable time for review and approval by the architect-engineer.

A typical submittal schedule contains the following information:

Specification reference

Description of required submittal

Date required for submittal to the owner

Date approval is required

Date to owner

Date required on site

Subcontract (if applicable)

Number

Submittal Transmittal

A submittal transmittal is used to document the flow of submittals to and from the contractor and the architect-engineer (see Fig. 16.19). It is used to document the dates submittal documents were transmitted to the architect-engineer for review and approval, when they were due, when they were received, and all required revisions and corrections.

Submittal Control Log

A submittal control log is a control logging system for tracking individual submittals and recording turnaround times (see Fig. 16.20). The system, when used in conjunction with the submittal schedule, should be capable of calculating the turnaround time from receipt of the submittal to receipt of the response and approval and of flagging any dates that are missing. Identification of missed submittal dates will provide the contractor with an early warning of potential delays.

A submittal control log can contain the following information:

Submittal number

Due date of submittal

Receipt date of the submittal

Contractor's requested return date

Distribution to the architect-engineer

Receipt of review from the architect-engineer

Utilizing the work activities used to develop basic cost information from the project estimate and budget, the contractor must establish his detailed construction schedule as soon as possible. This schedule must consider all basic activities from initiation of the contractor's activities for a project to final completion

SUBMITTAL TRANSMITTAL

Submittal No. _____   Page _____ of ___

A/E: _____   SPECIFICATION SECTION: _____

SUBCONTRACTOR/SUPPLIER: _____   DRAWING REFERENCE: _____

TRANSMITTAL RECORD	ATTN.	DATE SENT	DATE REC'D	DATE DUE	QUANTITY				REV'D BY (Init)
					REPRO.	PRINT	SAMPLE	MFG LT.	
SUBCONTRACTOR TO CONTRACTOR									
CONTRACTOR TO ARCH/ENG									
ARCH/ENG TO CONSULTANT									
CONSULTANT TO ARCH/ENG									
ARCH/ENG TO CONTRACTOR									
CONTRACTOR TO SUBCONTRACTOR									

REVIEW ACTION CODE:
1. REVIEWED/NO EXCEPTIONS TAKEN   2. MAKE CORRECTIONS NOTED   4. INCOMPLETE SUBMITTAL, RESUBMIT
                                       3. REVISE AS NOTED AND RESUBMIT   5. REJECTED/RESUBMIT AS SPECIFIED

1	2	3	4	5	DWG/ITEM	DATED	DESCRIPTION

CONTRACTOR REMARKS:	ARCH/ENGR REMARKS:

NOTE: Notations do not authorize changes to contract sum or time. If you are authorized to proceed with the work identified in this submittal, it is assumed that no change in the contract amount or completion date is required. If a change in the work afffecting your contract amount or completion date is involved, notify the CM immediately.

FIGURE 16.19 Submittal transmittal.

through startup and turnover. The contractor must also consider the activities of other parties that may restrain or potentially affect construction.

Several accepted scheduling techniques can be applied effectively by a contractor. A bar chart is an example of one type of scheduling tool for monitoring and controlling construction activities.

A bar chart generally shows all the basic work activities that make up the entire project overlaid by a calendar that covers the estimated duration for overall

SUBMITTAL CONTROL LOG

CONTRACT: _____ CONTRACT NO: _____ START DATE: _____ ENDING DATE: _____ PAGE ___ OF ___

| SUB. ID NO. | DESCRIPTION | SPEC. SECTION NO. | SCHEDULE RECEIVED | DATES | | | | | | REMARKS |
				TO A/E	DUE	FROM A/E	TO CONTR.	DAYS	CODE	

FIGURE 16.20 Submittal control log.

16.35

construction. The estimated duration for each individual work activity is indicated by a horizontal bar, usually a dashed or colored line, extending from the scheduled start to the completion date. As each item is accomplished, its progress is indicated immediately adjacent to the scheduled bar as a second line or bar, usually solid or of a different color. In many cases, the bar chart indicates the percent of completion for each work activity and the combined percent of completion for the project.

Truly effective project control occurs when the contractor considers both cost and schedule information together. In developing his cost breakdown and detailed construction schedule for a project, the contractor must call on all the experience and expertise available to him. He must carefully consider the length of time and resources required for each work activity. The number of building trades required, their charge rates, and the cost of equipment and other resources establish the estimated cost for that activity. Any variation in the resources used or the actual time required will directly affect the cost for that aspect of the project. The contractor must use his knowledge of manpower availability and the ease of procurement of materials and equipment in the project geographic area. The contractor must consider the time required to perform not only the on-site tasks but also mobilization and preparation.

A more comprehensive and perhaps the most widely used system of scheduling today is the critical path method. This technique permits a much more realistic projection and analysis of the construction process and the daily problems that can delay a project than does the bar chart. If contractors understand and apply the principles of CPM in conjunction with a cost-control system, they will be more efficient and enhance their competitive position in the industry.

In brief, CPM involves the development of a logical model of activities representing the various steps to be taken by each trade throughout the completion of a project. CPM requires the consideration of interdependent tasks and the sequential impact on future activities. CPM actually highlights the critical trades and tasks that control the schedule. It gives the contractor a current picture of the entire status of his project and highlights the controlling or "critical" items so he can put pressure where it will do the most good to expedite a project with the least cost.

One of the most common methods for using CPM is to create a work task flow diagram or project network that uses arrows and nodes. Each arrow represents a step for a particular trade or task. Each node is assigned a unique number and represents the completion of the steps or tasks illustrated by the arrows leading up to it. The node actually indicates the status of the project at that point. The great advantage of this type of network is that it shows what tasks can be done concurrently and what tasks must be done in sequence. The contractor must understand that a task shown after a node cannot be started until all tasks before that node have been completed.

The actual critical path in the network is the sequence of activities requiring more time than any other possible sequence. This critical path determines the total length of time for the project.

Another benefit of the CPM approach is the immediate recognition of "float time." Associated with noncritical activities, float time is the difference between the time required and the time available to execute a specific item of work. This information often enables a supervisor to delay noncritical activities, if necessary, and concentrate on critical activities.

The CPM approach is not complicated, but it does require training before it is best applied. It can be used in a very simple network form, or it can be applied in considerable detail to large and complex projects. Project status can be updated manually or with high-speed data processing. The latter method is extremely effective with a large number of tasks or frequent updating. With the advent of the personal computer and the availability of scheduling software programs, large and complex schedules can be easily tracked and updated in the field. CPM is discussed in more detail in Chap. 10.

SCOPE CONTROL

After discussing cost and schedule control, a brief discussion concerning *scope control* is necessary. Perhaps a better term would be *change control.*

The original contract between the owner and contractor specifies a particular quantity of work defined by plans and specifications for which the contractor is responsible. From time to time, the owner may request the contractor to perform extra work. These requests would constitute *formal* changes. Other instances may arise where the contractor may discover omissions by the owner or the architect-engineer which will necessitate that additional work be performed. Instances such as these would be referred to as *constructive* changes. In either case there may be reason for the contractor to seek additional compensation for the performance of work not included in the original plans and specifications and thus not covered by the contractor's estimate and bid. When this situation arises, a change to the original contract, or a *change order,* is initiated. Although changes are usually dealt with through the administrative provisions of the contract, a large number of changes can have a cumulative and disruptive effect on work performance, frequently referred to as the *ripple effect.* In some cases, individual changes may be so extensive and far-reaching as to completely alter the character and method of performance of the contract. Such changes may lead to claims for damages for breach of contract or, in extreme cases, to the contractor terminating the contract.

Contract law has always permitted the parties to a contract to modify it by mutual consent. Since a change order is a modification of the original contract, it cannot be unilaterally issued and approved. In construction contracts, change orders must be agreed to by both the owner and the contractor. Because of the almost universal need for owners to be able to incorporate changes in a contract, it has become common practice for owners to include a *change* clause to allow them to make necessary changes in the contractor's scope of work. Oftentimes the contract is worded such that further agreement or consent by the contractor is not required. The contractor's consent is implied by his signing of the original contract. At times the owner may have included contract language requiring the contractor to perform the changes as directed regardless of whether the contractor agrees with the changes or compensation for the changes has been agreed upon. In any case, the project manager and field superintendent need to be familiar with the contractual requirements for handling or initiating change orders and the associated documentation required.

This is particularly true when dealing with *constructive* changes. The concept of a constructive change is more difficult to deal with than formal, written change orders. As we noted earlier, a constructive change may result from words, acts, or omissions by the owner or his agents which are construed or inferred by the contractor to have the same effect as if a formal, written change order has been issued. This could involve something as simple as work that was rejected as not meeting contract requirements when in fact the work did comply with contract requirements. Nevertheless, the contractor incurred additional expenses correcting defects and deficiencies that did not exist. Or it could result from a formal change being issued that required the contractor to perform extra work but that did not allow a reasonable schedule extension for the extra work. The contractor would be forced to pay additional overtime to accelerate the work to meet the owner's schedule requirements. In either case the project manager should document the circumstances and attempt to have the owner agree to the changes in writing. Should the owner be unwilling to agree to the changes, the documentation can be used to support later claims.

When responding to requests by the owner to perform additional work, it is incumbent on the project manager to ensure that the scope of the change is clearly defined so that the owner can be given an estimate of the additional costs that will be incurred and/or the additional time that will be required. The owner must approve the extra charges or schedule extensions before they become part of the contract.

If the scope of the requested change is not clear or there is a question concerning contract documents, the project manager needs a vehicle to be able to obtain additional information. This can be accomplished via a request for information (see Fig. 16.5). An RFI is a document that can be used by the contractor to clarify plans and specifications that are not sufficiently detailed or explained. It can also be used to get answers to questions concerning interpretations of contract documents. Responses to RFIs should be made in a timely manner, otherwise project delays could result. Thus the status of all RFIs should be closely monitored and tracked. One method for doing this is the request for information log or RFI log (see Figs. 16.6 and 16.7). A typical RFI log contains the following information:

- Number of the RFI
- Brief description
- Specification or drawing reference
- Originator and date initiated
- Required response date
- Actual response date

Often, the time allowed for the owner to respond to an RFI is spelled out in the contract documents; however, in some cases the RFI can be critical in nature and require an immediate response. In these cases it is important that the contractor notify the owner of the critical nature of the RFI and do everything in his power to expedite a response. The owner may respond verbally to the RFI and back up his response in writing later. In any event, an RFI can be used as a precursor to a change order and, therefore, should be clear and concise.

Invariably, during the course of a project the contractor and owner will disagree in part or in whole on a submitted change order. The dispute could concern the estimated price of the change order or whether the change order is valid. In any case, it is wise for the contractor to document any and all dealings with the owner concerning a change order. For this purpose the record of change order negotiations (see Fig. 16.9) is an ideal mechanism. This document provides a summary of any discussions that have taken place and agreements reached regarding a given change order. Additionally, it provides a single source for identifying all pertinent documentation regarding the change; what initiated the change; and how any disputes concerning the change were resolved. They can be useful in justifying future progress payments.

To sum it up, changes are an inevitable part of the construction process. It is important for the contractor to document all changes to the contract documents and additions to the scope of the project. If there are questions concerning either the plans or specifications, it is incumbent on the project manager to obtain clarification. Changes to the scope can result in additional project costs and/or schedule extensions. It is important for the project manager to identify these additional costs and schedule extensions at the time they occur rather than at the project's completion. It is best to resolve disputes as they occur rather than after the project has long been completed, but in the absence of timely dispute resolution, proper documentation is essential to effective contract administration.

DISPUTES AND CLAIMS

Because the construction industry is so risky and the profits on projects often slim, it is in the interest of all parties involved to anticipate potential disputes and resolve them before they disrupt construction work in progress. Disputes are likely to arise on any project. It is up to the experienced contractor to recognize that certain areas or phases of construction are more likely to generate disputes and plan accordingly. When issues arise that cannot be readily resolved, procedures that resolve disputes and claims should be in place.

A construction claim is a request that is usually originated by the contractor for additional compensation for work related to a matter or event that the contractor considers to be outside the scope of the contract and not recognized by the architect-engineer as a change or extra work and that is not capable of ready resolution.

Construction claims arise for a variety of reasons, including:

- Changes during construction
- Defective contract documents
- Unforeseeable site conditions
- Improper rejection of installed work
- Wrongful termination of contract
- Loss of productivity
- Disruption
- Time-related issues

The general contractor has the duty to screen claims from subcontractors and to check that the owner is contractually responsible for the cost and that the amount claimed is reasonable. Claims are discussed in more detail in Chap. 25.

PROJECT CLOSEOUT

Punchlist Log

A punchlist log is a listing of items that are either deficient or have been omitted and require corrective action (see Fig. 16.21). It is used by the owner and contractor to track all items requiring correction of one form or another and to document their satisfactory resolution. In addition, reference to the appropriate specification and/or drawing is made to provide further guidance and clarification.

PUNCHLIST LOG

PAGE _____ OF _____

PROJECT _____

CONTRACTOR _____   PRELIMINARY INSPECTION DATE _____

LOCATION/STRUCTURE _____   INSPECTED BY _____

Spec./ Dwg. Ref.	Deficiency Item	Percent Complete/Date				Date Resolved
		1st Re-Insp		2nd Re-Insp		
		%	Date	%	Date	

FIGURE 16.21 Punchlist log.

Certification of Substantial Completion

The substantial completion certificate documents the completion and acceptance of major physical contract work items by the owner, the architect-engineer, and the contractor (see Fig. 16.22). It can also be used to establish the final date to which liquidated damages can be assessed and summarize the remaining nonphysical work items to be accomplished prior to final payment.

O'Brien-Kreitzberg   ATTACHMENT

CERTIFICATE OF SUBSTANTIAL COMPLETION

TO:_____ OWNER

DATE OF SUBSTANTIAL COMPLETION: PROJECT TITLE_____

_____   PROJECT NO._____

PROJECT OR SPECIFIED PART SHALL INCLUDE: LOCATION_____

_____   OWNER_____

_____   CONTRACTOR_____

_____   CONTRACT FOR_____

_____   CONTRACT DATE_____

The work performed under this contract has been inspected by authorized representatives of the Owner, Contractor, and Architect/Engineer, and the Project (or specified part of the Project, as indicated above) is hereby declared to be substantially completed on the above date.

> **DEFINITION OF SUBSTANTIAL COMPLETION**
> The date of substantial completion of a project or specified area of a project is the date when the construction is sufficiently completed, in accordance with the contract documents, as modified by any change orders agreed to by the parties, so that the Owner can occupy or utilize the project or specified area of the project for the use for which it was intended.

A tentative list of items to be completed or corrected is appended hereto. This list may not be exhaustive, and the failure to include an item on it does not alter the responsibility of the Contractor to complete all the work in accordance with the contract documents.

BY _____

_____
ARCHITECT/ENGINEER   AUTHORIZED REPRESENTATIVE   DATE

The Contractor accepts the above Certificate of Substantial Completion and agrees to complete and correct the items on the tentative list within the time indicated.

BY _____

_____
CONTRACTOR   AUTHORIZED REPRESENTATIVE   DATE

The Owner accepts the project or specified area of the project as substantially complete and will assume full possession of the project or specified area of the project at _____(time), on _____(date). The responsibility for heat, utilities, security, and insurance under the contract documents shall be as set forth under "Remarks" below.

BY _____

_____
                                               AUTHORIZED REPRESENTATIVE   DATE

REMARKS:

FIGURE 16.22 Certificate of substantial completion.

CHAPTER 17
ACCOUNTING

First Edition

Matthew J. O'Rourke

Price Waterhouse & Company
Independence Mall West
Philadelphia, Pennsylvania

Second Edition

Jack Weaver

Page, Weaver & Carter
North Crossing
Marlton, New Jersey

The success of any business is dependent upon its ability to achieve a common goal—profit. Profit is basically achieved by having excess revenues over expenses. Accounting constantly monitors the revenues and expenses and evaluates if the profit goal is being achieved.

Unfortunately, accounting is sometimes looked at as a necessary but routine business function which a contractor must implement for income-tax-reporting purposes, year-end financial reporting for banks, and so on. It is a proven fact that the lack of adequate accounting records or disregard of their informational value ranks high on the reasons for business failures. This is particularly true in the construction industry, where experts agree that the most common problem among contractors is not maintaining proper cost records on individual jobs and therefore not knowing the job's status on a timely basis. Properly maintained and integrated into the cost-estimating and operational-reporting phase of the contractor's business, accounting information is an invaluable management tool.

The accounting system implemented is dependent upon many factors, including size of contractor, type of contractor, management requirements, and so on. The optimum accounting system should produce information for the following uses:

Financial statements—monthly and annual

Income-tax reporting

Job costing

Budgeting and projections

Cost estimating

Detailed information on billing and expenses

The accounting system should communicate the information on a timely and accurate basis throughout the company to assist management in making the day-to-day decisions that are necessary to achieve the profit goal. With net income in the construction industry presently averaging between 1 and 2 percent of annual contract revenue, failure to adequately control expenses, both direct (job expenses) and indirect (administrative expenses) can often mean the difference between achieving the profit goal and incurring a loss.

The establishment of a clear recognition of the minimum and optimum records required is important to contractors. This is particularly true on cost-reimbursable contracts. However, all contractors must maintain accounting records for the purpose of income-tax reporting (minimum records). The optimum accounting records and related reports vary by company and are dependent on the size of the business and the sophistication and desires of management who will need and use the information developed from the accounting system.

FUNDAMENTAL CHOICES FOR ANY BUSINESS—CASH OR ACCRUAL BASIS OF ACCOUNTING

Perhaps the initial and very basic accounting decision to be made in any business enterprise is whether to employ the cash basis or accrual basis method of accounting. To make this decision there are certain tax considerations and internal-reporting conditions. For tax purposes, the accrual method must be used where inventories play an important part in the business operation. However, the Internal Revenue Service has determined that the construction industry derives income from contracts rather than from the sale of inventory in the normal course of business and therefore may elect either the cash or accrual method of accounting. The cash basis for tax purposes may only be elected under certain circumstances (see Chap. 24 to determine if your company may elect the cash basis for tax purposes).

Cash Basis of Accounting

Under the cash basis of accounting, income is recorded and reported for both financial and tax purposes on the basis of cash received during the year rather than earned. All costs and expenses are deducted from income when paid rather than when incurred. Accordingly, the financial statements of a business on the cash-basis method of accounting could erroneously present the results of operations as well as the financial condition of the company.

Some Advantages

1. Ease in use—cash receipts and disbursement books are all that are required.
2. Degree of "flexibility" in income-tax reporting—taxable income can be controlled by the taxpayer, i.e., the timing of cash receipts arising from billings as

well as the timing or "cutoff" of payments for expenditures. Also, under the cash basis, there is no requirement that prepaid expenses be recognized as they would be under the accrual method of accounting. These expenditures, such as a payment for an insurance policy that will benefit future periods, can be deducted in full from taxable income in the fiscal year that the expenditures are made.

3. Where accounts receivable exceed accounts payable and accruals, as occurs in most businesses, the contractor employing the cash method of accounting defers the payment of income taxes on income earned but not collected. Such income would not be included in taxable income until the year of collection.

Some Disadvantages

1. Does not properly reflect income (collections do not correspond to expenditures recorded for the fiscal period).

2. From an income-tax point of view, "bunching" of income is possible in some years because of heavy collections; correspondingly, losses may be sustained in other years because of this lack of proper matching of revenue earned with appropriate expenditures.

3. Separate record keeping of job cost records would have to be maintained on the accrual basis, otherwise the status of contracts would be misleading.

In summary, the cash-basis method of accounting should be considered advantageous only in certain circumstances, and then for tax purposes only. It serves no real purpose in a business where meaningful use is expected to be made of financial statements. This is particularly true in the contracting business, where financial statements are required continuously for banks, sureties, vendors, prospective customers, and other outside parties.

Accrual Basis of Accounting

Under the accrual method of accounting, revenues are recorded and reported as earned and not when received, while expenses are reported when incurred and not when paid.

Some Advantages

1. A fair financial presentation results since transactions are recorded in the period in which they occur rather than when they are paid or received.

2. In those particular situations where accounts payable and accruals would exceed accounts receivable, a favorable tax situation occurs when compared with the cash method of accounting as discussed above.

3. The job cost records can be integrated with the financial reporting system.

Some Disadvantages

1. The bookkeeping and related accounting tasks become much more involved than under the cash-basis method of accounting.

2. Although in certain instances favorable income-tax results will occur when accounts payable and accruals exceed accounts receivable, there is less control

over the timing aspects of the receipts and disbursements than is offered under the cash-basis method of accounting, i.e., billings must be prepared or accrued when the revenue is earned and not when received.

CONTRACT ACCOUNTING—ACCRUAL METHOD

Unique to the construction industry are two refinements of the accrual method of accounting: the percentage-completion method of accounting, which recognizes income on each contract as work progresses, and the completed-contract method, which recognizes income on contract when completed or substantially so. The percentage-completion method is generally recognized as the preferred method of accounting for contractors, at least from a financial-control concept of accounting. This method applies to long-term-type contracts, which are defined as those contracts which extend over two accounting periods or more (into more than 1 year).

The basis for recording income on construction contracts of short duration requires little discussion. Profits on these contracts are ordinarily recognized when the facilities are substantially completed and accepted by the owner. Few reasons, if any, can be found for departing from this accounting method for the relatively short-term contract.

Percentage-Completion Method

The percentage-of-completion method is preferable when estimates of cost to complete and extent of progress toward completion of long-term contracts are reasonably dependable and when the buyer and contractor are expected to satisfy their contracted obligations. The most common method of allocating the expected total profit under the percentage-completion method of accounting is on the basis of costs incurred to date in relation to budgeted total costs (cost-to-cost method). Other acceptable but less commonly used methods include the units-of-delivery method, the efforts-expended method, and the units-of-work-performed method.

Regardless of the choice of method in determining percentage completion, an up-to-date estimate of cost to complete is an absolute necessity if the percentage-of-completion method is to be employed.

Completed-Contract Method

Application of the completed-contract method presents little difficulty. However, realistic ground rules for determining the point of completion are essential. The completed-contract method is deemed preferable when there is a lack of dependable estimates to determine the percentage of completion or when the financial position and results of operations would not vary materially from the percentage-of-completion basis. As contractors on the completed-contract method of accounting may find themselves in peaks and valleys from a financial-reporting standpoint, the ground rules for determining the point of completion deserve careful and consistent application. The American Institute of Certified Public Accountants, commenting on this subject, states that income should be recognized at completion or "substantially so" and defines the latter as occurring "when remaining costs and potential risks are insignificant in amount."

Comparison of advantages under the two alternative methods could be summed up as follows: Percentage-of-completion basis more accurately reflects income earned on contracts under way during the fiscal period. Many of the assumptions that are interjected by the owners of the business and, more importantly, by outsiders such as banks and sureties who may be reviewing the contractor's financial statements are removed when percentage-completion financial statements are presented. The use of this method, of course, presupposes experience in the particular field and accurate estimating procedures.

The completed-contract basis is more conservative and exact as to revenues earned on contracts. Estimates of ultimate profit are avoided in the financial statements, since only known profit on completed jobs is reported. (Losses are reported in full for financial purposes as soon as such information is available under either method.)

For tax-reporting purposes, the contractor may be able to select either the completed-contract or the percentage-completion method. To select the completed-contract method, however, the contractor must meet certain tax requirements (see Chap. 24 concerning these requirements).

For financial-reporting purposes the authoritative accounting literature specifies which method should be used. Careful review of the requirements must be reviewed prior to adopting a method to ensure that the appropriate method has been chosen.

ACCOUNTING SYSTEMS

Fundamental Bookkeeping Method—Double-Entry Accounting

The double-entry bookkeeping method of recording transactions accounts for each transaction as a credit or debit to a corresponding asset, liability, income, expense, or capital account. The double-entry bookkeeping method would encompass the following:

1. Analysis of cash receipts, which would include

   - Collections from customers (on accounts receivable)
   - Straight cash sales
   - Other receipts (identify)

2. Cash disbursements analysis, which would reflect

   - Cash purchases
   - Payments made to vendors and subcontractors
   - Payments for expenses
   - Other disbursements (identify)

3. Sales analysis
4. Purchase analysis
5. Payroll analysis
6. General ledger

This information, together with information concerning customer accounts receivable, trade accounts payable, inventories in the normal course of business, and such other matters as accrued and deferred items at the beginning and end of the accounting period, would make it possible to prepare an income statement in double-entry form.

Suggested Accounting Records to Be Maintained by a Typical Contractor

Figure 17.1 contains a listing of the accounting records and related reports that a typical contractor would utilize, together with record-retention periods as promulgated by the Internal Revenue Service. Where appropriate, supporting exhibits of pertinent records and reports are presented within the chapter and indexed from Fig. 17.1. Figure 17.2 provides a suggested chart of accounts, Fig. 17.3 illustrates a cash receipts journal page, Fig. 17.4 a cash disbursements journal page, Fig. 17.5 a purchases journal page, and Fig. 17.6 a sales journal page.

Title	Figure reference	Record-retention period[†]	Management use
1. Principal books of account and related documents			
Chart of accounts	2	N/A[‡]	
Cash-receipts journal	3	Indefinitely	
Remittance advices		4 years	
Bank statements		7 years	
Cash-disbursements journal	4	Indefinitely	
Canceled checks		7 years	
Purchase journal	5 and 9	Indefinitely	
Paid invoices		7 years	
Sales journal	6	7 years	
Invoice copies		7 years	
General journal		Indefinitely	
General ledger		Indefinitely	
2. Subsidiary ledgers*			
Contract cost	9	7 years	
Accounts receivable		7 years	
Payroll register		5 years	
Payroll-earnings records (by employee)		5 years	
Perpetual (materials) inventory		7 years	
Equipment inventory		Indefinitely	
3. Management reports (monthly or more often)			
Action report—job control	10	N/A	X
Contract-cost analysis	7 and 8	N/A	X
Income statement with comparison to budget and other standards of performance	12	N/A	X
Projected statement of cash flow	13	N/A	X
4. Basic "conventional" financial statements			
Percentage-completion basis	14	Indefinitely	X
Completed-contract basis	15	Indefinitely	X

*Reconciled to the general ledger accounts monthly.
[†]As required by Internal Revenue Service regulations.
[‡]Not applicable.

FIGURE 17.1   Recommended contractor accounting records.

Assets	Liabilities and capital accounts
Current assets	Current liabilities
101 Cash in bank—general	201 Accounts payable
102 Cash in bank—payroll	203 Loans payable (one year and less)
103 Petty cash	215 Sales tax payable
111 Accounts receivable	220 Employee payroll deductions
111a Accounts receivable—retainage	221 Income tax withheld
120 Inventory—materials	222 FICA tax withheld
130 Costs incurred on contracts-in-process	225 FICA tax (employer's share)
140 Prepaid expenses	226 Federal unemployment tax
144 Estimated earnings on uncompleted contracts*	227 State unemployment tax
	230 Accrued payroll
	235 Other accrued liabilities
Property, plant, and equipment	236 Payable to subcontractors
150 Land	236a Payable to subcontractors—retainage
155 Buildings	240 Billings on uncompleted contracts
155a Accumulated depreciation on buildings	250 Income taxes payable
160 Furniture and fixtures	
160a Accumulated depreciation on furniture and fixtures	Long-term debt
165 Heavy equipment	260 Loans payable (due after one year)
165a Accumulated depreciation on heavy equipment	
170 Vehicles—other	Capital accounts
170a Accumulated depreciation on vehicles—other	280 Capital stock
	285 Paid in capital
	290 Retained earnings
Other assets	
180 Organization expense	
183 Miscellaneous other	

Income	Costs
300 Billings on completed contracts	400 Cost of completed contracts
305 Less: Estimated earnings on completed contracts recognized in prior periods*	401 Contract costs (postacceptance)
310 Current period estimated earnings on uncompleted contracts	Equipment operating expense
320 Miscellaneous income	500 Equipment rentals
	501 Tires
	502 Fuel
	503 Depreciation—heavy equipment
	504 Depreciation—vehicles: other
	507 Insurance, licenses, and taxes
	550 Miscellaneous equipment operating expense
	599 Equipment operating expense charged to contracts (cr.)

Indirect expenses	
600 Supervision	620 Payroll taxes
601 Indirect labor	621 Legal and audit
603 Small tools	622 Travel and entertainment
610 Office and clerical salaries	623 Dues and subscriptions
611 Officers' salaries	624 Depreciation—building
612 Office supplies	625 Building repair and maintenance
613 Utilities	626 Depreciation—office furniture and fixtures
614 Insurance—general	
615 Insurance—compensation	629 Contributions
616 Telephone and telegrams	650 Miscellaneous indirect expenses
617 Advertising	699 Indirect expense charged to contract (cr.)
619 Business taxes (other than payroll and income)	

*Elimination of these accounts would be necessary to place the contractor's accounts on the completed-contract basis of accounting.

FIGURE 17.2 Contractor chart of accounts.

CASH RECEIPTS JOURNAL

Date	Received From	Folio Ref.	Deposits	Amount Received	Discounts And Allowances	Accounts Receivable		Other Income			Other Accounts	
						Current	Retainage	Sub- account	Amount		Account	Amount

FIGURE 17.3 Cash receipts journal.

CASH DISBURSEMENTS JOURNAL

Date	Check No.	Payee	Folio Ref.	Amount	Accounts Payable	Contract Cost		Selling Expenses		General and Administrative Expenses		General Ledger	
						Account	Amount	Account	Amount	Account	Amount	Account	Amount

FIGURE 17.4 Cash disbursements journal.

17.9

PURCHASE JOURNAL

Invoice Date	Vendor	Folio Ref.	Accounts Payable	Contract				Contract				General Ledger	
				Material	Labor	Sub Con-tractor	Other Costs	Material	Labor	Sub Con-tractor	Other Costs	Account	Amount

FIGURE 17.5 Purchases journal.

SALES JOURNAL

Date	Customer	Invoice Number	Contract Number	Folio Ref.	Invoice Amount	Current	Retainage	General Ledger	
								Account	Amount

FIGURE 17.6 Sales journal.

Centralized and Decentralized Record-keeping Responsibilities

The need for on-site clerical personnel varies by contractor and by the size of his respective contracts. In some cases, such as the small and sometimes the medium-size contract or contractor company, there may not be a need for a full-time clerical employee(s) on the job site. However, the all-important field reports that indicate the employees working on the job and subcontractors employed, together with daily production reports, must be prepared for general office-management review or for use by the construction-company management while touring the job site on a regularly scheduled basis. Although the responsibilities of a field-office staff or individual clerk vary by size of job, the following on-site activities are characteristic of a medium-size to large contractor with an on-site clerk.

1. A petty cash account should be maintained for incidental purchases and expenditures.
2. A job-site checking account should be maintained on an imprest-fund (fixed-balance) basis. Such a checking account should be used for payroll and certain expenditures with an established limit as to amount and purpose. The bank account should be maintained in the name of the contracting company, and statements should be forwarded to the general office for reconciliation and review. Analysis of cash disbursements should be forwarded to the general office on a regular basis for review of transactions and for use in preparing the reconciliation of the cash account.

Since one of the prime purposes of an on-site job clerk is the reporting and control of payroll costs and labor effectiveness, the following procedures should be implemented:

1. The clerk or timekeeper should forward to the job superintendent time sheets for his approval prior to the preparation of the payroll.
2. The general office should deposit in the job payroll account funds which aggregate the amount of the current payroll net after withholdings. The job superintendent's approval of the payroll, prepared by the on-site clerk, is the basis for the general office control of disbursement to the job-site imprest account. The superintendent or someone in authority, independent of the person preparing the payroll, should make the "payoff" (distribution of checks) and return any unclaimed checks to the general office.

Maintaining an Effective Job Cost-Control System

Regardless of the type of contract—cost-plus, fixed-fee, or some refinement of either—a contractor wants to monitor the weekly and monthly progress on each individual contract. The ability to gather the expenditures by contract is, in its simplest form, a cost accounting system. Although regular field inspection of the contract while under way and a knack of gauging time elapsed with performance cannot be discounted as prerequisites for success in the contracting business, this technique can be supplemented with accurate quantitative information via a simple cost-control system. Unlike the contractor who has a general idea that the job is progressing satisfactorily based on his intuition, an effective cost-control system can pinpoint contracts or segments of particular jobs that need management attention and are not yet beyond repair. The steps to be followed and tools to be used in monitoring contracts while they are in progress and obtaining the information needed to take action would include the three concepts discussed below.

Recognize That the Contract "Estimate" Is the Financial Budget. Accurate and realistic estimating for contracts is one of the prime requisites for success in the contracting business. The estimate should be formally documented, preferably on a standard form, and should be thoroughly understood by key financial and cost accounting personnel as well as personnel from engineering and operation. The final estimate becomes the financial budget and should be the yardstick used to measure actual performance at frequent intervals during the course of the contract and not the focus of a postcontract ritual. The estimate, then, should contain information in sufficient detail to measure actual performance against the "budget." Methods of measure would include

1. Quantitative analysis of units completed versus the estimate by principal phase (i.e., cubic yards excavated, square yards surfaced, pounds of reinforcing steel placed)
2. Total cost by principal phase

The resultant unit cost becomes an important gauge of efficiency as work progresses. The unit cost includes the direct-cost items such as labor, material, and subcontracting and in a more sophisticated system might include certain indirect or overhead costs allocated to each phase for more precise control of total business expenses.

The Method of Compiling Cost within the Cost-Control System Should Be Compatible with the Detailed Estimate. The two preferable approaches used to measure actual results against the estimate (budget performance) are

1. The units-of-production concept, which accounts for cost by natural segment of construction, i.e., plumbing, foundation, electrical work, labor (see Fig. 17.7).
2. The line-item-cost approach, which records costs incurred and reduces the estimate to natural expenses, i.e., labor, material, equipment usage, and overhead, with little if any attempt to correlate with the natural segment of the contract (see Fig. 17.8).

The units-of-production method usually requires more detailed accounting records in the absence of a computerized accounting system (because of the refinement of, for instance, labor cost between numerous segments or phases versus the maintenance of a single labor-cost account under the line-item-cost approach). However, the units-of-production approach affords meaningful analysis and gives management insight into the wheres and whys of variances from the estimate.

The information available from the cost-accounting records (as to both units and dollars) maintained in the same form as the contractor's estimate should aid considerably in estimating on future contracts as well as pricing current change orders.

It should be noted that under the line-item-cost approach, careful analysis of total labor cost and further investigation of labor variances, say, by trade group within the direct-labor category from that estimated, can pinpoint the problem areas. However, much additional effort would be required. In-depth after-the-fact investigation is often precluded because of failure to identify labor charges with specific phase of construction in the basic field reports.

In addition to key cost-accounting personnel, complete job-cost analyses

CONTRACT COST ANALYSIS
(Under Units of Production Concept)

Contract No. _____
Period covered _____

Cost to Date (from contract cost ledger)			Phase No.	Classification		Cost to Complete			Forecast of Final Cost			Original Estimate			Over/Under Estimate		
Quantity	Unit	Amount				Quantity	Unit	Amount	Quantity	Unit	Amount	Quantity	Unit	Amount	+	−	
			1	Land preparation	1												1
			2	Excavation	2												2
			3	Masonry	3												3
			4	Carpentry	4												4
			5	Plumbing and heating	5												5
			6	Electrical work	6												6
			7	Lath, plaster and tile	7												7
			8	Painting	8												8
			9	Landscaping	9												9
			10	Extras	10												10
				(enumerate)	11												11
					12												12
					13												13
					14												14
					15												15
					16												16

FIGURE 17.7 Contract cost analysis—production concept.

CONTRACT COST ANALYSIS
(Under Line Item Cost Approach)

Contract No. _____
Month Ending _____

Cost to Date (from contract cost ledger cards)			Item No.	Classification		Cost to Complete			Forecast of Final Cost			Original Estimate			Over/Under Estimate		
Quantity	Unit	Amount				Quantity	Unit	Amount	Quantity	Unit	Amount	Quantity	Unit	Amount	+	−	
			1	Direct labor	1												1
			2	Material	2												2
			3	Subcontractors	3												3
			4	Indirect labor	4												4
			5	Fringe	5												5
			6	Equipment usage	6												6
			7	Indirect cost allocation	7												7
			8	Other	8												8
					9												9
					10												10
					11												11
					12												12
					13												13
					14												14
					15												15
					16												16

FIGURE 17.8 Contract cost analysis—item cost.

17.15

should be available to and regularly utilized by operations management, the job superintendent, and to the extent applicable, the project manager (at least in units if not dollars by the latter) for purposes of evaluating and appreciating estimated compared with actual performance.

Integrating Bidding, Cost Estimating, and Cost Accounting.   The lack of historic (actual) cost by natural phase of construction, for use in preparing a bid, exists in even many of the medium- and large-sized contracting companies. Instead of having cost information on similar structures, the educated guess of estimators and possibly top management often prevails. Estimates of the cost of future work should be based on past experience modified to fit the specifications of the new job. Historical costs should be recorded in sufficient detail to be helpful under the usual situations encountered on specific jobs. They are seldom identical but usually have common or similar elements.

This historical information could easily be converted to current cost if necessary, since both units and cost can and should be captured in the company's cost accounting system.

The units-of-production concept of cost control mentioned above anticipates complete and precise integration of the estimating and cost accounting functions.

While various types of construction require widely diverse "units" or work centers, an illustration might be useful. A simplified example is the contractor constructing individual residences, who might use the following:

1. Land preparation
   a. Erection of shack
   b. Clearing
2. Excavation
   a. Trenches
   b. Rough grade
   c. Backfilling
3. Masonry
   a. Forms
   b. Footings
   c. Block work
   d. Chimney
4. Carpentry
   a. Frame
   b. Shingles
   c. Clapboards
   d. Windows
5. Plumbing and heating
   a. Heating plant
   b. Pipes
6. Electrical work
   a. Outlet wiring
   b. Range circuit
   c. Oil-burner circuit
7. Lath, plaster, and tile
8. Painting
9. Landscaping
10. Extras (enumerate)

Each of these main classifications and possibly the subclassifications would be further categorized into material, direct labor, subcontractor, and such other expenses as can be directly related to the activity. The more costs that can be treated as direct, the less the uncertainties of allocation enter into the accounting. Compensation insurance, payroll taxes (fringe), and equipment rentals can usually be treated as direct costs. Overhead costs consisting of items such as general office expenses, automobile expenses, professional services, telephone, postage, and advertising are not usually allocated to detailed job-cost classifications but are normally allocated to jobs and included in the total cost upon which estimates are based. It is not uncommon for contractors working at less than full capacity to attempt to obtain business by bidding above direct costs but below full cost. This may be an appropriate temporary expedient but can lead to failure in the long run. It is the need for good historical cost figures that keeps the prudent contractor from entering into new construction areas where cost estimates and bids cannot be made on any sound historical basis.

ACCOUNTING RECORD-KEEPING SYSTEMS

"Write-It-Once" System

The contractor who relies on a conventional manual accounting system would find it virtually impossible to consider capturing contract cost by natural phase of construction. Maintaining the natural-cost elements of each contract, i.e., direct labor, material, and subcontractors as reflected in the purchase register (Fig. 17.5), and posting the data into the individual vendor or subcontractor subsidiary ledger cards or records is in itself a cumbersome, detailed task. Figure 17.9 illustrates how a popular "write-it-once" (pegboard) system works. This system relies on a single writing and posting from one record to another via carbonized forms. The illustration includes all the records needed to operate a contractor's cost accounting as well as accounts payable system under the units-of-production (natural segment or phase) concept.

Obviously, the simpler but less effective line-item-cost (natural-expense) classification is easily accommodated by the write-it-once system. Under either system of cost control, the write-it-once system is economical in terms of both time and money, lessens considerably the chance of clerical error in posting from one record to another, and should aid in providing more timely financial information.

Computerized System

With the introduction of microcomputers in the 1980s, and the steadily decreasing price of the computer along with the introduction of many turnkey software packages, a computerized system for maintaining accounting records is very cost-effective. For under $10,000, a small or medium-size contractor could install a very effective computerized system which would prepare and communicate, in an accounting format, management reports and financial statements.

These systems would produce the necessary project costing, estimating, billings, etc., from the original accounting entries on a very timely basis and at a much lower cost than a manual system. Several examples of reports which can be produced from these software packages are shown in Figs. 17.10, 17.11, and 17.12.

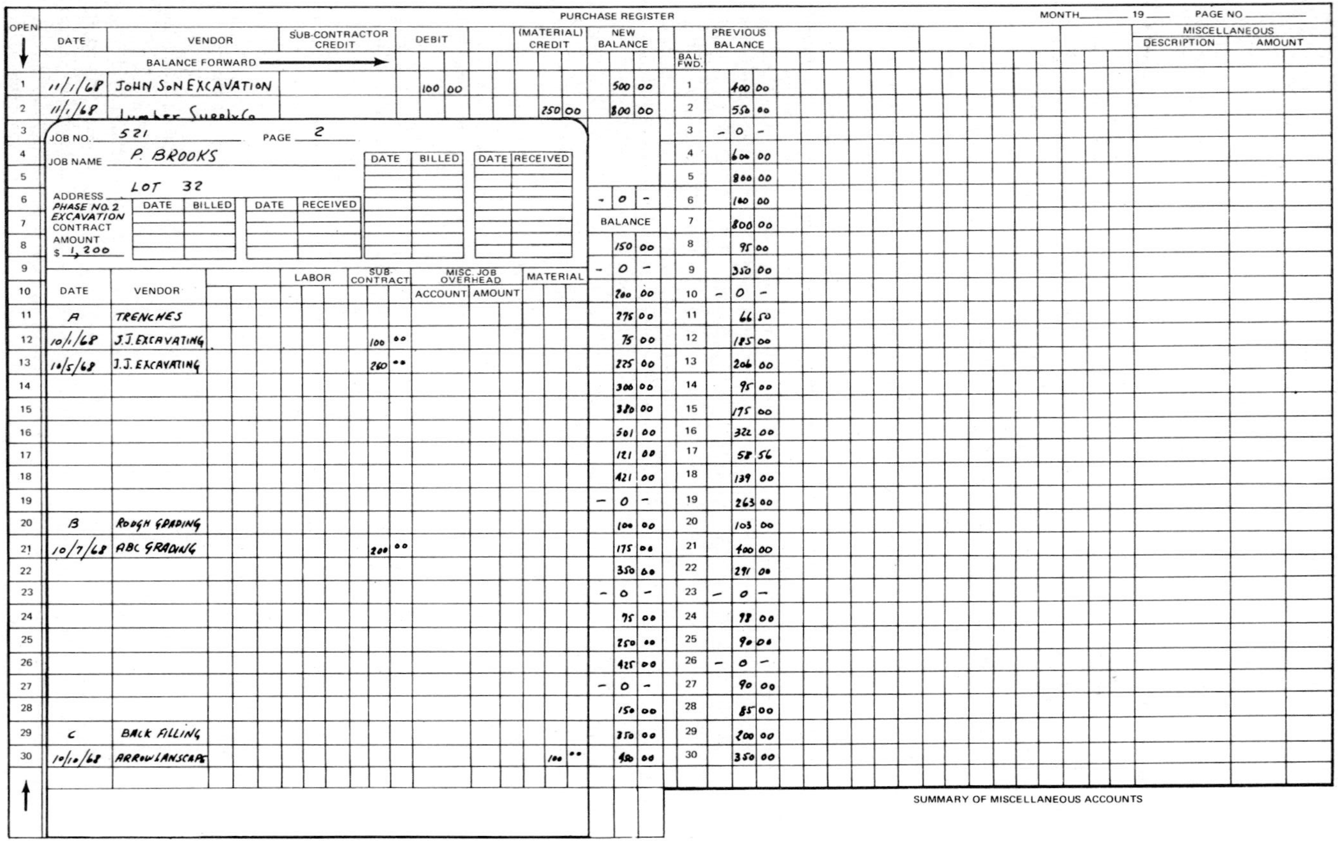

FIGURE 17.9 An example of a "write-it-once" accounting system.

CASH DISBURSEMENTS JOURNAL

DATE	CHECK ISSUED TO	DIRECT DISTRIBUTION	ACCOUNTS PAYABLE	DISCOUNT	CHECK AMOUNT	NEW BALANCE	PREVIOUS BALANCE	CHECK NUMBER	BANK BALANCE	DEPOSITS AMOUNT	DATE
	BALANCE FORWARD										
1	10/1/68	OFFICE SUPPLY Co	1,000.00		50.00	950.00	100.40	2216			
2	10/1/68	ARROW LANDSCAPE Co	500.00			500.00		2217			
3	10/3/68	T.J. EX CARATING	415.00			415.00	0	135.00	2218		
4		A.R. AND COMPANY, INC.							2219		
5									2220		
6									2221		
7						BALANCE		2222			
8						3.00		2223			
9						3.00		2224			
10						590.00		2225			
11						2.00	500.00	2226			

SBS CORPORATION
LANSDALE, PA.

60-220
313

N⁰ 2229

DATE	INVOICE	AMOUNT

GROSS AMOUNT   CHECK
OTHER   ACCTS PAYABLE   DISCOUNT   AMOUNT

PAY _____ DOLLARS

TO THE ORDER OF

NAME _____
STREET _____

SBS CORPORATION
SAMPLE
NOT NEGOTIABLE

CONTINENTAL BANK & TRUST COMPANY
LANSDALE OFFICE LANSDALE, PENNSYLVANIA

BY _____

TREASURER

SUMMARY OF MISCELLANEOUS ACCOUNTS

FORM NO AFL 7 NCR

SAFEGUARD BUSINESS SYSTEMS CORP
LANSDALE PA CHICAGO ILL LOS ANGELES CALIF

FIGURE 17.9 (Continued)

17.19

ABC COMPANY
JOB ANALYSIS REPORT BY COST TYPE

JOB NUMBER: 4102   XYZ Hospital Remodeling
JOB TYPE: 001 Contract Billing
JOB STATUS: O OPEN
CONTRACT NO: 2250-RTJ
% COMPLETE: 60.00%

CUSTOMER NO: 01-XYZ
BILL METHOD: F FIXED
STATUS DATE: 05/31/90
CONTR. DATE: 04/25/90
REPORTED DATE: 05/15/90

XYZ Hospital
ESTIMATOR: JONES   START DATE: 05/01/90
MANAGER: BROWN   COMPL DATE: 08/31/90
REV. CONTRACT: 36,450.0   SQ FEET: 10,000
EST PROFIT: 2,935.00
PROJ PROFIT: 7,843.33   PRJ PRFT%: 21.52%

COST TYPE	DESCRIPTION	THIS PERIOD	JOB-TO-DATE	ORIGINAL ESTIMATE	REVISED ESTIMATE	% OF ESTMT	CURRENT VARIANCE	PROJ COST TO COMPLETE	PROJ % OF EST
	BILLED TO DATE	11,120.00	18,870.00	30,000.00	36,450.00	51.8	(3,000.00)		
L	Labor	3,200.00	5,600.00	12,200.00	12,200.00	45.9	(175.00)	6,197.25	96.7
M	Material	2,500.00	5,075.00	12,025.00	12,025.00	42.2	897.50	3,782.31	73.7
S	Subcontract	3,355.00	3,495.00	5,000.00	5,440.00	64.3	53.00	2,132.78	103.5
O	Overhead	1,811.00	2,834.00	3,400.00	3,400.00	83.4	(350.00)	916.00	110.3
B	Burden	160.00	160.00	450.00	450.00	35.6	0.00	290.00	100.0
	COST TOTAL FOR 4102	11,026.00	17,164.00	33,075.00	33,515.00	51.2	425.50	13,318.34	91.0
	COST PER SQ FEET:	1.10	1.72	3.31	3.35	51.2	0.04	1.33	91.0

JOB NUMBER: 7918   BYN-17th Floor Buildout
JOB TYPE: 001 Contract Billing
JOB STATUS: O OPEN
CONTRACT NO: 4557-DTM
% COMPLETE: 85.00%

CUSTOMER NO: 01-BYN
BILL METHOD: F FIXED
STATUS DATE: 05/31/90
CONTR. DATE: 03/31/90
REPORTED DATE: 05/31/90

BYN Co.
ESTIMATOR: MILLER   START DATE: 04/20/90
MANAGER: ELLIOT   COMPL DATE: 07/30/90
REV. CONTRACT: 20,000.00   SQ FEET: 15,000
EST PROFIT: 4,250.00
PROJ PROFIT: 8,447.79   PRJ PRFT%: 42.24%

COST TYPE	DESCRIPTION	THIS PERIOD	JOB-TO-DATE	ORIGINAL ESTIMATE	REVISED ESTIMATE	% OF ESTMT	CURRENT VARIANCE	PROJ COST TO COMPLETE	PROJ % OF EST
	BILLED TO DATE	12,000.00	17,000.00	20,000.00	20,000.00	85.0	0.00		
L	Labor	2,167.50	3,967.50	7,250.00	7,250.00	54.7	50.00	2,969.35	95.7
M	Material	1,240.00	4,125.00	6,100.00	6,100.00	67.6	37.50	1,795.18	97.1
O	Overhead	681.50	1,618.50	2,050.00	2,050.00	79.0	0.03	431.46	100.0
B	Burden	108.38	108.38	350.00	350.00	31.0	0.00	241.62	100.0
	COST TOTAL FOR 7918	4,197.38	9,819.38	15,750.00	15,750.00	62.4	87.53	5,437.61	96.9
	COST PER SQ FEET:	0.28	0.65	1.05	1.05	62.3	0.01	0.36	96.9

FIGURE 17.10   ABC Company—job analysis report by cost type.

```
                          ABC COMPANY
                    JOB WORK IN PROCESS REPORT

JOB NUMBER: 4102    XYZ Hospital Remodelling       CUSTOMER NO:  01-XYZ          XYZ Hospital      START DATE: 05/01/90
  JOB TYPE: 001 Contract Billing                   BILL METHOD:  F FIXED         ESTIMATOR: JONES  COMPL DATE: 08/31/90
JOB STATUS: O OPEN                                  STATUS DATE:  05/31/90        MANAGER:   BROWN  SQ FEET:    10,000
CONTRACT NO: 2250-RTJ                               CONTR. DATE:  04/25/90        REV. CONTRACT: 31,450.00  LAST BILL: 5/15/90
% COMPLETE: 60.00%                                  REPORTED DATE: 05/15/90       BILLED TO DATE: 8,750.00
```

COST CODE/ COST TYPE	U/M	UNITS REV ESTIMATE	UNITS JOB-TO-DATE	DOLLARS REV ESTIMATE	DOLLARS JOB-TO-DATE	% OF ESTMT	ACTL % COMPLT		PROJ COST TO COMPLETE	PROJ % OF EST	OUTSTANDING WORK IN PROC
200-000-000 Interior Piping											
L Labor	Hour	160.0000	40.0000	4,000.00	1,000.00	25.0	25.0	05/15	3,000.00	100.0	0.00
M Material	Feet	2,500.0000	2,000.0000	2,500.00	2,250.00	90.0	95.0	05/15	118.42	94.7	1,250.00
CODE 200-000-000 TOTAL:				6,500.00	3,250.00	50.0			3,118.42	98.0	1,250.00
200-099-000 Interior Piping - Overhead											
O Overhead		0.0000	0.0000	0.00	650.00	0.0			0.00	0.0	250.00
PHASE 200 TOTAL				6,500.00	3,900.00	60.0			3,118.42	108.0	1,500.00
300-000-000 Wire Pull											
L Labor	Hour	100.0000	64.0000	2,500.00	1,600.00	64.0	65.0	05/15	861.54	98.5	1,000.00
M Material	Feet	5,500.0000	1,500.0000	825.00	225.00	27.3	30.0	05/15	525.00	90.9	0.00
CODE 300-000-000 TOTAL:				3,325.00	1,825.00	54.9			1,386.54	96.6	1,000.00
300-099-000 Wire Pull - Burden											
B Burden			0.0000		50.00	0.0	0.0	COST	0.00	0.0	963.00
				15,940.00	8,636.00	54.2			7,314.04	100.1	5,888.80
00-010-000 Fire Alarm - Installation											
L Labor	Hour	20.0000	0.0000	500.00	0.00	0.0	0.0	UNIT	0.00	0.0	0.00
M Material	Feet	10.0000	0.0000	1,200.00	0.00	0.0	0.0	UNIT	0.00	0.0	0.00
CODE 500-010-000 TOTAL:				1,700.00	0.00	0.0			0.00	0.0	0.00
500-020-001 Smoke Detectors - Initial Test											
L Labor	HOUR	8.0000	0.0000	200.00	0.00	0.0	0.0	UNIT	0.00	0.0	0.00
PHASE 500 TOTAL				1,900.00	0.00	0.0			0.00	0.0	0.00
JOB TOTAL				27,665.00	14,776.00	53.4	60.0	5/15	11,819.00	96.1	8,638.00

FIGURE 17.11 ABC Company—job work-in-process report.

ABC COMPANY
JOB COST CODE DETAIL REPORT

JOB NUMBER: 4102 XYZ Hospital Remodeling	CUSTOMER NO: 01-XYZ	XYZ Hospital	START DATE: 05/01/90
JOB TYPE: 001 Contract Billing	BILL METHOD: F FIXED	ESTIMATOR: JONES	COMPL DATE: 08/31/90
JOB STATUS: O OPEN	STATUS DATE: 05/31/90	MANAGER: BROWN	SQ FEET: 10,000
CONTRACT NO: 2250-RTJ	CONTR. DATE: 04/25/90	REV. CONTRACT: 31,450.00	PRJ % EST: 89.02%
% COMPLETE: 60.00%	REPORTED DATE: 05/15/90	COST J-T-D: 14,776.00	

COST CODE/ COST TYPE	DESC.	THIS PERIOD	JOB-TO-DATE	ORIGINAL ESTIMATE	REVISED ESTIMATE	% OF ESTMT	ACTL % COMPLT	DATE RPTD	CURRENT VARIANCE	PROJ COST TO COMPLETE	PROJ % OF EST
200-000-000	Interior Piping										
L Labor	COST:	0.00	1,000.00	4,000.00	4,000.00	25.0	25.0	05/15	0.00	3,000.00	100.0
M Material	COST:	1,250.00	2,250.00	2,500.00	2,500.00	90.0	95.0	05/15	125.00	118.42	94.7
CODE 200-000-000 TOTAL		1,250.00	3,250.00	6,500.00	6,500.00	50.0			125.00	3,118.42	98.0
200-099-000	Interior Piping - Overhead										
O Overhead	COST:	250	650.00	0.00	0.00	0.0			(650.00)	0.00	0.0
PHASE 200 TOTAL		1,500.00	3,900.00	6,500.00	6,500.00	60.0			(525.00)	3,118.42	0.0
300-000-000	Wire Pull										
L Labor	COST:	1,000.00	1,600.00	2,500.00	2,500.00	64.0	65.0	05/15	25.00		
M Material					825.00	27.3	30.0	05/15			
...erial	COST:	0.00	0.00	500.00	500.00	0.0	0.0 UNIT		0.00	0.00	0.0
	COST:	0.00	0.00	1,200.00	1,200.00	0.0	0.0 UNIT		0.00	0.00	0.0
CODE 500-010-000 TOTAL		0.00	0.00	1,700.00	1,700.00	0.0			0.00	0.00	0.0
500-020-001	Smoke Detectors - Initial Test										
L Labor	COST:	0.00	0.00	200.00	200.00	0.0	0.0 UNIT		0.00	0.00	0.0
PHASE 500 TOTAL		0.00	0.00	1,900.00	1,900.00	0.0			0.00	0.00	0.0
JOB 4102 TOTAL:		8,638.00	14,776.00	27,225.00	27,665.00	53.4	60.0	5/15	(1,830.50)	11,819.00	96.1

FIGURE 17.12 ABC Company—job cost code detail report.

Task-Force Approach to the Estimate and Bid

Unfortunately, most contracting companies—even those with sizable staffs—have not really implemented another of the methods available to eke out more profit from contracts. This is the *task-force approach*, under which a highly qualified group of administrative, accounting, and construction personnel, and other key management people are assigned to each contract at its inception. This group of specialists would first work together on preparing the bid. Then, being fully aware of the original cost estimate and contract terms on awarded work, they assume responsibility for organizing all procedures and assigning responsibilities prior to the commencement of any work under the contract. After the job program has been formulated and agreed to by the team, the job is turned over to the project manager (who preferably was a member of the team), and the task force goes on to another bid assignment. The benefits of the task-force method of operation can be realized by smaller contractors by expanding the bidding function to a team effort comprising representatives of operations and cost accounting as well as estimating personnel. The estimate and bid preparation in the smaller contracting firm usually ignores the accounting department as a source of assistance. Obviously, consideration must be given to the limitations of personnel as to both time and ability in the smaller firm.

Modern Operating Techniques—PERT, CPM, and PERTCO

PERT (program evaluation and review technique with respect to time factors in scheduling projects) or the critical path method (CPM) can aid in refining operating techniques. It is especially notable that the use of "prebid CPM or PERT" networks is now considered essential by some large contractors to aid in determining that estimates have been thoroughly evaluated prior to issuance. As success is obtained with PERT (involving only time factors) the cost factors (CO) can be added, and what is known as PERTCO can be used.

Basically, PERTCO requires a breakdown of the estimate, cost to date, and projected costs to completion into individual components or activities. In some cases, the breakdowns are so extensive and the details so fine that a computer operation is the only satisfactory method of obtaining timely and reliable information. There are software packages available which would enable a construction company to utilize these techniques with a small investment.

If used as theoretically contemplated, PERTCO is an ideal method of evaluating performance for each activity, for determining costs of alternative methods of construction, and for determining the effect on costs of alternate timing for completion of certain activities. However, as in any extensive administrative undertaking, the increased costs which are usually attendant to the administration of a PERTCO operation must be more than offset by the savings of more efficient construction work.

Maintaining the Major Elements of Cost under Constant Surveillance

Although most businesses close their books and make an in-depth cost analysis once a month, it is increasingly recognized that product cost is needed more frequently in certain businesses. These businesses are principally in manufacturing, where a job-order cost system is employed because of the lack of a production-line product where costs remain relatively constant. Similarly, the construction industry has a need for this more-frequent check on production efficiency and cost control. Each contract should be accounted for on a profit center for revenue recognition, cost accumulation, and income measurement.

The reports listed in Table 17.1 represent an ideal information flow for a contractor, from which he should be in a position to take action on a timely basis. The reports are described below.

Field Labor Report.   The field labor report prepared daily by each foreman would give the superintendent the following information:

- The type of work performed and in what areas of the structure (phase of job)
- Units of work completed
- Listing of men by trade or responsibility assigned and hours spent on job and elsewhere (explain when unusual)
- Extensions of hourly rate by hours charged to job (prepared by field clerk if practical)
- Cost of "work unit" in total and by trade or responsibility where applicable (superintendent would compare with estimate and discuss remedial action with foreman if conditions warrant) (prepared by field clerk if practical)

Field Progress Report.   The field progress report is a weekly compilation of the daily labor reports prepared by the foreman and represents the superintendent's initial report to operations management at the corporate level. Brief explanatory comments should accompany this report and would normally serve as the basis for a weekly meeting between the superintendent and operations management.

The weekly production report would also (1) account for quantities of materials delivered and used on the job (by phase of construction) and (2) provide information on equipment on-site, delivered, and removed during the week, together with hours actually in use (by phase of construction). More responsible personnel (operations management) now have the opportunity to take formal action where necessary.

Job Status Report.   The job status report is a compilation of the weekly field progress reports and includes operations management's formal update of units completed and forecast of units to complete the job.

TABLE 17.1   Reports Representing an Ideal Information Flow for a Contractor

Report	When prepared	Prepared by	Sent to
Field labor report	Daily	Foreman	Superintendent
Field progress report	Weekly	Superintendent	Operations management
Job status report	Monthly (at least)	Superintendent and engineering	Operations management and cost accounting
Contract cost analyses	Monthly (at least)	Cost accounting	Provides data for action report
Action report	Monthly (at least)	Cost accounting	Top management (financial, operations)

Contract Cost Analysis. (See Figs. 17.7, 17.8, 17.10, and 17.11.) In addition to the heavy emphasis on labor-cost control, which is without question the key to profit on most contracts, the complete cost analysis must include purchases of materials, equipment usage, and overhead both on the job site and for corporate office expenses. This analysis is prepared from the books of account (as to cost incurred), and units completed and to be completed are obtained from the job status report prepared jointly by operations and engineering management.

The cost accounting department would verify the labor-cost compilation reflecting cost for the period based on field reporting with that appearing in the payroll records. The cost accounting department would then price out the cost to complete the contract based on the current unit requirements indicated and applying most recent cost data.

Action Report. Figure 17.13 represents the culmination of all the various field reports and the cost-to-date and to-complete information contained in the contract status report. Explanations should be placed in writing for significant (say, 5 percent) change in the profit picture since the last action report as well as from the original estimate. This report would be included in the formal financial report package that is prepared monthly for top management's review. However, this report is not dependent upon the completion of other financial reports for issuance. It should be prepared and issued as swiftly as possible at prescribed intervals or on a when-needed basis.

GENERAL FINANCIAL CONTROL OVER THE BUSINESS

In addition to control over contract cost, the following areas need to be considered by the contractor as important to the overall financial success of the company:

1. Preparation of the annual budget
2. Monthly comparisons of the company's actual performance with the profit plan
3. Preparation of an annual cash-flow projection with monthly adjustment as required
4. Control over accounts receivable retainages and payments to subcontractors

The Annual Budget

Every business needs a plan to determine what its future financial needs are going to be, along with items such as future employee, office space, and equipment needs. Many contractors, particularly those involved in work for short duration, contend that a budget is of little value to them because of the uncertainties as to the number and dollar amounts of contracts a year away. This argument lacks sound judgment, since expenses, other than direct contract costs, will continue to be incurred regardless of contract income. For these reasons, it is incumbent

Contract Facts

Job number _____
Job type _____ Description _____
Owner _____
Site location _____
Date of contract _____
Work to begin _____

(000 of Dollars)

Through to Completion

Item or Phase No.	Original Estimate	% 100	Revised	% 100	Overrun (Underrun)	% 100
1.						
2. Preferably listed						
3. by natural phase						
4. of construction (units of production)						
5. or line item cost						
6. (see Exhibits 7 & 8)						
7.						
8.						

Billings
Costs

Profit
Profit reported on last report _____
Net change from last report dated _____
Explanation for profit change from last report (5% or greater) _____

Comments _____

Prepared by _____   Date _____

Final Data at Completion
(Stamp on final action report)

	Original Estimate	Actual
Completion date		
Profit		
One year "follow-up" cost		
True profit		

FIGURE 17.13 Action report.

upon the managers of a contracting firm, regardless of size, to reduce to writing their annual financial plan. Without such a plan, the amount of nondirect contact and general-office costs (burden) that must be recouped through contract income can easily be forgotten. This can result in faulty decisions as to the dollar amounts of volume and gross margin (contract revenue less direct contract expenses) that are required to break even or show a desired profit. The annual budget should determine the profit goal and everyone in the company should know what his responsibilities are to achieve it.

If the contractor's business is departmentalized, or if, in the case of the smaller contractor, a form of organization exists that assigns responsibilities to appropriate personnel for such areas as sales or contract revenues, operations control, and the other areas of expense within the company, these are the departments or individuals who should provide the raw data that will be used to compile the annual plan. Normally, the budget is divided into monthly periods for evaluation of monthly results against the plan. Figure 17.14 describes how the particular sections of the budget are pieced together into an overall plan.

Income and expense items	Based on following factors
Gross sales income	Sales forecast
Cost of houses sold	Cost estimate, and unit sales forecast
Gross profit on sales	Projected sales income less the projected cost of houses sold
Less: selling expenses and administrative expenses	Your past experience as reflected on your past profit and loss statements, balanced against standards of comparison. Then, adjust figures to meet the requirements of your selling plan.
Net operating profit	Projected gross profit less your projected operating expenses
Add: other income	Your past experience, as reflected on your past profit and loss statements
Total less: other deductions	Your past experience as reflected on your past profit and loss statements
Net profit (before taxes)	Projected net operating profit, plus projected other income, less projected other deductions
Less provision for taxes	Based upon current tax structure
Net profit (after taxes)	Is your estimated net profit adequate?

FIGURE 17.14 Preparation of annual budget for the contractor. *(National Association of Home Builders.)*

Monthly Review of Actual Operating Performance against the Budget

Once the annual plan is finalized and approved by management, it becomes the measurement of performance (similar to the job cost estimate). Aside from the direct contract costs which we have already dealt with at length, the indirect or overhead expenses must be reviewed monthly and deviations from budget justified. Figure 17.15 is an excellent example of the form the monthly internal income statement of a contracting firm should take and reflects the standards (historic industry experience or goals, for example) that should be compared with actual performance, in addition to the budget for the period (both monthly and

Account No.	General ledger account	Last year's actual	Standard of comparison	This year's budget	This year's actual	Over or under budget
	Gross contract sales	$	$	$	$	$
	Less: Cost of contract sales	$	$	$	$	$
	Gross profit on contracts	$	$	$	$	$
	Percent of gross sales	%	%	%	%	%
	Less: Selling expenses:	$	$	$	$	$
	Sales promotion					
	Advertising expense					
	Travel, auto, and entertainment expenses					
	Total selling expenses	$	$	$	$	$
	Percent of gross sales	%	%	%	%	%
	Less: General and administrative expenses:	$	$	$	$	$
	Management salaries (Including construction superintendent)					
	Office salaries					
	Rent					
	Insurance					
	Depreciation expense					
	Interest expense					
	Taxes					
	Utilities					
	Telephone and telegraph					
	Office supplies and expense					
	Legal and audit					
	Miscellaneous expenses					
	Total general and administrative expenses	$	$	$	$	$
	Percent of sales income	%	%	%	%	%
	Total operating expense	$	$	$	$	$
	Percent of gross sales	%	%	%	%	%

FIGURE 17.15 NAHB operating budget. (*National Association of Home Builders*.)

Net operating profit	$		$		$		$		$
Percent of gross sales	%		%		%		%		%
Interest income	$		$		$		$		$
Rental income	$		$		$		$		$
Total other income	$		$		$		$		$
Bad debts	$		$		$		$		$
Charges to completed jobs	$		$		$		$		$
Total other expenses	$		$		$		$		$
Net profit before income tax	$		$		$		$		$
Percent of gross sales	%		%		%		%		%
Provision for federal income tax									
Net profit after income tax	$		$		$		$		$
Percent of gross sales	%		%		%		%		%

year-to-date actual to budget should be reported each month and variances investigated).

The Cash Flow Projection

Once the budget is prepared, the statement of cash flow can easily be pieced together. The accrual-basis contractor's budget reflects contract revenues in the month billed and not when received. This, together with advance purchase of materials, payroll costs, income taxes, and possible debt repayments, usually requires that the contractor plot his inflow and outflow of cash, preferably on a monthly basis, so that he can decide if borrowings, additional capital, or possibly a cutback or increase in operations or overhead costs are called for. Figure 17.16 illustrates the form the statement of cash flow should take. This statement should be prepared at the time the annual budget is prepared and should be reviewed and updated regularly.

	January	February	December	Total for year
Projected cash receipts:				
Realization of billings				
Current month (90%)				
Prior months (90%)				
Retainage (10%)				
Collections of income items from other sources (list)				
Other (list)				
Total anticipated cash flow				
Projected cash disbursements:				
Payroll – net				
– related withholdings				
Trade account payable				
Vendors				
Subcontractors – 90% invoiced				
10% retainage				
Selling, administrative and general expenses				
(List or support with schedule)				
Borrowings				
Principle				
Interest				
Property and equipment purchases				
Other (list)				
Total anticipated cash outflow				
Cash receipts over (under) disbursements				
Add:				
Cash balance at beginning of the period				
Cash balance at end of the period				

FIGURE 17.16 Cash flow projection.

Control over Accounts Receivable Retainages and Payments to Subcontractors

An important difference in a contractor's mode of operation from most other businesses is the retainage requirement that exists on virtually all contracts. Generally, retainage is limited to 10 percent of each billing (payment of 10 percent of each invoice rendered by the contractor is held until the entire job is completed and accepted by the architect or owner). This retainage is commonly regarded as one of the chief reasons for the cash problems that plague many contractors, particularly those who perform services at the outset of the contract, i.e., excavation and structural steel contractors.

Where the general contractor employs subcontractors, this same percentage of retainage is normally held back from his invoice payments. Accordingly, the excavator, as well as the general contractor who does only a minimum amount of subcontractoring, may require a substantial amount of capital investment or borrowing to meet working-capital requirements. This problem, particularly as it applies to the "early" subcontractors on the job, has been dealt with over the years with some informal relief available depending on locale and the architect's preferences. However, the normal waiting period for collection of retainage is still dependent on final acceptance of the entire project by the architect or owner on most contracts.

FINANCING AND ACCOUNTING FOR EQUIPMENT USAGE

The use of heavy-construction equipment, such as cranes, bulldozers, and earthmovers, requires a substantial direct investment or rental cost to the general contractor or to subcontractors such as steel erectors and excavation contractors. These costs must be recouped through charges to contracts. Equipment cost should preferably be allocated to the job on the basis of hourly rental charges. This is appropriate whether the contractor owns the equipment or operates it under a lease or rental arrangement. The hourly rental charge is calculated by estimating total equipment cost (including costs for such items as depreciation, repairs, maintenance, operator, insurance, and moving) and dividing the total cost by the estimated number of hours that the equipment will be in use on job sites. Still another method employed, acceptable under many cost-plus-type contracts, is to charge the job at the rental rate that would be paid to an outside equipment-rental company, less the built-in profit that a leasing company would add onto cost.

An inventory of owned and leased equipment, supported by a history file on each piece of equipment, is highly desirable. The inventory would indicate job location, arrival date, and expected date of availability. Optimum usage can be preplanned and monitored with preciseness. The history file for each piece of equipment owned and equipment on long-term rentals would include a complete maintenance and repair record in addition to use (jobs and hours) and a performance evaluation. This information is essential for realistic repurchase and major-overhaul determinations. Manufacturer warranty or leased-equipment differences can often be resolved to the advantage of the owner or lessee when such detailed records are maintained.

Leasing versus Ownership

Leasing of equipment of all types continues to grow in popularity because it provides advantages to the lessee in placing certain of the risks of ownership on the lessor. Lessors of heavy-construction equipment realize such advantages as placing quantity orders, arrangements for ready resale of used equipment, and centralized servicing of these specialty pieces of equipment that enable them to minimize rental rates in their leases. Many contractors would rather consider the cost and bother of maintenance, obsolescence, and disposal someone else's problem and choose the lease route.

The choice between leasing and ownership, and in most instances, borrowing to finance the purchase, does not just involve a comparison of the effect of each on profits and cash flow. It also involves such matters as the freeing of management time and the effect on operating efficiency of having available prompt repair service for leased equipment that might otherwise sit idle and delay overall progress on an important contract.

Some Advantages of Leasing.   The leasing of equipment offers a number of advantages over ownership to a contractor. Among them are the following:

1. Leasing can finance up to the entire cost of new equipment, whereas only a percentage of the cost of owned assets is usually borrowed to finance their acquisition. This conserves funds for working-capital requirements, which the contractor is often forced to maintain at a set level for bidding and surety purposes.
2. Leasing may reduce both the investment in fixed assets and long-term borrowing. If prospective creditors take lease-rental charges fully into account, however, this advantage is minimized or, if the lease is considered a capital lease, the equipment must be capitalized and the debt recorded.
3. Immediate modernization and increase in equipment fleet are facilitated when assets can be acquired without down payment and merely by entering into a lease agreement.
4. Leasing may give a tax advantage, although this has become less significant as depreciation allowances have been liberalized and leases which are tantamount to purchases have been recognized as such by the IRS. (The accounting profession also recognizes leases that are purchases as such.)

Some Disadvantages of Leasing.   Reasons against leasing in lieu of ownership and related borrowing include

1. Higher cost, in the form of both a higher return on the lessor's investment during the primary lease period and the rental paid during the renewal periods after the investment has been amortized.
2. The loss of residual or terminal values after the end of the lease. If equipment is owned, these values are retained.
3. When assets leased for a long time become obsolete, there may be strong reluctance to abandon them when large rentals are payable for their use.
4. The tax benefit may be challenged when the lessee is given an option to purchase at other than market value at the time of purchase (as is common under conditional sales contracts). Some leases have been construed as sales or have been ignored for tax purposes if they were held to be mere devices for charg-

ing off excessive amounts against taxable income for depreciation under the guise of rentals.

Depreciation

In the past, accountants generally regarded depreciation as the physical deterioration of a tangible property caused by wear and tear. This concept of depreciation is now regarded by most accountants as outdated, for the following reasons:

1. Recognition that depreciation is related to economic as well as physical conditions, which ultimately terminate the economic usefulness of a property.

2. From the accounting standpoint, depreciation should apply to the investment in the asset, rather than to the asset itself. The emphasis on exhaustion of the investment rather than on exhaustion of the asset might not satisfy the contractor who is concerned with depreciation of his equipment as a physical function, but it is a useful emphasis from the standpoint of the accountant, who is concerned with the "use" of fixed-asset costs and their absorption as expenses, via charges against operations. Placing the accounting emphasis on the apportionment of cost rather than on physical deterioration gives recognition to the fact that depreciation charges are not intended to parallel physical decline. Depreciation charges are intended to spread the cost of the asset over the periods that benefit from the service of the asset; this result would not be accomplished if the accumulated depreciation charges followed physical depreciation. For one reason, physical depreciation usually is less during the early years than during the later years of an asset's life; if the accounting charges followed, the early years would be charged less for the use of the machine than the later years, although management often considers it desirable to replace fixed assets before physical depreciation is complete. Therefore, if income is to be properly measured, depreciation charged should equal cost less salvage value during the period of useful life.

The current conception of depreciation is expressed as follows by the American Institute of Certified Public Accountants.

> Depreciation accounting is a system of accounting which aims to distribute the cost or other basic value of tangible capital assets, less salvage (if any), over the estimated useful life of the unit (which may be a group of assets) in a systematic and rational manner. It is a process of allocation, not of valuation. Depreciation for the year is the portion of the total charge under such a system that is allocated to the year. Although the allocation may properly take into account occurrences during the year, it is not intended to be a measurement of the effect of all such occurrence.

Matters to Be Considered When Determining Depreciation Policy. In estimating the amounts to be charged to expense periodically for fixed-asset expirations, the following should be considered:

1. The depreciation base
2. Residual or salvage value
3. Estimated useful life

These factors determine the total depreciation to be provided and the period over which the total depreciation is to be spread. The amount charged to each period depends upon the apportionment method adopted.

The Depreciation Base.   The base generally used for the computation of depreciation is cost of the asset, which would include all costs incurred getting the asset ready for use.

Residual or Salvage Value.   The residual or salvage value of an asset is the amount which can be recovered by its disposal when it is taken out of service. The estimated residual value to be used in the computation of depreciation should be net after any estimated costs of dismantling or disposal are deducted.

Although residual value should theoretically be taken into consideration in determining the total amount of cost expiration to be charged to operations during the life of an asset, it is frequently ignored. This may be justified if the residual value is nominal (under 10 percent, a rate which the Internal Revenue Service also accepts) or not subject to reliable estimate, or if any dismantling and disposal costs cannot be accurately estimated.

Estimated Useful Life.   The life of any fixed asset is the total number of service units expected from the asset. Service units can be measured in the following ways:

1. Periods of time (years or months)
2. Operating periods, or production hours
3. Units of production

Estimating the useful life of an asset requires consideration of: (1) company's repair and maintenance policies, (2) prior experience with similar assets, (3) current condition of asset, (4) technological changes, and (5) future plans for the asset. For instance, heavy equipment used in mining may have an economic life limited to the life of the mine since it would be too costly to dismantle and remove the equipment.

Depreciation Methods.   The following are the principal methods of allocating equipment depreciation that should be considered by contractors.

- Straight-line
- Production-hours
- Production-output
- Accelerated-depreciation
- Declining-balance
- Sum-of-the-years' digits
- Charge-to-job-and-sell

The following symbols are used in depreciation formulas discussed below.

C = cost

S = scrap or residual value

n = estimated life (periods, working hours, or units of production)

r = rate of depreciation (per period, per working hour, or per unit of production)

D = depreciation per period

Basis of Illustrations.   For purposes of illustration, it will be assumed that:

- The cost of a piece of equipment is $60,000.
- The estimated residual value is $4,000.
- The estimated life is 8 years (except in two illustrations in which the life is stated in terms of production hours or units of production).

In the illustrations of methods in which the life is expressed in production hours or units of product, the necessary additional information is furnished.

Straight-Line Method.   This is the simplest and by far the most commonly used method. It results in spreading the total depreciation equally over all periods of life, unless the periodical charge is adjusted because of abnormal operating activities. The formula for computing the periodical depreciation charge is

$$\text{Using the assumed facts, } D = \frac{C - S}{n}$$

$$= \frac{\$60,000 - \$4,000}{8}$$

$$= \frac{\$56,000}{8}$$

$$= \$7,000$$

Table 17.2 shows the accumulation of depreciation under the straight-line method.

TABLE 17.2   Depreciation Table—Straight-Line Method

End of year	Depreciation expense	Total accumulated depreciation	Remaining value
			$60,000
1	$ 7,000	$ 7,000	53,000
2	7,000	14,000	46,000
3	7,000	21,000	39,000
4	7,000	28,000	32,000
5	7,000	35,000	25,000
6	7,000	42,000	18,000
7	7,000	49,000	11,000
8	7,000	56,000	4,000
	$56,000		

In practical applications of the straight-line method, the residual value usually is ignored and a rate determined from the estimated life of the asset is applied to cost. In the illustration, the rate would be 12½ percent and the depreciation would be 12½ percent of $60,000, or $7,500 each year.

The straight-line method has the advantage of simplicity. Suggested lives for various types of equipment are promulgated by the Internal Revenue Service, and most of the major equipment manufacturers make such information available in more detailed form.

Production-Hours Method. This method recognizes the fact that property, particularly machinery, depreciates more rapidly if it is used full-time or overtime than if it is used part-time. Not only is the wear and tear greater, but there is less opportunity for making repairs. Moreover, the full-time and overtime years get more benefit from the asset than do the part-time years. In the application of this method, the total number of working hours for which the machine is capable of operating is estimated, and a charge per hour is determined by the following formula:

$$r = \frac{C - S}{n}$$

If it is assumed that the asset used for illustrative purposes is expected to have an operating life of 22,400 working hours, the depreciation rate per hour of use is computed in the manner illustrated below.

$$r = \frac{\$60,000 - \$4,000}{22,240}$$

$$= \$2.50$$

Table 17.3 shows depreciation amounts per year for this method.

TABLE 17.3 Depreciation Table—Production-Hours Method

Year	Hours worked	Depreciation expense	Total accumulated depreciation	Remaining value
				$60,000
1	2,600	$ 6,500	$ 6,500	53,500
2	2,900	7,250	13,750	46,250
3	3,400	8,500	22,250	37,750
4	2,400	6,000	28,250	31,750
5	1,800	4,500	32,750	27,250
6	2,700	6,750	39,500	20,500
7	3,000	7,500	47,000	13,000
8	3,600	9,000	56,000	4,000
	22,400	$56,000		

Production-Output Method. This method is similar to the production-hours method in that it distributes the depreciation among the periods in production to the use made of the piece of machinery or equipment during each period. The estimated life is stated in units of product or service, and the rate of depreciation is a rate per unit. The figures in Table 17.3 for the production-hours method can serve as an illustration of this method also, if we assume that the estimated life is stated as 22,400 units of production (for example, cubic yards instead of production hours) and that the figures in the "Hours worked" column represent units of finished goods produced. The depreciation rate is then $2.50 per unit, and the depreciation each year is computed by multiplying the number of units produced by the rate per unit.

The production-output method is peculiarly suitable to the depreciation of assets for which the total service units can be rather definitely estimated and when the service is not uniform by periods. The method might, for instance, be appropriately applied in depreciating heavy-duty trucks or their tires or engines on a mileage basis.

If a piece of equipment is subject to obsolescence, the production-output method appears to be an illogical procedure for establishing a reserve intended to provide for both physical deterioration and obsolescence, because obsolescence presumably develops on a time basis rather than on the basis of units of output. During a period of small production, the depreciation charges might be less than the amount which should be provided for obsolescence on the basis of the lapse of time, and this inadequacy might not be compensated for in periods of larger production.

Accelerated-Depreciation Methods. There is increasing emphasis on the theory that, because new assets are generally capable of producing more revenue than old assets, a better matching of revenue and expense is achieved by larger depreciation charges in the early periods when assets have their greatest economic usefulness. Essentially, this procedure provides that depreciation charges follow a constantly decreasing pattern, although initially greater than those under the straight-line method.

The Internal Revenue Service recognizes various accelerated methods of depreciation. However, there is no requirement that a taxpayer must employ the same methods for financial- and tax-reporting purposes. It is commonplace in industry to use straight-line depreciation for financial-reporting purposes and the most liberal depreciation method and shortest life available under the law and regulations for income-tax purposes.

Declining-Balance Method. Under this method, a fixed or uniform rate is applied to the carrying value of the asset. The rate used is likely to be based on what is permissible for income-tax purposes. The law and regulations for the declining-balance method allow the use of a depreciation rate not exceeding twice that acceptable as a straight-line rate. The regulations also provide that scrap value need not be taken into account. Thus, if it is acceptable for income-tax purposes to use 12½ percent as a straight-line rate (this would agree with the 8-year use life being used in the illustrations), a rate up to 25 percent is acceptable for the declining-balance method. Assuming once again that a piece of equipment cost $60,000 and that the company adopted the 25 percent rate, the depreciation would be:

$15,000 for the first year	$60,000 × 25%
$11,250 for the second year	$45,000 × 25%
$8,437 for the third year	$33,750 × 25%

and so on. However, depreciation should not be continued when the result would be to reduce the carrying value below the estimated scrap value.

Sum-of-the-Years'-Digits Method. This method can best be explained as follows:

1. Add the numbers representing the periods of life:

Thus, $1 + 2 + 3 + 4 + 5 + 6 + 7 + 8 = 36$

2. Use the sum thus obtained as a denominator.

3. Use as numerators the same numbers taken in inverse order:

Thus, 8/36, 7/36, *etc.*

4. Multiply the total depreciation $(C - S)$ by the fractions thus produced.

TABLE 17.4   Depreciation Table—Sum-of-the-Years'-Digits Method

Year	Fraction of $56,000	Depreciation expense	Total accumulated depreciation	Remaining value
				$60,000
1	8/36	$12,444	$12,444	47,556
2	7/36	10,888	23,332	36,668
3	6/36	9,333	32,665	27,335
4	5/36	7,777	40,442	19,558
5	4/36	6,222	46,664	13,336
6	3/36	4,666	51,330	8,670
7	2/36	3,111	54,441	5,559
8	1/36	1,559	56,000	4,000
	36/36	$56,000		

Annual depreciation amounts under this method are shown in Table 17.4. The sum-of-the-years'-digits can be computed by using the following formula:

$$S = N \frac{N + 1}{2}$$

N equals the number of periods of estimated useful life. Applying the formula where the useful life is 8 years,

$$S = 8 \frac{8 + 1}{2}$$

$$= 8 \,(4.5)$$

$$= 36$$

Charge-to-Job-and-Sell.   On large-scale construction contracts, particularly where great distance and equipment which is impractical to move over the road are involved, it is not unusual for the contractor to charge the cost of certain types of equipment (heavy shovels, earth-movers, and specialty transportation equipment, for example) directly to the job at the outset and to credit (give allowance) to the job at completion of its on-site sale value. In these instances, the cost of dismantling, transporting, and reassembling makes it economically unfeasible for the contractor to use this equipment, which is usually well worn, on another job. It may be advantageous to the contractor as well as the owner to sell even at seemingly low scrap values rather than incur the additional costs cited.

ACCOUNTING FOR JOINT VENTURES

Contractors, not unlike major companies, such as those in the petroleum industry, have found that the joint-venture approach to large-scale projects enables them to spread the often tremendous financial risk and reap the benefits from sharing their respective areas of expertise. The joint venture is legally looked at as a form of partnership. The members of the joint venture may be either sole proprietorships, partnerships, or corporations, but the joint venture itself is a separate business entity for which separate accounts are usually kept. Each member of the joint venture usually contributes capital and may have accounts receivable from the joint venture for equipment rentals, engineering, architectural or other services, sales of material, and other items. It is also common for the participants to bill the joint venture for interest on capital invested and accounting and other overhead expenses incurred on behalf of the joint venture. The methods of reimbursing and compensating the participants are usually provided for in the joint-venture agreement.

The accounting for and reporting on joint-venture investments and operations in a contractor's financial statements has many unique accounting problems. The American Institute of Certified Public Accountants in its "Audit and Accounting Guide—Construction Contractors" discusses in detail the proper accounting treatment for joint ventures.

CORRELATION OF ACCOUNTING WITH OTHER BUSINESS FUNCTIONS

Operations

As with any other business, an organization structure with clear-cut lines of reporting and responsibilities is important to the success of a contracting company. Accounting is a staff function and as such can perform most effectively if provided with the full cooperation of operating management and personnel. The accounting section of a contractor's staff ideally translates operational data into understandable quantitative information (usually in the form of dollars) which operating management hopefully uses as an aid in making decisions and taking prompt action. This includes income-tax planning and return preparation, a discussion of which can be found in Chap. 24.

Claims Backup

The need for supporting data to backup of claims by a contractor usually arises out of change-order difficulties with the owner, architect, or general contractor (in the case of the subcontractor, usually with the latter). It cannot be repeated too frequently that the contractor should not perform any extra work or undertake change orders on contracts until this work is formally awarded via a properly authorized work order or contract change.

Should the contractor find himself in the dilemma of not having a formal change order, items such as his field reports and cost accounting records supported by labor tickets and/or material, and subcontractor invoices should prove helpful in supporting claims and "extras."

Although initially developed for planning and in-progress monitoring of contracts, PERT, CPM, and PERTCO (control techniques that formally document and interrelate contract events such as specification requirements, due dates, and costs which were covered earlier in the chapter) can probably provide the best form of support for large claims for or against the contractor. Particularly where litigation is involved, these techniques can provide third parties with a documented trail of performance or failure to perform by each phase or condition of the contract.

AUDITS

Internal Checks and Balances

As mentioned in an earlier section, dealing with the various field labor and production reports, monthly tie-in of detailed labor reports prepared in the field (which include payroll-cost extensions and totals) with the contractor's cost accounting and payroll records maintained at the general office constitutes an excellent system of checks and balances for the contractor. The importance of maintaining such a program of payroll-cost and labor-performance surveillance cannot be overemphasized.

Internal Audit

The larger construction companies, with operations in all parts of the United States and often abroad, employ a full-time internal audit staff which may function in one or more of the following roles:

1. Assist the company's independent (outside) accountants in the examination of the company's financial statements by performing certain audit tests under the supervision of the independent accountants (field inspections, test of payroll controls, and other finance-related work).

2. Perform more extensive examinations of various jobs in progress by determining that (a) all required field reports are being prepared properly and on time; (b) expenditures are being controlled at the field site (items such as payroll, small tools, equipment usage and maintenance); and (c) payroll tax, worker's compensation, and local tax requirements are being met. Where the job is very large, continuous on-site auditing is often performed.

The need and advisability of employing internal auditors is largely dependent on the size of the individual job or the contracting company. In the smaller contracting company, internal auditing is often replaced by more direct control by the general office and top management and/or the reliance on the company's outside accountants to perform more extensive work than is required in connection with their examination of the company's financial statements (such as those enumerated above).

Audit of Construction Cost by Contractor's Customer or His Representative

All cost-plus contracts and in certain cases other types of contracts which require an accounting of cost should contain a provision giving the internal and/or external accountants and auditors of the contractor's customer the right to review all records which generate charges to the company. A further provision should exist that all subcontracts contain the same clause.

Soon after the contract is signed, the auditors should visit the construction contractor and discuss the audit that the customer company will engage in, preferably continuing throughout construction. This preliminary meeting has considerable value, as it enables the auditors to make known to the contractor the various records that will be audited. Potential differences surrounding the availability and in some cases the need to maintain certain records can often be resolved at the outset before a problem actually arises.

Depending on the size of the contract, the audit will range from permanent on-site residence of the auditor to an audit at completion of the contract. The review and auditing at the offices of the contractor and/or his job-site office will consist principally of reviewing and checking records and documents which result in a charge to the customer company. The charges which can be billed vary according to each contract and are too numerous to cover here. Some of the more important, however, are discussed below.

Verification of Job Classification and Salary Rates. Job classifications and salary rates have to be verified by the contractor's records to ensure that each individual is paid by the contractor at the same rate charged to the company. A further audit of canceled payroll checks, after being cleared by the bank, provides evidence that payments were made in the amounts billed to the company.

Verification of Hours Worked on the Job Site. All contractors should have a system of checking construction workers on and off the job, and most of the larger construction companies have excellent procedures for accomplishing this. The auditor must be familiar with these procedures and should arrange for the contractor's resident accountant (where applicable) to observe checking in and checking out at frequent intervals, with the auditor himself participating to the extent deemed necessary to ensure compliance with this important procedure. The auditor should trace exceptions noted, such as lateness or absenteeism, to weekly time reports in connection with his payroll-audit work.

Verifications of Extensions. Verification of the basic payroll arithmetic is a simple and rather routine function that must be covered by the auditor. The degree of checking that is necessary, however, varies with the system employed by the contractor when computing his payroll charges to the customer company.

Other Payroll Charges (Taxes, Welfare, and Other Fringe Items). Though the entire contract may be cost-plus, this portion is sometimes agreed upon as a percentage of the labor cost, in which case calculation and auditing are simple. When standard rates are not agreed on, the auditor is compelled to review such items as the contractor's records and reports to governmental agencies to verify the payment of these costs.

One of the greatest causes of disagreement in contract interpretation is found in this area. For instance, an employee's FICA and unemployment taxes are computed only on the first so many dollars (base amount) paid an employee in a calendar year. Many contractors charge the company for payroll taxes on wages beyond the base amounts. Since in some contracting companies the contractor ceases to generate a cost, it is incumbent on the auditor to take exception to the excess charges. Some contractors will argue that their employees previously earned most of the base amount before they were assigned to the company's project and that the customer company should therefore not benefit as a result of a prior client's being charged. One cannot completely disagree with this argument. This position has merit particularly where large peak numbers of employees not otherwise on the payroll are on the job or transient workers are normally involved. However, utilizing an overall average rate based on annual employee earnings may be more equitable in those companies where the direct labor force remains rather constant throughout the year.

Small Tools. The terminology "small tools" is often used in contracts, and they are usually charged directly to the contract. Very few contracts, however, adequately define what is meant by small tools. Both the contractor and the customer would do well to have it spelled out so that both parties know what they are agreeing to. The absence of proper definition poses another dilemma to the customer company's accountants and auditors.

When it is decided exactly what "small tools" means, the auditor should review the procedures for the use of and, where applicable, the return in inventory of these tools. Despite the fact that the company is charged for these, they are usually in the possession of the contractor for use by his personnel. The auditor should also be aware of the method of accounting for these tools at the close of the project. (As a practical matter, small tools are usually well worn at the end of an extensive contract and of little dollar value.)

Discounts, Refunds, and Rebates. Refunds and rebates should be credited to the customer company when received by the contractor on cost-plus-type contracts. Cash discounts sometimes present a problem. It would appear reasonable for whoever does the financing of the particular charge to get credit for the cash discount. Thus, if the contractor takes the discount and withholds billing to the company until the normal time allowed by the vendor without benefit of cash discount, the contractor is doing the financing and the discount is not a reduction of purchase price. However, if the contractor takes the cash discount and immediately bills and receives payment from the customer company, the contractor is merely passing on the financing and in this instance should also pass on the cash discount.

Contracts may be written to solve this problem by requiring all cash discounts to accrue to the company, which in turn would require the contractor to take all cash discounts and pass them on to the company. The contractor in turn would then be permitted to bill and receive payment from the company immediately after his payment is made to the vendor. (Where there is a delay between submission of invoices by the contractor and payment by the customer, this pass-on-of-discounts concept should be reconsidered.)

On-site receiving procedures should be reviewed. Receiving information should be adequate for all the steel, bricks, lumber, concrete pipe, and other construction items that go into a new facility. Proper receiving reports form the basis for paying vendors' bills by the contractor and, ultimately, the charge to the company.

Job Residuals. Another point requiring careful attention is auditing the disposition of construction material and equipment left over at the end of the job. The value of these items may be significant. Proper handling requires maintaining a detailed inventory during construction and taking specific action at the completion of the job on all materials not used or equipment either usable or salvageable.

Rented equipment raises special problems. Adequate procedures must be established to record both its coming on and leaving the job (as discussed under equipment usage).

Other Expenses. Travel expenses, living allowances, telephone service, telegrams, permits, fees, and similar items are examples of miscellaneous billable items and, of course, will vary depending on the contract. The auditor should assure himself that these charges are in accordance with the terms of the contract.

Compliance-type Audits

In addition to having his books and records subjected to customer audits of construction costs and possibly an audit by a CPA, the contractor is subject to audits by other outsiders. These include

1. Taxing authorities:

   U.S. Internal Revenue Service (income and payroll taxes)
   State and local governments (payroll, unemployment, gross receipts taxes, etc.)

2. Insurance:

   Worker's compensation
   Bonding company (normally relies on financial statements audited by CPA)

3. Other compliance and regulatory audits:

   Unions—pension and welfare-fund payments
   Wages and hours laws (federal and state)

The contractor's books and records need to be maintained in an orderly fashion so that the above parties can be satisfied with a minimum of time and effort on the part of the contractor and his staff. The required retention periods for the various records maintained by a contractor are given in Fig 17.1.

Financial Statements for Use of Third Parties

The basic conventional financial statements are not the sole, and in many cases should not be considered the principal, medium of financial information for management purposes. The contractor should be just as interested in the action report (Fig. 17.13) and other management reports as in his overall earnings or cash position as set forth in the conventional financial statements. However, from the point of view of third parties such as bankers and sureties, the purpose of conventional financial statements is to furnish them with an inventory of assets, liabilities, and profits after an evaluation of all present conditions affecting the accounting, on as complete and accurate a basis as possible in a brief presentation (see Figs. 17.17 through 17.22). In addition, the construction industry, unlike most other businesses, must provide additional information to third parties. This information supplements the financial statements but is not as extensive as the internal information produced for management action.

The American Institute of Certified Public Accountants, in its "Audit and Accounting Guide—Construction Contractors," recognizes this need for additional information and suggests alternative presentations depending on the

Percentage Contractors, Inc.
Consolidated Balance Sheets
December 31, 19X8 and 19X7

Assets	19X8	19X7
Cash	$ 264,100	$ 221,300
Certificates of deposit	40,300	
Contract receivables (Note 2)	3,789,200	3,334,100
Costs and estimated earnings in excess of billings on uncompleted contracts (Note 3)	80,200	100,600
Inventory, at lower of cost, on a first-in, first-out basis, or market	89,700	99,100
Prepaid charges and other assets	118,400	83,200
Advances to and equity in joint venture (Note 4)	205,600	130,700
Note receivable, related company (Note 5)	175,000	150,000
Property and equipment, net of accumulated depreciation and amortization (Note 6)	976,400	1,019,200
	$5,738,900	$5,138,200

Liabilities and Shareholders' Equity	19X8	19X7
Notes payable (Note 8)	$ 468,100	$ 578,400
Lease obligations payable (Note 9)	197,600	251,300
Accounts payable (Note 7)	2,543,100	2,588,500
Billings in excess of costs and estimated earnings on uncompleted contracts (Note 3)	242,000	221,700
Accrued income taxes payable	52,000	78,600
Other accrued liabilities	36,600	36,000
Due to consolidated joint venture minority interests	154,200	26,200
Deferred income taxes (Note 13)	619,200	408,000
	4,312,800	4,188,700
Contingent liability (Note 10)		
Shareholders' equity		
Common stock—$1 par value, 500,000 authorized shares, 300,000 issued and outstanding shares	300,000	300,000
Retained earnings	1,126,100	649,500
Total shareholders' equity	1,426,100	949,500
	$5,738,900	$5,138,200

FIGURE 17.17 Percentage Contractors, Inc.—consolidated balance sheets.

Percentage Contractors, Inc.
Consolidated Statements of Income and Retained Earnings
Years Ended December 31, 19X8 and 19X7

	19X8	19X7
Contract revenues earned	$22,554,100	$16,225,400
Cost of revenues earned	20,359,400	14,951,300
Gross profit	2,194,700	1,274,100
Selling, general, and administrative expense	895,600	755,600
Income from operations	1,299,100	518,500
Other income (expense)		
Equity in earnings from unconsolidated joint venture	49,900	5,700
Gain on sale of equipment	10,000	2,000
Interest expense (net of interest income of $8,800 in 19X8 and $6,300 in 19X7)	(69,500)	(70,800)
	(9,600)	(63,100)
Income before taxes	1,289,500	455,400
Provision for income taxes (Note 13)	662,900	225,000
Net income (per share, $2.09 (19X8); $.77 (19X7))	626,600	230,400
Retained earnings, beginning of year	649,500	569,100
	1,276,100	799,500
Less: Dividends paid (per share, $.50 (19X8); $.50 (19X7))	150,000	150,000
Retained earnings, end of year	$ 1,126,100	$ 649,500

The accompanying notes are an integral part of these financial statements.

FIGURE 17.18 Percentage Contractors, Inc.—consolidated statements of income and retained earnings.

method of accounting for contracts and many other factors which might affect the practicality of the individual company presenting such data. It appears reasonable for bankers and sureties to request the following information in financial statements of contractors prepared for third-party use irrespective of their being submitted with or without audit:

1. Basic conventional financial statements:

   Comparative balance sheet
   Comparative statement of income and retained earnings
   Comparative statements of cash flow

2. Notes to financial statements containing, among other disclosures:

   Basic method of revenue recognition (generally either percentage-completion or completed-contract)
   Significant commitments and contingent liabilities
   Method of reporting affiliates and joint-venture investments

Percentage Contractors, Inc.
Consolidated Statements of Changes in Financial Position
Years Ended December 31, 19X8 and 19X7

	19X8	19X7
Source of funds		
From operations		
Net income	$ 626,600	$230,400
Charges (credits) to income not involving cash and cash equivalents		
Depreciation and amortization	167,800	153,500
Deferred income taxes	211,200	(75,900)
Gain on sale of equipment	(10,000)	(2,000)
	995,600	306,000
Proceeds from equipment sold	25,000	5,000
Net increase in billings related to costs and estimated earnings on uncompleted contracts	40,700	10,500
Decrease in inventory	9,400	
Decrease in prepaid charges and other assets		16,100
Increase in accounts payable		113,200
Increase in other accrued liabilities	600	21,200
Increase in amount due to consolidated joint venture minority interests	128,000	26,200
Total	1,199,300	498,200
Use of funds		
Acquisition of equipment		
Shop and construction equipment	100,000	155,000
Automobiles and trucks	40,000	20,000
Dividends paid	150,000	150,000
Increase in contract receivables	455,100	9,100
Increase in inventory		3,600
Increase in advances to and equity in joint venture	74,900	15,400
Increase in note receivable, related company	25,000	50,000
Increase in prepaid charges and other assets	35,200	
Decrease in notes payable	110,300	90,300
Decrease in lease obligations payable	53,700	9,700
Decrease in accounts payable	45,400	
Decrease in accrued income taxes payable	26,600	2,400
Total	1,116,200	505,500
Increase (decrease) in cash and certificates of deposit for year	83,100	(7,300)
Cash and certificates of deposit		
Beginning of year	221,300	228,600
End of year	$ 304,400	$221,300

FIGURE 17.19   Percentage Contractors, Inc.—consolidated statements of changes in financial position.

Completed Contractors, Inc.
Balance Sheets
December 31, 19X8 and 19X7

Assets	19X8	19X7
Current assets		
Cash	$ 242,700	$ 185,300
Contract receivables (less allowance for doubtful accounts of $10,000 and $8,000) (Note 2)	893,900	723,600
Costs in excess of billings on uncompleted contracts (Note 3)	418,700	437,100
Inventories, at lower of cost or realizable value on first-in, first-out basis (Note 4)	463,600	491,300
Prepaid expenses	89,900	53,900
Total current assets	2,108,800	1,891,200
Cash value of life insurance	35,800	32,900
Property and equipment, at cost		
Building	110,000	110,000
Equipment	178,000	163,000
Trucks and autos	220,000	200,000
	508,000	473,000
Less: Accumulated depreciation	218,000	203,200
	290,000	269,800
Land	21,500	21,500
	311,500	291,300
	$2,456,100	$2,215,400

Liabilities and Stockholders' Equity	19X8	19X7
Current liabilities		
Current maturities, long-term debt (Note 5)	$ 37,000	$ 30,600
Accounts payable	904,900	821,200
Accrued salaries and wages	138,300	155,100
Accrued income taxes	53,000	36,200
Accrued and other liabilities	116,400	55,550
Billings in excess of costs on uncompleted contracts (Note 3)	34,500	43,700
Total current liabilities	1,284,100	1,142,350
Long-term debt, less current maturities (Note 5)	245,000	241,000
	1,529,100	1,383,350
Stockholders' equity		
Common stock—$10 par value, 50,000 authorized shares, 23,500 issued and outstanding shares	235,000	235,000
Additional paid-in capital	65,000	65,000
Retained earnings	627,000	532,050
	927,000	832,050
	$2,456,100	$2,215,400

FIGURE 17.20 Completed Contractors, Inc.—balance sheets.

Completed Contractors, Inc.
Statements of Income and Retained Earnings
Years Ended December 31, 19X8 and 19X7

	19X8	19X7
Contract revenues	$9,487,000	$8,123,400
Costs and expenses		
Cost of contracts completed	8,458,500	7,392,300
General and administrative	684,300	588,900
Interest expense	26,500	23,000
	9,169,300	8,004,200
Income before income taxes	317,700	119,200
Income taxes	164,000	54,200
Net income ($6.54 and $2.77 per share)	153,700	65,000
Retained earnings		
Balance, beginning of year	532,050	525,800
	685,750	590,800
Dividends paid ($2.50 per share)	58,750	58,750
Balance, end of year	$ 627,000	$ 532,050

FIGURE 17.21　Completed Contractors, Inc.—statements of income and retained earnings.

Not unlike other facets of a contractor's business, the basic financial statements differ in many respects from those of other businesses. Figures 17.17 through 17.22 present basic conventional financial statements for two fictitious companies—Percentage Construction, Inc., and Completed Contractors Company, Inc., taken from the AICPA Guide "Audit and Accounting Guide—Construction Contractors."

Audit of Contractor's Financial Statements by an Independent Accountant (Outside Auditor)

Most bankers and sureties place much more reliance on audited financial statements than on those submitted unaudited. A banker would prefer and, depending on the size of the company and amount of the borrowing, would find it a necessary prerequisite to be furnished audited financial statements before lending to a contractor. Of course, the banker will also analyze the company's key financial ratios before approval of any loan.

Completed Contractors, Inc.
Statements of Changes in Financial Position
Years Ended December 31, 19X8 and 19X7

	19X8	19X7
Source of working capital		
Net income	$153,700	$ 65,000
Charge to income not requiring outlay of working capital—depreciation	54,800	50,300
Working capital from operations	208,500	115,300
Proceeds of notes payable	44,000	68,000
	252,500	183,300
Use of working capital		
Purchase of property and equipment	75,000	53,500
Reduction of long-term debt	40,000	28,000
Payment of dividends	58,750	58,750
Increase in cash value of life insurance	2,900	2,685
	176,650	142,935
Increase in working capital	$ 75,850	$ 40,365
Changes in components of working capital		
Increase (decrease) in current assets		
Cash	$ 57,400	$ (26,435)
Contract receivables	170,300	36,500
Costs in excess of billings on uncompleted contracts	(18,400)	49,100
Inventories	(27,700)	3,400
Prepaid expenses	36,000	(16,500)
	217,600	46,065
Decrease (increase) in current liabilities		
Current maturities, long-term debt		
Notes payable, bank	(6,000)	(12,000)
Mortgage payable	(400)	(500)
Accounts payable	(83,700)	(24,600)
Accrued salaries and wages	16,800	(24,300)
Accrued income taxes	(16,800)	6,300
Accrued and other liabilities	(60,850)	33,100
Billings in excess of costs on uncompleted contracts	9,200	16,300
	(141,750)	(5,700)
Increase in working capital	$ 75,850	$ 40,365

FIGURE 17.22 Completed Contractors, Inc.—statements of changes in financial position.

BIBLIOGRAPHY

American Institute of Certified Public Accountants, Audit and Accounting Guide, "Construction Contractors," 1981.

Bogen, Jules I., ed., *Financial Handbook,* 4th ed., rev. printing, 1968, New York: The Ronald Press Company.

Finney H. A., and Herbert E. Miller, *Principles of Accounting, Intermediate,* 6th ed., 1965, Englewood Cliffs, New Jersey: Prentice-Hall, Inc.,

Hoeflick, Charles J., NAA Management Accounting, September 1966.

CHAPTER 18

QUALITY ASSURANCE-QUALITY CONTROL

James J. O'Brien, P.E.
Chairman of the Board
O'Brien-Kreitzberg & Associates, Inc.
Pennsauken, New Jersey

Introduction

In the construction industry, the three control parameters for construction projects are quality, time, and cost. Until the advent of better project management tools in the late 1950s and early 1960s, quality was the element most controlled in the field. Since 1960, the focus has shifted to time and cost controls, with an emphasis upon computerized scheduling (CPM). Undoubtedly some of the increased emphasis upon schedule and cost has detracted from quality control.

Ironically, in the nuclear industry, where cost and time have literally run away in the later plants, quality control has been developed to a science. Quality control procedures in the nuclear industry are the most demanding quality control procedures in the construction industry.

The contractor construction manager (CM) is not oriented to inspection, relying on the contractors working for him to provide their own quality control. He depends on the business relationships—if problems are discovered, business leverage is applied to ensure that the problems are corrected. Otherwise, serious matters can go unresolved.

One way in which more attention will be given to quality control is development of a project quality control plan. Presently, testing and inspection requirements are scattered throughout the contract specifications. To develop a firm plan, the testing and inspection requirements can be combined into a new division of the specs. This would emphasize quality control and provide an organized location in which all quality control requirements are identified to the bidders.

The terms *quality assurance* (QA) and *quality control* (QC) are frequently used interchangeably. Since QC is a part of QA, maintaining a clear distinction between them is difficult but important. Quality assurance includes all planned and systematic actions necessary to provide adequate confidence that a structure, system, or component will perform satisfactorily.

Quality control procedures involved in the quality assurance process include planning, coordinating, developing, checking, reviewing, and scheduling the work. Quality is achieved by individuals performing work functions in conformance with the requirements.

Quality control of construction occurs only during the construction phase, which, while it is the most visible portion of the project, takes only about one-half or in some cases one-third of the total time from original concept and approval of the project through move-in and utilization. Although QC duties are confined to the construction period, it is helpful to the quality assurance (QA) program to understand the roles and attitudes of the various players within the project.

There are four major categories of project progress:

1. *Predesign activities,* in which the owner has primary responsibility for progress. Quality assurance policies and procedures should be in place.

2. *Design phase,* with the architect-engineer (A-E) or in-house staff having primary responsibility for progress and implementation of QA.

3. *Construction,* with the contractor responsible for progress, but the owner (and/or the owner's agents) responsible for QC.

4. *Furnish and move-in* (also termed *startup*), with the contractor having primary responsibility and the owner applying QC in accord with the QA procedures.

INSPECTION

Traditionally, inspection is provided by the owner or his agents (i.e., architect, engineer, staff, project manager, or construction manager).

General-contractor (GC)-type construction managers have added inspection to their role. A number of government agencies have specified that the GC shall be more involved in inspection.

Historically, government agencies tend to view the role of inspection in the traditional, ultranarrow sense. Nevertheless, this role is a base for the things that an inspector can and should do. The following description is from the manual *Construction Inspection Procedures* prepared by the General State Authority of Pennsylvania, discussing the role of the inspector.

The primary function of the field personnel of the construction division is inspection, and the persons assigned to this task are designated as inspectors. There are three classifications of field inspectors: general, mechanical, and electrical . . . .The Inspector must be able to look upon and view critically the particular phase of the construction project to which he is assigned. This requires some degree of experience in the construction field. In addition to experience, the Inspector must also have the ability to evaluate and analyze what he is inspecting. Therefore, a most important and necessary requirement is that the Inspector be able to fully read, comprehend and interpret the contract plans and specifications. It is also very important that the Inspector have the ability to maintain records that will fully reflect the inspection performed.

The Inspector must closely follow the progression of each stage of construction. He must be alert to existing conditions and be able to foresee future problems. When the Inspector notices through his daily inspections that certain phases of the work are not being done in accordance with the plans and specifications, or when other problems occur, he is to immediately report these errors, violations, or problems to "management" for further action.

In effect, the Inspector is not authorized to revoke, alter, substitute, enlarge, relax or release any requirements of any specifications, plans, drawings or any other architectural addenda. In addition, the Inspector must not approve or accept any segment of the work which is contrary to the drawings and specifications.''

The Corps of Engineers offers the following suggestions to the inspector on his role.

An Inspector should at all times be thoroughly familiar with all the provisions of the contract which he is administering. This includes familiarity with the plans and specifications including all revisions, changes, and amendments. In addition, the Inspector must be thoroughly familiar with pertinent Corps of Engineers, individual district, and supervisor's administration policies.

An inspector has different responsibilities and authorities dependent upon the organizational setup under which he is working and his own capabilities. Each inspector should know his (or her) part in the organization, and should be aware of the importance of high-quality construction. He should understand his own level of technical knowledge, and accept his responsibilities without overstepping his authority.

In order to do this, the inspector must be aware of the extent of his authority. To that end, the inspector always has the authority to require work to be accomplished in accordance with the contract plans and specifications.

The role of the inspector in construction management is important. The construction management team does not replace inspection, but incorporates it. Further, the inspector is management's contact with the job. Through the inspection process, the inspector develops not only knowledge of specific problems but a general awareness of the attitudes of the contractors in the various trades. The inspector can identify friction and problem areas, and should have knowledge of situations that could require management attention.

The inspection team becomes the five senses of the construction manager on the job site. Further, the inspection team provides a natural training ground for new construction-management staff. Recent emphasis on construction management should work in the long run to reduce the adversarial role between contractor and owner, by closing the communications gap.

QUALITY ASSURANCE PLAN

Several of the large contractors involved in nuclear projects have developed their own quality assurance plans, usually as required by the client. Of course, virtually all of these projects (at least since 1975) were on a cost-plus basis.

The remainder of this chapter presents a QA plan which a contractor might develop—especially for negotiated work.

POLICY STATEMENT

This quality assurance program plan establishes the quality assurance program, which is intended to control quality aspects of construction management and construction inspection services provided. The specific applicability of the requirement of this program plan shall be established in contract and project documents.

Personnel shall effectively implement this program plan, as a primary commitment, to assure the quality of construction.

The principal-in-charge of each project shall regularly review the adequacy of the project quality program. Personnel responsible for project quality activities shall have free access to the principal-in-charge to identify quality problems.

Table of Contents

1.0   QUALITY PROGRAM SCOPE

1.1   Construction Management and Inspection Services

1.1.1   This quality assurance program plan establishes the quality assurance program for construction management and inspection services.

1.1.2   The commitment to excellence in construction management includes vigorous controls for cost and schedule, which, although compatible with and supported by the quality requirements in this program plan, are established and implemented in separate corporate and project documents.

1.2   Quality Assurance Program Implementation

1.2.1   The specific application of the requirements of this program plan for a project shall be defined by contract documents, which shall establish

- Project organization and assignment of responsibilities
- Definition of external interfacing quality organizations and functions

- Project-unique requirements which supplement the program plan for a specific project

1.2.2   The quality assurance program is implemented in corporate and project procedures, specifications, and instructions.

1.2.3   Corporate procedures are approved by the principal-in-charge. Project procedures and instructions are approved by the project manager.

1.2.4   The project manager shall provide for preparation, listing, and distribution of applicable project control documents to project personnel.

1.2.5   The project manager shall provide for the indoctrination and training of project personnel in the requirements and application of the project control documents.

1.3   Definitions

The word "shall" is used to denote a requirement. The word "should" is used to denote a recommendation. The word "may" is used to denote permission: neither a requirement nor a recommendation.

2.0   APPLICABLE STANDARDS

2.1   The quality assurance program plan is responsive to the requirements of the following standards, as they apply to the construction management and construction inspection services:

- ANSI/ASME N45.2-1977, "Quality Assurance Program Requirements for Nuclear Facilities"
- Military Specification MIL-Q-9858A of 12/14/63, "Quality Program Requirements"
- Military Specification MIL-I-45208A of 12/16/63, "Inspection System Requirements .
- RDT F2-2/1973, "Quality Assurance Program Requirements"

3.0   QUALITY PROGRAM MANAGEMENT

3.1   Organization [see Fig. 18.1]

3.1.1   A typical project organization for construction management and inspection is shown below.

3.1.2   For each project, specific authority and lines of communication are estab-

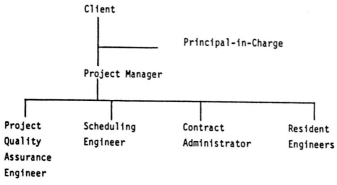

FIGURE 18.1 Typical project organization for construction management and inspection.

lished to report, control, and resolve problems that could affect the quality of the work effort. The project organization and a description of assigned responsibilities shall be documented and maintained current in the project procedures manual.

3.2   Management Review and Audit

3.2.1   The principal-in-charge shall regularly review the adequacy of the project quality program, and implement necessary program additions or changes. This review may be accomplished by:

- Review of project reports
- Discussions with project and client personnel
- Formal audit by an independent audit team

3.2.2   Formal audits shall include an evaluation of quality assurance practices, procedures, and instructions; the effectiveness of implementation; and conformance with policy directives. In performing this evaluation, the audits should include evaluation of work areas, activities, processes, and items; and review of documents and records.

3.2.3   The principal-in-charge shall define the scope of the audit and select an audit team experienced in auditing techniques, competent in the technical areas to be evaluated, and independent of project responsibilities. The audit shall be planned and accomplished in accordance with written procedures or checklists, with the results reported to the principal-in-charge, who is responsible for initiating and evaluating corrective action.

3.3   Construction and Inspection Planning

3.3.1   The project manager shall provide for the review of construction drawings and specifications with respect to:

- Constructability, including, but not limited to, conformance to generally accepted construction practices, enforceability of specifications, and avoidance of disputes
- Planning of inspection and testing requirements, methodology, and documentation

3.3.2   Inspection planning shall include

- Construction/inspection sequencing and identification of mandatory hold points
- Inspection procedure, personnel qualification, and equipment requirements
- Scheduling inspector training and certification
- Identifying inspection and testing to be subcontracted
- Scheduling inspections and tests
- Identifying individuals authorized to request and to approve inspections and tests

3.4   Inspection Procedures

3.4.1   The project quality assurance engineer shall prepare inspection procedures which establish

- The characteristics to be inspected
- The inspection methods
- The acceptance and rejection criteria

- The methods for recording inspection results
- Special preparation, cleaning, or measuring devices

3.5   Inspection Records

3.5.1   Inspection and testing records shall be identified, collected, and indexed to assure retrievability.

3.5.2   The records shall include the results of reviews, inspections, tests, audits, monitoring of work performance, materials analyses, and inspection logs. The records shall also include, as appropriate, closely related data such as qualifications of personnel, procedures, and equipment. Inspection and test records shall, as a minimum, identify the date of inspection or test, the inspector or data recorder, the type of observation, the results, the acceptability, and the action taken in connection with any deficiencies noted. Required records shall be legible, identifiable, and retrievable.

3.5.3   These records shall be reviewed to assure that they are legible and complete.

3.5.4   The records which have been identified and collected shall be suitably protected against fire, theft, and damage.

3.5.5   The project quality assurance engineer shall identify, collect, review, index, maintain, and arrange for the transfer of inspection records.

3.5.6   Inspection records shall be transferred to the client in accordance with project contract documents. Records may be transferred at various points in the project and at the end of the project. The project manager shall obtain the specific consent of the client prior to the destruction of any inspection records.

3.6   Corrective Action

3.6.1   Conditions Adverse to Quality

Conditions adverse to quality may be identified by a number of techniques:

- Audits by clients
- Internal audits
- Audits of sub-tier suppliers
- Project reports
- Principal-in-charge review of projects
- Discrepancy reports

Each of the above techniques has a mechanism to effect the correction of the condition adverse to quality: The audit technique has the audit report and response to the audit report mechanism; the project report and the principal-in-charge reviews result in management action; and the discrepancy report has the disposition mechanism.

3.6.2   Significant Conditions Adverse to Quality

Significant conditions adverse to quality are those which extend beyond a single condition or item. A significant condition adverse to quality must be generic in nature to a large number of items or must be a deficiency in the quality program.

Each condition adverse to quality shall be analyzed to determine if it represents a significant condition adverse to quality, as defined above. This analysis shall be performed by the individual making the disposition of the condition adverse to quality.

The principal-in-charge shall perform an analysis to determine if there are any broad programmatic problem areas or if any negative trends are detectable. This analysis shall be performed at least annually, as part of the management review.

4.0   CONSTRUCTION DOCUMENTS AND STANDARDS

4.1   Construction Documents and Standards

4.1.1   The project manager shall establish procedures to control design documents used for construction inspection activities, including drawings, specifications, procedures and instructions, and changes to these documents, to preclude the use of unapproved or outdated documents. These procedures shall control

- Defining the issuing authority for various documents and changes
- Establishing and updating distribution lists
- Verifying the use of current documents for inspection activities
- Removing obsolete drawings from use

4.1.2   The inspection program (discussed in section 6.3) shall include monitoring design document controls established by construction contractors, to verify that current documents and document changes are issued and used to control construction activities.

4.2   Design Changes

4.2.1   The project manager shall establish procedures to control engineering change request, approval, and issue for construction, in conformance with project contract requirements. These procedures shall include monitoring implementation of approved engineering changes.

4.2.2   The inspection program (discussed in section 6.3) shall include monitoring field changes accomplished by construction contractors, for compliance with applicable construction specification requirements. The verification of as-built drawings (discussed in section 4.3) shall include these field changes.

4.3   As-Built Records

4.3.1   The project quality assurance engineer shall provide for the collection and verification of as-built records as required by the construction specifications and contract documents.

4.3.2   Final as-built drawings shall include all approved engineering and field changes.

4.3.3   In addition to as-built drawings, as-built records shall include specifications, procedures, and instructions used in control of configurations or in construction, inspection records (discussed in section 3.5), and material certifications and test data.

4.3.4   The project quality assurance engineer shall provide for the indexing and transfer of as-built records to the client upon completion of the project, as required by the construction specifications.

4.4   Inspection and Test Equipment Calibration

4.4.1   The project quality assurance engineer shall provide for the control, calibration, and adjustment of inspection and test equipment, to assure that tools, gages, instruments, and other measuring and testing devices used for inspection and testing are properly controlled, calibrated, and adjusted at specific periods to maintain accuracy within necessary limits. These requirements are not intended to imply a need for special calibration and control measures on rulers, tape measures, levels, and such other devices, if normal commercial practices provide adequate accuracy.

4.4.2   The calibration of inspection and testing equipment shall be accomplished in accordance with written procedures, which shall include the following requirements:

- Identification of equipment and traceability to calibration data.
- Calibration methods, frequency, maintenance, and control.
- Labeling and marking of equipment to indicate due date for next calibration.
- Provisions for determining the validity of previous measurements when equipment is determined to be out of calibration.
- Use of calibration standards with an uncertainty (error) of less than one-fourth the tolerance of equipment being calibrated, within the state of the art.
- Traceability of reference and transfer standards to nationally recognized standards. When national standards do not exist, the basis for calibration shall be documented.

4.4.3   Calibration intervals shall be based on required accuracy, use of equipment, stability characteristics, or other factors affecting the measurement. Calibration may be performed on-site or by qualified laboratories utilizing competent personnel. Equipment which is found to be frequently out of adjustment shall be repaired or replaced.

4.4.4   Special calibration shall be performed when the accuracy of the equipment is suspect. When inspection or test equipment is found to be out of calibration, an evaluation shall be made and documented of the validity of previous inspection or test results and of the acceptability of items previously inspected or tested.

4.4.5   These requirements of inspection and test equipment calibration shall be imposed on sub-tier suppliers, including inspection and testing services.

4.4.6   Installed instrumentation used in acceptance testing shall be calibrated in accordance with project acceptance testing documents.

5.0   CONTROL OF PURCHASE

5.1   Supplier Evaluation

5.1.1   The project manager shall provide for the evaluation of the capability of a supplier to provide an item or service in accordance with engineering and quality requirements. This evaluation shall be based on one or more of the following:

- Supplier's capability to comply with the elements of the quality standard applicable to the type of material, equipment, or service being procured.
- Past records and performance for similar procurements to ascertain the capability of supplying a manufactured product (or services) under an acceptable quality assurance system.
- Surveys of supplier's facilities and quality assurance program to determine his capability to supply a product which satisfies the design, manufacturing, and quality requirements. This survey should include, as appropriate, facilities, production capabilities, personnel capabilities, process and inspection capabilities, and organization, in addition to the supplier's quality assurance program.

5.2   Control of Sub-Tier Suppliers

5.2.1   The project quality assurance engineer shall review purchase orders for items and services supporting construction inspection activities, to verify

- Complete and correct statement of the technical and quality requirements, including reference to appropriate standards and specifications.
- Identification of records to be prepared, maintained, submitted, or made available for review, such as drawings, specifications, procedures, procurement documents, inspection and test records, personnel and procedure qualifications, and material, chemical, and physical test results. Record retention and disposition requirements shall be provided.
- Provisions for extending applicable requirements of procurement documents to lower-tier subcontractors and suppliers, including purchaser's access to facilities and records, if appropriate.

5.2.2   The project quality assurance engineer shall assess the effectiveness of the control of quality by suppliers supporting construction inspection activities. This assessment shall be accomplished at intervals consistent with the complexity of the item of service, with the quantity of material furnished, and with the duration of the service furnished, based on one or more of the following:

- Direct source inspection (discussed in section 5.3)
- Reviews of objective evidence of quality furnished by the supplier, such as inspection and test records, personnel and procedure qualifications, material, physical, and chemical test results, and supplier licensing and certification
- Periodic audits of the supplier quality program and procedures
- Comparison or retest of supplier products or services, by independent testing facilities, and/or against known standards

5.3   Source Inspection

5.3.1   When specified in project contract documents, the project manager shall establish procedures for source inspection at supplier's facilities. The source inspection activities may include:

- Reviewing material acceptability, including associated expendable and consumable materials necessary for the functional performance of structures, systems, and components
- Witnessing in-process inspections, tests, and nondestructive examinations
- Reviewing the qualification of procedures, equipment, and personnel
- Verifying that fabrication or construction procedures and processes have been approved and are properly applied
- Verifying the implementation of the quality assurance/quality control systems
- Reviewing document packages for compliance to procurement document requirements, including qualifications, process records, inspection, and test records
- Reviewing certificates of compliance for adequacy
- Verifying that nonconformances have been properly controlled

5.3.2   The results of source inspection activities shall be documented and shall include copies of certifications, chemical and physical analyses, inspection reports, test results, personnel and process qualification results, code stamping, and nondestructive test reports as required by the applicable specification.

6.0   CONSTRUCTION CONTROL AND INSPECTION

6.1   Material and Inventory Controls

6.1.1   The inspection program (discussed in section 6.3) shall include monitoring material controls utilized by construction contractors, to verify that these controls are implemented in compliance with construction specification requirements. These material controls include

- Receiving and receiving inspection
- Material identification
- Storage and preservation
- Handling and rigging
- Identification, segregation, and disposition of nonconforming material

6.1.2   The project manager may establish an inventory control system for equipment and material received at the construction site as required by the project contract documents.

6.2   Construction Process Controls

6.2.1   The inspection program (discussed in section 6.3) shall include monitoring construction process controls utilized by construction contractors, to verify that these controls are implemented in compliance with applicable construction specification requirements. Construction process controls include

- Clear and complete instructions for performing work functions, appropriate to the complexity and importance of the activities involved
- Workmanship standards and criteria
- Control of special processes, such as welding, heat treating, and application of coatings, including qualification of personnel, procedures and equipment
- Documentation of correct construction sequence and material identification, such as concrete lift release cards, wire pull and termination cards, and mechanical alignment data

6.3   Inspection Control

6.3.1   The project quality assurance engineer shall implement construction inspection activities in accordance with project contract and specification requirements. These inspections shall be accomplished using approved inspection and test procedures (as discussed in section 3.4). Inspection and test results shall be documented, and reviewed by the project quality assurance engineer.

6.3.2   The project quality assurance engineer shall document the training, qualification, and certification of inspection personnel, in accordance with project contract and specification requirements.

6.3.3   The project quality assurance engineer shall maintain a system for identifying the inspection status of equipment, systems, and structures subject to construction inspections. Inspection status shall be indicated by stamps, marks, tags, or labels attached to the item, or on documents such as drawings, construction travelers, or inspection records traceable to the item.

6.3.4   The inspection procedures shall include monitoring the following construction contractor activities for compliance with project contract and specification requirements:

- Design document control (discussed in section 4.1)
- Field changes (discussed in section 4.2)
- Material controls (discussed in section 6.1)
- Construction process controls (discussed in section 6.2)

CHAPTER 19

CONTRACTOR FINANCING

Robert D. Falese

President and Chief Executive Officer
Sterling Bank
Mt. Laurel, New Jersey

Financing is a critical issue for any contractor. Bankers (or sureties) who provide capital must carefully analyze the fundamental elements of the contractor's business in order to invest funds or to ensure performance. For this reason, it is vitally important for any contractor to understand how a bank analyzes the business and financial risks, and ultimately determines the appropriate type and amount of financing which can be provided.

Initially, the bank receives a loan request and obtains the last 3 years' financial statements from the contractor. The usual corporate lending routine is set in motion with a focus on a contractor's profile. In that regard, the following items are pertinent when evaluating a contractor relationship.

1. Does the contractor have a history of frequent loss jobs? Excessive volume?
2. Are there unusually high overhead expenses? Inadequate construction volume?
3. Is there a history of slow or poor-quality receivables? Overinvestment in fixed assets?
4. Is there a trend toward participation in certain types of risky joint ventures? Investments in outside ventures?
5. Does the contractor plan entry into new lines of construction with inadequate preparation?
6. Does the contractor plan entry into new geographical areas with inadequate knowledge?
7. Does the contractor have sufficient estimating skills and a track record?

- Financial statement analysis
- Cash flow analysis
- Types of financing
- Solid working relationship with banker

A HISTORY OF FREQUENT LOSS JOBS

A history of frequent loss jobs suggests that a company has difficulty operating profitably. However, most contractors have experienced at least one loss job, due to any of the following:

1. Poor bidding
2. Inadequate field supervision
3. Unanticipated labor strikes
4. Cost escalations
5. Sluggish material deliveries
6. Unanticipated weather conditions
7. Subcontractor performance failures
8. Difficult relationships with owners or architects
9. Poor management of change orders ("bad documentation")
10. Unfamiliar requirements in a new work endeavor

Because the banker expects some jobs to be losses, it is important to the relationship with your banker that you discuss these fully and openly. The contractor should be alert to the positive steps he can take to avert the possibility of loss jobs, such as:

- Including escalation clauses in contracts with owners
- Requiring subcontractors to be bonded
- Assuring that the contract price is sufficient to cover most contingencies

EXCESSIVE VOLUME

Creditors view excessive volume with concern equal to that with which they view inadequate volume: Excessive volume can strain a company's supervisory resources and lead to loss of control over field work; profit erosion or actual loss becomes more likely. The company's capital may be inadequate to finance the levels of work in progress, receivables, and retentions required to carry an excessive volume of work.

UNUSUALLY HIGH OVERHEAD EXPENSES

Overhead expenses that appear unusually high concern the bank because of a perception that this will stimulate a contractor to take on a greater volume of work than he is prepared to manage profitably.

INADEQUATE CONSTRUCTION VOLUME

Inadequate construction volume may result in total gross profits which are insufficient to cover general and administrative and other fixed costs of the contractor's business. Inadequate volume can also stimulate the contractor to bid more closely and increase the risk of taking on unprofitable contracts. Bidding to cover overhead in a cyclical business is a real trap. It is better to reduce overhead than to bid and lose money.

SLOW OR POOR-QUALITY RECEIVABLES

Because one of the contractor's largest assets frequently is accounts receivable, bankers and sureties will be disturbed by an indication that collection of receivables is slow or unlikely. To avoid an uncollectable receivable, the contractor should exercise care in selecting his customers. He should also exercise care in agreeing to lien waives, as the liens may be the ultimate source of collection of his receivables.

OVERINVESTMENT IN FIXED ASSETS

Too great an investment in equipment or in other fixed assets, such as office buildings, leasehold improvements, or equipment yards, presents potential long-term risks which may affect the future financial condition and profitability of a company. The contractor faces reduced working capital, the expense of servicing the required debt, and possible capital loss upon ultimate disposal of the assets.

PARTICIPATION IN CERTAIN TYPES OF JOINT VENTURES

Participation in joint ventures may provide certain advantages to the contractor: The contractor does not bear the full risk of the undertaking, he gains another check on his estimates, and he may eliminate a potential competitor for a specific project. However, joint ventures may present increased risk, particularly if the contractor's joint-venture "partner" is financially weak and unable to make his cash or equipment contributions, if the partners do not have a clear understanding of their individual rights and duties, or if there is poor communication between the partners leading to a lack of project control and direction.

INVESTMENTS IN OUTSIDE VENTURES (ESPECIALLY REAL ESTATE)

Having a significant portion of the company's capital committed to an outside and unrelated activity reduces the company's available working capital—often reducing cash and credit availability as well—and strains the contractor's ability to effectively manage the company. If cash flow from normal operations is "pledged" to real estate ventures, it's a safe bet that management's attention is also similarly "pledged."

ENTRY INTO A NEW LINE OF CONSTRUCTION WITH INADEQUATE PREPARATION

The courts are replete with cases of contractors entering bankruptcy after failing at a type of construction in which they had no previous experience. Excavators have lost money paving; road builders constructing sewage treatment plants; high-rise builders contracting for hospitals; and marine contractors trying land-based operations. The contractor should diversify only after developing a thorough understanding of the problems and hazards involved in entering a new field and after successfully completing small, low-risk jobs in the field.

ENTRY INTO NEW GEOGRAPHICAL AREAS WITH INADEQUATE KNOWLEDGE

Entry into new geographical areas, domestic or international, without adequate preparation can also result in critical job losses. Unfamiliarity with local labor, site, or material conditions can take the unprepared contractor by sorry surprise.

ESTIMATING SKILLS

Last, but certainly not least, is an analysis of the contractor's estimating skills coupled to an analysis of how much of the present reported income is actually based on estimates (see Exhibit A).

The contractor's estimating skills are of critical importance. The more evidence there is of the contractor's competence in estimating, the more confidence the bank will have in his estimated gross profit figures for work in progress. (See Exhibit B, Schedule 16.)

The banker should look to the schedule of contracts completed (Exhibit B, Schedule 1a) for the information needed to assess the contractor's estimating skills. A properly prepared schedule of completed contracts will present total revenue, cost, and gross profit for each job as of the end of the immediately prior reporting period; and revenue, cost, and gross profit realized during the reporting period in which the work is completed. At this point an analysis should be made of the percentage of income recognized on the income statement from completed or nearly completed (90 percent or more) jobs in relation to the income recognized from work in progress (see Schedule 1). Overly optimistic job results on interim statements can be very misleading.

EXHIBIT A *Percent Completion Schedules*

As reported on income statement (000s omitted)		Contractor A		Contractor B		Contractor C	
		Completed	% Estimate	Completed	% Estimate	Completed	% Estimate
Sales (revenue)	$20,000	$19,000	$1,000	$1,000	$19,000	$10,000	$10,000
Cost of revenues	18,000	$17,100	$ 900	$ 900	$17,100	$12,000	$ 6,000
Field (gross) Profit	$ 2,000	$ 1,900	$ 100	$ 100	$ 1,900	$(2,000)	$ 4,000

19.5

EXHIBIT B *Simple Contractor, Inc.*

Earnings from Construction (Schedule 1)
Year Ended December 31, 19X1

	Revenue earned	Cost of construction	Gross earnings
Contracts completed (Schedule 1a)	$2,504,100	$2,204,900	$299,200
Contracts in progress (Schedule 1b)	2,101,700	1,887,000	214,700
Indirect construction cost (Schedule 1c)		4,400	(4,400)
Callbacks and adjustments		6,800	(6,800)
	$4,605,800	$4,103,100	$502,700

Exhibit C presents abbreviated schedules of contracts completed for contractors D and E. A banker would use these schedules to assess the two contractors' relative estimating skills. After reviewing these schedules the banker should reach the following conclusions:

1. Contractor D's schedule of contracts completed demonstrates good takeoff and interim estimating skills. There are no loss jobs reflected in the first three columns, "Job Totals at Completing," and the interim gross profit rates derived from the second three columns, "Job Totals from Prior Years," were in fact achieved when the jobs were competed as shown by the third set of columns, "Job Totals for Year of Reporting."

2. Contractor E's schedule of contracts completed suggests the opposite. The contractor experienced losses on 40 percent of the jobs completed. The gross profit rates on the loss jobs were positive, however, at the end of the interim period. This indicates that neither of the loss jobs was recognized by estimators, superintendents, or the company president until the jobs were complete.

FINANCIAL ANALYSIS

An analysis of a contractor's financial condition utilizes all the usual tools in evaluating any other credit request, including trend analysis, careful reading of footnotes, and a reconstruction of cash flow. If a reliable accounting firm has prepared the presentation, a meaningful analysis can be achieved. Exhibit D contains Simple Contractor's financial statements. The following is a checklist of items that are particularly important to financial statement analysis of a contractor. Each of these items can be located in the Simple Contractor statement.

Contractor Analysis Checklist

- Accounting method used to determine income recognition
- Method of determining income recognition for tax purposes
- Extent of litigation or contingencies against the contractor
- Related party transactions

Exhibit B (Continued)
Simple Contractor, Inc.

Contracts Completed (Schedule 1a)
Year Ended December 31, 19X1

Contract number	Contract totals			Prior to January 1, 19X1			During the year ended December 31, 19X1		
	Final contract	Cost of construction	Gross earnings (loss)	Revenue earned	Cost of construction	Gross earnings (loss)	Revenue earned	Cost of construction	Gross earnings (loss)
X1-6	$ 398,500	$ 345,800	$ 52,700	$265,800	$229,900	$35,900	$ 132,700	$ 115,900	$ 16,800
X1-9	33,000	29,400	3,600	2,000	2,000		31,000	27,400	3,600
X1-10	47,300	56,100	(8,800)	30,000	38,000	(8,000)	17,300	18,100	(800)
X1-11	58,500	50,400	8,100	23,000	20,200	2,800	35,500	30,200	5,300
X1-18	120,100	108,500	11,600	10,100	10,100		110,000	98,400	11,600
X1-19	1,048,000	950,500	97,500	59,600	53,200	6,400	988,400	897,300	91,100
X1-24	460,000	408,800	51,200				456,100	404,900	51,200
X1-25	238,000	213,000	25,000				238,000	213,000	25,000
X2-1	148,300	118,900	29,400				148,300	118,900	29,400
X2-3	26,900	23,400	3,500				26,900	23,400	3,500
X2-8	88,300	71,900	16,400	3,900	3,900		88,300	71,900	16,400
Contracts under $25,000	268,100	216,100	52,000	36,500	30,600	5,900	231,600	185,500	46,100
	$2,935,000	$2,592,800	$342,200	$430,900	$387,900	$43,000	$ 2,504,100	$ 2,204,900	$299,200
							(Schedule1)	(Schedule1)	(Schedule 1)

19.7

Exhibit B (Continued)
Simple Contractor, Inc.
Contracts in Progress (Schedule 1b)
December 31, 19X1

	Contract to date						Year ended December 31, 19 × 1			Future workload (backlog)		
Contract number	Contract	Revenue earned	Cost of construction	Gross earnings	Progress billings	Under-(over-)billed	Revenue earned	Cost of construction	Gross earnings	Backlog remaining	Estimated cost to complete	Estimated gross earnings
X1-20	$ 285,000	$ 276,000	$ 253,300	$ 22,700	$ 282,000	$ (6,000)	$ 256,000	$ 235,300	$ 20,700	$ 9,000	$ 8,300	$ 700
X2-4	146,000	135,000	116,300	18,700	134,300	700	135,000	116,300	18,700	11,000	10,000	1,000
X2-6	1,681,300	841,200	773,900	67,300	872,100	(30,900)	841,200	773,900	67,300	840,100	773,100	67,000
X2-12	630,000	415,600	385,700	29,900	401,200	14,400	415,600	385,700	29,900	214,400	199,000	15,400
X2-16	416,000	204,100	177,700	26,400	249,000	(44,900)	204,100	177,700	26,400	211,900	184,400	27,500
X2-21	210,200	61,300	41,900	19,400	80,000	(18,700)	61,300	41,900	19,400	148,900	101,900	47,000
X2-24	161,000	102,900	86,400	16,500	131,000	(28,100)	102,900	86,400	16,500	58,100	48,800	9,300
X2-31	29,500	5,100	5,100			5,100	5,100	5,100		24,400	21,400	3,000
X2-33	37,800	1,000	1,000			1,000	1,000	1,000		36,800	32,800	4,000
X2-34	66,500	800	800			800	800	800		65,700	60,700	5,000
Under $25,000	163,200	78,700	62,900	15,800	31,500	51,500	78,700	62,900	15,800	84,500	68,500	16,000
						(4,300)						
	$3,826,500	$2,121,700	$1,905,000	$216,700	$2,181,100	$ (59,400)	$2,101,700	$1,887,000	$ 214,700	$1,704,800	$1,508,900	$195,900
		(Note B)	(Note B)	(Note B)		$ 73,500	(Schedule 1)	(Schedule 1)	(Schedule 1)			
						$(132,900)	(Note B)	(Note B)	(Note B)			
						$ (59,400)						
						(Exhibit A)						
						(Note B)						

Work contracted for after December 19X1 but before February 10, 19X2

										Backlog remaining	Estimated cost to complete	Estimated gross earnings
X3-2										$ 747,900	$ 682,300	$ 65,600
X3-3										195,000	173,500	21,500
X3-4										851,200	791,200	60,000
X3-5										25,200	21,700	3,500
										$1,819,300	$1,668,700	$150,600

EXHIBIT C *Schedule of Contracts Completed*
(in Thousands)

Contractor D

Job number	Job totals at completion			Job totals from prior years			Job totals for year of reporting		
	Revenue	Cost	Gross profit	Revenue	Cost	Gross profit	Revenue	Cost	Gross profit
1	$1,000	$ 900	$ 100	$ 500	$ 450	$ 50	$ 500	$ 450	$ 50
2	540	486	54	180	162	18	360	324	36
5	800	720	80	450	405	45	350	315	35
7	700	630	70	300	270	30	400	360	40
13	1,200	1,080	120	800	720	80	400	360	40
	$4,240	$3,816	$ 424	$2,230	$2,007	223	$2,010	$1,809	$ 201

Contractor E

Job number	Job totals at completion			Job totals from prior years			Job totals for year of reporting		
	Revenue	Cost	Gross profit	Revenue	Cost	Gross profit	Revenue	Cost	Gross profit
1	$1,000	$ 900	$ 100	$ 500	$ 450	$ 50	$ 500	$ 450	$ 50
2	540	560	(20)	180	162	18	360	398	(38)
5	800	920	(120)	450	405	45	350	515	(165)
7	700	630	70	300	270	30	400	360	40
13	1,200	1,080	120	800	720	80	400	360	40
	$4,240	$4,090	$ 150	$2,230	$2,007	$223	$2,010	$2,083	$ (73)

CHAPTER NINETEEN

EXHIBIT D *Simple Contractor, Inc.*

Balance Sheet
December 31, 19X1

Assets	
Current assets:	
Cash	$ 94,200
Certificates of deposit	200,000
Notes receivable	14,600
Accounts receivable, including retention of $135,100 (Note C)	530,700
Unbilled amounts on completed contracts (Note A-1)	21,600
Material and supplies inventory (Note A-6)	39,300
Costs and estimated earnings on contracts in progress in excess of related billings	
(Notes A-1, B and C and Schedule 1b)	73,500
Prepaid expenses and other current assets	18,900
Total current assets	992,800
Other assets:	
Land held for investment	10,000
Cash surrender value of life insurance, net of policy loans of $31,100 (Note G)	3,600
	13,600
Property and equipment (Notes A-7 and D):	
Land	10,600
Building and improvements	115,200
Construction equipment	165,000
Vehicles	41,000
Office equipment	14,500
	346,300
Less accumulated depreciation	131,200
	215,100
Total assets	$1,221,500

Liabilities and stockholders' equity	
Current liabilities:	
Accounts payable, including retention of $72,700	$ 275,500
Accrued payroll, payroll taxes, union benefits and amounts withheld from employees	8,000
Additional costs on completed contracts (Note A-1)	8,600
Amounts billed in excess of costs and estimated earnings on contracts in progress (Notes A-1 and B and Schedule 1b)	132,900
Other current liabilities	11,000
Income taxes (Notes A-5 and F):	
Current	15,000
Deferred	105,600
Current portion of long-term debt (Note D)	15,000
Total current liabilities	571,600
Long-term debt (Note D)	182,700
Commitments (Note H)	

Exhibit D (Continued)
Simple Contractor, Inc.

Balance Sheet
December 31, 19X1

Liabilities and stockholders' equity	

Stockholders' equity (Note G):
Common stock, par value $10 per share, authorized 10,000

shares, issued and outstanding 1,850 shares	18,500
Additional paid-in capital	11,200
Retained earnings	437,500
	467,200
Total liabilities and stockholders' equity	$1,221,500

Earnings from construction (Notes B and C and Schedule 1):	
Revenue earned	$4,605,800
Cost of construction	4,103,100
Gross earnings	502,700
Selling, general, and administrative expense (Schedule 2)	332,400
Earnings from operations	170,300
Other income (expense):	
Interest income	16,200
Gain on sale of assets	18,800
Interest expense	(23,300)
Other expense—net	(1,900)
	9,800
Earnings before income taxes	180,100
Income taxes (Notes A–5 and F)	68,800
Net earnings	111,300
Retained earnings, beginning of year	326,200
Retained earnings, end of year	$ 437,500

Source of working capital:	
Operations:	
Net earnings	$ 111,300
Add expenses not requiring the outlay of working capital—	
depreciation	19,600
Working capital provided from operations	130,900
Proceeds from long-term borrowings	148,000
Increase in loans on life insurance policies	31,100
Sale of land held for investment	15,200
Net carrying amount of equipment disposals	7,600
	332,800

Application of working capital:	
Additions to equipment	78,500
Payments and current maturities on long-term debt	25,600
Increase in cash value of life insurance	6,100
	110,200
Increase in working capital	$ 222,600

Exhibit D (Continued)
Simple Contractor, Inc.

Balance Sheet
December 31, 19X1

Liabilities and stockholders' equity	
Changes in components of working capital:	
Increase (decrease) in current assets:	
Cash and certificates of deposit	$ 106,200
Receivables	200,600
Underbillings	58,000
Other current assets	26,200
	391,000
(Increase) decrease in current liabilities:	
Accounts payable	(60,000)
Overbillings	(26,900)
Income taxes	(76,600)
Other current liabilities	(4,900)
	(168,400)
Increase in working capital	222,600
Working capital, beginning of year	198,600
Working capital, end of year	$ 421,200

See notes to financial statements (Exhibit E).

- Size of and 3 years of trend information for:

  Total assets
  Long-term debt
  Equity
  Annual volume
  Backlog
  Over- and underbillings
  Jobs (contracts) in progress

- Supplementary information:

  Detailed job schedules that tie to the financial statements
  Amount of unallocated indirect costs

- Other disclosures such as:

  Joint ventures
  Stock repurchase agreements
  Lease commitments
  Claims and adjustments
  Pension, profit sharing, and other employee benefit plans

Accounting Methods

In the construction industry the one distinguishing characteristic which makes accounting different is that the object (a project) that is sold *does not exist* at the time of the sale (contract), and the ultimate cost to produce it is not yet known. This means that no matter what the basis of the company's recognition of income, the true financial condition of an ongoing operation is based on yet-to-be-accomplished work. That is to say that if the backlog of contracts in progress (both completed and uncompleted) bears a significant relationship to net worth, then the financial health of the organization rests in its present work. There are few exceptions.

With this condition in mind, bankers must understand not only the various acceptable methods of accounting for contracts, but also the basis for measurement of contract performance. During any one accounting period, under the same accounting method, the following can affect revenue recognition.

1. Physical performances (cost of complete)
2. Economic activity or effort expended (cost to cost)
3. Amelioration of risk
4. A combination of the above

There are two generally accepted accounting methods of allocating contract gross profit, cost, and revenue among periods: the completed contract method and the percentage of completion method.

Completed Contract Method. The completed contract method is primarily used only for tax reporting. However, it may be appropriately used for financial statements under some circumstances. For example, if contract income cannot be reasonably estimated because of unmeasurable incentive clauses or if the contractor has a high volume of short-term contracts, the completed contract method may be appropriate. The completed contract method is based entirely on the concept of amelioration of risk.

Percentage of Completion Method. Although the completed contract method is acceptable for reporting contract revenues and expenses on financial statements in the construction industry, the percentage of completion method is preferred by the American Institute of Certified Public Accountants (AICPA). Percentage of completion is also the method favored by most banks and sureties.

The percentage of completion method recognizes gross profit, cost, and revenue throughout the life of each contract based on a periodic measurement of progress. In the simplest sense, a ratio, or "the percentage of completion," is determined, and applied to the expected gross profit on the contract to determine the gross profit to be recognized in the financial statements.

Three typical methods of measuring the "percent complete" are:

1. The cost ratio method, which uses the ratio of actual contract costs incurred during the reporting period to total estimated contract costs.

$$\frac{A}{A + B} \quad (C) = E$$

where A = known costs
B = cost to complete
C = contract
E = estimated profit plus cost to date

2. The effort expended method, or "cost-to-cost" method, which uses the ratio of some measure of the work input during the reporting period, such as labor hours, labor cost, machine hours, or material quantities, to the total units of that measure of work required to complete the contract. The use of this method assumes that profits on the contract are derived from the contractor's efforts rather than from the acquisition of materials or other tangible items.

3. The units of work method, which uses the ratio of units of work performance to total units of work to be performed under the contract. For contracts under which discrete units of output are produced, progress may be measured on the basis of units completed; a typical unit of work would be cubic yards of materials excavated.

Many other techniques will be found in practice, including combination of the above, or the application of one or more of these methods to different elements of the same contract, even with differing rates of gross profit between the elements. The well-run contractor will always know the "indicated outcome" or gross profit on a job as well as the cost to complete.

Unacceptable Methods

Two other methods of income recognition, the cash basis and the accrual basis, are available for tax reporting but are not generally accepted methods of financial reporting. For a going concern, the cash basis of reporting does not result in a meaningful measure of gross profit at any one point in time. To the extent that a contractor successfully accelerates billings and cash collections and delays cash disbursements, the cash method distorts actual performance. The accrual method also produces a distorted gross profit figure since billings which are not a measure of contract performance are considered as revenue.

While these two methods are not acceptable for financial reporting, they may be used for tax determination. Contractors frequently use different accounting methods for financial statements than for tax reporting. The use of different methods generally creates the need to recognize deferred income taxes in the financial statements.

CASH FLOW ANALYSIS

A contractor's cash flow is difficult to analyze, particularly when cash is comingled. In order to understand the cash flow, an understanding of the accounting treatment for costs in excess of billings, and billings in excess of costs, is critical.

Costs in Excess versus Billings in Excess

Because amounts billed on contracts may be independent of the amount to be recognized as revenue, the posting of these journal entries to the progress billing accounts will ordinarily not exactly offset the balances in these accounts. This gives rise to two accounts which appear on the balance sheet of contractors which are unique to contractors, Costs in Excess of Billings and Billings in Excess of Costs.

Cost and Estimated Earnings in Excess of Billings. A debit balance will appear in the Progress Billings account if the value of a contractor's performance exceeds what he has actually billed. This is reported on the financial statements as a current asset, called "Cost and estimated earnings in excess of billings" (also referred to as "Underbillings"). It does not represent either ownership or a tangible object, and may potentially be a capitalized but unrecoverable expense.

To illustrate, let's assume Doitnow Contractors, Inc. enters into a fixed price contract with a municipality in Vermont to install 100,000 feet of 48-inch drain pipe at $20 per linear foot including excavation and backfill. Contract price is predicated on fully installed product. Unknown to Doitnow, there is a granite rock formation just beneath the surface of where the pipe is to go. (Doitnow is headquartered in Paradise, Pennsylvania, and has no knowledge of subsoil conditions in Vermont.) On day one, a loss should probably be recognized on Doitnow's books; however, 2 weeks into the job the bank asks for a statement and Doitnow reports the job on a cost/cost basis.

Total contract	$2,000,000
Bidder's anticipated gross profit	200,000
Cost to complete	$1,800,000
Two weeks into job:	
Costs to date: $200,000 Cost/cost % complete = 11%	
(Pipe in place: 8,000 × physical completion = 8%)	
Reported on the balance sheet:	
Cost and estimated earnings in excess of billings: $200,000 (11% of $2,000,000)	
Income	$ 220,000
Gross profit	22,000

Actually, in this not-too-far-fetched example, the cost of the job based on the physical conditions would be $25 per linear foot or $2.5 million in total. The contractor, or their bonding company, would assume a $500,000 estimated loss.

Billings in Excess of Cost and Estimated Earnings. On the liabilities side of the balance sheet, a credit balance in the Progress Billings account is reported as "Billings in excess of cost and estimated earnings" (also referred to as "Excess" or "Overbillings"), and classified as a current liability, although there is some debate as to whether it is in fact a liability or simply a derivative number representing an obligation to perform that should actually be considered as an offset to accounts receivable.

At the very least, it is a record of work to be performed for which a bill (perhaps not yet paid) has been generated. This entry can signal trouble in front-end-loaded contracts (contracts which permit "pre-bidding") if the contractor consumes the cash for other jobs not so "loaded" or otherwise fails in its ability to complete that for which it has been paid.

Examples of Cash Flow Analysis

Historical cash flow from the statement of changes in financial position (in Exhibit D) provides an indication of change in working capital over the last year. However, estimates of future cash flow are more important. Utilizing the information about Simple Contractor, Inc. provided in the notes to the financial statements (Exhibit E), an estimate of future cash flow can be obtained as shown in Note B to Exhibit E and notes to the financial statement.

EXHIBIT F   *Simple Contractor, Inc.*

Notes to Financial Statements
Year Ended December 31, 19X1

A. Significant Accounting Policies:
   1. Method of accounting for long-term construction contracts:

The company is engaged in the construction of commercial and light industrial buildings under long-term construction contracts. The accompanying financial statements have been prepared using the percentage-of-completion method of accounting and, therefore, take into account the cost, estimated earnings and revenue to date on contracts not yet completed.

The amount of revenue recognized at statement date is the portion of the total contract price that the cost expended to date bears to the anticipated final total cost, based on current estimates of cost to complete. It is not related to the progress billings to customers.

Contract cost includes all direct labor and benefits, materials unique to or installed in the project, subcontract costs, and allocations of indirect construction cost.

As long-term contracts extend over one or more years, revisions in estimates of cost and earnings during the course of the work are reflected in the accounting period in which the facts which require the revision become known.

At the time a loss on a contract becomes known, the entire amount of the estimated ultimate loss is recognized in the financial statements.

Contracts which are substantially complete are considered closed for financial statement purposes. Revenue earned on contracts in progress in excess of billings (underbillings) is classified as a current asset. Amounts billed in excess of revenue earned (overbillings) are classified as current liabilities.

   2. Operating cycle:

Assets and liabilities related to long-term contracts are included in current assets and current liabilities in the accompanying balance sheet, as they will be liquidated in the normal course of contract completion, although this may require more than one year.

   3. Selling, general and administrative expense:

These expenses are charged to operations as incurred and are not allocated to contract costs.

   4. Allocation of indirect construction cost:

Indirect construction cost is allocated as follows:
   Shop and yard—shop orders
   Trucking and equipment—hours of use
   Benefits—dollars of labor incurred
The difference between actual expenditures for indirect construction cost and the amount allocated is charged to operations for the current year.

Exhibit E   Simple Contractor, Inc. (Continued)

Notes to Financial Statements
Year Ended December 31, 19X1

A. Significant Accounting Policies: (*Continued*)
   5. Income taxes:

   Deferred income taxes are provided for differences in timing in reporting income for financial statement and tax purposes arising from differences in the methods of accounting for construction contracts.

   Financial statements are prepared according to the percentage-of-completion method with projects considered closed when they are substantially complete. Construction contracts are reported for tax purposes when they are finally completed and accepted.

   Investment tax credits are applied as a reduction to the current provision for federal income taxes using the flow-through method.

   6. Inventories:

   Inventories are stated at the lower of cost (first-in, first-out method) or market.

   7. Property, equipment and depreciation:

   Property and equipment are carried at cost. Depreciation is computed on the straight-line method based on the estimated useful lives of the related assets.

B. Contracts in Progress:

   Contract amounts, accumulated costs, estimated earnings and the related billings to date on contracts in progress as of December 31, 19X1 are as follows (see Schedule 1):

	Contract amount	Contract revenue	Contract cost	Gross earning
Total construction activity	$ 6,761,500	$ 4,605,800	$ 4,103,100	$ 502,70
Contracts completed during year	(2,935,000)	(2,504,100)	(2,204,900)	(299,20
Unallocated indirect construction cost			(4,400)	4,40
Callbacks and adjustments			(6,800)	6,80
Activity during the year on contracts in progress		2,101,700	1,887,000	214,70
Activity in prior years on contracts in progress		20,000	18,000	2,00
Contracts in progress December 31, 19X1 (Schedule 1b)	$ 3,826,500	2,121,700	$ 1,905,000	$ 216,70
Less progress billings to December 31, 19X1		2,181,100		
		$ (59,400)		

The above is included in the accompanying balance sheet under the following captions:

Costs and estimated earnings on contracts in progress in excess of related billings	$ 73,500
Amounts billed in excess of costs and estimated earnings on contracts in progress	(132,900)
	$ (59,400)

Exhibit E   Simple Contractor, Inc. (Continued)

Notes to Financial Statements
Year Ended December 31, 19X1

C. Related Party Transactions:

Accounts receivable and underbillings at December 31, 19X1 include $127.400 and $14,400, respectively, due from a stockholder on a contract in progress. The contract is for $630,000 of which the Company has reflected revenues of $415,600 and gross earnings of $29,900 during the year ended December 31, 19X1. Of this receivable, $85,000 was collected during January 19X2.

D. Long-Term Debt:

Long-term debt at December 31, 19X1 is as follows:

11¾% mortgage note, collateralized by land and building with a carrying value of $94,500, payable in monthly installments of $750, plus interest, to December 19Yl when the balance is due	$137,400
11½% installment note, collateralized by equipment with a carrying value of $79,200, payable in 60 monthly installments of $500, plus interest, with the balance due on January 1, 19X6	60,300
	197,700
Less current portion	15,000
	$182,700

E. Pension and Profit Sharing Plans:

Union employees are covered by industry pension plans to which the Company contributes monthly based upon hours worked by each eligible employee. Pension expense for these plans amounted to $46,500.

The Company maintains a noncontributory profit sharing plan covering substantially all salaried employees. The discretionary contributions were $20,000 for the year.

F. Income Taxes:

The Company has elected to pay federal and state income taxes on income derived from completed contracts only. A provision is made for the estimated taxes, at current rates, which will be paid in the future on income reflected in these statements on jobs not yet completed. The components of the provision for income taxes are as follows:

Provision for income taxes:	
Currently payable income taxes:	
Federal	$23,400
State	5,700
	29,100
Deferred	39,700
	$68,800

The Company has also elected to account for the investment tax credit as a reduction of federal income tax expense on the flow-through method. Accordingly, Federal income tax expense was reduced $7,100.

Exhibit E   Simple Contractor, Inc. (Continued)

Notes to Financial Statements
Year Ended December 31, 19X1

G. Stock Repurchase Agreement:

The Company is obligated under an agreement dated January 8, 19W6 to re-purchase the outstanding shares of stock held by the stockholders upon their death, disability or retirement at a value per share based on the book value of the preceding year plus a proportional share of the amount by which the appraisal value of the property and equipment exceeds the net book value.

The terms of the repurchase agreement relating to timing of payments differ for death, disability and retirement. The liability under this agreement is partially funded by life insurance, payable to the Company, on the lives of the stockholders.

H. Lease Commitments:

The Company leases certain vehicles from leasing companies. Rent expense for the year amounted to $15,300.

At December 31, 19X1, aggregate net minimum annual rental commitments of more than one year are as follows:

19X2	$15,300
19X3	12,100
19X4	8,200
19X5	1,600
	$37,200

I. Backlog:

Following is a reconciliation of backlog of signed contracts:

Balance January 1, 19X1	$1,754,200
New contracts and change orders during 19X1	4,556,400
	6,310,600
Less contract revenues earned during 19X1	4,605,800
Balance December 31, 19X1	$1,704,800

In addition, between January 1, 19X2 and February 10, 19X2, the Company entered into contracts approximating $1,800,000.

Exhibit E Simple Contractor, Inc. (Continued)

Notes to Financial Statements
Year Ended December 31, 19X1

Contract number	Contract	Contract to date					Year ended December 31, 19X1			Future workload (backlog)		
		Revenue earned	Cost of construction	Gross earnings	Progress billings	Under (over) billed	Revenue earned	Cost of construction	Gross earnings	Backlog remaining	Estimated cost to complete	Estimated gross earnings
X1-20	$ 285,000	$ 276,000	$ 253,300	$ 22,700	$ 282,000	$ (6,000)b	$ 256,000	$ 235,300	$ 20,700	$ 9,000	$ 8,300	$ 700
X2-4	146,000	135,000	116,300	18,700	134,300	700 a	135,000	116,300	18,700	11,000	10,000	1,000
X2-6	1,681,300	841,200	773,900	67,300	872,100	(30,900)b	841,200	773,900	67,300	840,100	773,100	67,000
X2-12	630,000	415,600	385,700	29,900	401,200	14,400 a	415,600	385,700	29,900	214,400	199,000	15,400
X2-16	416,000	204,100	177,700	26,400	249,000	(44,900)b	204,100	177,700	26,400	211,900	184,400	27,500
X2-21	210,200	61,300	41,900	19,400	80,000	(18,700)b	61,300	41,900	19,400	148,900	101,900	47,000
X2-24	161,000	102,900	86,400	16,500	131,000	(28,100)b	102,900	86,400	16,500	58,100	48,800	9,300
X2-31	29,500	5,100	5,100			5,100 a	5,100	5,100		24,400	21,400	3,000
X2-33	37,800	1,000	1,000			1,000 a	1,000	1,000		36,800	32,800	4,000
X2-34	66,500	800	800			800 a	800	800		65,700	60,700	5,000
Under $25,000	163,200	78,700	62,900	15,800	31,500	51,500 a (4,300)b	78,700	62,900	15,800	84,500	68,500	16,000
	$3,826,500	$2,121,700 (Note B)	$1,905,000 (Note B)	$216,700 (Note B)	$2,181,100	$(59,400) $73,500 a $(132,900)b $(59,400) (Exhibit A) (Note B)	$2,101,700 (Schedule 1) (Note B)	$1,887,000 (Schedule 1) (Note B)	$214,700 (Schedule 1) (Note B)	$1,704,800	$1,508,900	$195,900

Work contracted for after December 19X1 but before February 10, 19X2

X3-2	$ 747,900									$ 747,900	$ 682,300	$ 65,600
X3-3	195,000									195,000	173,500	21,500
X3-4	851,200									851,200	791,200	60,000
X3-5	25,200									25,200	21,700	3,500
	$1,819,300									$1,819,300	$1,668,700	$150,600

This analysis indicates an excess of cash available to pay debt, pay overhead, or distribute to shareholders if the firm completes its contract as scheduled, on time and on budget; collects its receivables/retainages; pays future costs directly associated with the contracts; and pays current obligations for trade and taxes. If any of these items are questionable, then the estimates must be researched further.

Another way to analyze cash flow is to look at the individual terms of each contract, and project the cash flow on the basis of the firm's contractual obligations to perform, collect, and pay out. Exhibit F analyzes the cash flow effect on six contractors for the same contract based on their individual production methods for performing the contract, collecting receivables and retainages, and paying their bills.

As you can see, there is a dramatic cash impact on each firm using the same contract. A banker (or surety) must understand the dynamics of cash inflows and outflows on a month-to-month basis like this if credit or bonding is to be provided.

EXHIBIT F BACKGROUND

Six businessmen started separate contracting firms, each with $100,000 in cash. The illustration assumes that each contractor has been awarded one contract:

- The contract price is $1,350,000.
- Cost of construction will be $1,215,000.
- Each contractor will require nine months to complete the contract work.
- The cost of construction will be divided evenly between labor and material.
- Costs and progress billings will be spread evenly over the nine months of work.
- Each contractor will maintain a $10,000 minimum cash balance throughout the life of the project.
- Each contractor employs different production and cash management methods.

Exhibit F (Continued)
Contractor A

Comparative Pro Forma Balance Sheet

Starting Date and Representative Cash Needs for Nine Months

Assets	Starting date	Month 1	Month 2	Month 3	Month 4	Month 5	Month 6	Month 7	Month 8	Month 9
Current assets:										
Cash	$100,000	$ 90,000	$ 93,500	$ 92,500	$ 96,000	$ 99,500	$ 98,500	$102,000	$105,500	$104,500
Accounts receivable	—	135,000	135,000	135,000	135,000	135,000	135,000	135,000	135,000	135,000
Retention receivable	—	15,000	30,000	45,000	60,000	75,000	90,000	105,000	120,000	135,000
Costs and estimated earnings on contracts in excess of related billings	—	—	—	—	—	—	—	—	—	—
Total current assets	100,000	240,000	258,500	272,500	291,000	309,500	323,500	342,000	360,500	374,500
Property and equipment	—	—	—	—	—	—	—	—	—	—
Total assets	$100,000	$240,000	$258,500	$272,500	$291,000	$309,500	$323,500	$342,000	$360,500	$374,500
Liabilities and equity										
Current liabilities:										
Notes payable to bank	$ —	$ —	$ —	$ —	$ —	$ —	$ —	$ —	$ —	$ —
Accounts payable	—	121,500	121,500	121,500	121,500	121,500	121,500	121,500	121,500	121,500
Retention payable	—	13,500	27,000	40,500	54,000	67,500	81,000	94,500	108,000	121,500
Amounts billed in excess of costs and estimated earnings on contracts in progress	—	—	—	—	—	—	—	—	—	—
Income tax payable	—	1,500	3,000	—	1,500	3,000	—	1,500	3,000	—
Total current liabilities	—	136,500	151,500	162,000	177,000	192,000	202,500	217,500	232,500	243,000
Stockholders' equity:										
Capital stock	100,000	100,000	100,000	100,000	100,000	100,000	100,000	100,000	100,000	100,000
Retained earnings	—	3,500	7,000	10,500	14,000	17,500	21,000	24,500	28,000	31,500
Total liabilities and equity	$100,000	$240,000	$258,500	$272,500	$291,000	$309,500	$323,500	$342,000	$360,500	$374,500
Working capital	$100,000	$103,500	$107,000	$110,500	$114,000	$117,500	$121,000	$124,500	$128,000	$131,500

Comparative Pro Forma Balance Sheet
Starting Date and Representative Cash Needs for Nine Months

Assets	Starting date	Month 1	Month 2	Month 3	Month 4	Month 5	Month 6	Month 7	Month 8	Month 9
Current assets:										
Cash	$ 75,000	$ 31,250	$ 28,000	$ 20,250	$ 17,000	$ 13,750	$ 10,000	$ 10,000	$ 10,000	$ 10,000
Accounts receivable	—	135,000	135,000	135,000	135,000	135,000	135,000	135,000	135,000	135,000
Retention receivable	—	15,000	30,000	45,000	60,000	75,000	90,000	105,000	120,000	135,000
Costs and estimated earnings on contracts in excess of related billings	—	—	—	—	—	—	—	—	—	—
Total current assets	75,000	181,250	193,000	200,250	212,000	223,750	235,000	250,000	265,000	280,000
Property and equipment	25,000	25,000	25,000	25,000	25,000	25,000	25,000	25,000	25,000	25,000
Total assets	$100,000	$206,250	$218,000	$225,250	$237,000	$248,750	$ 260,000	$275,000	$290,000	$ 305,000
Liabilities and equity										
Current liabilities:										
Notes payable to bank	$ —	$ —	$ —	$ —	$ —	$ —	$4,000	$7,250	$10,500	$18,250
Accounts payable	—	94,500	94,500	94,500	94,500	94,500	94,500	94,500	94,500	94,500
Retention payable	—	6,750	13,500	20,250	27,000	33,750	40,500	47,250	54,000	60,750
Amounts billed in excess of costs and estimated earnings on contracts in progress	—	—	—	—	—	—	—	—	—	—
Income tax payable	—	1,500	3,000	—	1,500	3,000	—	1,500	3,000	—
Total current liabilities	—	102,750	111,000	114,750	123,000	131,250	139,000	150,500	162,000	173,500
Stockholders' equity:										
Capital stock	100,000	100,000	100,000	100,000	100,000	100,000	100,000	100,000	100,000	100,000
Retained earnings	—	3,500	7,000	10,500	14,000	17,500	21,000	24,500	28,000	31,500
Total liabilities and equity	$100,000	$206,250	$210,000	$225,250	$237,000	$248,750	$ 260,000	$275,000	$290,000	$ 305,000
Working capital	$ 75,000	$ 78,500	$ 82,000	$ 85,500	$ 89,000	$ 92,500	$ 96,000	$ 99,500	$103,000	$ 106,500

Exhibit F (Continued)
Contractor C
Comparative Pro Forma Balance Sheet
Starting Date and Representative Cash Needs for Nine Months

Assets	Starting date	Month 1	Month 2	Month 3	Month 4	Month 5	Month 6	Month 7	Month 8	Month 9
Current assets:										
Cash	$ 50,000	$ 10,000	$ 10,000	$ 10,000	$ 10,000	$ 10,000	$ 10,000	$ 10,000	$ 10,000	$ 10,000
Accounts receivable	—	135,000	135,000	135,000	135,000	135,000	135,000	135,000	135,000	135,000
Retention receivable	—	15,000	30,000	45,000	60,000	75,000	90,000	105,000	120,000	135,000
Costs and estimated earnings on contracts in excess of related billings	—	—	—	—	—	—	—	—	—	—
Total current assets	50,000	160,000	175,000	190,000	205,000	220,000	235,000	250,000	265,000	280,000
Property and equipment	50,000	50,000	50,000	50,000	50,000	50,000	50,000	50,000	50,000	50,000
Total assets	$100,000	$210,000	$225,000	$240,000	$255,000	$270,000	$285,000	$300,000	$315,000	$330,000
Liabilities and equity										
Current liabilities:										
Notes payable to bank	$ —	$ 37,500	$ 47,500	$ 62,000	$ 72,000	$ 82,000	$ 96,500	$106,500	$116,500	$131,000
Accounts payable	—	67,500	67,500	67,500	67,500	67,500	67,500	67,500	67,500	67,500
Retention payable	—	—	—	—	—	—	—	—	—	—
Amounts billed in excess of costs and estimated earnings on contracts in progress	—	—	—	—	—	—	—	—	—	—
Income tax payable	—	1,500	3,000	—	1,500	3,000	—	1,500	3,000	—
Total current liabilities	—	106,500	118,000	129,500	141,000	152,500	164,000	175,500	187,000	198,500
Stockholders' equity:										
Capital stock	100,000	100,000	100,000	100,000	100,000	100,000	100,000	100,000	100,000	100,000
Retained earnings	—	3,500	7,000	10,500	14,000	17,500	21,000	24,500	28,000	31,500
Total liabilities and equity	$100,000	$210,000	$225,000	$240,000	$255,000	$270,000	$285,000	$300,000	$315,000	$330,000
Working capital	$ 50,000	$ 53,500	$ 57,000	$ 60,500	$ 64,000	$ 67,500	$ 71,000	$ 74,500	$ 78,000	$ 81,500

Exhibit F (Continued)
Contractor D
Comparative Pro Forma Balance Sheet
Starting Date and Representative Cash Needs for Nine Months

Assets	Starting date	Month 1	Month 2	Month 3	Month 4	Month 5	Month 6	Month 7	Month 8	Month 9
Current assets:										
Cash	$ 50,000	$ 10,000	$ 10,000	$ 10,000	$ 10,000	$ 10,000	$ 10,000	$ 10,000	$ 10,000	$ 10,000
Accounts receivable	—	150,000	150,000	150,000	150,000	150,000	150,000	150,000	150,000	150,000
Retention receivable	—	—	—	—	—	—	—	—	—	—
Costs and estimated earnings on contracts in excess of related billings	—	—	—	—	—	—	—	—	—	—
Total current assets	50,000	160,000	160,000	160,000	160,000	160,000	160,000	160,000	160,000	160,000
Property and equipment	50,000	50,000	50,000	50,000	50,000	50,000	50,000	50,000	50,000	50,000
Total assets	$100,000	$210,000	$210,000	$210,000	$210,000	$210,000	$210,000	$210,000	$210,000	$210,000
Liabilities and equity										
Current liabilities:										
Notes payable to bank	$ —	$ 37,500	$ 32,500	$ 32,000	$ 27,000	$ 22,000	$ 21,500	$ 16,500	$ 11,500	$ 11,000
Accounts payable	—	67,500	67,500	67,500	67,500	67,500	67,500	67,500	67,500	67,500
Retention payable	—	—	—	—	—	—	—	—	—	—
Accounts billed in excess of costs and estimated earnings on contracts in progress	—	—	—	—	—	—	—	—	—	—
Income tax payable	—	1,500	3,000	—	1,500	3,000	—	1,500	3,000	—
Total current liabilities	—	106,500	103,000	99,500	96,000	92,500	89,000	85,500	82,000	78,500
Stockholders' equity:										
Capital stock	100,000	100,000	100,000	100,000	100,000	100,000	100,000	100,000	100,000	100,000
Retained earnings	—	3,500	7,000	10,500	14,000	17,500	21,000	24,500	28,000	31,500
Total liabilities and equity	$100,000	$210,000	$210,000	$210,000	$210,000	$210,000	$210,000	$210,000	$210,000	$210,000
Working capital	$ 50,000	$ 53,500	$ 57,000	$ 60,500	$ 64,000	$ 67,500	$ 71,000	$ 74,500	$ 78,000	$ 81,500

19.25

Exehibit F (Continued)
Contractor E
Comparative Pro Forma Balance Sheet
Starting Date and Representative Cash Needs for Nine Months

Assets	Starting date	Month 1	Month 2	Month 3	Month 4	Month 5	Month 6	Month 7	Month 8	Month 9
Current assets:										
Cash	$ 50,000	$ 10,000	$ 10,000	$ 38,000	$ 10,000	$ 10,000	$ 10,000	$ 10,000	$ 10,000	$ 10,000
Accounts receivable	—	45,000	315,000	—	90,000	315,000	—	90,000	315,000	—
Retention receivable	—	5,000	40,000	40,000	50,000	85,000	85,000	95,000	130,000	130,000
Costs and estimated earnings on contracts in excess of related billings	—	100,000	—	50,000	100,000	—	50,000	100,000	—	50,000
Total current assets	50,000	160,000	365,000	128,000	250,000	410,000	145,000	295,000	455,000	190,000
Property and equipment	50,000	50,000	50,000	50,000	50,000	50,000	50,000	50,000	50,000	50,000
Total assets	$100,000	$210,000	$415,000	$178,000	$300,000	$460,000	$195,000	$345,000	$505,000	$240,000
Liabilities and equity										
Current liabilities:										
Notes payable to bank	$ —	$ 37,500	$137,500	$ —	$117,000	$172,000	$ 6,500	$151,500	$206,500	$ 41,000
Accounts payable	—	67,500	67,500	67,500	67,500	67,500	67,500	67,500	67,500	67,500
Retention payable	—	—	—	—	—	—	—	—	—	—
Amounts billed in excess of costs and estimated earnings on contracts in progress	—	—	100,000	—	—	100,000	—	—	100,000	—
Income tax payable	—	1,500	3,000	—	1,500	3,000	—	1,500	3,000	—
Total current liabilities	—	106,500	308,000	67,500	186,000	342,500	74,000	220,500	377,000	108,500
Stockholders' equity:										
Capital stock	100,000	100,000	100,000	100,000	100,000	100,000	100,000	100,000	100,000	100,000
Retained earnings	—	3,500	7,000	10,500	14,000	17,500	21,000	24,500	28,000	31,500
Total liabilities and equity	$100,000	$210,000	$415,000	$178,000	$300,000	$460,000	$195,000	$345,000	$505,000	$240,000
Working capital	$ 50,000	$ 53,500	$ 57,000	$ 60,500	$ 64,000	$ 67,500	$ 71,000	$ 74,500	$ 78,000	$ 81,500

Exhibit F (Continued)

Contractor F

Comparative Pro Forma Balance Sheet

Starting Date and Representative Cash Needs for Nine Months

Assets	Starting date	Month 1	Month 2	Month 3	Month 4	Month 5	Month 6	Month 7	Month 8	Month 9
Current assets:										
Cash	$ 50,000	$10,000	$10,000	$10,000	$10,000	$10,000	$10,000	$10,000	$10,000	$10,000
Accounts receivable	—	135,000	135,000	135,000	135,000	135,000	135,000	135,000	135,000	135,000
Retention receivable	—	15,000	30,000	45,000	15,000	30,000	45,000	15,000	30,000	45,000
Costs and estimated earnings on contracts in excess of related billings	—	—	—	—	—	—	—	—	—	—
Total current assets	50,000	160,000	175,000	190,000	160,000	175,000	190,000	160,000	175,000	190,000
Property and equipment	50,000	50,000	50,000	50,000	50,000	50,000	50,000	50,000	50,000	50,000
Total assets	$100,000	$210,000	$225,000	$240,000	$210,000	$225,000	$240,000	$210,000	$225,000	$240,000
Liabilities and equity										
Current liabilities:										
Notes payable to bank	$ —	$37,500	$47,500	$62,000	$27,000	$37,000	$51,500	$16,500	$26,500	$41,000
Accounts payable	—	67,500	67,500	67,500	67,500	67,500	67,500	67,500	67,500	67,500
Retention payable	—	—	—	—	—	—	—	—	—	—
Amounts billed in excess of costs and estimated earnings on contracts in progress	—	—	—	—	—	—	—	—	—	—
Income tax payable	—	1,500	3,000	—	1,500	3,000	—	1,500	3,000	—
Total current liabilities	—	106,500	118,000	129,500	96,000	107,500	119,000	85,500	97,000	108,500
Stockholders' equity:										
Capital stock	100,000	100,000	100,000	100,000	100,000	100,000	100,000	100,000	100,000	100,000
Retained earnings	—	3,500	7,000	10,500	14,000	17,500	21,000	24,500	28,000	31,500
Total liabilities and equity	$100,000	$210,000	$225,000	$240,000	$210,000	$225,000	$240,000	$210,000	$225,000	$240,000
Working capital	$ 50,000	$53,500	$57,000	$60,500	$64,000	$67,500	$71,000	$74,500	$78,000	$81,500

19.27

Exhibit F (Continued)
Comparative Production Methods and the Effect on Cash Flow

Production method	Results
Contractor A	
The owner withholds 10% retainage. Contractor A subcontracts the entire contract	Exhibit F (A) presents the pro forma balance sheet for A. Contractor A has the following results: Cash, $104,500 Working capital, $131,500 Notes payable, $0
Withholds 10% retainage from the subcontractor	Contractor A had no need to borrow during the project because the retainage on his subcontractor provided sufficient cash to cover his outlays.
Contractor B	
The owner withholds 10% retainage. B subcontracts 50% of the contract,	Exhibit F (B) presents the pro forma balance sheet for B. Contractor B has the following results: Cash, $10,000 Working capital, $106,500 Notes payable, $18,250
Withholds 10% retainage from the subcontractor; Performs 50% of the work using his own crews; Pays labor and benefit costs as incurred;	Because B could withhold retainage on only 50% of the costs incurred, a loan was necessary in the last four months of the contract.
Purchases $25,000 of tools to equip his labor force; Pays for materials the month following delivery.	
Contractor C	
The owner withholds 10% retainage. C performs 100% of the work using his own crews; and	Exhibit F (C) presents the pro forma balance sheet for C. Contractor C has the following results: Cash, $10,000 Working capital, $81,500 Notes payable, $131,000
Pays labor and benefit costs as incurred; Purchases $50,000 of tools to equip his labor force; Pays for materials the month following delivery.	Because C used only his own crews, cash outlays for labor could not be delayed. The result was the lowest ending working capital of the six contractors and relatively high outstanding debt.

Exhibit F (Continued)

Comparative Production Methods and the Effect on Cash Flow

Contractor D

The owner withholds no retainage.
D performs 100% of the work using his own crews, and

Pays labor and benefit costs as incurred;
Pays for materials the month following delivery.

Exhibit F (D) presents the pro forma balance sheet for D.
Contractor D has the following results:

Cash, $10,000
Working capital, $81,500
Notes payable, $11,000

D would have concluded the job in the same position as C except that cash receipts were accelerated by eliminating the owner's retainages.

Contractor E

The owner withholds 10% retainage.
E performs 100% of the work using his own crew; and

Pays labor and benefit costs as incurred;
Pays for materials the month following delivery;
Does not bill evenly over the 9 months of the project. Every fourth month E repeats the following cycle:
—the first month $100,000 is underbilled.
—the second month $100,000 is overbilled.
—the third month, nothing is billed.

Exhibit F (E) presents the pro forma balance sheet for E.
Contractor E has the following results:

Cash, $10,000
Working capital, $81,500
Notes payable, $41,000

Underbillings created the need for interim loan balances, which would have eroded profits if interest had been considered in the illustration

Contractor F

The owner withholds 10% retainage.
F performs 100% of the work using his own crews, and

Pays for materials the month following delivery;

Splits the contract into three smaller contracts, each requiring 3 months for completion.
Retainage on each of the contracts is collected in the fourth month of that contract.

Exhibit F (F) presents the pro forma balance sheet for F.
Contractor F has the following results:

Cash, $10,000
Working capital, $81,500
Notes payable, $41,000

Because F worked on smaller jobs and was able to accelerate the receipt of retainage, he finished the job with a lower balance of borrowing than either C or E.

TYPES OF FINANCING

Having completed his analysis, a banker is in a position to provide various types of financing to support contractors. The typical types of financing and expected sources of repayment are

- *Short-term loans or lines of credit:* These financings are intended to be repaid in less than one year and are tied to the collections of receivables and retainages as supported by the analysis of the financial statements, jobs-in-process schedule, and month-to-month projected cash flow.
- *Long-term loans:* These financings are intended to carry long-term fixed assets such as machinery and equipment. They are typically tied into the useful life of the asset and are repaid out of cash generated by profits. Long-term debt used to support the job cycles (specifically receivables or retainages) is *not* a good use of bank financing and is generally rejected by the banker. The contractor's capital base and its payment and collection practices should carry the normal cash needs for jobs in progress. Bank lines should provide short-term support for increases in job activity or changes in the firm's collection or payment terms. Therefore, a banker will also look to a strong relationship between the net worth and the total debt in order to provide credit. Sureties providing bonding support also view contractors' ability to "carry their jobs" as well as their net worth in relation to their total debt as a key criterion for extending bonding support.

Other types of long-term credit, such as mortgages, require the banker to analyze the value of the underlying asset as well as the ability of the contractor's cash flow to handle payments.

Finally, bankers will provide joint-venture financing for projects or developments. However, be aware that this is a highly specialized type of financing which requires the banker to thoroughly analyze the underlying project, as well as the resources and overall credit standing of the joint-venture partners utilizing the process outlined in the preceding paragraphs.

MEETING WITH THE BANKER

As you can see, the banker (or surety) should become intimately familiar with the contractor, the jobs, and the methods of operation, as well as the financial information. This requires a great deal of time to be spent between the contractor and the banker, walking the jobs, and confirming the financial information and the analysis. Contractors should expect to use the banker in a consultative manner once he has learned the business. Remember, even if you don't need financing today, if the banker isn't spending time with you, he will not be up to speed when you do need him.

Supply the banker with regular (quarterly) financial statements, cash flow estimates, jobs in progress schedules, receivables/retainage agings, and payable agings. This is a very good way to facilitate the discussion analysis and concluding financial evaluations that will result in a common view by the banker and contractor on the term and amounts of financing which each can expect.

CHAPTER 20
CONSTRUCTION LAW

Thomas P. O'Callaghan, Esq.
James J. O'Brien, P.E.
O'Brien-Kreitzberg & Associates, Inc.
Pennsauken, New Jersey

No separate body of law exists for construction projects. The law is really a massive heterogeneous mixture of laws, statutes, ordinances, and regulations prepared by the various independent and overlapping jurisdictions of legislature. In the United States' system of government, these legislated bodies of law are administered by executives. Where problems occur, the judiciary system is utilized to adjudicate the problem.

In criminal justice, when a law has been broken there is a recognized procedure for apprehending, trying, and sentencing those who perpetrated the crime or misdemeanor. The rules of evidence are well established, and the criteria for conviction generally well structured. The system is one which deals with extremes.

Civil law is designed to handle disputes rather than crimes. In a dispute there tends to be less black and white, and much more gray area to study. While the rules of evidence are the same, the question most often occurring is, what was the agreement between the parties? Once that is established, the next question to be addressed is, how did the parties respond to their obligations?

The rules of law under which these two questions are addressed have evolved through the English common-law system. Through usage, the general common-sense laws laid down have become structured. The precedent case is an indispensable part of our legal system. It is complicated, however, because given the same set of facts, courts in various jurisdictions have come up with different answers. Generally speaking, therefore, precedent cases in the jurisdiction in which the project dispute is to be heard would have priority or precedence over those from other jurisdictions. Nevertheless, precedent cases with analogous facts or situations are considered by the courts in arriving at findings. Thus, *construction law* really is a term which applies to a loosely structured set of procedures that have evolved within the specific jurisdiction within which the contract has either been agreed upon or is being implemented.

When the parties to a contract have not been able to settle their disputes through the machinery established in the contract or inherent in their situation, then they may litigate. There are levels of litigation, and beyond the basic litigation—appellate courts and higher courts.

In litigation, juries determine the facts, while the jurists interpret the law. In nonjury trials or during appeal, jurists review both findings of fact and interpretations of the law.

THE CONTRACT

The contract for construction is the basis for all legal interpretations, judgments, and resolutions of the impact of construction delay. Yet, in the preconstruction phase, it is the area perhaps least understood by the principal parties. Contractors, owners, architects, and engineers all refer to the contract portion of the specifications as the boilerplate.

The owner, usually through the architect-engineer, prepares the construction contract. The term *contract documents* includes not only the actual contract form, but the various additional forms used to describe the contract requirements as well as the response forms which the contractor executes as part of his bid. Construction documents generally include the following:

Advertisement for bids	Payment bond
Information for bidders	Contract form
Bid form	General conditions
Notice of award	Supplementary or special conditions
Notice to proceed	Plans
Performance bond	Specifications

Under common law, the intent of contracts is that the parties thereto shall have had a meeting of the minds. However, in the case of most prime construction contracts, the reality is a case of take it or leave it.

In public works, the contractor bids on a set of documents which will become the contract. If the contractor conditions potential acceptance, the bid is considered nonresponsive and will be rejected. More than that, it must be rejected. Similarly, in most of the negotiated contracts, the owner (usually on the advice of architect-engineer's legal counsel) states the basic legal language which must be included in the contract. The contractor may be able to negotiate, but in most cases will not, does not, or cannot. Often, the contractual language in the general conditions is mandated by the agency or organization, having been developed through prior experience. The courts take the position that the contractor was not forced to accept the contract, and therefore there was a meeting of the minds.

An owner may downplay the legalese portion of the contract by noting that the owner can always relax or interpret the specifications. Since a contractor cannot change the boilerplate section, it is accepted in the trust that the contractor will never be exposed to litigation in regard to performance. Even when warned that there are certain hazards in accepting certain phraseology, the contractor has the choice of either accepting it or not bidding. Further, a contractor suffers from chronic optimism and expects to either meet the contract or beat it on legal terms if necessary. The contractor preparing a bid is in the romance stage, and hopes for a marriage, and is not interested in studying the litigation rules involved in an ultimate divorce.

Contract Components

The contract documents include many different components, each with its own purpose. In the interpretation of the documents, definite requirements will govern over general requirements.

Where the components of the contract document are in conflict, there is either a gap in information (the basis for a claim for extra work) or an overlap. Where information overlaps, ambiguity often results. The law holds generally that, given two interpretations, the courts will find against the drafter of the ambiguous information.

In the general conditions, it is usual to find exculpatory clauses. These clauses seek to avoid responsibility for unanticipated situations, with a view toward shifting all risks to the contractor. Exculpatory clauses are usually unenforceable, but if the contractor has taken them seriously in the bid, there may be a substantial contingency to cover the risk of either litigation or actual damage in the field.

Plans and Specifications

Plans and specifications are the tools prepared by the designer that the constructor uses to build the building. The terms have very definite, well-recognized connotations to both the design and construction professional. The attorney recognizes plans and specifications as a part (by reference) of the legal contract between the parties.

The nature of the plans and specifications varies with the type of contract contemplated. The range includes, but is not limited to

In-house design: With plans and specifications; generally outline form

Design-build: More detailed than in-house design, but still very performance-oriented

Cost plus fixed fee: More in-depth, but not as much concern on scope or limitations

Competitive bid: Must completely define the scope of the work to preclude extras or additional work costs

Generally speaking, the plans are graphic and provide a quantitative description of the work. The specifications are qualitative and specify the level of quality required. Good practice indicates that the plans and specifications should not overlap. *Overlapping,* that is, mentioning something both in the plans and specifications, can cause confusion, particularly when the overlapping statements are in conflict.

Most of today's specifications are organized into 16 technical divisions as described by the Construction Specifications Institute (CSI). Part 1 is the legal section known as general conditions. The remaining 15 divisions are as follows:

Division 2   Site work

Division 3   Concrete

Division 4   Masonry

Division 5   Metals

Division 6   Carpentry

Division 7   Moisture protection

Division 8   Doors, windows, and glass

Division 9   Finishes

Division 10   Specialties

Interpretation of Contract

It is an accepted principle that the specifications should be viewed in the whole with meaning given to every part, if it is possible to do so. Thus, it is reasonable, helpful, and certainly permissible to view other paragraphs when attempting to interpret a single section or paragraph.

In *Drainage District 1 v. Rude* (21 F. 2d 257, Neb.; 1927), the court stated:

> Courts of law must enforce written contracts according to the language used by the contracting parties, giving, however, to such language a rational interpretation and one which will, as far as possible, effectuate their mutual intention, and not defeat the object and purpose sought to be accomplished. The intention of the parties as expressed by, and not divorced from their language, is what a court must seek to discover in constructing a contract. It is elementary, of course, that, where language is plain and its meaning clear, there is no room for construction. In cases of doubt, however, as to the meaning of the language of contracts, preliminary negotiations, subject matter, and surrounding circumstances should be considered, not to vary the terms or change the language of the contract, but to enable the court to determine in what sense words of doubtful meaning were used.

This leads to the use of evidence regarding preliminary meetings between the parties before the execution of the written contract. While the court holds that the written contract represents the best evidence of the parties at the time of execution of the contract, where there is doubt as to the intent of the language parol evidence may be presented. In *Hawkins v. United States* (96 U.S. 607; 1877), the court ruled that this type of evidence is: "in general inadmissible to vary its [i.e., contract] terms or to affect its construction, the rule being that all such verbal agreements are to be considered as merged in the written instrument." However, the courts will hear such evidence as an indication, but not controversion, of the intent of the contract.

This was further expressed in *Harnett Co., Inc. v. Throughway Authority* (3 Misc. 2d 257 N.Y.; 1956) where the court stated:

> If the court finds as a matter of law that the contract is ambiguous, evidence of the intention and acts of the parties plays no part in the decision of the case. Plain and ambiguous words and undisputed facts leave no question of construction except for the courts. The conduct of the parties may fix a meaning to words of doubtful import. It may not change the terms of the contract.

The language above applies principally to acts of the parties during the execution of the contract, but can also be interpreted to apply to their acts (written as well as verbal) prior to the execution of the contract.

SUBCONTRACTORS

The subcontractor presents a legal paradox. In the aggregate, subcontractors do most of the work on the average construction project. Nevertheless, there is no privity of contract between the owner and the subcontractor; they are legally isolated from one another.

In *Guerini Stone Co. v. P. J. Construction Co.* (240 U.S. 264; 1915), this isolation was noted:

> [The] prime contract specifically provided that none of its provisions shall be constituted as creating any contractual relation between the [owner] and any subcontractors . . . and . . . there is no provision in the prime contract which would allow a subcontractor to appear or participate in any way before the [owner] . . . in a dispute which affect it . . .Indeed, the [owner], as any other owner, may not wish to deal with a subcontractor at all, and we do not criticize this mode of doing business.

Subcontractors range from the very small to the very large. Traditionally, the subcontractor subcontracted to the general contractor. However, in those states in which there must be separate prime contracts under the law, and more recently in the construction management form of contracting, prime contracts for HVAC, plumbing, and electrical can easily exceed the value of the general contract. These larger prime-subcontractors are experienced in working either way, and are experienced in the contractual differences between the two approaches.

Smaller subcontractors, who have traditionally always subcontracted to a prime contractor, may find that the contractual differences in working on a prime contract directly with a construction manager involve substantially different contract administration techniques and requirements. Actually, this type of contract is, in effect, a contract between the owner and the former subcontractor, since the typical construction management contract places the construction manager in the role of "owner's representative."

The Subcontract

In subcontracting, there is a greater opportunity for the prime contractor and subcontractor to have a meeting of the minds, because of the opportunity for negotiation. Also, because of the more frequent opportunity to select subcontractors rather than to have to accept the lowest bidder, prime contractors often have a longtime relationship with their subcontractors. Usually, a prime contractor will accept prices from a limited number of qualified subcontractors with whom he has worked in the past. Thus, reputation and prior working relationships do become factors in the selection process for subcontractors. This tends to limit the risk in the actual working relationship in the field, generating few litigation problems. Conversely, there are many more subcontracts than there are prime contracts, so that there is, nevertheless, a substantial number of suits involving subcontracts.

Most prime contractors have developed a standard form of contract that they use as their general conditions, adding any specific or special clauses appropriate to the particular subcontract. These general conditions tend to be carefully drawn, but often the individual subcontract is somewhat loose. Also, subcontracting arrangements can become quite complex.

In *International Erectors v. Wilhoit Steel Erectors* (400 F. 2d 465, 5th Cir.;

1968) a prime contractor for the construction of an industrial plant subcontracted the fabrication and erection of the structural steel frame. The subcontractor was Southern Engineering, who fabricated the steel, but sub-subcontracted the erection to Wilhoit. Wilhoit, in turn, sub-sub-subcontracted the erection to International Erectors. Southern did not deliver the steel on time, and International suffered delay damages, and sued Wilhoit. The suit also named Southern as a party.

The court did not find assurances of delivery as part of the contractual obligations that were transferred from party to party. Finding against International, they stated: "Prudence and perhaps foresight might have insisted that a provision creating such an obligation (i.e., guarantee of delivery) be included in the written contract, but the written [contract] expressly and unequivocally negated any such obligation. This was an arms-length transaction between contractors of considerable experience in such matters, and we cannot rewrite the contract just because one of the parties would in retrospection have written it differently."

Incorporation of Prime Contract

It has long been practice to incorporate the construction documents into the subcontract, so that the subcontractor is bound by the same terms as is the prime contractor. This was the case in the contract between Guerini Stone and P. J. Carlin, in which Guerini was hired to do floor and wall concrete work for a post office on which Carlin was the general contractor. Carlin was slow in supplying materials, which delayed Guerini's work. Carlin attempted to avoid liability for a delay damage claim because the prime contract precluded damages for delay. The court refused the defense, holding that: "The reference in the subcontract to the drawings and specifications was evidently for the mere purpose of indicating what work was to be done, and in what manner done, by the subcontractor."

However, a more complete incorporation clause is enforceable. Following is a typical subcontract incorporation clause: "Work performed by subcontractor shall be in strict accordance with Contract Documents applicable to the work to be performed and materials, articles and/or equipment to be furnished hereunder. Subcontractors shall be bound by all provisions of these documents and also by applicable provisions of the principal contract to which the Contractor is bound and to the same extent." With this clause, the prime contractor stands in the same position to the subcontractor as the owner does to the prime contractor where applicable.

In *Johnson Inc. v. Basic Construction* (429F.2d 764, D.C. Cir; 1970), general contractor, Basic, attempted to force subcontractor, Johnson, to follow the disputes procedure in the prime contract between the owner and Basic. Basic had received a direction to accomplish extra work, and had imposed that same obligation upon Johnson. Johnson brought suit claiming that Basic was obligated to give it a commitment for payment for extra work even though Basic had not received a similar commitment from the owner for the same work. Johnson argued that it was justified in abandoning its work and in being compensated for the work it had performed. Basic argued that it did not have such an obligation because Johnson was bound to the same terms and conditions of the prime contract as was Basic. The court disagreed and found that the disputes clause was incorporated into the contract only insofar as it was applicable to the work performed, and that the clause, by its terms, did not extend to require an adherence by a subcontractor to an administrative remedy designed to be used only by the parties to the prime contract. This limited application is explained by the fact that the incorporation clause made no mention of binding the subcontractors to the general contract provisions containing the disputes clause, to the same extent that the prime contractor was bound. Accordingly, on the basis of a loosely worded clause, the court refused to force the contractor to relinquish a common-law right to abandon the work. However, if the incorporation clause had been more specific, the subcontractor would have been required to respond to the procedures agreed to by the prime contractor. (In the *Johnson Inc. v. Basic* construction case, the incorporation of the prime contract, however, would not have been presumed to have been a waiver of Johnson's statutory right to sue Basic, unless such right was specifically waived in the contract.)

LITIGATION

Pretrial

Litigation is not an automatic process. Specific actions must be undertaken by the party desiring to institute suit. During the life of a project, the contractor has limited opportunity to terminate or abandon the work. Although it is the contractor's common-law right to abandon the work in the face of certain compelling situations, most construction contracts include a completion bond—which then puts the contractor's surety in the position of completing the work. A construction firm that plans to stay in business cannot afford to deliberately trigger a default, since this would negatively influence his ability to get a bond in the future from this surety, or from any other. Further, the contractor has usually a separate indemnification deal with the surety.

If the contractor does default by abandoning the work during the process of the project, the contract is breached, and the owner looks to the surety to finish. If the relationship between the surety and the contractor remains amiable, which is often the case where the contractor had no choice but to default, as in cases of bankruptcy, the surety will often reassign the work to the contractor (or in the case of a joint venture to the most stable member of the team).

Recognizing this proclivity for reassignment of the same contractor, many owners are reluctant to actually default the contractor—even when he is performing poorly. The owner may, in concert with his default action, attempt to preclude the return of the bonded contractor to the job.

Default during the construction period is not a common occurrence, since the legal arrangements and remobilization of the job with another contractor involve substantial delays. Most owners would prefer to accept the situation until substantial completion, and then seek damages through litigation.

In New York City's Department of Public Works, under the standard construction contract, Article 45, the commissioner or the Department of Public Works has the right to declare the contractor in default of the whole or any part of the work if:

1. The contractor fails to begin work when notified to do so by the commissioner; or if

2. The contractor abandons the work; or if

3. The contractor refuses to proceed with the work when and as directed by the commissioner; or if

4. The contractor without just cause reduces his working force to a number which, if maintained, would be insufficient, in the opinion of the commis-

sioner, to complete the work in accordance with the approved progress schedule, and fails or refuses sufficiently to increase such working force when ordered to do so by the commissioner; or if

5. The commissioner believes that the contractor is or has been unnecessarily or unreasonably or willfully delaying the performance and completion of the work, or the award of necessary subcontracts, or the placing of necessary material and equipment orders; or if

6. The commissioner believes that the contractor is willfully or in bad faith violating any of the provisions of this contract; or if

7. The commissioner believes that the contractor is not executing the contract in good faith and in accordance with its terms; or if

8. The commissioner believes that the work cannot be completed within the time provided or within the time to which such completion may have been extended, provided that the impossibility of timely completion is, in the commissioner's opinion, attributable to conditions within the contractor's control; or if

9. The work is not completed within the time provided or within the time to which the contractor may be entitled to have such completion extended.

The procedures in New York City for commencing default action involve three specific steps:

1. Field order from resident engineer to contractor
2. Second warning to contractor from director, building construction
3. Notice from corporation counsel to contractor to appear at a default hearing

Contracts by the State of New Jersey include a provision for a 3-day notice prior to institution of default proceedings.

Judicial Structure

The judicial systems in the United States are divided basically into the two major areas of sovereignty under the Constitution: federal and the individual states. While the states may delegate certain judicial powers to the local government, these courts handle minor areas and misdemeanors, and would not normally handle delay matters.

In the federal system, most contracts for construction directly involving the federal government include the standard disputes clause, and litigation must be entered in the U.S. Court of Claims, with a review by the Supreme Court if appropriate. However, many cases involving construction are heard in the federal court system, because federal courts have jurisdiction over civil actions between citizens of different states (where the amount in question exceeds $10,000).

The basic trial court for suits in the federal system is the district court, which is presided over by a district court judge. A case may be heard in front of the judge alone, or in certain situations a jury trial can be requested. It is quite usual in involved litigation for the presiding judge to urge that the parties forgo the jury trial with a view toward expediting the proceedings.

Decisions by the federal district courts may be appealed to the circuit court of appeals with jurisdiction. There are 11 separate circuit courts of appeal in the

United States. The next court of appeal is the U.S. Supreme Court, which usually hears only cases that it feels are significant in terms of national interest, or where a conflict between rules of different federal courts is involved. Appointment to the bench for federal court judges is by the executive branch (the President) with confirmation by the Senate. Appointments are lifetime.

The state judicial systems vary considerably. The basic trial court may be called the district, circuit, or superior court, depending upon the state. The presiding judge may either be elected or appointed by the governor of the state.

There may be a jury for certain categories of suits. Again, the judge will often encourage the parties to forgo the layman jury option. In some states, such as the Commonwealth of Virginia, the laws permit the use of a professional jury, often a three-person jury. Each party has the prerogative of appointing one professional member, with the court and the parties agreeing on a neutral third member. The juries are experienced in the specific matter to be covered, and are compensated at appropriate professional fees by the parties.

There is usually at least one appeal court above the basic court, usually known as the appellate court. In those states not having an appellate court, the decision of the basic trial court can be reviewed by the state supreme court.

Formal Litigation

The first step in the actual litigation is the preparation of a complaint and service of that complaint upon the defendant. The complaint is also filed with the court having appropriate jurisdiction. (In some cases, the plaintiff has an option of courts, and obviously selects the one that provides the best opportunity for presentation of his case in the most favorable circumstances.)

Once served, the defendant has a specified amount of time to respond. His response may assert that the complaint is incorrect in its factual statements, or that the defendant has legal defense, even when the allegations in the complaint are true.

Filing of the suit must be undertaken within a specified time period. State law usually specifies a statute of limitations regarding contracts that would apply to the time frame within which litigation would have to be initiated to recover damages for delay. The statute of limitations may start either when an act, such as specific delay, occurs or from the time when the plaintiff became aware that he had suffered a loss. Thus, in a delay claim, the statute of limitations might start running from either the initiation of the delay or from substantial completion, at which time the dimensions of the delay would be known. In construction delay, the statute of limitations would usually start to run when the contract has been substantially completed, or formally completed as evidenced by final payment.

The time frame varies between the states, but is usually in the range of 2 to 5 years. Once suit is filed and the litigation is permitted to continue, it is clearly important for a party to a construction contract to undertake a suit promptly, or a valid claim may be forfeited.

Pretrial Preparation: Discovery

The time period between the initial pleading and the trial varies considerably, dependent principally upon the caseload of the court in which the suit has been filed, and the various maneuvers of the parties. The plaintiff, who seeks to recover, is usually the better prepared and the more aggressive in terms of moving the process forward. The defense, unless they happen to have a strong countersuit or counterclaim, are in a position where they can tie or lose—so they are in no great hurry to come to trial.

The process of developing the case includes a specific legal process known as *discovery*. It is a mutual process, and each party has a number of processes through which they can request additional information on the other party's case. One such method included in discovery is the *interrogatory*. This is usually initiated by the defendant to request specific information in regard to the complaint. The complaint is a concise document, while the interrogatory seeks to expand the information regarding the complaint and if possible, to identify the legal nature of the arguments that the plaintiff intends to undertake, although the interrogatories are intended to disclose fact and not to argue the law. The interrogatory is prepared and forwarded via the court to the other party. It must be answered within a reasonable time, or the offending party will face the displeasure of the court.

The response to the interrogatory is under oath. It is prepared in the privacy of the plaintiff's offices, and with the assistance of his counsel. In fact, usually the party provides information, which is then developed into the answers by legal counsel. The answers to the interrogatories must be careful, truthful, and complete. However, there is considerable latitude in the nature of the response. In areas where the respondent is not certain of an answer, his answer can be general—but it must not be incorrect. Usually, the response to the first interrogatories leads to a second, and even third, round of interrogatories and responses. The process cannot be prolonged too much, or the court will question the productivity of the time investment.

Following the interrogatories, the parties may request the process of deposition. The witnesses are summoned usually by subpoena or court order requiring appearance at a particular time and place. Attorneys for both parties are in attendance, and if the individual giving the deposition is a third party, he is well advised to have legal counsel available. The deposition process may also include the furnishing of records and documentation related to the case. If this type of information is anticipated by counsel preparing the subpoena, he will request a subpoena duces tecum which compels the production of documentation under the witness's normal control.

The deposition is taken with a court reporter in attendance and is subsequently transcribed and furnished to the parties. The counsel conducting the deposition conducts the direct examination, which is under oath. Counsel for the other party can subsequently ask additional questions for the purpose of amplifying or reorienting the impression given by the initial series of questions on direct examination. The examination is a miniversion of the actual trial testimony procedure, but without judge or jury in attendance. The deposition process provides a means of preserving evidence in a legal suit, in the event of either death or inaccessibility of a witness at the time of trial.

The deposition process serves certain other purposes. It provides both counsel with a direct impression of the value of the individual as a witness, both in terms of the type of performance that can be anticipated by the witness in the trial, as well as defining the actual admissible testimony that the witness has. During the trial, if a witness changes his testimony, away from the specific information given during deposition, the deposition can be used as a means of impeaching the credibility of the trial testimony.

In some states, a pretrial conference is a step in the litigation system. This conference is usually conducted in chambers in the presence of the judge, the counsel, and the parties. The purpose is to review the issues stated now through pleadings, interrogatories, and depositions with a view toward reducing the number of issues through stipulation of situations that are obviously irrefutable. Also, certain portions of the complaint may be settled without prejudice to proceeding with the balance.

The interrogatory and deposition procedures can limit the range of the evidenciary process. For instance, if a particular record or document is requested, either in the interrogatory or during the deposition, and cannot be produced, it will probably be precluded as a possible part of the evidence during the trial unless the circumstances can be clearly documented—and even then the judge may preclude its admission on the basis of its previous unavailability to the other party.

During the pretrial conference, the judge may request that the counsel for each side state his legal argument to support the pleading, as well as the evidence (as supported by the interrogatories and deposition(s) that he intends to submit. The judge has great power of persuasion implicit in his position. Thus, if during the pretrial conference, he suggests that certain weak arguments and/or potential evidence would best be dispensed with, counsel affected is well advised to follow that specific suggestion.

Trial

In a jury trial, the judge acts as the enforcer of the courtroom rules of decorum, in accordance with the laws governing the court. He also rules on the law regarding evidence and other legal matters as the trial proceeds. He has the power to cite individuals for contempt of court if they fail to follow his direction. The parties may agree to try the case without a jury, and in many jurisdictions civil trials do not have a jury. In either case, the judge rules upon both the law and the facts of the case.

In a jury trial, the counsel for the plaintiff usually makes an opening statement in which he states the salient features of the case, including those areas that he is setting out to prove through the development of evidence. In a nonjury trial, the opening statement may be omitted, or will be more brief. The defendant's attorney may be allowed to make an opening statement following that made by the plaintiff's attorney.

Following the opening remarks, the attorney for the plaintiff presents the case. The facts are developed through the questioning of witnesses under oath. Physical evidence and exhibits, including documents, are usually offered in evidence during the questioning of a witness who can validate their authenticity, and correlate them to the case in hand. In civil actions, the other party may be called as a witness by the opposition (since there is no question of incrimination per se).

Immediately following the examination (direct), a counsel for the opposing party (defendant) may cross-examine the witness. This cross-examination is limited to matters that were covered in the direct examination. During cross-examination, the attorney may not open up new areas of evidence. During cross-examination, the attorney will attempt to develop additional information favorable to his view of the case, or may attempt to impeach the credibility of the witness by showing that his statements are contradictory or incorrect.

After the plaintiff's case has been presented, including the cross-examination of witnesses, the defense is given an opportunity to present his view of the case.

This is done in a similar manner with the attorney for the defendant calling witnesses and examining them (direct examination) through questioning. Each witness may be cross-examined by the attorney for the plaintiff. Again, questions on cross-examination can relate only to the direct examination immediately preceding. Following cross-examination, the attorney who conducted the direct examination is usually given the opportunity to ask questions in redirect.

After the case for the plaintiff and then the case for the defendant have been presented, the plaintiff is given the opportunity to present evidence in rebuttal of the defense case. Following this, the attorney for the plaintiff may make a closing statement, followed by a closing statement by the defense. The plaintiff gets the last opportunity to make concluding remarks in rebuttal to the defense closing statement.

In the jury trial, this is the point at which the judge makes his instructions to the jury. In preparing these instructions, the judge may ask the collaboration of the two counsels with a view toward presenting instructions that will not result in a mistrial or defective verdict. The instructions by the judge are usually quite specific in terms of the questions of fact that the jury should decide upon. He also instructs the jury on the law of the case, and the latitude which they, as finders of fact, have in reaching a verdict.

The jury meets privately to review the cases presented. This review includes discussions until the jurors are ready to attempt ballots. The jury first decides on the findings of fact. Following this, the jury must decide upon the amounts to be awarded to the winning litigant or litigants. (The jury may find for one party on some of the specifications and charges, and for the other on others.)

If the trial is nonjury, then it is usual practice for the judge to request briefs from the opposing counsel. In preparing a brief the counsel usually prepares a summary of facts as presented in evidence, extracting those that tend to support their view of the case. The brief is a separate document that lists legal arguments for their position, and against the position of the opposition. The briefs are exchanged at the same time as they are presented to the judge, and both parties have the opportunity to file counterbriefs.

Evidence and Procedures

To the layman, the procedures followed to develop the evidence in a case appear very stilted and time-consuming—and from one point of view, they are. There are proponents of a more narrative form of testimony that, they claim, would permit the facts to be developed more readily, and in a form much more easily understood by the jury, in particular, and even by judges. However, experience indicates that the narrative form permits the introduction of inadmissible evidence or prejudicial information that might not otherwise be allowed into evidence.

In a trial, almost nothing can be assumed. It is a long-recognized principle of law that the judge and jury must base their verdict upon evidence that was actually presented, and not on assumptions. Further, if the court recorder misses the information—then, in effect, it doesn't exist. This is particularly a problem if key information is omitted from the record of a case that goes to appeal. In order to expedite the proceedings, the court can take judicial notice of commonly recognized facts. Further, the counsel for the parties can mutually stipulate to any agreed-upon information or facts.

It is the purpose of the court to provide an environment within which the facts of the case can be developed from evidence available. It is an important rule of evidence that hearsay information cannot properly be submitted as evidence. The most common example of hearsay is a witness stating the facts that someone else told him were true, but that he did not personally observe through sight, sound, touch, taste, or smell. The law holds that it should be presented with the best source of information. Therefore, rather than accept hearsay information, it insists that the source of the information be made available to testify as to what had been specifically and personally observed.

There are exceptions to the hearsay rule. One is that of the dying declaration, where the person who made the statement has knowledge that he is mortally sick or injured, and makes the statement knowing that it will be used. Another exception is an admission made by an individual. Hearsay statements may be admitted as evidence to impeach a witness. Thus, the hearsay statement is not admitted for its content, but rather to demonstrate that a witness had spoken differently in a different situation.

Another purpose of the hearsay rule is to permit the party adversely affected by the evidence to cross-examine and question the bearer of that evidence. This cannot be done through a third party, so it is preferred that the witness be made available. A deposition made by a person without giving the other party an opportunity to cross-examine during the deposition has a built-in flaw, and may not be admitted. If admitted, the judge may direct that a lesser weight be given to the evidence.

Documents are actually hearsay testimony in the sense that they are writings made by persons who are not present. Thus, the best approach in introducing documents is to have them introduced by witnesses who either prepared the documents or observed their preparation. It is important in evaluation of documents to develop evidence showing that they were prepared in the normal course of business—and not as a self-serving document specifically for the case at hand. In civil cases, courts are generally inclined to be flexible in their acceptance of documents, particularly those that are official records or that can be identified as normal business entries.

In jury trials, federal judges often comment on the relative weight of evidence, the state courts generally less so. In a nonjury trial, judges tend to admit information into evidence that might be precluded from a lay jury. This is done on the basis that the judge has experience in the law, and can assign to each piece of information the weight that it deserves.

In the course of testimony, counsel will object at certain points to the admission of evidence or to statements by a witness, or to questions posed by the opposition counsel. These objections have a number of purposes. One is to register the objection, even if it is overruled, so that the objection can be carried into an appeal action if appropriate. If the objection is not made, there is nothing on the record to indicate or provide a foundation for the appeal. Counsel will often, after being overruled on an objection, request that his exception be noted in the record.

If records are being submitted into evidence, the custodian of the records or someone else normally working with them, such as an accountant, is often used as a witness to describe the contents. If a summary of the contents is to be used, the witness is well advised to have the original records at hand for review by the opposition. In the absence of the actual source documents, opposing counsel may successfully object to the presentation of the summary—since it does not represent the best source.

ARBITRATION

The following description of arbitration in the construction industry is taken from am American Arbitration Association publication:

> Under the Construction Industry Arbitration Rules, arbitration can be provided for in the original contract. This provision is expressed in a future dispute arbitration clause of a contract. A clause reading:
>
> > Any controversy or claim arising out of or relating to this contract, or the breach thereof, shall be settled in accordance with the Construction Industry Arbitration Rules of the American Arbitration Association, and judgment upon the award may be entered in any court having jurisdiction thereof.
>
> can be used to take advantage of new procedures.
>
> In the absence of such a clause, parties can bring an existing dispute to arbitration by means of a signed statement in which both parties briefly describe the issue between them and agree to arbitrate under the Construction Rules.
>
> On receiving the Demand for Arbitration or Submission Agreement, the Arbitration Association sends each party a copy of a list of proposed arbitrators technically qualified to resolve the controversy. In a construction dispute, these names may include builders, contractors, engineers, architects, other businessmen familiar with the construction industry, and attorneys who customarily represent such clients. In cases involving lesser sums one arbitrator is generally appointed. But in larger cases, it may be preferable to have three neutral arbitrators.
>
> Parties are allowed seven days to study the list, cross off any name objected to, and number the remaining names in order of their preference. Where parties want more information about a proposed arbitrator, such information is given on request.
>
> When these lists are returned, the American Arbitration Association compares them and appoints the arbitrator whom the parties have approved. Where parties were unable to find a mutual choice on a list, additional lists may be submitted at the request of both parties.
>
> If parties cannot agree upon an arbitrator, the Association will make administrative appointments, but in no case will an arbitrator whose name was crossed out by either party be appointed.
>
> Arbitrators on AAA panels are generally willing to serve without fee. They volunteer an occasional day as a public service. But after spending two days on a case, the arbitrator must be compensated by the parties. The rate of compensation will then be based upon the amount of service involved and on the number of hearings. Any arrangement for the compensation of an arbitrator is made through the AAA, not directly by him with the parties.
>
> After the arbitrator is appointed, the AAA consults with the parties to determine a mutually convenient time and place for the hearing. Arrangements are made through the Association, rather than directly between the arbitrator and the parties. The reason for this is twofold: it relieves the arbitrator of routine burdens and it eliminates the danger that, in the course of conversations outside the hearing room, one party may offer arguments on the merits of the case that the other has not had an opportunity to rebut.
>
> Arbitration hearings are less formal than court trials. Arbitrators are not required to follow legal rules of evidence. Rather, they are empowered to listen to all evidence that is relevant and material. Arbitrators often accept evidence that might not be permitted in court. But this does not mean that all evidence is believed or given equal weight.
>
> Each party has a right to be represented by counsel, and the hearing is conducted in a businesslike manner. It is customary for the complaining party to proceed first with his case, followed by the respondent. This order may be varied, however, when

the arbitrator thinks it advisable. Each party must try to convince the arbitrator of the correctness of his position and the hearing is not closed until each has had a full opportunity to present his case.

The purpose of the award is to dispose of the controversy finally and conclusively. It must be handed down within thirty days after the close of the hearing. The power of the arbitrator ends with the making of the award; the decision cannot be changed unless both parties agree to reopen the case, unless the applicable law provides for reopening.

CHAPTER 21
CONTRACTOR OFFICE STAFF

Rita G. O'Brien
Executive Vice President
Personnel & Administration
O'Brien-Kreitzberg & Associates, Inc.
Pennsauken, New Jersey

The construction contractor home office runs by a different set of circumstances than the construction site. For the beginning contractor working from kitchen table and pickup truck, setting up the home-office function can require a quantum leap. Instead of journeyman and craft skills, the contractor has to deal with secretaries, accountants, bookkeepers, personnel specialists, data processors, and other nonconstruction types.

At some point, every contractor's success must depend at least partially on an efficient administrative support staff. This staff can sometimes make the difference between a loss and a profit for a small contractor.

The small contractor's office usually starts with no full-time secretarial support, gradually growing into a one-person office. More success for the company demands additional staffing. Surprisingly, quite often the next plateau is not one additional person, but several.

The small construction office is totally production-oriented—and office work is viewed as a necessary evil. Inefficient office support can be expensive and detrimental to morale, even adding a cliff-hanger atmosphere. In bottom-line terms, the single most important area affected by the office support staff is in the processing of progress payments and other billings. Slowdown of a few weeks or even days can spell the difference between red ink and black ink.

The primary resource of an office is people, and the full utilization of each person's time is the mandate for cost-effectiveness.

OFFICE ORGANIZATION

Four basic systems are found in contractors' offices for administrative staffing patterns: one-person office, area assignments, functional assignments, and secretarial pools.

One-Person Office

In small or medium-sized offices, a single capable secretary-administrator can handle all the important office functions, including routine bookkeeping and accounting, as well as correspondence and telephone. Although telephone reception and placing of calls is the least of these in terms of effective work, it is in many cases important because of the client image created. In an efficient office, it is obvious that the requirements of the job rapidly overburden one secretary. Expansion of the secretarial staff can be postponed by moving bookkeeping and accounting work to either a new department or an accounting service. This serves two functions—it shifts an important function to more qualified hands and concentrates the secretarial staff effort on a less sophisticated, but equally important function.

Area Assignments

Area assignments represent the expansion of the single-person office into a larger capability, usually in response to pressures of expansion. Generally, a receptionist/switchboard operator is added. Beyond that, secretaries are assigned to individuals or small groups of individuals on a dedicated basis. A secretary is assigned to a specific person or group of people. This approach presents minimum friction, except at peak loadings of one department or another. At these times, problems can often be solved by a trade-off system, borrowing assistance from secretaries in other areas not quite as busy.

As attractive as the trade-off approach appears, it rarely works well. Each secretary functions within a cluster as a satellite to the group being served. There is little incentive for a secretary to indicate availability of time—particularly if there is ever any possibility of reduction in force. No one wants to appear idle or slow. The psychology of the area assignment does not lend itself to easy interchange. Accordingly, temporary-assistance agencies such as ADIA, Staff Builders, or Kelly may be utilized during peak periods. A fair amount of slow-time or poorly utilized secretarial capability will occur under area organization. Delineation of responsibility is clear, but at the cost of turf mentality.

Functional Assignments

In the functional office, secretaries are assigned on the basis of specialties or responsibilities. This overlaps the area assignment, since many of the areas are also broken down by function. This approach tends to have many of the same characteristics, but fewer difficulties in coordination within a functional area. For instance, if the marketing area has a high typing load, assistance can be sought from other functional areas. This coordination effort is handled by a lead secretary or office manager. The burden of coordination is substantial and should be recognized by management. The office manager may utilize peak assistance in meeting peak loadings. Each functional staff area will tend to be parochial in terms of its own work, and reluctant in regard to crossing into other functional lines.

Choice of the office manager is clearly an important one, and many factors must be considered. Characteristics of leadership are most important, as this person will be a member of the executive staff with substantial responsibilities, usually at a lower salary than other management-level personnel.

Secretarial Pool

One of the most effective ways to cut the operational costs in an office is via the establishment of a secretarial-pool operation. This system employs a group of secretaries for all transcription, typing, reproduction, and production-type secretarial work. It establishes a more even distribution of work among the staff, saves space, and reduces overhead. Also, it is easier to supervise the quality of the work produced.

The secretarial pool increases production, with less personnel requirement, resulting in savings in both time and money. It is estimated that in a company numbering more than 20 employees, the secretarial-pool approach reduces stenographic staff by almost 50 percent.

Unfortunately, the pool approach almost inevitably produces a lower staff morale. Jobs in the pool are generally relegated to the newest and least experienced clerical personnel. Well-trained secretaries resist the idea of multifaceted work required by the pool—even at salaries suitable for their experience.

Also, there is a definite loss of status by lack of identification with professional staff, and by loss of responsibility for functional roles such as the receiving and placing of telephone calls.

In the short range, the traditional pool will work and will save money. However, a fairly high turnover rate can be anticipated, and intangible losses through the requirement for additional training must be anticipated.

Integrated Approach

An integrated approach to office organization can be most successful. In the medium-size or large construction organization, a combination of functional assignments with a pool-oriented operation can be effective. There must be a system, and its organization and responsibilities must be promulgated—preferably by a documented office procedure. The keystone of this system is a lead office manager or executive secretary to establish the system and make it work.

The office manager reviews all work to be processed by the organization, and establishes priorities—then delegating work to the proper areas.

While the office should be organized along functional lines, the secretarial staff reports directly to the office manager, who assigns new work and clears work as it is completed. This provides instant coordination, and also a desirable quality control.

In turn, the office manager is familiar with the capabilities of each of the secretarial staff and makes assignments in keeping with individual talent, attitudes, and aptitudes. In larger organizations, the office manager may utilize an office coordinator to interface directly with the secretaries.

The office manager also coordinates activities of the secretarial group with other functional areas such as accounting, not only to provide more efficient work, but also to avoid redundant work and/or omission.

The integrated pool is governed by the office coordinator maintaining a constant understanding of the workload handled by each of the secretarial staff. Accordingly, the overload in any area can be handled by either applying unused capacity or calling in peak-load help. However, in this case, the office coordinator must also be business-oriented—recognizing the cost of outside help versus overtime, as well as the morale factors involved. By positive scheduling of work, a higher morale can be anticipated, since each individual has a sense of achievement, as well as a specific person to receive the work. The office manager/coordinator is thus a true member of the management team with pressure from higher management for adequate production at reasonable cost, while necessarily remaining sympathetic to personal attitudes and feelings of the staff. In this regard management experience is typical of the experience of others in the field, including general superintendents, area superintendents, and trade superintendents.

Figure 21.1 illustrates the combination approach for a large office, and illustrates the functional distribution of six secretaries. Their duties would be as follows:

Executive secretary A: Reports directly to the office of the president. Responsibilities include all personal work of the president, including personal filing, telephone screening, etc. Heads up central pool. Typing as required during peak loading and confidential work for accounting and office of the president.

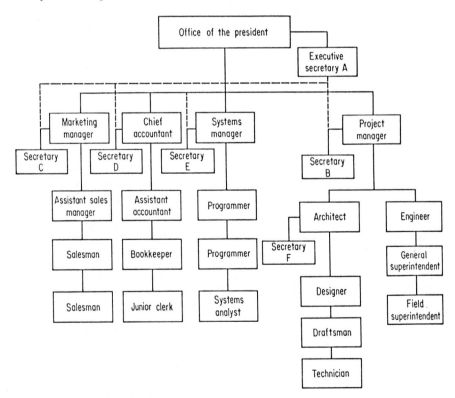

FIGURE 21.1 Office organization.

Secretary B: Screens telephone calls for the engineering staff. General typing. Relief switchboard operator.

Secretary C: Screens telephone calls for the sale division. Maintains the personal file for marketing manager. Maintains corporate files.

Secretary D: General typing, light bookkeeping, invoice typing, check writing, in charge of office supplies, ordering and checking of the deliveries thereof.

Secretary E: Secretary-keypunch operator for in-house systems work. General typing.

Secretary F: General typing, including typing of specifications, change orders, etc. Maintains personal file of the architect. Screens telephone calls for technical staff. Is trained in basics of the drafting department.

OFFICE LAYOUT

The most permanent image of a company is often based on the physical impression it creates. In this regard, the office staff must be presentable and must create an atmosphere of good organization. The arrangement also has a direct impact on the efficiency of the secretarial team, directly affecting both the morale and communication.

The secretarial group must necessarily fit within the existing space and must aspire only to that which is practical for the corporate income level. However, it is usual for the successful organization to grow, even though growth may be unplanned.

Equipment

Mechanization will not replace people, but when utilized in the proper balance, it can be cost-effective. Also there is a certain level of mechanization indispensable to the operation of an effective office, including telephones, reproduction equipment, transcription devices, typewriters, PCs, and fax machines.

Telephone. The single most important equipment item in an office is the telephone and the telephone system. The system is oriented around the physical arrangement of the office, which in turn reflects the organizational attributes.

The cost of an average business letter is approximately $25 and is escalating every day. Accordingly, it is often less expensive and more convenient to answer a letter with a telephone call, unless a written record is necessary. Additionally, telephoning has the advantage of the personal touch—if each call is properly handled.

As an office grows, the contractor should be certain to have enough trunk lines so that callers are not discouraged with constant busy signals. Tie lines to branch or field offices are indicated where long in-house discussions may tie up trunk lines.

The telephone company will monitor the telephone system to determine circuit loads, including calls not placed because of overload. As the company grows, so should the telephone system. When a contractor is experiencing "growing pains," a survey from the telephone company once a year would be in order to determine how much upgrading is necessary to keep abreast of the growth.

The size will dictate the need for a switchboard operator who is free from other duties and can give pleasant, courteous, timely service. To ensure good telephone service, telephone companies conduct PBX schools free of charge to train and place operators. They also maintain lists of substitute operators who will work when a regular operator is ill or vacationing or an emergency situation develops.

Dictating Equipment. Any contractor's office turning out a sizable volume of writing should consider the use of dictating equipment. In recent years dictating equipment has been greatly refined. Any of the top brands can be a successful adjunct to the efficient operation of an office. Statistics indicate that any executive can become sufficiently proficient at dictating to cut writing time by 50 percent. More important, portable machines should be available 24 hours a day, at home or at the office as well as in the field.

Some personnel will be more successful than others in the use of dictating equipment. Thus, in an initial effort to introduce the equipment, arrangements should be made with top companies for trial-use periods. For some contractors' personnel, one type of equipment will be easier to use than another. It is therefore well worth the effort to try several brands until the one most acceptable is determined.

Typewriters. Electronic typewriters and word processors have been supplanted by personal computers.

The computer is the all-purpose office tool. The key idea behind the computer as a mind tool is that is performs *all* the operations performed by the adding machine, typewriter, file cabinet, television, and telephone. The versatility of the computer as an office tool cannot be overemphasized. Once the contractor's office has grown beyond the manual, one-person-type office, purchase of a computer or several PCs should definitely be considered. A recent study indicates that a PC can transform a business and the return on investment can be as much as 1000 percent.

Management should realize that computers are in the TOM category (totally obedient moron). The key to directing the TOM is the development of programs that direct the computer to produce the necessary results—meaningful, accurate, and timely reports.

Standardization

If more than one office is planned, standardization of equipment is a *must*. For example, when a contractor has multiple offices in different cities—with personnel traveling between the various offices—the dictation can be done in one city and transcribed in another, if equipment is standardized. This also applies to typewriters, PCs and word processors. If a report is begun in one office, it can be finished in another, if all the company's transcribers have the same typeface capabilities. This is particularly effective when one office is carrying a peak load and another office can help.

A fax machine can send and receive a copy of an original document via a dedicated telephone line. The components of the fax machine—the internal modem, the scanner, and the recorder—all vary by manufacturer and determine the quality and transmission speed of the reproduction.

Many options, such as built-in telephones with memory for frequently called numbers, automatic paper cutters, user reports, voice request capabilities, as well as plain paper fax machines, are available.

Any company or business, with or without multiple locations, would need a fax machine. Facilitating communications is, after all, one of the determining factors for success.

FILES

No business office can do business without files. The filing components are the management information system (MIS) of an office. The complexity and extent of the filing system are a function of the amount of data being filed. Files are the memory of a business, and they are useful only when they can produce the facts accurately and expeditiously.

Tickler File

This day-to-day file is particularly beneficial in ensuring proper follow-up. Ideally, these files should be kept in a convenient place, with the folders checked daily and marked either for "action" or for "no action" and redated. When the transaction has been completed, the documents can be filed in the permanent file.

Chronological or Reading File

This file is a must in any office—from the smallest to the largest. An extra copy of all documents should be made and kept in this file by date—the latest date on top. Depending on the volume, these can be kept current on a one-month basis and then stored by month. After 6 months these copies can be disposed of. This system is very convenient when the general filing has fallen behind, someone has removed material from the corporate file, or the corporate file copy is lost.

Maintenance of File

When a file folder's thickness exceeds half an inch, the contents should be divided and new files made. Miscellaneous folders should be checked and individual folders prepared for all names which have four or more letters filed.

For general use the "out" card should be filed in place of the record withdrawn from the file. A supply of printed "out" cards should be available on top of the file cabinets. The information given on the card should state the nature of the document and the date removed. The "out" card should be easy to fill out to facilitate the procedure.

Kinds of Files

Generally speaking, the contractor's office could use the following file categories:

1. General file: A to Z miscellaneous.
2. Personnel file: Figure 21.2 is a sample of a new employee memo for the personnel file. It can be enlarged to fit any corporate need but is designed to provide all the pertinent information at a glance.
3. Resume file.
4. Proposal file.

New Employee Memo

Name: _____
Address: _____
Change of address: _____
Soc. Sec. no.: _____
No. of exemptions: _____
Status — hourly or salaried: _____
Site: _____
Position: _____
Full time: _____ Part time: _____
Start Date: _____
Rate: _____
Rate increase: (1)_____ (2)_____ (3)_____
               (4)_____ (5)_____ (6)_____
Number assigned: _____
Amount advanced: _____
Application: _____ Resume: _____
Attach W–2: _____
Hosp., life ins., major medical: _____
Req. company credit cards issued: _____
_____
_____

Misc. information: _____
_____
_____

Notice of Employee Termination

Location: _____
Last day worked: _____
Distribution: Company credit
Personnel _____   cards returned: _____
_____   _____
_____   _____
_____   _____
_____   _____

FIGURE 21.2   New employee memo.

5. Sales file (by state) (or combine items 4 and 5).
6. Contract file.
7. Unpaid bills (by supplier and A to Z miscellaneous).
8. Paid bills (by supplier name and A to Z miscellaneous).

As the office grows, the files must be centralized and carefully controlled, with only authorized persons allowed access to them.

Converting files to microfiche can be very cost-effective where files have to be stored for many years and storage becomes a problem. A four-drawer filing cabinet can be reduced to a 3 × 5-inch area. However, if this type of file storage is anticipated, the microfilming should begin early on. It is extremely difficult to attempt to film, store, and retrieve a large backlog of files. An analysis of cost of film versus physical storage should be made to determine break-even points. Variables will include cost of storage per cubic foot; length of storage—legal minimum and company policy; cost of filming; and frequency of retrieval.

STAFFING

The staff is the heart of the successful office. In a growing organization, a fair amount of turnover must be anticipated. Therefore, recruiting is a continuing function—and can be handled by the office manager or personnel person. A number of important considerations include characteristics desired, methods of recruiting, compensation, and working environment.

Characteristics

Each secretary must be interviewed on the basis of capability as well as potential for becoming an executive secretary or an administrative assistant. Success often finds the growing firm committed in terms of seniority to personnel who have reached their maximum level of competence. In interviewing, characteristics such as superior intelligence, sense of responsibility, and tactfulness are of equal importance with ability to type and accomplish the basic requirements of the position. Leadership characteristics are important, though not necessarily compatible with the basic staff. Accordingly, the expanding office can afford to consider a variety of talents. Some of these might be the ability to delegate or an innate feeling for handling people from employees to clients; even personal responsibilities might be a consideration if the job requires overtime.

The administrative assistant will be part of management. Orders must be issued and work delegated. In this regard, grooming and a sense of humor are important adjuncts to assure recognition of the management role.

The administrative assistant should be well versed in all the secretarial disciplines and should have at least 10 years' experience as an executive secretary or senior secretary. Familiarity with stenography, use of dictating equipment, electric typewriters, PCs, word processors, and other equipment which the office may use is a must. Involvement with the administrative functions rather than basic secretarial duties is required, but a positive attitude in regard to joining the work team during peak loads is also needed. The importance of selecting an administrative assistant who will not be outgrown by the company cannot be overestimated.

Recruiting

Recruiting can generally be accomplished by newspaper advertisements and contact with local federal or state employment agencies. In certain metropolitan areas it is difficult to attract competent staff applicants, and consideration can be given to direct contact with business schools and recruiting agencies.

A good application form is of inestimable value in weeding out applicants who cannot practically fill the position. From a good form, the following information can be derived:

- Is the applicant recently educated? If this is a first position, there is a high risk of turnover, and this should be evaluated in considering the selection of a person who may leave soon after the training period is over.
- Newly married people have a tendency to leave for various reasons related to either family or reassignment of spouse.
- A maturity consideration is involved when hiring persons in the post-school-age range of 18 to 24, who often live at home and are not overly concerned with the job. People in this bracket are often uninterested in overtime work or pay.

The personnel manager should take an objective view, keeping certain basic qualities in mind:

Appearance and manner

Availability for work

Education, as required by job description

Experience in the field

Physical condition

Certainly a telephone check should be made with employers given as references. Some firms give psychological tests to a prospective employee. These may be useful but should not be the sole basis for acceptance or rejection.

Procedures

A new employee should receive a company handbook outlining fringe benefits, salary-review dates, incentive plans, and other important general information. Further, a complete written job description should be given to the employee, including responsibility, managers, and specific job assignments. If the job is to include overtime, this should be made clear from the outset. Other duties, including secondary ones, should be clearly outlined to avoid any misunderstandings after work is started. It is also important that the personnel manager explain not only the advantages of the job but the disadvantages—and any potential problem areas.

If a prospective employee is employed at the time of the interview and anticipates working out a notice, a periodic check should be made to reaffirm the job-start date. Many times prospective employees, intentionally or as a matter of circumstance, utilize the new job as a lever to obtain a better position from their present employer—with the result that an expected position is not filled in a timely fashion.

Newspaper Advertising

Depending upon the area of the country, many people will answer a well-worded newspaper advertisement. Often, they will respond even though they do not fit the job description, resulting in substantial interruptions during the workday. A secretary can do a superficial job of screening on the telephone and should attempt to meet all potential interviewees. This can be done by asking them to visit the office to fill out an application. Further screening should be done using the application form, and the executive secretary or personnel manager can be utilized at that point. Figure 21.3 shows a sample application form.

Employment Agencies

Employment fees vary throughout the country, but the norm is 3 months' to 6 months' salary. For this, the employer is supposed to receive only prospects already tested and screened, but unfortunately, this is not always the case. There is a problem which should be anticipated in the turnover of an employee who is accepted but leaves within a month or two. One method of circumventing this is reimbursement of the agency fee on the 6-month anniversary date, or more equitably, one-half of the total fee.

Schools

Business schools and high schools are often quite willing to place their more exceptional students directly. If a job description calls for a proficient and skilled secretary, schools may offer a ready source of talented but inexperienced young people.

Bulletin Board

A job notice posted on the bulletin board will often bring specific references. This is good from the viewpoint of direct knowledge of the applicant but can be a drawback, since employee interpretation of attributes does not always equate with that of management.

Handicapped Personnel

Every consideration should be given to the hiring of handicapped personnel, from the business as well as the humanitarian viewpoint. It has been proven that employers hiring the handicapped have developed many excellent relationships and have received specific rewards through less turnover or absenteeism, less tardiness, and a high degree of loyalty. As in any group of human beings, there are exceptions. If the personnel manager does an intelligent and realistic job of

Application For Employment

We consider applicants for all positions without regard to race, color, religion, sex, national origin, age, marital or veteran status, the presence of a non-job-related medical condition or handicap, or any other legally protected status.

(PLEASE PRINT)

Position(s) Applied For	Date of Application

How Did You Learn About Us?

☐ Advertisement   ☐ Friend   ☐ Walk-In

☐ Employment Agency   ☐ Relative   ☐ Other _____

Last Name	First Name	Middle Name

Address	Number	Street	City	State	Zip Code

Telephone Number(s)	Social Security Number

If you are under 18 years of age, can you provide required proof of your eligibility to work?   ☐ Yes   ☐ No

Have you ever filed an application with us before?   ☐ Yes   ☐ No

If Yes, give date _____

Have you ever been employed with us before?   ☐ Yes   ☐ No

If Yes, give date _____

Are you currently employed?   ☐ Yes   ☐ No

May we contact your present employer?   ☐ Yes   ☐ No

Are you prevented from lawfully becoming employed in this country because of Visa or Immigration Status?
Proof of citizenship or immigration status will be required upon employment.   ☐ Yes   ☐ No

On what date would you be available for work? _____

Are you available to work: ☐ Full Time   ☐ Part Time   ☐ Shift Work   ☐ Temporary

Are you currently on "lay-off" status and subject to recall?   ☐ Yes   ☐ No

Can you travel if a job requires it?   ☐ Yes   ☐ No

Have you been convicted of a felony within the last 7 years?   ☐ Yes   ☐ No
Conviction will not necessarily disqualify an applicant from employment.

If Yes, please explain _____

WE ARE AN EQUAL OPPORTUNITY EMPLOYER

FIGURE 21.3 Application for employment form.

Education

	Elementary School					High School				Undergraduate College / University				Graduate / Professional			
School Name and Location																	
Years Completed	4	5	6	7	8	9	10	11	12	1	2	3	4	1	2	3	4
Diploma / Degree																	
Describe Course of Study																	
Describe any specialized training, apprenticeship, skills and extra-curricular activities																	
Describe any honors you have received																	
State any additional information you feel may be helpful to us in considering your application																	

Indicate any foreign languages you can speak, read and / or write			
	FLUENT	**GOOD**	**FAIR**
SPEAK			
READ			
WRITE			

List professional, trade, business or civic activities and offices held.
You may exclude memberships which would reveal sex, race, religion, national origin, age, ancestry, or handicap or other protected status:

_____

_____

_____

_____

References

Give name, address and telephone number of three references who are not related to you and are not previous employers.

1. _____

2. _____

3. _____

Have you ever had any job-related training in the United States military?

☐ Yes ☐ No

If Yes, please describe _____

Are you physically or otherwise unable to perform the duties of the job for which you are applying? ☐ Yes ☐ No

FIGURE 21.3 *(Continued).*

screening, the company will not be acquiring handicapped persons who are ill-equipped to fit in psychologically with the company group. If the proper selection has been made by company management, the staff often finds many rewards in working with the handicapped, and personal achievement in seeing them blossom on a job.

The term *handicapped* is becoming less of a liability as equipment such as hearing aids and artificial limbs are readily accepted. Conditions formerly considered handicaps, such as epilepsy, can now be controlled with drugs—and people in this category are not even considered handicapped.

Assignment of the handicapped must be carefully considered in terms of the job description. For instance, the reproduction center, including duplicating machines, postage machines, blueprint machines, and other centralized equipment, can be operated by a person in a wheelchair. However, this person should not be expected to handle concomitant collateral assignments.

Offices of the federal employment agencies and local Easter Seal and other organizations conduct workshops for pretraining of handicapped people. Often, the director of a workshop will be able to give specific assistance not only in the selection but also in the on-site testing of personnel. These people are equally concerned with successful assignments and are very much against precipitous assignments, which will tear down the morale of the handicapped person. Usually, the workshop maintains a relationship with the handicapped person for several months after the job assignment. Even though there is a tremendous waiting list for jobs (often as many as 20 people for every employer willing to consider the handicapped), a competent director will be reluctant to assign a person about whom there are doubts.

COMPENSATION

Office personnel are usually salaried rather than paid hourly. Base salaries vary geographically, but all employees, regardless of locale, expect to get merit increases. After the first 6 months—or an established trial period—the new employee should be reviewed. A policy of periodic reviews should be outlined in an administrative policy statement. A method commonly used by many contractors is a review after 6 months from date of hire and a yearly anniversary review thereafter. The government has developed strict laws pertaining the employees' rights. In hiring a new employee, a probationary period should be established to protect the employer. If the company manual states a date for review of the employee, this does not mandate an increase in salary or continuation of employment. The probationary period extends to the employer as well as the employee.

Often as important as salary is the appropriate increase in status. There are many titles that can accompany these periodic reviews and subsequent increases, including clerks, typists, stenographers, secretaries, executive secretaries, administrative specialists, and supervisors.

A rule of thumb to use with the clerical staff could be what is commonly known as the "minimum range," encompassing three levels of staffing:

1. Training period for beginners
2. Range for average employees
3. Special range for outstanding employees

Within this minimum range, there can be a 50 percent spread between the minimum and the maximum. In a company of 10 people (clerical) in a department, the following formula might apply:

Two employees: above average

Six employees: meeting the company average

Two employees: below average

Based on this formula, at employee-review time, it would not be necessary to make an adjustment in salary for the employees who are considered below average. These employees can be replaced. In the company average range, it might be worthwhile to consider an increase, making it known to the employees what they can do to improve their average rating. Figure 21.4 is an illustration of an employee review sheet depicting the areas for improvement.

To keep above-average employees, the contractor should consider more frequent reviews so that he is fully aware of their goals and aspirations.

How to Keep a Secretary

In a recent nationwide survey, the following four reasons were given for discontent on the job by clerical help:

1. *85 percent:* salary and recognition
2. *80 percent:* immediate supervisors
3. *60 percent:* general working conditions
4. *58 percent:* promotions

Obviously, all these conditions are subject to control. There are many ways to make the general working conditions more palatable, in fact even enviable. Certainly, there is no formula for making everybody happy all the time. If a contractor is fortunate enough to have an administrator who has initiative, a sense of responsibility, and other attributes that are extremely valuable to the company, it is in the company's best interests to keep the person. Basic salary is not the only criterion. One company enrolled a key secretary in a travel club at a weekly cost of only $9 plus additional annual vacation. The resulting sense of responsibility, with no additional salary, more than offset this direct cost.

There cannot and should not be one hard-and-fast system for an office operation. Flexibility is the key to growth. The old way is not always the best way, nor is the indiscriminate purchase of the latest office equipment always the most efficient answer to expansion. One very basic rule is that if the office functions are being performed well and with a minimum of personnel—then maximum efficiency has been accomplished.

HOW TO SET UP A FIELD OFFICE

Facilities Required

The most advantageous place for these facilities is directly at the job site. This enable members of the project team to interface with the contractors and agen-

SALARY REVIEW FORM

Employee Name: _____   Dept. _____

Type Review: Performance:

First (six months) _____   Fair   _____
Annual   _____   Good   _____
Special/Merit   _____   Excellent   _____
Combined   _____   Outstanding _____

Employment Date: _____   Last Review Date: _____

Current Salary: Increase to:

Hourly _____   Hourly _____

Annual _____   Annual _____

Effective: _____   Effective Date: _____

Is This Retro-Active? Yes___ No ___   If so, Effective Date: _____

Approved: _____   Date: _____

Approved: _____   Date: _____

- -

Payroll Department:

_____   Effective Date:

_____   Effective Payroll Date:

_____   Effective Retro-Active Date:

_____   _____
   Payroll Coordinator's Signature   Date

Personnel Department: Processed and Entered   _____   _____
                                                  (Initial)   (Date)

- -

Computer Department: Processed and Entered   _____   _____
                                                  (Initial)   (Date)

- -

FIGURE 21.4 Salary review form.

SALARY REVIEW COMMENTS: PAGE 2

_____

_____

_____

_____

_____

_____

_____

_____

_____

_____

_____

_____

_____

_____

_____

_____

_____

_____

_____   _____
Manager/Supervisor Signature   Date

CC: Employee

cies directly on the site. Projects that cover large areas require a centrally located field office for convenience and to minimize travel. Sometimes it would be necessary to establish a main field office and a secondary support facility. This would enable various field engineers to have limited facilities for preparing various reports with the necessary utilities to, again, minimize travel time for field engineers, which will enable them to spend more time in the field providing inspection and necessary clarification. All project records should be maintained in the general area of the project secretary or project clerk for use by the project team. A reproduction machine should also be included in this general area.

Facility requirements for a project office must be evaluated during the design phase to determine

Location

Square footage required

Offices required

Conference space required

Electrical and sanitary requirements

Parking requirements

Type of facility desired

The time given the contractor to establish the project field office should be as short as possible and yet must be realistic with respect to the facilities and equipment he must provide. This must be evaluated on a project-by-project basis. Project demands dictate project equipment. While not essential, many field office locations have other equipment for the convenience of the project team, such as water coolers, coffee makers, microwaves, and refrigerators. These do provide a real convenience for the project team, especially when the project is located at a remote location.

CHAPTER 22
CONSTRUCTION PRODUCTIVITY ANALYSIS

Robert G. Zilly, P.E., M.A.S.C.E., A.I.C.
Professor of Construction Management
Emeritus
University of Nebraska
Lincoln, Nebraska

The sorry state of construction productivity is well described in the January 1983 Business Roundtable Report "More Construction for the Money":

> By common consensus and every available measure, the United States no longer gets its money's worth in construction, the nation's largest industry. Since the closing years of the 60's, productivity in construction has been declining at a rate many industry leaders find appalling. The figures should not be regarded as precise because of statistical deficiencies in the data on which they are based, but they all contain the same disturbing message: a large and increasing gap has opened between the performance of construction and that of U.S. industry as a whole. In 1981, for example, the Commerce Department reported that productivity in new construction put-in-place had dropped from an index number of 100 in 1972 to an index of 82.9 in 1979—a debilitating decline of nearly 20%. The Houston-based American Productivity Center, measuring labor productivity in 11 large sectors of the U.S. economy over a span of three decades, found construction to be the most laggard performer by a wide margin. Since 1955, according to the Center, construction has been the only industry with consistently negative productive growth. The average annual rate of change was minus 0.9% from 1965 to 1973, then dropped 3% a year from 1973 to 1979 and an alarming 8% a year in 1979–80.
>
> One ominous consequence is that construction's share of gross national product has been declining. Historically it has run about 10% of GNP, but since 1975 that share has dropped to less than 6%. On physical terms, that gap may be even larger, since the Department of Commerce index of construction costs has risen from an index number of 100 in 1967 to 304 in 1980, while the consumer price index has climbed from the same index of 100 in 1967 to a 1980 level of 247.
>
> The creeping erosion of construction efficiency and productivity is bad news for the entire U.S. economy. Construction is a particularly seminal industry. The price of every factory, office building, hotel or power plant that is built affects the price that must be charged for the goods and services produced in it or by it. And the effect generally persists for decades. . . .

PRODUCTIVITY DEFINED

Starting from the premise that each construction project is unique, many practitioners argue that productivity standards for construction work are impossible to establish within precise limits. Others, pointing out that most projects have common elements that are subject to analysis, have established a variety of productivity definitions and standards that they find useful within their own firm. Overall productivity in construction is defined by the U.S. Department of Commerce as dollars of output divided by labor hours of input, with the dollars adjusted to compensate for variations in the Consumer Price Index. Data are available for various types of construction and installation of some specific products, but few construction firms find it useful for evaluating their own workers' productivity.

For those practitioners and researchers who are concerned about productivity analysis, the preferred definition of productivity seems to be either units of output divided by hours of labor input or its inverse, hours of labor input divided by units of output. However, even this approach must be used with caution. Did the carpenter nail boards in place with a hand-held hammer or a nail gun? Was paint applied with a brush, a roller, or a spray gun? Comparative productivity figures are often invalid because no consideration was given to capital investment in the form of laborsaving tools and equipment. Indeed, productivity figures can also be affected by poor management, poorly packaged materials, and a host of other variables. Thus, measuring construction productivity is a difficult task at best. But the fact that productivity in construction is widely believed to be below that in other industries requires that contractors make a serious effort to measure it and set achievable goals for their employees.

HISTORICAL BACKGROUND

The giants of productivity analysis in the United States are Frederick W. Taylor, Henry L. Gantt, and Frank B. Gilbreth. Taylor's work at the Midvale Steel Plant was readily applicable to construction because much of his early work was in the field of bulk materials handling. Gantt, who was oriented toward planning and worker training, is closely associated with construction because of its adoption of the Gantt or bar chart as a tool for project planning. Gilbreth, who had become a master craftsman in several construction trades in his youth, ran his own construction company and applied many of his theories on productivity to his own construction activities.

Although none of the "big three" appears to be responsible for coining the phrase, it was the work of Taylor, Gantt, and Gilbreth which became the basis of "scientific management" in the early 1900s. Unfortunately, many practitioners of this new "science" forgot that its founders believed that productivity gains resulting from the application of their theories should be shared with the workers. Indeed, the writings of Gilbreth indicate that he offered as incentives to his construction crews such rewards as financial bonuses, time off, and a variety of other forms of recognition for superior performance. Ultimately, the Congress made it illegal to use federal funds for time and motion studies in government plants. Passed in 1914, this law was the result of a worker strike in a federal arsenal and the general resentment of workers across the country who saw their productivity rise while their pay remained constant and they received little recognition for superior performance. It was not until the 1940s that the law was repealed.

In 1918 the book *Modern Management Applied to Construction* by D. J. Hauer was published, but it was poorly received by the industry. It was not until the 1950s that productivity analysis in construction began a slow revival under the aegis of a group in the civil engineering department at Stanford University. Several of these people came directly from the construction industry and their work soon gained support from some of the nation's largest construction firms. In the early 1960s the National Association of Home Builders sponsored a series of studies with the support of the Stanley Works and several large home-building firms. Also worthy of mention from this era is a set of four books on construction management authored by George E. Deatherage, which embodied much of what was then known about construction productivity analysis. But, it was not until the late 1970s that the Business Roundtable studies began to significantly impact on the construction industry's failure to be concerned with its reputation for low productivity. In fact, much of the success of these studies was dependent on owners' writing productivity study requirements into their construction contracts.

COLLECTING PRODUCTIVITY DATA

"How many bricks does a bricklayer lay?" was one question addressed in a major study of masonry work sponsored by the Department of Housing and Urban Development in the early 1970s. Answers to that question ranged from a low of 125 per day from one general contractor to 1500 per day from an engineer. The study itself came up with a figure of 660 per 8-hour day. Thus, in spite of the fact that the size of brick, the type of joint, and other details were meticulously specified, the industry really did not have a fix on what was expected of a skilled mason in the way of productivity. However, it must be recognized that the wide-ranging productivity estimates were probably not so much due to the variability of production among individual bricklayers as to such things as job setup, management, materials handling, and crew composition. Thus, it appears that productivity data must be gathered by each construction firm on an individual basis. Once a firm has gained confidence in its own data, it is ready to go on to the task of improving on its own performance.

In addition to serving as the base for a productivity improvement program, productivity data are useful to the contractor in many other ways. They can be used to:

1. Evaluate the merit of new methods or explain results due to changed conditions
2. Detect and possibly explain variances from one project to another
3. Quickly detect and correct adverse trends in the field
4. Measure the effectiveness of the project management team
5. Tighten up the estimating process

According to a supplemental study from the Business Roundtable Report, good site-productivity data-collecting systems (see Fig. 22.1) should include the following elements.

1. Establish cost accounts
Divide project into
logical blocks of work.
Example: Acct 2.640 sidewalks

2. Quantity take-off
Measure quantity of work for
each cost account.
Example:

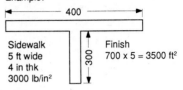

Sidewalk
5 ft wide
4 in thk
3000 lb/in²

Finish
700 x 5 = 3500 ft²

3. Establish budget
Use historical data on
hours/unit to develop
budget for each account.
Example: Acct 2.640 sidewalks-finish
     ft²   h/ft²
3500 x 0.040 = 140 h

4. Measure progress
Monitor at planned intervals.
Example: 1500 ft² complete
2000 ft² remaining

5. Collect actual costs
Charge labor to cost account
Example: 70 h to 2.640

6. Report status
Check status at planned intervals.
Example: Acct 2.640
- Original quantity - 3500 ft²
- Completed quantity -1500 ft²
- % complete - 1500/3500 = 43%
- Actual hours charged - 70
- Budget hours/ft² - 0.040
- Actual hours/ft² - 70/1500 = 0.047
- Required to complete at current
  rate - 2000 x 0.047 = 94 h
- Predicted total - 70 + 94 = 164 h
- Budget over-run = 164 −140 = 24 h
- Over-run − 17%

7. Review status report
Management review of SR
followed by action

PM   "How come?"
FRMN   "Screed breakdown
         forced hand labor"
PM   "Rent a power screed"
FRMN   "OK with new screed.
         We can finish in 60 h"

9. Return to step 4
Measure progress
under new plan.

8. Revise prediction
Required to complete - 60 h
Revised prediction - 70 + 60 = 130 h
(+ cost of screed rental)
7% reduction on labor

FIGURE 22.1 Outline of a basic site productivity system from a supplementary report for the Business Roundtable "Construction Industry Cost Effectiveness Project Report."

1. *A good labor cost account code:* Where crew members are expected to fill out their own time cards with assigned cost codes, the system must remain simple yet detailed enough to ensure proper distribution of hours to specific tasks. On projects large enough to support a timekeeper, codes can be crafted to provide finer detail.

2. *Quantity take-offs based on labor cost account code:* Quantity of work must be measured for each used code, a discipline that some estimators may find inhibiting.

3. *Work budget:* Based on historical data of labor hours per unit of work or units of work per labor hour, develop budgeted labor hours for each cost account code.

4. *Progress measurement:* At planned intervals, progress should be monitored and recorded on a percent complete basis. Percent complete may be established on the basis of an informed judgment or on actual physical measurement of work accomplished. For some work it may be necessary to establish "rules of credit." For example, the fact that all columns and beams are in place does not necessarily indicate that 100 percent of steel erection is completed. There may be additional hours required for final alignment and bolting.

5. *Collection of actual costs:* Labor hours must be gathered from time cards or accounting records and charged to specific cost account codes.

6. *Status report:* Based on progress measurement (percent complete) and actual labor costs in hours, is the work over or under budget?

7. *Status report review:* If work is under budget, find out why. If it is over budget, consult with field personnel and develop improved methods to get the work back on budget or, at least, minimize losses.

8. *Budget revision:* With the cooperation of field personnel, establish a revised budget using improved methods, equipment, or management controls.

9. *Return to step 4:* Resume monitoring work, possibly at shorter intervals, to ensure corrective measures have met requirements of the revised budget.

There are many tools available for gathering productivity data in the field. They range from careful observation of the work by a qualified group or individual to sophisticated use of photographic or TV recordings. For some work, stopwatch studies may be appropriate as well as work sampling. Above all, data gathered in the field must be coordinated with carefully crafted labor-cost code data to be sure that valid measurements are obtained. While the overall use of job cost codes can and should result in productivity improvement, contractors are well advised to make detailed studies of work activities which are common to all or most of their projects. Too often productivity assumptions for specific work are based on what is being done in the field rather than what could be done. And, data from accounting may be out of date or may not clearly reflect job conditions or changes in methods and equipment.

One man with a stopwatch and clipboard can readily gather data when small crews are working in a relatively small area. Two men, with synchronized watches, can also do accurate studies of earth-moving operations when one is located at the borrow pit and the other at the fill area. However, as crew size increases above four or five, time-lapse photography becomes almost mandatory. Whether using film or TV, time-lapse cameras allow pictures to be taken at fixed time intervals ranging from 1 to 6 or more seconds. The finer the detail involved, the shorter the time interval. Most construction work can be studied with the time interval set at 4 seconds.

With the time-lapse camera properly located, preferably above the work area and far enough away so that workers are always in the picture, 4 hours of work can be filmed on a typical 50-foot roll of conventional film. Once the film has been processed—not necessary with TV equipment—a half day of work can be reviewed in minutes. And, unlike the situation with stopwatch and paper, instant replays are readily available. In addition, the time factor is built in, for every frame represents the number of seconds elapsed between shots. With a projector equipped with a frame counter, cycle times can be readily determined. Since the film can be replayed as often as necessary, the film can readily pinpoint the activity of each member in the crew. In fact, work sampling of a single crew can readily be done using time-lapse records. Finally, if the camera is in a safe location, it can be left unattended while doing its recording job.

PREPLANNING

Regardless of how well a constructor may have planned and scheduled the overall project, failure in the area of short-term planning appears to be a primary contributor to low productivity. In the early 1980s, John D. Borcherding and his colleagues at the University of Texas performed work-sampling studies on 41 construction projects in Austin, Texas. The percentage of time crews spent at direct work ranged from a low of 32 percent on a university pharmacy building to a high of 72 percent on an apartment complex. A typical pie chart (Fig. 22.2) shows how workers' time was spent during a typical project day. Note that waiting and idle time in this example accounts for 32 percent of the workers' time. In fact, on industrial and power plant projects, waiting and idle time often account for an even greater percentage of workers' time.

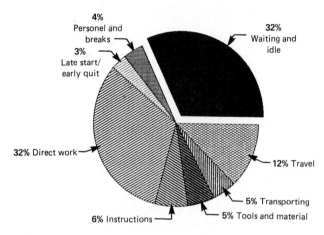

FIGURE 22.2 A typical construction workday breakdown. Percent of time for "waiting and idle" varies widely and tends to be higher on industrial and power plant projects.

It is easy to blame the construction worker for these low productivity scores, but recent studies tend to point the finger at management as being equally culpable. It is also reasonable to assume that some delay and idle time is simply a "built-in" factor in construction work. For example, a contractor may consciously increase the size of a concrete crew to be sure that work is not damaged when early set occurs on a hot, windy day. However, there is clear evidence that work crews can perform more productively if management has done a good job of planning for the short term.

One of the keys to good productivity is preplanning. A good superintendent should know today what will be going on in two weeks, and even more important, what will be going on tomorrow morning. This introduces the concept of the short-interval production schedule (SIPS). Even though a project may have been planned and scheduled using the critical path method (CPM), and the plan is workable and has been applied in the field, there is still a need to fine-tune the plan on a day-to-day basis. The short-interval production schedule is a useful tool for this purpose.

The format for a SIPS can vary to meet specific project needs. The illustrations in (Fig. 23a and b) are used by Alvin F. Burkhart, director of productivity

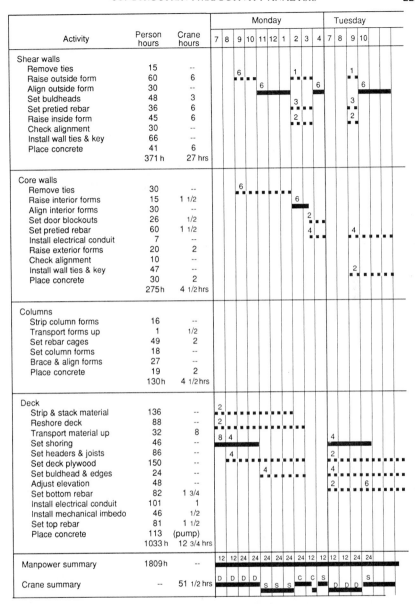

Activity	Person hours	Crane hours
Shear walls		
Remove ties	15	--
Raise outside form	60	6
Align outside form	30	--
Set buldheads	48	3
Set pretied rebar	36	6
Raise inside form	45	6
Check alignment	30	--
Install wall ties & key	66	--
Place concrete	41	6
	371 h	27 hrs
Core walls		
Remove ties	30	--
Raise interior forms	15	1 1/2
Align interior forms	30	--
Set door blockouts	26	1/2
Set pretied rebar	60	1 1/2
Install electrical conduit	7	--
Raise exterior forms	20	2
Check alignment	10	--
Install wall ties & key	47	--
Place concrete	30	2
	275h	4 1/2 hrs
Columns		
Strip column forms	16	--
Transport forms up	1	1/2
Set rebar cages	49	2
Set column forms	18	--
Brace & align forms	27	--
Place concrete	19	2
	130h	4 1/2 hrs
Deck		
Strip & stack material	136	--
Reshore deck	88	--
Transport material up	32	8
Set shoring	46	--
Set headers & joists	86	--
Set deck plywood	150	--
Set buldhead & edges	24	--
Adjust elevation	48	--
Set bottom rebar	82	1 3/4
Install electrical conduit	101	1
Install mechanical imbedo	46	1/2
Set top rebar	81	1 1/2
Place concrete	113	(pump)
	1033 h	12 3/4 hrs
Manpower summary	1809h	--
Crane summary	--	51 1/2 hrs

FIGURE 22.3 (a) Portion of a short interval production schedule as developed by Alvin F. Burkhart, Director of Productivity, Phelps, Inc. Note that manpower and crane usage are scheduled on an hourly basis.

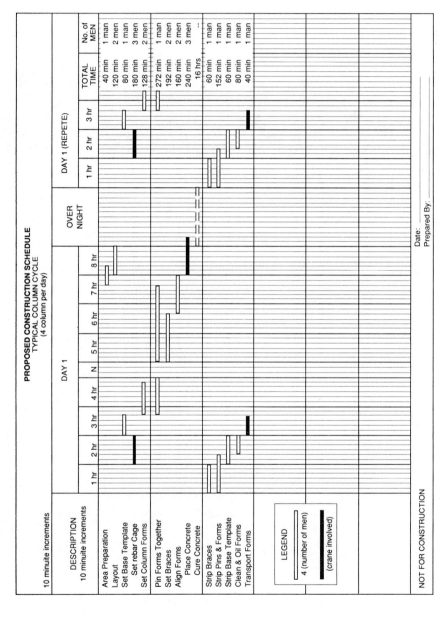

FIGURE 22.3 (*Continued*) (*b*) A detailed short interval production schedule for the column work shown in (*a*). Note that time is broken down into 10-minute intervals.

at Phelps, Inc. Developed for a reinforced concrete high-rise project, the schedule shown is the result of numerous prior planning discussions involving selection of both methods and equipment. The first illustration shows the workday broken into hours, the second into 10-minute intervals for a typical column cycle. It is important to note that the SIPS is not graven in stone and with the cooperation of both labor and management, improvements can often be made during the progress of the work.

In addition to SIPS, some contractors are using job assignment sheets to provide written instructions to crews. These sheets tell workers where the work is to be done, specifically, what is to be done and how to do it. For large projects, the assignment sheet can include skeleton plans and elevations to indicate the precise location of the work area. For experienced workers these sheets require a minimum of information, but for the benefit of new workers or workers using equipment or materials for the first time, they may include detailed written descriptions and sketches. Finally, it is advisable to include instructions on the assignment sheet to advise the crew where the foreman can be located if questions arise or when the assignment is completed.

FOREMAN DELAY SURVEYS AND CRAFTSMAN QUESTIONNAIRES

Most people performing specific tasks are aware that there are better ways to do them. Unfortunately, they are seldom asked to express themselves. Thus, in construction and most other industries, a gold mine of productivity nuggets remains undiscovered. The foreman delay survey and the craftsman questionnaire are tools that can be used to expose productivity problems in construction. Although used informally in the past, they made a formal appearance on the construction scene about 1979.

There is no standard format for these surveys and most of them are tailored to particular situations. The craftsman questionnaire may involve questions ranging from likes and dislikes in the work situation to how to help the worker do his job better and easier. The foreman delay survey has evolved because of a growing recognition that various delays that occur on the typical construction project have a tremendous impact on productivity. The use of these tools by management can make a significant contribution to productivity if the tools are understood by workers to be used to improve working conditions rather than as performance evaluations.

The sample foreman delay survey form shown in (Fig. 22.4) is taken from a supplementary report from the Business Roundtable study of the construction industry. A variety of problems causing delay are listed along with space for the foreman to add others which were overlooked or which occur more rarely. The list would probably vary from project to project and contractor to contractor and should be carefully planned and tested before formal use. The foreman is expected to fill in this form (Fig. 22.5) at the end of each working day, recording the number of hours and the number of men involved in each delay. It is obviously a task that does not make heavy demands on his time. The forms are collected each day and the tabulated results are returned to the foreman along with summary reports at planned intervals.

FOREMAN DELAY SURVEY

DATE: _____		NAME: _____				
		GEN. FOREMAN: _____				
NUMBER IN CREW: _____		FOREMAN NAME: _____				

PROBLEMS CAUSING DELAY						
	NUMBER OF HOURS	×	NUMBER OF MEN	=	MANHOURS	
CHANGES/REDOING WORK (DESIGN ERROR OR CHANGE)	_____	×	_____	=	_____	
CHANGES/REDOING WORK (PREFABRICATION ERROR)	_____	×	_____	=	_____	
CHANGES/REDOING WORK (FIELD ERROR OR DAMAGE)	_____	×	_____	=	_____	
WAITING FOR MATERIALS (WAREHOUSE)	_____	×	_____	=	_____	
WAITING FOR MATERIALS (VENDOR FURNISHED)	_____	×	_____	=	_____	
WAITING FOR TOOLS	_____	×	_____	=	_____	
WAITING FOR CONSTRUCTION EQUIPMENT	_____	×	_____	=	_____	
CONSTRUCTION EQUIPMENT BREAKDOWN	_____	×	_____	=	_____	
WAITING FOR INFORMATION	_____	×	_____	=	_____	
WAITING FOR OTHER CREWS	_____	×	_____	=	_____	
WAITING FOR FELLOW CREW MEMBERS	_____	×	_____	=	_____	
UNEXPLAINED OR UNNECESSARY MOVE	_____	×	_____	=	_____	
OTHER: _____	_____	×	_____	=	_____	
_____	_____	×	_____	=	_____	

COMMENTS: _____

FIGURE 22.4   Format for a foreman delay survey as presented in a supplementary report for the Business Roundtable "Construction Industry Cost Effectiveness Project Report." The list of delays may vary from project to project and should be tailored to meet conditions of a particular study.

Some of the many advantages of the foreman delay survey are

1. It is cheap, requiring only about 5 minutes of the foreman's time.
2. It can easily provide information from the entire project.
3. It is a way of getting current information.
4. It can pinpoint specific delays causing the greatest damage to productivity.

FOREMAN DELAY SUMMARY

PROJECT: _____ DATE: _____

GENERAL FOREMAN: _____ CRAFT: _____

DELAY CAUSE	CRAFT	CARPENTERS	ELECTRICIANS	INSULATORS	MANAGERS	LABORERS	MILLWRIGHTS	OPERATORS	PIPEFITTERS	TEAMSTERS			SUM	%
	MANHOURS WORKED	909	810	90	432	1088	32	560	999	200			5120	
REWORK - DESIGN		16	5				8		60				89	1.7
REWORK - PREFAB						5			20				20	0.4
REWORK - FIELD									2				7	0.1
WAITING FOR MATLS. (WHSE.)		9	1		32				74	2			118	2.3
WAITING FOR MATLS. (VENDOR)		8			64				8				80	1.6
WAITING FOR TOOLS					40		9		22				66	1.3
WAITING FOR EQPT.		2			6				17				25	0.5
EQPT. BREAKDOWN								13	10	7			30	0.6
WAITING FOR INFORMATION									28	2			30	0.6
WAITING FOR OTHER CREWS			6	3					24				33	0.6
WAITING FOR SAME CREW			6	4									10	0.2
UNNECESSARY MOVE			1	3		7			6	2			14	0.4
OTHER		15	4						20	1			40	0.8
OTHER														
TOTAL		50	23	10	142	12	12	13	291	14			567	11.1
		5.5%	2.4%	11.9%	32.9%	1.1%	37.5%	2.7%	30.8%	7%				

FIGURE 22.5 Typical summary report from a foreman delay survey. This information should be discussed with the foremen as soon as possible to confirm that efforts are being made to eliminate problems.

5. It specifically identifies crews and crafts.

6. It opens an avenue of communication between the foreman and management.

To have an impact on productivity, the foreman delay survey must follow a thorough indoctrination and orientation session for the foremen. They must be assured that the effort will make their jobs easier and that there is no punitive element in the program. Once the program is under way, reports must be collected daily and reviewed with the foreman on a regular basis. Summary reports should be provided, but, most important of all, management must take strong, positive action to correct problems and do it in a highly visible style.

On large projects, it is usually not necessary or desirable to run the foreman delay survey daily over a long period. Preferably, it should occur on a 1-week-per-month frequency. Proper response from management can soon spread the word to foremen and crews alike that the company they are working for is sincerely interested in removing the roadblocks that frustrate them in the pursuit of their daily assignments.

WORK SAMPLING

Work sampling is a technique that can be used both economically and effectively to study productivity on construction projects. It can be applied to all of the workers on a site or to a specific crew performing a specific task. Worker status may be categorized simply as "working" or "not working" or in a variety of ways, ranging up to the limits of the human observer's ability to make instantaneous category classifications. Studies often zero in on delays attributed to various causes or the specific activities required to complete a task such as concrete forming.

The work-sampling process involves sending a trained observer out to observe the workers and record what he sees on a simple form. The accuracy of the data is dependent on the number of observations and, in the case of the simple "working" "not working" observations, the percentage of each recorded. From statistics we obtain the formula:

$$SE = \sqrt{\frac{P \times Q}{N}}$$

SE = sampling error

P = percent working

Q = $(1 - P)$ or percent not working

N = number of observations

The confidence level and sampling error (95 percent and 5 percent are considered adequate for construction) may be established by using the formula:

$$N = \frac{Z^2 + (P \times Q)}{SE^2}$$

Z = 1.65 for a confidence level of 90 percent

2.00 for a confidence level of 95 percent

2.60 for a confidence level of 99 percent

It is important that observations be random to avoid hitting cyclical work at the same point in every cycle and to prevent workers from "performing on cue." However, many observers point out that workers soon adjust to their presence and they can therefore make observations at set intervals with little loss of accuracy. Difficulties with work sampling are primarily the result of human limitations. There is bound to be variation among observers in the way they read workers' actions, and bias can seriously distort data. For example, sending an anti-union observer to study a union project would obviously stack the deck against the workers.

Preplanning should include the establishment of standard routes through the project and the times they should be traveled. In addition, the population to be studied should be clearly defined and an identification system (colored hard hats for example) should be used to be sure that the proper people are being observed. Since the observers are making snap judgments continuously as they tour the site, it is important to limit duration of tours to avoid observer fatigue. Finally, during periods of abnormal worker behavior (rumors of a strike or impending lay-off) it is inadvisable to attempt work-sampling studies.

Formal work-sampling studies should be preceded by a pilot program which includes enough observations to ensure that all subjects have been covered. The activity underway for each observation should be noted and this information used to establish categories for the forms to be used by the observers. In addition, the percent working and not working should be calculated and used to establish the proper number of observations needed to achieve the desired confidence level and sampling error. Once the pilot study has been completed, standard forms can be prepared, tour routes and times established, and a worker identification system put in place.

The illustrations shown in Figs. 22.6 and 22.7 cover a one-man study of a pan-wrecking operation done by John D. Dornblaser of Arthur Young & Company's Tulsa office. The forming work on this project was a first for the contractor and his primary concern was with delays. For the pan-wrecking operation a five-man crew was observed at 2-minute intervals for a period of 4 hours as shown on the first sheet (Fig. 22.6). The second sheet (Fig. 22.7) is a summary sheet pulling together observations from four half days and one full day. With a total of 3600 observations, it is obvious from the statistical formulas that a low sampling error and a high confidence level were achieved. While the nondelay production rate of 13.9 pans per man-hour is probably unachievable, it clearly indicates that there is room for improvement on the 6.1-pans-per-hour observed production rate. In addition, the delay problems can be rated on the basis of the cumulative record and there is an obvious need to reduce the problem of "wait for other crew."

While such detailed studies are valuable, it should be noted that shorter work sampling studies can also be helpful in the "shakeout" period when newly formed crews begin an activity. Sometimes referred to as "5-minute ratings," these might involve observation of a five-man crew at 5-minute intervals for only an hour or two, and sometimes less. While not statistically valid, these short-term studies can be helpful in identifying problems of crew balance and individual productivity.

FORMATS FOR ANALYZING DATA

Breaking down the "we've always done it that way" syndrome is one of the keys to successful productivity analysis. Thus, it is important to have groups and individuals look at construction work data in as many different ways as possible. The flow process chart is one way to achieve this and involves following the material or the worker (or both) from the inception of an activity to its completion using symbols to represent operation, transportation, inspection, delay, and storage. The diagrams in Fig. 22.8 based on placing timbers to stabilize the walls of an excavation illustrate several techniques appropriate to flow process charting.

JOBSITE SAMPLING OBSERVATION FORM									DATE 8/24/81	
JOB NO. 909	ACTIVITY WRECK PANS			PRODUCTION UNIT PAN WRECKED				SAMPLING RATE 2 MIN.		
CREW SIZE 5	PERIOD OBSERVED 7:30a — 11:30a			TOTAL HRS. SAMPLED 20				OBSERVER JDD		
		DELAY CATEGORIES								
SAMPLED PERSONNEL	PRODUCTIVE TIME	WAIT FOR CREW MEMBER	WAIT FOR OTHER CREW	WAIT FOR TOOLS	WAIT FOR HOIST	WAIT FOR INSTRUCTIONS	STRAIGHTEN BENT PAN		NOT OBSERVED TIME	TOTAL OBSERVATIONS
Dave	60	13	19	3	2	5	15		3	120
Brian	53	16	28	10		10			3	120
Steve	42	16	44		2	3	13			120
James	56	13	11	4	1	33	2			120
Randy	40	14	23	10		9	18		6	120
TOTAL OBSERVATIONS	251	72	125	27	5	60	48	—	—	12 600
PRODUCTION UNIT COUNT	123 Pans									

FIGURE 22.6   A work sheet covering a 4-hour period from a work sampling study conducted by John D. Dornblaser out of the Tulsa office of Arthur Young & Company. The emphasis of the study is on delays involved in removal of pan forms.

JOBSITE SAMPLING SUMMARY FORM

JOB NO. 909 ACTIVITY WRECK PANS PRODUCTION UNIT PANS WRECKED SAMPLING RATE 2 MIN.

DAY (COUNT) CATEGORIES	NO PANS	PROD.	CREW MEMBER	OTHER CREW	TOOLS	HOIST	INSTR.	STRAT. PAN	FIRE		'N'	TOTAL
8/24	123	251	72	125	27	5	60	48			12	600
8/25	112	210	60	110	35	22	84	62			17	600
8/26	209	481	161	199	74	53	41	79	63		49	1200
8/27	131	301	41	112	22	6	79	30			9	600
8/28	141	278	37	15	66	39	53	110			2	600
TOTALS	716	1521	371	561	224	125	317	329	63		89	3600
% OF TOTAL OBSERVATIONS LESS 'N'		43.3	10.5	16.0	6.4	3.6	9.0	9.4	1.8		−	3511 / 100%
TOTAL MINUTES OBSERVED		3042	742	1122	448	250	634	658	126			7022
MINUTES PER UNIT		4.3	1.0	1.6	0.6	0.3	0.9	0.9	0.2			9.8

OBSERVED PRODUCTION RATE: $\left(\dfrac{1 \text{ unit}}{9.8 \text{ minutes}}\right)\left(\dfrac{60 \text{ minutes}}{\text{hour}}\right) = 6.1$ units/manhour

NON-DELAY PRODUCTION RATE: $\left(\dfrac{1 \text{ unit}}{4.3 \text{ minutes}}\right)\left(\dfrac{60 \text{ minutes}}{\text{hour}}\right) = 13.9$ units/manhour

PRODUCTIVITY: observed production rate / non-delay production rate = 43.9 %

FIGURE 22.7 Summary sheet covering 4 half days and 1 full day of work sampling observations covering removal of pan forms. Note that if delays could be eliminated, productivity would more than double. With 3600 observations, this study has a high confidence level and a very low sampling error.

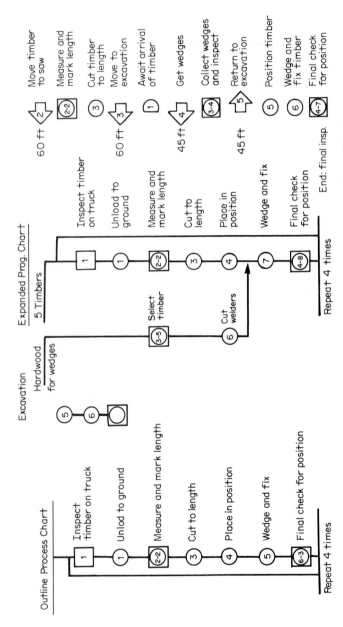

FIGURE 22.8 Several formats, including a site layout, for flow process charts. (*Source: Roy Pilcher, Principles of Construction Management, London: McGraw-Hill*)

A tabular format is also shown (Fig. 22.9), which allows for some alternatives in method when the questions of why, what, who, where, and how have been thoroughly analyzed.

Pie charts, crew balance charts, and man/machine charts are also useful forms of data presentation. Figure 22.10 shows a man/machine chart for a simple, hypothetical situation where one laborer has been assigned to mix and deliver mortar for a masonry crew. Since the mixing cycle is a fixed duration, the machine tends to set the pace of each cycle. In the original plan it is assumed that the value added by converting raw materials into finished mortar is $8.00 per yard. With a half cubic yard mixer costing $16.00 per hour and labor $8.00 per hour, the original plan produces 3CY (6 cycles per hour at 0.5CY per cycle) of mortar per hour at a cost of $16 plus $8, or $24. Thus, the contractor breaks even since he is getting $24 in value added. However, study reveals that the mason crew is being held up because of a shortage of mortar. It was determined that the addition of a second laborer would speed up the operation by reducing loading time and idle time of the mixer because the second laborer could help load and also could deliver a batch of mortar during the mixing cycle. With the revised plan, the cycle was reduced to 6 minutes, and 5CY of mortar was produced each hour. The new hourly cost was $32 and the value added was increased to $40. Thus the demand for mortar from the mason crew was satisfied and a net of $8 was contributed as the difference between cost and value added.

CASE STUDY

The following case study is based on a report by Alvin F. Burkhart, director of productivity at Phelps, Inc.

This study covers the installation of some job-site fabricated forming required in several areas on each floor of a high-rise building. The purpose of this summary is to show various formats for data presentation and to emphasize that productivity analysis is an ongoing rather than a one-shot process. In brief, three sets of time-lapse films were studied to increase square foot production per manhour from 3.58 to 33.34.

Initially, a three-man crew was assigned to the forming task. However, it soon became evident that, while their nonproductive time was probably within normal limits, their output was extremely low. This led to a time-lapse film study of the operation (film no. 1). Each man was followed on the film through one complete cycle, with frames in which he appeared counted for productive work, support work, and nonproductive time. Since the time interval between each frame was known, these data could be converted into time units or percentage of total observations (frames). The pie chart shown in Fig. 22.11 was then drawn.

Obviously, this does not help much in trying to find clues to the cause of low productivity by the three-man crew. So, a more detailed classification was used to develop data for the pie chart shown in Fig. 22.12.

This picture clearly indicates that over 60 percent of the men's time was spent going for materials and waiting on others. Material location, operation sequence, and overmanning emerged as problems, based on the expanded pie chart and the crew balance chart shown in Fig. 22.13.

Here it is evident that the third man is idle almost half of the time and that "going for material" is consuming a great deal of time for all three crew members. At this point it was decided to reduce the crew to two men and some

FLOW PROCESS CHART

DATE _____   PAGE ___ OF ___

WHY ? WHAT? WHO ? WHERE ? WHEN? HOW?

INVESTIGATOR _____

PROJECT_____

RECAPITULATION

ACTIVITY_____

CREW_____

MATERIALS_____

MACHINES_____

START_____ STOP_____

		NOW		REVIS.		DIFF.	
		NO	TM	NO	TM	NO	TM
◯	OPERATIONS						
▷	TRANSPORTATIONS						
☐	INSPECTIONS						
⟱	DELAYS						
▽	STORAGES						
DISTANCE TRAVELED		FT		FT		FT	

ALTERNATIVES CHANGE

DESCRIPTION OF METHOD	OPER.	TRANS.	INSPEC.	DELAY	STOR.	DIST.	QUANT.	TIME	ELIMINATE	COMBINE	IMPROVE	SEQUENCE	PLACE	PERSON	NOTES
1	◯ ▷ ☐ ⟱ ▽														
2	◯ ▷ ☐ ⟱ ▽														
3	◯ ▷ ☐ ⟱ ▽														
4	◯ ▷ ☐ ⟱ ▽														
5	◯ ▷ ☐ ⟱ ▽														
6	◯ ▷ ☐ ⟱ ▽														
7	◯ ▷ ☐ ⟱ ▽														
8	◯ ▷ ☐ ⟱ ▽														
9	◯ ▷ ☐ ⟱ ▽														
10	◯ ▷ ☐ ⟱ ▽														
11	◯ ▷ ☐ ⟱ ▽														
12	◯ ▷ ☐ ⟱ ▽														
13	◯ ▷ ☐ ⟱ ▽														
14	◯ ▷ ☐ ⟱ ▽														
15	◯ ▷ ☐ ⟱ ▽														
16	◯ ▷ ☐ ⟱ ▽														
17	◯ ▷ ☐ ⟱ ▽														
18	◯ ▷ ☐ ⟱ ▽														
19	◯ ▷ ☐ ⟱ ▽														
20	◯ ▷ ☐ ⟱ ▽														
21	◯ ▷ ☐ ⟱ ▽														

FIGURE 22.9 A typical flow process chart worksheet. Note recapitulation chart which may give clues for change in methodology or elimination of activities.

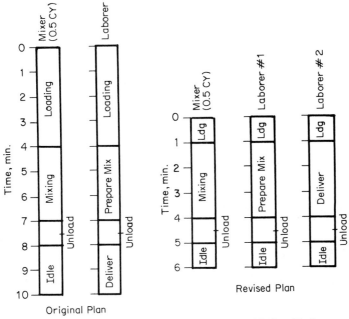

Man / Machine Chart — Mix and Deliver Mortar

FIGURE 22.10 Simple man/machine chart. Fixed mixing time tends to put machine in control. Addition of second laborer reduces loading time and increases productivity of machine even though worker idle time is created.

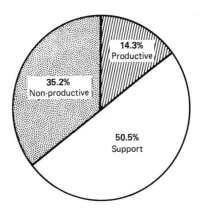

Efficiency = productive + support

14.3% + 50.5% = 64.8%

Effectiveness = quantity / manhours

2.94 S.F. / 0.82 MH = 3.58SF/MH

FIGURE 22.11 Pie chart showing percentages of productive, support, and nonproductive time for three-man forming crew, from time-lapse film study 1.

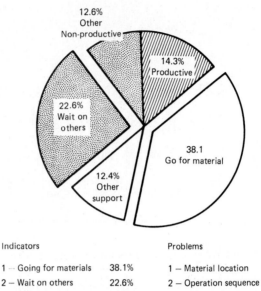

Indicators

1 — Going for materials   38.1%
2 — Wait on others   22.6%
                           ―――――
                           60.7%

Problems

1 — Material location
2 — Operation sequence
3 — Over manned

FIGURE 22.12 Expanded pie chart showing breakdown of support and nonproductive activity for three-man forming crew.

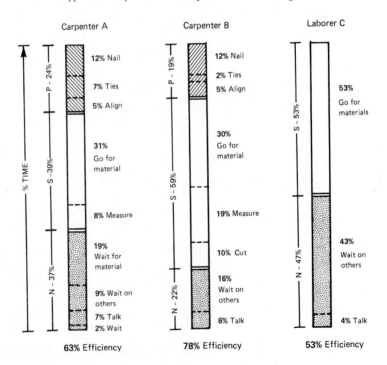

FIGURE 22.13 Crew balance chart for three-man forming crew.

improvements in material location and work technique were made. The activity was again subjected to a time-lapse study (film no. 2) and the new, simple pie chart shown in Fig. 22.14 produced.

As can be seen from the comparison pies in Fig. 22.15, efficiency remained about the same, but effectiveness was almost doubled.

The more detailed pie chart for film no. 2 (see Fig. 22.16) gives some indicators that there may still be problems with work technique and, as a result, overmanning.

The crew balance charts shown in Figs. 22.17 and 22.18, in both percentage of total time and in actual time elapsed in minutes formats, were then studied and further improvements in the task environment were made.

Material storage was further improved and a special work area was provided. This was followed by film no. 3, the final time-lapse film of the

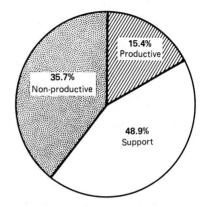

Efficiency = productive + support
          15.4% + 48.9% = 64.3%

Effectiveness = quantity / manhours
          4.09 S.F. / 0.63 MH = 6.49 SF/MH

FIGURE 22.14   Revised pie chart showing percentages of productive, support, and nonproductive time for two-man crew under improved conditions, from time-lapse film study 2.

activity. Note in the sample pie chart in Fig. 22.19 that efficiency has risen significantly and there has been a tremendous rise in effectiveness.

Figure 22.20 presents a comparison of the three simple pie charts from the three time-lapse films followed by Fig. 22.21, the final crew balance chart.

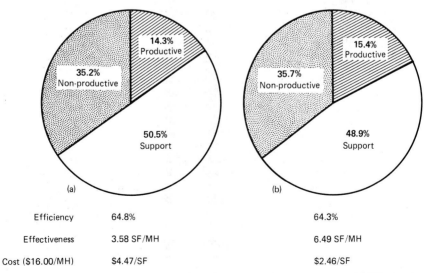

Efficiency	64.8%	64.3%
Effectiveness	3.58 SF/MH	6.49 SF/MH
Cost ($16.00/MH)	$4.47/SF	$2.46/SF

FIGURE 22.15   Comparison of efficiency and effectiveness of three-man crew. (*a*) Film no. 1, (*b*) film no. 2.

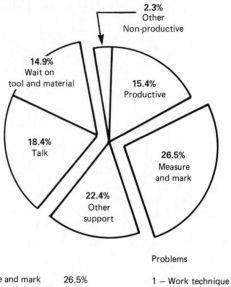

Indicators

1 — Measure and mark	26.5%
2 — Talk	18.4%
3 — Wait on tools and mat.	14,9%
	59.8%

Problems

1 — Work technique

2 — Over manned

FIGURE 22.16 Detailed pie chart analyzing productivity problems for two-man crew.

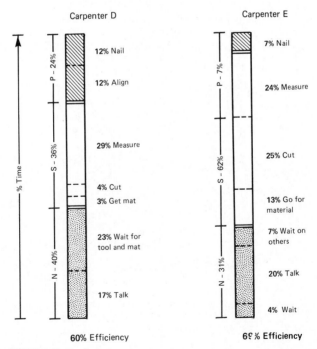

FIGURE 22.17 Crew balance chart for two-man crew, percentage of time format.

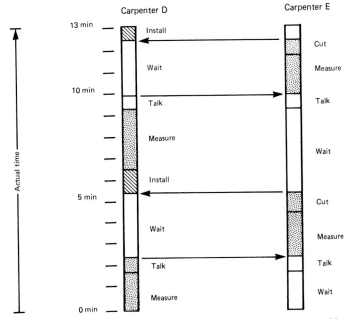

FIGURE 22.18 Crew balance chart for two-man crew, actual time elapsed in minutes format.

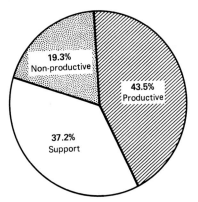

Efficiency = productive + support
          43.5% + 37.2% = 80.7%

Effectiveness = quantity / manhours
          14.67 S.F. / 0.44 MH = 33.34 SF/MH

FIGURE 22.19 Revised pie chart for two-man crew after improvements in task environment, from time-lapse film no. 3.

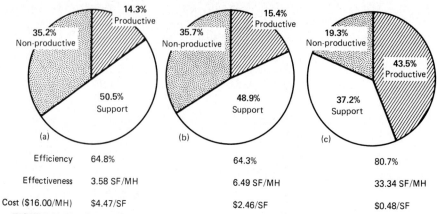

Efficiency	64.8%	64.3%	80.7%
Effectiveness	3.58 SF/MH	6.49 SF/MH	33.34 SF/MH
Cost ($16.00/MH)	$4.47/SF	$2.46/SF	$0.48/SF

FIGURE 22.20 Comparison of pie charts from the three film-lapse studies. (*a*) Film no. 1, (*b*) film no. 2, (*c*) film no. 3.

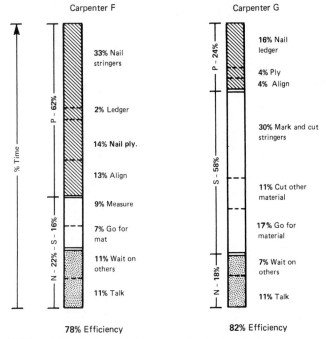

FIGURE 22.21 Final crew balance chart for forming crew.

   While the above case-study summary has been oversimplified, it clearly demonstrates the value of productivity analysis in construction. At the same time, it
demonstrates that there are no panaceas to cure low productivity. The contractor
who commits to productivity analysis cannot be halfhearted. He must be willing
to make the necessary investment in money, manpower, and equipment before

he can reap the benefits. But, once intelligently and enthusiastically committed, a contractor can not only improve his own fiscal position, he can contribute to the necessary task of enhancing the reputation of his industry.

MATHEMATICAL MODELING

As the result of efforts during World War II, many new mathematical techniques were developed and old ones improved that are gradually finding their way into the construction industry. Queuing is a technique that has many applications in earth moving and in such site service facilities as toolsheds and material storage. It is not unusual to see a line of scrapers on an earth-moving project waiting to be served by a tractor pusher. Nor is it unusual to see a line of craftsmen waiting to be issued tools or materials by a clerk. The balance between the rate of service and the rate of arrival of people or machines to be served can often be established using queuing theory so that waiting time is significantly reduced.

General theories of linear programming are also applicable to many construction situations and a variety of computer programs are available that do not require users to be expert mathematicians. A typical problem is to minimize scrap when cutting a variety of lengths from standard lengths of wood, steel, plywood, and other materials. It is one that can readily be solved using linear programming. Transportation problems, a special case of linear programming, often occur in construction. They involve minimization of shipping costs when supplies of material or equipment must be shipped from several warehouses to several job sites. Another special case of linear programming is the assignment problem. This involves minimizing cost or maximizing profit when several machines or men must be assigned to several tasks. Each machine or man can perform all of the tasks, but at different costs. While computer programs can be used for many of these problems, many of them are amenable to simple rule-of-thumb solutions which require nothing more than pencil and paper.

Interested contractors are referred to the following sources:

References

M. S. Makower, and E. Williamson, *Operational Research*, London: The English University Press Ltd., 1967.

Pilcher, Roy, *Principles of Construction Management,* London: McGraw-Hill Book Company (UK) Limited, 1967.

CHAPTER 23
WORKER MOTIVATION

Robert G. Zilly, P.E., M.A.S.C.E., A.I.C.
Professor of Construction Management,
Emeritus
University of Nebraska
Lincoln, Nebraska

Interest in construction worker motivation has accelerated rapidly in the past 20 years, even though most construction management personnel have not been well enough educated in the subject to develop programs for their companies. This has led to a proliferation of "experts" in the field who may or may not function competently as consultants to the construction industry. This situation brings to mind a favorite story of Victor Riesel, the well-known labor news columnist. An old fable begins with a grandfather and his grandson trudging along a dusty road with their burro. A stranger approaches them and asks, "Old man, why don't you ride the burro instead of walking?" So, the grandfather clambers aboard.

A little later, another stranger approaches them and says to the old man, "Aren't you ashamed of yourself letting the little boy walk while you ride?" The grandfather immediately helps his grandson mount and the two ride on. At this point a third stranger approaches and lectures the pair on cruelty to animals, suggesting that they should be carrying the burro. They immediately dismount, find a long pole, and sling the burro from it by binding his front and rear legs together and sliding the pole through. Soon they come to a fast-moving stream which could be crossed only by walking a slippery log. They proceed across, slip, and all are thrown into the stream. The boy and his grandfather easily swim to shore, but the burro drowns.

The moral of the story: You could lose your burro taking the advice of strangers! And the moral applies particularly in the area of worker motivation, where it behooves the contractor to select a consultant who is not only well qualified but also sincere. Construction workers are quick to detect incompetence and even quicker to reject a phony.

Despite this cautionary note, there is strong evidence to support the use of worker motivation programs in the construction industry. A good introduction to the subject appears in the Business Roundtable Report A-2, "Construction Labor Motivation," a special report from the Construction Industry Cost Effectiveness Project.

Productivity in the U.S. is not keeping pace with that of many other countries. Quantity as well as quality of production has become a major area of concern for many manufacturers. The construction industry is among those faced with reports of low productivity by its work force. In nuclear power plant construction, for example, studies have revealed an annual productivity loss of 5% per year over the past decade. Since construction labor amounts to an average of 25% of the direct capital costs of a project, ways and means must be found by the industry to arrest declining productivity.

Many items contribute to falling productivity, i.e. ineffective management and supervision that leaves material unavailable when it is needed, incompetency in staff personnel, delays in transmitting engineering information, communication breakdowns, rework; the unavailability of tools and equipment, lack of recognition and little participation in decision making by foreman and their crews. On the union side, restrictive work practices in collective-bargaining agreements hamper contractors' efforts to employ and deploy their labor force efficiently. Also in the union sector, productivity problems are worsened by the fact that foreman and general foremen are members of the same bargaining unit as the employees they supervise. This is frequently cited as a major reason why the management role of foremen is limited and often ineffective, especially on large construction projects built by transient contractors—that is, contractors who are not locally based. In these situations, the motivation and actions of foremen often conflict with management's efforts to improve productivity.

One area of concern in this multifaceted problem is worker motivation. Construction workers seem to take less pride in their work than was true in past years. The work ethic seems to have weakened considerably, possibly because of social welfare programs, unemployment benefits or, at least in some years, economic prosperity.

The nature of construction work also may have changed in recent years to reduce worker morale. During the 1970s, the increasing number of "super projects" involving high technology brought new management problems. Some workers suddenly found themselves in work environments they did not understand, some work took on the appearance of repetitive factory-type labor. Workers might be employed for years on a single project, though they might prefer more mobility and more variety. In any case, a lack of worker motivation appears to be a factor in reduced productivity, increased absenteeism, and increased turnover.

A LAYMAN'S HISTORICAL REVIEW OF MOTIVATIONAL THEORY

Although they did not coin the term, Frederick W. Taylor, Henry L. Gantt, and Frank B. Gilbreth are generally conceded to be the founders of "scientific management" (see Chap. 22). Their efforts, primarily oriented toward measuring and improving worker productivity, may have left us with a heritage that they did not intend: an inherent resistance by the work force to efforts to increase its productivity. This is of particular importance to the construction industry, since Gilbreth ran his own construction firm, Gantt invented the bar chart which is widely used by contractors to plan and schedule their projects, and Taylor dealt with work in the steel mills which was closely akin to some work on construction projects.

It was primarily Taylor and Gilbreth who managed to separate planning from doing by seeking out better ways to use a shovel and lay brick. No longer, under their system of management, could the worker develop a personal style in his daily work routine. Taylor told his people what shovel to use and how many shovelsful they should deliver in an hour. Gilbreth told his bricklayers how to lay brick and how many they were to lay per hour.

Initially, most workers accepted Taylor's and Gilbreth's approach because both were "naturals" in the field of worker motivation. They sincerely believed that if their methods improved productivity, the workers using those methods should share in the gain—either through paid time off or an increase in hourly pay rate. In addition, Gilbreth made an athletic contest out of work on his construction projects, often pitting an Irish crew against an Italian and flying the American flag over the workplace of the winning crew the next day. Unfortunately, the spread of scientific management bred many consultants who put the founder's ideas to work, but forgot or deliberately ignored (often at the request of their clients) the concept of motivation. The result was worker resentment which has probably remained a factor in labor-management relations to this day.

As the term "scientific management" gradually gave way to "industrial engineering," two new concepts began to work their way into the industrial scene: human relations and behavioral science. Human relations in its most simplistic form sought to create "happy" workers on the assumption that a happy work force would be a productive one. Unfortunately, that premise proved to be largely false. Behavioral science, on the other hand, sought to analyze the goals of the individual worker, how that worker functioned within a work group, and how that work group functioned within the total organization.

According to most authorities, the relationship between the behavioral sciences and industry had its beginning in the work of Elton Mayo and his colleagues at the Hawthorne Works of the Western Electric Company. These studies, begun in 1927, remain controversial. However, at the risk of oversimplification, two key ideas seem to have emerged. One, known as the "Hawthorne effect," implied that behavior is changed simply because the subjects are being observed and that the change is usually positive. This conclusion was reached from a study of female workers who were subjected to a variety of changes in working conditions, mostly involving lighting. The study showed that when lighting was improved, production rose. But when lighting was deliberately reduced, production also rose! However, in another area of the plant, a study dealing with male workers who were union members provided a different perspective. Members of a crew were given the opportunity to earn premium pay through higher productivity. They rejected the opportunity, presumably because they feared being ostracized or harassed by the members of other crews. In other words, they were unwilling to become "rate busters," a tradition that remains strongly embedded in workers on both union and non-union construction projects.

The Hawthorne study had little impact on industry until many years later. As one authority put it, "The study was 20 years before its time." Thus, it was not until the 1940s that the relationship between industry and the behavioral sciences really began to flourish. With apologies to the many other contributors in this field, this discussion will be confined to the work of three men: Abraham H. Maslow, Douglas M. McGregor, and Frederick Herzberg. It is their work that has attracted the greatest interest among those attempting to develop an approach to worker motivation in the construction industry.

Maslow's Hierarchy of Needs

Maslow's systematic theory of human motivation was published in 1954. He believed that people were motivated by a specific set of needs that could be arranged by the following hierarchy:

Need for self actualization

Need for esteem

Need for belongingness and love

Safety needs

Physiological needs

Physiological Needs.   These involve bodily needs such as food, water, warmth, shelter, sex, and sleep.

Safety Needs.   Included here is both the need for a feeling of physical safety as well as emotional security.

Need for Belongingness and Love.   Unlike the two previous needs, which are centered around the individual's own person, this implies a need for other people. The individual wishes to be part of a group and to love and be loved.

Need for Esteem.   This involves an individual's need for a feeling of personal worth, adequacy, and competence as well as a need for respect, admiration, recognition, and status from others.

Need for Self-Actualization.   This involves an individual's desire to achieve in reality what that person perceives of as "self." In other words, one wants to be the best that one can be.

In setting up this hierarchy, Maslow assumes that most if not all of us will move up the ladder in orderly procession. Of course, the neurotic is excluded and it is well to remember "the starving artist" syndrome. Certainly, there are individual differences which must be taken into account in the practical application of Maslow's theory, but in general it appears to be a reasonable concept. Maslow himself described the first four needs on his list as deficit needs. They come into play only because we lack what they demand. Self-actualization, however, is a growth need which comes into play when all the deficit needs are satisfied. For some it may never come into play, for others it may be an all-consuming drive, with each step forward creating a need for further progress.

Herzberg's Satisfiers and Dissatisfiers

Drawing heavily on Maslow's ideas, Frederick Herzberg worked with his colleagues to survey various worker groups to find out what made them feel exceptionally good or bad about their jobs. He found that what he called "satisfiers" involved job content, whereas "dissatisfiers" involved job environment. In terms of human needs in the workplace, his discoveries (circa 1959) can be tabulated as shown on the following page.

It is important to note that the left- and right-hand lists are not opposites. Herzberg found some overlap, but it was not statistically significant. Thus, es-

Security and fairness group (rights) *Dissatisfiers*—seldom *motivate* but may *demotivate*	Recognition and self-satisfaction group (ambitions) *Satisfiers*—all potential *motivators*
Administrative policy	Achievement
Managerial expertise	Recognition for accomplishments
Social relationships on the job	Meaningful work
Fairness in job placement	Responsibility
Working conditions	Advancement
Job security	Personal growth (learning)
Fair compensation	

sentially what he is saying is that if every item on the left were as nearly ideal as possible on the job, workers would not be motivated to extend themselves to achieve high productivity. On the other hand, if all or many of those left-hand items are less than ideal, workers might become demotivated and productivity would suffer. Thus, what Taylor, Gilbreth, and Gantt saw as motivators in the early 1900s are no longer functional, perhaps because of minimum wage laws, unemployment compensation, and OSHA and other governmental programs that have essentially wiped out Maslow's first three stages and impacted on his fourth. In fact, if Herzberg is right, he has uprooted the foundations of scientific management, which were built on the idea of "experts" telling the worker how to do his job. It is apparent that job enrichment is the key to Herzberg's approach to improving productivity through worker motivation. Today's employee wants to feel that work is meaningful and that pursuing it will give a sense of personal achievement. In addition, work must carry responsibility, a chance for advancement, and the opportunity to learn. Finally, today's worker seeks recognition for a job well done. If these conditions are met, workers will be motivated and productivity should improve.

McGregor's Theory X and Theory Y

Douglas McGregor is credited with being the first behavioral scientist to bridge the gap between laboratory research and managerial applications. He is best remembered for his theory X and theory Y categorization of the human nature of the worker.

He stressed the idea that one person's influence on another person's behavior was affected by the influencer's concept of the person to be influenced. Briefly, he felt that if the influencer was a proponent of theory X he would treat workers as if they were unwilling to work and assume that their abilities were essentially static, unimprovable, and not very impressive to start with. On the other hand, theory Y proponents would treat workers as if they really wanted to work, had a desire to learn, and had innate potential to improve. Further, he believed that the influencer's initial assumption created a "self-fulfilling prophecy." Clearly, McGregor's theory X person was the one addressed by Taylor in his early work and, though he treated his people fairly, he often displayed little respect for their capabilities.

McGregor recognized that individual workers operated under a blend of theory X and theory Y. Thus, when management assumes all workers to be in the theory X camp it attempts to compensate for their human deficiencies by means of threats, punishments, discipline, and surveillance. The normal worker reaction to such an assumption is resistance, apathy, and a deliberate reduction in output. On the other hand, when management assumes that all workers are theory Y types it resorts to coaxing them through rewards, praise, and permissiveness. It does so at great risk, for the concept of theory Y is foreign to many managers and its application in the workplace involves continuous effort over a long period of time. Job enrichment was emphasized by McGregor, and his approach to motivation recognized that human nature was indeed more complex than most managers were willing to concede.

As a closing footnote to this brief history, a review of the practical approach to worker motivation by James F. Lincoln of the Lincoln Electric Company is appropriate. Many years ago the author visited with Lincoln and made an unescorted tour of the production area. One good example of a theory Y–type worker was the employee assigned to the task of assembling the gasoline tank and fittings for the engine driving an electrical generator which provided the power for electric welding. This individual was paid on a piecework basis, but operated almost as if he were running his own business. He proudly described innovations he had made in the assembly process and was extremely excited about the testing system he had devised to ensure that none of his output would be rejected because of errors or omissions in his work.

This attitude was prevalent throughout the plant and the record of the company over a period from the late 1930s to the 1950s seems to indicate that something was being done "right" at Lincoln Electric. The company's labor costs were well above those of its competitors, but the costs of its products were lower. In addition, Lincoln's motivational program had reduced labor turnover, increased worker output in terms of dollar sales value of products, and allowed the company to maintain an enviable position in the market.

Lincoln wrote a number of books detailing his approach to motivation; a brief quotation from one of them, (*A New Approach to Industrial Economics*, New York: The Devin-Adair Co., 1961,) is sufficient to get a feel for his approach:

> The problem that management has in applying incentive is to make sure that the program it uses is an incentive in the mind of the worker. Does he want to go along? It does not follow that because managers think they are applying a good program to the workers, the workers necessarily think so too. If the plan does not inspire the individual worker to feel that he wants to do his best on the job, and keep on doing so, the incentive is far from successful. The attitude of the wage-earner absolutely determines the success of any incentive program.
>
> What then are the components of a successful incentive? First, the worker must feel that he actually wants to work more efficiently and produce more. He must feel that greater efficiency will reward him in a satisfactory way. He will feel this only when his greater efficiency does in fact bring him greater rewards, both in money and other ways as well....
>
> The worker also must feel that greater efficiency will not in any way endanger his employment....Any incentive plan is useless if fear of a lay-off exists. That is still true even if the threat is imagined only in the worker's mind and does not actually exist.
>
> The incentives that are most potent when properly offered and believed in by the worker are the following:

First: Money in proportion to production.
Second: Status as a reward for achievement.
Third: Publicity of the worker's contribution in skill and imagination and the reward that is given for it. This results in added status for the worker.

APPLICATION OF MOTIVATION IN CONSTRUCTION

Starting with Gilbreth at the turn of the century, there are many examples of contractors using various forms of motivation. However, most of these were random, trial-and-error approaches using premium pay, bonuses, and other forms of recognition for work well done. Researchers seeking to develop organized programs for motivating construction workers really began to proliferate in the 1970s, often with the support of large construction clients and large construction firms. For the Business Roundtable's Construction Industry Cost Effectiveness Project, a contract was given to the University of Texas to conduct a literature review of motivational studies. The work was done by Dr. John D. Borcherding and Dr. Jimmie M. Hinze and reported in the brochure "Construction Labor Motivation," Report A-2, August, 1982. Most of the following information was taken from that report.

Borcherding's early studies were patterned after the approach of Herzberg and are reflected in a 1978 study for the Department of Energy by the University of Texas. More than 1000 craftsmen at 12 large industrial construction projects were interviewed and filled out questionnaires which were used to determine 11 motivators and 17 demotivators affecting work on construction projects. The results are summarized on the following page. It should be noted that valid data were not obtained from all of the projects.

It is important to note that many of these items played dual roles as both motivators and demotivators. Also, there is some similarity between several items on both lists. But, the lists can provide useful guidance to contractors interested in improving the productivity of their crews.

The Business Roundtable report indicates that the majority of motivational programs can be grouped under the following five categories: (1) goal setting, (2) incentives, (3) positive reinforcement (i.e., recognition for a job well done), (4) work participation, and (5) work facilitation. The report discusses each in terms of its use in other industries and in construction. The following is a quotation of the comments for construction.

Goal Setting The best way to set goals is for management to agree on attainable targets, based on the best historical performance for both quality and productivity. Unfortunately, few studies have been published about construction firms that have used this technique. But, the following two examples suggest some advantages of goal setting in construction projects:

Sixty 17- to 23-year-olds were hired to work individually on a two-hour construction task. They were assigned to one of two pay conditions (piece-work or hourly) and one of three goal setting conditions (no goal, quantity or quality). As expected, the method of payment was found to affect quantity performance and effort; goal setting affected quantity and quality performances and direction of behaviors.

Individual goals may be meshed with organizational goals through such rewards as money, promotion, work environment, praise or recognition. Yeargin Construction Company of Greenville, South Carolina used company goal setting to encourage new and higher working standards among its employees. The philosophy was:

Motivators	Number of projects with ratings of		
	Somewhat important	Major importance	Extremely important
Good craft relations	3	2	
Good orientation program	4	2	2
Good safety program	3	3	1
Work itself		6	1
Overtime			2
Ray	2	7	
Recognition	2		
Goals defined	4		
Open house and project tour	1	2	
Well-planned project	1	2	
Suggestions solicited	4	1	

Demotivators	Number of projects with ratings of		
	Somewhat important	Major importance	Extremely important
Disrespectful treatment	1	2	4
Little accomplishment	1	2	
Material availability	4	6	1
Tool availability	5	4	
Redoing work	7	2	
Crew discontinuity	2	3	
Project confusion	12		
Lack of recognition	5	2	
Productivity urged but no one cares	3	2	
Ineffective use of skills	3	2	
Incompetent personnel	7	4	
Lack of cooperation among crafts	3		2
Overcrowding	2		
Poor inspection programs	4		
Communications breakdown	6	5	
Unsafe conditions	4	4	
Lack of participation in decision making	5	1	

"What's good for our customer is good for us." New construction jobs secured by Yeargin meant more work for its employees.

Incentives Profit sharing appears to be the most frequent type of incentive program among construction companies. But the effectiveness of company-wide incentive systems is virtually impossible to determine. A University of Texas study issued in 1980 pointed out two drawbacks inherent in profit sharing programs: 1) profit is controlled more by outside than inside forces, and 2) such rewards are irregular and infrequent.

Worker Participation We endorse structured work-management programs through labor-management committees or quality circles, because they let workers identify and solve work problems. Quality circles programs lead, among other things, to cost-saving ideas, more job satisfaction, a more cohesive work unit, and improved quality control.

Writing in the American Society of Civil Engineers' "Construction Journal," John D Borcherding, a consultant to this study team, notes that construction may be the only industry where participative decision making should occur naturally because of the challenge of the work environment. Foremen have to make many day-to-day decisions; they must also participate with project management in establishing such job site policies as coffee breaks and crew sizes. Journeymen have an opportunity to participate in method selecting decisions and help to mesh the work done by different trades. Construction Contracting Magazine reported in 1979 that more than 50% of the work force believes it has a right to share in decision making about issues that affect them. In a recent productivity improvement survey of more than 500 managers, employee participation programs were ranked as the most effective way to boost productivity in construction.

Positive Reinforcement On average, craftsmen receive little or no recognition for their efforts. But studies based on extensive interviews indicate that it is very important for workers to know that management formally recognizes their work and especially that management appreciates extraordinary efforts.

Non-monetary recognition appears to be more effective than financial incentives for construction, because of the many difficulties associated with the latter, notably, of course, union objections. There appears to be only a few existing monetary incentive programs, mostly in residential construction. Non-monetary recognition can include craftsman-of-the-month awards. Individuals or crews can be recognized for outstanding quality and productivity by commendation letters or stickers—a subtle form of adult merit badge. An entire project can be recognized by banners, posters or newsletter articles aimed at instilling a sense of pride in the job.

Construction executives should consider motivational programs that recognize extra effort and resolve problems that lower productivity. The key elements of current construction management motivations include: 1) improved management efficiency and effectiveness, 2) eliminating demotivators and minimizing productivity constraints, 3) more planning and training, 4) improved communications through newsletters, posters, meetings, etc., 5) recognition, awards and monetary incentives. Some craftsmen may be less concerned about the dollar value of an award than with the visibility and prestige it confers.

Work Facilitation Construction workers can best be motivated through the satisfactions inherent in construction work itself. Dissatisfaction must be eased before any added motivators become effective because an individual construction worker will not be motivated if he is strongly dissatisfied. For journeymen and apprentices, managerial insistence on good workmanship should provide considerable motivation. Though a productive day may leave some workers physically exhausted, there are offsetting benefits such as good social relations on the job. Demotivation is caused by strained interpersonal relationships among crew members and unfair job assignments, and usually results in a poor work performance.

Job motivators for foremen should include the challenge of running the work, maintaining the job schedule, good workmanship, and the physical taking shape, and good work relationships within a crew. Job demotivators would include uncooperative workmen, union problems, lack of initiative in workmen, lack of management support (i.e., absence of engineering information or the timely availability of materials and equipment).

The report concludes with recommendations stating, "It is fully recognized that contractors have the primary responsibility for the execution of onsite work activities of their craftsmen. Owners, on the other hand, have a self interest in these matters because of the direct effect on the cost of these activities." The following recommendations established the basic role of owners and contractors in order to obtain a cost effective construction labor motivation program.

For owner action

1. Enthusiastically support a labor motivation program. Provide site management supportive of motivation concept principles

2. Assist in eliminating demotivation items such as late design, design changes, work environment, etc.

3. Establish clear, open, and effective communication systems to the project.

4. Provide representation on the site motivation steering committee.

5. Provide opportunities for recognition for efficient work practices.

6. Insist on and/or provide good working conditions.

7. Insist on and support an effective safety program.

8. Consider the use of consultants to assist in program development and implementation.

For contractor action

1. Implement a construction labor motivation program and provide site management supportive of motivation concept principles.

2. Establish a steering committee.

3. Effectively choose and train first- and second-level supervision.

4. Incorporate the use of the foreman delay survey concept to identify those demotivators affecting the work force. After identifying demotivators, the contractor should diligently pursue opportunities for eliminating the demotivators and provide feedback information to the foreman and crews.

5.. Provide open communication lines. Consider project orientation, newsletters, suggestion boxes, bulletin boards, etc.

6. Provide and maintain good working conditions.

7. Establish an effective safety program.

8. Formally recognize efficient work practice.

DO MOTIVATIONAL PROGRAMS WORK?

Monsanto is one of several large corporations that have insisted on its contractors using motivational programs. They have brought in consultants to work with their own staff and their contractors' staffs to develop sound motivational programs on their projects, following all of the recommendations listed above. They have achieved success on both union- and open-shop projects and on lump-sum contracts and time and materials contracts under such program names as:

TOPS: Teamwork-Optimum Performance-Skills

PULL: Performance with Union Labor and Leadership

CHAMP: Craftsmen Helping America Maximize Production

The following comments from both union officials and craftsmen on a CHAMP project are worth noting.

Union official: "I've never seen anything like it in my 40 years in the building trades. I can only speak for the men, you could not pry them off the job. Monsanto deserves five stars for what they have done."

Union official: "I talked to various trades on the job and was really impressed. I hope what Monsanto and Fruin-Colnon have done rubs off on other clients and contractors."

Craftsman: "This is the first time I've been thanked for anything."

Craftsman: "It will be up to us to show other contractors the good work we've always done. CHAMP just makes us feel better about getting there and getting the job done."

Craftsman: "If half of what we do here on this job spreads to the other general contractors, St. Louis will be a better place to live."

On a more quantitative level, Monsanto officials report that on one of their projects absenteeism averaged less than 3 percent in spite of the worst winter weather in decades. Turnover rates averaged less than 1 percent and foreman delay survey trends indicated delay reductions from approximately 20 percent per man per week to approximately 5 percent. Most of the credit for these positive statistics is directly attributed to the motivation program in operation for the duration of the project.

CHAPTER 24
TAXES

Arnold S. Page, CPA
Page, Weaver & Carter, P.A.
106F Centre Boulevard
Marlton, New Jersey

INTRODUCTION

A general understanding of the tax system is extremely important to contractors. Taxes have a major impact on business operations, not only in terms of cash flow and budgeting, but also as a major component of a firm's overhead, also referred to as selling, general, and administrative expenses. The ability to accurately analyze and calculate overhead rates is essential to the process of competitive bidding. Moreover, the ability to manage and control overhead costs plays a crucial role in the firm's profitability. As discussed in this chapter, taxes are subject to varying degrees of management and control, and should not be viewed as a fixed cost about which nothing can be done.

For purposes of this discussion, business taxes are grouped into three major categories: federal income tax, state and local taxes (income, sales and use, property), and employment taxes. There are also various types of excise and special-purpose taxes which may apply to some businesses, but these are usually minor or incidental to other costs. Foreign taxes are, of course, a concern of multinational operations but are beyond the scope of this chapter.

FEDERAL INCOME TAX

It is assumed that the contractor's business is incorporated. A small start-up business may initially operate as a proprietorship or partnership, but the exposure to potential litigation in today's environment normally encourages incorporation very early in the firm's existence. The legal authority to operate as a corporation is granted by the respective states. The corporation's tax status, on the other hand, is determined by federal statute, currently the Internal Revenue Code of 1986 (the Code). There are two types of corporations that the contractor must consider for tax purposes: a regular corporation under Subchapter C of the Code (referred to as a "C" corporation), or an electing corporation under Subchapter S of the Code (referred to as an "S" corporation).

With respect to C corporations, the current federal income-tax rates (in 1989) are as follows:

15 percent on the first $50,000 of taxable income

25 percent on the next $25,000

34 percent on the next $25,000

39 percent on the next $235,000

34 percent on income in excess of $335,000

The effect of this tax system is to impose a 5 percent surtax on income between $100,000 and $335,000, so that all income in excess of $335,000 will be taxed at a flat rate of 34 percent from the first dollar. It should be mentioned at this point that a C corporation may have the misfortune of being categorized as a personal service corporation (PSC) if its owners provide a significant amount of the services delivered by the firm to clients. Architect and engineering firms, but not construction firms, might fall into this category. The result is that all income of a PSC is taxed at the 34 percent rate from the first dollar, eliminating any benefit derived from lower rates on income less than $100,000. Being a PSC would not be disadvantageous for firms whose annual taxable income consistently exceeds $335,000.

It can be seen from the tax rate structure described above that the most beneficial rates for a closely held corporation (where reported earnings per share may not be a primary concern) occur when taxable income falls below $100,000, or at least below $335,000. This can sometimes be accomplished by judicious use of bonuses to key employees and contributions to qualified pension plans. There are, of course, both statutory and practical limitations on the use of these techniques, and expert tax advice should be sought before implementing any plan which may have tax implications.

Another tax alternative is to elect S-corporation status. Various criteria must be met to qualify for this election, for example, no more than 35 shareholders who generally must be U.S. individuals, and only one class of stock issued (different voting rights are allowed). The tax result is similar to that of a partnership, in that net income or loss and credits flow through to the owners and are not taxed at the corporate level. Rather, the owners (shareholders in the case of S corporations) report these items on their individual income-tax returns and are taxed at their individual tax rates. This can be a major advantage for shareholders subject to the 28 percent individual rate (or the 21 percent alternative minimum tax rate). Under current law, the difference between the C corporation rate of 34 percent and the individual rate of 28 percent can result in substantial aggregate tax savings over time.

The federal income tax is not deductible for tax purposes, and thus it must be added back to the C corporation's net book income in determining taxable income. Similarly, the federal income tax is not allowable as a cost in determining overhead rates under government accounting principles. This is not the case for state and local or employment taxes discussed below, most of which are allowable as federal tax deductions and as includable costs in the overhead rate.

STATE AND LOCAL TAXES

State and local taxes can in many cases impose a significant cost on the business. Most state corporate income tax rates are in the range of 5 to 10 percent. If business is conducted in more than one state, the corporation is required to allocate its income to the various states. This is done by an apportionment formula, usually based on three factors: sales, payroll, and property. Ideally, the apportionment factors for all the states in which business is conducted should add up to 100 percent, resulting in no double tax. In practice, the total factors often exceed 100 percent because the states have different methods of calculating the factors and require different types of adjustments to the federal income tax base. These different methods and adjustments are usually designed to maximize the allocation which must be made to each state. Thus, it is important for the multistate contractor to make sure that sufficient tax expertise is brought to bear in this area to minimize the overall tax burden. It should be noted here that most states follow the federal treatment of S corporations (i.e., income taxed at the shareholder rather than corporate level). Nevertheless, several states do not recognize this status, so contractors should be advised as to where in their area of operations they may be responsible for state corporate income tax despite the federal election.

Many cities impose their own income or business tax. Some, such as New York City, base the tax primarily on net income. Others, such as San Francisco and Los Angeles, base it on payroll or gross receipts factors. Philadelphia bases its tax on both net income and gross receipts. For contractors doing business in cities which impose tax, the combination of state and city taxes can often exceed 15 percent of allocated taxable income. The city allocation calculations obviously deserve the same degree of tax expertise as those of the state referred to above.

Sales and use taxes are imposed by most states and some cities, typically in the range of 4 to 8 percent. Sales tax is no longer tax-deductible, and therefore this cost is added to the cost of the asset purchased (e.g., office equipment, furniture, vehicles). Most states do not impose sales tax on professional services or on the sale of real property. Thus, many contractors are spared the administrative chore of collecting sales tax from customers and paying it over to the state. There are exceptions to this general rule, however; contractors should make sure they are informed about their sales tax collection responsibilities, as penalties for noncompliance can be very onerous.

Taxes on real estate owned by the business are levied by virtually every local jurisdiction. Some cities also impose tax on the value of tangible personal property (e.g., equipment and furniture), and other jurisdictions may tax intangible assets (e.g., stocks, bonds, and notes, and mortgages receivables). These types of local taxes are generally deductible for income-tax purposes.

EMPLOYMENT TAXES

Both the federal and state governments require employers to fund certain benefit programs. At the federal level, the employer payed social security tax at a rate of 7.51 percent in 1989 (this increased to 7.65 percent in 1990) on the first $48,000 of each employee's wages. Both the tax rate and the wage ceiling have increased substantially in recent years, and additional increases are scheduled for the future. The federal unemployment tax rate (net of state unemployment tax credit) is a relatively modest 0.8 percent on the first $7,000 of each employee's wages.

The states generally impose both an unemployment and disability tax on employers. In many states the employee is required to pay a portion (usually a minor portion) of these taxes via payroll withholding. The rates of these taxes are based on experience factors (i.e., the amount of benefit claims filed by the employer's employees), and these rates can vary significantly. High employee turnover and/or disability can result in tax rates in the 5 to 7 percent range, whereas 3 to 4 percent would normally be expected.

Employers must also pay worker's compensation premiums, which are based on job description categories. This cost is technically not a tax, but it is directly attributable to employment and is considered part of payroll overhead along with the other taxes described above.

In summary, employment taxes are a significant overhead item which can add 10 percent or more to the gross payroll cost. Contractors should have a knowledgeable person oversee the administration of this area. Proper handling of claims can help keep rates from escalating. Timely deposits of payroll taxes and filing of reports are essential; penalties are automatically imposed on late payments and on late report filing.

TAX PLANNING

As indicated above, there are opportunities for the contractor to influence, and in some cases control, the amount and timing of various tax payments due. At the outset, it should be emphasized that taxation is a complex discipline, subject to frequent statutory change. It is imperative for the contractor to avail himself of expertise, through either outside professionals (CPA and/or tax attorney) or in-house staff, or both. Tax planning cannot effectively be done in a vacuum; it must be based on the actual situation and circumstances of each business. This is why it is important to obtain specific advice from advisers thoroughly familiar with the contractor's business.

Tax planning begins with the initial decisions reached as to form of business (i.e., proprietorship, partnership, S corporation, C corporation) and methods of tax accounting. Accounting methods are discussed in detail in Chap. 17. The same methods are often used for tax purposes, but there can be significant differences. For example, it may be possible to use the accrual method for financial statement purposes and the cash method for tax purposes. Another difference may involve the method of accounting for long-term contracts. Under the percentage-completion method, estimated profits are reflected as income as the work progresses, whereas under the completed-contract method, profits are only reflected as income upon completion of the work. The latter method results in a deferral of taxable income, and therefore it has been widely used by contractors for tax purposes. However, recent tax legislation has significantly curtailed the benefit of using this method for firms with over $10,000,000 in annual gross receipts.

There also can be differences in book and tax accounting for specific items, such as depreciation, bad debts, inventory, leases, etc. The objective of using a tax-specific accounting method is usually to minimize or defer tax payments. Contractors should satisfy themselves that these methods are being used advantageously if appropriate to their particular business. This is perfectly legitimate as long as the method is a recognized one which is used consistently; the company cannot arbitrarily swing from one type to another from year to year.

Many other aspects of business also involve tax considerations. This is particularly true with respect to executive compensation, retirement programs, health plans, and other fringe benefits. As companies grow, increased attention must be focused on this whole area from a budgetary point of view, because costs can easily escalate out of control. Employers cannot afford the additional cost of a retirement or health program that does not comply with the tax law requirements as to eligibility, funding, and various nondiscrimination aspects. Noncompliance can result in disqualification of the benefit plan, which means that tax deductions for plan expenses are disallowed.

Despite the technical complexities of our tax laws, the fundamentals of how much is due and when should be determined and budgeted reasonably in advance. Tax planning with the contractor's tax advisers is a requisite to sound financial management. Regular liaison between the contractor's internal accounting/tax department and the external tax advisers is important. This close relationship can generate cash flow protection for a growing business and help conserve cash for an established one.

TAX ADMINISTRATION AND COMPLIANCE

Tax Department

As the company increases in size and tax requirements become more complex, it becomes difficult, if not impossible, for the contractor to effectively administer corporate taxes without trained personnel. The cost of making errors can be substantial; in attempting to follow technically written rules and regulations, mistakes can be made in either direction. If taxes are inadvertently overpaid, they may never be recovered. This is particularly true if the overpayment occurs due to a judgmental interpretation rather then an arithmetical error. Even if the error is detected within the statute of limitation period, costs are incurred for the preparation and filing of the claim for refund and for the use of money while held by the government. If taxes are underpaid, the consequences can be more severe. If the underpayment is discovered during an audit, penalties and interest are usually assessed, and additional tax periods may be audited in depth to determine whether similar underpayments occurred; if discovered by IRS or state computer review, it could generate an audit that may not otherwise have occurred.

To cope with these potential pitfalls, the contractor should establish a specialized tax department or group. At the small company level, this can be accomplished by utilization of clerical or accounting help to organize and maintain basic records such as receivables, payables, general ledger, and so on. Outside expertise (such as a CPA) can be retained to prepare or review tax filings and for consultation, as needed. An outside payroll-tax service could also be retained for processing payroll and generating the required payroll-tax reports. These outside services are generally very cost-effective. With the complexity of payroll taxes, particularly for multistate operations, usually only the largest companies can justify the cost of hardware, software, and expert personnel required to adequately maintain in-house payroll capability.

Larger companies generally establish tax departments, either as part of the controller's group or as a separate group reporting directly to the chief financial officer. Outside expertise, CPAs, and/or tax attorneys, can be used as necessary to augment the contractor's staff when dealing with complex issues or audits. The centralization of expertise and decision-making capability in one group is important in the development of cohesive information and documentation for the preparation of required tax reports and conduct of audits.

TAX-FILING COMPLIANCE

Businesses are required by statute to file returns and report information to the various government agencies. Income taxes in our country are basically self-assessed; it is the responsibility of each taxpaying person or entity to accurately report, in an organized fashion, the items of income and expense that determine taxable income. The taxpayer then pays tax on that self-determined income. The tax reporting and paying system is not left to chance, however. As discussed below, IRS and other government agencies conduct periodic audits to ensure proper compliance with the law.

In addition to filing income tax and other types of returns, businesses also have been assigned the responsibility of collecting taxes and fees for the various government agencies. Our tax system relies on employers to withhold and pay over federal and state income taxes, as well as the social security (FICA) tax. When applicable, sales and use taxes must also be collected and paid over to the state. It is the responsibility of the contractor to determine the applicability of all tax collection and filing in its geographical areas of operations.

COMPLIANCE AUDITS

Contractors become involved in various types of compliance audits relatively frequently. With this business fact of life in mind, the accounting system should be designed, and refined as necessary, to produce effectively the types of summarized information and reports responsive to these audits. A properly organized system can save countless hours of both clerical and professional time. Some commonly encountered audits are briefly discussed below.

Tax-Authority Audits and Examinations

In addition to maintaining and recording information for use by the contractor's management, the accounting personnel must record data and information in a manner that will meet with the various tax authorities' requirements. The IRS will audit the income-tax returns as filed on behalf of the contractor and will also review and examine the quarterly reports of payroll taxes remitted. In addition, each of the respective states and local subdivisions may audit the income, gross receipts, capital stock, and franchise taxes levied on companies doing business within their jurisdiction.

Of all the problems inherent in business, few are viewed with more distaste and apprehension by the taxpayer than the "tax audit," involving a review of income-tax-return files with either the IRS or some state or local authority. In the normal course of time, a contractor, like any other taxpayer, may expect a routine examination of the income-tax returns filed on its behalf. Such examinations should be accepted in the context of their true relationship to all business activities and met with proper preparation and the correct attitude. Whether the examination is to be held at the offices of the tax authority or in the field—that is, at the place of business, the general process will be similar. Revenue agents conducting an examination can be expected to be professional, impersonal, and quite equitable in their questioning and seeking of data. With few exceptions, these agents are competent, specific, and direct and reasonable in making determinations. Areas where deductions are prescribed by the law and code requiring strict records and supporting data will be fully examined (e.g. travel, meals, entertainment, promotion, donations), and a complete adherence to the requirements will be necessary to sustain deductions. Backup data and records necessary to support all such deductions must be made available to sustain a complete allowance of expenses. It is usually unwise for a company to conduct a tax examination of its returns with its own personnel exclusively. The problem of personal emotional involvement precludes the professional deportment and expertise which will present the contractor's records and their import in the best light. The services of the contractor's tax consultant should be obtained and utilized to prepare the information for presentation and to conduct the actual audit, since he is more familiar with tax audit procedures than the average financial officer of a taxpayer.

Every audit by a cognizant tax authority will be based solely on the law and the applicable code insofar as interpreted by the courts. Examining agents do not indulge in personal animosities; nevertheless, there are occasions when there is a divergence of opinion between the agent and the taxpayer and his representatives as to the correctness or propriety of items as claimed. When such an impasse arises, there are mechanics available, using the IRS as an example, to have the information in dispute reviewed at higher administrative levels. Assuming the contractor's audit is being conducted in an IRS office and he does not agree with the findings (conclusions) of the examining agent, within a stipulated time (presently 15 days) he has a right to request a conference with a member of the conference staff. If his audit has been conducted entirely by mail, as some office audits are, he should commence his discussions of the findings with an auditor who will be assigned to hold a meeting with him before any conference staff meeting is requested. If the contractor has disagreed with the findings of an agent who has conducted the audit either at his office or at the office of his accountant, upon receipt of his report he may also request a conference with the conference staff. In either event, the contractor must specifically write and request the additional meetings and discussions. The time limit for objecting to or "protesting" an agent's report in these circumstances is 30 days. Subsequent to the conference level, should the contractor still not agree with the original findings as reviewed, he has a right to continue to the appellate section for a hearing. Should this level of review not conclude a finding that is acceptable, the taxpayer has recourse to the federal court system, either through the tax court or the federal district court depending upon the advice of tax counsel.

In addition to the disallowance of expenses or the inclusion of income which gives rise to income-tax assessments, the IRS may assess penalties for negligence or for civil fraud in connection with an audit. The assessment of penalties is statutory and can be the subject of requests for review; however, the basis for review will be limited to the law applicable—hence more narrow in concept and discussion than those associated with the review of tax-deficiency assessments.

Insurance Audits

Worker's compensation insurance is mandatory for all contractors in every state. Usually such insurance is placed on a contractor-furnished estimate of total wages by general category for a given period times a rate factor determined by the insurance carrier. As a requirement of the policy issued, an audit of the contractor's records is utilized to determine the accuracy of the estimate, revise the billing, and determine the correct final invoicing for a period. This type of policy is issued on an annual basis with audit cognizance on the anniversary date. Normally, this audit includes reference to payroll-tax returns as filed and is conducted with the contractor's internal staff. Bonding-company requirements for issuance of the required performance or surety bonds for certain types of work are usually met with the furnishing of the company's financial statements. Should any audit reliance be required, the contractor's independent accountant can augment any support required by the contractor's staff.

Customer Cost Audits or Cost-Auditable Prime Contracts

Contracts issued to a contractor on a "cost-plus" or "time and material" basis as well as other contracts often contain a clause granting the customer a right of audit of costs incurred. The contractor himself may use such a contract clause with his own subcontractors. When the contractor is granted a contract which contains accounting provisions for costs and audit of records, any contracts issued by the contractor to his subcontractors should contain and repeat these clauses, as the customer has a right to audit the subcontracts issued in the performance of his contract. The usual audit program contains the following principal examinations.

Verification of Wage Rates and Classifications. The propriety of charges for wages paid is determined by examination of the contractor's records to determine the job classifications and rates assigned to each employee regardless of his assignment and to ensure equality of charge to every contract in performance by the contractor. Canceled payroll checks and supporting pay-time records are examined as well to determine the accuracy of time charges, extensions of rates and hours, and completeness of records. A check of employees on the job as part of an unannounced audit may also be undertaken as part of the audit of reliability of payroll records.

Payroll-Tax and Fringe-Benefit Costs. Where the basic contract specifies a "fringe and payroll tax factor or rate," the assessment of costs to a specific contract presents no auditing problem. Where the basic contract is silent as to rate, the actual payroll-tax returns and payments to various health plans and other benefit payments must be examined. In the case of "fringes," the usual payment is expressed as either a percentage of wages paid or per capita assessment by a specific pay period. In the case of federal and state payroll taxes, since both tax bases have an exclusion after an employee reaches a predetermined amount of earnings each year, wages paid during the latter part of a calendar year may be excluded from taxable reporting of a contractor because of the wage base reportable. Where the labor force of a contractor is fairly stable, the most equitable basis for payroll-tax cost assessment is the overall average rate based on annual earnings. Where there are wide variations in employment levels, specific calculations should be used.

Depreciation and Amortization Charges. While most contracts are silent as to the specific method, depreciation usually will be allowable as a cost to the contracts as part of the overhead rate. As a general rule, the depreciation and amortization charges established by a contractor may be reviewed in the light of being allowed as part of the overhead cost as long as the method of charging for them is in conformity with generally accepted accounting principles (GAAP) and is uniform in application.

Discounts, Refunds, and Allowances. All discounts, refunds, and allowances should be recorded to indicate clearly the source and type on the books of the contractor. As a part of the audit procedure for discounts, adequate receiving reports for all vendor-delivered material properly supported by invoices and purchase orders or contracts to verify prices and terms must be maintained and will be audited as part of this program.

Inventory Credits and Rental Cutoff. The contractor's records must clearly indicate the inventory of material and supplies purchased for a contract on hand at the completion of the work effort, and its location, condition, and value. The inventory records maintained by the contractor must be self-supporting and capable of audit and the method of valuation must be in conformity with GAAP. The cutoff date for rental items should be clearly defined and supported by documents; any final credits or charges should be defined and related to the rental contracts which will be examined.

Other Direct Charges. Depending on the terms of the basic contract, certain items of travel, telephone, permits, site costs, etc., are permitted as direct charges to the customer. Such items should be examined and audited to determine the accuracy of charges made and to preclude inclusion of same in the allowable overhead pools for charging. The contract may also allow certain overhead charges as expenses to be recovered, as well as direct wages, materials, subcontracting, etc. The audit should rigidly adhere to the allowing of only those items specifically contained in the overhead pool to be recovered as part of the cost.

Regulatory Audits

Contractors are subject to federal and state wage and hour laws as well as specific statutes pertaining to contracts issued by various governmental agencies. From time to time these agencies will audit the records of a contractor to determine compliance with the federal or state wage and hour or equal employment opportunity (EEO) laws. The records of the contractor, hiring and firing practices, time cards, payroll sheets, payroll checks, and all other relevant data will be audited. Every contractor should seek counsel from his accountant and attorney continuously to prevent inadvertent failure of compliance with these rules and regulations. In addition to the wage and hour audits, certain union fringe-benefit requirements give the union the right of audit to determine the correctness of payments made. Such audits are limited to the subject of the payment and the supporting payroll records and can usually be conducted by the contractor's office staff.

As a general summary, most cost auditing is assigned to the internal staff auditors, if the contractor's business is large enough to warrant it, or to the contractor's outside accountant. In either case, the contractor's professional consultants should be utilized in determining the method of audit and the audit program and in reviewing areas of disagreement.

CHAPTER 25
CLAIMS AND LITIGATION

James J. O'Brien, P.E.
Chairman of the Board
O'Brien-Kreitzberg & Associates, Inc.
Pennsauken, New Jersey

The critical path method can be utilized to evaluate actual claims situations through the reconstruction of a project's history or the use of an existing CPM plan to indicate the effects of change on the original schedule.

In one example, a contractor consortium was asked by a bridge authority to show cause why it should not be pressed for $550,000 in liquidated damages. Actually, the authority felt the contractor had done a good job, but because of the public trust involved, the authority also felt that it needed tangible proof of this good performance. To respond, the contractor used a construction CPM plan to demonstrate the effects of three different unforeseen circumstances: unusually bad weather, loss of special equipment by fire, and time lost in doing work claims as extra. The presentation demonstrated the combined effect of the three causes (which, of course, was less than the serial effect) and the effects of any one or two of them alone and together. Thus, if any one or two of the factors had been deemed unacceptable, the effect of the remaining factor or factors was still quantified. On the basis of this finite presentation, the bridge commission did not press for the liquidated damages.

In negotiating extra work, contractors often neglect the effects the change order will have on working time, so that they have requested either no time extension or an extension equaling the total period they estimate the additional work will required. Generally speaking, however, extra work on a project affects float areas, and any time extension granted should be less than the total incremental time needed to complete the additional work. At Cape Canaveral, the combined emphasis on time and public pressure for completion of projects reversed this situation. Contractors recognized the time-money relationships and usually made substantial requests for additional time as well as for extra money to implement changes. The Corps of Engineers and NASA required network analysis for the basic work on most of the major projects undertaken there. Thus most of the contractors prepared network-oriented fragnets to demonstrate the effects that additional work would have on scheduling. Although there were abuses, in the long run CPM was used by both parties to evaluate requests for time extensions, and many claims were settled without the drudgery of formal legal suits.

The type of contract originally signed for a project has an impact on whether or not there is a potential for easy resolution or settlement of claims should they arise. Claims relating to construction management and negotiated contracts in the private sector can often be resolved by means of an objective report, based upon schedules and other factual information. Such objective evaluation is important not only in regard to the legalities of the settlement proceedings, but as documentation for proving to both plaintiff and defendant that a proper settlement has been reached. However, claims in the public sector are usually not so easily settled, and disputes there are increasingly running the full course of litigation.

DELAY

The principal dimension measured by schedules is delay. In years past, delay in the completion of construction used to be a mutually accepted condition; even the courts on occasion recognized that delay was a normal situation in the construction process.

Today, however, with tight budgets on the part of owners, who usually want to expend their funds right up to the limits of their budgets but no further, and the real costs contractors encounter in staying on the job longer than planned, delay is a very problematic area. When delays occur during construction, the parties involved attempt to shift the costs that result onto each other. If litigation results after negotiating fails, the lawsuits are between two (or more) losers, both of whom are attempting to mitigate their losses. There are no winners in delay.

To the private owner, delay can mean a loss of revenues through the resulting lack of production facilities and rentable space, as well as through a continuing dependence on present facilities. To the public owner, it can mean that a building or facility is not available for the use to which it needs to be put at the proper time. The service revenues lost through delay can never be recovered. To the contractor, delay means higher overhead costs that result from the longer construction period, higher prices for materials resulting from inflation, and escalation costs due to labor cost increases. Further, working capital and bonding capacity are tied up so that other projects cannot be undertaken.

Responsibility for Delay

The assignment of responsibility for delay after the fact is usually difficult, and the courts have often remarked that delay should be anticipated in any construction project. Traditionally, the courts have protected owners more than contractors. No-damage-for-delay clauses have often been enforced, with the contractors receiving only time extensions when delays occurred. However, the granting of time extensions avoids another owner-oriented remedy for problems connected with delay: liquidated damages. Even with courts that are included to consider recovery of damages for owner-caused delays, the burden is on the contractor to prove active interference on the part of the owner in order to receive a favorable decision.

There are four general categories of responsibility

1. Owner (or owner's agents) responsible
2. Contractor (or subcontractors) responsible

3. Neither contractual part responsible

4. Both contractual parties responsible

In cases where the owner (or owner's agents) has (have) caused the delay, the courts may find that the language of the contract, in the form of the typical no-damage-for-delay clause, protects the owner from having to pay damages but requires a compensatory time extension to protect the contractor from having to pay liquidated damages. If the owner can be proven guilty of interfering with the contractor's progress on the project or has committed a breach of contract, however, the contractor can probably recover damages from the owner.

If the contractor (or subcontractors) causes (cause) the delay, the contract language does not generally offer the contractor protection against litigation on the part of the owner to recover damages.

If the delay is caused by forces beyond the control of either party to the contract, the finding generally is that each party must bear the brunt of its own damages.

If both parties to the contract contribute to the delay or cause concurrent delays, the usual finding is that the delays offset one another. An exception to this would occur in those instances where the damages can be clearly and distinctly separated, although the courts are not quick to allow such distinctions.

Types of Delay

There are three basic types of delay: classic, concurrent, and serial.

Classic delay occurs when a period of idleness and/or uselessness is imposed upon the contracted-for work. In *Grand Investment Co. v. United States* (102 Ct. Cl. U.S. 40; 1944), the government issued a stop order by telegraph to the contractor that resulted in a work stoppage of 109 days. The contractor sued for damages caused by the delay, basing the suit on a claim of breach of contract. The court found that the stop order was not justified and thus resulted in a breach of the government's obligations in the contract. The court allowed, among other things, a damage due to the loss of utilization of equipment on the job site, finding inability to utilized equipment on the job site, and stating

> When the government in breach of its contract, in effect, condemned a contractor's valuable and useful machines for a period of idleness and uselessness . . . it should make compensation comparable to what would be required if it took the machines for use for a temporary period.

Johnson v. Fenestra (305 F. 2d 179, 181; 3d Cir. 1962) also involved a classic delay: Workers were idled by the failure of the general contractor to supply materials. This type of delay, to be legally recognized as such, must be substantial, involving an essential segment of the work to be done, and it must remain a problem for an unreasonable amount of time.

Generally, if two parties claim *concurrent delays,* the court will not try to unravel the factors involved and will disallow the claims by both parties. In *United States v. Citizens and Southern National Bank* (367 F.2d 473; 1966), a subcontractor was able to show delay damages caused by the general contractor. However, the general contractor in turn was able to demonstrate that portions of the damages were caused by the factors for which he was not responsible. In the absence of clear evidence separating the two claims, the court rejected both, stating: "As the evidence does not provide any reasonable basis for allocating the additional costs among those contributing factors, we conclude that the entire claim should have been rejected."

Similarly, in *Lichter v. Mellon-Stuart* (305 F. 2d 216; 3d Cir. 1962), the court found that the facts supported evidence of delay imposed upon a subcontractor by a general contractor. However, it also found that the work had been delayed by a number of other factors including change orders, delays caused by other trades, and strikes. The subcontractor had based its claim for damages solely upon the delay imposed by the general contractor, and both the trial court and the appeals court rejected the claim on the following basis:

> Even if one could find from the evidence that one or more of the interfering contingencies was a wrongful act on the part of the defendant, no basis appears for even an educated guess as to the increased costs . . . due to that particular breach . . . as distinguished from those causes from which defendant is contractually exempt.

It should be noted, however, that in recent decisions, the courts increasingly have demonstrated a willingness to allocate responsibility for concurrent delays.

Serial delay is a linkage of delays (or sometimes of different causes of a delay). Thus, the effects of one delay might be amplified by a later delay. For instance, if an owner's representative delays reviewing shop drawings, and the resulting delay causes the project to drift into a strike or a period of severe weather resulting in further delays, a court might find the owner liable for the total serial delay resulting from the initial incremental delay.

Force Majeure Causes

Force majeure causes include what are known as "acts of God." The general contract usually provides a list of such events: fires, strikes, earthquakes, tornadoes, floods, and similar unforeseen circumstances. Should they occur, the contract provides for a mutual relief from demands for damages due to delay and the owner is obligated to provide a reasonable (usually a day-for-day) time extension.

In the case of weather-related delays, usually only those occurrences shown to be beyond the average weather conditions expected for the area based upon past records can be considered as a reason for time extensions. However, this can vary with contract language. A number of states and cities allow a day-for-day extension (noncompensable) for all bad weather.

Many contracts have clauses stating that time extension for delay caused by "acts of God" shall be granted only to those portions of the projects that are specifically affected by such events. Thus, a severe downpour after a site has been graded and drained and the building closed in may cause no actual delay, so that claims for time extensions because of it would not be accepted even though it would qualify under other methods of evaluation as a force majeure act.

CPM-ORIENTED ANALYSIS

The critical path method (CPM) can be useful in establishing the facts, and also the intentions, of the parties to a contract. This is the most important part of the

CPM network, because it describes the manner in which the contractor intended to meet the requirements of the contract at the start of the project. The network can be used by the owner to demonstrate areas of failure on the part of the contractor, and can be used by the contractor to demonstrate points of interference on the part of the owner (or owner's agents).

A project involving regular (usually monthly) reviews or updatings of the CPM plan should provide a good basis, through the CPM reports, for evaluating the progress of the work done on it. Unfortunately, many such projects have only a collection of CPM diagrams and computer runs to show for those reviews. The CPM reports are far more valuable if each updating is accompanied by a comprehensive narrative. These narratives, which should be normal portions of the project documentation, are prepared in the normal order of business—and therefore can be accepted later at face value, with due weight given to their origins.

It is not unusual for the CPM scheduling team to periodically readjust the schedule of a project to attempt to maintain the end date or to accommodate problems and unexpected situations. When looking at those periods of rescheduling, it can appear that the project either was on schedule or had not fallen further behind schedule, while in reality the dates were being revised in terms of the overall plan but did not necessarily reflect the true progress on the project.

As-Planned and As-Built Schedules

A first step in utilizing CPM to analyze what happed on a project is to set up the initially approved plan in network form. If the original network was small (1000 or fewer activities), it is merely recomputerized to confirm the initially scheduled dates. If the network was larger, particularly in the range of 5000 to 10,000 activities, milestone points should be identified and a summary of activities prepared. A summary CPM network of 1000 or fewer activities equivalent to the detailed major network can be developed.

When the activities on the as-planned network have been identified, work can start on an as-built network. This second network should include the same activities as the first, for comparison purposes, but should be based upon actual performance dates. These dates are researched from the updatings of the original CPM plan, the progress reports, and any other documentation available. Sparse or faulty project documentation makes development of an accurate as-built network difficult. (For this reason, CPM updating should plug in actual dates for all activities as they start and are completed.) The as-built network is drawn to the same time scale, and organized in the same arrangement, as the as-planned network. The two can now be compared directly.

The work involved in preparing these two schedules will vary with the input information available, its organization, and the information on the levels of the work provided by the client and/or the client's attorney. From two to five people will be needed to work on them, over a period of 1 to 3 months. The work should be under the direction of a CPM scheduling professional who is qualified to testify in regard to the final products.

With the completion of the as-planned and as-built schedules, a uniform format for the evaluation of the causative factors in the delay is now available. The identity of most of the causative factors should be readily apparent, but the specific impact of different factors may not be as obvious.

Identification of Causative Factors

One of the first areas to be identified is force majeure. The most common areas for this in construction projects are strikes and bad weather. Strikes should be documented in terms of their lengths, the remobilization time it takes when they are over, and the trades and areas of work affected by them. Most contracts provide for time extensions due to strikes, but not for compensation. In the case of a contractor making a claim, it would be important to be able to demonstrate that a strike had little or no impact on the critical path of a project, so that other compensable factors could be shown to be the cause of the damages being claimed. Conversely, an owner defending against claims should be able to demonstrate that strikes did indeed cause the delays, and other problems were at worst concurrent.

Change Orders.   Change orders are evaluated in terms of the specific impacts they have on the progress of a project. This is done in two ways. First, a determination is made of the point in the network at which a particular change order impacted on the field work. In addition, activities are identified which were preparatory for implementing the change order, such as change-order proposals, the ordering of material, mobilization, and any other preimplementation factors. Next, the change order's impact is identified in terms of the amount of the labor portion of the work activity being evaluated if it is identified either in the bid estimate or approved progress payment breakdown. The worker-hours involved in implementing the change are then determined by multiplying the typical crew size by the number of hours it took to complete the work item.

A separate evaluation is done for every change order in the project. In addition to identifying the basic impact each has had on the plan, it is necessary that the analysis also identify the times of issue of the individual change orders' notices to proceed. In each case, if that is later than the late start date of the affected activity, it is obvious that the change order had the potential to delay the project. And in fact, it probably did delay it unless there were methods to work around the change—methods that must themselves be demonstrated to have been used.

Stop Orders.   Another area to be researched is stop orders or suspensions. These are applied to a network in the form of actual dates, or as activities inserted in the stream of activities affected.

Time Impact Evaluation

When all the causative factors have been identified, a time impact evaluation (TIE) is prepared for each one. The information is assembled as described previously, and prepared in a format such that the impact of each factor on the as-planned network can be determined and applied to it. When the impacts of all the causative factors have been correctly determined and applied, the result should be an approximation of the as-built network. Then the impacted, as-planned network should be compared with the as-built one, and any major disparities between them should be examined to identify whether TIEs were incorrectly applied, or whether there were additional causative factors not identified.

The theoretical effects of the impacting factors on the as-planned network must be explainable in terms of the as-built network, or the proposed analysis is probably incorrect. Some professionals take a different position, however. One well-known scheduling consultant expounds the theory of the "500 bolts": If an owner is to provide 500 bolts, and has delivered only 499, in the consultant's opinion the activity involved will be impacted until that 500th bolt has been delivered. But it appears more logical to examine the function of the 500th bolt. For instance, if it is a spare or there is a readily acceptable substitute which permits construction to proceed, then it is not, theoretically speaking, proper to claim that the as-planned network has been impacted by its absence.

Another position, often taken by schedulers who conduct impact analyses on as-planned networks for contractor evaluations, is that all float belongs to the contractor. This has been a continuing argument in the profession. In fact, some recent owners' specifications, in order to counteract such claims, state outright, "All float belongs to the owner." Neither position is tenable, however. Float is a shared commodity. Like a natural resource, it must be used with common sense. The owner should be permitted to use float for order changes, shop drawing reviews, and other owner-responsible areas. On the other hand, it is obvious that owners should not use float excessively to the point that the entire project becomes totally critical. This would be an overreach on the part of owners. Conversely, contractors should be expected to utilize float only to balance their work forces and to work efficiently, in order to complete projects on time and at the optimum budgets.

Standard CPM Calculation

When all of the TIE information has been imposed on the as-planned network, a standard CPM calculation is made. This calculation should correlate, as discussed previously, with the as-built network. When such a correlation is observed, the TIEs are selectively zeroed out by category. For instance, the force majeure changes are zeroed out, and a run is made to determine the overall impact of their absence on the network. Similarly, contractor-related TIEs are zeroed out, and whatever further improvement their absence makes in schedule is noted. Then the owner-related TIEs, involving changes and any hold orders, etc., are zeroed out, and this final result should bring the network back to its as-planned status.

Since the various categories of changes are each zeroed out concurrently, the effects of concurrency due to combined impacts can be observed from the results of the three separate runs. This can provide an arbitrator or a court with the means to allocate delay damages and impacts caused by the various parties.

Examples of CPM Application

The first application of this approach was in regard to a major airport project. The airport authority had contracted for the installation of a $12 million underground fueling system. The contractor for the work, who was the low bidder by several million dollars, prepared a construction CPM plan that was never accepted by the owner and all the milestone dates were completely missed. The airport authority took under advisement the matter of whether or not to enter suit for delay damages due to losses in interest on money and in airport operating efficiency, as well as for other direct delay damages. But when the contractor filed a $6 million delay suit against the authority, the authority promptly filed a counterclaim and litigation ensued.

In the absence of a mutually acceptable CPM plan representing what actually happened, the owner directed that one be prepared to evaluate the real causes of the delays. The daily, weekly, and monthly reports, as well as personal observations by the owner's field team and the CPM consultant, were utilized in developing this comprehensive plan. It contained milestone points reflecting actual dates of accomplishment for various activities. Between the milestone points, the estimate for the time that the work should have taken were inserted, and the CPM team then divided the delay proportionally by its causes. The causes were: either by contractor, owner, combined, or neither. The first computer run of the network showed the actual dates for all the events. The next computation established the amount of delay due to the contractor alone. The third established the amount of delay due to the owner alone. The fourth identified the amount of delay due to both. But his total delay was less than what the combined total was when the amounts caused by the owner alone and the contractor alone were added together.

Using this very specific information, the managing engineer for the owner was able to direct efforts toward an out-of-court settlement that took more than a year to negotiate. (Part of the willingness to negotiate on the part of the owner's management personnel arose out of a recognition of the very real delays caused by slow shop-drawing review. Many of these delays were due to the high workload that the owner's engineering department was carrying at the time, but many were also identified as coming from attempts by the owner's engineers to redesign the shop-drawing submissions, a common mistake made in the course of many shop drawing reviews.)

While it is best to start with an as-planned network, there are situations where a good as-planned network did not exist, or in which the one utilized had flaws or was inadequate. In those cases, one approach is to produce an as-should-have-been network. In some cases, the as-should-have-been network has a bar graph to utilize as a guideline.

In one major project, the new Library of Congress building (James Madison Memorial Library), it was recognized by both the owner, the Architect of the Capitol, and the contractor, Bateson Construction Co., that there would be delay claims as a result of certain delay problems in the project. It was mutually agreed that it would be advantageous to convert the contractual as-planned bar graph into a CPM network which would be more useful in evaluating the effects of delay impacts. The contractor's scheduling consultant, A. James Waldron, converted the network into a CPM diagram and printout. This was reviewed for the Architect of the Capitol by O'Brien-Kreitzberg & Associates (OKA), and after some adjustments a mutually agreed upon baseline was stipulated. The network was useful to both sides in determining the responsibility for delays and the costs resulting from them.

Usually the use of an as-should-have-been network is more of an uphill situation. Lacking the agreement by both parties to a previously approved as-planned network, those producing the as-should-have-been network must be prepared to provide a foundation for it, and to justify the use of same.

Take the 34-day CPM plan for the initial portion of the John Doe project as a schedule, and use it to measure delays or impacts. If, for instance, the well pump required a 6-week delivery time, the equivalent number of working days would be 30. The impact area is measured by adding an activity starting at 0 and going to event 4. The activity would be titled "late delivery of well pump," and adding it would produce the result shown in Fig. 25.1, the time scale version of the initial part of the John Doe project. Since the well work was on the critical path, the delay would force the late start of activity 4–5, install well pump, to await the delivery of the well pump. In this example that would be 30 minus 22, or a delay of 8 working days. Of course, it is necessary to view the entire contractual universe. For instance, if there were a 2-week delay in the notice to proceed for reasons other than the pump delivery, then the pump delivery delay would be better represented by disconnecting the initial or i end of the delay arrow from the 0 event and bringing it into the network as a new starting point with a specified date. Thus, if there were a 2-week force majeure delay imposed on the start of the site work, the additional time needed for delivery of the well pump would become concurrent delay.

Figure 25.2 shows a TIE form describing the delay in the delivery of the well pump. Figure 25.3 shows a TIE form describing a 60-day delay in the delivery of steel. This is applied to the phased construction network, which incorporates both design and procurement phases with the construction phase, and procurement, in this case, is the owner's responsibility. (The owner, in turn, may have a claim against the construction manager, or the architect-engineer, if the fault for late delivery lies with either of those parties.) When the two problems are imposed upon the overall network, it is seen that the critical path as shown in Fig. 25.4 now goes through procurement of the structural steel, and even with the slow delivery of the well pump, the initial site-work network now has float as shown in Fig. 25.5. There are, however, an additional 8 days of float in the early activities prior to the installation of the well pump. The 8-day differential in float along the well-drilling path is still imposed by the late delivery of the well pump. However, there is no impact upon the overall project because the late steel delivery takes precedence.

To determine the cumulative effect of all delays, all TIEs should be developed and impacted against the network simultaneously. To evaluate the impact of any one category, just the TIEs representing that category (i.e., owner's responsibility, force majeure, contractor responsibility, etc.) should be applied to the network.

EVIDENTIARY USE OF CPM

During the 1960s, CPM schedulers, technicians, and engineers anticipated that the critical path method would be utilized as a tool in construction claims and litigation at some point in time. In fact, as early as 1962 to 1965, consultants to the litigants on both sides of a case involving the Atomic Energy Commission utilized CPM to prepare their positions, although a case citation is not available, and no wide exposition of the results was made. (The firm providing consultants to both sides was Mauchly Associates.)

In the 1970s, CPM techniques were used in presenting, and defending, delay claims cases in many instances. In no case where O'Brien-Kreitzberg & Associates OKA was involved was the use of CPM questioned by opposing counsel or the court. Some of these cases include the following (dates are approximate):

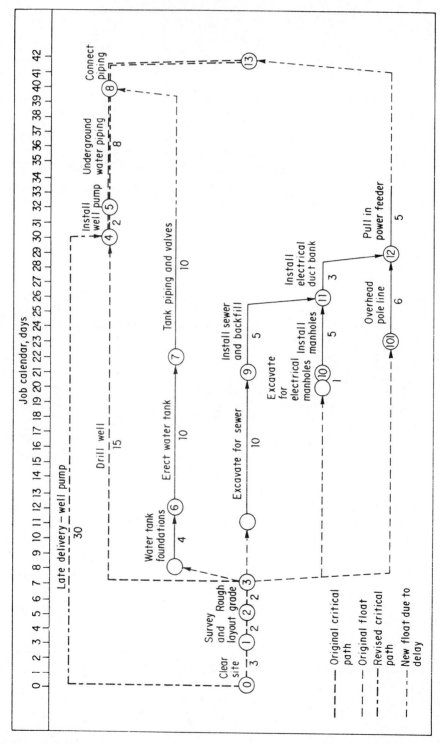

FIGURE 25.1 Late delivery of well pump, time scale.

TIME IMPACT EVALUATION

PROJECT: *John Doe*   TIE #: *1*

PREPARED BY: *J. J. O'Brien*   DATE: *9/15/83*

DESCRIPTION: *LATE WELL PUMP DELIVERY — DELIVERY WAS SIX WEEKS AFTER CONTRACTOR NOTICE TO PROCEED. CONTRACTOR WAS READY FOR PUMP AT DAY 22.*

ACTIVITIES AFFECTED:

4-5 "INSTALL WELL PUMP"

TYPE OF IMPACT:

INCREASED DURATION: _____   AMOUNT: _____

DELAYED DATE/SUSPENSION OF WORK: *DELIVERED @ DAY 30*

FRAGNET:

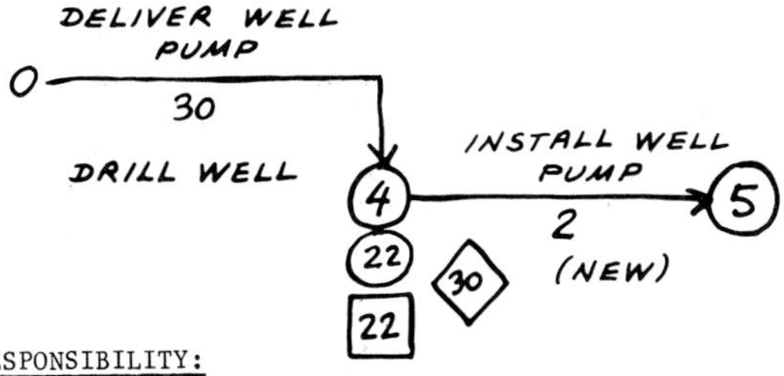

EVALUATION/RESPONSIBILITY:

L.S. OF 4-5 WAS 22; ACTUAL START 30, THEREFORE 8 WORK DAYS DELAY ON CRITICAL PATH

RESPONSIBILITY: A-E (FAILED TO DELIVER SPECIFICATIONS)

FIGURE 25.2   Time impact evaluation [TIE] describing delay of well pump.

TIME IMPACT EVALUATION

PROJECT: *John Doe*   TIE #: *2*
PREPARED BY: *J. J. O'Brien*   DATE: *1/31/89*

DESCRIPTION: *STRUCTURAL STEEL DELIVERED IN 123 WORK DAYS RATHER THAN SCHEDULED 80*

ACTIVITIES AFFECTED:

29-30 "ERECT STRUCTURAL STEEL"

TYPE OF IMPACT:

INCREASED DURATION: *43*   AMOUNT:

DELAYED DATE/SUSPENSION OF WORK: *DELIVERED @ DAY 123*

FRAGNET:

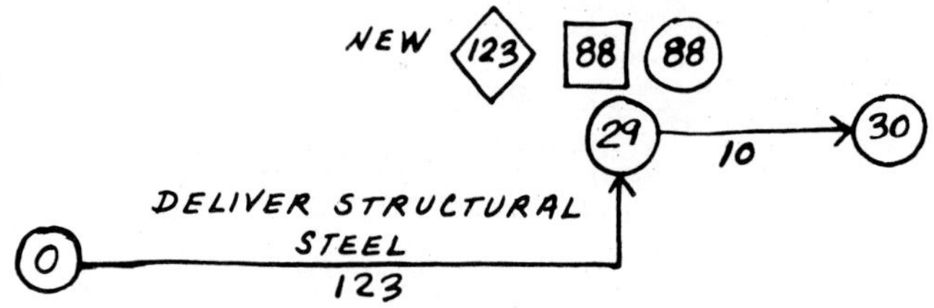

NEW ◇*123* ☐*88* ◯*88*

◯*29* ──── *10* ────▶ ◯*30*

DELIVER STRUCTURAL STEEL
◯*0* ───────────────── ▲
123

EVALUATION/RESPONSIBILITY:

STEEL DELIVERY HAD 8 DAYS FLOAT.
THEREFORE DELAY IS (123 - 88) = 35

OWNER REQUIRED CHANGES. RESPONSIBILITY
AS FOLLOWS: DESIGN CHANGES   15 DAYS
                    FABRICATION CHANGES 15 "
                                OWNER   30
            FABRICATOR   5

FIGURE 25.3   TIE for 60-day delay in delivery of structural steel.

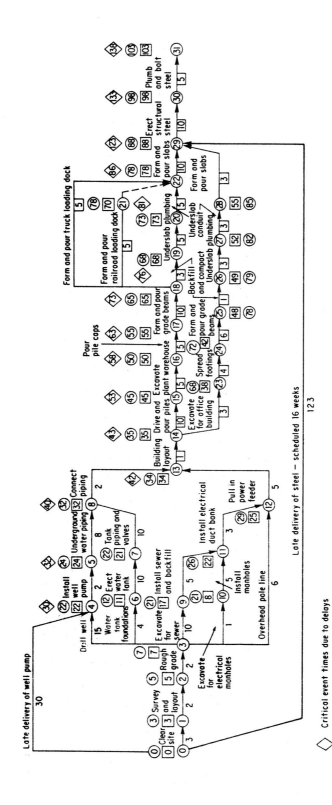

FIGURE 25.4 Time scale network showing steel delay.

25.13

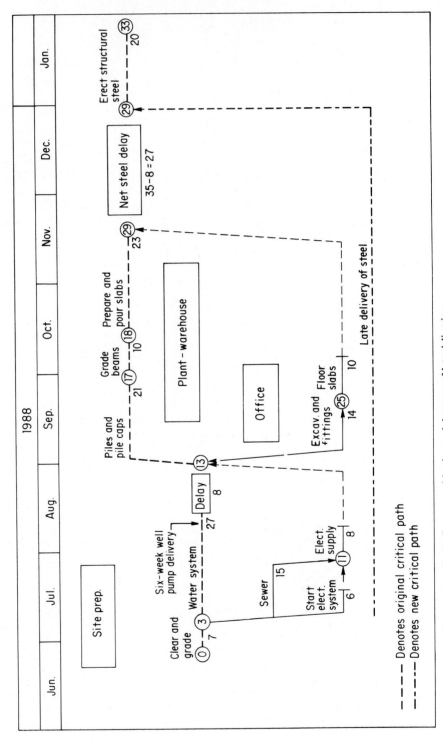

FIGURE 25.5 Overview showing relative float created in site work because of late deliveries.

- *IBM v. Henry Beck Construction;* Federal Court, Florida, 1973
- *Somers Construction v. H. H. Robertson;* arbitration, Philadelphia, 1973
- *E. C. Ernst v. City of Philadelphia;* Eastern Federal District Court, Philadelphia, 1976
- *Arundel v. Philadelphia Port Corp.;* Commonwealth Court, Pennsylvania, 1979
- *Buckley v. New York City;* New York State Court, 1979
- *Federal Construction v. Blake Construction;* Federal District Court, Washington, D.C., 1980
- *Kidde-Briscoe v. University of Connecticut;* Connecticut State Court, 1980–1982
- *Keating v. City of Philadelphia;* Eastern District Court, Philadelphia, 1981
- *Glasgow v. Commonwealth of Pennsylvania;* Commonwealth Board of Claims, 1982–1983
- *PT & L Construction v. NJDOT;* New Jersey State Court, 1983.

On many more OKA cases which had been entered and were en route to trial, CPM was a factor in settlement.

In the early 1970s, several lawyers researched the question of CPM as an evidentiary tool. A series of articles and presentations followed, a number of which used the same thread, starting with the article "The Use of Critical Path Method Techniques in Contract Claims" by Jon M. Wickwire and Richard F. Smith in the *Public Contract Law Journal* of October 1974. Excerpts from the article follow

> Judicial acceptance of CPM analyses as persuasive evidence of delay and disruption has been slow to develop, primarily due to technical errors in the analysis submitted or a failure of a presentation to realistically portray the work as actually done. In spite of the early reluctance to accept CPM presentations, the current state of the law is that use of CPM schedules to prove construction contract claims has become the standard, rather than the exception. Scheduling techniques which cannot display activity interrelationships are not favorably regarded as evidence of delay and disruption.
>
> In Minmar Builders, Inc., GSBCA, 3430, 72-2 BCA 9599 (1972) the General Services Administration Board of Contract Appeals commented upon Minmar Builder's construction schedules (bar charts) which were offered to show project completion delay due to government's failure to timely issue ceiling change instructions:
>
> "Although two of Appellant's construction schedules were introduced in evidence, one which had been approved by the government and one which had not, neither was anything more than a bar chart showing the duration and project calendar dates for the performance of the various contractual tasks. Since no interrelationship was shown as between the tasks the charts cannot describe what project activities were dependent on the prior performance of the plaster and ceiling work, much less whether overall project completion was thereby affected. In short, the schedules were not prepared by the Critical Path Method (CPM) and hence are not probative as to whether any particular activity or group of activities was on the critical path or constituted the pacing element for the project.
>
> The greatest difficulty encountered by contractors using CPM techniques in claim presentation is the requirement for the presentation to be thoroughly grounded in the project records. The failure of contractors to properly document CPM studies has been held controlling in many board decisions....

Guidelines for the use of CPM presentations were set forth in the General Services Administration Board of Contract Appeals decision in Joseph E. Bennett Co. (GSBCA 2362, 72-1 BCA 9364 (1972) which . . . affirms the need to properly update a CPM and support the study with accurate records. The contractor's claim in this appeal was founded on a letter from the contracting officer ordering completion of the work by the contract completion date. The contractor argued this requirement was an acceleration order, which was denied by the contracting officer because of lack of meaningful evidence. The contracting officer rejected the accuracy of the contractor's critical path method construction plan on the basis of errors in the interrelationships of activities.

At the board, the appellant presented a computer analysis of the CPM used on the project to isolate the delays caused by government activities. The board held that the usefulness of this analysis was dependent upon three things: 1) the extent to which the individual delays are established by substantial evidence—this requirement is concerned with the project records and evidence available for the appellant to show the underlying causes of delay; 2) the soundness of the CPM system itself—this requires the contractor to demonstrate the logic of the CPM and show that its theoretical and scheduling analyses are sound; and 3) the nature of and reason for any changes to the CPM schedule in the process of reducing it to a computer program—this relates to the exactness and accuracy with which the appellant has reduced the CPM network to a computer analysis and how effectively this analysis can be used in a claim presentation.

As expected, the appellant in Bennett argued that the CPM was the proper basis for any analysis of the project since the plan was submitted by the appellant and approved by the government.

However, the board rejected the appellant's CPM analysis because it: 1) contained numerous mathematical errors; 2) failed to consider foreseeable weather conditions; 3) changed the critical path and float times without reason; and 4) was prepared without the benefit of any site investigation and after the project was already completed. . . .

The gradual acceptance of CPM presentations when properly documented is demonstrated in the case of Continental Consolidated Corp. ENG BCA 2743, 2766, 67-2 BCA 6624 (1967). . . .

In this case a claim was submitted for extra costs due to suspension of work and subsequent acceleration directed by the government. The appellant alleged it was entitled to time extensions due to government delay in approving shop drawings. The government's failure to grant time extensions for these delays made the work appear to be behind schedule as of certain dates when in fact, if proper time extensions had been granted, the appellant would have been on schedule. As a result, government directives to work overtime and/or extra shifts would have been unnecessary. . . .

The contract set completion dates for various elements of the work which in effect required a critical path for each element within an overall work plan. With the use of the appellant's CPM analysis, the board was able to separate out the delay costs due appellant and the additional costs incurred due to a compensable acceleration order. This evidentiary tool allowed the board to identify the periods of delay and actual progress on the job and thereby determine when an acceleration order was properly issued from the point in time when such an order was compensable because the contractor was back on schedule.

Thus the boards have recognized the value of a CPM developed contemporaneously with the work or subsequent to the work so long as it's based upon the relevant records available.

The records may include daily logs, time sheets, payroll records, diaries, purchase orders.

While the boards have accepted the CPM as an evidentiary tool, this tool cannot rise above the basic assumptions and records upon which it is founded. The board can accept the theoretical value of a CPM presentation, but reject its conclusion for failure to base the analysis on the actual project records. (See C. H. Leavell & Co.,

GSBCA 2901, 70-2 BCA 8437 (1970); 70-2 BCA 8528 (1970) [on reconsideration] where the contractor failed to establish the accuracy of the input date for its computer analysis of delays due to design deficiencies.)

Where the board has received persuasive evidence that the CPM network is either logically or factually inaccurate, incomplete or prepared specifically for the claim, the board will discount its evidentiary value. A CPM must be linked to the job records, as a CPM analysis is primarily concerned with visually portraying the job records to establish the cause of delay or disruption.

The extent to which a CPM presentation may be used to document a claim can be seen in Canon Construction Co. (ASBCA 16142, 72-1 BCA 9404 1972) where the contractor gained total acceptance of its CPM schedule to establish a delay claim. In this opinion, the board recognized the underlying logic and evidence presented in the appellant's original CPM schedule and the value of CPM techniques to prove extended overhead costs.

In Canon, the contractor was awarded his overhead costs determined by the difference between the actual date of completion and the date the contractor would have completed the work absent government fault and performance of changed work. But the recovery for extended overhead costs was held to be limited by either the extended period of performance time or the aggregate net extent of delays caused by government fault or changed work, whichever is the lesser. Using this formula the board recognized that the contractor was not entitled to recovery for the group of excusable but noncompensable delays including weather delays, reasonable suspensions of work, etc. . . .

The Canon decision is extremely important since it shows that a properly prepared and presented CPM schedule will be accepted by the board as the basis for computing project delays. In this regard it is noted that the board clearly indicated that it was "relying principally on the CPM chart and only using the witness' testimony to ascribe an aspect of reasonableness to the chart."

The Canon decision is also significant since it provided further guidance as to the application of CPM principles to claims. For example, the board acknowledged that delays incurred off the critical path would not delay ultimate performance. Further, the board found that where the sequence established by the network was violated, costly start and stop operations would result and implied that the contractor's planned network operations need not be the only way to accomplish the work shown, but must be shown to be economical in both cost and time. (Reference: Stagg Construction Co., GSBCA, 2664, 69-2 BCA 7914 (1969); 70-1 BCA 8241 (1970) [on reconsideration]).

In 1975, Paul J. Walstad, Jon M. Wickwire, Thomas Asselin, and Joseph H. Kasimer wrote a book titled *Project Scheduling and Construction Claims, a Practical Handbook,* published by A. James Waldron Enterprises. The authors note:[1]

There was reluctance at first to accept the use of CPM analysis as evidence of delays and disruption. Of paramount concern were possible technical errors in the system or a failure of the system or analysis to realistically portray the work as actually done. *See e.g., A. Teichert & Sons, Inc.,* ASBCA No. 10265, 68-2 BCA 7151 (1968). . . .

This concern no doubt stemmed from early presentations which based CPM analysis to a great extent on speculation, inferences, or innuendo rather than hard, documented facts. Thus, even though the CPM has become recognized as a competent source of evidence . . . its usefulness in providing a claim has been held dependent upon at least four factors:

---

[1]Permission to quote courtesy A. James Waldron.

1. The soundness of the CPM schedule itself. . . . This requires proof of the reasonableness and feasibility of the schedule so as to show that on a theoretical basis the scheduling was sound;
2. The extent to which any individual delays can be established by substantial evidence. This goes to the basic records and evidence available to the claimant to show the underlying causes of delay or disruption;
3. The nature of any changes to the CPM schedule made during the claim analysis process. This relates to the exactness and accuracy with which the claimant has analyzed the project scheduling in making his presentation;
4. Proof that the work sequence shown was the only possible or reasonable sequence by which the work could be completed on time.

In the late 1970s and early 1980s, *Engineering News-Record* presented a series of professional seminars in regard to claim and litigation. Paul J. Walstad, Esq., has been a leader in the formulation and presentation of a number of these. The comments on evidentiary value of CPM continue as previously described. By 1980, Walstad had added the following in this regard.[2]

In *Blackhawk Heating & Plumbing Co., Inc.,* GSBCA No. 2432, 75-1 BCA, the contractor claims 403 days as a result of ductwork design deficiencies. The Board found the deficiencies were the fault of the Government. However, the Board indicated the main question was whether the ductwork delay had extended contract completion; the Government contended a delay involving electrical fixtures was the critical item.

In support of its position, the Government produced its own CPM analysis, which had been prepared after the delays had occurred. The Government CPM showed the ductwork design problems were not on the critical path; the activities which the contractor had contended were delayed actually had "float" time remaining even after the delay was considered, and the critical path ran through the electrical fixture approval, delivery and installation cycle.

The Board carefully analyzed the Government's CPM, and found it . . . established a sound network diagram and computer run showing just how the project was actually constructed up to the date of substantial completion on December 7, 1970. . . .

After reviewing the delay analysis set forth in the Government CPM, the Board further concluded it had provided "a sound basis upon which to evaluate various project delays." Based upon the finding the electrical fixture delay was the factor which delayed ultimate completion, the Board then proceeded to allocate responsibility for the fixture delays. Upon reconsideration, the Board refused to modify its original decision, indicating the as-built CPM was the best evidence of delay.

The use of CPM as an evidentiary tool in claims and court proceedings is not confined to administrative boards. In the *Brooks Towers Corporation vs. Hunkin-Conkey Construction Company,* 454 F. 2d 1203 (10th Cir. 1972), the owner claimed delay damages from the contractor. The Tenth Circuit Court of Appeals affirmed an award in favor of the contractor, and in so doing placed great weight on the CPM analysis provided by an expert witness:

The testimony of Richard N. Green, a Construction Consultant, is corroborative of Ratner's grant of some 185 days extensions and significant in relation to the 'clockwork' scheduling of work components required to accomplish the original contract completion schedules. Green's study took into consideration the plans and specifications, *the computerized Critical Path Scheduling program,* all Bulletins, formal Change Orders; related correspondence, Daily Progress Report and Monthly Pay Requests. He computed some 394 days involving requests for ex-

[2]See page 269 of Material on ENR's "Advanced Course on Construction Claims," Arlington, VA, May 1 and 2, 1980. Permission to quote courtesy *Engineering News-Record,* copyright McGraw-Hill, Inc., and Construction Education Management Corporation.

tensions. He eliminated those of an "overlapping" nature and those which were not critical. He did not consider delays resulting from labor disputes or severe weather conditions. He arrived at a total of 180 days extension of time to which the Contractor was entitled.

In its decision of July 18, 1983, the General Services Administration Board of Contract Appeals (GSA BCA) complained about the misuse of CPM schedules in the presentation of a claim by Welch Construction, Inc. Welch filed a claim for damages as a result of owner delay in the modification of a geological survey center. Presenting its claim, Welch utilized CPM diagrams which purported to present as-planned and as-built schedules. In its opinion, GSA BCA, denying the claim, stated:

Candor compels us to admit that we may not have figured our what it was that Appellant thought its exhibit would show. If so, Appellant has only itself to blame . . . [One] of the surest ways of losing a case for lack of proof is submitting complex exhibits to a tryer of facts with no attempt to explain what they show or how they relate to the other evidence in the record.

The Board believed that the schedules used in presenting the claim ignored both contractual and actual completion dates.

INDEX

About the Editors

JAMES J. O'BRIEN, P.E., is Chairman of the Board of O'Brien-Kreitzberg & Associates, Inc., the construction management firm that handled the renovation of San Francisco's cable car system. Mr. O'Brien's firm is program manager for the redevelopment of New York's John F. Kennedy International Airport.

ROBERT G. ZILLY, P.E., M.A.S.C.E., is Professor Emeritus of Construction Management at the College of Engineering and Technology, University of Nebraska, Lincoln.